COSMETICS PROCESSES

and Formulations Hand Book With Herbal Cosmetics Technology and Formulae

OTHER RELATED BOOKS

- Candle Making Processes & Formulations Hand Book
- Complete Technology Book on Detergents with Formulations (Detergent Cake, Dish Washing Detergents, Liquid & Paste Detergents, Enzyme Detergents, Cleaning Powder & Spray Dried Washing Powder)
- Cosmetics Processes & Formulations Hand Book with Herbal Cosmetics Technology & Formulae
- Hand Book Of Adhesives With Their Formulaes
- Hand Book of Synthetic & Herbal Cosmetics (How to Make Beauty Products)
- Hand Book Of Synthetic Detergents With Formulations
- Herbal Cosmetics & Beauty Products with Formulations
- Manufacture of Disinfectants, Cleaners, Phenyl, Repellents, Deodorants, Dishwashing Detergents and Aerosols with Formulations
- Manufacture Of Household Soaps, Toilet Soaps And Other Soaps With Formulations
- Manufacture of Washing Soap, Toilet Soap, Detergent Powders, Liquid Soap & Herbal & Paste Detergents and Perfumes with Formulations
- Manufacturing Technology & Formulations Hand Book on Thinners, Putty, Wall& Industrial Finishes and Synthetic Resins
- Modern Inks Formulations & Manufacturing Industries
- Modern Small & Cottage Scale Industries
- Modern Technology of Acid Slurry, Surfactants, Soap and Detergents with Formulae
- Paint Pigment Varnish & Lacquer Manufacturing
- Paint Varnish Solvents & Coating Technology
- Paint, Pigment, Solvent, Coating Emulsion, Paint Additives & Formulations
- Powder Coating Technology Hand Book
- Profitable Businesses To Start For Entrepreneurs
- Profitable Small Cottage Tiny & Home Industries
- Profitable Small Scale Manufacture of Cosmetics (Synthetic & Herbal)
- Rubber Chemicals And Processing Industries
- Start Your Own Export Business (How To Export)
- Start Your Own Small Business And Industry
- Stationery, Paper Converting & Packaging Industries
- Technology of Coating, Resins, Pigments & Inks Industries
- Technology of Herbal Cosmetics & Toiletries Products with Formulae
- Technology of Paints and Coatings with Formulations
- Technology of Synthetic Resins and Emulsion Polymers

COSMETICS PROCESSES

and Formulations Hand Book With Herbal Cosmetics Technology and Formulae

Written By

EIRI Board of Consultants and Engineers

ENGINEERS INDIA RESEARCH INSTITUTE

4449, Nai Sarak, Main Road, Delhi - 110006 (India)

Ph: +91-11-23918117, 23916431, 45120361, 23947058, 64727385

* E-Mail: eiritechnology@gmail.com & eiriprojects@gmail.com

*Website: www.eiriindia.org & www.industrialprojects.in

PRINTED & PUBLISHED BY

ENGINEERS INDIA RESEARCH INSTITUTE

4449, Nai Sarak, Main Road, Delhi - 110006 (India)
Ph: +91-11-23918117, 23916431, 45120361, 23947058, 64727385
*** E-Mail: eiritechnology@gmail.com & eiriprojects@gmail.com**
***Website: www.eiriindia.org & www.industrialprojects.in**

Distributors:

EIRI PROJECT CONSULTANTS AND PUBLISHERS
4/54 Roop Nagar, Delhi-110007
and
Industrial Technologies, India
Nai Sarak, Delhi-110006

Revised and Enlarged Edition

ISBN: 9788186732410

Printed in New Delhi (INDIA)

₹ 1475/- US$ 150

Printed & Published by Sudhir Gupta for "Engineers India Research Institute", 4449 Nai Sarak, Main Road, New Delhi -110006

Contents and Subject Index

OTHER RELATED BOOKS

- Candle Making Processes & Formulations Hand Book
- Complete Technology Book on Detergents with Formulations (Detergent Cake, Dish Washing Detergents, Liquid & Paste Detergents, Enzyme Detergents, Cleaning Powder & Spray Dried Washing Powder)
- Cosmetics Processes & Formulations Hand Book with Herbal Cosmetics Technology & Formulae
- Hand Book Of Adhesives With Their Formulaes
- Hand Book of Synthetic & Herbal Cosmetics (How to Make Beauty Products)
- Hand Book Of Synthetic Detergents With Formulations
- Herbal Cosmetics & Beauty Products with Formulations
- Manufacture of Disinfectants, Cleaners, Phenyl, Repellents, Deodorants, Dishwashing Detergents and Aerosols with Formulations
- Manufacture Of Household Soaps, Toilet Soaps And Other Soaps With Formulations
- Manufacture of Washing Soap, Toilet Soap, Detergent Powders, Liquid Soap & Herbal & Paste Detergents and Perfumes with Formulations
- Manufacturing Technology & Formulations Hand Book on Thinners, Putty, Wall& Industrial Finishes and Synthetic Resins
- Modern Inks Formulations & Manufacturing Industries
- Modern Small & Cottage Scale Industries
- Modern Technology of Acid Slurry, Surfactants, Soap and Detergents with Formulae
- Paint Pigment Varnish & Lacquer Manufacturing
- Paint Varnish Solvents & Coating Technology
- Paint, Pigment, Solvent, Coating Emulsion, Paint Additives & Formulations
- Powder Coating Technology Hand Book
- Profitable Businesses To Start For Entrepreneurs
- Profitable Small Cottage Tiny & Home Industries
- Profitable Small Scale Manufacture of Cosmetics (Synthetic & Herbal)
- Rubber Chemicals And Processing Industries
- Start Your Own Export Business (How To Export)
- Start Your Own Small Business And Industry
- Stationery, Paper Converting & Packaging Industries
- Technology of Coating, Resins, Pigments & Inks Industries
- Technology of Herbal Cosmetics & Toiletries Products with Formulae
- Technology of Paints and Coatings with Formulations
- Technology of Synthetic Resins and Emulsion Polymers

EQUIPMENT USED IN THE MA

INTRODUCTION

Cosmetics m… processes, there a… overall view of th… principles of cos… is convenient… manufacture… (i) Mixing…

MANUFAC…

A conver… in table 1. Every single… one mixing…

Chapter - 1

EQUIPMENT USED IN THE MANUFACTURE OF COSMETICS

INTRODUCTION

Cosmetics manufacture is concerned with a very broad range of processes, there are enough common elements to allow a relatively simple overall view of the subject; this helps considerably in a study of the basic principles of cosmetic production technology. The manufacture of cosmetics is conveniently divided into two parts: (i) Bulk manufacture; and (ii) Unit manufacture. The bulk manufacture is carried out in three steps. They are: (i) Mixing; (ii) Pumping; and (iii) Filtering. The most important step is mixing.

MANUFACTURE OF BULK PRODUCT

A convenient way of classifying the mixing processes is represented in table 1. Every single cosmetics manufacturing process contains minimum one mixing operation.

Table - 1

Scope of mixing operations within the cosmetics industry

	Type of mixing	*Examples*
1.	Solid/Solid	
	(a) Segregating	None
	(b) Cohesive	Face powders, eye shadows and all dry mixing
2.	Solid/Liquid	(i) Dissolution (of water–soluble dyes, preservatives, powder surfactants, etc.)
		(ii) Suspensions and dispersions (pigments in castor oil and in other liquids)
3.	Liquid/Liquid	
	(a) Miscible	(i) Chemical reactions (formation of soaps from acid and base)

(Cont'd)

Type of mixing	Examples
	(ii) pH control
	(iii) Blending (spirituous preparations, clear lip gloss products)
(b) Immiscible	(i) Extraction (none)
	(ii) Dispersion (emulsions)
4. Gas/Liquid	(i) Absorption (none)
	(ii) Dispersion (aeration and de-aeration)
5. Distributive	
(a) Fluid motion	Heat transfer (during emulsion and other manufacture)
(b) Limited flow	Pumping (pastes and other highly viscous products)

e.g. The manufacture of pigmented emulsion–based cream include four mixing steps. They are :

1. Preliminary dry blending of pigments and excipient (type Ib).
2. Dissolution of oil–soluble and water–soluble materials separately in their appropriate phase (type 2 example i and type 3a).
3. Dispersion or suspension of pigments in the oil or water phase (type 2, example ii).
4. Mixing of the two phases to form an emulsion, possibly with the formation *in situ* of a soap as part of the emulsifier (types 3a and 3b).
5. Adjustment of pH (type 3a).
6. De-aeration of the bulk (type 4).
7. Cooling to ambient temperature and pumping into a storage vessel (type 5a).

The subject of pumping is not clearly separated from that of mixing since pumping implies the forced flow of product. Any flow will naturally introduce an element of mixing if the product is not already homogeneous. Further, since flow is a common element of both processes, the same product characteristics (for example, rheological behaviour) must be taken into account.

Filtering is not usually a unit operation of major importance in cosmetics manufacture except in the production of spirituous preparations (colognes, aftershave and perfumes). It is possible to regard filtering as un-mixing and certainly the flow characteristics of the filtered product are again of prime importance.

Unit Manufacture

Most cosmetic products are filled from bulk in machines specifically designed to handle the units of a particular product type. While it is true that great care must be taken in the choice and the setting up of such machines, the main problems encountered are often concerned with the characteristics of the machines themselves rather than with the manufacture or processing of the product. There are at least two areas, however, where special understanding of the product units and their characteristics are essential for the achievement of efficient production: these are the moulding processes (lipsticks, wax–based sticks, alcohol–stearate gels) and compression processes (compressed eyeshadow, blushers and face powders). A description of unit manufacture could include all filling and packaging operations.

THE MANUFACTURE OF BULK COSMETIC PRODUCTS

Mixing

The object of a mixing operation is to reduce the inhomogeneities in the material being mixed. As Table - 1 shows, inhomogeneity may be of physical or chemical identity or of heat. Further, in the processes demanded by cosmetic manufacture, the mixing is designed to be permanent–or as permanent as it is possible to make it.

The reduction in inhomogeneity depends on the efficiency of the mixing apparatus used and also on the physical characteristics of the materials constituting the mixture. For miscible liquids, homogeneity can be produced at a molecular level whereas for mixture of powders homogeneity is limited to the sizes of the powder particles themselves. When examining a mixture for quality, therefore, the *scale of scrutiny*–the magnification at which the mixture is examined–must vary from product to product. At an acceptable scale of scrutiny, *perfect mixing* implies that all samples removed from the mixture will have exactly the same composition. This is rarely achievable. *Random mixing* is achieved if the probability of finding a particle of a given component in a sample is the same as the proportion of that component in the whole mixture. Random mixing is the aim of all industrial mixing operations and whereas samples removed from such a mixture will not be identical, the variations should be very small. If the scale of scrutiny is reduced sufficiently, however, this may no longer be true.

Mixing can only occur by relative movement between the particles of the constituent components of the mixture. Three basic mechanisms for achieving this relative movement have been identified: bulk flow, convective mixing and diffusive mixing. *Bulk flow* (which includes shear mixing, cutting, folding and tumbling) occurs in pastes and solids, when relatively large volumes of mixture are first separated and then redistributed to another part of the mixing vessel. *Convective mixing* involves the establishment of circulation patterns within the mixture. Finally, *diffusive mixing* occurs by particle collisions and deviation from a straight line. In miscible liquids of sufficiently low viscosity, the thermal energy which is possessed by the constituent molecules may be enough to achieve a good mixture quality by thermal diffusion without additional energy being applied, although this process is usually too slow for industrial purposes.

Many mixing problems arise from the tendency of mixture particles to segregate during attempts to mix them. *Segregation* is defined as the preference of the particles of one component to be in one or more places in a mixer rather than in other places. The size of the non–uniformities in an imperfect mixture is sometimes referred to as the 'scale of segregation' and the difference in composition between neighbouring lumps of volumes is the 'intensity of segregation'. Segregation is not, fortunately, a major problem in cosmetics manufacture although it does manifest itself occasionally (as, for example, in the flotation of pigments during lipstick processing).

SOLID–SOLID MIXING

Solid–solid mixing is of two types: (i) Segregating; and (ii) Cohesive. Free flowing powders exhibit many process advantages (such as easy storage, easy flow from hoppers, smooth flow of product), but have the disadvantage that they tend to segregate unless all the constituent particles are of very similar shape and size. Cohesive powder, on the other hand, lacks mobility, and individual particles are bonded together and move as clumps or aggregates. Although segregation does not appear to be a problem (except, as will be seen, at very small scales of scutiny), cohesive powders are difficult to store and do not easily flow from hoppers.

MANUFACTURE OF PIGMENTED POWDER PRODUCTS

Powder eyeshadows, face powders and powder blushers are commonly composed of the following types of material : Talc, Pigments, pearl agents, Liquid binder and preservative.

The order in which these ingredients are mixed and the process by which the mixing is carried out depend largely upon the type of equipment that is available.

Hammer Mill

The processing of bulk pigmented powder products is carried out using the hammer mill Fig. 18.1. The hammer mill was designed as a comminution machine. It consists of a fast rotating shaft fitted with freely swinging hammers mounted in a cage which is equipped with a breaker plate against which the feed is disintegrated, chiefly by impact from the hammer. The very high speed at which the hammers move (60–100 ms^{-1}) increases the chance of a hammer making contact with each particle and the dwell–time of particles within the chamber is increased by the placement of a variable size screen over the exit.

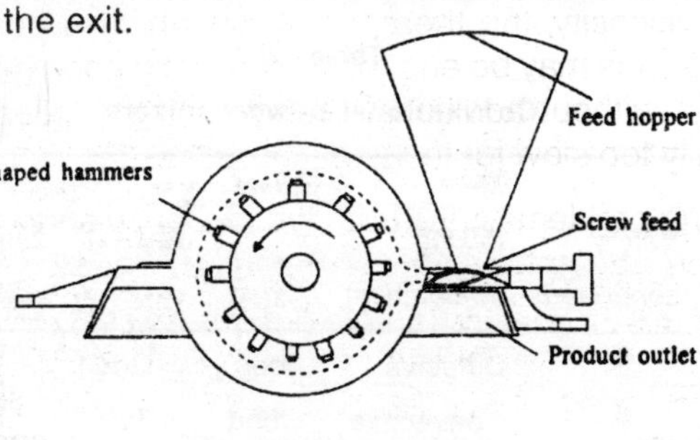

Fig. 18.1. Hammer mill.

Hammer mills are very efficient in the comminution of brittle particles in the range of 1500–50 μm but below this size their efficiency (the probability of direct impact) falls off rapidly. The very high rotational speed of the hammers and the air flow within the chamber ensure that there are enough weak secondary impacts (particle-wall and particle-particle) to break the much weaker pigment agglomerates–which may be up to 50 μm in diameter. The disintegrated agglomerate fractions then stabilise by becoming coated on a larger talc particles and should not be further changed by subsequent passes through the mill.

Hammer mill, has certain disadvantages. For example, from the viewpoint of energy consumption, a hammer mill used is very inefficient. The feed-rate and therefore, the processing time for all but the smallest batch sizes of powder is very slow. Increasing the residence time of powder within the grinding chamber by decreasing this mesh size can cause the screen to become blocked with compacted powder, resulting in overheating and damage to machine and product. The hammer mill is a continuous processing device being used for batch processing. For this reason, it must be fed with a powder mixture which has already been effectively mixed, otherwise the colour of the milled product changes as each section of unmixed bulk passes through. This preliminary mixing must be efficient although it is not necessary for any extension to be achieved at this stage.

The most widely used is the 'ribbon blender' which comprises a horizontal drum containing a rotating axial shaft which carried ribbon-like paddles. In such a device, the pre-mix can take anything between 20 and 60 minutes. Other mixers are now available which utilise higher energy input but are quicker. Table - 2 summarises the properties of some of the more conventional powder mixers. Since it is relatively easy to achieve good mixture quality (at a large scale of scrutiny) in cohesive powders, any mixing device will eventually produce a satisfactory even distribution of components provided that it contains no dead spots where mixing does not take place.

Table - 2

Conventional powder mixers

Type of mixer	*Batch/ continuous*	*Main mixing mechanism*	*Speed of mixing*	*Ease of cleaning*	*Energy consumption*	*Quality of extension*
Horizontal drum	B	Diffusive	Poor	Good	Low	Poor
Loedige-type	B	Convective	Good	Fair	Medium	Fair
Ribbon blender	B or C	Convective	poor	Fair	Low	Poor
Nauta mixer	B	Convective	Good	Poor	Low	poor
V-mixer (with cutters)	B	Diffusive	Poor	Good	Medium	Unknown
Airmix	B	Convective	Good	Fair	Low	Unknown

It is usual to add the liquid binder during this preliminary mixing stage. The binder may be poured into a suitable orifice in the mixer although many production chemists prefer to spray it into the mixer cavity as an aerosol through a venturi or similar device. This procedure helps to distribute the liquid more evenly and avoids the formation of wet, lumpy areas in the powder body. The separation of large agglomerates which takes place subsequently in the mill normally assures the completion of the wetting process provided only that the binder is correctly chosen. Should the binder still appear to be unevenly distributed after the passage of the powder through the mill, the product can often be rescued by passing it through as fine a mesh sieve as possible.

Batch Colour Correction

It is not unusual for the bulk powder product, even though it has been correctly processed, to require colour correction in order to obtain a satisfactory match to the standard. Since any addition of pigment or talc needs to be extended, a passage through the mill is necessary. A common procedure is as follows. After the preliminary coarse mix has been completed, a small amount of the bulk (usually about 5 kg), which is assumed to be representative of the whole, is passed through the mill. This is examined in the laboratory, and if necessary, a pigment addition specified. This correction is added to the 5 kg of milled product, mixing in roughly by hand and the 5 kg is re-milled. The twice-milled sample is returned to the remainder of the bulk and re-mixed in the original mixer. A further 5 kg is then removed and the process is repeated until a match is obtained. The use of pigments previously extended on talc and stored as such. This has the merit of speeding up the correction process.

When pearl agents are part of the formulation, unless an un-pearlised standard is provide, the pearl must be added in the correct proportion to the laboratory sample before colour can be assessed. Pearl is only added to the bulk in the last stage of the manufacturing procedure. The ideal equipment would probably have the following properties :

1. It would be capable of breaking up weak particles in the size range 50–0.5 μm without damaging talc or mica particles of similar diameter.
2. It would be a low energy device, consuming little power itself without heating the powder mixture excessively.
3. It would be a batch processing device capable of mixing and extending in one operation.
4. It would be rapid: processing times of less than 10 minutes would be acceptable.
5. It would not cause excessive aeration of the powder (since this causes further processing problems in later processing).
6. It would be easy to clean.
7. Its efficiency would not vary with the cohesiveness of the powder; it would not be affected by poor flow characteristics.
8. It would be quiet and clean in operation.

Other comminution devices have been shown to produce extension, particularly pin mills and fluid energy mills, yet none seems to work as efficiently as the hammer mill. Recently two types of mixers have been developed. They are : (i) Vertical vortex mixer; (ii) Plough-shear.

Vertical vortex mixer

The powder mixture is placed in a vertical, cylindrical chamber and is then accelerated outwards and upwards into a fluidised vortex motion. The motion may be produced by compressed air blasted sequentially from a series of nozzles contained in a lower cone-shaped section; alternatively, a propeller-shaped tool of 'poor aerodynamic' design may be used which rotates rapidly in the dished base of the mixing bowl. Mixing and dispersion occur at the point of conversion of the powder particles (in the upper point of the mixing bowl) by particle-particle collisions.

Plough–Shear

The high-speed mixer is often referred to as a 'plough-shear' device, because of the unusual shape of the mixing paddles which rotate on an axial shaft in a cylindrical horizontal mixing chamber. These paddles cause the powder from all parts of the chamber to be thrown about in such a way that it all passes rapidly through a zone occupied by a series of rapidly revolving blades on a separate shaft, referred to as a 'chopper'. The chopper is largely responsible for the powder extension and may be switched on or off independently of the main axial drive.

Both types of mixer have been used as partial or complete replacement for the traditional blender-hammer mill combination. The plough-shear type may also be used for wet-processing.

MIXING PROCESSES INVOLVING FLUIDS

Although there are similarities between the flow of powders and the flow of liquids it is obviously easier to set up and sustain flow patterns in the latter. On the whole this makes the mixing processes easier to perform and a much larger variety of equipment is consequently available to choose from.

General principles of Fluid Mixing

Some mixing operations can be thought of as simple blending – for example, the blending of colour solutions into miscible bulk liquids and the blending of oils, alcohol and water in perfumes and colognes. On the other hand, the formation of an emulsion, the suspending of a gelling agent and the distribution of pigment agglomerates in a viscous liquid all involve the breaking up of one of the constituents of the mixture into finer particles during the mixing process. For this reason, it is referred to as 'dispersive' mixing to distinguish it from simple blending.

On the industrial scale, mixing occurs as the result of forced bulk flow within the mixing vessel. Two types of flow can be distinguished, laminar and turbulent. Laminar flow occurs when the fluid particles move along streamlines parallel to the direction of flow. The only mode of mass transfer is by molecular diffusion between adjacent layers of fluid (Brownian motion). In turbulent flow, the fluid elements move not only in the parallel paths but also on erratic and random paths, thus producing eddies which transfer matter from one layer to another. For this reason, turbulent mixing is rapid compared with other mixing mechanisms.

When a quiescent liquid is slowly stirred the flow is laminar but as the velocity increases it may become turbulent; thus the velocity is a significant factor in determining the type of flow set up in the mixing vessel. A valuable aid in describing the critical point at which laminar flow becomes turbulent is due to Reynolds who, in 1883, first demonstrated turbulence. The dimensionless number which bears his name, Re, can be calculated for agitated vessels as follows :

$$Re = \frac{D^2 N p}{\eta} \qquad 18.1$$

Where *D* is the diameter of the impeller, *N* the impeller speed (rpm), *p* the density of the mixture and h its viscosity.

Although little is known about the mechanism of turbulence, experience has shown that in agitated tanks the onset of turbulence occurs at Reynolds numbers of about 2×10^3. For fully developed turbulence, Reynolds numbers greater than 10^4 are required and are found in many cosmetic mixing processes. The majority of products exhibit non-ideal (non-Newtonian) behaviour which can often be more appropriately described by the expression

$$F = (\eta_{app})^n A \times \text{velocity gradient} \qquad 18.2$$

In this case η_{app} is termed as the 'apparent viscosity' and n usually has a value between 0 and 1. The name given to this type of behaviour is 'pseudoplastic' and the basic difference between materials exhibiting this property and ideal or 'Newtonian' fluids is illustrated in Figure. 18.2. As can be seen, pseudoplasticity is manifested by a fall in viscosity with increasing shear rate at constant temperature. Many cosmetic liquids exhibit this behaviour – especially emulsions and suspensions of particles of the order of 1 mm or less in size.

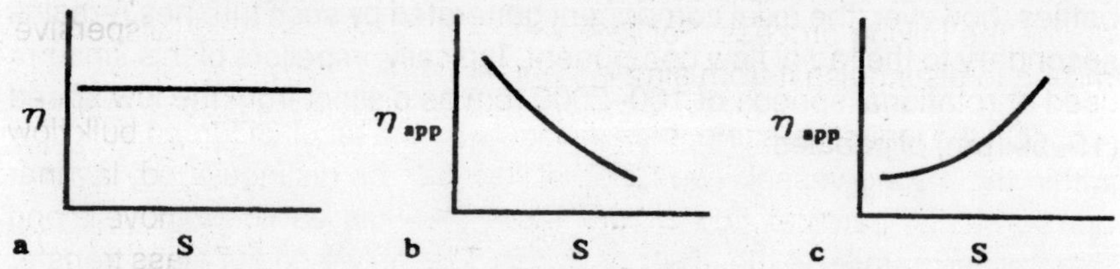

Fig. 18.2 Rate of shear (S) plotted against viscosity (η) or apparent viscosity (η_{app}).

Mixing Equipment for Fluids

In the mixing of fluids, all three mixing mechanisms – bulk flow, turbulent diffusion and molecular diffusion – are usually present. As viscosity increases, however, and turbulence becomes correspondingly more difficult to establish, the parts played by turbulent and molecular diffusion become less important.

Mixing equipment can therefore be divided into two categories, laminar shear and turbulent mixers.

Laminar shear/distributive mixers	*Turbulent mixers*
Helical screw/ribbon blenders	Turbine-agitated vessels
Two-blade mixers	Pipes
Kneaders	Jet mixers
Extrusion devices	Sparged systems
Calenders	High-speed shear mixers
Static mixers: low Re	Static mixers: high Re

Paddle mixers

Paddle mixers are simple and cheap but very inefficient for all but very low viscosity liquids. They produce mainly tangential flow and are usually mounted centrally because of their large diameter compared with that of the tank.

Turbines

Turbines are probably the most common impeller type used in cosmetic processing since they can cope with a wide range of viscosities and densities. For liquids of low viscosity, the flat-blade impeller is sometimes used Figs. 18.3 (a) and (b). For very viscous materials the blades may be curved backwards in the direction opposite to the rotation, since these require a lower starting torque and seem to give better energy transfer from impeller to liquid Fig 18.3 (c).

Fig. 18.3 (d) illustrates a fixed-pitch *axial flow* impeller. Used without baffles, however, the axial component generated by such turbines remains secondary to the radial flow component. Typically, impellers of this kind are used at rotational speeds of 100–2000 rpm as distinct from the low speed (15–50 rpm) of paddles.

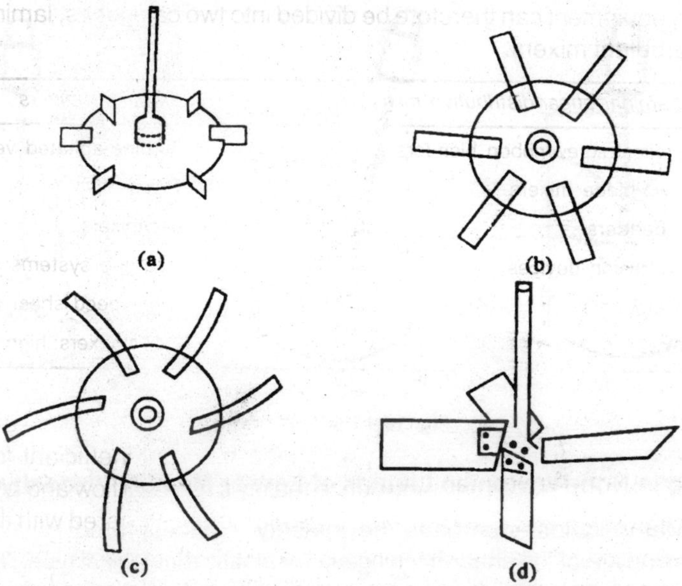

Fig. 18.3 Various designs of turbine impeller.

Propeller mixers

Propeller mixers are restricted to use with low viscosity fluids. They have pitched blades of which the blade angle varies along the length from centre to tip. Flow patterns developed by propeller mixers have a high axial component and the rate of circulation is high. They are usually of relatively small diameter, typically three-bladed, and are used at speeds between 450–2500 rpm. Such stirrers are used extensively in the cosmetics industry for simple blending operations but are not suitable for the suspension of particles which settle rapidly or for the dissolution of sparingly soluble heavier materials.

Many portable mixers are of the propeller type. If the mixer is mounted centrally in the mixing tank Fig. 18.4 (a), because of the entrainment of liquid above the impeller, the surface becomes depressed and a vortex is formed. Generally, vortices are to be avoided because of the low order of turbulence and the air-entrapment which they cause. When they are mounted eccentrically, however Fig. 18.4 (b) turbulence is increased and vortices avoided.

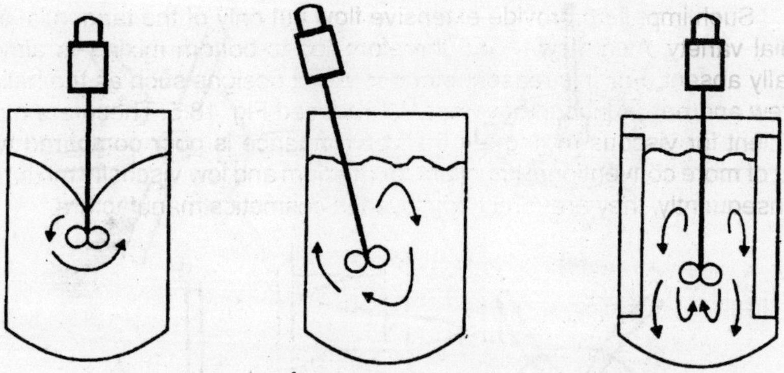

a b c

Fig. 18.4 Portable mixers

Mixing in Non-Newtonian Liquids of Low or Medium Viscosity

Many liquids – perhaps the majority – encountered in cosmetics processing are of the shear-thinning and/or elastic rheological type. Naturally, if the liquid is already of low viscosity, the effect of shear-thinning may not be noticeable. On the other hand, more viscous liquids showing these characteristics present considerable problems to the cosmetics processor. The fluid close to the rotating impeller of a mixer is sheared at a high rate and so becomes relatively mobile, but as this is pumped away from the impeller it encounters regions of less intense flow and hence of much higher viscosity. Turbulence is therefore rapidly damped out, decreasing the turnover in the vessel and slowing down the mixing process. Moreover any elasticity shown by the liquid results in the absorption of energy by deformation of a recoverable variety, thus damping out turbulence even further.

Impeller Types and Mixers for High Viscosity Fluids

Propellers and turbines, as already mentioned, work best under turbulent conditions at relatively high rotational speeds. In viscous products, given that such speeds are attainable at all, flow is confined to the regions very close to the impeller, and large stagnant regions in the mixer exist where no mixing can occur without the employment of some secondary mechanism. To eliminate these stagnant regions, large impellers such as paddles, gates, anchors and leaf impellers may be used; these sweep a much greater proportion of the vessel and produce more extensive flow. Usually such impellers are designed to have close clearances with walls, giving a degree of wall-scraping. This help to eliminate build-up of unmixed materials at walls provides a region of high shear for dispersing aggregates and lumps, and may improve the wall heat transfer to and from the bulk.

Such impellers provide extensive flow but only of the tangential and radial variety. Axial flow – and therefore top-to-bottom mixing–is almost totally absent. For this reason, more complex designs such as the helical screw and helical ribbon have been introduced Fig. 18.5. These are more efficient for viscous mixing but their performance is poor compared with that of more conventional impellers for medium and low viscosity mixtures. Consequently, they are rarely employed in cosmetics manufacture.

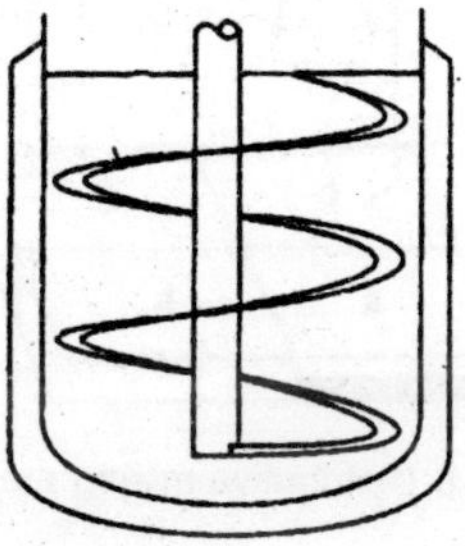

Fig. 18.5 Helical impeller

Axial flow cannot be achieved by the introduction of baffles as when mixing lower viscosity fluids, but some success has been achieved by the use of impeller-draught tube combinations. As the name implies a draught tube is a tubular, axially orientated enclosed space within the main mixing chamber containing an impeller or some other means of forcing the flow of mixture along it. Small impellers or helical screws designed to fill most of the cross-section of such a tube have been successfully used to promote axial flow in most liquids, even those of very high viscosity.

An alternative approach to the problem created by lack of flow in viscous media is the use of impellers which progressively sweep the whole contents of the vessel while the mixture remains stationary. Examples of this include the 'Nauta'-type mixer in which a helical screw sweeps the wall of a conical mixing chamber.

For even more viscous products such as mascara and very thick pastes, equipment which exhibits a greater degree of distributive mixing may be utilised. Such mixers are designed to produce bulk flow and laminar shear by spatial redistribution of elements of the mixture. Perhaps the most commonly encountered mixers of this type are of the single or double action planetary type or the two-blade 'dough' mixer. Their essential feature involves the cutting and folding of a volume of the mixture and the physical replacement of it into another part of the mixer where it is cut and folded again. An example of this distributive mechanism is illustrated in Fig. 18.6, in which for clarity a volume of a mixture has been isolated and divided into six equal segments, one of which consists of a black minor component. The cube is compressed to one quarter of its initial height, cut and reassembled as shown. Redistribution of the minor component has been achieved which, were the process to be repeated often enough, would eventually achieve the desired level of homogeneity.

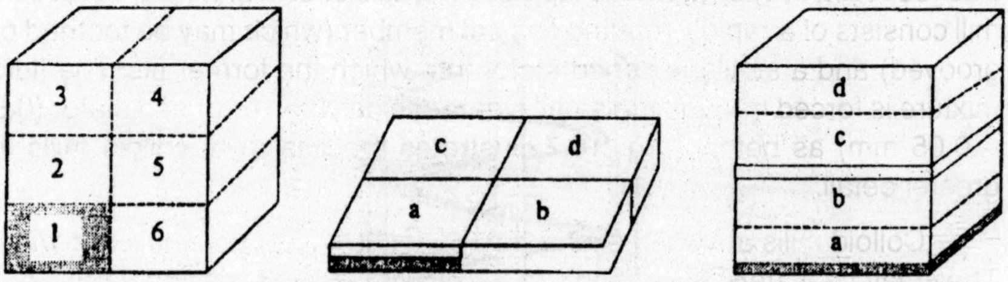

Fig. 18.6 Distributive mixing mechanism

A more recent innovation is the so-called static mixer, of which several designs are now commercially available. Static mixers are essentially in-line mixing devices in which mixtures flowing through a pipe are cut and folded by a series of helical elements in a circular tube Fig. 18.6. These elements (which do not move – hence the name 'static') turn the flowing mixture through an angle of 180°. since alternative elements have opposite pitch and are displaced 90° to each other, this causes the bulk flow to reverse direction at each junction, and thus the leading edge of each element becomes a cutting device, splitting ;and re-folding the mixture in on itself.

Finally, mention must be made of extruders, in which a helical screw forces the bulk mixture to flow down a tube. Here, the pressure generated can be enormous, as in soap-plodding, and such energy can cause materials with the viscosity of toilet soap to undergo laminar flow. The actual flow pattern produced is complex, being a combination of pressure and drag flow within the tube.

High Shear Mixers and Dispersion Equipment

Generally, a high shear rotor-stator mixer may be used either for batch processing all-enveloping chamber. Used as a batch mixer, it is capable of generating considerable turbulence because of the great velocity with which fluid is pumped out of the mixing head. As with other devices, however, this high energy is increasingly converted into heat with increasing viscosity of the mixture. A serious disadvantage for certain processes is the tendency of the mixer to cause aeration when used in the top-entry mode. For this reason such devices are often incorporated into the bottom of processing vessels.

Another high shear rotor-stator device in common use is the colloid or stone mill. Such equipment is commonly thought of as a comminution device; this serves to illustrate the fineness of the dividing line between mixing and comminution with high shear equipment. While it is true that colloid mills may be used for the comminution of very soft materials in a slurry, they find application in the cosmetics industry for the dispersion of pigments and the size reduction of internal phase droplets in emulsions. In principle, the colloid mill consists of a rapidly rotating conical member (which may be toothed or grooved) and a similarly coned stator into which the former fits. The fluid mixture is forced through the small clearance between rotor and stator (0.5 – 0.05 mm) as before. Fig. 18.7 illustrates the design of colloid mills in greater detail.

Colloid mills are used exclusively as an 'in-line' or continuous device. They may be water-cooled and can be adjusted as the moving parts wear down.

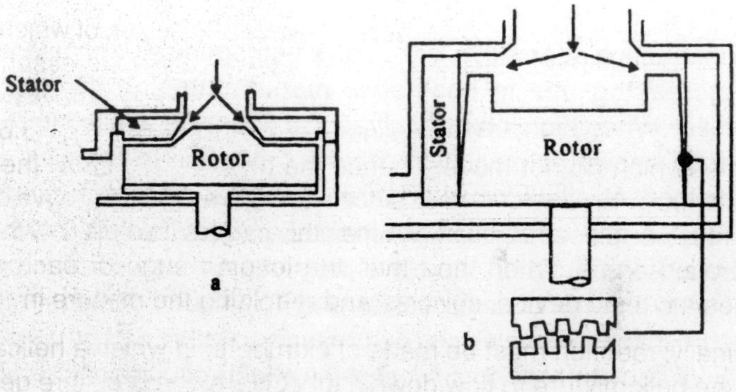

Fig. 18.7. Colloid mills (a) Stone (b) Toothed.

for more viscous products, an alternative device is the triple roll mill Fig. 18.8. The device consists of three steel rollers which rotate in the directions indicated in the diagram. Each roller is water-cooled and machined to great accuracy so that the gaps between each pair of rollers can be set very fine. The product is applied at the top of roller A, passes between A and B and round the underside of B between rollers B and C. As it traverses each gap, the product is subjected to enormous compression forces which are particularly effective in breaking down pigment agglomerates. Strictly speaking, therefore, the triple roll mill is not a high shear device but a compression device. It is included here, however, as a real alternative to the rotor-stator mixers in bringing about effective pigment dispersion in liquids – particularly in viscous liquids.

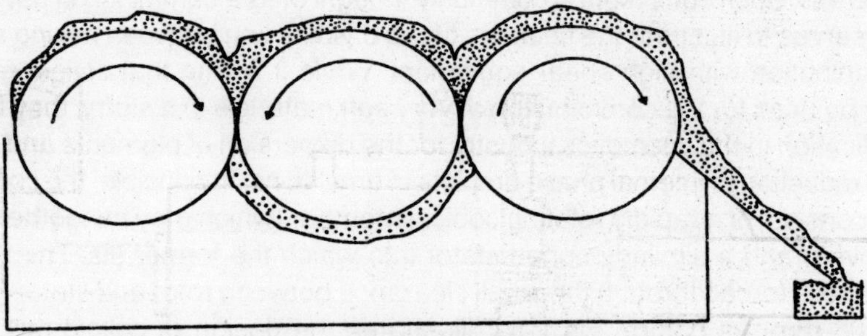

Fig. 18.8. Triple roller mill.

Perhaps the highest shear stress of all is generated by a valve homogeniser, which is still extensively used in the production of emulsions with very fine internal phase droplets.

An interesting alternative to the valve homogeniser, and one which is finding increasing use in cosmetics manufacture, is the ultrasonic homogeniser. When high intensity ultrasonic energy is applied to liquids, a phenomenon known as cavitation occurs. Cavitation is complex and not fully understood. As ultrasonic waves are propagated through the fluid, areas of compression and rarefaction are formed and cavities are produced in these rarefied areas. When the wave passes on, these cavities collapse and change to an area of compression and it has been demonstrated that the pressure in these cavities just before their collapse can be as much as several thousand atmospheres. Most of the effects of ultrasonic radiation in liquids are attributed to the powerful shock waves produced immediately following the collapse of such cavities. One design of ultrasonic homogeniser is illustrated in Fig. 18.9.

No description of dispersing equipment would be complete without mention of ball mills and sand mills. In both these devices the breakdown of agglomerates is achieved by attrition between rapidly moving grinding elements which take the form of pebbles, balls or (in the case of sandmills) finer sand-like particles < 1 mm diameter. The movement of these grinding particles may be achieved in a number of ways. In a tumbling mill, the elements tumble over each other as a horizontal drum is rotated on trunnions Fig. 18.10. Sand mills may be horizontal or vertical cylinders in which the grinding medium is stirred by a rotating agitator (Fig. 18.11), whereas in vibration mills movement of the whole chamber may be caused by eccentric cams, by out-of-balance weights on a drive shaft, or electrically.

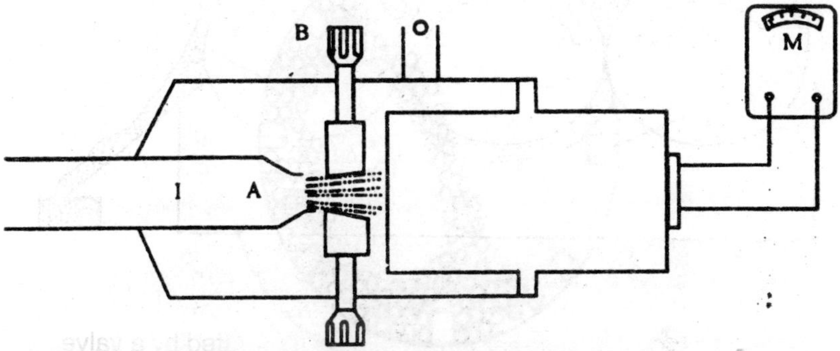

Fig. 18.9. Ultrasonic homogeniser.

The roughly premixed product enters at I and, on passing through orifice A, is subjected to intense ultrasonic energy by vibrating blade B. The treated product leaves via O. The meter, M, and 'tuning' devices at B combine to allow the operator to achieve maximum effect with each different product type.

Small ball mills and sand mills are used extensively in the dispersion of pigments into liquids (as, for example, in the production of castor oil lipstick pastes) and for the dispersion of bentone into nail varnish media. Although they are very effective, their chief disadvantage is the extremely protracted cleaning time required when changing from one colour to another. For this reason many users prefer to keep separate sets of grinding media for each different colour they wish to produce.

The basic mechanism by which mills of this kind produce their effect is attrition between grinding elements. Very little shear is developed.

SOLID-LIQUID MIXING

The production of a cosmetic product often involves the incorporation of a powdered solid material into a liquid. The objective may be to dissolve the powder completely (as with salt or preservatives in water), to effect a colloidal dispersion of water-swellable particles (as with bentones and other gelling agents) or simply the dispersion of insoluble materials such as pigments. To do this efficiently with a wide range of powder particle size and surface characteristics and with a range of different liquids of varying viscosity, quite a variety of mixing equipment is available.

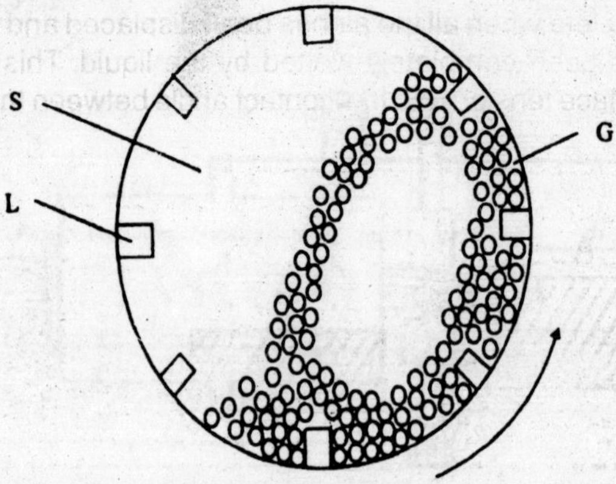

Fig. 18.10. Ball mill showing ball pattern in rotating drum. (G–Grinding medium; L–Lifter elements; S–Slurry).

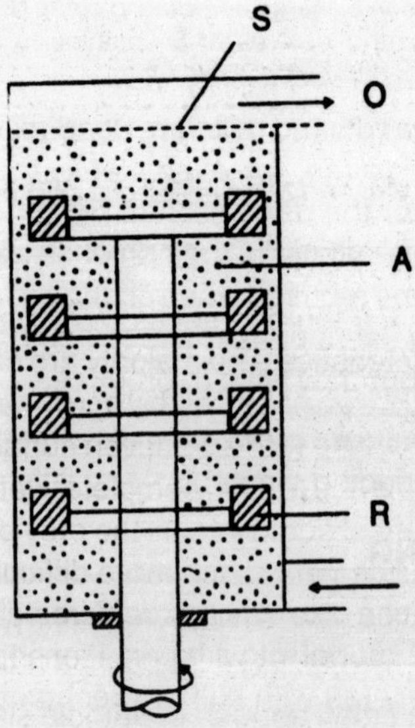

Fig. 18.11. Sand mill. (I-Slurry in; O-Slurry Out; S-Screen; R-Rotating agitator; A-Glass beads, sand or shot).

Perhaps the easiest of these processes to carry out is the dissolution of a fairly large size, smooth-faced solid, such as salt. The initial incorporation of each crystal into the liquid involves the complete replacement of the air-solid surface with a liquid-solid surface. This may be considered to be a three-stage process of adhesion, immersion and spreading Fig. 18.12. Immersion is complete when all the air has been displaced and the surface of the crystal has been completely wetted by the liquid. This process is aided by a low surface tension and low contact angle between the liquid and solid.

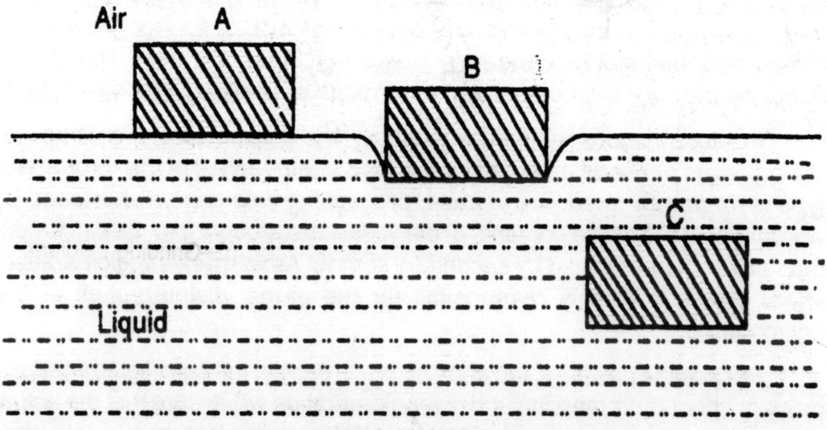

Fig. 18.12 Immersion of a solid in a liquid.

(A) Adhesion (B) Immersion (C) Spreading).

Not all powders used in cosmetics, however, have such favourable size and surface characteristics. The majority are of extremely small particle size and, as has already been noted, highly agglomerated. Each agglomerate will have a complex structure with an uneven surface and will be perforated by cavities of irregular shape. The complete wetting of such structures, involving the penetration of liquid into all the crevices and cavities together with the expulsion of air, is very much more difficult. It should be noted, for example, that penetration into cavities requires a low contact angle but a high surface tension – in conflict with conditions for easy wetting.

Powders that are small enough in particle size to form agglomerates are by far the most commonly used in cosmetics processing. In the dry state they entrap ;an enormous quantity of air (a bag of cosmetic-grade titanium dioxide, for example, contains only 25 per cent of powder together with 75 per cent of air). The majority of this air must be expelled if a smooth uniform mixture is to be obtained.

Immersion is only the first stage in the production of cosmetic quality dispersions. Even if the agglomerates were evenly distributed, the larger of them would give rise to 'grittiness'. Further, for pigments maximum colour can only be developed when these agglomerates are broken up and the maximum possible surface area of pigment is exposed. Disagglomeration is therefore the next step in the production process.

In cosmetic processes, the disagglomeration of solid particles in liquid media can be brought about by a variety of machines. In lipstick processing, for example, pigments are 'ground into' castor oil by preparing a coarse mixture which is then passed over a triple roll mill, or further ground in a colloid mill, ball mill or sand mill. These machines are used specifically because they will deal effectively with media of lipstick-paste viscosity.

For less viscous media (for example, the dispersion of pigments into the aqueous phase of an emulsion), a high shear device of the rotor-stator type is frequently used. In this case, processing time can be shortened by ensuring that the whole contents of the vessel are brought into the catchment area of the shearing head by secondary stirring. As with all disagglomeration, shear stress is largely responsible for the partial disintegration of the agglomerate.

For soluble powders, the enormous increase in the solid-liquid interface brought about by immersion and disagglomeration will ensure that the actual process of dissolution can proceed at the maximum possible rate. For insoluble powders, however, there remains the problem of maintaining a good stable dispersion.

Disagglomeration is usually a reversible phenomenon and it can usually be assumed that the opposite process–'flocculation'–will be simultaneously taking place.

It was noted when considering powder-powder dispersion that stabilisation could be achieved by the introduction of particles of larger size to which the disintegrated agglomerates could adhere. In some cases this can be applied to solid-liquid systems – for example, by pre-extending pigments onto talc before adding them to a liquid foundation base – but in many instances all the solid particles are of too small a size for this to be done. Under these circumstances rules similar to those used in emulsion technology can be applied. Thus the rate of flocculation can be slowed by some or all of the following means. :

1. The use of surface-active agents (sometimes as polymer coating of the powdered solid) to inhibit flocculation by steric hindrance.
2. The manipulation of electrostatic charges on the surface of the powder particles.
3. The manipulation of the viscosity of the dispersion.

Surface-active agents have a part to play at two stages in the process of manufacturing a stable dispersion. It has already been seen that the lowering of the solid-liquid contact angle speeds up the wetting process. In practice, the best results are often achieved not with a surfactant, which measurably lowers the surface tension of the liquid, but with what is sometimes described as a 'surface activator' which reduces the interfacial tension between solid and liquid. These surface activators (which are also described as 'dispersants' or 'wetting agents') can, if correctly chosen, cause an immediate improvement in the quality of the dispersion which is made manifest by a sudden increase in the colour intensity.

Suspension of Solids in agitated Tanks

If a particulate solid is dispersed in a liquid in which it does not dissolve and the suspension so formed is allowed to stand undisturbed in a vessel, provided that the densities of the two components are dissimilar some degree of settlement or flotation will eventually take place. Where the particles are present in sufficiently low concentration to have a negligible effect on the viscosity of the suspension, re-suspension can be achieved by the establishment in the liquid of flow patterns of sufficient turbulence. The suspension of solids in agitated tanks is frequently encountered in cosmetics processing, as an aid to dissolution or as a means of obtaining a good dispersion of particles prior to a change of viscosity of the liquid medium by gelling or cooling.

Three conditions can be recognised during the production of a suspension, namely complete suspension, homogeneous suspension and the ;formation of bottom or corner fillets.

Complete Suspension

Complete suspension exists when all particles are in motion and no particle remains stationary on the bottom or surface for more than a short period. Under these conditions, the whole surface of the particles is presented to the fluid, thereby ensuring the maximum area for dissolution or chemical reaction.

Homogeneous Suspension

Homogeneous suspension exists when the particle concentration and (for a range of sizes) the size distribution are the same throughout the tank. The homogeneous suspension speed is always considerably higher than 'complete suspension speed' and more difficult to achieve and to measure. Nevertheless, homogeneous suspension is very desirable for certain types of cosmetics applications and particularly so for continuous processing. In practice, for such processes the requirement is only that the particle size distribution and concentration in the discharge and the vessel are the same.

Sometimes heavier particles are allowed to collect in corners or on the bottom of the vessel in relatively stagnant regions to form *fillets.* This may have the practical advantage of very large saving in power consumption compared with the energy that may be needed to achieve complete suspension (provided, of course, that this saving offsets the loss of active solids in the fillets).

In general, it may be said that propeller or 45^0 - angle turbines offer the best advantage for rapid suspension for low power consumption – particularly if draught tubes are introduced. If, on the other hand, radial flow agitators need to be used, these should be of relatively large length-to-diameter ratio, be placed close to the bottom of the tank and have turbine blades extending to the shaft to prevent problems with central stagnant regions.

LIQUID-LIQUID MIXING

As indicated by Table 18.1, it is convenient to consider separately the case in which the liquid components are all mutually soluble and the case in which some or all of them can coexist as separate phases (that is to say, they are sparingly or partly soluble in each other).

Miscible Liquids

The mixing of miscible liquids (Blending) represents perhaps the simplest mixing operation in cosmetics manufacture. Several examples have already been cited and no further elaboration is needed except to reiterate that it is important to choose the mixing apparatus best suited to the viscosities of various components in order to carry out the operation efficiently.

Immiscible Liquids

Practically the only representatives of this category of mixing operation are emulsions. All cosmetic emulsions consist of two major immiscible liquids, one dispersed as fine droplets in the other and separated by a layer of surface-active agent at each liquid-liquid boundary.

The emulsification Process

The two major phases (these will be referred to as 'oil' and 'water') together with the emulsifier are brought together under turbulent conditions. Depending on the prevailing conditions, one major phase is broken up into droplets (predominantly by the action of shear stress imparted by turbulent eddies) and distributed throughout the other major ('continuous') phase.

While the droplets remain larger than the eddies, they will continue to break up into ever smaller droplets. Eventually a point is reached in this process when the available power giving rise to the turbulence cannot provide the shear stress necessary to reduce the droplet size any further. All this stage there exists an emulsion containing droplets of a certain mean diameter but over a range d_{min} to d_{max}. Provided that it is correctly chosen, the emulsifier prevents the rapid coalescence of these droplets and a stable emulsion is formed.

Orientation of Phases

In any emulsion the orientation of the phase (that is, whether the oil or the water phases is continuous) is determined principally by the choice of emulsifier and the volume ratio of oil to water. Usually, however, there is a range of volume ratio over which either phase may be dispersed, depending upon the method of manufacture. If a quiescent mixture of two phases coexisting as two simple layers (one upon the other) is agitated, the phase into which the agitator is placed is most likely to form the continuous phase in the resulting emulsion. In other words, drops are drawn into the phase in which the impeller is placed. If initially only one phase is present in the mixing vessel containing the impeller, an added second phase will inevitably form the disperse or discontinuous phase. If, however, the continued addition of the second phase combined with the choice of emulsifier eventually leads to a volume ratio at which the system is more stable with the added phase being continuous, then the emulsion will spontaneously invert to achieve this end result. When inversion takes place, it is very often accompanied by a change in droplet size. Where this change is a decrease, then inversion leads to a more stable emulsion and gives rise to a valuable method of manufacture.

Addition of Surfactant

In a batch manufacturing process for emulsions, there are four possible methods of adding the emulsifier. The first of these involves dissolving (or dispersing) the emulsifying agent in water, to which the oil is added. An oil-in-water emulsion is initially produced but inversion to water-in-oil may take place if more oil is needed.

Alternatively, the emulsifier may be added to the oil phase; the mixture may then be added directly to water to form an oil-in-water emulsion or water may be added to the mixture to form a water-in-oil emulsion. Many emulsions, on the other hand, are stabilised by soaps which are formed at the interface between the two phases. In this case, the fatty acid end of the soap is dissolved in the oil and the alkaline component is dissolved in the water. The two phases can be brought together in any order.

Finally, a less used method is one in which water and oil are added alternately to the emulsifying agent. Usually, the improvement in product quality obtained by the use of this method does not warrant the complication it causes in the manufacturing procedure.

Batch Processing Equipment

It will be evident from the discussion so far that there are at least two important elements of emulsion processing, namely shear (for the emulsification and particle size reduction process) and flow (in order to bring the whole contents of the vessel through the region of the high shear). Flow is also important in the heating and cooling of the emulsion. Most emulsion processing vessels are equipped with a jacket through which steam or hot water can be circulated to heat the contents and cold water circulated to cool them. Evidently then, to be effective, the mixing circulated to cool them. Evidently then, to be effective, the mixing mechanism must be able to provide adequate flow and from the vessel walls.

For these reasons, most emulsion batch processing vessels contain a high shear turbine or rotor-stator device (typically bottom or side entry rather than top entry, to decrease the likelihood of air entrapment) and a high flow, low shear mixing device which may be driven by a separate motor. This high flow device is of variable design, the most popular being a gate stirrer in which the arms are inclined at about 45° to the horizontal so as to give an element of axial flow. In more complicated designs, a central shaft carries more blades which sweep the area between the first set, the sets of blades rotating in opposite directions. Whatever the design, the frame holding the outer blades normally carries spring-loaded plastic scraper blades to prevent the build-up of product on the inner vessel wall, which would interfere with efficient heat exchange across the surface (Fig. 18.13).

The main motor may be driven electricity or by air (up to about 100 psi or 9 bar). The advantages of air-driven motors are that they are infinitely variable in speed, torque-sensitive (and therefore less likely to become damaged when subjected to sudden loads), they do not constitute a hazard in the processing of low flash-point materials and generally they require less maintenance. Electric motors can be built to match some of these advantages (with slipping clutches and flameproofing), but only at considerable expense.

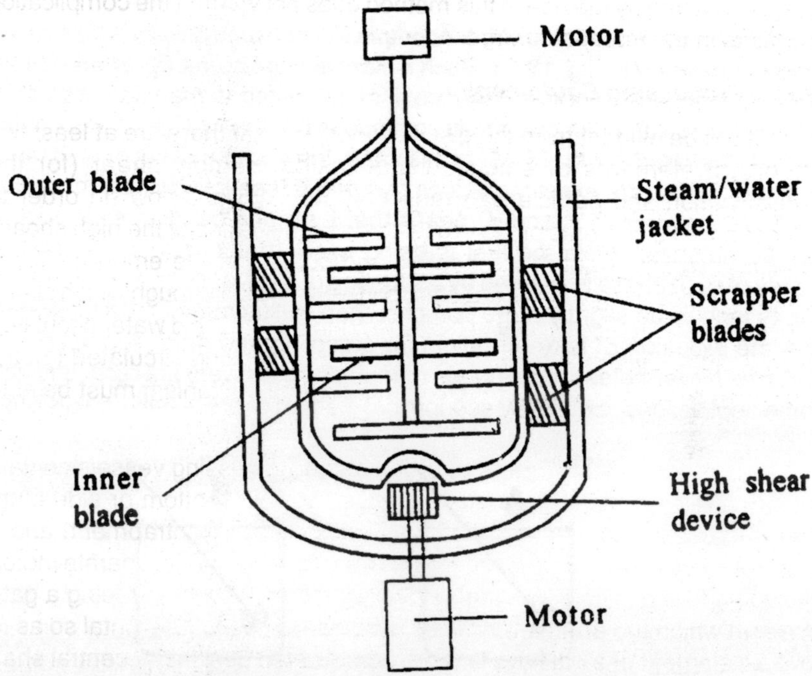

Fig. 18.13 Batch emulsion processing plant

This traditional gate-type impeller system suffers from the grave disadvantage of limited axial flow. This is not noticeable in smaller vessels (below 600 liters capacity) but becomes a major problem in large tanks. One approach to the problem is to provide top-to-bottom transfer for the contents by means of a pump and an external pipe. A more satisfactory arrangement for the manufacture of emulsions of medium and low viscosity is to replace the gate stirrer by one or more axial flow impellers mounted centrally on a single central shaft. Although it becomes more difficult to provide wall-scrapers, the excellent flow around the vessel walls makes scraping less necessary.

The problem of ensuring that all the product passes through the region of high shear has led to the idea of passing the batch through an external circuit containing an in-line homogeniser; this may be a rotor-stator device, colloid mill or valve homogeniser.

Continuous Processing

In view of the difficulties encountered in manufacturing large batches of emulsion, a logical extension of an external circuit with in-line homogeniser is a continuous processing plant. A simple form of such a plant is illustrated diagrammatically in Fig. 18.14. Such a plant is more correctly referred to as 'batch-continuous' since in essence a single batch is manufactured at a time. For long-run products, a truly continuous plant would be suitable, such as that illustrated in Fig. 18.15. In this case, the addition of second vessels A' and B' (which are exact duplicates of A and B respectively) together with the three-way valves V_1 and V_2 means that a second batch of each phase can be prepared while the first is being used. In this way, a continuous supply of each phase is assured by the turning of a valve. In reality, continuous plants tend to be slightly more complex than is illustrated in the diagrams with the inclusion of take-off points for sampling and other sophisticated features. Nevertheless, continuous manufacture is a very practical and, for some applications, extremely economical method of processing emulsions.

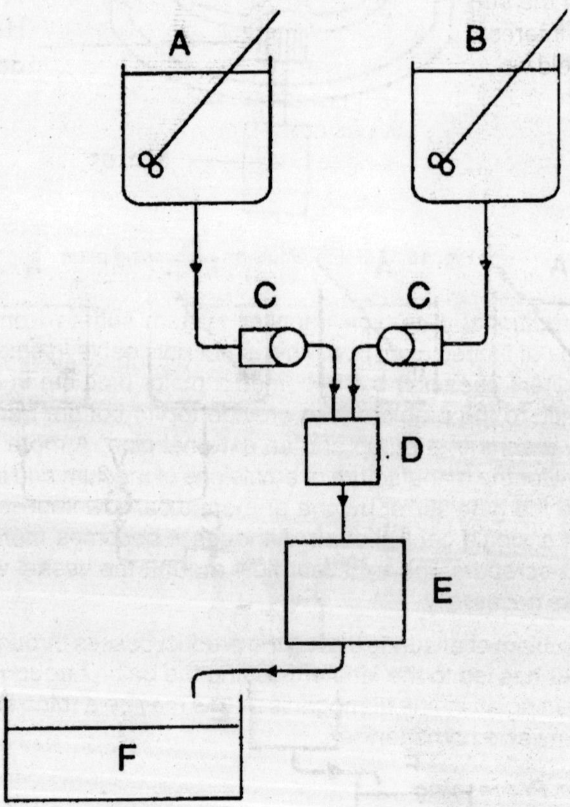

Fig. 18.14 Simple continuous-processing emulsion plant. (The two phases are prepared separately in tanks A and B, then pumped in correct proportions via metering pumps, C, into an in-line premixer, D (such as a static mixer), and then through a

homogeniser, E. Finally, the formed emulsion is pumped into F, which may be a storage tank or the hopper of a filling vessel. A heat exchanger can be incorporated between E and F for rapid cooling.)

Emulsion Temperature

The primary reason for raising the temperature of the phases during emulsion manufacture is to ensure that both are in the liquid state. In particular, the oil phase may contain fats and waxes that are solid at room temperature; there is very little point in raising the temperature of the oil phase much above that at which these liquefy. Excessive heating of the phases during manufacture prolongs the manufacturing time and wastes energy.

If the water phase is liquid at room temperature, it is customarily heated to approximately 5°C above the temperature chosen for the oil phase (so as not to cause the sudden solidification of the latter on blending). There is, however, an interesting alternative – namely, emulsification between hot oil phase and cold water phase. The plant for this procedure is illustrated in Fig. 18.16, which shows that mixing of the phases and homogenisation take place simultaneously. The obvious advantage of such a method is the saving of time and energy in not having to heat the aqueous phase.

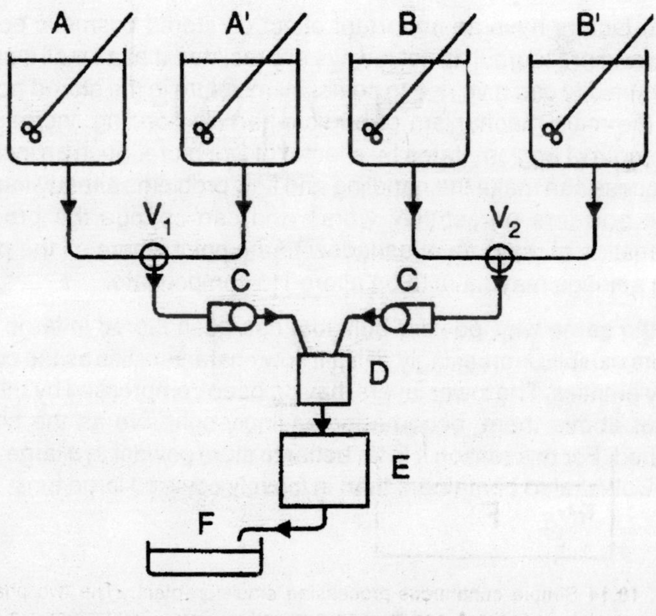

Fig. 18.15 Continuous-processing emulsion plant for long-run products.

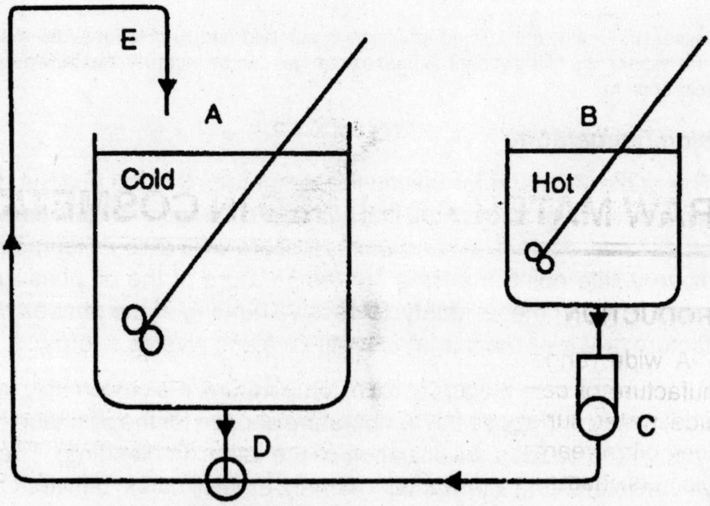

Fig. 18.16 Hot/Cold processing emulsion plant.

(The hot oil phase from tank A and the cold water phase from tank B are pumped into an in-line homogeniser at D and thence into the main tank B at E).

Storage of Cosmetic powders

Two factors have an important effect on stored cosmetic powders : moisture and pressure. It is not always appreciated that a small increase in relative humidity can give rise to sufficient moisture in the stored powder to change the main mechanism of particle-particle bonding, increasing the bond strength of agglomerates by a factor of 2 or more. Such an increase in cohesiveness can make the handling and flow problems already inherent in cosmetic powders perceptibly worse and can change the processing characteristics of (say) an eyeshadow to the point where all the pressing machine settings may have to be altered to compensate.

In the same way, powder bulk that has been stored in large vertical containers exhibits increasingly difficult flow characteristics as the container gradually empties. The lower layers, having been compressed by the weight of powder above them, become increasingly cohesive as the bottom is approached. For this reason it is far better to store powder in a large number of small well-sealed containers than in loosely covered large bins.

Chapter - 2

RAW MATERIALS USED IN COSMETICS

INTRODUCTION

A wide range of chemical and natural materials are used in the manufacture of cosmetics. Some of the most commonly used materials include; water, surfactants, shampoos and bath additives, oil components, silicone oils, cream bases, oil-in-water (o/w) emulsifiers, water-in-oil (w/o) emulsifiers, humectants, aerosol propellants, antioxidants, colours and perfumes.

Water

Water is highly reactive substance. In biochemical process, oxidation, reduction, condensation, and hydrolysis occurs. The water is also used as solvent for many ingredients of cosmetics. The water is always associated with many impurities hence it is purified by techniques such as, ion-exchange process, distillation, reverse osmosis, microbial technique, uv-radiation and filtration.

Surfactants

Surfactants are surface active agents which reduces the surface tension of the liquids. Anionic, cationic and non-ionic surfactants are used in cosmetics and toiletries due to their balanced properties. They are excellent foamers. The basic or primary surfactants are the backbone of the cleansing products. They include alkyl ether sulphates, linear alkyl benzene and alkane sulphonates. Mild anionic surfactants are sulphosuccinates, cocoyl isethionates, acyl amides, alkyl; ether carboxylates, and magnesium surfactants. Amphoteric surfactants include, alkyl betaines alkyl amide betaines, amine oxides, and ethoxylated products, alkyl polyglycosides are non-ionic surfactants. The list of cationic surfactants include monoalkyl, dialkyl, trialkyl, benzyl and ethoxylated quaternaries.

SHAMPOO AND BATH ADDITIVES

Thickeners

A high viscosity is often very important both for product stability and for handling of a cosmetic product. A different principle of thickening is obtained by the use of special, high molecular weight thickeners such as distearate, myristy; glycol methy; glucose dioleate. A side-effect of all these thickeners is that they modify the flow properties, leading to increased Newtonian flow. This contrasts with salt-or polymer-thickened systems, which show typically pseudoplastic flow behaviour. Another type of rheological modifier is the inorganic bentonites, which can be used to obtain a yield point.

Foam Stabilisers

The stability of shampoo foam is reduced in the presence of oily soils such as sebum. The so-called foam boosters act as stabilisers and also modify the foam structure to give a richer, dense foam with small bubbles e.g. monoethanolamides, diethanolamides.

Pearlescent agents

Ethylene glycol mono-and distearates (EGMS, EGDS) are most often used as pearlescent agents in surfactant formulations. They have to be incorporated at high temperatures (approx. 70–75°C). Direct contact with perfume oils can result in coagulation of the polystyrol, and must be avoided.

Conditioning Agents

The addition of conditioning agents improves the wet-combability and reduction of static charge build-up. These are especially effective if the formulation also contains amphoteric surfactants such as betaines or amines oxides. Cationic surfactants used in hair rinses are normally incompatible with anionic surfactants and cannot be used in shampoo formulations. This problem can be overcome by the use of quaternised polymers.

Emollients

Emollients are added to overcome possible harsh effects of shower and foam baths on the skin. Real lipids like isopropyl; myristate are difficult to incorporate due to their limited solubility in water-based formulations. Water-soluble lipids, which still have a certain lipophilic character can be obtained by ethoxylation to HLB of approx. 6 to 8. They do not interfere with the foaming of the surfactants.

Sequestering Agents

Sequestering agents are used to prevent the formation and deposition of Ca and Mg soaps. Hard water along with these agents can be used for the production of shampoo and bath preparations. As a positive side-effect they can also give support to the preservation system.

Oil Components

Mineral Oil

Mineral oils for cosmetic use are high-boiling fractions obtained from crude oil distribution that are purified and refined by treatment with sulphuric acid. Two types are of importance: (i) liquid paraffin (viscosity 110 to 230 mPas); and (ii) light liquid paraffin (viscosity 25 to 80 mPas). Mineral oils are colourless, clear and odourless liquids, insoluble in alcohol or water. They are excellent cosmetic emollients because they are inert and do not penetrate into the skin. They therefore have excellent skin compatibility and little or no comedogenic potential. Since they are not considered 'natural', mineral oils have been attacked repeatedly but are still the most widely used oil component in skin-care formulations.

The fatty character of mineral oils help to form a film on the skin which increases hydration by blocking the normal evaporation of water. Combinations with synthetic esters such as isopropyl stearate are recommended in order to open the film, and to guarantee the right balance for water evaporation.

Natural Oils

Triglycerides

Natural oils from vegetable sources are mainly glycerol esters based on mixtures of fatty acids. The most important are the saturated lauric, myristic, palmitic and stearic acids and the unsaturated oleic and linoleic acids. These fatty acids are derived from natural sources and typically have even numbers of carbon atoms in their chains.

Important characteristic values for triglycerides are the saponification number and the iodine number. The latter indicates the amount of unsaturated fatty acids present.

Triglycerides are relatively fatty and spread very little on the skin. They generally show moderate comedogenicity, exceptions being sunflower oil and safflower oil where no comedogenic effects have been found. Castor oil is used in lipsticks and also in alcoholic preparations.

Jojoba oil

It is a liquid, unsaturated wax from the esters of long carbon-chain fatty acids and long carbon-chain unsaturated alcohols. Jojoba oil has a very fatty character and shows excellent cosmetic properties.

Synthetic Oils

Synthetic oils are esters, usually obtained by direct reaction of fatty acids with alcohols. A wide range of combinations to produce different synthetic esters is possible, and the list of synthetic oils available to the cosmetic industry is long.

Isopropyl Esters

The most important synthetic ester for cosmetics is isopropyl myrisate. It has a very dry character and shows good spreading on the skin. It can open films of mineral oil or other fatty oils in order to let water evaporate, and it is an excellent solvent for perfumes, ultraviolet filters, etc. The isopropyl esters can cause difficulties when used in formulations that are filled into polystyrene or polyethylene containers since it is good solvent.

Ethylhexyl Esters

Ethylhexyl esters of palmitic acid have become important products for the cosmetic industry. Compared with isopropyl esters, the molecular weight is higher, but spreading properties are similar.

Oleic Acid Esters

The two most important oleates are decyl oleate and oleyl oleate. The character of these esters is relatively fatty and, as with unsaturated esters, they can become rancid. The advantage of the oleates is that, even at high molecular weight, the esters are liquid.

Caprylic/Capric Acid Esters

The most important caprylic/capric esters are the triglyceride and the propylene glycol diester. The glycerol ester is mainly used as a replacement for natural triglycerides, with the advantage that it is stable against oxidation.

N-Butyl Stearate

N-butyl stearate is an excellent skin-compatible ester with very good emollience. The character is not very fatty compared with the isopropyl esters.

Isocetyl Stearate

Isocetyl stearate is a saturated liquid ester of high molecular weight and good emollience. Water can evaporate easily through the ester and even small amounts can perforate a hydrophobic film of mineral oil.

Octyldodecanol

Octyldodecanol is not an ester but may be used as a cosmetic oil component. It combines a fatty character with good spreading properties.

Di-Isopropyl Adipate

Di-isopropyl adipate is an ester of a dicarbonic acid. Contrary to most other oils, it is soluble in alcohol and is therefore used, for example, as a refatting agent in aftershave formulations.

Pentaerythritol Tetraisostearate

Pentaerythritol tetraisostearate is a high molecular weight, highly branched ester of pentaerythritol and isostearic acid. It has a very fatty character and shows no comedogenic effects. Consequently, it is an ideal ester for skin-protection formulations such as baby products and, due to its water-repellent properties, water-resistant suntan preparations.

WAXES

The word wax has two different meanings. From a chemical point of view it means an ester of a fatty acid and a fatty alcohol. Jojoba oil is therefore a liquid wax. In this section, however, the word wax is considered from a physical point of view, and means compounds having a high melting point (approx. 50–100°C).

Natural Waxes

The most important wax, and a classical component for creams, is beeswax, which is the construction material of honeycombs. Chemically, it consists of mixed esters of long-chain alcohols plus fatty acids and hydroxy fatty acids of chain length of 16–26. At room temperature the beeswax is very hard. The melting point is around 61 to 66°C. Untreated beeswax is dark-yellow and is usually treated to improve the colour.

Beeswax is a very good consistency regulator in creams and ointments and is also used in stick formulations. The addition of approx. 6 per cent of borax, calculated on the beeswax, results in partial saponification and provides the beeswax with some emulsifying properties.

Two other natural waxes that are harder and therefore mainly used in stick formulations are carnauba wax (melting point approx. 85°C) and candelilla wax (melting point approx. 70°C).

Synthetic Waxes

These are often mixtures of different chemicals. An example of a beeswax replacement is the mixture of glyceryl hydroxystearate (and) cetyl palmitate (and) micro-crystalline wax (and) trihydroxy stearine. This product, which shows very similar behaviour compared with beeswax, is easy to emulsify and can be used as a general consistency regulator for cosmetic emulsions.

Silicone Oils

The high molecular weight organo polysiloxanes (dimethicone) are hydrophobic oils with good skin protection and non-sticky skin-feel. They show very high spreading and are used in small amounts in stearate creams to avoid the soap-up effect. To prevent eye-sting, non-volatile oils should not be used in products that are applied to the eye area. Due to their water-repellent properties, silicone oils are important for waterproof sun products. They are usually classified by viscosity.

CREAM BASES

Fatty Alcohols

Fatty alcohols are important raw materials for surfactants, emollients and emulsifiers. Pure fatty alcohols, mainly cetyl alcohol and stearyl alcohol, are also used *per se* as consistency regulators and co-emulsifiers in creams, lotions and hair rinses. The so-called natural fatty alcohols are obtained by hydration of fatty acid methyl esters.

Polyol Esters

The most important polyol ester is glycerol monostearate (GMS). Generally, it is not a pure product but a mixture of mono-and diesters of stearic and palmitic acids. The main distinguishing feature is the content of monoester. Products with approx. 40% monoester are obtained by direct esterification of stearic acid and glycerol. Products with approx. 60% monoester are produced by glycerolysis of triglycerides with glycerol. The 90% material can be obtained by molecular distillation but is seldom used in cosmetic formulations because the mono/diesters provide the best applicational properties. Typical combinations are :

1. GMS plus potassium stearate ('GMS self-emulsifying')
2. GMS plus sodium lauryl sulphate
3. GMS plus ethoxylated fatty alcohols ('GMS self-emulsifying, acid stable')

Fatty Acids

Fatty acids, like the fatty alcohols, are important raw materials for cosmetic ingredients such as surfactants, emulsifiers and emollients. They are seldom used in emulsions. They act as consistency regulators but tend to crystallise in the formulation.

Fatty acids especially stearic acids, are mainly used in the form of soaps. As the pH increases, they become truly anionic and at as oil-in-water (O/W) emulsifiers, forming a group of so-called stearate creams.

OIL-IN-WATER (O/W) EMULSIFIERS

Anionic O/W Emulsifiers

Anionic O/W emulsifiers can be used to obtain very stable emulsions because they can build an electrical double layer around the droplets, which prevents the droplets from coalescing. On the other hand, anionic emulsifiers are sensitive to low pH and electrolytes.

The most important anionic O/W emulsifier is soap, which forms the stearate creams. The use of triethanolamine as a neutralising agent is more comon. A disadvantage of stearic acid is the typical 'soap-up' effect, a type of foaming that occurs when the cream is rubbed into the skin. To prevent this, silicone oil is frequently added to the formulations.

Other very effective anionic emulsifiers are alkyl sulphates, particularly sodium cetearyl sulphate. In principle, all anionic surfactants can be used. However, due to the fact that the soaps are relatively alkaline and fatty alcohol sulphates are irritant to the skin, the mild surfactants are of more interest. These include sodium cocoyl isethionate as an extremely mild emulsifier, and phosphoric acid esters, like potassium cetyl phosphate which are very effective at low concentrations.

Cationic O/W Emulsifiers

Cationic emulsifiers have generally been avoidea in skin-care products because they are often more irritant compared with anionic emulsifiers. They are important in hair-care formulations, where they act as conditioners and anti-static agents. Their advantage, particularly distearylammonium chloride, is that they produce emulsified products with excellent cushion feel on skin and mitigate the heavy feel imported by glycerine.

Non-Ionic O/W Emulsifiers

A wealth of non-ionic O/W emulsifiers is available. These are mainly PEG derivatives such as ethoxylates or PEG esters. Typical O/W emulsifiers are :

1. Ethoxylated fatty alcohol
2. PEG esters of fatty acids
3. Ethoxylated sorbitan esters
4. Ethoxylated monoglycerides
5. Ethoxylated castor-oil derivatives

The degree of ethoxylation determines the primary properties of that part of the molecule that results in the HLB classification. Good O/W emulsifiers can be found in the HLB range between 8 and 18. However, the type of hydrophobic moiety is also very important for the stability of the emulsions. Contrary to anionic emulsifiers, the non-ionics are unaffected by changes in pH and, in the case of pure ethers, they can also be used at extreme pH values.

O/W Stabilisers

Carbomers are very efficient and widely used stabilisers for O/W emulsions. These are polyacrylate resins which have to be neutralised in order to form gels, usually by the use of triethanolamine (TEA). Amounts up to 0.5% are recommended for cosmetic emulsions. Too much can leave an unpleasant feel on the skin. The principle of stabilisation is the thickening of the outer phase. The use of preneutralised copolymers, e.g., acrylamide/ sodium acrylate copolymer can make incorporation and handling easier.

WATER-IN-OIL (W/O) EMULSIFIERS

From the dermatological point of view, W/O emulsions are preferable to O/W emulsions. The natural lipid film on the skin is also a W/O emulsion. W/O emulsions can improve the hydration of the skin and are an ideal base for lipid-soluble active ingredients. A problematic point is that they usually leave a 'fatty-feeling' on the skin, and this is not particularly appreciated by customers. Another problem can be 'oiling-off' or separation of the oil phase on storage. Viscosity and stability are extremely process sensitive.

Single W/O Emulsifiers

A limited number of W/O emulsifiers are available. This is because ionic emulsifiers will not work in the case of W/O emulsions and, since very low HLB is required, variations using ethylene oxide are not possible. W/O emulsifiers have HLB values between 3 and 6. However, the type of the alkyl chain is also important. In practice, oleyl derivatives have shown good effects. The most widely used W/O emulsifiers are sorbitan monooleate, sorbitan sesquioleate and glycerol monooleate, and with increasing importance, polyglycerol esters.

Lanolin Derivatives

Lanolin or wool wax obtained from sheep wool is a mixture of different esters from higher alcohols, mainly cholesterol, with higher fatty acids. Since lanolin can cause allergies, lanolin alcohols extracted after saponification of the wool wax are now mainly used. Due to the high amount of cholesterol, they are better emulsifiers than lanolin itself.

Absorption Bases

Since it is relatively difficult to obtain stable W/O systems, pre-mixtures, which are able to bind high amounts of water are available. Relatively simple absorption bases are, for example, mineral oil (and) lanolin alcohol or petrolatum (and) lanolin alcohol. Very complex systems are also offered and include petrolatum (and) decyl oleate (and) sorbitan sesquioleate (and) beeswax (and) mineral oil (and) ceresin (and) aluminum stearate, or mineral oil (and) petrolatum (and) ozokerite (and) glycerol oleate (and) lanolin alcohol. Using these premixtures it is relatively simple to obtain stable emulsions, although the resulting emulsion often behaves more like an ointment than a cosmetic product.

W/O Stabilisers

The stable W/O emulsion is obtained using block copolymer like dodecyl glycol. These products, with molecular weights of 2000 to 4000, can improve the stability of W/O emulsions by protection of the droplets from coalescence. The hydrophilic middle part is responsible for a good anchorage in the water phase, while the highly branched ends give a steric hindering effect. The high molecular weight imparts excellent skin compatibility. These co-polymers typically reduce the viscosity. It is possible to obtain light, highly stable W/O lotions that are good bases for sun preparations and which give a skin-feel very close to emulsions.

HUMECTANTS

Humectants protect emulsions or toothpaste from 'drying-up'. The most important humectants are glycerol, obtained from saponification of triglycerides, and sorbitol, a hexa-alcohol. Sorbitol is a hygroscopic powder but is most often used in the form of a 70% aqueous solution. Glycerol is typically used at 99% with a density of 1.26 or at 85% with a density of 1.22. Both are non-toxic and have a sweet taste, which makes them ideal for the use in toothpastes.

Other humectants for emulsions are lactates, 1,3-butylene glycol and 1.2-proplene glycol. The latter should be of high quality as it has occasionally been implied as a skin irritant. A positive side-effect of humectants is a reduction of the freezing point. Humectants are also important in moisturising products.

AEROSOL PROPELLANTS

The fluoro-carbons were popular aerosol propellants however, it is banned due to reduction in ozone layer. Hydrocarbons and dimethyl ether are used now-a-days.

Hydrocarbons

The hydrocarbon propellants are propane (freezing point – 42.1), *n*-butane (freezing point – 0.5) and isobutane (freezing point – 11.7). Commercial butane is always a mixture of *n*-butane and isobutane. Propane mixtures with different rations are usually used to adjust the pressure. Hydrocarbons are cheap, stable and of low toxicity, but are highly flammable.

Dimethyl ether

Dimethyl ether (DME) has been known as a propellant and, it is a gas (freezing point – 24.8) with a vapour pressure of 4.2 bar at 20°C. It shows very low toxicity and does not damage the ozone layer. Like hydrocarbons it is inflammable, but unlike hydrocarbons it is miscible with water. This can reduce or prevent the risk of flammability of DME aerosol sprays, since 6% water can be solved in DME, or 34% DME can be solved in water. Alcohol/DME mixtures are good solvents for PVP/PVA resins for hair sprays, whereas hydrocarbon propellants are difficult to use in this field.

ANTIOXIDANTS

Cosmetic preparations containing fats and oils particularly those have unsaturated linkage are susceptible to oxidative deterioration. Even a very small quantity of highly unsaturated ingredient is sufficient to start a typical oxidative deterioration. Some of the most commonly used antioxidants are:

1. Phenolic Type
2. Quinone Type
3. Amine Type
4. Organic acids, alcohols and esters
5. Inorganic acids and their salts

Selection of Antioxidant

The selection of antioxidant depends on the following :

1. The Nature of the fat/or oil present as ingredient of cosmetics
2. The physical form of cosmetic
3. pH of cosmetics
4. Intended use of cosmetics
5. Expected shell life of cosmetics
6. Conditions of storage of cosmetics

An ideal antioxidant would be one which is stable and effective over a wide range of pH and is soluble in its oxidised form. The reaction products of antioxidant should be colourless and odourless.

COLOURS

Colours have been used in cosmetics from the very beginning. Basically a desire to buy a cosmetic product is controlled by three senses, namely, sight, touch and smell. As such colour is an important ingredient of cosmetic formulation.

Colours which can be used in cosmetics can be classified into three classes: (i) Natural Colours; (ii) Inorganic Colours; and (iii) Coal tar Colours.

Natural Colours

Some of the important natural colours used are :

Cochineal

Cochineal is a red dye stuff.

Saffron

Saffron is dried stigma of flowers of plant.

Chlorophyll

Chlorophyll occurs abundantly in nature. Green colour to leaves is imparted by chlorophyll. Chlorophyll can be extracted from plant leaves.

Inorganic Colours

A number of inorganic colour pigments which are used in cosmetics are : Iron oxides, chromium oxides, ultramarines, carbon black, titanium dioxide, zinc oxide, aluminium hydrate.

PERFUMES

There may be only few types of cosmetics which may not contain perfume. A perfumer blends a number of natural and synthetic materials to make a perfume. This mixture is usually known as perfume compound. These blends may contain two or three materials (which is very rare) or may contain many (about dozen or more) materials. Raw materials of perfume compound can be classified as : Plant oil, Animal Secretions, Chemical Substances.

Plant Oil

Plant oil may be essential oils, flowers oils or resins, gums etc.

Animal Secretion

Many animals secrete odourous materials. Some of the materials of importance are : Musk, Civet, Ambergris and Castoreum.

Chemical Substances

The chemical substances used in perfumes and cosmetics may be isolates from plants. There are certain chemical substances which are derived from either isolates or essential oils, by chemical reactions. Examples of such substances are : esters, geraniol, terpineol. The other synthetic materials may be those which occur in nature, e.g., phenylalcohol, (found in jasmine oil) or those which do not occur in nature.

Chapter - 3

PACKAGING OF COSMETICS PRODUCTS

INTRODUCTION

The packaging of any product and cosmetics have same principle. However, in case of cosmetics for successful marketing more importance is given to package design and development.

Packaging utilises a wide variety of materials such as plastics, glass, paper, board, metal and wood combined with wide range of technologies including printing, machinery design and tool making.

Packaging has been defined as the means of ensuring the safe delivery of a product to the ultimate consumer, in sound condition at the minimum overall cost. Other definitions are :

1. Packaging is the art or science of, and the operations involved in, the preparations of articles or commodities for carriage, storage and delivery to the customer.
2. Packaging sells what it protects and protects what it sells.

PRINCIPLES OF PACKAGING

Packaging must contain the product, restrain the product, protect the product, identify the product, sell the product and give information about the product, and do this within a cost related to the marketing, profit,margin, selling price and image of the product.

Marketing and Packaging

The package projects the style and image, not only of the product, but often of the company which markets the brand. The pack must therefore project the image that it has been designed for, not only to the customer through advertising and point of sale but also to the retailer and wholesaler chain.

Packaging is particularly important in the self-service retail trade. The package designer has a responsibility to ensure not only that the pack has the type of appeal that will make the customer pick it up and be encouraged to purchase on impulse, but also to ensure that the pack will stack on self-service shelves and give the retailer the maximum profit per linear unit of shelf space.

Advertising has ensured that the package is now more widely seen than ever before. With the predominance of colour in advertising – in television, cinema and press advertisements and on posters – the package must be made of materials that have good aesthetic appeal and which will take the hold colour.

TECHNOLOGY AND COMPONENTS

Plastics

The use of plastics for producing primary components and point-of-sale material now dominates packaging technology. Two main groups are used–thermoplastic resins and thermosetting resins. Thermoplastics can be extruded at their melt temperature and then blow moulded or injection moulded. After cooling, the resin can be remelted by heating to the limits of thermal fatigue and oxidation. Thermosetting resins, by contrast, are moulded using an irreversible chemical reaction and the resins tend to be rigid, hard, insoluble and unaffected by heat up to decomposition temperature.

Metals

Metals are suited in cosmetics packaging are aerosol containers, powder dispensers, shallow tins and collapsible tubes. Tin plate is the most commonly used metal for the rigid packs, although aluminium also finds widespread use. The impervious nature of the metal gives me collapsible tube the great advantages of reduced risk of contamination of the product and reduced losses of volatile materials from the contents.

Laminates

The various requirements of packages for cosmetics and toiletries (such as attractive appearance; impermeability to water and volatile oils) are not always available from a single material. In such case the use of composite material in laminar form can be made. Laminates have found particular application in the production of sachets and of collapsible tubes as alternatives to pure metal tubes for toothpastes.

Laminates are used for *flat sachets* that are heat sealed around the periphery (as distinct from the fatter *pillow sachets* which are made from PVC tube and sealed ultrasonically). The laminate must be able to withstand the pressure of the contained product and provide leak-proof seals.

Glass

Glass containers are still used widely in the toiletries industry by virtue of the basic packaging characteristics of glass. Glass is chemically very inert and generally will not react with or contaminate high quality cosmetic and perfume products. Glass is manufactured in many different formulations but the most common in packaging is soda lime glass.

Paper and Board

Practically every cosmetic and toiletry products uses paper or paperboard in some form. Many grades of paper and board are available. Uses of paper and board in cosmetics packaging include labels, leaflets, corrugated cases, printed cartons and soap wraps.

Printing and Decoration

All packaging components can be printed to give a wide range of decorative effects. Different processes are used depending on the application. The five main processes used in the printing of packaging components are screen printing, letter press, flexographics, offset lithography and gravure printing.

Package Development And Design

Package development has the aim of increased sales and profit through the correct design of the package. Packaging must be considered as early as possible in the development of a new product to allow time to ensure that pack and product are compatible. The development process begins with a detailed analysis of the product so that a pack can be designed to give protection. Finally, in the development of the package the environmental aspects of the pack should be considered in terms of disposability and litter. It should also consider the re-use of scarce raw materials.

Technical Aspects of Design

The packaging material must be sufficiently strong to survive any treatment that it is liable to receive from the time to first delivery at a factory, through to filling, distribution, sale and actual use. It is essential that failure rate due to accident must be very low. Hence very strict testing and quality control of packs is essential in a factory producing toiletries or cosmetics.

A pack must be attractive to the consumer and contain the product in an efficient manner and render the product available as soon as the consumer desires to use it.

Closures

Unless it has an efficient closure, container has no value. Ideally the closure should be easy to remove and replace. However, it should give a seal that prevents the diffusion of gases and vapours and the seepage of liquids. Many bottle and tube closures consist of a screw cap containing a compressible wad. But wadless closures–achieved by new designs of thermoplastics screw and snap–on–are now extensively used for liquid products such as shampoos and hair conditioners.

PACKAGE TESTING AND COMPATIBILITY

Testing

The testing of packaging material and finished pack is required :

1. For effective material selection;
2. For assessing performance of material; and
3. For checking quality.

The packaging industry examines the properties like, mechanical, physical chemical and compatibility.

Mechanical properties for example, compression, tensile, flexural and impact strengths. *Physical properties* for example, water absorption, moisture vapour transmission rates, accelerated aging, flammability and thermal conductivity. *Chemical properties* for example, resistance to the product or the chemical environment, and corrosion testing. *Compatibility testing* is performed when the final product formulation and packaging system have been decided. Samples of the product should ideally be taken from trial batches, and the complete packaging system should be assembled using actual samples or pilot tooling samples representing the final component.

The general compatibility of the pack and product needs to be checked by storage testing which will enable an assessment to be made of the effect of the pack on the product as well as that of the product on the pack. It is important to remember that the effect of spillage on the outside of the pack is important, and should certainly be included in any testing schedule.

Shelf-life testing is also necessary in order to determine the rate at which volatiles may be lost and this includes not only water or alcohol but the perfume. The assessment of loss of perfume can only sensibly be done by nose, although weighing will obviously allow determination to be made of the loss of solvents.

Finally, the convenience of any cosmetics pack must be tested by in-use tests as well as by laboratory tests and for this purpose it is necessary to take into account both the local customs and the climate of the country in which the product is to be marketed : for instance, bathrooms in the UK tend to be cold, and tests for pourability should reflect this; similarly, products for tropical countries should be tested in conditions of high temperature and humidity.

Chapter - 4

SKIN CREAMS, ASTRINGENTS AND SKIN TONICS

INTRODUCTION

The human body is protected from the surrounding the skin. The entry of radiations, bacteria, fungi and water is controlled by the dead outer layer of the skin. The skin also absorbs oxygen (it does breathe), eliminates waste, secretes protective lubricants, grows hair, and manufactures new skin cells at a furious rate. No simple organism could do all this.

The layer of dead corneal cells does not feel like a rough, splintered board because it is coated with an oily liquid secreted by underlying sebaceous glands and by moisture from sweat glands. This film coats the scales, smoothing and sealing them. The fatty secretions and sweat combine to create an "acid mantle" of pH 4–6 on the skin. This mantle–or film – keeps the skin's surface supple and regulates the moisture content of the deeper as well as the outer skin strata. Most dermatologists believe that the mantle also inhibits the growth of bacteria and fungi on the skin's surface, most of which flourish at higher pH (6.0–7.5) and moisture levels than those of the corneal layer. This may explain why people whose skin cannot maintain normal pH and moisture ranges are prone to skin problems.

Age and Skin

as the body ages, its functions change and its needs alter. Some cosmetics can meet the skin's changing needs and cover ageing effects. In no case do they "cure."

In old age the output of sebum from the sebaceous glands drops and the skin dries out. The skin becomes flaky and itchy, particularly on the lower legs. Household cleaning products, which can strip sebum off the skin, can cause a similar condition in younger people. Furthermore, since many household cleansers are alkaline, they can swell and damage the keratin of the corneal cells.

Wrinkles are another change. Wrinkles occur when the connections between the epidermis and the dermis loosen. No known cosmetic can eliminate wrinkles by filling it in or by swelling, pinching, or oiling the skin. However it makes unnoticeable.

Cosmetics and Skin

Most skin cosmetics fall into two categories : those with a purely decorative effect, and those which have subsurface effect. The decorative cosmetics, such as eye make-up, face make-up, and fragrances, should affect only the surface of the skin. A good product should not irritate or sensitise the skin, or cause infections, or harm the health of the user in any other way. On the other hand, no special benefits to the skin can be expected from even the best of decorative skin cosmetics. Cosmetics with a subsurface effect, such as moisturisers and cleansers, are usually intended to alleviate or change some skin condition. Since judgements concerning the effectiveness of make-up or fragrances are largely subjective the chapters on decorative cosmetics will focus on alerting consumers to potential health problems associated with the use of such products. In our treatment of subsurface beauty preparations, we will show how they act upon the skin to help users evaluate their efficacy and safety.

SKIN CREAMS

In the context of cosmetics, the term 'cream' usually signifies a solid or semi-solid emulsion. It is also applied to non-aqueous products such as wax-solvent-based mascaras, liquid eyeshadows and ointments.

Classification of Skin Creams

Traditionally, cosmetic creams have been marketed and sold on the basis of their 'function'. Thus customers have come to learn what type of emulsion they can expect from a jar marked 'cold cream' or 'night cream'. The customer, therefore, is likely to make her own judgement on the basis of subjective features, using the manufacturers functional labels as a guide to end-use and quality. The characteristics of various skin creams are given in Table 21.1.

Table 21.1

Characteristics of skin creams

Functional	*Phusico-chemical*	*Subjective*
Cleansing creams	Medium-to-high oil content	Oily
Cold creams	Oil-in-water or water-in-oil	Difficult to 'rub in'
Massage creams	Low slip-point oil phase	May be stiff and 'rich'

(Cont'd)

Night creams	Neutral pH may contain surfactants to improve penetration and suspension properties	Also popular as lotions
Moisturising creams	Low oil content	Easily spreadable and 'rub in' quickly
Foundation creams	Usually oil-in-water	
Vanishing creams	Low slip-point oil phase Neutral to slightly acidic pH may contain emollients and special moisturising ingredients	Available as creams or lotions
Hand and body protective	Low-to-medium oil content Usually oil-in-water	Easily spreadable but do not 'rub in' with the ease of vanishing creams
	Medium slip-point oil phase May have slightly alkaline or acidic pH may contain 'protective factors', especially silicones and lanolin	Very popular in lotion form
All-purpose creams	Medium oil content Oil-in-water or water-in-oil	Very often slightly oily but should be easy to spread.

Cleansing Creams

The regular cleaning removes grime, sebum, and other secretions and keeps skin healthy. Water is a very cheap and effective cleansing agent for certain types of facial soil but fails to remove oils. By the process of emulsification, soaps and other detergents are able to improve the cleansing properties of water dramatically. However, this combination suffers from disadvantages; it is inconvenient to use outside the bathroom, and it may remove too much oil from the surface, leaving it feeling dry and rough. The alkalinity of soap, may cause the outermost cells to lift and separate from their neighbours.

Cleansing creams and lotions can, by a combination of water and the solvent action of oils, effect the cleansing of the skin surface efficiently and pleasantly. Moreover, if they are properly formulated they can accomplish this without completely degreasing the skin (indeed, by leaving behind a very thin emollient layer of clean oil, they may give a healthy supple feel to the skin surface).

A cleansing cream or lotion is spread onto the skin, using the fingertips, and massaged onto the surface. This action serves to loosen and suspend the grime and soil in the emulsion. A subsequent wipe with a tissue or cotton wool pad removes the majority of the applied cleansing emulsion, and with it the skin soil, grime or make-up. The cream should have a medium-to-high percentage oil phase and easily spreadable, should not 'rub in' and should not irritate the skin. In addition, it can also leave a residual emollient film on the skin, so much the better.

Today, beeswax–borax emulsions are still popular and commercially viable, although the development of secondary or alternate emulsifiers has enabled the formulator to produce a wider range of emulsions around the beeswax-borax theme.

Beeswax itself suffers from two disadvantages as an ingredient in skin creams. It has a distinctive smell which usually has to be masked in the final product. The beeswax odour is not unpleasant, but it is not compatible with the sophisticated skin-care image which many manufacturers now-a-days build into their products. Nevertheless, the qualities of neutralised beeswax as an emulsifier are such that it will continue to be used in cleansing and cold creams for the foreseeable future.

The sodium salts of wax acids are formed when borax solution is mixed with molten bees-wax at the oil water interface. A stable and textured cream is obtained using borax quantity less than theoretical value, i.e. 5–6%. The amount of borax–neutralised beeswax in a cold cream can vary from 5 to 16 per cent. The lower levels produce softer creams which can be stiffened (if required) by incorporating other waxes. Formulae 1, 2 and 3 are all water-in-oil emulsions.

Formulae	*1*	*2*	*3*
Constituents	*Percent*	*Percent*	*Percent*
Beeswax	5.0	16.0	12.0
Mineral oil	45.0	50.0	–
Borax	0.2	0.8	0.5
Micro-crystalline wax	7.0	–	–
Spermaceti	–	–	12.5
Sesame oil	–	–	40.0
Water	32.8	32.8	35.0
Perfume, preservative	q.s.	q.s	q.s.
Paraffin wax	10.0	–	–

Alternative to waxes as thickeners for a continuous oil phase are bentones (quaternary hectorites and related chemical species); formula 4 is a product of this type :

Formula 4

Constituents	*Percent*
Beeswax	12.0
Mineral oil	53.0
Quaternium-18 hectorite	0.7
Borax	0.7
Water	33.2
Isopropanol	0.4

Procedure

Mill the bentone with the isopropanol and some of the mineral oil. Heat the resultant gel with the beeswax and the remainder of the oil to 75°C. Dissolve the borax in the water, bring to 70°C and slowly pour into the oil phase with stirring. Continue stirring to 45°C, adding perfume at a late stage.

It is a peculiarity of the beeswax–borax system that both water-in-oil and oil-in-water creams may be produced without the aid of secondary emulsifiers. The ratio of oil to water, the proportion of the beeswax that is saponified, the constituents of the cream (which will affect the HLB. requirement) and the temperature have influence on the type of emulsion.

It has been found that preparation at high temperature tends to produce cold creams of the water-in-oil type and phase inversion may occur during processing. Phase inversion also occurs on the skin when an oil-in-water emulsion is spread onto the skin surface and the water phase begins to evaporate.

Non-ionic emulsifiers like sorbitan fatty acid esters can be used to increased flexibility and stability to the emulsion. Formulae 5 and 6 illustrate the point; formula 5 is a water-in-oil emulsion whereas 6 is oil-in-water.

Formulae	*5*	*6*
Constituents	*Percent*	*Percent*
Beeswax	10.0	16.0
Mineral oil	50.0	20.0
Lanolin	3.1	3.0

(Cont'd)

Borax	0.7	0.7
Hydrogenated vegetable oil	–	25.0
Antioxidant	–	0.5
Sorbitan sesquioleate	1.0	–
Sorbitan stearate	–	5.0
Polysorbate	–	2.0
Water	35.2	33.8
Perfume, preservative	q.s.	q.s.

If required, the external phase of oil-in-water cleansing creams may be thickened by the use of cellulose derivative alginates and other hydrocolloids formula 7.

Formula 7

Constituents	*Percent*
Beeswax	8.0
Mineral oil	49.0
Paraffin wax	7.0
Cetyl alcohol	1.0
PEG-15 Cocamine	1.0
Borax	0.4
Carbomer-934	0.2
Water	33.4
Perfume, preservative	q.s.

A number of beeswax derivatives are manufactured with modified emulsifier properties, for example, a range of ethoxylated beeswax derivatives available with HLB values ranging from 5 to 9. Although they still have the beeswax odour, it is claimed that creams made from them are softer, liquefy readily, allow the incorporation of larger amounts of water, are neutral and are stable at 50°C. Formulae 8 and 9 both oil-in-water creams.

Formulae	*8*	*9*
Constituents	*Percent*	*Percent*
Mineral oil	50.0	50.0
Beeswax	–	7.0

(Cont'd)

PEG-8 Sorbitan beeswax	12.0	–
PEG-20 Sorbitan beeswax	3.0	8.0
Polysorbate-40	–	2.0
Water	35.0	33.0
Perfume preservative	q.s.	q.s.

Night and massage Creams

Night or massage creams are designed to be left on the skin for several hours or to remain mobile on the skin even after vigorous rubbing. They are composed with a substantial oil phase which will spread easily without disappearing but also without rubbing off onto clothing or bed linen in use. Such creams tend to be high-oil-content, water-in-oil, soft solid or viscous liquid creams.

A moisturising effect is resulted due to formation of the occlusive layer on the skin surface thereby reducing the rate of trans-epidermal water loss. Hence the skin surface feel smooth by lubricating action and allowing any 'saw tooth' cells in the outer layer of the stratum corneum to be smoothed down.

Massage has a valuable part to play in skin care. It is well-known that vigorous rubbing of the skin helps to prevent the build-up of excessive numbers of dead surface cells and keeps the epidermal blood supply in good condition.

The term 'moisturising' has also been applied to water-in-oil creams of this type. The recent research has broadened the concept of moisturising from the simple occlusive skin barrier principle. Many modern mosisturising creams are comparatively light and easy to rub in compared with those of the overnight and massage types, although there still remains a market for the heavier moisturising creams.

Vitamins in Skin Creams

It has been found that fat-soluble as well as water-soluble vitamins are capable of being taken up through the skin. The use of stablised vitamins in cosmetic preparations for external application is justified.

Pantothenic acid, a part of the water-soluble vitamins B complex. Its precursor and the related materials panthenol, pantethine and pangamic acid have all been quoted as having a beneficial action on the skin and being useful in skin and/or hair preparations. Although there is no certain proof that they penetrate the skin and reach the location where they might exert an influence, vitamin B complex, panthenol and vitamin B_6-pyridoxin are used in some cosmetics.

Vitamin D, like vitamin a, is oil-soluble and is essential for skin health, but deficiencies are best corrected by oral administration to achieve a systemic effect. However, vitamins D_2 and D_3 (calciferol) are used, sometimes in conjunction with vitamin A. A mixture of vitamins A, E and D_3 has been claimed to be synergistic.

Vitamin E is said to enhance percutaneous resorption, and vitamin H is claimed to help fat and cholesterol synthesis.

Other vitamins having some use in topical preparations include the so-called vitamin F, now known as essential (unsaturated) fatty acids (EFA), which can undoubtedly heal the skin symptoms characteristic of rats brought to a chronic state of EFA deficiency. The relevant point here is that it would be virtually impossible to bring the human to a corresponding EFA-deficient state.

Oil Phase Constituents

The predominant oil phase constituents in massage and night creams are petrolatum, mineral oil, lanolin and low-melting-point waxes such as beeswax and low-melting mineral waxes (ceresins and paraffin). Esters such as isopropyl palmitate, iso-propyl myrisate and purcellin oil are reserved for lighter 'vanishing cream' types of product.

Moisturising, Vanishing and Foundation Creams

As the term 'vanishing' implies, creams and lotions falling within this category are designed to spread easily and to seem to disappear rapidly when they are rubbed into the skin.

Moisturisers

Of all the beneficial properties claimed for cosmetic creams, 'moisturising' is possibly the most widely used. Water is the only material which will plasticise the outer dead layers of the epidermis to give the much desired attribute we call 'soft, smooth skin', hence the turn moisturiser.

If water is lost more rapidly from the stratum corneum than receiving from epidermis, the skin dehydrates. Hence loses flexibility which can not restored by oil alone.

Dry skin is of two types. (i) It is due to prolonged exposure to low humidity and air movement, which modifies the normal hydration gradient of the stratum corneum; and (ii) It is due to ageing, continual degreasing. Ageing occurs due to influence of ultra-violet rays.

The dry skin is hydrated using three different routes–occlusion, humectancy, and restoration of deficient materials–which may be (and often are) combined.

Occlusion

Occlusion reduces the rate of transepidermal water loss through old or damaged skin or in protecting otherwise healthy skin from the effect of a severely drying environment. It instantly decreases the rate of water loss through the epidermis. This results the stratum corneum to become more hydrated, making it softer and more supple. However, this extra hydration increases the diffusion coefficient of water across the ;epidermis. After application of petroleum jelly within three hours rate of water loss actually increases to a value higher than the pre-treatment value. (This, of course, in no way detracts from the usefulness of this approach to moisturisation, since it achieves the desired hydration of the stratum corneum.) Examples of occlusive are : mineral and vegetable oils, lanolin and silicones. Their effect is increased by the use of mixtures of lipids and other fatty chemicals which have been designed to imitate the composition of the skin's natural oily secretions.

More recently, skin substantive barrier materials (mainly based on quaternary ammonium complexes) have become available which seem to be able to influence the rate of transepidermal water loss without putting an occlusive or greasy barrier layer on the surface. These materials can be shown to be substantive to skin (and hair) and act not only as moisturisers, but as emollients and skin conditioning agents. Example are quaternium, a hydroxyethyl-cellulose derivative.

Humectants

A second approach to the moisturising problem is the use of humectants to attract water from the atmosphere, so supplementing the skin's water content. Although popular in use, such a concept is, to say the least, somewhat doubtful from the physiological viewpoint. It is, after all, easy to demonstrate that externally applied water will not increase the flexibility of the stratum corneum-in fact, it can have precisely the opposite effect.

The humectants most frequently used as moisturisers are glycerol, ethylene glycol, propylene glycol and sorbitol. They can be used alone or in admixture at various levels. Whether or not they penetrate the skin surface is a moot point, but at least they will attract moisture to the skin.

Moisturisation

The moisturisation of skin is to determine the precise mechanism of the natural moisturisation process, to assess what has gone wrong with it in the case of dry skin and to replace any materials in which such research has shown damaged skin to be deficient.

Emollients

'Emollience' is another ill-defined term often used in connection with skin creams. Emmollient means imparting of a smoothness and general sense of well-being to the skin, as determined by touch. (In a sense, therefore, water is an emollient).

Every liquid, semi-solid or low-melting-point solid of a bland nature and cosmetic quality has been used as emollients. Among the most popular water-soluble emollients are glycerine, sorbitol, propylene glycol, and various ethoxylated derivatives of lipids. Oil-soluble emollients include hydrocarbon oils and waxes, silicone oils, vegetable oils and fats, alkyl esters, fatty acids and alcohols, together with ethers of fatty alcohols (including polyhydric alcohols). The choice is determined by personal preference, data on potential skin irritation, the degree of 'greasiness' and apparent residual film on the skin, cheapness and availability.

Mineral oils and silicone oils do not 'disappear' from the skin very readily when used in any quantity and are therefore useful, in cleansing and night creams. Propylene glycol is an efficient preservative against certain micro-organisms at concentrations of more than 8 per cent, but it is a potential sensitiser.

The alkyl esters represent a range of interesting emollients ranging, as they do, through lactates, oleates, myrisates, adipates, linoleates with the possibility of straight-chained, branch-chained, unsaturated, or saturated precursors. Some are almost water-thin liquids which rub quickly into the skin (decyl and isodecyl oleates, isopropyl myristate) and others are waxy solids which melt near body temperature and give 'body' to creams. Lanolin was considered once to be an extremely desirable emollient and the claim 'contains lanolin' was felt to be a product 'plus'.

Vanishing and Foundation Creams

In order to achieve their rapid 'rub-in' effect, vanishing creams are composed, in the oil phase. A low percentage oil phase is usually chosen of emollient esters which leave apparent film on the skin.

Foundation creams posses many of the same properties. These creams are for day-time use to protect and 'condition' the cleansed skin. They must therefore leave the; skin surface non-greasy and preferably matt so that other make-up can easily be applied over it. Modern foundation creams are of excellent appearance and stability. They contain emollients and moisturisers. Sun-scree agent present helps to protect the consumer's skin from the harmful, ageing effects of short-wave solar radiation. A typical 'simple' vanishing cream formula is as under :

Formula 10

Constituents	*Percent*
Stearic acid	15.0
Potassium hydroxide	0.7
Glycerine	8.0
Water	76.3
Perfume, preservative	q.s.

Pigmented Foundation Creams

Pigmented foundation creams can contain from 3 to 25 per cent of pigments. Those with between 3 and 10 per cent form a suitable substrate for the subsequent use of powder, whereas those with higher pigment concentrations can be used as complete make-up and are often termed powder creams. They can be water-continuous or oil-continuous systems in liquid or solid form. The difficulties encountered in the preparations are : (i) The preferential absorption of emulsifier in the high surface of the pigment may sometime cause inversion of emulsion; (ii) the inadequate dispersion of the pigment for reproducible colours. Pigments can be suspended by the use of cellulose derivatives or inorganic silicates such as bentonite or hydrated magnesium silicate. The basic type of tinted foundation cream are illustrated by the following examples.

Formulae (Water-in-oil creams)	*11*	*12*
Constituents	*Solid*	*Liquid*
	Per cent	*Per cent*
Light mineral oil	4.0	30.0
Isopropyl myristate	8.0	–
Lanolin	–	8.0
Ceresin	19.2	–
Micro-crystalline wax	–	1.0
Sorbitan Sesquioleate	2.8	2.3
Polysorbate	–	0.1
Powder base	q.s.	8.0
Titanium dioxide	3.0	–
Glycerine	–	5.0
Water, perfume, preservative to	100.0	100.0

Formulae (Oil-in-water solid creams)	*13*	*14*	*15*
Constituent	*Per cent*	*Per cent*	*per cent*
Mineral oil	30.0	–	–
Stearing acid	3.0	8.0	12.0
Isopropyl palmitate	–	–	1.0
Glyceryl stearate	3.0	–	–
Sorbitan Sterate	–	–	2.0
Polysorbate-60	–	–	1.0
Cetyl alcohol	2.0	–	–
Triethanolmine	1.0	–	–
Glycerine	–	10.0	–
Sorbitol	–	–	2.5
Propylene glycol	–	–	12.0
Lenette wax	–	8.0	–
Pigment and powder base	5.0	10.0	11.0
Water, perfume, preservative, etc.	to100.0	100.0	100.0

Formulae 16 (Oil-in-water liquid make-up)

Constituents	*Per cent*
Mineral oil	20.0
Cetyl alcohol	1.0
Spremaceti	1.0
Sodium lauryl sulphate	0.5
Glyceryl stearate	1.0
Bentonite	2.5
Powder base and colour	8.0
Water, perfume, preservative, etc.	to 100.0

The foundation preparations which do not contain water, for example :

Formulae 17

Constituents	*Per cent*
Sesame oil	64
Zinc oil	11

(Cont'd)

Oxycholesterol	2
Triglyceryl stearate (polyglyceryl-3-stearate)	1
Perfume and colouring	6
Titanium dioxide	16
Preservative	q.s.

Hand Creams and Hand-and-body Creams

The hands are the main unprotected area of the body other than the face. It is important that the skin which covers them should remain soft and smooth. The main features of good hand creams or lotions are therefore that they should be easy and quick to apply without leaving a tacky film, They should also soften the hands and perhaps help them to heal without interfering with normal hand perspiration. They are usually coloured and are lightly perfumed to make their use pleasant.

The most popular healing agent is allantoin (2,5-dioxo-4-imidazolidinyl-urea) one weak metal complexes such as aluminium dihydroxy alltoinate. Additionally, some of the newer, skin-substantive quaternary salts have also been shown to have healing and soothing effects-for example, Quaternium, a hydroxyethylcellulose derivative.

Further examples of formulations suitable for the starting -point of a hand lotion or cream are given below.

Formula 18

Constituents	*per cent*
Glyceryl stearate SE	2.7
Cetyl alcohol	1.5
Dimethicone	1.5
Lanolin oil	2.0
squalene	3.0
Sodium lauryl sulhpate	0.3
Water, perfume, preservative	q.s.

Formula 19

Constituents	*per cent*
DEA-oleth-3 phosphate	0.5
Lanolin alcohol	1.0

(Cont'd)

Mineral oil	4.0
Stearic acid	1.0
Glycerine	3.0
Triethanolamine	0.5
Carbomer 941	0.1
Dimethicone	1.0
Water, perfume, preservative	q.s.

Formula 20

Constituents	*per cent*
Stearic acid	7.0
Lanolin	0.5
Sorbitan oleate	0.5
Polysorbate-60	0.5
Sorbitol	10.0
Water, perfume, preservative	q.s.

Formula 21

Constituents	*per cent*
Cetrimonium bromide	1.5
Isopropyl myristate	3.0
Cetyl alcohol	2.5
Lanolin	2.0
Glycerine	8.0
Water, perfume, preservative	q.s.

All-purpose creams

All-purpose creams should comply with the following requirements :

1. It must provide a satisfactory foundation base for make-up without being too greasy as foundation cream.
2. It should be oily in nature, liquefy readily and not readily absorbed by skin as a cleansing cream.
3. It should be emollient yet not leave a greasy or sticky film on the skin as a hand cream.

4. It should leave a continuous but non-occlusive oil film on the skin as a protective and emollient cream.

Some suggested starting formulae for all-purpose creams are given in formulae 22-24.

Formula 22

Constituents	*per cent*
Trieolyl phosphate	3.0
Petrolatum	18.0
Glyceryl stearate	5.0
Isopropyl palmitae	4.0
Cetyl alcohol	2.0
Stearyl heptanoate	0.5
Cetearyl octanoate	0.5
Sorbitol	5.0
Water, perfume, preservative	q.s.

Formulas	23	24
Constituents	*per cent*	*per cent*
Stearic acid	15.00	15.00
Lanolin	4.00	2.00
Beeswax	2.00	2.00
Minearl oil	23.00	24.00
Polysorbate-85	1.00	-
Sorbitan trioleate	1.00	-
PEG-40 stearate	-	5.00
Sorbitol	12.00	10.00
Water, perfume, preservative	q.s.	q.s.

PROTECTIVE CREAMS AND HAND CLEANSERS

The chemicals that are in everyday use and are capable of inflicting damage on unprotected skin. The list include domestic materials such as detergents, floor and metal polishes, bleaches, oven cleaners, paints and varnishes. Industrial hazards include acids, alkalies, organic solvents, resins, dyestuffs, weedkillers, insecticides, lubricants and many more.

The types of hazard from which the skin is to be protected are :

1. Dry solids, dust and dirt.
2. Aqueous solutions or suspensions.
3. Non-aqueous materials, including oils, fats and solvents.
4. Emulsions.
5. Physical hazards, such as heat, cold, uv radiation and abrasion.

Barrier Materials – Protective Creams and Gels

The use of barrier material in protective creams and gels provide protection from water borne hazards. There are many hydrophobic substances that can be spread upon the skin in a continuous film to form a water-repellent occlusive film These include petrolatum, paraffin waxes, vegetable oils, lanolin, silicones and occlusive esters. The water-repellent materials added are capable of modifying the film-forming agent to improve its aesthetic or functional qualities. These include alumina, zinc oxide, zinc stearate, talc, titanium dioxide, kaolin and stearic acid. Oil-repellent films can be formed from water-swellable polymers such as alginates, cellulose derivatives, bentonites and natural clays. The combination of water- repellent and oil-repellant can form the basis of a general purpose barrier cream.

Formulae – creams and lotions

The barrier properties of lanolin, petrolatum and kaolin are used in formula 25. It also contains a small amount of sodium stearate to facilitate easy wash-off. Such a cream might best be used to protect the skin against dust and dry powders.

Formula 25

Constituents	per cent
Stearic acid	6.0
Cetyl alcohol	3.0
Lanolin	3.0
Petrolatum	2.0
Sodium hydroxide	0.65
Water	67.35
Kaolin	18.0
Colour, preservative, perfume	q.s.

The presence of stearic acid thickens water-in-oil emulsion of non-ionic emulsifier. The barrier properties of silicon oil are used in formula 26 and the water-repellent properties of zinc stearate together with a film- forming material, methylcellulose are used in formula 27. The presence of sorbitol in each case prevents 'rolling' on application and provides an additional emollient effect. (Formula 26 can be used as an aerosol if packaged in a nitrogen-pressurised container.)

Formulae (Protective hand creams)	26	27
Constituents	*per cent*	*per cent*
Stearic acid	20.00	15.00
Dimethicone	5.00	-
Zinc stearate	-	5.00
Isopropyl myristate	2.00	-
Sorbitan stearate	1.50	1.50
Polysorbate	3.50	2.00
Sorbitol	20.00	6.00
Methylcellulose (4% aqueous)	-	25.00
Water	48.00	45.00
Perfume, colour, preservative	q.s.	q.s.

The barrier properties of silicones are used in formulae 28 and 29. The emulsifier system consists of a mixture of polyethylene glycol esters of cetyl alcohol and the viscosity is controlled by the presence of another film-forming agent, Carbomer (neutralised with triethanolamine).

Formulae (Protective hand lotion)	28	29
Constituents	*per cent*	*per cent*
Dimethicone	10.00	10.00
Catech	7.50	4.00
Triethanolamine	0.20	0.20
Carbmer	0.20	0.20
Water	82.10	82.00
Perfume, colour, preservative	q.s.	q.s.

A simple cream containing silicone, mineral oil and sodium magnesium sulphate is represented by formula 30.

Formula 30 (Barrier cream)

Constituents	*per cent*
Dimethicone	19.00
Mineral oil	19.00
Glyceryl oleate	2.00
Sodium magnesium silicate	2.00
Water	58.00
Colour, preservative, perfume	q.s.

There have been attempts, however, to utilise film-forming materials of a type completely impervious to and unaffected by water. A method of using such polymeric films is to apply the material in a water-soluble form and then to convert it, in situ, into an insoluble analogue. The use of acid polymers that are soluble as alkaline salts but insoluble in the free acid form could be considered. If the substance were to be presented as an ammonium salt, the volatile alkaline end of the molecule would detach itself leaving the polymer behind in the free acid form. Similarly, soluble sodium salts of certain film-formers (for example, alginates) can be converted into an insoluble form by the subsequent application of calcium or other suitable ions.

Non-aqueous barrier products

The protection against water-soluble irritants can be given by film-forming materials applied from a non-aqueous medium. The non- aqueous protective product of al! is the zinc and castor oil ointment which has been smeared onto the more vulnerable skin surfaces of countless babies and young children. The following anhydrous formulation is suggested as protection against flash burns in formula 31.

Formula 31 (Protective base)

Constituents	*per cent*
Dimethicone	50.00
Titanium dioxide	30.00
Magnesium stearate	18.00
Iron oxide	2.00

A much more pleasant and sophisticated product is the gelled oil formulation given in formula 32.

Formula 32 (Protective gel)

Constituents	*per cent*
Lanolin oil	12.00
Lanolin wax	2.50
Mineral oil	50.48
Olive oil BP	20.00
Sorbitan oleate	5.00
BHT	0.02
Silica	10.00

Testing of protective preparation

Although laboratory screening tests to determine the relative efficacy of protective creams have been described. No test can predict the behaviour of the protective cream. Some of them give some useful indications, particularly in the negative aspect, which can eliminate unsuitable preparations.

The simplest test is described here. A film of the barrier or protective cream is applied to a series of clean glass microscope slides. After drying for specified period slides are immersed in solvents like alcohol, acetone, water and oil to obtain resistance of the product. The slide may be subjected to standardised conditions of agitation, and the integrity of the barrier film after such treatment examined, preferablys against a control preparation.

An apparatus for measuring the permeability of films of barrier cream was devised. Here the passage of the test solution through the barrier could be measured by reading the meniscus from time to time in a glass tube of fine bore, graduated in hundredths of a millilitre.

Barrier creams will usually remain effective for at least 4 hours, and they are usually applied twice a day. However, when dealing with particularly corrosive substances or whenever the cream is likely to be rubbed off more regularly, more frequent applications of the barrier cream are indicated in order to provide full protection for the hands.

All protective creams should be properly labelled. The substances against which protection will be conferred should be clearly indicated. Hence the user may avoid contact with irritants against which a particular cream will not protect him.

Hand Cleansers

Skin cleansers of various types are now considered to be a valuable part of the skin care regime along with toners and moisturisers. Such cleansers are formulated to remove everyday grime, secretions and make-up. They may not be equally effective against the heavy stains, greases, resins, adhesives, oils, paint, tar, and dyestuffs with which the skin (particularly the hands) may get covered in the modern home, garage or workplace. Heavy-duty cleansers offer the possibility of removing many of these contaminants with little risk of permanent damage to the skin.

The first heavy-duty skin cleaners other than soap and water are sulphonated oils. These being particularly valuable in the removal of oils and solvents where the habitual and frequent use of soap had caused skin irritation. Sulphonated oils have now been largely superseded by the so-called waterless hand cleansers. The term 'waterless' is misleading because many of them contain water in the formulation, and 'waterless' refers to the fact that they can be used without the use of additional water (although a final rinse-off in water is often recommended by thes manufacturer).

Waterless hand cleansers can be formulated as pastes, creams, gels, lotions or clear liquid and consist of a cleansing agent, a thickener, an emulsifier and (usually) water.

The heavy-duty cleansers are not water soluble. Aliphatic solvents are used as cleansing agents. These solvents are effective, cheap, innocuous and readily available. Thus the majority of formulae given below contain odourless kerosene, mineral spirits or mineral oils.

Any agent which will thicken either the water phase or oil phase of the product may be used as a thickener. The soaps used as emulsifiers to produce gels may be the sodium, triethanolamide or monoethanolamide salts of stearic or oleic acids or a mixture of both.

Emollients are added improve the application properties and to prevent the defatting of the skin. The emollient used in the following formulae are lanolin (formula 33), ethoxylated lanolin (formula 34), myristyl myristate (formula 41) and propylene glycol (formula 34) :

Formulae (Waterless hand gels)	33	34
Constituents	*per cent*	*per cent*
Deodorised kerosene	35.00	25.00
Lanolin	10.00	-
Cocamide	4.00	-
Stearic acid	2.43	6.00

(Cont'd)

Oleic acid	3.64	8.00
Sodium hydroxide	0.38	0.80
Amphoteric	-	2.00
PEG Lanolin	-	0.50
Water	44.55	57.70
Perfume, colour, preservative	q.s.	q.s.

Formula 35 (Waterless hand gel)

Constituents	*per cent*
Deodorised kerosene	20.00
Alkylaryl sulphonate (amine neutralised)	5.00
Cocamide	2.00
Oleic acid	8.00
Monoethanolamide(20%)	8.00
Water	57.00
Perfume, colour, preservative	q.s.

Formulae (Waterless hand cleansers)	36	37
Constituents	per cent	per cent
Deodorised kerosene	20.00	55.00
Minearl oil	20.00	-
Glyceryl stearate	3.00	-
Stearic acid	5.00	-
Oleic acid	-	4.50
Stearamide stearat	-	6.00
Propylene glycol	5.00	-
Triethanolamine	1.50	1.50
PEG-Cocoate	-	3.00
Water	45.50	30.00
Perfume, colour, preservative	q.s.	q.s.

Formula 38 (Skin cleansing gel)

Constituents	*per cent*
Mineral oil	15.50
Stearic acid	4.40
Triclosan	0.10
Sodium magnesium silicate	2.00
Triethanolamine	1.60
Water	76.40
Perfume, colour, preservative	q.s.

Formula 38 illustrates the possibility of using antiseptic agents (such as triclosan) and other additives to provide additional benefits to the product.

Formula 39 is soapless, utilising non-ionic emulsifiers to produce a cream. Such a formulation might be favoured by users who find that alkaline products are irritating to their skin. Formula 40 is a much milder form of cleanser in simple liquid form :

Formula 39 (Waterless hand cleansing cream)

Constituents	*per cent*
Magnesium aluminium silicate	2.50
Sorbitan stearate	2.00
Polysorbate	8.00
Deordorised kerosene	35.00
Mehtylcellulose	0.50
Water	52.00
Perfume, colour, preservative	q.s.

Formula 40 (Liquid hand cleanser)

Constituents	*per cent*
PVM/MA polymer	0.40
PEG	5.00
Octoxynol	5.00
Water	89.60
Potassium hydroxide	to pH 7
Perfume, colour, preservative	q.s.

The formula is 41 unusual. It comprises a base which may be turned into a number of different products of varying consistency by the addition of solvent together with variable amounts of oleic acid :

Formula 41 (Waterless hand cleanser)

A Base (smooth paste)	*per cent*
Cocamidopropylamine oxide	18.00
Cocamide	38.00
Dioctyl sulphosuccinate	15.00
Myristyl myristate	15.00
Oleic acid	14.00
Mix until smooth at 45-55°C.	

B. Finished products	*Gel*	*Cream*	*Lotion*
	per cent	*per cent*	*per cent*
Base	15.00	13.90	12.95
Odourless kerosene	30.00	27.70	25.90
Oleic acid	1.50	1.40	1.40
Water	53.50	57.00	59.75
Perfume, colour, preservative	q.s.	q.s.	q.s.

All the ingradients are stirred and heated except water at 55-65°C. Gradually add water at 55°C with stirring till homogeneous and smooth product is formed.

Astringents and skin tonics

Astringents are a class of materials which are identified by their local effect on skin when applied topically. These effects may include all or some of the following (not all astringents are equally active) : the erection of hairs, the tightening of skin (or at least the sensation of tightening), the temporary reduction of pore size, antiperspirancy, the mitigation of 'oily skin', the rapid coagulation of blood from a fresh wound, skin healing, the promotion of tissue growth and other, more subjective sensations such as a refreshing or invigorating feeling. While these beneficial properties ensure that astringents are regarded as important and valuable cosmetic materials, not all the claims made for them can be substantiated by careful experiment.

TYPES OF ASTRINGENT

Metal Salt Astringents

The astringent effects of many metal ions have long been known. The list of active metals includes iron, chromium, aluminium, zinc, lead, mercury, tin, copper, silver and zirconium, although they vary in their degree of astringency. Of these only useful are the salts of zinc, aluminium and zirconium.

The effect of the anion in metal salt astringents is not entirely passive. It can be shown, for example, that the astringency of a metal ion is partially dependent upon the identity of the anion. Furthermore, the anion will also help to determine the solubility of the salt in various cosmetic media.

Organic Acids

Low-molecular-weight organic acids with an ionisable proton show astringent properties. Most commonly encountered are lactic and citric acids.

Alcohols

Both ethanol and (less frequently) isopropanol are used as astringents, usually as aqueous solutions of strength up to 60 per cent w/v. Solutions of ethanol greater in strength than 20 per cent may cause stinging when first applied although this may be regarded as beneficial in certain types of product.

Auxiliary Additives

The materials added to astringent preparations to assist or enhance their effect are referred as auxiliary additives. Menthol included to produce a cooling effect in an after-shave, an antibacterial in a styptic stick, and rose water as a refreshing adjunct to a skin toner are various agents added to tonics to promote soothing and the healing of damaged skin.

Astringent Products

Many products contain raw materials with astringent properties. It is possible to categorise these various products according to the particular astringent feature which they utilise. Antiperspirants, for example, exploit the property which some zinc, aluminium and zirconium compounds have of causing 'anhidrosis' or decrease in activity of the sweat glands.

Astringent lotions may be subdivided into a number of related products. These include pre-shave and after-shave lotions, skin tonics, toners, colognes and fresheners.

Astringent emulsion include antiperspirant creams as well as plain astringent creams and milks together with emulsion colognes and after-shaves.

Stick astringents are generally formed from sodium stearate - alcohol gels. Among the products presented in this form are antiperspirants, deodorants, colognes, after-shaves and styptic pencils. Some astringents are made in gel form, including some cleansing products and face masks.

Aqueous and Aqueous – Alcoholic Lotions

Toners

Toners have become an accepted part of the facial skin treatment regime. They are normally recommended for use after cleansing and before the application of a moisturising cream. The primary purpose of such a product is to tighten the skin , reduce the pore size and reduce any tendency of areas of the face and neck to oiliness Formulae 42-44 are shown below. In some product ranges, toners are offered in a series of increasing alcoholic strength for dry, normal and oily skins (formulae 45, 46 and 47).

Formulae (Skin toners- aqueous)	42	43	44
Constituents	*per cent*	*per cent*	*per cent*
Potassium alum	1.00	-	4.00
Zinc sulphate	0.30	1.00	-
Glycerin	5.00	-	6.00
Zinc phenolsulphonate	-	2.00	-
Rose water	50.00	57.00	35.00
Orange flower water	-	-	35.00
Water	43.70	40.00	20.00
Perfume, preservative	q.s.	q.s.	q.s.

There is a variety of water-soluble or alcohol-soluble emollients that can be used to offset the drying effect of ethanol. IN formulae 45, 46 and 47 use is made of an ethoxylated lanolin derivative, together with propylene glycol.

Formulae (Skin toners-aqueous-alcoholic)	45	46	47
Constituents	*per cent*	*per cent*	*per cent*
Denatured ethanol	20.00	35.00	50.00
Water	72.00	58.00	42.00
Propylene glycol	5.00	5.00	2.00
Laneth-10 acetate	3.00	3.00	1.00
Perfume, preservative	q.s.	q.s.	q.s.

Skin tonics

Skin tonics can be made by the addition of auxiliary additives and perhaps menthol or camphor to produce a slightly 'medicated' fragrance. Possibly the most commonly used skin healing and soothing additive is allantoin, a chemical of the purine group. Allantoin has been shown to have regenerative, healing, softening, soothing and keratolytic properties. More recently, two allantoin combination compounds, chlorodydroxyaluminium allantoinate and dihydroxyaluminium allantoinate have become available. These possess mild astringent qualities in addition to the healing and soothing properties of allantoin itself and their use has been specifically recommended in astringent lotions of the 'tonic type' .

Azulene and its derivatives, particularly guaiazulene, have long been accredited with healing and soothing properties. Newer soothing ingredients to become available include a cationic cellulose polymer. No doubt other skin-substantive cationic polymers will be found to have similar desirable properties.

The various benefits to be derived from the use of such additives make them logical ingredients of pre-shave and after-shave sproducts. Pre-shave lotions-especially those designed to be used before electric shaving - make use of the ability of astringents to make facial hairs stand erect. After-shave lotions may be designed to soothe and cool the skin. Also to tighten it, to close the pores, to sterilise and stem the flow of blood from any inadvertent nicks or cuts. Formulations of skin tonic/after shave are given in formulae 48 and 49.

Formulae (Skin tonic/after-shave)	48	49
Constituents	*per cent*	*per cent*
Alcohol	40.00	20.00
Water	55.30	77.75
Allantoin	0.20	-
Polysorbate	1.50	-
Sorbitol	1.50	-
Glycerine	1.50	2.00
Quaternium	-	0.25
Perfume, colour, preservative	q.s.	q.s.

The normal pH of skin is slightly acid; body lotions and shaving preparations often make use of acids to 'restore' this acidic condition as well as for reasons of astringency, as in formulae 50 and 51.

Formulae (Skin tonic/shaving lotions)	50	51
Constituents	*per cent*	*per cent*
Alcohol	10.00	45.00
Zinc sulphate	0.40	-
Citric acid	1.00	-
Sorbitol	6.00	5.00
Water	82.50	48.90
Lactic acid	-	1.00
Menthol	-	0.10
Perfume, colour, preservative	q.s.	q.s.

Astringent lotions such as these may be thickened with cellulose ethers (formulae 52 and 53) or carbomer (formulae 54 and 55) or any other suitable agent, such as an alginate.

Formula 52 (Body lotion)

Constituents	*per cent*
Alcohol	43.00
Aluminium chlorhydroxyallantoinate	0.20
Propylene glycol	3.00
Menthol	0.05
Aluminium chlorohydrate(50%)	5.00
Hydroxypropylmethylcellulose(3%)	47.75
Mica (and) titanium dioxide	1.00
Perfume, colour, preservative	q.s.

Formula 53 (body lotion)

Constituents	*per cent*
Magnesium aluminium silicate	1.50
Hydroxypropylmethylcellulose	0.75
Water	80.00
Acetylated monoglyceride	3.00
Di-isopropyl adipate	5.00
Camphor	0.40

(Cont'd)

Menthol	0.80
Methyla salicylate	6.50
Zinc phenolsulphonate	1.00
Mica (and)titanium dioxide	1.00
Perfume, colour, preservative	q.s.

Formulae 52 and 53 contain a small quantity of titania coated micas to give a 'pearly' effect, which is slightly unusual in products of this kind.

Formula 54 (Skin freshener)

Constituents	*per cent*
Carbomer 940	2.00
Alcohol	73.00
Propylene glycol dicaprate	1.00
PEG-25 castor oil	5.00
Di-(2 ethyl hexyl) amine	2.00
Water	17.00
Perfume, colour, preservative	q.s.

Formula 55 (Astringent gel)

Constituents	*per cent*
Alcohol	50.25
Water	47.26
Carbomer 940	0.70
Menthol	0.04
Di-isopropylamine	0.50
Octoxynol-9	1.25
Perfume, colour, preservative	q.s.

Astringent emulsions

Astringent creams or lotions (of the emulsion variety) serve many purposes in the cosmetic field. Specifically as antiperspirants, shaving products and perfumed creams. The following formulae (56 and 57) illustrate a few of the ways in which astringents can be used in emulsions. Formula 58 is non-ionic and formula 59 is anionic. Formulae 60 and 61 shows the formulation of astringent lotion and creams.

Formula 56 (Alcoholic astringent cream {anionic})

Constituents	*per cent*
Sodium magnesium silicate	2.00
Isopropyl myristate	5.00
Triethanolamine	0.80
Glycerine	2.00
Stearic acid	3.00
Cetyl alcohol	0.50
Triclosan	0.10
Alcohol	30.00
Water	56.60
Colour, perfume	q.s.

Formula 57 (Alcoholic after-shave lotion{non-ionic})

Constituents	per cent
Laneth-40	0.50
Oleth-10	0.50
Mineral oil	1.00
Alcohol	15.00
Water	72.50
Glycerine	1.00
Di-isopropylamine(10% aqueous)	1.50
Carbomer 941 (91% dispersion)	8.00
Perfume, colour, preservative	q.s.

Formuale(Astringnet/antiperspirant creams)	58	59
Constituents	*per cent*	*per cent*
Stearic acid	14.00	10.60
Mineral oil	1.00	1.00
Beeswax	2.00	1.00
Sorbitan stearate	5.00	-
Polysorbate 60	5.00	-
Aluminium chlorohydrate(50% aqueous)	40.00	32.00

(Cont'd)

Water	33.00	42.70
Glyceryl stearate	-	6.40
Propylene glycol	-	5.00
Sodium lauryl sulphate	-	1.30
Colour, perfume, preservative	q.s.	q.s.

Formula 60 (Astringent lotion non-ionic/cationic)

Constituents	*per cent*
Glyceryl stearate	5.00
Quaternium-7	5.00
Aluminium chlorohydrate	15.00
Water	67.00
PEG-20 stearate	3.00
PEG-8	5.00
Colour, perfume, preservative	q.s.

Formula 61 (Astringent cream with witch hazel)

Constituents	per cent
Water	69.00
Witch hazel extract	10.00
Cetyl alcohol	3.00
Propylene glycol stearate	12.00
Sorbitol	5.00
Isopropyl myristate	1.00
Colour, perfume, preservative	q.s.

Chapter - 5

SKIN PRODUCTS FOR BABIES AND YOUTH

INTRODUCTION

The skin of the child undergoes extensive change and development – during the very earliest weeks after birth. Therefore, the skin of the young child differs from that of the adult and from that of the older child. The very young skin is very thin, less cornified, less hairy and contains a relatively high proportion of water in comparison with the adult. Sebaceous glands are not only present in the newborn skin, but begin to function very early. Apparently, transpidermal water loss at this time is lower than for adults (at least for some body areas).

Typically, the skin of babies and very young caucasian children is pink, very soft and smooth to the touch. The majority of skin products purchased by young people in this age group are concerned with the treatment, prevention or camouflage of blemishes or of oily skin.

FUNCTIONAL REQUIREMENTS OF BABY PRODUCTS

The baby skin care products need to protect the skin from a hostile environment, to cleanse the skin thoroughly from sebum, grime and excreta and to keep the skin surface as dry as possible. Within few days of birth most baby skins come into contact with soap and water. Although there is no evidence that ordinary soap has a bad effect on the baby, most baby soaps are white and free from perfume.

Zinc and castor oil creams or ointment provides the protection to baby skin. Zinc oxide is mildly antiseptic, astringent and anti-inflammatory. This accounts for its use in protective products, in the concentration range 2-10 per cent. Petrolatum, castor oil, beeswax, lanolin, silicone oil and polyethylene wax gives protective, occlusive barrier. These may be used as anhydrous preparations or as the oil phase of protective baby creams. Inorganic salts of stearic acid and oleic acid are used to improve the water-repellent effect of creams while stabilising the emulsion.

Baby powder is another traditional and valuable toiletry product. It provides a dry and lubricated surface to skin that has been cleaned and protected with oils or lotions. The main constituent of baby powder is talc, but since this lacks the absorbency of other powders it is often blended with such materials as kaolin, hydrated aluminium silicate, magnesium and calcium carbonates, starches and pyrogenic silica. The grades of materials used are naturally important - particularly talc, which should be the very purest available and devoid of any fibrous materials. The adhesive power of baby powders as well as their water repellency can be improved by the incorporation of aluminium, zinc and magnesium stearates; cetyl and stearyl alcohols and zinc oxide perform a similar function.

One of the main problems associated with the use of talc is its susceptibility to contamination by micro-organisms. Various methods are available for the sterilisation of talc, some being more suitable and successful than others. Ethylene oxide treatment may leave irritating residues, while heat treatment is not always sufficient to sterilise the material completely.

The use of boric acid and borates in baby powders as a mild antiseptic and as a neutralising buffer, although once popular, has now largely ceased because of the potentially toxic nature of these substances.

Safety of Baby Products

It is extremely important to ensure that all baby products are free from bacteria. They contain adequate preservative systems to prevent accidental contamination during use. Such principles should apply equally to all cosmetic and toiletry products.

The logical conclusions to be drawn from these considerations is that the raw materials used in baby products should, wherever possible, be chosen for their low toxicity and their non-irritating character when applied topically.

Example Formulations

The first two formulae for baby creams and lotions illustrate the use of a comparatively new type of mild, non-toxic emulsifier based on sucrose esters of palmitic and stearic acids. Formula 1 is a lotion and formula 2 a cream.

Formulae	1	2
Constituents	*per cent*	*per cent*
Mineral oil	25.00	35.00
Cetearyl alcohol	-	0.50

(Cont'd)

Petrolatum	-	4.20
Lanolin alcohol	-	1.25
Mono-ester	3.00	-
Di-ester	0.50	-
Tri-ester	-	3.00
Hydroxyethylecellulose	0.20	-
Water	71.30	55.05
Glycerine	-	1.00
Perfume, preservative	q.s.	q.s.

Baby creams and lotions are based upon the triethanolamine stearate (anionic) emulsifier system, of which formulae 3 and 4 being representative.

Formulae	3	4
Constituents	*per cent*	*per cent*
Mineral oil	26.00	15.00
Lanolin	1.04	5.00
Stearic acid	0.94	2.00
Triethanolamine	0.52	1.00
Water	69.68	52.00
Stearyl alcohol	0.94	-
Cetyl alcohol	0.52	-
Sodium alginate	0.36	-
Isopropyl palmitae	-	2.00
Beeswax	-	8.00
Propylene glycol	-	5.00
Stearate	-	10.00
Perfume, preservative	q.s.	q.s.

The use of some of the non-ionic emulsifiers based upon sorbitol in baby creams and lotions is shown in formulae, 5 to 7 :

Formula 5

Constituents	*Per cent*
Cetearyl alcohol	1.00
Mineral oil	4.00
Polysorbate	1.70

(Cont'd)

Sorbitan isostearate	1.00
Glyceryl stearate	1.00
Liquid lanolin	0.25
Water	83.35
Hydroxyethylcellulose	0.20
Glycerine	7.50
Perfume, preservative	q.s

Formula 6

Constituents	*per cent*
Mineral oil	35.50
Lanolin	1.00
Cetyl alcohol	1.00
Sorbitan oleate	2.10
Polysorbate	4.90
Dimethicone	5.00
Water	50.50
Perfume, preservative	q.s.

Formula 7

Constituents	*per cent*
Pertrolatum	20.00
Sorbitan isostearate	2.10
Micro-crystalline wax	3.34
Mineral oil	10.55
Glycerine	3.14
Water	60.87
Perfume, preservative	q.s.

Formulae 5 and 6 are of oil-in-water creams , whereas formula 7 is water-in-oil. The last cream formulation (formula 8) illustrates the use of polyoxyethylene sorbitan lanolin derivatives, which are also thought to be fairly mild.

Formula 8

Constituents	*per cent*
Mineral oil	15.00
Stearic acid	15.00
Beeswax	2.00
Lanolin	1.00
PEG-20 sorbitan lanolate	5.00
PEG -40 sorbitan lanolate	1.00
Sorbitol	10.00
Water	51.00
Perfume, preservative	q.s.

In view of its potentially irritating nature, the use of lanolin itself in baby products should be carefully considered.

In the transition from emulsions to baby oils, the use of anhydrous ointments (of which the zinc and castor oil cream is an example) should be considered. The following formulation (formula 9) is a little less sticky and more pleasant to use than zinc and castor oil, while still affording excellent barrier protection against excreta.

Formula 9

Constituents	*per cent*
Mineral oil	83.50
Acetylated lanolin alcohol	1.50
Silica	5.00
Zinc oxide	10.00

Baby oils are composed predominantly of a very pure grade of mineral oil. Small amounts of fatty acid esters, vegetable oils, lanolin derivatives and other compatible materials should be included only after careful consideration of safety and irritation potential.

Baby powders functions is to lubricate, dry and perhaps to impart a slight perfume to the skin. The absorbency and adhesiveness of talc can be improved by the blending in of other materials is shown by formulae 10-13.

Formulae	10	11	12	13
Constituents	*per cent*	*per cent*	*per cent*	*per cent*
Sterilised talc	80.00	74.00	95.00	90.50
Magnesium stearate	10.00	4.00	-	2.50
Calcium carbonate	10.00	-	-	-
Kaolin	-	20.00	-	5.00
Glyceryl stearate	-	1.00	-	-
Cetyl alcohol	-	1.00	-	-
Starch	-	-	5.00	-
Zinc oxide	-	-	-	2.00
Perfume	q.s.	q.s.	q.s.	q.s.

Chapter - 6

BATH PRODUCTS PREPARATIONS

INTRODUCTION

Now-a-days of bath product are available. They have undergone considerable change in terms of volume. The product range include, bath oils, shower gels, after bath body lotions and newer hydro-alcoholic products like bath satins.

FORAM BATHS

Foam baths are most popular bath preparations, which enjoyed a very healthy growth in recent years. Generally, they are available in liquid, gel and powder forms. Body cleansing, the primary function of a bath, is performed very well by a bubble bath. In addition it offers the opportunity to apply many desirable health and beauty ingredients to the skin, although not necessarily so efficiently as when these aids are used individually. Functioning as a body cleanser, a bubble bath soaks off and suspends dirt, grime and body oils. It prevents the formation of the 'bath-tub ring' that usually results from the use of soap. Therefore a bubble bath is superior to the traditional soap and water bath. Additionally, a well formulated bubble bath will condition the skin, deodorise, perfume the body and the bathroom, stimulate the senses, yet promote relaxation.

A good foam bath has following characteristics :

1. It should provide copious foam at minimal detergent concentration.
2. The foam should be stable, particularly in the presence of soap and soil and within wide limits of temperature. The foam stability should be reasonable and not excessive. It is possible to prevent premature breakdown of the foam, by late use of soap. This will satisfy the aesthetic requirements of the bather and facilitating the subsequent removal of the dirty water from the bath.
3. It should prevent bath-tub ring formation.
4. It must be non-irritant to the eyes, skin and mucous membranes. Bubble baths have been claimed to produce symptoms of irritation

in the lower urinary tract and it is essential to check the irritation potential of all these products before marketing.

5. It should have adequate detergent power so that it will cleanse the body efficiently. In order to counteract any excessive harshness to the skin it is advisable to include a low level of skin emollient.

Formulation of Foam Baths

As already mentioned, foam baths are available in several physical forms and clearly the choice of raw materials is highly dependent on the final products. Before discussing the product types in detail, it is of interest to examine the raw materials available.

Foaming agents

The foaming agent is the most important ingredient in all foaming bath products. While selecting a surfactant it is important to bear in mind the properties the good foam baths should exhibit. The anionics are the most widely used; both non-ionics and amphoterics are also of considerable interest. Due to eye irritancy and incompatibility with soaps and anionic, cationies are not advisable to use in bath formulations.

The anionic surfactants used are the sodium, ammonium and alkanolamine salts of fatty alcohol sulphates, fatty alcohol ether sulphates and (sometimes) alkyl benzene sulphonates. Soaps are not suitable surfactauts for use in foam baths, since in hard water calcium and magnesium soaps precipitate as a dirty hard scum.

Perhaps the most popular surfactants used in foam baths are the fatty alcohol ether sulphates, especially the sodium salts and in particular, those based on lauryl-myristyl alcohols and containing 2-3 moles of ethylene oxide per mole of the alkyl ether sulphate. Copious foaming in hard water, reasonable foam stability in the presence of soap, fragrances, oil additives and body debris, together with a good skin compatibility, make these materials an obvious choice for bath products. A high degree of proficiency as a lime soap dispersant prevents bath-tub ring even in very hard water. Other advantages of these surfactants are good colour, which permits the use of very delicate pastel colours if required, a good viscosity response to electrolyte and unusual solubilising powers for perfumes.

Primarily for reasons of cost, alkyl benzene sulphonates (mainly branched-chain dodecyl benzene sulphonates) soon found their ways from household detergent uses into toiletry items such as bubble baths. Of all the synthetic surfactants, the sodium alkyl benzene sulphonates are probably the most suitable for spray drying and until recently most of the commercial products on the market in bead form consisted of this material and various salt builders and extenders. When biodegradability considerations became critical, the importance of linear alkyl benzene suphonates grew.

The alpha-olefin sulphonates are commercially attractive and have been used as alternatives to linear alkyl benzene suphonates in powder foam baths. Lauryl sulphoacetates are sometimes used in high-priced powder or granular bubble baths but limited solubility has greatly restricted their use in liquid products.

The sulphosuccinates, particularly the monoesters such as the di-sodium lauryl alcohol polyglycol ether sulphosuccinate, are considered to be very mild detergents with good foaming properties. They are free from any tendency to irritate the skin and mucous membranes. Furthermore, they are also claimed to increase the tolerance of the skin to other detergents such as fatty alcohol ether sulphates and alkyl benzene sulphonates.

The paraffin sulphonates produced by the sulphoxidation of *n*-paraffins are relatively cheap, in particular, the secondary alkane sulphonates. This material, in addition to being biodegradable and exhibiting good physiological properties, is also a good foamer with high solubility in water. The use of alkane sulphonate with alkyl ether sulphates prevent excessive degreasing of the skin and easy thickening of finished product.

The non-ionic components of bubble baths are used to stabilise foam, to enhance the viscosity of the product, or to solubilise skin care ingredients and fragrances. The non-ionic surfactants used in bubble baths are alkanolamide and amine oxides. In addition, ethoxylated derivatives such as ethoxylated fatty alcohols, ethoxylated fatty acids, alkyl phenol ethoxylates, ethoxylated alkanolamides, ethoxylated propylene oxide condensates (Pluronics) and ethoxylated sorbitan fatty acid condensates are occasionally utilised.

Emollients

Special ingredients known as emollients are often added to the formulation to achieve and maintain a healthy and attractive skin. The value of many of these conditioners has been challenged but they continue to be used with apparent success. Although it has been argued that the bather stays in the bath for too short a time to receive any real benefit, equally strong opinions have been expressed that, even in this short time, the skin absorbs active substances. Many such ingredients are available. The following list gives some of the most popular in common use : branched chain esters, for example isopropyl myristate; decyl oleate; ethoxylated partial glyceride fatty acid esters protein derivatives; lanolin derivates; and fatty alcohol ethoxylates; etc.

Perfumes

There si no question that the perfume used in a foam bath is extremely important. Most of the larger companies marketing foam baths spend a great deal of time and money in selecting the perfumes for their products. A good perfume must of course, convey the marketing image of the brand and it should also fulfil the following requirements :

1. It should be acceptable when sniffed in the bottle.
2. In use it should be fresh and have sufficient volatility to give a strong impact.
3. It should linger on the skin to give feeling of freshness and wellbeing.
4. It must have an acceptable shelf-life in the product.

The level of perfume used will vary between 1 and 5 per cent, depending on the cost. The nature of the perfume ingredients may require the use of additional solubilisers; the most commonly used are non-ionics such as ehtoxylated fatty alcohols, ethoxylated fatty acid esters, ethoxylated sorbitan fatty acid esters and ethoxylated propylene oxide condensates (for example, pluronics).

Perfumes often cause problems of product instability. They not only affect odour stability, but can cause discolouration, upset preservation systems and cause instability in clear, opacified and emulsion products. The need to test the shelf life of all new products adequately cannot be overstressed. The ingredients used in perfumes should also be adequately tested before use for safety.

Herbal extracts are used in bath preparations, usually to help convey the brand image and to justify therapeutic claims with respect to minor skin disorders. Herbal extracts of most living plants can be obtained if required, but their medicinal nature is open to speculation.

Viscosity controllers

The problem of achieving the required viscosity of liquid products depends on the choice and level of surfactant and foam booster. Even certain perfumes have been found to have significant effect on viscosity. Generally, inorganic salts such as sodium and potassium chloride are used to thicken the product where possible, whereas alcohol, hexylene glycol, propylene glycol and polyethylene glycols are used to lower the viscosity certain thickening problems, however, can only be solved by the use of natural gums such as tragacanth and gum acacia, or synthetic gums such as methyl cellulose and hydroxyethyl cellulose.

Colour

Colour of foam baths is clearly important in marketing and care should be taken to select colours that are stable in the chosen product. Obviously, if the products are marketed in clear bottles adequate light testing should be carried out. Interesting colour effects in the bath can be achieved by the use of indicator colours and fluorescein. The colour should be selected as per the legislative requirement of the country.

Preservatives

Foam baths are easily attacked by moulds and bacterias, particularly Pseudomonas. Hence, they should have sufficient amount of preservative. Bacterial attack can produce opacity in products that are intended to be clear, separation in emulsified and pearlescent products and can cause changes in both perfume and colour system. Suitable preservatives include ethanol; methyl, propyl and butyl hydroxy benzoate; phenylmercuric nitrate; formaldehyde; Bronopol; and may others. The best preservative for a particular foam bath can only be determined by properly designed microbiological testing. Good housekeeping in the manufacturing unit is, however, just as important as choice of preservative if product contamination is to be avoided.

Opacifying agents

When an opaque liquid foam bath is required, an opacifier is needed. Higher alcohols such as stearyl or cetyl alcohols; ethylene glycol mono- and distearates; glyceryl and propylene glycol stearates and palmitates; and the magnesium, calcium and zi nc salts of stearic acid are opacifier used

Clearly, viscosity is an important factor in the stability of such systems. The manufacturing technique used is vitally important in achieving maximum stability. Ideally, when using tho opacifies mentioned above, all the ingredients (except perfume) should be heated to 65°-70°C and allowed to cool slowly to ambient temperature with gentle mixing, when the pearl will develop. Rapid cooling will produce less pearly products that may be unstable. It is possible, however, to obtain blended opacifier- detergent concentrates of some of these opacifiers which eliminate the need to heat the batch.

TYPES OF PRODUCT

Liquids

Liquids can be further divided into clear, translucent, opaque, pearlescent and multi-layer products. The formulation possibilities for a medium-priced clear liquid foam bath are endless. A typical and very simple product formula is shown below :

Formula 1

Constituents	*per cent*
Sodium lauryl ether sulphate(28% active)	50
Coconut diethanolamide	3
Perfume	1-2
Citric acid	q.s. to pH 7
Colour, preservative, emollients, solubiliser	q.s.
Sodium chloride	q.s. to required viscosity
Water	to 100

More expensive but milder formulations can be achieved by replacing part of the sodium lauryl ether sulphate by a coconut imidazoline betaine.

Translucent and pearlescent products can be created by the addition of insoluble stearates. These are readily available from all major surfactant manufacturers and the depth of opacity is governed by the level of incorporation, which is usually between 1 and 5 per cent. Opaque non-pearlescent products are achieved by the use of polymeric materials.

Multi-layer products can be achieved and a typical formulation is as follows :

Formula 2

Constituents	*per cent*
Sodium lauryl ether sulphate (28%)	50.0
Coconut diethanolamide	9.0
Hexylene glycol	14.0
Neutral monoethanolamine citrate	13.0
Citric acid	3.0
Perfume, colour, preservative	to 100.0

Gels

Basically gels are very similar to liquid products, having much higher viscosity. This is achieved by increasing the level of detergent, foam stabiliser or electrolyte content, depending on the particular formulation. Shower gels are virtually identical in formulation to the highly viscous liquid bath products; however, because they are sold for direct application to the body they must be very mild. It is usual to adopt for shower gels the types of formulation, already mentioned, that have a milder action on the skin and eyes.

Dry bubble baths

Dry bubble baths of considerably less importance than liquid bubble baths. Basically they consist of a mixture of one or more foaming agents, fillers and water softeners to add bulk or act as carriers, perfume, colour and free-flow agents.

The major surfactant ingredients are usually dry products, sometimes fortified with liquid surfactants, for example sodium lauryl ether sulphate, to give good flash foam. The principal surfactants employed are benzene sulphonates. Other surfactants that have been used include sodium lauryl sulphate, sodium lauryl sulphoacetate and isethionate derivatives.

Inorganic fillers such as sodium chloride and sodium sulphate are often used in the more inexpensive products. These can, however, be replaced by functional fillers also have water-softening properties. These include sodium hexametaphosphate, sodium sesquicarbonate and tetrasodium pyrophosphate. Free-flowing and anti-caking is obtained by tri-calcium phosphate, calcium silicate, or sodium silica aluminate to powdered bubble bath. Bentonite or starch is usually employed to absorb the perfume, in order to disperse it throughout the product. The colour is usually incorporated by premixing with one of the fillers. Formulae 3 and 4 are given as under :

Formula 3

Constituents	*per cent*
Alpha-olefin sulphonate(40% active spray-dried beads)	20
Lauric isopropanolamide	3
Sodium sesquicarbonate (low density)	60
Sodium chloride	14
Perfume	3
Colour	q.s

Formula 4

Constituents	*per cent*
Sodium lauryl sulphate	30
Sodium lauryl sulphoacetate	10
Lauric isopropanolamide	3
Sodium sequicarbonate(low density)	50
Calcium silicate	4
Perfume	3
Colour	q.s.

Product Assessment

A large consumer panel is required for complete assessment of foam bath products. As it involves complete interpretation of the initial and residual feel of skin, efficiency of special ingredients, fragrance, amount of texture of foam. The laboratory testing is limited to the assessment of foam volume and stability.

Of the stabilisers examined on alkylamido betaine was shown to be the best stabilsing agent against soap, with N-alkyldimethyl betaine second.

BATH SALTS

Ingredients and Formulation

Salts

Sodium sesquicarbonate ($Na_2Co_3.NaHCO_3.2H_2O$), which is a mixed salt, is probably the most popular material used in the preparation of bath salts. It is available in uniformly sized, elongated, attractive translucent crystals which are extremely stable, non-caking and free-flowing. It dissolves rapidly and completely in water, is easy to colour and perfume. It si an excellent water softener and quite mild to the skin, having a pH value of about 9.8 for a 1 per cent solution.

Other carbonates that have been used are sodium carbonate decahydrate, $Na_2CO_3.10H_2O$ (Washing soda), and the monohydrate, $Na_2CO_3.H_2O$. The decahydrate, is a good water softener and consists of large attractive crystals that are readily soluble in warm water. Unfortunately, it has several serious disadvantages including a low melting point of 35°C, at which temperature it dissolves in its sown water of crystallisation. This clearly precludes its use in hot climates. Even under ordinary storage conditions it tends to effloresce to become powdery and unsightly, although this can be overcome by coating the crystals with a film of humectant such as glycerine. It is also more highly alkaline than the sesquicarbonate. The monohydrate is the most stable form of sodium carbonate and is available in attractive crystal agglomerates with excellent stability its main disadvantages are its slow rate of dissolution and the fact that it is more alkaline than the sesquicarbonate.

Phosphates like the hexametaphosphate (Calgon), tetrasodium pyrophosphate and sodium tripolyphosphate are used to improve softening. Trisodium phosphate is a good water softener but because of its highly alkaline nature it cannot be used without buffering. However, it can be used in combination with either sodium sesquicarbonate or borax, both of which buffer it quite effectively.

Borax ($Na_2B_4O_7.10H_2O$) is less alkaline than the carbonates and possesses a mild detergent action. Although it is less effective as a water softener than the carbonates and is slow to dissolve.

Rock salt, NaCL, is used in bath salts of the type that provide fragrance only. It is very stable and its large crystals are attractive and easily coloured. It is of course non-alkaline and mild to the skin. Its disadvantage are that it has no water-softening properties interfere with soap lathering the large crystals do not dissolve easily.

For effervescent systems, sodium bicarbonate and tartaric or citric acid are included.

Fragrance

The instability of fragrance is attributed to its distribution in a thin film on the surface of an inorganic salt which can be quite alkaline. Hence, the perfume must have good fixative properties in addition to adequate stability to alkalies, light and oxidation. The deposition, retention and stability of the fragrance and they may also improve the flow characteristics of the product is achieved by using calcium silicate or fumed silica.

Colour

As with fragrance, the choice of colour is limited by stability to both alkalies and light. Colour stability may also be affected by perfume. Insoluble colours have been recommended because of their better stability to alkalies and light. These are best dispersed at a concentration of about 1 per cent in a suitable medium such as a glycol or liquid non-ionic surfactant.

Example formulations

Formula 5 (Bath salts-fragrance only)

Constituents	*per cent*
Sodium chloride	95-99
Perfume	1-5
Colour	q.s.

Formula 6 (Water-softening bath salt)

Constituents	*per cent*
Sodium sesquicarbonate	95-99
Perfume	1-5
Colour	q.s.

Formula 7 (Effervescent bath salts)

Cosntituents	*per cent*
Sodium sesquicarbonate	25
Sodium bicarbonate	50
Tartaric acid	20
Perfume, colour	5

The manufacture of bath salts is a straightforward process and can be carried out in most types of dry powder blender. Colouring is done either by spraying with colour solution, mixing and drying or by immersing the salts in the colour solution, followed by drying. Colour solutions should be hydro-alcoholic or, if possible, alcoholic. Alcohol, in addition to reducing the drying time, helps to prevent solution of the bath salts. Fragrance is added colour solution. Perfume can also be mixed with oil-absorbent powders. Clearly, in colouring effervescent salts no water can be used.

Bath Cubes and Tablets

Bath cubes and Tablets employ the same materials as bath salts, but in powder form. The powdered bath salts are first granulated with starch and a small amount of alcohol-soluble gum binder is normally added. The granules are then compressed into tablets or cubes. A suitable disintegrating material like sodium lauryl sulphate or starch should be included to aid the dissolving process before compressing.

BATH OILS

The primary function of a bath is to cleanse the body. The function of bath oil is not only cleansing but of skin lubrication. In addition, they are used to impart fragrance to the body.

The oil bath has emerged as the simplest and most effective method of lubrication for generalised skin dryness. Dry skin affects both young and old and, in its mildest form, appears as a slight roughening and scaling of the skin. Severe dryness can result in disturbing itching and both the incidence and serverity of itching becomes Progressively worse as the individual becomes older. Clinical efforts to overcome skin dryness are based on the concept that a surface oil or lipid film on the skin retards water loss through evaporation - hence the importance of oil baths in combating dry skin.

Various investigations have been conducted, aiming to quantify the absorption of different oils by skin. Recently, the first objective attempt to quantify all deposition on skin using the technique of arm emersion in a bath of oil stipulates that product based on mineral oil adhere to skin better than vegetable oil formulation. Further, an oilated oatmeal preparation (colloidal oatmeal combined with mineral oil and lanolin) can be adsorbed very poorly by the skin. The likely explanations for this being that oatmeal is a better adsorptive substrate for oils than is the skin. It is also observed that adsorption increased as the temperature of the bath was raised and as the concentration of oil increased. Soaking for longer than 20 minutes, however, did not cause a significant increase in oil adsorption.

Classification of Bath Oil

Bath oils can be classified into four main categories: floating or spreading bath oils which are water-immiscible; a dispersible or blooming type which turns milky on addition to water; a soluble type which forms a clear dispersion in water; and a foaming type similar to the foam bath.

Floating or Spreading Oils

Floating or spreading bath oils are hydrophobic in nature. They have low specific gravity. Hence, they float on top of the bath water, which covers the bathers skin with an oily film on emergence from the water. It provides the bather with a luxurious emollient coat. This type of product is ideal for augmenting the aesthetic nature of the bath with pleasant fragrance to the bathroom, since the oil layer on top of the hot bath water allows the fragrance to distil readily into the atmosphere. One problem with this type of product is the occurrence of an unsightly 'ring' around the bath caused by the oil deposit. This deposit is compounded by a soap scum if the bather also uses a true soap in conjunction with hard water. Furthermore, since oils are natural foam depressants, the floating oil layer is likely to impede the lathering performance of the soap. Ideally, a floating bath oil should fully cover the surface of the water and be deposited on the skin in a very thin film, covering as much of the skin surface as possible. A lubricating bath oil should not be deposited in a heavy greasy layer, which is unattractive to the user, nor should it leave in the bath a heavy oily film that is difficult to remove.

Perfume is obviously an important ingredient. Other ingredients sometimes included are antioxidants, colours and sunscreens.

Typical formulae for floating bath oils are given below :

Formula 8

Constituents	*per cent*
Arlamol	49
arlatone	1
Light mineral oil	45
Perfume	5

Formula 9

Constituents	*per cent*
Light mineral oil	46
Isopropyl myristate	48
Arlatone	1
Perfume	5

Dispersible or Blooming Oils

Dispersible bath oils consist of emollient oils, perfume oils and contain a surfactant. To emulsify the oils in the water instead of making them spread on the surface surfactant is used. When poured into the bath water they bloom into a milky cloud. They are sometimes preferred to the floating type because the oils are dispersed uniformly throughout the bath water, providing thorough contact with the body during the bath. When properly formulated they leave very little oily stickness or ring in the tub after the water is drained. The emollient oils used tend to be similar to the ones used in floating bath oils, with perfume levels between 5 and 10 per cent. A typical formula for a dispersible bath oil would be as follows (formula 10).

Formula 10

Constituents	*per cent*
Mineral oil	65
Isopropyl myristate	20
Brij	10
Perfume	5

Soluble Oils

Soluble bath oils contain large quantities of surfactants to solubilise the high-fragrance oil concentrations. And also to dissolve or disperse these oils readily in the bath water. They leave no residue in the bath and have no emollient effect on the skin. Soluble bath oils are either anhydrous concentrates consisting of perfume and surfactant or solubilised products consisting of perfume, surfactant and water. They contain 5 to 20 per cent perfume oil, which can usually be solubilised by means of a hydrophilic surfactant. A typical formulation is shown in formula 11.

Formula 11

Constituents	*per cent*
Perfume	5
Polyoxyethylene	
Sorbitan monolaurate	5–25
Preservative	q.s.
Water	to 100

The quantity of tween (polyoxyethylene sorbitan monolaurate) is clearly dependent on the type of perfume used.

Foaming Oils

Foaming bath oils can be considered either as bubble baths with high fragrance levels or as soluble bath oils with foaming agents and stabilisers. These products provide both fragrance and foaming action. They also serve to eliminate the bath-tub ring. Like the soluble bath oils they generally have no emolliency properties. The foaming agents and stabilisers discussed under foam baths are used. Polyoxyethylene sorbitan monoalaurate is often used to solubilise the fragrance in the foaming bath oil. Thickeners such as carboxymethyl cellulose, methyl cellulose and other gums are commonly added, as are sometimes sequestrants. A typical formulation is shown in formula 12.

Formula 12

Cosntituents	*per cent*
Perfume	5
Polyoxyethylene	
Sorbitan monolaurate	20
Sodium lauryl ether sulphate (28% active)	40
Coconut diethanolamide	2
Preservative	q.s.
Water	to 100

Very occasionally emollient oils are included in these products at significant levels but most of these have such a foam-depressing action that the final product can barely be considered to be a foam bath.

AFTER–BATH PRODUCTS

After-bath products are body or dusting powders and the various lotions

Body or Dusting Powders

Body or dusting powders are also known as body talcs or talcum powders. They have a wide appeal because of the smooth feeling and cooling effect which they impart while they temporarily absorb moisture. The extra heat loss from the large surface area of the talc particles creates cooling effect.

Talc used in these formulations, must have good slip characteristics, covering power, body adhesion and absorbency. The slip and texture properties are essentially based on the talc. It is essential, therefore, that grit-free, alkali-free high quality cosmetic talc is used. Talc should be free of bacteria and sterilised grades should always be used. In order to improve adhesion properties, metallic stearsate such as zinc or magnesium stearate and kaolin are incorporated. Whereas magnesium carbonate, starch, kaolin and precipitated chalk all improve asorbency. Zinc and titanium oxides at low levels along with earth colours can be incorporated for tinting purposes when required. Perfume oils are easily incorporated and should be sufficiently powerful to cover the base odour yet not interfere with other perfumes that may be used. Other ingredients sometimes included are boric acid to act as a skin buffering agent and fumed silica to give a powder of lower density. A typical formulation (formula 13) is as follows :

Formula 13

Constituents	*per cent*
Talc	75
Kaolin	10
Fumed silica	2
magnesium carbonate	6
Zinc stearate	6
Perfume	1

After-bath Emollients

After-bath emollients or moisturisers are applied to the body to replace natural skin liquids removed during bathing . Their function, therefore, is to prevent the occurrence of dry skin. Basically four types of products exist, anhydrous oil-based systems , water-in-oil emulsions; oil-in-water emulsions;

and hydro-alcoholic emulsions. The first two types are less popular due to their greasy nature. Oil-in-water emulsions are perhaps most widely used. Generally, they are sold in lotion form and are usually formulated to give good 'rub-in' and feel properties. Atypical formulation (Formula 14) is shown below :

Formula 14

Constituents	*per cent*
Crodafos N-3 acid	0.5
Emollient oil	5.0
Carbopol 9.41	0.4
Denatured ethanol (95%)	40.0
Triethanolamine	q.s. to pH 6.5
Perfume	1-5
EDTA	q.s.
Water	to 100.0

Such a product could be made without heat by hydrating the Carbopol in the water with efficient mechanical agitation, followed by the addition of a mixture of emollient oil, perfume and Crodafos. Finally, the emulsion is completed by the addition of the alcoholic solution of triethanolamine. EDTA or other suitable sequestrant is included to stabilise the Carbopol gel, since metal ions can depolymerise Carbopol and this can lead to loss in viscosity and hence emulsion instability.

The higher concentration of alcohol, above 50% should be avoided as it may destabilise due to coagulation of the carbopol. It may destabilise the emulsion unless the levels of emulsifier and gelling agent are increased at the same time. Increasing the level of alcohol serves to provide greater perfume lift and quicker drying but produces a thinner, less apaque and sometimes a more unstable emulsion.The rise in the level of emollient oil increases emolliency which produces more opaque product.

Chapter - 7

DEODORANTS AND ANTIPERSPIRANTS PREPARATIONS

INTRODUCTION

Antiperspirants are used primarily to reduce (axillary) wetness. Deodorants (except soaps) are employed to reduce axillary odour. Since this is considered a non-therapeutic purpose and a function of the body is not considered to be altered, they are classed as cosmetics.

Several metal salts have astringent properties including those of aluminium, zirconium, zinc, iron, chromium, lead, mercury and several rarer metals.

MECHANISM OF DEODORANTS AND DEODORANT INGREDIENTS

Since axillary odour is largely produced by the action of bacteria on nutrients present in apocrine secretion, any compound which inhibits, the growth of those micro-organisms found in the axillae will, in theory, exhibit deodourant properties.

A formulation (Formula 1) of a deodorant composition is as follows:

Formula 1

Constituents	*per cent*
hexamethylenetetramine	14-20
Zinc oxide	16-23
Starch	16-23
Petroleum jelly	38-43
Perfume	0.5-1.2

The effect of this deodorant remains for 15 days.

Sodium bicarbonate (baking soda) is used as a deodorant. It is an acid salt which can act chemically as either a mild alkali or a mild acid. Underarm odours are largely caused by volatile acidic compounds which are absorbed by baking soda to form stable odourless salts.

EVALUATION OF ANTIPERSPIRANTS

Efficacy of Antiperspirants

The range of effectiveness (average sweat reduction) in laboratory hot-rooms tests of OTC antiperspirant submitted to the Antiperspirant Review Panel is given in Table 24.1

Table 24.1 Range of average sweat reduction – US FDA OTC antiperspirant review panel.

Dosage form	*Average reduction %*
Aerosols	20-23
Creams	35-47
Roll-ons	14-70
Lotions	28-62
Liquids	15-54
Sticks	35-40

The efficacy of an antiperspirant is best defined as the percentage reduction in the rate of sweating in the axilla that may be achieved after a realistic application or series of applications of the test product. The preferred methods for the determination of efficacy are gravimetry or the use of electronic hygrometers.

Product Formulation – Antiperspirants

Aerosols

The antiperspirant in powder suspension, are prepared using micronised powdered aluminium carbohydrate and oil base 3-4% active ingredient. Many combinations of raw materials are available for the formulation of aerosol antiperspirants. In addition, formulations must provide maximum antiperspirant and deodorant effectiveness, maximum safety, cosmetic elegance and minimum staining. A typical powder-in-oil formulation (Formula 2) is given below :

Formula 2

Constituents	*per cent*
Aluminium chlorhydrate (micronised)	4.50
Isopropyl myristate	3.70

(Cont'd)

Fumed silica	0.15
Perfume	q.s.
Propellants (65.35)	to 100.00

The emollient or carrier for the aluminium chlorhydrate is used to produce a smooth feel on the skin and to help the powder to adhere. Commonly an ester such as isopropyl myristate is used although some products contain volatile silicones to reduce staining of clothes.

A suspending agent is added to prevent agglomeration of the aluminium chlorhydrate which could lead to valve blockage and leakage. Typical suspending agents are silica and 'Bentone' derivatives. Fumed silica has an extremely fine particle size and forms a coating over the powder particles to prevent the development of hard caking.

Antiperspirant sticks

the antiperspirant stick usually consists of a wax-like matrix which serves as a carrier for aluminium chlorhydrate powder and volatile silicone. A low-melting matrix and a high-boiling volatile silicone are necessary in order to conserve the latter during processing. For this reason stearyl alcohol is preferred over stearic acid because of its lower melting point (58.5°C vs 69.9°C).

Typical formulations are as follow (Formulae 3 and 4) :

Formulae	*3*	*4*
Constituents	*per cent*	*per cent*
Volatile silicone	46	46
Aluminium chlorhydrate powder	20	20
Stearyl alcohol	24	24
Polyethylene glycol distearate	6	6
Carbowax	4	4

Procedure : heat the stearyl alcohol, carbowax and polyethylene glycol distearate 6000 to 80°C. when melted, add the aluminium chlorhydrate and mix thoroughly. Cool to 70°C and rapidly mix in the volatile silicone 7158. When mixing is complete, pour the mixture into a stick container. Allow the mixture to cool undisturbed for 24 hours.

Antiperspirant creams

While oil-in-water emulsions provide a convenient vehicle for storing and delivering antiperspirant actives, compositions of this type tend to produce an undesirable wet, cold and/or sticky sensation when they are applied to and rubbed into the skin. This can be minimised somewhat by utilising compositions in anhydrous form. The formulations (Formula 5) is given as under :

Formula 5

Constituents	*per cent*
Isopropyl myristate	32.0
Bentone 38 (thickening / suspending agent)	7.0
Ethyl alcohol (gel-promoting agent)	3.0
Zirconium hydroxychloride/aluminium chlorhydroxide/glycine complex	47.0
Silicone (antisyneresis agent)	10.0
Perfume	1.0

This is a substantially anhydrous antiperspirant composition in the form of a cream and is resistant to syneresis. A normal oil-in-water cream antiperspirant formulation (Formula 6) is given as under :

Formula 6

Constituents		*parts by weight*
A	Neo-fat	10.6
	Mineral oil	1.0
	Beeswax	1.0
	Glyceryl monostearate (pure)	6.4
B	Chlorhydrol (50% solution of aluminium chlorhydrate)	32.0
	Perfume	q.s.
C	Propylene glycol	5.0
	Sodium lauryl sulphate	1.3
	De-ionised water	to 100.0

Procedure

Heat A to 70°-80°C. Add C with agitation and cool to 35° - 40°C. Add B and mix thoroughly.

Roll–on Antiperspirants

They are generally either emulsion products or aqueous alcoholic solutions thickened with cellulose gums. The aqueous alcoholic products generally dry quicker and are less sticky than the emulsion products. The viscosity of the final product is important to avoid leakage around the roll-ball.

The volatile silicone reduces the sticking of the roll-ball due to the drying out of the aluminium chlorhydrate (Formula 7) is given as under :

Formula 7

Constituents		*per cent*
A	Magnesium aluminium silicate	1.0
	De-ionised water	49.0
B	Glyceryl monostearate (acid stable)	8.0
C	Aluminium chlorhydrate (50% soln.)	40.0
D	Volatile silicone	2.0
E	Fragrance	q.s.

Product Formulation–Deodorants

Deodorant soaps

Among the deodorants, the toilet soap market is important market in the world. The most frequently used antimicrobial agents in soaps at the present time are trichlocarban (TCC), cloflucarban (CF3) and triclosan. Hexachlorophene and tribromsalan (TBS) occupied the key spots in this application before they are ban. All but triclosan are active only against Gram positive organisms in the presence of soap. Triclosan is active against both gram positive any many gram negative organisms.

Deodorant sticks

A typical formulation (formula 9) is given below :

Formula 9

Constituents	*per cent*
Sodium stearate	8.0
Ethyl alcohol	74.8
Propylene glycol	10.0

(Cont'd)

Isopropyl myristate	5.0
Triclosan	0.2
Perfume	2.0

The alcoholic sticks shrink if the packaging is poor. Hence, to avoid shrinkage non-alcoholic deodorants sticks are prepared. The formulation (Formula 10) is given below :

Formula 10

Constituents	*per cent*
Sodium stearate	8.0
Propylene glycol	10.0
Perfume	1.0
Coconut diethanolamide	5.0
PPG-3-myristyl ether	68.8
Triclosan	0.2
Water	7.0

Aerosol Deodorants

The alcoholic solution of bactericide is the base of aerosol deodorants. A product called a 'deo-cologne' is based on alcoholic solution of perfume. It si used as body spray. A typical formulation (Formula 11) for an aerosol deodorant is given as under (Lacquered monobloc aluminium or tinplate containers can be used) :

Formula 11

Constituents	*per cent*
Triclosan	0.05
Propylene glycol	2.00
Alcohol(99% v/v)	57.45
Perfume	0.50
Propellant	40.00

Chapter - 8

DEPILATORIES

INTRODUCTION

The depilatory are those preparations applied for the removal of superfluous hair, specifically on the face, legs and axilla with no injury. A distinction must be drawn between the mechanical removal of hair by either plucking it with tweezers or by embedding it in an adherent material which can then be pulled away from the skin bringing the hair with it (a process referred to as epilation), destruction of hair by electrolysis, and the removal of hair after it has been sufficiently degraded by chemical means.

EPILATION

Epilatory preparation are based on mixtures consisting essential oil of rosin and beeswax, modified in some instances by the addition of mineral oil and or waxes. The following formulations (Formulae 1 and 2) are given as under :

Formula 1

Constituents	*per cent*
Rosin	75.0
Beeswax	25.0

Formula 2

Constituents	*per cent*
Light coloured rosin	52.0
Yellow beeswax	25.0
Paraffin wax	17.0
Petrolatum	5.0
Perfume	1.0

In addition to rosin and waxes, mineral or vegetable oil may be included (for example at a level of about 15 per cent). The discomfort experienced when the hair is pulled off is reduced by addition of camphor. A local anaesthetic, for example benzocaine, to enhance this effect and an antibacterial compound will reduce the chance of infecting the skin after damage or exposure.

CHEMICAL DEPILATION

The term 'depilatory' refers to preparations intended for the chemical breakdown of superfluous hair without injury to the skin. The essential requirements of a depilatory are :

1. Non-toxic and non-irritant to the skin;
2. Efficient in action, removing hair rapidly (prfefably in 4-6 minutes);
3. Preferably odourless;
4. Stable on storage;
5. Harmless to clothing; and
6. Preferably cosmetically elegant.

Depilatory preparations usually contain as their active component an alkaline reducing agent. The latter will cause the hair fibres to swell and produce a cleavage of the cystine bridges between adjacent polypeptide chains as a preliminary to the complete degradation of the hair.

Sulphides

Compositions based on alkali and alkaline earth sulphides are capable of producing rapid depilation, when used with a suspension of lime.

Strontium sulphide is a much milder depilatory, but must be used at a higher concentration than sodium sulphide to produce an equivalent dehairing action. Preparations containing strontium sulphide. Although largely replaced by those based on thioglycollates, are still available. They are very effective and work within 3-5 minutes after application.

In addition to the active agent, a depilatory preparation may contain a humectant such as glycerine or sorbitol. A thickening agent, methyl cellulose incorporated, so as to thicken the solution sufficiently to allow it to remain in contact with the hair as long as necessary. For a sulphide depilatory, the following formula (3) will be found effective :

Formula 3

Constituents	*per cent*
Strontium sulphide	20.0
Talc	20.0
Methyl cellulose	3.0
Glycerin	15.0
Water	42.0

This is prepared using an emulsion base for smoothness and stability. The formulation of depilatories depends upon very careful adherence to detail; slight departures from formulation in the process of manufacturing can produce remarkable differences between the efficacies of different batches of supposedly the same product. For this reason any formulation a general guide.

Despite their disadvantages, sulphide-based depilatories are preferred by many black-skinned men for removing facial hair because of their comparatively rapid action.

Stannites

The stannites have no appreciable odour, they suffer from instability, forming stannites in the presence of water. The triethanolamine, dextrine sugar, can be used as stabilisers of water-soluble organic compounds having three or more carboxyl group. They are also used for soluble silicates.

Substituted Mercaptans

The majority of depilatories available today are substituted mercaptans. They are used in the presence of alkaline reacting materials, For example calcium thioglycollate, in conjunction with calcium hydroxide. These preparations possess less odour than the sulphide but slow to act. They are safer on the skin than sulphides. They are therefore used on the face - an area where superfluous hair can cause great distress and where women have a strong psychological aversion to using a razor. In general, thioglycollate preparations are more attractive than the sulphide type. However, their slowness in attacking the coarse resistant hair of the underarm has left a market open for sulphide depilatories used for this purpose only.

It is often said that depilatories can be used for smoothing the legs, but so much of the product is required to cover each leg that it becomes uneconomic for most users. In any case, the legs are easy to shave.

Thioglycollates

Thioglycollate-based preparations are non-toxic and stable at concentrations between 2.5 and 4 per cent. At these concentrations they may produce depilation in 5-15 minutes at pH 10.0 and 12.5 to produce depilation within a fairly short time and without irritating the skin. Basic formula 4 for preparing cream, semi-fluid and powder depilatories is given below :

Formula 4 (Depilatory cream)	
Constituents	per cent
Evanol	6.5
Calcium thioglycollate	5.4
Calcium hydroxide	7.0
Duponol paste	0.02
Sodium silicate	3.43
Perfume	q.s.
Distilled water	to 100.0

Procedure

Add with stirring Duponol and Evanol to hot water (70°C) till it melts and disperse. After cooling add calcium hydorxide, perfume and calcium thioglycollate until uniform solution obtained. Formulae 5 and 6 are given below :

Formulae (Semi-fluid depilatories)	*5*	*5*
Constituents	*per cent*	*per cent*
Cream base		
Distilled water	60.0	60.0
Cetyl alcohol	6.0	6.0
Brij		
Final product		
Distilled water	17.3	17.2
Calcium thioglycollate	5.4	5.4
Calcium hydroxide	6.6	10.4
Strontium hydroxide	3.7	
Perfume	q.s.	q.s.
Cream base (as above)	67.0	67.0

Procedure

Prepare the cream base at 70°C and allow to cool to room temperature. Add the calcium thioglycollate to the bulk of the water and mix well; add the calcium hydroxide slowly with stirring, followed by the strontium hydroxide and any remaining water. Combine the two parts and stir well, adding the perfume at this point. Formula 7 for powder depilatory is given below :

Formula 7 (Powder depilatory)

Constituents	*per cent*
Calcium thioglycollate	20.0
Calcium hydroxide	23.1
Strontium hydroxide	8.9
Sodium lauryl sulphate powder	1.5
Cellosize	1.0
Magnesium carbonate	45.2
Perfume	0.3

Procedure

Mix the calcium thioglycollate, calcium hydroxide, strontium hydroxide, sodium lauryl sulphate and sellosize. Blend the perfume thoroughly with the magnesium carbonate. Add the latter to the former and blend thoroughly.

Other 'Thio' Compounds

A non-irritant, rapid-acting depilatory 'soap' bar formula 8 is given below :

Formula 8

Constituents	*per cent*
Thiolactic acid	30.5
Urea-sorbitol complex	25.5
Strontium hydroxide	4.5
Calcium hydroxide	4.5
Sodium lauryl sulphate	35.0

Enzymes

Depilatory preparations based on the enzyme keratinase have also been developed. They have the unpleasant odour of sulphide or even thioglycollate depilatories, and are non-irritant, but are not quite as effective.

Keratinase is used in depilatory preparations in a purified form, buffered to a pH within the range of 7-8, with an activity of 200k units per mg. The k unit is defined as the amount of enzyeme which will digest wool keratin so as to produce an increase in optical density of 0.04 at 280 nm.

Facial Depilatories for Black Skin

Conventional thioglycollate-based depilatories take 15-20 minutes to remove beard hair which is regarded as far too long. Effectiveness outweighs cosmetic elegance. The tendency is to use a powder depilatory which must be mixed with water before use but which effects adequate hair removal in 3-7 minutes.

The active ingredients commonly used in powder depilatories are barium sulphide and calcium thioglycollate. The former is the most popular because of its effectiveness and despite its offensive odour.

However, powders based on calcium thioglycollate are said to be gaining favour since they are less odourous and therefore more easily perfumed, though less effective.

EVALUATION OF DEPILATORY EFFICACY

The procedure for determining the efficacy of depilatories, involves the measurement of the cross-sectional diameter and the length of a hair immersed in a solution of a depilatory, and observing the time of maximum hair swelling. Sigmoid curves are obtained when both the length and width of swelling hair are plotted against time.

The slope maxima of these sigmoid curves amy be used to define an index of depilatory effectiveness in vitro.

Table 25.1. Relative efficacy of 'thio' compounds at 5 per cent concentration, adjusted to pH 11.0 - 12.0.

'Thio' compound	*Average depilation time* (min)*
2-Mercapto-ethanol	4.0
Thioglycerol	6.5
Thioglycollic acid	7.5
3-Mercaptopropionic acid	8.0
2-Mercaptopropionic acid	11.0
Thiodiglycol	15.0
Thiomalic acid	15.0

* Average of times for all alkalies used for neutralisation. Some combinations are found to be more effective than others.

Table 25.1 summaries the relative efficacy of various 'thio' compounds at a concentration of 5 per cent pH 11.0 - 12.0. It has been found that a concentration of 5 per cent 'thio' compound is sufficient.

The increase in concentrations do not increase the speed of depilation appreciable. Table 25.2 highlights the activities of thio-glycollic acid and thio-lactic acid neutralised with various alkalies.

Table 25. 2
Depilatory activity of thio-glycollic acid and thio-lactic acid neutralised with various alkalies (mercapto-acid concentration 0.4M, pH 12.5)

Cation	*Thio-glycollic acid*		*Thio-lactic acid*	
	Depilation time (min)	*Effect on skin*	*Depilation time (min)*	*Effect on skin*
Calcium	7	0	10	0
Barium	12	0	7	0
Strontium	5	0	7	0
Sodium	4	+	5½	+
Potassium	3½	+	4	++
Lithium	3½	0	5	0

Chapter - 9

PREPARATIONS OF FOOT COSMETICS

INTRODUCTION

Foot discomfort is common among a large population in different form. Although foot fatique affects adversely which sharply reduces individuals effort, very little attention is a paid to it. It is really amazing how little personal attention is lavished upon the much maligned human foot, although foot fatigue affects adversely both the physical and mental well-being of the sufferer, and leads to a sharp decline in the individual effort. Man-made materials impermeable to moisture vapour and thus to sweat have considerable influence on foot health. Wear trials have shown that it is the properties of the upper material which have by far the greatest effect on sweat accumulation in shoes.

Sweet accumulation in footwear has a direct effect :

1. On mechanical properties of foot skin;
2. On physicochemical properties of the shoe material; and
3. On encouragement of micro-biological growth in the skin and the shoe materials.

Foot Malodours and Foot Ailments

A musty or mouldy odour to the shoe and foot is due to fungi and breakdown of perspiration due to bacteria. However, other odours can arise by interactions with the material of the shoe. This will lead to penetration of odour of sweaty feet, burning and itching sensation between the toes; painful, tired and swollen feet; softening of the toe-nail bed; moist skin irritation, creating ideal conditions for fungla infections.

Foot Infection, Care & Hygiene

The feet spend long periods covered with socks or stockings and encased in footwear. This results in persistently warm and moist conditions which form an ideal environment for microbial proliferation and activity. The use of communal washing and bathing facilities is a major cause of spread of such infections. The supreme importance of hygienic cleansing of communal bathrooms, showers,etc., is clear; regular cleansing with germicidal products to remove skin debris and microbial contaminants is essential. The most prevalent kinds of foot infection are caused by fungi- mycosis. The well known mycosis 'athlete's foot' has almost become an international disease.

The feet should be washed at least once a day with soap and water. After washing it should be dried thoroughly, especially between the toes, and dusted with a talcum or foot powder. If infection is suspected or likely to have been encountered, both the soap and the powder should certainly contain an antiseptic agent.

There are many types of foot preparation in existence. Some are used to provide relief for tired and aching feet , others to soften cornified skin or to combat foot perspiration, and there are those used for alleviating skin irritations, eruptions and infections and for providing an anti-bacterial or anti-fungla effect.

Bathing the Feet

The reduction of bacterial infection, stimulation of blood circulation, and elimination of sweat secretions can be done by bathing foot in hot water. If the bath is alkaline it softens the hard keratinous layer of the skin, corms, calluses, etc. Artificial sea-salt powders are used in foot baths (formula 1). One part of artificial powder of prepared by mixing is enough for 20 parts of water for foot bath.

Formula 1

Constituents	*parts*
Potassium iodide	1
Potassium bromide	2
Magnesium chloride	250
Calcium chloride	125
Magnesium sulphate	250
Sodium sulphate	500
Sodium chloride	1500
Colour, perfume	q.s.

A bubbling foot bath tablet releases oxygen and carbon dioxide. The composition of Deo-foam bath for the feet is shown in formula 2.

Formula 2

Constituents	*per cent*	
Lathanol	26.0	
Tartaric acid powder	26.0	
Salicylic acid	1.0	
Sodium bicarbonate powder	25.0	
Sodium sesquicarbonate powder	9.0	
Sodium hexametaphosphate	4.0	
Sodium perborate	5.9	
Perfume	1.5	or q.s.
Calflo	1.5	
Colour :FD & C Blue NO. 1	0.1	or q.s.

Formula 3

Constituents	*per cent*
Texapon extract N25	55
Comperlan KD	6
Salicylic acid 20% solution*	25
Foromycen F10	2
Water	7
Neo-PCL water-soluble	1
Perfume oil	4
Salicyclic acid 20% solution :	
Borax	8
Salicylic acid	20
Water	72

(Heat to near boiling point to obtain a clear solution)

Foot Powders

Foot powders keep the feet dry. If they contain a fungicidal or fungistatic agent a better opportunity is presented for a more continuous application as perspiration dissolves the medicament. In shoes they help to prevent reinfection (formula 4). They are recommended in the Indian Army.

Formula 4

Constituents	*per cent*
Thymol	1
Boric acid	10
Zinc oxide	20
Talc	69

Another simple fungicidal dusting powder for the feet is given below in formula 5 :

Formula 5

Constituents	*per cent*
Zinc undecenoate	10.00
Undecenoic acid	2.08
Pine oil	0.47
Starch	50.00
Light kaolin	37.45

The main constituents of aerosol spray form foot powders are deodorant and antiperspirant. The different compositions are given in formulae 6 and 7.

Formula 6 (Aerosol foot powder)

Constituents	*per cent*
Talc	92.0
Zinc stearate	1.0
Irgasan	0.2
Santocel	2.8
Span	2.0
Isopropyl myristate	1.0
Perfume oil	1.0
Powder base	15.0
Propellants	85.0

Formula 7 (Women's foot spray)

Constituents	*per cent*
Fragrance	0.35
Menthol crystals	0.10
Talc 'lo micron'	8.35
Acetol	1.00
Chloroxylenol	0.20
Propellants 12/11 (40 : 60)	90.00

Foot Sprays

Foot sprays are intended principally to cool and refresh the feet. They contain anti-microbial agents, and an antiperspirant material, an absorbent powder. They may be sprayed through socks or stockings and therefore are suitable for 'emergency' treatment.

The following three formulae, two for aerosol sprays respectively and onē for a non-aerosol pump spray, illustrate modern products. The formula 9 is sooting and cooling spray. It provides relief for hot tired feet and leaves them feeling soft and smooth. ' A clear liquid solution for packing in a munually operated spray dispenser which dries quicly and tack tree leaving the feet cool and refreshed is formula 10 :

Formula 8 (Antiperspirant foot spray)

Constituents	*per cent*
Talc	34.0
Cab-o-sil	2.0
Microdry	5.0
Procetyl	4.0
PVP-VA Co-polymer	4.0
Menthol	0.5
Ethanol anhydrous	50.5
Concentrate	15.0
Propellant	85.0

Formula 9 (Aerosol foot deodorant spray)

Constituents	*per cent*
Ammonyx	0.125
Menthol (racemic)	0.125
2-Ethyl-1, 3-hexanediol	2.25
Laneto	0.25
Ethanol anhydrous	27.25
Perfume	q.s.
Propellants	70.00

Formula 10 (Foot deodorant spray solution for pump spray)

Constituents	*per cent*
Ethanol 96%	28.00
Versene	0.03
Perfume	q.s.
Hyamine	0.25
Laneto	2.00
Deionised water	68.62
Silicone fluid	0.10
Camphor	0.50
Menthol (racemic)	0.50

Foot Creams

Foot massage is extremely relaxing. Foot creams are a suitable adjunct to massage and may contain antimicrobials, antiperspirants, mildly keratolytic agents, vasodilators to stimulate circulation, cooling agents, as well as providing emolliency and skin-softening properties. A simple emollient and deodourant foot cream may be formulated (Formula 11) as given below :

Formula 11

Constituents	*per cent*
Glyceryl monostearate	15.00
Lanolin	1.00
Sorbitol syrup 70%	2.50
Glycerine	2.50
Antimicrobial agent	0.25-0.50
Water	to 100.00

The foundation creams formulae may be applicable to foot creams. Many of the formulae given under foundation creams may be adapted for foot creams. Some spermaceti substitute or high- melting wax, or fatty acid such as stearic acid, may be included to give a waxy film rather than a greasy layer on the foot. Camphor methyl salicylate and menthol are commonly included to give a cooling sensation. The formula 12 is given below :

Formula 12

Constituents	*per cent*
Glyceryl monostearate	12.0
Minearl oil	2.0
Glycerine	5.0.
Spermaceti substitute	5.0
Camphor	1.0
Methyl salicylate	1.0
Water	73.9
Preservative	0.1

Formula 13 (Foot cream)

Constituents		*per cent*
A	Ottasept extra	1.00
	Lexemul AR	16.00
	Cetyl alcohol	1.00
	Amerchol L-101	3.00
	Solulan 98	0.50
	Mineral oil	3.00
B	Alcloxa	0.25
	Propylene glycol	5.00
	Distilled water	69.95
C	Perfume	0.30

Formula 14 (Oil-in-water foot massage emulsion)

Constituents		*per cent*
A	Self-emulsifying	25.0
	Propyleneglycol dipelargonte	3.0
	Hostaphat	0.5

(Cont'd)

B	Water	65.9
	Propylene glycol	5.0
	Preservative	0.3
	Borax	0.1
C	Perfume oil	0.2

Corn and Callus Preparations

Corn cures or paints contain salicylic acid in collodion either with or without cannabis extract. Other preparations include lactic acid, trichloracetic acid, glacial acetic acid is as given in formulae 15 and 16 :

Formula 15

Constituents	*per cent*
Salicylic acid	10
Lactic acid	10
Flexible collodion	80

Formula 16

Constituents	*per cent*
Salicylic acid	10
Cannabis extract	10
Flexible collodion	80

Five per cent castor oil may be added to the above if desired, for its plasticising effect. For callus softening, alkaline products are used, such as given formulae 17 and 18 :

Formula 17

Constituents	*per cent*
Tribasic sodium phosphate	8
Triethanolamine	12
Water	80
Perfume (alkali stable)	q.s.

Formula 18

Constituents	*per cent*
Potassium hydroxide	0.5
Glycerine	15.0
Water	84.5

Formula 18 should be used with care and must not be left in contact with the skin as it is caustic. The composition of corn remover in gel form is shown in formula 19 :

Formula 19 (Corn remover)

Constituents	*per cent*
Salicylic acid	12
Benzoic acid	6
Pluronic	47
Water	35
Perfume, colour	q.s.

The product is effective on clean skin but the presence of oil or grease may cause it to 'smear' rather than 'roll'. The emulsion can be made pressure-sensitive by using minimal quantities of the correct type of emulsifier. The following formula (formula 20) will serve as a basis.

Fromula 20

Constituents	*per cent*
Stearic acid	1.0
Beeswax	4.0
Cetyl alcohol	0.5
Paraffin wax	12.0
Triethanolamine	0.6
Sorbitol syrup	5.0
Veegum	0.5
Water	76.4

Chilblain Preparations

Chilblains are a condition resulting from poor circulation and an inadequate supply of blood to the hands and feet. The constituents for ointment (Fromula 21) is given below :

Formula 21

Constituents	*per cent*
Phenol	1.0
Camphor	6.0

(Cont'd)

Balsam of Peru	2.0
Soft paraffin	25.0
Hard paraffin	7.5
Anhydrous lanolin	58.5

Athlete's Foot Preparations

Since the introduction of aerosol sprays and powders the number of preparations for the treatment of athlete's foot has been increased. The antiseptics that are mainly present in aerosol foot preparations are selected primarily for the control of fungi, but they have also an important function as deodourising agent to inhibit the growth of odor-producing bacteria.

Salts of certain fatty acids such as propionic and undecylenic acids, often used in conjunction with the free acids, have been claimed to give good results in the treatment of Trichophyton and other dermatophytes. The formulae 22 and 23 are given for foot ointments.

Formula 22 (Propionate ointment)

Constituents	*per cent*
Sodium propionate	16.4
Propionic acid	3.6
Propylene glycol	5.0
n-propyl alcohol	10.0
Carbowax	35.0
Zinc stearate	5.0
Water	25.0

Formula 23 (Undecylenate ointment)

Constituents	*per cent*
Undecylenic acid	10.0
Triethanolamine	6.00
Propylene glycol	14.00
Carbowax 1500	10.00
Carbowax 4000	40.00
Water	20.00

These acids rarely cause any adverse reaction on the skin. Undecylenic acid is often used in conjunction with zinc undecylenate, which is similar to zinc stearate. It would be more suitable for use in aerosol powders than in pressurised lotions.

The antifungal foot powder based on a mixture of salts of propionic and caprylic acids is illustrated by the following formula 24 and gel form by formula 25.

Formula 24

Constituents	*per cent*
Calcium propionate	15.00
Zinc propionate	5.00
Zinc caprylate	5.00
Propionic acid	0.25
Talc	74.75

Formula 25

Constituents	*per cent*
Ethanol 96%	72.00
Water	21.00
Undecylenic acid	5.00
Carbopol	1.00
Di-isopropanolamine	1.00

Other Developments

Among newer developments are 'odour-destroying insoles' with absorbent and deodorant properties, a foot care kit with 'everything you need' for the care of the feet and a synthetic fibre 'foot sponge' for use with soap to remove thick hard skin. A recent patent describes a deodoriser for the foot, etc., based upon an ion-exchange material such as ion-exchange cotton.

Chapter - 10

SHAVING PREPARATIONS

INTRODUCTION

A wide range of preparations are now available which prepare beard or face for shaving. These preparations increase speed and comfort during and after-shave. The shaving preparations has been divided into three types, wet-shaving, dry-shaving and after-shave.

WET SHAVING PREPARATIONS

Wet-shaving preparations are to soften the beard, to lubricate the passage of the razor over the face and to support the beard hair. The Preparation should be non-irritating, assist in removing shaving debris from the face, should be stable over a range of temperatures, resistant to rapid drying out and collapse, non-corrosive to the razor blade and easily rinsed from the razor and face. There is good evidence for the hair softening and lubrication functions of the shaving preparation, but little has been reported on the hair-supportive role.

Lather Shaving Cream

Criteria for a Good Lather Shaving Cream

Reasons for successful shaving preparations are economic use, supply of water to beard, and maintaining hair in fully water saturated condition. The requirements of a good lather shaving are, it must produce rich copious lather, composed of small bubbles, non-irritant, good wetting properties, smooth, soft, adhere readily and retain texture at all temperatures. The following points evaluate shaving preparations.

1. Ease of transfer to and spreading on the face.
2. Wetting and drainage properties of foam.
3. Comfort and closeness of shave.
4. Foam texture, rigidity rheology and stability.

5. Easy removal of the other shaving debris from the razor basin.
6. Acceptability on perfume and life of razor blade.

Formulation

Lather shaving creams are concentrated dispersions of alkali metal soaps in glycerol and water. To maintain the desired level of foamability, consistency and product stability, careful control of the manufacturing process is essential. Even the slightest change to the formulations or manufacturing procedure can result in a disastrous phase separation of the cream at slightly elevated temperatures.

Lather shaving creams normally contain 30 to 50 per cent soaps. To produce voluminous lather, it is usual to add some coconut oil fatty acids or stearic acid. The satisfactory ration of stearic acid to coconut oil is 75:25. A mixture of sodium and potassium hydroxides is used to saponify the fatty acids. It has been suggested that a 5:1 ratio of potassium hydroxide to sodium hydroxide with 3-5 per cent free fatty acids will give shaving creams of the correct degree of plasticity. A cream containing a high level of sodium soaps tends to be thick and stringy, from which it is often difficult to produce a good lather. Lather creams can be made with potassium soaps alone, but these tend to be less stable. Formulae 1 and 2 given below show the formulation of lather shaving cream :

Formulae	*1*	*2*
Constituents	*per cent*	*per cent*
Stearic acid	30.0	36.0
Coconut oil	10.0	9.0
Palm kernel oil	5.0	-
Potassium hydroxide	7.0	8.0
Sodium hydroxide	1.5	1.0
Glycerine	10.0	-
Water	36.5	43.0
Perfume	q.s.	3.0
Sorbitol (70% solution)	-	3.0

saponification of mixture of half of stearic acid with oil at 75 – 80°C using alkali water and glycerine with agitation. Later on add left out stearic acid and perfume at 35°C. In second process saponify coconut oil using alkali at 75 – 80°C. Then add melted stearic acid, sorbitol, preservative and water. Add perfume after cooling at 35°C.

Lather Shaving Stick

A lather shaving stick can be prepared from a mixture containing 80 per cent fatty acid soaps, 5–10 per cent glycerol and 8 –10 per cent water. The ratio of the fatty acids and the ration of potassium to sodium soaps should be similar to those described under lather shaving creams. After mixing, the composition is chipped, dried and milled with perfume, colour or an opacifier. The soap flakes are packed to the desired shape using a soap plodder.

Aerosol Shaving Foams

Aerosol shaving foams are oil-in-water emulsions in which propellant droplets, liquefied under pressure, form a substantial part of the oil phase. When the emulsion is discharged to the atmosphere, the dispersed propellant droplets vapourise, producing a foam consisting of propellant vapour bubbles surrounded by an aqueous surfactant phase. The formula 3 of foam contain from 4 to 15 per cent soaps, mainly triethanolamine stearate with minor proportions of potassium and sodium stearates.

Formula 3

Constituents	*per cent*
Triethanolamine stearate	8.0
Sodium stearate	1.0
Potassium stearate	4.6
Water	72.5
Perfume	0.9
Borax	0.5
Propellant (fluorocarbon)	12.5

The composition of shaving foam concentrate is given in formula 4 :

Fromula 4

Constituents	*per cent*
Potassium soap from stearic acid /coconut oil fatty acids (80:20)	1.5
Potassium Polyacrylate (polyacrylic acid mol, wt, 100 000-200 00)	1.0
Polyvinylpyrrolidone	0.5
Stearic acid /coconut oil fatty acids (80:20)	3.0
Castor oil	3.0

(Cont'd)

Lauric acid diethanolamide	0.5
Polyoxyethylene sorbitan monolaurate	0.5
Perfume	0.5
Water	89.5

Guidance on Formulation

The hydrocarbon propellent base and scum-free aerosol shaving form (formulae 5,6) is prepared by heating parts A and B separately at 75°C. Then adding A to B at 35°C with stirring, also add perfume. At room temperature charge the aerosol container. The process for the preparation of soap free aerosol shaving foam (formula 7) except adjustment of pH of concentrate using citric acid remain same.

Formula 5

	Constituents	*per cent*
A	Palmitic acid	5.0
	Lauric acid	1.0
B	Sodium lauryl sulphate	1.0
	Polyethylene glycol (400) monolaurate	0.5
	Polyacrylic acid (40% aq.) mol.wt. 100 000	1.5
	Triethanolamine	2.0
	Potassium hydroxide	0.8
	Glycerol	5.0
	Water (deionised)	83.2
	Perfume	q.s.
	Concentrate	96.9
	Propellants, isobutane/ Propane	3.1

Formula 6

	Constituents	*per cent*
A	Palmitic acid	1.95
	Myristic acid	0.62
	Myristyl alcohol	2.10
B	Polyoxyethylene (20) cetyl ether	5.23
	Lauric diethanolamide	5.23

(Cont'd)

	Propylene glycol	0.82
	Glycerol	3.54
	Triethanolamine	1.54
	Water (deionised)	78.97
	Perfume	q.s.
Or	Concentrate	91.5
	Propellants 12/114(40:60)	8.5
Or	Concentrate	97.0
	Propellants (Butane 48)	3.0

Formula 7

Constituents		*per cent*
A.	Myristyl Alcohol	2.1
B.	Dicarboxylanted lauric imidazoline 40% solution	5.1
	Polyethylene glycol (1000) monolaurate	5.5
	Propoxylated polyol	0.7
	Glycerol	5.0
	Water (Deionised)	81.6
	Perfume	q.s.
	Citric acid	q.s.
	Concentrate	97.0
	Propellant (Butane 48)	3.0

Brushless or Non-Lathering Cream

Brushless or non-lathering shaving creams are oil-in-water emulsions. They contain components similar to those in vanishing creams. The main difference being that the concentration of oils and emulsifying agents tends to be higher in the shaving preparations. Ideally, the cream should vanish on completion of the shave, leaving the face free from irritation and with a matt appearance. Since a too rapid disappearance of the cream would be deleterious to the comfort and closeness of the shave, it should be possible at least to rub any remaining cream into the skin after the shave.

The composition of a typical brushless shaving cream is given in formulae 8-10. The preparation is done by heating the oil and stearic acid at 75°C. Then disperse the carbopol in cold water and add the glycerol, surfactant and triethanolamine. Add the oil phase to the aqueous phase 75°C with vigorous stirring. Cool the mixture rapidly, and add the perfume.

Formulae	8	9	10
Constituents	*per cent*	*per cent*	*per cent*
Mineral oil	9.0	-	5.0
Lanolin	0.5	4.0	-
Stearic acid	14.5	18.0	18.0
Carbopol	0.5	-	-
Triethanolamine	2.5	1.0	1.0
Triethanolamine lauryl sulphate	1.0	-	-
Glycerol	5.0	2.0	-
Water	67.0	66.8	63.0
Preservative, perfume	9.5	0.2	9.5
Propylene glycol monostearate-	-	4.0	-
Isopropyl palmitate	-	4.0	-
Silicone fluid	-	-	1.0
Polyoxyethylene	-	-	5.0
Sorbitan monostearate			
Borax	-	-	2.0
Sorbitol (70%)	-	-	5.0

Brushless Shaving Stick

Brushless shaving stick can be applied directly to the face. The continuous thin smear left on wetted skin provides adequate lubrication for the shaving operation. The stick is composed of fatty or waxy materials to which hydrophilic properties have been imparted soap or a partial fatty acid ester of a polyhydric alcohol. This ensures that the product is readily wetted. It is not more sparingly soluble in, water. Pigment, dyestuff or opacifier is incorporated to indicate the presence of the composition on the face formulae 11 and 12 are given as under :

Formula 11

Constituents	*per cent*
Sesame oil	35.35
Spermaceti	45.80

(Cont'd)

Stearin	7.60
Soap	5.00
Monoglycerides of coconut oil fatty acids	3.00
Titanium dioxide	2.00
Perfume	1.25

Formula 12

Constituents	*per cent*
Mineral oil	95.97
Dioctyl sodium sulphosuccinate (Aerosol OT)	1.44
Lanolin	0.96
Silicone fluid	0.67
Octadecanol	0.48
Fragrance	0.48
Preservative	q.s.

DRY SHAVING PREPARATIONS

It is generally recognised that electric shavers do not cut beard as close to the skin surface as a razor blade. Both electric and blade shaving result in there removal of skin, the amount removed for an individual being dependent on the pressure applied to the face. Generally, the closer the shave the greater the amount of skin damage. It has been suggested that pre-electric shave preparations may not increase the quality of the shave but may assist in reducing skin damage.

Lotions of the oily type aim to deposit on the face a film of lubricant which reduces the drag of the cutting head against the skin. It has been shown that a film of silicone oil substantially reduces the frictional force between skin and a smooth steel probe formulae 13-15 are given below :

Formula 13

Constituents	*per cent*
Ethanol	45.0
Sorbitol	5.0
Lactic acid	1.0
Water	49.0

Formula 14

Constituents	*per cent*
Zinc phenolsulphonate	1.0
Distilled extract of witch hazel	40.0
Ethanol	40.0
Water	18.8
Menthol	0.1
Camphor	0.1

Formula 15

Constituents	*per cent*
Alumuminium chlorhydroxide (50%)	5.0
Isopropyl myristate	5.0
Ethanol	80.0
Perfume	q.s.
Colour	q.s.
Water	to 100.0

AFTER-SHAVE PREPARATIONS

The purpose of an after-shave preparation is to relieve the slight irritation or 'after-glow' and confer a pleasant of comfort and well-being after shaving. This is achieved by giving a slight coolness, anaesthesia, mild astringency or emolliency to the skin. At the same time, the preparation should be antiseptic and help to keep the skin free from bacterial infection during the short time it takes to recover from to the slight degree of injury inflicted during the shaving operation.

After-shave Lotion

An after-shave lotion is a clear aqueous ethyl alcohol solution containing a perfume. They contain 50-70 per cent by weight ethyl alcohol. The controlled ratio of ethyl alcohol to water produces balanced mild astringency and coolness. Perfume or solubiliser is also used. Non-ionic surfactants with a hydrophile-lipophile balance (HLB) number in the range 15-18 are often found to be the most effective solubilisers, although anionic surfactants have also been used. Humectants and emollients are at levels not exceeding 5 per cent. Polyols such as glycerol, sorbitol and propylene glycol help to maintain the water content of the skin. Glycerol has the best humectant properties of the group, but propylene glycol is often preferred because of its greater solvent power, lower viscosity and higher volatility. The feel of the skin can be improved by the addition of long-chain fatty esters, for example, isopropyl myristate or lanolin. Quantities are often limited by their low solubility in aqueous alcohol solutions. Water-soluble lanolin derivatives can be used at higher levels to provide emolliency and to assist in the solubilisation of the perfume oil.

The level of menthol should be kept below 0.1 per cent because of its lachrymatory properties and because its odour can upset the balance of the perfume. Odouless cooling agents may be more appropriate for this type of product. Menthol is also said to cause slight surface anaesthesia of skin; however, it is preferable to achieve this effect with lignocaine at a level of 0.025-0.05 per cent. A basic after-shave lotion, composition is given in formula 16.

Formula 16

Constituents	*per cent*
Ethyl alcohol, specially denatured	60
Propylene glycol	3
Water, demineralised	36
Perfume	1

It is prepared by dissolving the perfume and propylene glycol in the alcohol and add the water slowly with stirring. Allow the solution to stand or several hours at about 4°C, then filter. Formulae 17-19 given below show the formulation of antiseptic after-shave lotion :

Formula 17

Constituents	*per cent*
Hyamine	0.250
Ethyl alcohol	40.000
Menthol	0.005
Benzocaine	0.025
Water	59.720
Perfume	q.s.

Formula 18

constituents	*per cent*
With hazel extract	15.00
Ethyl alcohol	10.00
Alum	0.50
Menthol	0.50
Ethyl p-amino benzoate	0.05
Glycerol	5.00
Water	69.40

Formula 19

Constituents	*per cent*
Hyxadecyl alcohol	0.8
Ethyl alcohol	53.7
Distilled water	33.0
Polawax	2.0
Perfume	0.5
Propellant	10.0

Some perfumes are unstable to ultra-violet light. Therefore after exposure to direct sunlight for few months, an after-shave lotion in clear glass bottles develops a characteristic 'bottle-odour', quite unlike the original fragrance. Accelerated testing of the ultra-violet light stability of the packaged product should therefore be included in the evaluation of after-shave preparations. Many manufacturers circumvent the problem by using opaque or chromium-containing glass bottles to package the lotion.

After-Shave Gel

An aqueous alcohol gel can be formed by neutralising a carboxyvinyl polymer with a base. The amount of gelling agent (usually less than 1 per cent) and the degree of neutralisation controls the stiffness of the gel. The gel may optionally contain a physiological cooling agent an emollient which is soluble in the alcoholic solution. It is prepared by dissolving perfume and menthol in alcohol and stirred in water to get clear solution. Disperse the Carbopol 940 in the aqueous alcoholic solution. Reduce the speed of the mixer and slowly add the di-isopropylamine dissolved in the small quantity of retained water. The resulting product should be a crystal-clear gel, to pack it in coloured or opaque containers. The formula 20 is given below :

Formula 20

Constituents	*per cent*
Ethanol	45.1
Water	53.0
Carbopol	1.0
Menthol	0.1
Di-isopropylamine	0.8
Perfume oil	q.s.

After-Shave Cream and Balm

The astringency of after-shave preparations containing more than 50 per cent by weight alcohol can be irritating to skin which has been excessively damaged by shaving or over-exposure to sun and wind. Formula 21 gives soap-free after-shave cream.

Formula 21 (soap-free after-shave cream)

Constituents		*per cent*
A.	Glycerol monostearate	10.0
	Mineral oil	10.0
	Petrolatum	6.0
	Tegiloxan	0.5
	Lanolin	3.0
	Cetyl alcohol	3.0
B.	Glycerol	3.0
	Citric acid	0.2
	Potassium aluminium sulphate	0.1
	Water	64.2
	Perfume	q.s.

Formula 22 (Opaque hydro-alcoholic balm)

Constituents		*per cent*
A.	Amerchol	5.0
	Isopropyl lanolate	10.0
	Poly-thylene glycol	3.0

(Cont'd)

B.	Carbopol	0.5
	Water	60.0
	Tiethanolamine	0.5
	Ethyl alcohol	30.0
	Perfume	q.s.

Procedure

Add the Carbopol slowly to the water at room temperature with rapid agitation until cloudy dispersion is obtained. Heat the carbopol solution and the oil phase separately to 75°C. Add the carbopol solution to the oil phase and stir for 5 minutes before adding the triethanolamine. Cool with stirring to 38°C. Add the alcohol and perfume.

Chapter - 11

SUNSCREEN, SUNTAN AND ANTI-SUNBURN PRODUCTS

INTRODUCTION

The sunlight has both beneficial and harmful effects on the human body, depending on the length and the frequency of exposure, the intensity of the sunlight and the sensitivity of the individual concerned. Erythema of the skin is obvious effect of sun rays. It is followed by the formation of tan. Factually tan is a protective reaction of the human body to minimise any damaging effect of solar irradiation. The intensity of erythema (reddening) produced depends on the amount of uv energy period of 2–3 hours and reaches its maximum intensity within 10 to 24 hours after exposure.

SUNLIGHT AND THE HUMAN BODY

Tanning

The tanning ability of an individual is genetically predetermined and depends on his capacity to produce melanin pigment within the melanocytes. The energy from 300 and 660 nm rays stimulates tanning immediately. Its maximum efficacy lies between 340 nm and 360 nm. It entails the immediate darkening of unoxidised melanin granules present in the epidermal layer of the skin, near its surface. It reaches a maximum about one hour after exposure to radiation and begins to fade within 2–3 hours after exposure.

The erythemogenic radiation (wavelength 295 to 320 nm) stimulates delayed and true tanning. True tanning starts about two days after exposure and reaches a maximum about two to three weeks later.

Beneficial and Adverse Effects of Sunlight

Beneficial effects

the moderate exposure of human body to sunshine gives sense of fitness, peace of mind and well-being. It stimulates blood circulation, increases the formation of haemoglobin, and may also promote a reduction in blood pressure. It plays a vital part in the prevention and treatment of rickets by producing through the activation of 7-dehydrocholesterol (provitamin D3) present in the epidermis. This enhances the absorption of calcium from the intestine.

It has been used in the treatment of certain types of tuberculosis, such as the tuberculosis of glands and bones, and the treatment of certain skin diseases such as psoriasis. A beneficial influence on the autonomous nervous system and reduction in the susceptibility of individuals to various infections is observed. Finally, by producing melanin and causing thickening of the skin, it plays an essential part in the formation of the body's natural protective mechanism against sunburn.

Adverse Effects of Sunlight

Solar irradiation can have short-term and long-term adverse effects.

Sunburn

The known symptoms of sunburn are temporary damage of the epidermis. These may range in severity from a slight erythema to painful burns and blistering accompanied in more severe cases, when large amounts of the skin have been affected, by shivering, fever and nausea, and sometimes pruritus. The symptoms of sunburn are the direct result of damage or destruction of cells in the prickle cell layer of the skin, possibly through denaturing of its protein constituents. The four degrees of sunburn are observed with exposure to mid-day sunshine. They are minimal perceptive erythema, vivid erythema, painful burn and burn and blistering burn.

Chronic exposure

It may also produce degenerative changes in the connective tissue of the corium and result in the so-called premature ageing of the skin. This is evidenced by the thickening of the skin, the loss of natural elasticity and the appearance of wrinkles, all resulting from the loss of the skin's water-binding capacity. There is also an increased tendency to form skin blemishes.

SUNSCREENS AND SUNTAN PREPARATIONS

The sunscreens and suntan are prepared to prevent or minimise the harmful effects of solar radiation or to assist in tanning the skin without any painful effects. Sunscreens are classified on the basis of applications as :

1. Sunburn preventive agents are defined as sunscreens which absorb 95 per cent or more of uv radiation within wavelengths 290-320 nm.

2. Suntanning agents absorb at least 85 per cent of uv radiation within the wavelength range from 290 nm to 320 nm but which transmit uv light at wavelengths longer than 320 nm and produce a light transient tan. These agents will produce some erythema but without pain. Both agents are defined as sunscreens. These are chemical sunscreens absorbing a specific range of uv radiation. In some instances the same sunscreen may be employed in both product classes but at different concentrations (lower in a suntan product).

3. Opaque sunblock agents aim to provide maximum protection in the form of a physical barrier e.g. Titanium dioxide and zinc oxide. Titanium dioxide reflects and scatters practically all radiation in the uv and visible range (290–777nm), there by preventing or minimising both sunburn and suntan.

Sunscreen Agents

Sunscreens should either scatter the incident light effectively, or they should absorb the erythemal portion of the sun's radiant energy. Opaque powdered materials, when applied to the skin either in the dry state or with suitable vehicles, will serve to scatter the ultra-violet light falling upon them.

The most important class of sunscreens are those which operate by absorbing the erythemal ultra-violet radiation. Sunscreen must have following properties :

1. It must be effective in absorbing erythmogenic radiation in the 290-320 nm range without breakdown would reduce its efficiency or give rise to toxic or irritant compounds.

2. It must allow full transmission in the 300-400 nm range to permit the maximum tanning effect.

3. It must be non-violet and resistant to water and perspiration.

4. It must possess suitable solubility characteristics to allow the formulation of a suitable cosmetic vehicle to accommodate the requisite amount of sunscreening.

5. It must be non-odourous or at least sufficiently mild to be acceptable to the user and be satisfactory in other relevant physical characteristics such as stickiness, etc.

6. It must be non-toxic, non-irritant and non-sensitising.

7. It must be capable of retaining its protective capacity for several hours and stable under conditions of use.

8. It must not stain clothing.

A number of proprietary products have been based upon menthyl salicylate. It is non-irritant, odourless and initially acts as a satisfactory sunscreen at concentrations of about 10 per cent.

The level of five sunscreen agents recommended by the US department of health, education and welfare to use in a base like mineral oil, cold cream or ethyl alcohol is, Isobutyl p-aminobenzoate 5% Propylene glycol p-aminobenzoate 4.0% monoglyceryl p-aminobenzoate 2.5%, diagalloyl trioleate 5.0% and benzyl salicylate and benzyl cinnamate 2% each.

Evaluation of Sunscreen Preparations

All sunscreen preparations are necessarily assessed for their efficiency. The absorption characteristics measured in terms of concentration, thickness and wavelength which decides efficiency of products. In other words absorption is called as optical density. It is the logarithm of the ratio of the intensities of the radiation before and after passage through the solution. It is directly proportional to the concentration and to the thickness of the material, hence calculation is simple. These three categories of ingredients of sunscreen with concentration are tabulated in Table 28.1.

Table 28 .1

Classification of sunscreen ingredients.

I Safe, Effective Compound	*Discount limit %*
p-Aminobenzoic acid	5-15
2-Ethoxyethylpmethoxy cinnamate	1-3
Diethanolamine-p-methoxy cinnamate	8-10
Digalloyl trioleate	1-5
2,2-Dihydroxy4methoxybenzophenone	3
Ethyl-4-bis-(hydroxypropyl) aminobenzoate	1-5
2, Ethylhexyl 2-cyano-3, 3-diphenyl acrylate	7-10
Ethylhexyl-p-methoxy cinnamate	2-7.5
2-Ethylhexyl salicylate	3-5
Glyceryl aminobenzoate	2-3
3, 3, 5-Trimethylcyclohexyl salicylate	4-15
Lawsone with dihydroxyacetone Lawsone	0.25
(DHA)	3.0
Menthyl anthranilate	3.5-5
2-Hydroxy-4-menthoxy benzophenone	2-6

(Cont'd)

Amyl-p-dimethylamino benzoate	1-5
2-Ethylhyexyl-p-dimethylamino benzoate	1.4-8
2-Pehnyl benzimidazole-5-sulphonic acid	1-4
Red petrolatum	30-100
2-Hydroxy-4-methoxybenzophene-5 sulphonic acid	5-10
Titanium dioxide	2-25
Triethanolamine salicylate	5-12
II Not safe, not effective	
2-Ethylhexyl-4-phenyl benzophenone-2'-carboxylic acid	
3-(4-methylbenzylidence)-camphor	
Sodium 3, 4-dimethylphenyl glyoxylate	
III Unclassified	
Allantoin combined with aminobenzoicacid	
5(3,3 Dimethyl 2-nonrbornylidence)-3- penten-2-one	
Dipropylene glycol salicylate	

The absorption characteristic of a chemical is frequently expressed as the molar extinction coefficient. Sunscreen index based on optical density is shown in Table 28.2.

Table 28 . 2

Sunscreen index (SI) based on optical density of 1 per cent solution at 308 nm.

Compound	*SI*
Ethyl p-dimethylaminobenzoate	14.8
Ethyl p-aminobenzoate	9.6
Isobutyl p-aminobenzoate	9.2
Propyl p-aminobenzoate	9.0
n-Butyl p-aminobenzoate	8.0
ß-Methyl umbelliferone	7.7
p-Aminobenzoic acid	7.4
Dehydroacetic acid	7.0
3-Carbethoxycoumarin	6.6
Benzilidine camphor	6.6

(Cont'd)

Heliotropine	6.5
Umbelliferone acetic acid	6.0
Salicylic acid	4.3
Sodium p-aminosalicylate	4.3
Menthyl salicylate	4.0
Salicylamide	3.9
Methylenedisalicylic acid	3.0
3-Carboxycoumarin	3.0
Thiosalicylic acid	2.7
Brightener W/450	2.7
p-Hydroxyanhranilic acid	2.6
Sodium salicylate	2.4
Digalloyltrioleate	2.4
μ-Resorcylic acid	2.2
Salicylaldehyde	2.2
p-Aminosalicylic acid	1.9
Dipropyleneglycol salicylat	1.9
Pyribenzamine	1.8
Pyrianisamine maleate	1.7
Sodium gentisate	1.7
Fluorescent white	1.6
Ethanolamide of gentisic acid	1.5
Ethyl gallate	1.4
Sodium sulphadiasine	1.2
Ethylvanillate	1.1
sodium sulphapyridine	0.95
Lauryl gallate	0.85
Totaquine	0.80
Barbituric acid	0.19
Chlorophyll	0.15
Amberlite IR–4–B	0.15
Salicyl alcohol	0.05
Anisic acid	0.01
Uvitex RBS	0.01
Uvitex RS	0.005

Water Resistance and Perspiration Resistance of Sunscreens

The efficacy of sunscreen preparations also depends on their ability to form substantive films on the skin, which are resistant to removal by water or perspiration. Hence, the evaluation of sunscreen preparations is done by assessing their water and perspiration resistance.

An appropriate test for determination of resistance to perspiration is to obtain sweating within 30 min. under controlled environmental conditions. Such a claim will be allowed if the sunscreen preparation under test retains its original PCD after the test. The claim 'resists removal by sweating' is also appropriate if the product proves to be water resistant, since water immersions a more severe test than sweating.

Tests for water resistance and waterproof is conducted. It is reproducible if carried out in an indoor pool. It is carried out after 40 minutes of moderate activity in water, and that to test the claim that a given product is waterproof after 80 minutes of moderate activity.

Efficacy of Sunscreens

The efficacy of a sunscreen preparation depends on the amount of harmful (erythemogenic) solar radiation, the absorption range of the active sunscreen, its absorption peak, concentration employed, its resistance to water and perspiration, the solvent employed and other constituents present.

The molar absorptivity of a sunscreen in the erythemogenic and photosensitisation ranges of the uv spectrum is another a criterian to know effectiveness of a sunscreen agent. The larger its value at a specified wavelength, the greater the ability of the sunscreen agent to absorb uv radiation at this wavelength. The effectiveness of sunscreens with a low molar absorptivity can be increased by raising the concentration of the active ingredient in the preparation. The factors which can influence the effectiveness of a sunscreen preparation are :

1. pH;
2. The solvent system employed;
3. The thickness of the residual film on the skin; and
4. The stability of the product during the time it is employed.

A change in the pH, will change the ratio of ionised and nonionised fractions of the sunscreen agent and result in a shift in the absorption range (and absorption peak) away from the erythemogenic range of 290-320 nm with a consequent reduction in efficacy.

In practically all aromatic uv absorbers, addition of solvents can also produce a shift of their absorption range. Thus the absorption peak of p-aminobenzoic acid in 100 per cent isopropanol was moved from 287.5 to 267.5 nm in 100 per cent water. Mineral oil can produce a shift of the absorption range of sunscreens to a lower wavelength. Change of solvent, adversely affect the protection given by the sunscreen agent. On the other hand, 2-ethylhexyl palmitate is very stable to uv radiation and has practically no effect on the absorption peak.

Formulation of Sunscreens

Consider the following points for formulation. It should be convenient to use effectively with sufficient quantity. It should be soluble in aqueous or non-aqueous solvent. The film of non-volatile material left on the skin must have desirable properties. The various composition of sunscreens is given in formulae 1-11.

Formula 1 (Lotion, primarily aqueous, with a small amount of thickener)

Constituents	*per cent*
Filtosol	7.0
Methyl cellulose	0.5
Glycerine	2.0
Ethyl alcohol	10.0
Water	80.5
Perfume	q.s.

Formula 2 (Lotion, primarily alcohol, with oleyl alcohol as residual lipid)

Constituents	*per cent*
Giv-tan	1.5
Ethyl alcohol (denatured)	65.0
Oleyl alcohol	10.0
Water	23.5
Perfume	q.s.

Formula 3 (Clear sunscreen lotion)

Constituents	*per cent*
Isobutyl p-aminobenzoate	5.0
Tween	9.0
Alcohol SD-40	45.0
Water	41.0

Formula 4 (Alcoholic lotion including silicone as the residual vehicle)

Constituents	*per cent*
Sunscreen agent	1.0
L-43 silicone (Union Carbide)	5.0
Ethyl alcohol	94.0
Perfume	q.s.

Formula 5 (Gel with a hydrophilic residue)

Constituents	*per cent*
Sunscreen (water soluble)	5.0
1,2,6-Hexanetriol	15.0
Distilled water	80.0
in addition :	
Carbopol	0.1
Sodium hydeoxide 10%	0.42

Formula 6 (Non-greasy oil based on isopropyl palmitate and silicone)

Constituents	*per cent*
Sunscreen (oil-soluble)	1.0
Silicone fluid	10.0
Isopropyl palmitate	89.0

Formula 7 (Water-in-oil emulsion with an oil-soluble sunscreen)

Constituents	per cent
Sunscreen (oil-soluble)	3.0
Mineral oil	34.0
Atlas	2.0
Avitex	5.0
Beeswax	2.0
Isopropyl myristate	0.5
Petroleum jelly	7.5
Water	46.0

Formula 8 (Oil-in-water emulsion with a low oil content of now-greasy character)

Constituents	*per cent*
Giv-tan	1.5
Diethylene glycol monostearate	2.0
Stearic acid	3.5
Cetyl alcohol	0.4
Isopropyl myristate	4.0
Triethanolamine	1.0
Triethanolamine lauryl sulphate	0.75
Water	86.85
Perfume, preservative	q.s.

Formula 9 (Low oil content vanishing cream containing veegum)

Constituents	*per cent*
Filtrosol A	5.00
Stearic acid	6.00
Cetyl alcohol	0.50
Veegum	2.28
Water	85.42
Borax	0.50
Potassium hydroxide	0.30
Perfume, preservative	q.s.

Formula 10 (Oil-in-water cream with a moderate oil content of mixed character)

Constituents	*per cent*
Sunscreen, etc.	q.s.
Glyceryl monostearate	16.0
Cetyl alcohol	1.0
Mineral oil	10.0
Seasame oil	10.0
Glycerine	7.0
Water	to 100.0
Antioxidant, preservative, perfume	q.s.

Formula 11 (Water-in-oil cream with an oil : water ratio similar to formula 10)

Constituents	*per cent*
Ethyl p-diethylaminobenzoate	1.0
Mineral oil	9.0
Ozokerite	2.0
Micro-crystalline wax	1.0
Paraffin wax	5.0
Petroleum jelly	2.0
Lanoline	3.0
Isopropyl myristate	10.0
Arlacel	1.5
Glycerine	5.0
Preservative, perfume	q.s.
Water	to 100.0

Formulae 12 and 13 are aerosol sunscreen oils. Formula 12 is based on mineral oil, while formula 13 is alcohol-based, contains silicone and is non-greasy and aerosol quick breaking foam non-greases is shown in formula 14.

Formula 12

Constituents	*per cent*
Filtrosol	3.0
Mineral oil	75.0
Eutanol	8.0
Lantrol	2.0
Isopropyl myristate	12.0
Perfume	q.s.
Concentrate	40.0
Propellants	60.0

Formula 13

Constituents	*per cent*
Sunscreen agent	5.0
Isopropyl myristate	25.0
Silicone	5.0

(Cont'd)

Perfume oil	1.25
Lanolin oil	2.5
Menthol Racemic	0.25
Absolute alcohol	61.0
Concentrate	20.0
Propellants	80.0

Formula 14 (Aerosol quick-breaking foam, substantially non-greasy)

Constituents	*per cent*
Myristic acid	1.3
Stearic acid	5.0
Cetyl alcohol	0.5
Isopropyl myristate	1.3
Glycerine	5.0
Sunscreen agent	1.0
Silicone fluid	1.0
Triethanolamine	3.0
Distilled water	80.6
Benzyl alcohol	1.0
Perfume oil	0.3

The release of histamine due to exposure to sun increases sensitivity of the skin. It is well-known that perfume may have irritant effect. There fore the perfume selected should be only below 0.2%.

Heavy Sunscreens

Sunscreens are used to resist pigmentation completely. This class of products also includes preparations which are applied to the skin with the sole object of providing a mechanical barrier to sunlight, such as calamine lotion or heavy make-up. Many attempts have been made to develop cosmetic products which would inhibit the formation of freckles or any skin lesions resulting from exposure to sunlight or other uv light sources. Like other sunscreen preparations, these products are commercially available in cream, lotion or aerosol foam form. Heavy sunscreen creams constitutes :

1. 2-hydroxy-4-methoxy-4'-methylbenzophenone;
2. 3-benzoyl-4-hydroxy-6-methoxybenzophenone (1%);
3. *p*-aminobenzoic acid (3-15%);
4. aesculin (5-10%);

5. salol in yellow vaseline (10%);
6. Methyl salicylate in an ointment base (10%); and

Heavy sunscreen lotions constitutes :

1. *p*-aminobenzoic acid in 70 per cent alcohol (10-50%); and tannic acid in 25-30 per cent alcohol (5-10%).

PALLIATIVE PREPARATIONS

Preparations for the relief of sunburn may be formulated on the basis of calamine lotion, or other zinc preparations.

Formula 15 (Calamine lotion type)

Constituents	*per cent*
Colloidal calamine	20.0
Glycerine	5.0
Water	75.0
Antiseptic	q.s.

The following improved calamine lotion (formula 16) is suggested :

Formula 16

Constituents	*per cent*
Zinc oxide	8.0 g
Prepared calamine	8.0 g
Polyethylene glycol	8.0 cm^3
Polyethylene glycol (monostearate)	3.0 g
Lime water	60.0 cm^3
Water	to 100 cm^3

Triethanolamine stearate milks are also soothing (Formula 17) :

Formula 17

Constituents	*per cent*
Triethanolamine stearate	4.80
Liquid paraffin	10.00
Water	85.20
Antiseptic	q.s.

Greasy preparations should not be used in the treatment of sunburn. They only retain the heat of the burn and prevent the use of an antiseptic capable of mixing with the secretions and preventing bacterial infection. These preparations should be either aqueous solutions or oil-in-water emulsions which are capable of exerting both a protective and cooling effect.

ARTIFICIAL SUNTAN PREPARATIONS

Stains

The enhanced colour of suntan may be regarded as functional, to prevent skin damage by absorption of erythemal radiation, or as cosmetic, to indicate the health and well-being of the subject. In either case the effect may be obtained by the use of staining materials. From ancient times materials such as walnut juice have been used. Water-soluble dyes, however, will streak on exposure to rain or moisture, and oil-soluble materials have been recommended. A vegetable product may be obtained by extracting a mixture of cudbear and henna with ten parts of warm deodorised olive oil, the ration of the vegetable dyestuffs being adjusting to give the desired shades. A more modern practice is to use suitable oil-soluble dyestuffs in less greasy lipid material. Heavily pigmented face powders or modifications of the 'cosmetic stocking' may also be used. In conjunction with suitable shades of make-up, excellent effects may be obtained.

Systemic Materials

Alkoxypsoralens, and methoxsalen (8-methoxypsoralen) photosensitiser has been investigated extensively both as a treatment for vitiligo and also as a possible cosmetic tanning preparation. Local application, probably the most pigment-stimulating method of use, causes severe oedema, erythema, blistering and pain when the skin is subjects to natural or artificial ultra-violet radiation. Increased pigmentation is said to occur after ingestion of 10-20mg of methoxsalen when the skin is exposed to sunlight within 2-4 hours.

Chapter - 12

FACE POWDERS AND MAKE-UP

INTRODUCTION

The smooth finish to the skin can be obtained using face powder. The visible imperfections or shining due to moisture or grease either from perspiration or formulation used on the skin can be masked. The aim is to make the skin pleasant to touch. The face powder is blend of several constituents.

Covering Power

The covering power of face powders should be sufficient so as to conceal various defects of the facial skin including scars, blemishes, enlarged pores and excessive shine. It is increased by use of titanium dioxide, zinc oxide, kaolin and magnesium oxide.

Absorbency

The second important function of face powders is to eliminate shiny skin in certain facial areas by absorbing sebaceous secretions and perspiration. A high absorptive capacity is a essential property of material. The colloidal kaolin starch, precipitated chalk and magnesium carbonate have this property hence used in face powders.

Hewitt method is used to determine water absorbent properties. In this method, filter, a known weight of powder shaken with excess water, through buchner funnel. Weight the wet powder and find out increase in weight.

Besides absorbancy of water, powder must be grease absorbent. If a person's face is inclined to dryness a more greasy foundation is usually employed. A powder which is not grease-absorbent will show a shiny nose or face which will necessitate re-powdering. Constituents of higher opacity such as zinc and titanium oxides tend to mask greasiness, while starch, chalks and kaolin absorb only a certain amount of grease. Oil absorption and water absorption capacities of powder bases are shown in Tables 29.1 and 29.2.

Table 29 .1

Oil absorption capacities of powder bases

Substance	*Oil take-up (ml per g of substance)*	*Saturation time (min)*
Oracid (urea-formaldehyde foam)	11.11	15
Aerosil	6.00	15
Magnesium carbonate	5.40	15
Magnesium oxide	3.30	15
Kieselguhr	2.70	15
Kaolin	2.80	15
Talc	2.50	15
Rice starch	2.10	15
Zinc stearate	0.40	15

Table 29 .2

Water absorption capacities of powder bases

Substance	*Water take-up (ml per g of substance)*	*Saturation time (min)*
Oracid (urea-formaldehyde foam)	16.60	30
Aerosil	8.70	45
Magnesium carbonate	4.03	28
Kieselguhr	3.20	12
Magnesium oxide	2.60	20
Titanium dioxide	2.30	30
Kaolin	1.50	5
Talc	1.40	10
Zinc oxide	1.10	18
Rice starch	0.75	15
Zinc stearate	0.05	120

Slip, Adhesion and Bloom

Slip

Slip is the quality of easy spreading and application of powder to produce a characteristic smooth feeling on the skin. Slip is mainly imparted by talc and also by metallic soaps such as zinc stearate and, to a lesser extent, starch.

Talc

Talc is a hydrated magnesium silicate. It is the major component of face powders, and in high class products it may be used in amounts of up to 70 per cent or more. Its main function is to impart slip and good adhesion. However, the covering power and the moisture absorbing capacity of talc are low. It must therefore be combined with other powders to modify these deficiencies. Talc is also used in talcum powders.

The most suitable physical form of talc for use in cosmetics is the foliated variety, the flat platelets of which slide readily over each other, thus accounting for the high slip characteristics of the product.

Adhesion

Adhesion is another important property of face powder constituents, determining how well the powder will cling to the face. The magnesium stearates are used in face powders in amounts ranging between 3 and 10 per cent. They also render the ultimate product soft and fluffy and furthermore impart to powders some water-repellent characteristics. The adhesion of powders to the skin can also be improved by the addition of 0.5 to 1.5% of certain emollients such as cetyl or stearyl alcohols and glyceryl monostearate.

Powdered silica and silicates

Very finely divided pure silica has been introduced for cosmetic purposes. The use of this substance obviates the need for zinc and magnesium stearates. The addition of 10 per cent to an ordinary powder mix exerts a marked effect in increasing its fluffiness. Up to 20 per cent may be used in a face powder or 30 per cent or more in talcum and baby powders. The small amount of such an ultrafine silica is very efficient as an anticaking agent in body powders.

The number of ultrafine synthetic silicates having high oil and water absorption preparation can be added to face powders.

Bloom

The materials chiefly used to impart bloom, the requirement for which may vary according to fashion, are chalk, rice starch and prepared starch. These have been described above.

Powdered silk

The silk powder spreads easily and adheres tenacioulsy to the skin, producing a velvet matt finish. It will absorb as much as three times its volume of water and still retain the appearance of a powder. The addition of large amounts of such materials as kaolin or chalk is not advised, as it is claimed that they tend to make the final product too dense and compact.

Colour

The solubilisation by sweat and lipid secretions makes water soluble or oil soluble dye-stuffs unsuitable. Face powders are coloured due to inorganic, organic pigments and organic lakes. Inorganic pigments include natural and synthetic iron oxides which give yellows, reds, browns and black; ultramarines which give green and blue, and chrome hydrate and chrome oxide which give green.

The choice of colour is usually a matter of taste. It is advisable to keep colour formulations as simple as possible so that matching with fresh batches of raw material is made easier. The colour effect produced by a powder applied to the skin will depend inter alia upon the opacity of both tinted and white pigments, their particle size, the degree of dispersion, the thickness of the applied film and the colour of the skin.

Perfume

The importance of the perfume on the sales appeal of the product cannot be over-emphasised. Usually the powders are perfumed very lightly. The odour of the face powder must be fragrant and pleasant, and a preference is shown today for either a flowery fragrance or that of a synthetic bouquet.

The compatibility of perfume with other constituents of the product must be carefully checked. Talc, for example, usually contains a little free lime, magnesia or iron which may adversely affect the perfume depending on the amount of these substances present. The perfume may also be affected by Precipitated chalk, by kaolin, magnesium carbonate or a metal stearate, if these contain impurities, or indeed by some of the pigments used in colouring the powders. Finally, it should be remembered that the perfume note in a powder will be different from that, for example, in an alcoholic solution, particularly in the case of floral bouquets, and any tests on perfume acceptance must be carried out on the final product.

Formulation

The powder given in formula 1 is very transparent, 'light' powder, and is favoured by persons who wish to impart some colour and bloom to the face without appearing to be 'made-up'. The starch may be replaced with precipitated chalk.

Formula 1

Constituents	*per cent*
Talc	80.0
Zinc oxide	5.0
Zinc stearate	5.0
Rice starch	10.0
Perfume, colour	q.s.

Formula 2 has high opacity and gives a very definite opaque matt finish which tends to hide minor skin defects. It is more popular with certain people who like to have a definite powdered appearance without being over-powdered.

Formula 2

Constituents	*per cent*
Talc	30.0
Zinc oxide	24.0
Zinc stearate	6.0
Precipitated chalk	40.0
Perfume, colour	q.s.

The formulae 3 and 4 are popular variations of powder.

Formula 3

Constituents	*per cent*
Talc	65.0
Precipitated chalk	10.0
Zinc oxide	20.0
Zinc stearate	5.0
Perfume, colour	q.s.

Formula 4

Constituents	*per cent*
Talc	60.0
Kaolin	20.0
Zinc oxide	15.0
Zinc stearate	5.0
Perfume, colour	q.s.

As previously stated, both starch and precipitated chalk tend to impart bloom; formula 5 is a powder of medium weight, that is medium opacity or coverage and bloom.

Formula 5

Constituents	*per cent*
Talc	50.0
Rice starch	15.0
Precipitated chalk	15.0
Zinc oxide	15.0
Zinc stearate	5.0

The following formula (formula 6) is prepared from precipitated chalk and a high proportion of zinc stearate is incorporated. To provide some grease-resistance, kaolin and titanium dioxide are employed.

Formula 6

Constituents	*per cent*
Water-proof chalk base	50.0
Zinc or magnesium stearate	10.0
Kaolin	20.0
Titanium dioxide	6.0
Talc	14.0
Perfume, colour	q.s.

The following formula (formula 7) gives a good medium powder, characterised by excellent slip, absorbency, adequate coverage, good velvety feel and adherence – and an indefinable improvement in mattness, etc., which is attributed to the rice starch :

Formula 7

Constituents	*per cent*
Zinc oxide	16.0
Talc	37.0
Zinc stearate	5.0
Precipitated chalk	18.0
Rice starch	8.0
Kaolin (best cosmetic grade)	16.0

A special kind of 'fatty powder' is much favoured by persons afflicted with a rough or dry skin (Formula 8) :

Formula 8

Constituents	*Parts*
Vaseline	50
White beeswax	40
Petroleum jelly	40
Stearin	20
Glyceryl monostearate	75

The modern trend with face powder is to apply it over foundation to achieve special effects, for example, matt or shimmer. The following complete formula illustrates a light shimmering effect : (Formula 9)

Formula 9

Constituents	*per cent*
Talc	77.00
Zinc stearate	5.00
Zinc oxide	2.00
Kaolin	5.00
Mica	10.00
Red iron oxide	0.36
Yellow iron oxide	0.36
Black iron oxide	0.03
Perfume	0.25

MANUFACTURE

In a horizontal mixer with a screw agitator mixing of ingredients in face power is completed. If lakes are used they may be mixed with a small quantity of one of the constituents, chalk, zinc oxide or talc, and the colour concentrate so formed mixed with the main bulk. Water-soluble or alcohol-soluble dyes are best sprayed on to the mix or alternatively on to one of the constituents which possesses good absorbency such as chalk, kaolin or magnesium carbonate, then dried an mixed into the main bulk.

Machines are available which mix, sift and spray the perfume automatically. The perfume can also be added by meter pump by feeding a long tube with a multitude of small holes fitted along the top of the blender (for example, on to magnesium carbonate or chalk in the ribbon blender) before mixing with the remainder of the powder.

The use of water-soluble or oil-soluble colours should be avoided as they lead to streaking, darkening and staining of the skin. In the pebble mill method of mixing which obviates the making of a colour base. All the ingredients, including the colour and perfume, are milled together in a pebble mill for six hours, discharged. Such a mill delivers an excellent product and is widely employed in preference to mixers. This method, however, is too slow to be recommended for large-scale production. Micro-pulverisers are being increasingly employed since the material obtained is finely ground and uniformly mixed and only a rough pre-mixing is required. Various other pulverisers such as disintegrators, hammer mills, attrition mills,etc., may also be used.

Pin-disc mills give good results, especially in respect of colour dispersion, provided that the material is first given a rough pre-mix. Such mills are often applied in conjunction with a turbine sifter. The Air Spun process is described briefly is as follows.

Pass purified and cold air, under great pressure (100 psi; 700 kPa) in a continuous stream into a closed drum-shaped chamber. This chamber or mill is called a microniser as it reduces particles to micron (μm) size. The speed of the air stream, the manner in which it is directed and the shape of the chamber itself, cause air to revolve about this chamber at a rate somewhat is excess of 1000mph. In this super cyclone all the ingredients are hurled against each other until they reduce themselves to the desired size and fluffiness. When this is attained such particles are emitted through a central exit while the heavier particles are forced to remain. It is claimed that the particle size was selected after numerous experiments had shown it to be the best for the appearance effect and adhesiveness of a face powder.

There are various methods available for preparing powders of a desirable particle size. These depend upon elutriation by means of air or water. Control of such separated fractions may be carried out by microscopic examination of the fractions, but this method involves the visual or photomicrographic inspection of a very large number of fields in the microscope and is tedious. A useful variation is the method of Andreason in which volumes of the suspension, after definite times of setting (calculated from Stokes' Law) are pipetted into a tared dish, evaporated to dryness and weighed. Various air permeability methods are also widely used.

The most modern method of particle size analysis applicable to cosmetic powders entails the use of a Coulter Counter. Packaging is usually carried out by automatic vacuum filling devices, which minimise dusting. In choosing powder boxes, care should be taken to see that these are prepared with an odourless glue, otherwise the fragrance of the powder will be ruined in storage.

COMPACT POWDER

Compact powders enjoy wide popularity. They are prepared by either a damp or a dry compression process. The moulding process used originally, which entailed the use of plaster of Paris, has fallen into disuse.

In the damp process, the powder, is milled to the required plasticity after mixing intimately mixed with a suitable binding agent. Then compressed into suitable containers, usually metal godets, and dried for the requisite period in a current of warm air. In the dry process the mass is subjected to compression without being wetted to any appreciable extent. This process, although difficult to achieve satisfactorily at first, is probably the best to use for manufacturing compacts on a large scale. Because it can be rigidly adhered to once the mix and suitable conditions have been determined. Hydraulic or reciprocating presses may be used for the manufacture of compact powders. They range from foot operated presses producing one cake at a time, to fully automatic presses which may produce up to 60 units per minute.

The requirement of good covering power, adhesion and uniformity in compositions mentioned in respect of conventional face powders also applied to compact powders. The adequate binding properties to the compressed powder mixture is attained in order to remove easily from cake for application using powder puff. Furthermore, the powders used for compacts should be free-flowing so that they do not adhere to punches or dies during compression; otherwise, air pockets will be formed which will result in an uneven compression and cause the cakes to break. From this it can be seen that one of the main aims during manufacture of compact powders is to ensure that the compressed cakes are of uniform density.

The actual pressing can also affect the shade of the product so quality control can be a problem. In fact, if large volumes are anticipated it is always best to conduct an extended manufacturing trial rather than go straight from the laboratory bench into full-scale production.

The composition of compact powders is generally very similar to that of loose powders. The differences which exist arise from the need to meet the requirement of greater cohesion and are largely evident in terms of percentages of some of the components present. In compact powders, colloidal kaolin, zinc oxide and metallic stearates are usually present at a higher level than in loose face powders, and starch is sometimes incorporated to facilitate compression. A binding agent to improve their cohesion is added so that on compression a firm cake is produced. Water-soluble and water-insoluble binding agents may be used. The former are natural and synthetic gums which are used in amounts ranging from 0.1 per cent to about 3 per cent by weight of the product, and are usually of a 5-10 per cent aqueous solution is mixed. A very much favoured binding agent for this purpose is low-viscosity carboxymethylcellulose. A small amount of a humectant is usually added to the solutions. A water-insoluble binding agent should be use in the form of oil-in-water emulsion, for example glyceryl monostearate, cetyl or stearyl alcohols, Isopropyl esters of fatty acids, lanolin and its derivatives or ozokerite, paraffin wax and microcrystalline waxes.

In the dry compacting process, it is usual to employ zinc or magnesium stearates at a level of 5-15 per cent by weight, as well as a lubricant such as mineral oil in similar proportions.

Considerable changes have taken place in formulation during the last fifty years or so; an ammoniastearinstarch compounds containing white petrolatum, ammonia, starch and stearin (Formula 10) for the manufacture of compact powder and rouge has been recommended.

Formula 10

Constituents	*per cent*
Stearin	100 g
White petrolatum	20 g
Ammonium hydroxide solution, 0.97 s.g.	50 cm^3
Rice or maize starch	250 g

Formula 11 gives a formula to which the damp compression process is applicable.

Formula 11

Constituents	*per cent*
Kaolin	20.0
Zinc oxide	15.0
Precipitated chalk	25.0
Talc	32.0
Compact binder	8.0
Perfume, colour	q.s.

The dry compression method is suitable for mass production, but necessitates the use of higher pressures than are employed in the damp compression process. The composition of a compressed face powder cake by the dry compression process is given in formula 12.

Formula 12

Constituents	*per cent*
Talcum	61.25
Sodium lauryl sulphate	0.75
Titanium dioxide	7.50
Zinc stearate	11.25
Inorganic pigments	1.00
Mineral oil	4.50
Spermaceti	3.00
Cetyl alcohol	1.50
Lanolin	1.00
Glycerine	7.50
Hexachlorophene	0.25
Alkyldimethylbenyl ammonium chloride	0.20
Methyl-p-hydroxybnzoate	0.09
Propyl-p-hydroxybenzoate	0.09
Perfume	0.12

Procedure

Talc, sodium lauryl sulphate, titanium dioxide, zinc stearate and inorganic pigments are first mixed together in a ribbon mixer for an hour. The premixed hexachlorophene, quaternary ammonium base and preservative are added to the mixer and the batch is mixed for about two hours, before passing through a micro-pulveriser, using a no. 0.013 screen. The temperature of the material should not be allowed to rise more than 37°C during this operation. After cooling , the powder blend is repassed through the micro-pulveriser. The mineral oil, spermaceti, lanolin and glycerine, mixed with heating until liquid, are then sprayed into the dry batch which is mixed in the ribbon mixer for a further half hour. The batch is passed through comminuter and once again through a pulveriser, using a 3 / 16 in screen. When cool, the powder is passed through the micro-pulveriser using a no.0.027 screen, and finally, having been cooled once more, is passed through a 40 mesh screen ensuring that no heat is generated during this final screening. The resulting material is filled into containers and 40-50 psi pressure is applied to convert the powder into cake. It is usually advisable to keep the powders for several days in a suitably humid atmosphere before pressing, to facilitate the escape of any trapped air, and to ensure that the powder blend will not be too dry when compressed. During the dry compression process, it is usual to apply a small pressure initially to squeeze out the air, and thus avoid the formation of air pockets in the powder cakes. Pressure is then gradually increased up to 150 psi or even more 1000 + kPa before the die is removed from the surface of the cake.

CAKE MAKE-UP

The modern cake make-up originates from theatrical grease-paint and has acquired popularity because of its ease of application and stability and also because more product cant be applied to the face and thus deeper shades and effects can be achieved. The cake make-up is also made from talc, kaolin, zinc oxide and precipitated chalk. In addition it has inorganic pigment such as titanium dioxide and iron oxides. Humectants such as sorbitol or propylene glycol may also be incorporated together with other additives such as sorbitan sesquioleate, lanolin or mineral oil and perfume. Humectants and other liquid constituents are usually combined and sprayed on to the powder constituents while these are mixed in the ribbon mixer. The resulting blend is granulated and finally compressed.

A dry cake-form make-up which can be applied with a moistened pad or sponge. The cake contains oily and waxy ingredients (0.8-24 per cent), a water-soluble dispersing agent (1-13 per cent) and fillers (35-80 per cent) and pigments (12-50 per cent) whose particles are coated with the oils and waxes to make them water-repellent. The make-up is prepared by adding the afillers (talc, chalk) and pigments (zinc, titanium and Ferric oxides) to the oils and waxes dispersed in water. After drying mixture is pulverised and compressing it into cake-form.

In case a much higher ratio of powder to emulsion used drying is not needed. For example approximately 12 to 1, and mixing with a Duplex mixer. The mixing operation takes between 30 and 60 minutes and the mix is compacted after granulating through fine screen. The following formulae can be made in this fashion (formula 13) :

Formula 13

Constituents	*parts*	
Powder base (perfume)	100	
Emulsion :		
Stearic acid	34.5	8.5
Mineral oil	21.5	
Triethanolamine	10.5	
Water	33.5	

For deep shades with good coverage, zinc oxide is replaced by titanium dioxide (this also facilitates better pressing characteristics) formula 14 :

Formula 14

Constituents	*per cent*
Colour mix :	
Talc	89.75
Titanium dioxide	9.00
Yellow iron oxide	0.75
Red iron oxide	0.40
Black iron oxide	0.10
Base :	
Stearic acid	15.0
Acetylated lanoiin	3.0
Stearyl alcohol	3.0
Glyceryl monostearate	2.2
Sulphonated castor oil	1.2
Triethanolamine	3.0
Mineral oil	35.0
Polyethylene glycol	10.0

(Cont'd)

Water	27.6
Completion ratio :	
Base	20.0
Colour mix	79.8
Perfume	0.2

Pressing of this product can be very rapid as for compact powders, although it is important to check that there is consistent dispersion of the base in the colour mix throughout long manufacturing runs.

Application of Cake Make-up

The application of cake make-up is recommended in the following manner : To apply cake make-up correctly, wet and squeeze out a sponge and rub it lightly over the face. Before drying smooth cake make-up on the face blend in the rouge. Carefully squeeze all water out of the sponge and rub it lightly over the face until the make-up is dry. It is recomended that people who not like a heavy make-up should blot off the excess of water with a dry towel or facial tissue.

The cake make-up is satisfactory for the younger woman; and persons in the later thirties, and even younger persons who suffer from dry skin.

MAKE-UP CREAM

Foundation make-up preparations in cream form are essentially suspensions of pigments in an emulsified lotion. The suspension is usually homogenised and milled. The addition of the pigment is usually made at about 50-55°C as the emulsion is slowly cooled with agitation. The following formula for a cream make-up (Formula 15) :

Formula 15

Constituents	*parts*
Glycerol mono- and distearate (pure)	2.0
PEG monostearate	1.0
Stearic acid	11.5
Cetyl alcohol	0.5
Isopropyl myristate or palmitate or palmitate	2.0
Propylene glycol	12.0
Sorbitol syrup	2.5
Preservative	0.1
Titanium dioxide	2.2

(Cont'd)

Talc	8.0
Colour pigments	1.0
Water	57.4

LIQUID POWDER

Liquid powders have been used as a base for ordinary powder or to replace such powder for evening wear, dances or similar occasions. They have also included a theatrical product, 'Wet white', which is used for whitening the neck and arms. Its basic components are zinc oxide and bismuth oxychloride, subnitrate and carbonate incorporated into a liquid consisting of a mixture of glycerine and water in varying proportions. Glycerine is employed in amounts of up to 30 per cent and the water is often replaced by triple rose water or other fragrant waters; starch is also used sometimes to suspend heavier constituents. To prepare 'wet white' the constituent powders are mixed and glycerin is added. Surfactants could also be included to assist in dispersing the powders. A 'wet white' formula on these lines, is given in formula 16 :

Formula 16

Constituents	*per cent*
Bismuth subnitrate	5.0
Starch	5.0
Zinc oxide	10.0
Glycerine	15.0
Rose water	65.0

Instead of bismuth salt and starch, pigments, fillers and colours are added in modern formulae (formulae 17 and 18) :

Formula 17

Constituents	*per cent*
Zinc oxide	3.0
Chalk	15.0
Kaolin	2.0
Colouring matter	q.s.
Glycerine	15.0
Water	65.0
Preservative, perfume	q.s.

Formula 18

Constituents	*per cent*
Zinc oxide	10.0
Titanium oxide	10.0
Talc	10.0
Colouring matter	q.s.
Gum tragacanth (0.5 solution)	25.0
Glycerine	15.0
Water	30.0
Preservative, perfume	q.s.

Liquid powder formulation is given in formula 19 :

Formula 19

Constituents	*per cent*
Sodium carragheenate	2.0
n-Propyl alcohol	2.0
Propylene glycol	5.0
Water	68.5
Veegum HV	0.5
Talc	10.0
Magnesium carbonate	4.0
Titanium dioxide	1.0
Colour pigments	7.0
Perfume	q.s.

LIQUID MAKE-UP

Liquid make-up consists essentially of pigments dispersed in a viscous base. The liquid make-up preparations were suspensions of pigments in an aqueous alcoholic solution. They require vigorous shaking prior to use to ensure uniform distribution of the product during application.

The main trouble in preparing this product is that to prevent the sedimentation of constituent pigment. It si done by dispersing them in a hydrocolloid base or in a liquid emulsion. The hydrocolloids used for thickening the preparations may be selected from cellulose derivatives, carragheenates, etc. The pigments used are talc, kaolin, zinc oxide, titanium dioxide, calcium or magnesium carbonates and others.

In emulsified products, raw materials used included propylene glycol monostearate, glyceryl monostearate, fatty alcohols such as cetyl or oleyl alcohols, isopropyl myristate, lanolin and its derivatives, polyethylene glycols, humectants and others. A liquid make-up composition is shown in formulae 20-21.

A liquid make-up formulae is given in formula 20. Viscosity may be adjusted by varying the amount of gum and bentonite.

Formula 20

constituents	*per cent*
Propylene glycol	4.40
Polyethylene glycol	1.92
Preservative	0.32
Gum tragacanth	76.68
Bentonite	0.96
White oil	1.20
Oleyl alcohol	6.72
Stearic acid	4.20
Triethanolamine	1.92
Perfume	q.s.
Titanium dioxide plus powdered pigments	q.s.

Pigments and titanium dioxide are usually 5-10% as in the formula 21.

Formula 21

Constituents	*per cent*
Isopropyl lanolate	3.50
Isopropyl myristate	4.20
Squalane	1.40
Purcellin oil	2.10
Mineral oil	12.80
Sorbitan oleate	1.00
Veegum (5% solution)	30.00
Propylene glycol	8.00
CMC (1% solution)	20.60
Polyoxyethylene sorbitan mon-oleate	4.00

(Cont'd)

Water	6.04
Titanium dioxide	4.60
Yellow iron oxide	0.56
Red iron oxide	0.55
Black iron oxide	0.10
Perfume	0.25
Preservative	0.30

STICK MAKE-UP

This stick concept can be extended further to give the cover-up product, used to disguise birthmarks and blemishes. The product is heavily pigmented and is applied like a lipstick.

Formula 22

Constituents	*per cent*
Lanolin alcohols	2.8
Ozokerite wax	8.0
Paraffin wax	6.0
Mineral oil	20.2
Isopropyl myristate	10.0
Lanolin	2.8
Titanium dioxide	36.8
Kaolin	8.0
Yellow iron oxide	2.5
Black iron oxide	0.6
Red iron oxide	2.0
Perfume	0.3

FACE PACKS AND MASKS

The use of face packs by women dates back to early antiquity when some of the earths used in them were credited with almost miraculous healing powers. These preparations are applied to the face in the form of liquids or pastes. They are then allowed to dry or to set with the object of improving the appearance of the skin, by producing a transient tightening effect as well as by cleansing the skin. Such a preparation should possess the following properties :

1. It should be a smooth paste without gritty particles and without an 'earthy' or other objectionable odour.

2. When applied to the face by immediate drying must form adherent coating on the skin which can be peeled off the face.
3. It should produce a definite sensation of tightening of the skin after application and cleansing of the skin.
4. It must be dermatologically innocuous and non-toxic.

The five basic systems based on wax, rubber, vinyl resins, hydrocolloids and earth respectively gives satisfactory properties.

Wax-based Systems

Wax-based masks generally consist merely of paraffin wax of a suitable melting point. It may be mixtures of wax with the addition of a little petroleum jelly and cetyl and stearly alcohols. The use of microcrystalline waxes may assist the continuity of a suitable 'wax mask'. The following formula 23 illustrates the use of this material :

Formula 23

Constituents	*per cent*
Micro-crystalline wax	13.0
Paraffin wax	60.0
Cetyl alcohol	5.0
Mineral oil	20.0
Bentone	1.4
Isopropyl alcohol	0.6

Rubber–based Systems

Rubber masks are removed from the skin very easily by mere pulling. Slight plumping of the skin becomes noticeable which disappears after skin respiration has been restored to normal. Formula 24 illustrates the composition of face packs based on rubber latex.

Formula 24

Constituents	*per cent*
Latex emulsion	25
Sorbitol	5
Methylcellulose	10
Kaolin	3

Borax	1
Water	56
Preservative	q.s.m

Vinyl–based Systems

Vinyl - based systems are generally based on polyvinyl alcohol or vinyl acetate resin as film-former. The use of polyvinyl alcohol in face packs is illustrated by formula 25.

Formula 25

Costituents	*per cent*
Veegum	0.5
Kaolin	0.5
Titanium dioxide	0.3
PVA	12.0
Propylene glycol	8.0
Ethanol	20.0
Water	58.7

Hydrocolloid–based Systems

Hydrocolloid-based systems are high-viscosity sols which after application lose water and form a flexible gel film. They are also solid gels which are melted before application to the face. The sensation of tightness is produced by the eventual shrinking of the gel on loss of further moisture. The formula 26 for a 'gelanthum' mask containing gelatin and tragacanth is given below :

Formula 26

Constituents	*per cent*
Gum tragacanth	2.2
Glycerine	2.5
Gelatin (white)	2.3
Water	90.5
Zinc oxide	2.5

For a 'gleanthum mask with honey', is replacement of about 4.5 parts of the water in the above formula by honey is recommended. The formula 27 is given below :

Formula 27

Constituents	*parts*
Casein	20.0
Borax	0.5
Glycerine	5.0
Water	100.0
p-Hydroxybenozic acid propyl ester	0.1

The following composition for a face pack is given in formula 28.

Formula 28

Constituents	*parts*
Gelatin	10.00
Water	50.00
Camphor	0.05
Zinc oxide	3.00
Kaolin	5.00
Titanium dioxide	2.00

The preparations given in formulae 27 and 28 are heated before use and applied in a warm state. The use of alcohol as part solvent is shown in formula 29.

Formula 29

Constituents	*per cent*
Carbopol	2.0
Water	42.0
Alcohol	50.0
Glycerol	2.0
Di-isopropanolamine	4.0

Earth–based Systems (Argillaceous Masks)

Earth-based systems are referred as paste masks. They include clay facial packs and the so-called mud packs and a high percentage of solids. These products can either be presented in bulk, or packed in sachets, for mixing with water when required, or they can be presented ready mixed for use. The ready mix should be sterilised using heat or ethylene oxide and should contain preservative. The presence of bentonite produces a genuine cleaning effect, particularly on very greasy skins. China clay, colloidal kaolin, fuller's earth, bentonite, etc., may be used as the 'argillaceous' material. The colour of fuller's earth or bentonite is modified by blending with kaolin and/or the addition of zinc oxide or titanium dioxide.

Bentonite has strong affinity for water and its thixotropic properties as it is derived from volcanic clay. Certain bentonites will absorb up to fifteen times their volume of water. The addition of a small quantity of magnesium oxide, or some other substance possessing a similar pH increases absorption capacity.

The consistency of bentonite gels is influenced by concentration and pH of the gels. A gel containing 6 per cent bentonite has the consistency of glycerin, while a 20 per cent gel has the consistency of lanolin. The formulae 30-31 are examples of earth based systems.

Formula 30 (All-purpose masks)

Constituents	*per cent*
Kaolin	35.0
Bentonite	5.0
Cetyl alcohol	2.0
Sodium lauryl sulphate	0.1
Glycerine	10.0
Nipagin M	0.1
Perfume	q.s.
Water	to 100.0

Formula 31

Constituents	*per cent*
Glyceryl monostearate	3.0
Lanolin oil	2.0
Sodiumlauryl sulphate	2.0
Veegum	8.0
Kaolin	10.0
Propylene glycol	7.0
Titaniumdioxide	4.0
Ethanol	6.0
Isopropyl myristate	2.0
Water	56.0

The following two formulations (formulae 32 and 33) for face packs for dry and greasy are given below :

Formula 32 (Face pack for dry skin)

Constituents	*parts*
Kaolin	80.0
Starch	10.0
Cold cream	20.0
Cetyl alcohol	2.0
Hydrophilic oil	5.0
Water, boric water or infusions	q.s.

Formula 33 (Face pack for greasy skin)

Constituents	*parts*
Kaolin	80.0
Magnesium carbonate	15.0
Starch	5.0
Tragacanth gum	1.0
Water	q.s.

For oily, sallow skin or skin blemishes 'oxygenated' mask is recommended, after conducting trail on a small area of the skin. An 'oxygenated' face mask, based on kaolin. Bergwein has the following composition (formula 34) :

Formula 34

Constituents	*parts*
Colloidal kaolin	800
Salicylic acid	20
Aluminium lactate	5
Magnesium peroxide	200

Anti-Wrinkle Preparations

Face packs are usually left on the face for about 10-25 minutes, to allow most of the water to evaporate and the resulting film to contract and harden, after which they are removed. The anti-wrinkle preparations are based on bovine serum albumin, and form an 'invisible' mask over the skin. They are allowed to remain in contact with the facial skin for about 6-8 hours, that is, for the period of time during which they remain effective, and are then removed by washing.

Sterile solution containing a suitable preservative and ready for immediate us without dilution; as a 30 per cent solution to be diluted with an equal volume of water prior to use; and also in the form of a freeze-dried powder which before use is reconstituted with water. The smoothing effect would seem to be a purely physical one entailing the 'filling-in' of facial wrinkles and the formation of a tight occlusive film which stretches the skin. How long this effect lasts will largely depend on how much the facial muscles are used.

A wrinkle-smoothing composition disclosed in an American patent contains proteins obtained from cow's milk whey, namely a-lactalbumin and some b-lactoglobulin. The film produced with this composition is claimed to be effective for about four hours and can be re-activated by moistening it with a little water. Both the component proteins are under natured and water-soluble, are present in the aqueous composition in a ratio of 4:1. It may constitute 10-30 per cent by weight of the total composition. Water may be present within a range of 70-90 per cent by weight, together with 2-4 per cent by weight (of the composition) glycerin or propylene glycol, ot increase the flexibility of the dried films. Bacteriostatic and Fungistatic preservative must not precipitate the lactalbumin or the lactoglobulin. The pH of the final preparation is maintained within the 5-7 range.

Apart from the ability to re-activate films produced, other advantages claimed for this preparation are that when it is dry it is not shining in appearance, that is does not flake away after drying and that no make-up is required to conceal the film.

Chapter - 13

COLOURED MAKE-UP PREPARATIONS

LIPSTICK

Lipsticks, the lip cosmetics moulded into sticks. They are essentially dispersions of colouring matter in a base consisting of a suitable blend of oils, fats and waxes.

Lipstick is used to impart an attractive colour and appearance to the lips, accentuating their good points and disguising any bad ones. Narrow bad-tempered lips may be widened, and broad sensual lips made to appear narrower by its use. In fact, if applied intelligently it is capable of entirely altering the apparent facial characteristics.

Since lips are considered to be more alluring when they possess a slightly moist appearance, this is always achieved by the use of a greasy base which also exerts an emollient action.

Characteristics Required in a Lipstick

A good lipstick should have the following characteristics :

1. It should have retainable smooth surface of uniform colour, free from defects such as pinholes or grittiness due to colour or crystal aggregates. It should not exude oil, develop a bloom, flake, cake, harden, soften, crumble nor become brittle over the range of temperatures likely to be experienced.
2. It should be innocuous, both dermatologically and if ingested.
3. It should be easy to apply. A film on the lips that is neither excessively greasy nor too dry, that is reasonably permanent. But capable of deliberate removal, and which has a stable colour.

Ingredients of Lipsticks

Colour

The colour of a lipstick is one of the major selling points. It can only be dealt with in general terms, since the precise shades are dictated by ephemeral fashion. It is usual for the colour to contain red and this allows shades ranging between orange-yellow and purple-blue, although even greens are not unknown. The colour is imparted to the lips in two ways :

1. By staining the skin, which requires a dyestuff in solution, capable of penetrating the outer surface of the lips.
2. By covering the lips with a coloured layer which serves to hide any surface roughness and give a smooth appearance. It is met by insoluble dyes and pigments which make the film more or less opaque.

Typical proportions for the colours in a lipstick are as under :

Constituents	*per cent*
Staining dyes (bromo acids)	1/2-3
Oil-soluble pigment	2
Insoluble pigment	8-10
Titanium dioxide	1-4

Staining dyes

The most widely used staining dyes are water-soluble eosin and other halogenated derivatives of fluorescein called as 'bromo acids' a term originally applied to acid eosin, tetrabromofluorescein.

Eosin

Eosin is an insoluble orange compound which changes to an intense red salt at pH above 4. It is also known as D & C Red No. 21. When applied to the lips in the acid form, it produces a relatively indelible purple red stain on neutralisation by the lip tissue.

Eosin and some of its derivatives can give rise to sensitisation or Photosensitisation, leading to cheilitis (inflammation of the red portion of the lips) or more general allergic reactions.

Difficulties may be encountered when using bromo acid dyestuffs in obtaining entirely homogeneous dispersions of these dyes in the lipstick mass. This could result in shade variations in lipsticks. Novel compositions have been disclosed which aim to overcome these difficulties and to ensure that the colours of the lipsticks sold are indentical with those conferred by them on the skin. These compostitions comprise amine salts of bromo acid dyestuffs and fatty substances which are at least partial solvents for such components. The amines employed in the preparation of these compositions are selected from non-aromatic primary, secondary or tertiary monoamines, in which the groups attached to the nitrogen atom contain at the most 6 carbon atoms. Some of them may contain hydroxy radicals, others may be heterocyclic compounds. Specifically mentioned in patent claims have been triethanolamine, diethanolamine, 2-amino- 2methyl-propanediol–1,3, monoisopropanolamine, trihy droxymethylamino- methane, diglycolamine and morpholine.

To prepare these compositions the bromoacids are dispersed in a fatty material, preferably soya lecithin, and the amine is added with mixing. The resulting mixture may be optionally heated and allowed to cool. The amine salts of the bromoacid dyestuffs are then dissolved in a mixture of waxes (for example carnauba wax, beeswax and ozokerite) and oils (for example various lanolin derivatives and vaseline).

Non-eosin Staining Dyes

Non-eosin staining dyes are an interesting development in view of the restrictions applying to some of the fluorescein derivatives. It is claimed that water-soluble FD&C and D & C dyes. They are useless in lipsticks, when converted to the free sulphoacid form become water-insoluble, lipophilic, and suitable for use as staining dyes in lipsticks, covering a wide colour range.

Pigments

Inorganic and organic pigments are metallic lakes used to give intensity and variation of colour. When selecting lakes the possibility of reaction with the base, for example soap formation with free fatty acid, must be borne in mind.

Titanium dioxide

It is the most effective white pigment for obtaining pink shades and giving opacity ot the film on the lips. Its concentration used is upto 4 per cent. However, the use of titanium dioxide requires great care in the grade of material selected (anatase or rutile) and the surface treatment it has received to make it lipophilic, and also in the method of incorporation, if unexpected troubles such as oily exudation, streaking, dullness and coarse texture are to be avoided.

Although two D&C colours, D&C Red No. 36 and D&C Orange No 17, are metallic lakes, insoluble in both water and oil. They may be considered as pigments. Similarly, the amount of staining dye used often exceeds the solubility in the base and the insoluble portion will act as a pigment.

Lakes

Of many of the D&C dyes with metals such as aluminium, barium, calcium and strontium are potential pigments for lipsticks. However, some strontium and zirconium lakes are banned. Aluminium lakes are not usually favoured because of their lack of opacity, but this very property would seem to suggest their use in transparent lipsticks.

The following lakes are considered to be the most useful lipstick colourants :

1. Calcium lakes of D&C Red No 7, 31 and 34.
2. Barium lakes of D&C Red No 9 and Orange No 17.
3. Aluminium lakes of D&C Red No 2, 3 and 19 and FD&C Yellows No 5 and 6.

When the parent D&C colour is subject to restriction the lakes are also restricted in the same way.

As noted above, pigments and lakes are used at levels between 8 and 10 per cent or perhaps over a wider range, say 5-15 per cent. Iridescent lipsticks utilise either mica coasted with titanium dioxide or bismuth oxychloride at levels of up to 20 per cent, depending upon the effect desired.

Base

The quality of the lipstick during manufacture, storage and use will be determined for the most part by the composition of the fatty base and colour. The quality is also concerned with the rheology of the mixture at various temperatures. For instance, during manufacture (usually while warm) it must be possible to mill and grind the mass, and to pour and mould it while holding the insoluble colours evenly dispersed without settling. In the moulds it must set quickly with a good surface and good release properties. During shelf life and usage life the stick must remain rigid and stable, and generally in good condition. In use the stick must soften sufficiently in contact with the lips, and be sufficiently thixotropic to spread on the lips to form an adherent film which will not smear nor, ideally, transfer to cups or glasses.

Dyestuff Solvents

Some part of the base must act as the necessary solvent for the staining dyes. Many of the normal fatty materials are too non-polar to dissolve the dyestuffs. It is convenient to consider first those ingredients which do have solvent properties for eosin, and which must form some part of the base.

Caster oil

It is a traditional material for dissolving bromoacid. This is due to its high content of ricinoleic (hydroxyoleic) acid, which is unique among natural oils. Its other properties include a high viscosity, even when warm, which delays pigment settling. The oiliness which helps with gloss and emollience, although too high a quantity causes drag during application and an unpleasant greasy film. The level of castor oil is 25-50%. The disadvantages of castor oil include an unpleasant taste and potential rancidity.

Fatty Alcohols

The hexadecyl alcohol is a good solvent for bromoacid dyes. Lipsticks containing it is applied with very little drag do not bleed or smear. Its presence lessens any tendency to develop an unpleasant taste during storage.

Esters

They are lipophilic liquids of low oiliness giving lubricating and emollient effects with some dye solvent properties.

Glycols

They are more polar than the fatty alcohols and might be expected to be better dye solvents with two hydroxy groups.

Polyethylene glycols (Carbowaxes)

They have good dyestuff solvent power, which correlates to some extent with water solubility and this is a detraction. These materials would seem to have considerable possibilities in lipstick formulation, if correctly selected.

Monoalkanolamides

They have good dye-dissolving properties. They have also no action on the plastic material of the lipstick cases. The pre-dissolved in Loramine wax is kept as a concentrate for more convenient dispensing when required.

Other base ingredients. The ingredients quoted so far have had the high melting points or hardness which give satisfactory moulding properties, i.e. quick setting and good release with a glossy surface and a rigid stick. This function is generally fulfilled by the inclusion of waxes or wax-like materials.

Carnauba wax

It is a very hard vegetable wax used for raising the melting point imparting rigidity, hardness and contraction properties in the moulding process.

Candelilla

It is another hard vegetable wax serving the same functions as carnauba wax but has a lower melting point and is less brittle.

Amorphous hydrocarbon waxes

In mineral oil, for example ozokerite wax, gives a short-fibred texture to the product.

Petroleum-based waxes

Microcrystalline wax, are also used to modify the rheology of the product.

Beeswax

It is the traditional stiffening agent for castor oil, but it can give a grainy and dull effect if used in large quantities.

Hydrogenated vegetable oils having wax like properties are more solid and less prone to rancidity than the unhardened oils. Of particular interest is hydrogenated castor oil, still retains eosin solvent properties. Some other softer materials will be found to be of use in lipstick manufacture.

Lanolin and lanolin absorption bases

They have eosin solvent properties and also act as binding agents for the other ingredients, tending to minimise sweating and cracking of the stick and acting as plasticisers. Absorption bases are recommended to enhance the gloss on the lips. They are useful upto 10%.

Petroleum jelly

Paraffin oils they act as lubricants and improve spreading properties. Large amounts tend to impair the adhesion properties and can be difficult to blend if much polar material such as castor oil is present.

Lecithin

It acts as a dispersing agent for pigments, in addition to facilitating the application of the lipstick and improving the adhesion to the lips.

Silicone waxes

They are largely insoluble in water, ethanol and organic fats and oils. The compositions containing them have improved viscosity, stability and a sharper melting point. They are said to be superior to compositions with no silicone wax, retaining their form plus all the properties of the silicone wax, over a wider temperature range. They are also said to have good shelf stability.

Perfumes

Perfumes selected should mask the fatty odour note of the base and should be non-irritant to the lips. The flavour as well as odour must be considered as consumer is likely to apprehend it in the mouth and nose. Perfumes should be stable and compatible with the other constituents of the lipstick base. The amount of perfume used is 2-4%.

The preferred perfumes are of the light floral or light sophisticated type with no single essential oil predominating. Rose alcohols and esters are often used as well as other essential oils, preferably terpeneless, such as aniseed, cinnamon, clove, lemon, orange and tangerine. The following formulae illustrate some lipstick formulations in existence. It is prepared by : first melt the ingredient by heating. Then add 7 parts of pigment to 92 parts and run the mixture through heated mill. Run the final blend into the mould with 1 part of perfume.

Formula 1

Constituents	*per cent*
Loramine	20.0
Lanolin	10.0
Cocoa butter	5.5
Refined beeswax	4.0
Ozokerite	18.0
Carnauba wax	4.2
Oleyl alcohol	7.0
Mineral oil (high viscosity)	29.3
Perfume	2.0 or q.s.
Insoluble lake	10.0 or q.s.
Bromo acid (or eosin salt)	2.0

Formula 2

Constituents	*per cent*
Castor oil or bromoacid solvents	30.0
Mineral oil	15.0
Beeswax	15.0
Paraffin	10.0
Carnauba wax	10.0
Ceresin wax	10.0
Silicone-Fluid	10.0
Perfume-flavour compound	q.s.

Formula 3

Constituents	*per cent*
Hexadecyl alcohol	26.0
Castor oil	20.0
Propylene glycol monolaurate	15.0
Anhydrous lanolin	2.0
Ceraphyl	5.0
Candelilla wax	32.0c

Formula 4

Constituents	*per cent*
Hexadecyl alcohol	44.0
butyl stearate	2.0
Isopropyl palmitate	3.5
Anhydrous lanolin	7.0
Petrolatum	12.0
Candelilla wax	11.0
Carnauba wax	11.0
Stearic acid, triple pressed	8.0
Cetyl alcohol	1.5
Nordihydroguaiaretic acid (antioxidant)	0.02
Citric acid	0.006

Formulae	*5*	*6*
	Deep stain lipstick	*Creamy lipstick*
Constituents	*per cent*	*per cent*
Castor oil	60.0	65.0
Lanolin	5.0	10.0
Isopropyl myristate	-	5.0
Propylene glycol monoricinoleate	10.0	-
Polyethylene glycol 400	5.0	-
Beeswax	7.0	7.0

(Cont'd)

Candelilla wax	7.0	7.0
Carnauba wax	3.0	3.0
Ozokerite	3.0	3.0
In addition:		
p-Hydroxybenozoic acid propyl ester	0.2	0.2
Bromo acids	3.0	3.0
Colour lakes and pigments	12.0	12.0

Manufacture of Lipsticks

Lipstick manufacture employed will depend to some extent on the formulation and the plant available. In general, the manufacture of lipsticks consists of three stages :

1. The preparation of component blends, that is the oil blend, colour dispersion and wax blend.
2. The blending of these intermediates to form the lipstick mass.
3. The moulding of the lipstick mass into sticks.

Preparation and Blending

The colours, that is the bromoacids, pigments and lakes, are blended separately and dispersed in the complete lipstick base. The object of the operation is to produce a completely homogeneous dispersion of colourants conducive to the preparation of a smooth stick. A finely ground colours are used to wet fatty mixture and taken to milling to grinding process. Ball mills, sand mills, roller mills, colloid mills, edge or end runner mills has been used. It is desirable that the portion of the base used should be a plastic semisolid during the milling and it may sometimes be necessary to mill under warm conditions.

The soluble dyes are first dissolved in dye-solvent using heat. If solution is complete, this portion can be left on one side while the pigments are dispersed, but if not, the dye blend must at some point be ground with the pigment dispersion.

In preparing the pigment dispersion the colours are first milled with wetting chemicals like lanolin, polyglycol compounds and then add the completely non-polar materials.

The remainder of the base materials, for example the high melting waxes which may not have been used in the dye or pigment blends, are melted and blended together and then blended with the others. In order to secure an intimate mix a final milling operation is desirable.

Vacuum processing of the lipstick melt facilitates dispersion of pigments by removing the film of absorbed gas on the pigment particles, which is a barrier and causes incomplete wetting. It has been established that petroleum jelly, will dissolve 10 per cent air by volume at 90°C but only 5 per cent at 20°C. therefore the mix has been held at high temperature and allowed to absorb its full quota of air and then cooled. The air is not released until the viscosity of the mass is too great to allow to escape completely. It may collect round the pigment particles, displacing the oil and giving the effect of incomplete wetting.

The manufacture of lipsticks conducted at the lowest temperature. It is desirable that when mixing is complete the mixture should be transferred to a jacketed closed vessel. The fluid mixture is stirred gently while sufficient vacuum is applied to remove all occluded air. When the air has been removed, vacuum is shut off, the mass is stirred and the perfume is added and mixed through. The mass is then ready for moulding immediately. Else can be set into blocks which are stored and moulded as required.

In one of the two methods described, the wax blend is prepared and stored in a molten state while all constituents oils are metered into a storage tank fitted with a suitable mixer. A part of the oil blend is then mixed with the dry pigments in a pre-mix pan attached to a sand mill and the resultant slurry passed through the sand mill into the steam pan fitted with a combined mixer and pump. The remainder of the oil blend is then passed through the pre-mix pan and sand mill to flush any residual colour.

The wax blend is metered into the steam pan simultaneously and thoroughly mixed with the other constituents. The resulting base is tested for shade, perfume and flavour are added, and the lipstick mass is pumped into storage trays, using the mixer as a pump.

Moulding

For moulding first lipstick mass is remelted in a jacked pan. The entrapped air si removed by slow agitation for 30 minutes. The molten mass is then run into moulds for casting. Moulds are usually filled to excess to prevent the formation of a depression in the centre of the stick. This excess is scraped off and the mould is then carefully cooled to allow the mass to set. The overcooling will affect the removal of stick from the moulds.

The moulds are made of brass and aluminium. They may be of the vertical split type (with a split down the centre to allow for the easy removal of the sticks) or the automatic ejection type. A cooling cabinet is required with the split moulds. A preheating device in moulds can raised a temperature of about 40°C before filling with the lipstick mass. This prevents 'flow marks' which would otherwise be visible on the moulded stick. With the water-jacketed automatic ejection mould a cooling cabinet is unnecessary. The jacket is filled with warm water prior to pouring the lipstick mass. Then the cold water is introduced and kept running to chill the lipstick mass. When cooled, the moulds are opened and the sticks are pushed out automatically or with a rubber-covered finger.

Automatic ejection mould (whether air-cooled or water-cooled) will not produce a good bullet-shaped stick, because a small ring or ridge is left near the tip of the stick caused by the thickness of the metal edge of the ejection plunger. It is considered that such moulds are best for the wedge-shaped stick. After moulding, the sticks should be stored for about a week before being filled into the lipstick holders. Then lipstick is passed rapidly through a small gas flame to melt the surface layer, in order to remove any surface spots and to produce a bright, smooth and glossy surface. This process is called as flaming.

Transparent Lipsticks

A lipstick can be described which uses soluble or solubilised dyes. This allows light to shine through it, giving it a sparkle. The suitable solvents such as a monoalkyloamide of mixed fatty acids or dipropylene glycol methyl ether enhances staining action of dyes. Standard lipstick case is shown in Fig. 30.1.Fig. 30.1.

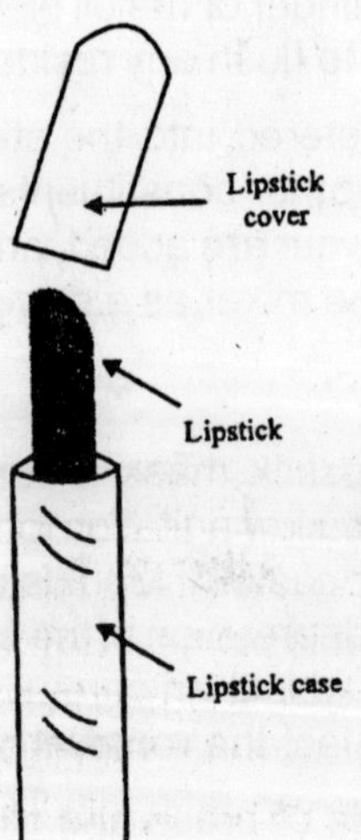

Fig. 30.1. Lipstick case.

Water–soluble dyes may be used for additional colour effect. The compatibility of such dyes is improved by using anhydrous lower alcohols such as ethanol or isopropanol as co-solvents. These alcohols control syneresis and improves stability at 2 to10 per cent.

Polyamide resins or blend of solid polyamide resin with liquid polyamide resin of molecular mass 2000 - 10,000 and 600 - 800 are used for moulding lipstick to give solid stick.

Ensure that the resulting sticks are not brittle. These materials can be used with softening agents like a lower aliphatic alcohols in conjunction with other polyamide solvents like fatty acid esters, to prevent brittleness the glycol ester of higher fatty acids, particularly those used are between C_{13} and C_{18}. The formulations are given to illustrate transparent lipsticks in formula 7 :

Formula 7

Constituents	*per cent*
Polyamide resin (average MW 8000)	20.0
Polyamide resin (average MW 600-800)	5.0
Propylene glycol monolaurate	28.0
Castor oil	12.6
D&C Red 21	0.3
Lanolin alcohols	8.0
Dipropylene glycol methyl ether	10.0
Ethoxylated lanolin alcohols (5 mol Et_2O)	10.1
Anhydrous isopropanol	5.0
Perfume	1.0

Lip Salves

The lip salve is used, not for decoration, but for protection against exposure to cold, in winter or sub-arctic conditions. The requirement is simply for a fairly substantial, flexible, adherent, moisture-resistant film on the lips and there is no need for staining dyes. The base can be made largely from mineral oils, jelly and waxes. It is necessary to include a proportion of a more hydrophilic material to promote adherence, perfume blending and general properties. In some cases a small amount of antiseptic can be added. Some users prefer a coloured salve in which case the colour is provided by a small amount of oil-soluble dye or dispersed lake not necessarily of a staining type. Suitable base formulation are given in formulae 8 and 9 :

Formula 8

Constituents	*per cent*
Paraffin wax	30.0
White petroleum jelly	35.0
Technical white oil	20.0
Beeswax	15.0

Formula 9

Constituents	*per cent*
Cetyl alcohol	5.0
Eutanol	30.0
Beeswax, white	25.0
Paraffin wax, 52°C	15.0
Liquid paraffin	25.0

A lip-protective pomade is made up as follows formula 10 :

Formula 10

	Constituents	*per cent*
A	Mineral oil	25.0
	Petroleum	7.0
	Ceresin wax	24.0
	Beeswax	7.0
	Atlas G-2859	3.5
	Tween 60	0.5
	Union Carbide L-45 Silicone Fluid (1000 cS)	5.0
B	Water	28.0
	Preservative	q.s.
C	Perfume	q.s.

A lip salve which is used as a decorative item has become known in recent years as a lip gloss. This popular item can be applied to the lips without other make-up or over the normal lipstick. Lip gloss preparations take the form of a stick, or a salve for finger application, or a liquid for roll-on or brush application. These compositions may also contain pearl pigment to confer a transparent sheen in addition to the normal gloss. Formulation of finger applied lip gloss & liquid lip gloss are given below in formulae 11 and 12 :

Formula 11 (Finger-applied lip gloss)

Constituents	*per cent*
Syncrowax HRC	5.0
Syncrowax HGLC	5.0
Timica silk white	8.0
Fluilan	8.0
Liquid paraffin	74.0
Perfume, antioxidant	q.s.

Formula 12 (Liquid lip gloss)

Constituents	*per cent*
Polybutene	30.0
Lanolin oil	20.0
Mineral oil	24.8
Oleyl alcohol	25.0
Saccharin	0.2
Perfume, antioxidant	q.s.

Liquid Lipsticks

Liquid lipsticks have been developed with the object of providing more permanent films than can be obtained with conventional lipsticks. These liquid lipsticks consist of ethanolic solutions of alcohol-soluble dyes, film-forming resins like ethyl cellulose, polyvinyl alcohols and polyvinyl acetate and plasticisers like triethyl citrate, dioctyl acetate, methyl abietate or polyethylene glycols. The dyestuffs employed are alcohol-soluble halogenated fluoresceins and also other alcohol-soluble dyes.

The dyes and perfume are dissolved in the alcohol. Then resulting solution is filtered. The disadvantage associate with the use of these alcoholic preparations is 'smarting' produced on the lips on application. Excessive drying of the lips may also result. Persons affected in this way should discontinue the use of these Preparations. Apply occasionally a 40 per cent solution of aqueous glycerine and use an emollient lip salve. The manufacture of liquid lipsticks based on ethyl cellulose, the formulations are given in the following illustrative formulae 13 and 14 :

Formula 13

Constituents	*per cent*
Ethyl cellulose	3.1
Ethyl alcohol	68.4
Petroleum ether	20.0
Hydrogenated methyl abietate	7.5
Rhodamine	1.0

Formula 14

Constituents	*per cent*
Ethyl cellulose	3.06
Bleached wax-free shellac	4.94
Ethyl alcohol	65.00
Petroleum ether	14.66
Hydrogenated methyl abietate	12.00
Fuchsine	0.30
Saccharin	0.04

The accessory agents like perfumes, preservatives, antioxidants, etc., may be added. The preparations are preferably clear and transparent and are of a viscosity ranging between 3 and 500 cP, while best results are obtained in a range between 20 and 50 cP. Another lipstick formulation is given below in formula 15 :

Formula 15

Constituents	*per cent*
Ethyl cellulose	1.0
PVA (high viscosity)	3.0
Triethyl citrate	1.0
Alcohol-soluble lanolin	0.5
PEG	1.0
Isopropyl alcohol, pure	40.0
Bromoacid dyes	3.0
Flavour	0.5
Ethanol	50.0

ROUGE

The oldest make-up preparations used to apply colour to the cheeks is rouge. The preparations are available in liquid, cream and solid forms, of which the pressed powder or dry rouge is the most popular.

Dry Rouge (Compact Rouge)

Compact rouge differs from an ordinary compact powder in being more highly tinted. The properties of compact rouges are therefore virtually identical with those of ordinary compact powders. The finished product must be smooth, free from grittiness and should be easy to apply. It should have good adhesion to the skin and a good covering power. Because these products are highly tinted and may be conspicuous if not adequately blended. It is essential that component colours are distributed evenly throughout the product. A component liable to impart undesirable opacity must be used in moderate amount which has no deleterious effect on the appearance of product. e.g. at lower concentration zinc oxide is used. The hygroscopic nature of kaolin are liable to produce colour streaking in damp weather.

Grinding and shade-matching stages are included in the manufacture of compact rouges. The component raw materials must be very finely divided to facilitate their intimate blending as a prerequisite to a uniform distribution of component colours.. The constituents are, therefore, intimately mixed and simultaneously ground in hammer mills or attrition mills rather than just blended in ribbon mixers. This operation is carried out in the absence of large quantities of liquids. The presence of a little water or oil will ensure better colour distribution. The binder is either sprayed into the powders while they are being mixed, or incorporated in dry form.

The raw materials used in the manufacture of compact rouges are talc, kaolin, precipitated chalk, magnesium carbonate, titanium dioxide, zinc stearate, inorganic oxides, certified colourants and perfumes. Zinc oxide between 5 to 10% is used to increase the adhesion of the rouge, confers opacity to the product. Titanium dioxide has an appreciably greater covering powder than zinc oxide, and it also gives brighter and more stable colour shades.

Metallic stearates between 4-10% are used extensively as dry binders for compact rouges as they improve the adhesion with skin.

Compact Rouge Formulation

Typical compact rouge formulations are given in formulae 16 and 17:

Formula 16

Constituents	*per cent*
Talc	48
Kaolin	16
Zinc stearate	6
Zinc oxide	5
Magnesium carbonate	5
Rich starch	10
Titaniumdioxide	4
Colours	6

Formula 17

Constituents	*per cent*
Talc	67.5
Zinc stearate	5.0
Titanium dioxide	4.0
Red ion oxide	11.5
Black ion oxide	0.3
D&C Red 9 – barium lake	0.2
Mica coated with titanium dioxide	6.8
Perfume	0.2
Base	4.5
Base:	
Beeswax	12.00
Lanolin	2.00
Mineral oil	86.00

The colour lakes used for lighter and deeper shades are 1.5 and 6%. Colour lakes provide wide range of shades. Water-soluble and oil-soluble dyes are not suitable as colourants in compact rouges.

Wax-based Rouge

W-based rouge are in many respects similar to lipsticks. Formulae for bases resemble the drier type of lipstick. The shape is sometime larger in diameter (≈ 2 cm), colour is red or pink shade, or white. It is known as 'glemers' as it is used to disguise the colours of the face. The bromoacid type staining dye is not due to possibility of dermatitis. The formulae 18 and 19 are examples for wax-based rouges :

Formula 18

Constituents	*per cent*
Candelila wax	8.6
Carnauba wax	5.4
Beeswax	4.0
Mineral oil	17.0
Lanolin	2.0
Isopropylmyristate	33.0
Inorganic pigments and colour lakes	30.0

Formula 19

Constituents	*per cent*
Carnauba wax	10.0
Paraffin wax	2.5
Ozokerite wax	5.0
Petrolatum	4.0
Mineral oil	68.5
Titanium dioxide	1.9
Red iron oxide	1.0
Bismuth oxychloride	7.0
Perfume	0.1

Cream Rouge

Two types of cream rouge are available: anhydrous products and emulsified products.

Non-Aqueous Cream Rouge

Cream rouges are more difficult to apply than compact rouge. It is claimed that their use gives better results, in that there is no obvious line of demarcation when they are correctly applied. This gives a more natural effect. An effective anhydrous cream rouge has following formula 20. It is prepared by first grinding colours with the powder constituent, and then mill this into the warmed fatty base. Alternatively, mix all the ingredients and mill in a warmed ointment mill.

Formula 20

Constituents	*per cent*
Petroleum jelly	70.0
Kaolin	30.0
Colour, perfume	q.s.

Hexadecyl alcohol is claimed to impart a smooth and soft feeling to the skin during application and use. It also facilitates the spreading of a cream rouge. Such an anhydrous rouge may be prepared with the composition given in formula 21 :

Formula 21

Constituents	*per cent*
Hexadecyl alcohol	27.0
Light mineral oil	23.5
Talc	10.0
Ozokerite	10.0
Carnauba wax	6.0
Titanium dioxide	20.0
D&C Red No. 9 lake	3.0
Perfume	0.5

Emulsions

Cold cream or vanishing cream are emulsion products. The composition of emulsified cold cream is given in formula 22. The process involves dispersion of finely powdered colour base with melted fat. Add borax solution at 75°C, mix and finally mill.

Formula 22

Constituents	*per cent*
Lanolin	5.0
Cocoa butter	5.0
Beeswax	14.0
Liquid paraffin	30.0
Cetyl alcohol	1.0
Water	44.2
Borax	0.8
Colour	q.s.

The composition shown in formula 23 of cream rouge provides a product which is soft, creamy, and possesses excellent spreading properties. Because it is of the water-in-oil type it has less tendency to dry out than emulsified creams of the oil-in-water type.

Formula 23

Constituents	*per cent*
Arlacel C	2.0
Lanolin (anhydrous)	2.0
Mineral oil 65/75	16.0
Petrolatum	30.0
Preservative	q.s.

Cream rouge of the vanishing cream type has following composition is shown in formula 24 :

Formula 24

Constituents	*per cent*
Stearic acid	15.00
Water	76.32
Potassium hydroxide	0.50
Sodium hydroxide	0.18
Glycerine	8.00
Colour, preservative	q.s.

The solution of water soluble-dye in water or glycerin is used in emulsion products. After saponification add to main bulk of cream. In formula 25, diglycol stearate is employed as emulsifying agent.

Formula 25

Constituents	*per cent*
Diglycol stearate	20.0
Water	70.0
Glycerin	10.0
Water-soluble colour	q.s. (from 0.6 to 1.0)
Preservative	q.s.

The concentration of the colour darkens the cream surface as water soluble dyes are difficult to evaporate. Therefore it is necessary to incorporate glycerine, or *d*-sorbitol. Since it possesses a much narrower humectant range than glycerien, that is, it absorbs less moisture in a moist atmosphere, but holds it better in a dry one. A further improvement might be the packing of such products in a tightly capped tube.

Most of the colours employed in cream rouge are insoluble lakes, although sometimes oil colours are used. In the vanishing cram type, however, these lakes may be supplemented by fluorescein dyestuffs it is necessary to incorporate a non-volatile solvent.

Example of a vanishing cream type of rouge, has the following composition in formula 26 :

Formula 26

Constituents	*per cent*
Cetyl alcohol	2.00
Stearin	18.00
Propylene glycol	4.00
Isopropyl myristate	8.00
Carbowax	4.00
Potassium hydroxide	0.70
Water	54.65
Perfume	0.50
Preservative	0.15
Lakes	8.00

Liquid Rouge

Liquid rouge yield extraordinarily good results when skilfully applied and maintain a degree of favour. The essential requirements of such a preparation are that it has sufficient viscosity to permit easy and even application and that it dries reasonably rapidly.

The requisite amount of water soluble dye is dissolved by adding a gum or synthetic thickener for viscosity. A small portion of wetting agent helps to promote spreading. Formulae 27 and 28 shows composition of liquid rouge :

Formula 27

Constituents	*per cent*
Methylcellulose	2.0
Wetting agent	0.1-0.2
Water	to 100.0
Water-soluble red, preservative	q.s

Formula 28

Constituents	*per cent*
Sodium alginate	0.45
Calcium citrate	0.13
Wetting agent (dermatologically acceptable)	0.1-0.2
Water	to 100.0
Water-soluble red, preservative	q.s.

In order to shorten the drying time, 10-20 per cent alcohol or more may be added to gum mucilages, but high concentrations must not be used with alginate products otherwise precipitation may occur.

The preparations of liquid lipstick with a plasticiser to obtain the requisite flexible film, can also serve as liquid rouge. No wetting agent is necessary. By the use of suitable dyes more permanent preparations are obtainable than with aqueous mixtures. Since evaporation of alcohol will lead to an increase in the viscosity of the product. It is particularly important that containers should be provided with a well-fitted wick built into, or screwed into, the neck of the container, the whole being enclosed in a screw dust-cap. This enable ready and even application without sticking users hand with Varnish.

The resultant rouge film is readily removed with a little alcohol with little high boiling solvent to prevent too rapid evaporation of the rouge remover. The following formula represents composition.

Formula 29

Constituents	*per cent*
Tincture of styrax, 5%	38.0
Alcohol, 95%	60.0
Castor oil	2.0
Spirit-soluble red	q.s.

The above solutions are prepared by simple mixture. Proportions of film-forming material, plasticiser and dye may be altered to suit particular requirements.

EYE MAKE-UP

since many years eye make-up is us used. Now-a-days Mascara, eyeshadow and eyebrow pencils are effective if applied properly. Mascara pencil is shown in Fig. 30.2.

Mascara (Eyelash Cosmetic)

Egyptian women soon discovered that smearing the eyelids with unguent and stibium (that is, powdered antimony) not only eased the pain in the eyes and rested them but also added to the natural beauty of their faces. The whiteness of the whites of the eyes was emphasised by the darkened eyelids and the large pupils appeared like black pools in their midst, the whole effect being very striking.

Mascara is a black pigmented preparation for application to the eyelashes or eyebrows to beautify the eyes. It has been claimed that by correctly applying mascara to darken the eyelashes and to increase their apparent length, the brightness and expressiveness of the eyes is enhanced. Mascara bottle is shown in Fig. 30.3.

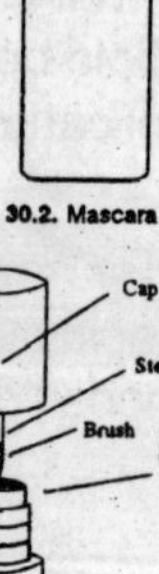

Fig. 30.2. Mascara Pencil.

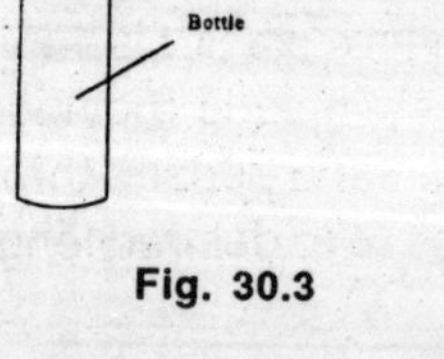

Fig. 30.3

Characteristics of Mascara

1. It must be capable of easy and even application;
2. It must have no tendency to run and thereby cause smudging;
3. It must not cake, causing the eyelashes to stick together;
4. It must not dry too rapidly to interfere with the evenness of the application, but should nevertheless dry fairly rapidly and be reasonably permanent once applied; and
5. It must be neither toxic nor irritant.

Umbers (brown ochres), burnt sienna (a mixture of hydrated ferric oxide $Fe_2O_3.H_2O$ with some manganic oxide) and synthetic brown oxides have been used for brown shades, and yellow ochres for yellow shades. For bluish shades soluble oil blue is employed, while for green shades chromium oxides and for red shades carmine, the aluminium lake of cochineal, have been used. Salts of cobalt may be used only if they are insoluble salts and will not react with other ingredients of the preparation to form soluble cobalt compounds. Finely powdered metals, such as silver and aluminium, have been widely employed in eyeshadow and may be used if they are insoluble salts and will not react with other ingredients of the preparation to form soluble cobalt compounds. Finely powdered metals, such as silver and aluminium, have been widely employed in eyeshadow and may be used if they consist entirely of the pure metal. If they contain an appreciable content of copper they are considered to be harmful. White pigments such as titanium dioxide and zinc oxide may also be sometimes included to lighten shades.

Cake (Block) Mascara

Cake mascara is a very common form of product. Since 1960s softer cream or liquid preparations were popular due to special container-dispensers with a brush. These products essentially consist of a soap (generally triethanolamine stearate) modified in consistency with oils and waxes, and colour. Modern cakes may be produced by melting together the waxy materials, adding the colour and mixing them in thoroughly to obtain an even distribution. The resultant mixture is then cooled and worked in a heated roller-mill. It is subsequently re-melted in a pan and cast into cakes. A composition quoted (formula 30) is very similar to a large majority of block mascara. The process include melting, mixing and extruding in proper form Or it may be milled and passed through a warm plodder after mixing. Then mascara strip is cut to desired lengths, and cake mascara in formulae 31-33 :

Formula 30

Constituents	*per cent*
Staric acid	27.0
Triethanolamine	12.0
Beeswax	30.0
Carnauba wax	50.0
Colour (bone black)	25.0

Formula 31

Constituents	*per cent*
Triethanolamine stearate	40.0
Paraffin wax	30.0
Beeswax	12.0
Anhydrous lanolin	5.0
Lampblack	13.0

Formula 32

Constituents	*per cent*
Glyceryl monostearate	60.0
Paraffin	15.0
Carnauba wax	7.0
Lanolin	8.0
Lampblack	10.0

Formula 33

Constituents	*per cent*
Triethanolamine stearate	50.0
Carnauba wax	24.0
Paraffin wax (MP 45°C)	12.5
Anhydrous lanolin	4.5
Silicone fluid	5.0
Carbon black	3.8
Propyl-p-hydroxybenzoate	0.2

Cream Mascara

Cream mascara may be prepared by milling the pigment into a vanishing cream base, or by the use of a suitable oil-soluble dye. In such cases a suitable wetting agent lowers surface tension and prevents adherence of colour to brush. The coloured pigment may be incorporated into the base immediately after emulsification has been completed. When the product is cooling continue the agitation which allows air to escape and product is filled into tubes. Alternatively, a previously prepared base is melted in order to incorporate the pigment.

The composition of reliable cream mascara which does not dry up in the tube and which adheres well to the eyelashes is given in formula 34. A modern equivalent of this formula would employ a synthetic hydrocolloid such as hydroxyethylcellulose to replace the quince seed. A process include grinding the gum and the ivory black (or umber, etc.) with the syrup (3 per cent sugar to 2 per cent water). Then adding the mucilage containing a preservative, such as methyl-p-hydroxybenzoate.

Formula 34

Constituents	*per cent*
Mucilage of quince seeds	35.0
Sugar syrup	35.0
Gum arabic	7.5
Ivory black (or umber)	22.5

Recent cream mascara are shown in formulae 35, 36 and 37. The application on eyelashes is free from the tendency to run or cake have good performance properties.

Formula 35

Constituents	*per cent*
Polyethylene glycol 400 stearate	10.0
Diglycol stearate	8.0
Lanolin	3.0
Stearyl alcohol	13.0
Isopropyl palmitate	2.0
Triethanolamine lauryl sulphate	1.5
Water	54.5
Colour	8.0

Formula 36

Constituents	*per cent*
Triethanolamine stearate	45.0
Carnauba wax	15.0
Glyceryl monostearate	5.0
Anhydrous lanolin	10.0
Unbleached beeswax	5.0
Lampblack	20.0

Formula 37

Constituents	*per cent*
Hexadecyl alcohol	7.3
Propylene glycol	9.1
Stearic acid	11.2
Glyceryl monostearate	4.5
Triethanolamine	3.6
Ultramarine blue	9.1
Methyl-p-hydroxybenzoate	0.2
Water	55.0

The incorporation of 10 % pigment or dyestuff into greasy base renders easy removal formulae 38 and 39. It is warmed for application with a brush.

Formula 38

Constituents	*per cent*
Beeswax	4.0
Spermaceti	4.0
Cetyl alcohol	2.0
Cocoa butter	6.0
Petroleum jelly	64.0
Oil-soluble blue	20.0
Preservative	q.s.

Formula 39

Constituents	*per cent*
Cocoa butter (odourless)	5.0
Petroleum jelly	50.0
Paraffin wax (uncrystallisable)	5.0
Lampblack	40.0

Procedure

Melt and mix.

The new process include, suspension of carbon black in alcoholic solution of resins is formed. A little castor oil is often included which dry rapidly, producing a semi-permanent waterproof colour. The composition is shown in following formula (formula 40) :

Formula 40

Constituents	*per cent*
Rosin (10% alcohol solution)	3.0
Castor oil	3.0
Ethyl alcohol	84.0
Lampblack	10.0

Eyeshadow

An attractive 'moist'– looking background for the eyes is produced using eyeshadows. The use of gold leaf, bronze powder and powdered aluminium produce silver or gold effect. Various pearlescent pigments, for example those based on bismuth oxychloride or mica coated with titanium dioxide may also be used. Eyeshadow preparations available, are for example :

Liquefying or emulsifying type; emulsions; stick eyeshadow; liquid suspensions or dispersions; and as pressed powders.

Cream eyeshadow

Cream eyeshadow may be made by mixing first of all the selected colours and blending these pigments with petroleum in a roller mill. This mass is then stirred into the blend of fatty and waxy constituents which have been previously blended by melting them together in a pan. After through agitation, the product is then poured into suitable containers. Alternatively, the pigments in powder form may be stirred directly into the molten mass of fats and waxes. Then passed through a roller mill to ensure thorough distribution of colours and remove any lumps from the formulation. The second mixing operation may follow before the product is poured into the containers. As in the case of mascara, the eyeshadow base should be capable of easy and smooth application. It should also be waterproof to avoid streaking. Sometimes, in order to facilitate liquid filling of the product into containers, the product requires to be kept warm in a jacketed steamheated pan and, gently stirred to prevent the sedimentation of any heavy pigments. The composition of eyeshadow creams of the anhydrous type include cocoa butter. Mix 85 parts parts of this base with (say) 12 parts of titanium dioxide and 3 part of a mineral pigment or earth colour as given in formulae 41-43 :

Formula 41

Constituents	*per cent*
Cocoa butter (odourless)	2.0
beeswax	3.0
Spermaceti	5.0
Lanolin	5.0
Petroleum jelly	55.0
Zinc oxide	30.0
Cosmetic lake, preservative	q.s.

Formula 42

Constituents	*per cent*
Petroleum jelly	75.0
Cocoa butter (odourless)	8.0
Lanolin	7.0
Cetyl alcohol	3.0
Paraffin wax (uncrystallisable)	7.0
Cosmetic lake, preservative	q.s.

Formula 43

Constituents	per cent
Bleached beeswax	4.5
Spermaceti	9.5
Lanolin absorption base	13.0
Paraffin of low melting point	73.0

To obtain a grey shade, suggested a mixture of 1 part of ultramarien blue, 1 part of lampblack and 2 parts of titanium dioxide for a brown shade, a mixture of 3 parts of an umber and 1 part of titanium dioxide. And then heating the colours with the mixture of fats and waxes (Formula 43) and passing them through a roller mill. Another eyeshadow cream formula is also suggested.

Formula 44

Constituents	*per cent*
White petroleum jelly	59.0
Glycerol monostearate	17.0
Lanolin	4.0
Beeswax	8.0
Candelilla wax	4.0
Pigment	8.0

Emulsion-type eyeshadow creams are produced by mixing suitable pigments into an emulsion and distributing them evenly throughout the base. The products should be filled into containers when cold. Emulsions based on triethanolamine stearate can be used as bases for such preparations (Formula 45).

Formula 45

Constituents	*per cent*
Stearic acid	1.5
Glyceryl monostearate	1.5
Lanolin	4.0
Isopropyl myristate	5.0
Veegum (5% solution)	30.0
Triethanolamine	0.75
Water	38.25
Propylene glycol	4.0
Ultramarine blue	4.5
Black iron oxide	1.2
Chrome hydrate	0.8
Mica coated with titanium dioxide	8.5

Stick Eyeshadow

The sticks contain a fairly high proportion of waxes such as ceresin, ozokerite or carnauba. The formulation is given in formula 46.

Formula 46

Constituents	*per cent*
Castor oil	43
Mineral oil 75/85	6
Hydrogenated cottonseed oil	5
White ceresin MP 76°C	26
Carnauba wax	4
Titanium dioxide	8
Iron oxide ochre shade	4
Iron oxide sienna shade	4

Pressed Powder Eyeshadow

Pressed powder eyeshadow can be regarded as compact rouge with a much higher colour levels than the rouge products. For example, with products containing high levels of an iridescent material such as mica coated with titanium dioxide, care must be taken that, in dispersing the product, the platelets are not shattered by the hammer mills. The product is usually applied by means of a sponge-tipped plastic rod, although finger-tip application is popular. Typical formulae illustrating a matt shade (formula 47) and a high iridescent shade (formula 48) are given below :

Formulae	*47*	*48*
Constituents	*per cent*	*per cent*
Talc	82.5	41.7
Zinc stearate	6.0	7.0
Ultramarine blue	5.4	-
Black iron oxide	0.1	-
Chrome hydrate	2.0	-
Yellow iron oxide	-	2.0
Mica coated with titanium dioxide	-	40.0
Base (see formula 17 above)	4.0	9.3

Liquid Eyeshadows

Liquid eyeshadows take the form of either a liquid suspension or a liquid dispersion. In the former case the pigments are suspended in a mixture of oils, but they usually settle and have to be shaken before use. The liquid dispersions are prepared from dilute solutions of alcohol in water thickened with a synthetic gum such as methyl cellulose. It is suitably preserved and containing a wetting agent in which the pigments have been dispersed. However, liquid eyeshadows are not very popular.

Eyeliner

Eyeliners used on eyelids, particularly the upper eyelids, close to the eyelashes to enhance expressiveness. They are available in liquid, cake and pencil form. The compressed powder form is similar in composition to cake mascara. The following composition is suggested (formula 49) for dry eyeliner is given as under :

Formula 49

Constituents	*per cent*
Mineral oil	5
Colour	30
Titanium dioxide	5
Talc	60

Liquid eyeliners may be used to apply colour to the tissue around the eyes. Usually a brown colour is considered a good colour for daytime wear. A liquid eyeliner composition is given in formula 50 :

Formula 50

Constituents	*per cent*
Water	40.00
Methocel HG 60-50V	1.00
Veegum	1.00
Shellac	1.08
Oleic acid	0.50
Triethanolamine	0.40
Water	3.02
Pigment	18.20
Alcohol	5.00
Water, preservative	to 100.00

Eyebrow Pencils

Eyebrow pencils may be either of a wax crayon type pigmented black or brown, in which the pigments are present at a higher level than in cream eyeshadow preparations. They may be in the form of an extruded eyebrow pencil similar to an ordinary lead pencil, in which a crayon-type formulation has been enclosed in a wooden casing. In the latter form they are even more readily applied than the stick type. Eyebrow pencils are used either to accentuate the line of the eyebrows, or to modify their outline after plucking. The proportion of beeswax or other high-melting constituent may be optionally increased to produce a somewhat firmer pencil in the lipstick type. However, such sticks must be capable of ready and uniform application as given in formula 51 below :

Formula 51

Constituents	*per cent*
Hydrogenated castor oil	46.0
Hydrogenated cottonseed oil	12.0
Cocoa butter (odourless)	8.0
Castor oil	8.0
Lanolin absorption base	17.0
black iron oxide	9.0

If a brown stick is required the black iron oxide may be partially replaced by the red and yellow versions. An eyebrow pencil composition prepared by stirring the colours into the molten fat phase and mill until uniform. Fill the warm batch into the moulds.

Formula 52

Constituents	*per cent*
Ozokerite (MP 70°-75°C)	45.0
Unbleached beeswax	24.0
Cocoa butter	22.5
White petrolatum	6.0
Absorption base	1.5
Anhydrous lanolin	1.0
In addition :	
Pigment or lake colours	10.0
Oil-soluble colour	1.0

Formula 53

Constituents	*per cent*
Beeswax	21.0
Carnauba wax	5.0
Paraffin	29.0
Cetyl alcohol	8.0
Vaseline	18.0
Lanolin	9.0
Pigments	10.0

Chapter - 14

SHAMPOOS

INTRODUCTION

Almost all the people use shampoos which are required for washing of hair. They constitute suitable detergents. They are packed in special package convenient to use. The primary function remains that of cleansing the hair of accumulated sebum, scalp debris and residues of hair- grooming preparations. The cleansing should be selective and should preserve a quantity of the natural oil that coats the hair, and above all, the scalp.

The process of shampooing is a cleansing , purifying activity, designed to free them from daily accumulation and maturation of grease, dirt, perspiration, cooking smells, dandruff, environmental pollution and so on. In fact, it seems sensible to retain the definition of a shampoo as a suitable detergent for washing the hair with the corollary that it should also leave the hair easy to manage and confer on it a healthy look.

Detergency

The ambiguous objective, variability of substrate and the process made the development of detergent system adopted to hair complex. The substrate to be cleaned is made of the relatively hard but porous keratin of the hair. The soft keratin of the scalp is sensitive to drying and defatting. While there exists very large individual variation in fibre number and diameter, the average surface area of a female head of hair is calculated to be between 4 and 8 m2 - that is, 50 to 100 times the average scalp area.

The kind of soil to be removed, either natural or captured, varies greatly according to the weather, the life style, the type of work, the physiological functions, the haircare practice and so on.

The problem of cleaning hair is particularly one of grease removal although shampoo removes more soil than oil. Hair pick-up dirt without the help of greasy layer as it represents hard surface. As long as the grease can be removed, it is quite easy to remove the dirt. To remove grease from the hair, one must find some agent with a greater affinity for the grease found suitable. This function can be accomplished by absorbent solids such as fuller's earth or flour, but solutions of surface-active materials (Surface-active Agents) are much more convenient and more commonly employed.

The mechanism of detergent action involves a number of complex physical phenomena - wetting, foaming , emulsifying and peptisation – several of which are imperfectly understood. The removal of dirt, involves the following processes :

1. The detergent solution must be able to wet both the dirt and the substrate, hence it must lower the surface tension.
2. The dirt or oil particles are displaced by the detergent solution due to reduction of interfacial tension.
3. The dirt particles to be kept dispersed in order that they may readily be washed away.

The most important property in hair washing is the ability of polar group of the detergent to displace oil from a surface.

EVALUATION OF DETERGENTS AS SHAMPOO BASES

The screening test for evaluation of detergents and as shampoo bases is measurement of surface tension and interfacial tension. The trial on the head must be conducted for detergent selection because the after-effects of the shampoo may often be the deciding factor. With the wide range of materials available it is a relatively easy task to find materials that will adequately clean hair and allow for adequate lather. The final criterion which them applies in the selection of the detergent is its effect on the hair, These effects are best observed in comparative tests on the same head, as hair diameter, quantity, greasiness and previous treatments may all affect the results.

RAW MATERIALS FOR SHAMPOOS

Originally the shampoos were made from soap or soap mixtures. But today, the shampoos are made from synthetic detergents. Ingredients of present shampoos can be classified as under :

Surfactants, Foam boosters and stabilisers, Conditioning agents, Special additives, Preservatives, Sequestering agents, viscosity modifiers, Opacifying or clarifying agents, Fragrances, and Colour.

Non-ionic detergents does not have sufficient foaming properties, hence it can not be used in shampoos. While cationic detergents are ideal due to foaming , cleaning power. Anionic and ampholytics are suitable due to low cost foaming, and conditioning properties.

From the list of anionic surfactants alfa olefin sulphonates, alkyl sulphates, alkyl polyethylene glycol sulphate. Sulphoccintates and acyl lactylates are used in shampoos. Among the non-ionic surfactants fatty acid alkanolamides, polyalkoxylated derivatives and amine oxides are used. N-alkylamino acids, betains are amphoteric surfactants used in shampoos.

Additives

Conditioning Agents

Conditioning agents are placed to improve manageability, feel and lustre of the hair. The materials which have been claimed to have conditioning effect on hair include fatty materials like lanolin, mineral oil; natural products like polypeptides, egg derivatives, herbal extracts; and synthetic products like specifically designed surfactants and resins.

Viscosity Modifiers

Thickening of shampoo can be achieved by a number of compounds. Compounds which can be used to modify viscosity of shampoos include : Electrolytes, Natural gums, cellulose derivative and carboxyvinyl polymers and others. The list includes, ammonium chloride, sodium chloride, gum karaya, gum tragacanth, alginates, hydroxycellulose, hydroxypropyl cellulose, carboxy methyl cellulose, carbopol 934, phosphate ester, TEA soap, poly vinyl alcohols, and alkanolamides.

Opacifying And Clarifying Agents

A number of materials can be used for opacifying or giving pearlescent effect. Non-ionic solubilisers, alcohols, phosphates improve transparency. The opacifying agents are : Alkanolamides of higher fatty acids, glycol mono – and di-stearates, propylene glycol – and glycerol-monostearates and palmitates, fatty alcohols (Cetyl, stearyl), Milky emulsions of vinyl polymers and latexes, magnesium calcium or zinc salt of stearic acid,finely dispersed oxide or titanium dioxide, and magnesium aluminium silicate.

The clarifying Agents are : Ethanol, isopropanol; propylene glycol, hexylene; glycol, dimethyl-octyne diol phosphate; polyethoxylated alcohols and esters.

Sequestering Agents

These materials are used to prevent deposition of calcium and magnesium salts of soaps on to the hair. EDTA salts (Ethylene diamine tetracetic salts) and polyphosphates are the most commonly used sequestering agents in shampoos.

Preservatives

Bacterial growth in shampoos can lead to breakdown of detergents in shampoos resulting in discolouration of the product. The surfactant in shampoos interfere with bactericidal activity of anti-bacterials. This fact should be considered while selecting preservatives. Therefore, higher concentration of preservatives are necessary in shampoos. The most effective antimicrobial agent is formaldehyde. Formaldehyde remains unaffected by surfactants and can be used in concentration of 0.1 - 0.15%. But it is not compatible with certain ingredients of shampoos, e.g., protein hydrolysates.

Esters of parahydroxy benzoic acid are quite effective against fungi, but these are inactivated by non-ionics. These are also not effective against Pseudomonas.

Perfumes

The fragrance selected must be soluble and compatible with shampoo. It means that, viscosity and stability should remain unaffected. Herbal, fruity or floral fragrances can be used in shampoos.

FORMULATION

The shampoos can be classified into the following main groups : (i) clear liquid shampoos; (ii) Liquid cream/lotion shampoos; (iii) Cream shampoos; (iv) Jelly shampoos; (v) Powder shampoos; (vi) Aerosol foam shampoos.

Clear Liquid Shampoos

Clear liquid shampoos can be prepared with detergents having lower cloud point. These can also be made with detergents and alkanolamides. The different compositions of clear liquid shampoos is given in formulae 1-3.

Formulae	*1*	*2*	*3*
Constituents	*per cent*	*per cent*	*per cent*
Sodium lauryl ether sulphate	40.0	-	-
Sodium chloride (to desired viscosity)	2.0-4.0	-	-
Triethanolamine lauryl sulphate	-	50.0	45.0
Lauric isopropanolamide	-	2.0	-
Coconut monoethanolamide	-	-	2.0
Water	to make 100	100	100
Colour, Perfume and Preservatives	q.s.	q.s.	q.s.

Concentrated clear liquid shampoo can be prepared with more soluble monoethanolamine lauryl sulphate. These shampoos may be used by hairdressers by diluting at the time of use. The composition of such shampoo is monethanolamine lauryl sulphate (70.0%), coconut diethanol amide(2.0%), colour, perfume, preservative in small quantity made to 100% with water.

Liquid Cream or Lotion Shampoos

These can be prepared by adding opacifier like ethylene glycol monostearate or ethylene glycol distearate to clear liquid shampoos. Detergent manufacturers also make preformulated concentrated materials which can be diluted, coloured and perfumed. Ethylene glycol monostearate, ethylene glycol distearate can be used as opacifiers. These however, have tendency to redissolve in shampoo in hot weather. Insoluble magnesium stearate can be added to overcome this problem. Formulae 4 and 5 are examples of liquid cream shampoo with pearly sheen.

Formula 4

Constituents	*per cent*
Monethanolamine lauryl sulphate	45.0
Ethylene glycol monostearate	5.0
Water	to make 100.0
Perfume, Colour & Preservatives	q.s.

Formula 5

Constituents	*per cent*
Triethanolamine lauryl sulphate	35.0
Glyceryl monostearate	2.0
Magnesium stearate	1.0
Water	to make 100.0
Colour, Perfume & Preservatives	q.s.

An alkanolamide can be added to such formulation as foam booster as exemplified in formula 6.

Formula 6

Constituents	*per cent*
Monoethanolamine lauryl sulphate	38.0
Ethylene glycol monostearate	5.0
Lauric isopropanolamide	2.0
Water	to make 100.0
Colour, Perfume and Preservatives	q.s.

Cream Shampoos

Professional hair dressers demand cream shampoos. These products can be packed in collapsible tubes. These products are also known as shampoo pastes. Generally, these constitute sodium alkyl sulphates (38%) which give products of firm consistency. Cetyl alcohol (7.0%) can be added as builder. An alkanolamide such as coconut diethanolamide, lauric isopropanolamide can be added in concentration of 1-2% as foam stabiliser.

The disadvantage is that mass of crystals present in shampoo may dissolve in hot weather making the product runny and translucent. On cooling, recrystallisation takes place and crystals formed may be large appearing as lumps or fibrous mass.

Jelly Shampoos

Jelly shampoos are formulated with detergent alone or in combination with soap. By varying the proportions of triethanolamine coconut soap, triethanolamine lauryl sulphate and sodium lauryl sulphate different texture can be prepared.

Jellies can also be prepared by thickening the conventional clear liquid shampoos with hydroxy-alkyl or methyl cellulose ethers or alkanolamides. Appropriate combination of anionic and amphoteric surfactants can also produce gels. Formula 7 is example where methyl cellulose ether has been used as thickening agent.

Formula 7

Constituents	*per cent*
Alkyl dimethyl benzalammoium chloride	15.0
Triethanolamine lauryl sulphate (40%)	28.0
Coconut diethanolamide	7.0
Hydroxy propyl methyl cellulose	1.0
water	to make 100.0
Perfumes, Colour & Preservatives	q.s.

Powder Shampoos

The powder shampoos were prepared with soap powder and diluents like sodium carbonate, sodium bicarbonate, disodium phosphate or borax or their combination. The composition is given below in formula 8 :

Formula 8

Constituents	*per cent*
Soap Powder	35.0
Sodium Bi-carbonate	45.0
Di-sodium Phosphate	20.0
Perfume	q.s.

Such formulations were also available with herbal ingredients which were supposed to give slight colouring effect to the hair. Formulae 9 and 10 are examples of these.

Formula 9

Constituents	*per cent*
Henna Powder	5.0
Soap Powder	50.0
Sodium Carbonate	22.5
Potassium Carbonate	7.5
Borax	15.0
Perfume	q.s.

Formula 10

Constituents	*per cent*
Camomile Flowers Powder	5.0
Soap Powder	55.0
Sodium Powder	15.0
borax	25.0
Perfume	q.s.

The soap powder was replaced with detergents. Formula 11 is an example.

Formula 11

Constituents	*per cent*
Sodium lauryl sulphate	20.0
Sarcoside	5.0
Sodium bicarbonate	10.0
Sodium sulphate	65.0
Perfume	q.s.

The disadvantage of powder shampoo is difficult ot use and these leave the hair in poor condition.

Aerosol Shampoos

Shampoos available in aerosol packaging are called aerosol shampoos. Shampoos for aerosol packing are required to be specially formulated. When sprayed, the foam should be manageable and should have enough staying power. The aerosol shampoos are applied by spraying on the palm of the hand. Then it is thoroughly rubbed into the hair which have been wetted in advance. Thereafter, these may be removed as is done in the case of conventional shampoos. They constitute shampoo base 90% and propellent 10%.

Shampoo base may be prepared by mixing : ammonium/triethanolamine lauryl sulphate 60.0%; coconut diethanolamide 2.0%; and water, perfume, colour and preservatives.

Some Special Shampoos

Shampoos formulated for a specific purpose are dandruff and shampoos for conditioning effect. These two are, by far the most important groups of shampoos which are marketed for their special effects.

Anti-dandruff Shampoos

As a result of cell division in deeper layers of epidermis, some cells are being always pushed up towards the surface of the skin. The cells farthest from the dermis are keratinised and subsequently are shed off. This is true of scalp also. A process of keratinisation and shedding off increases to an abnormal rate due to any reason in case normal function do not synchronise. Such a condition causes dandruff. In another condition there is abnormal secretion of sebum from sebaceous glands. The former condition is known as *seborrhoea sicca* and the latter as *seborrhoea oleosa*. These abnormal conditions of scalp are generally associated with an increase in the growth of bacteria and fungi. This may lead to skin diseases like acne and psoriasis. The above-mentioned conditions should, therefore, be treated. One of the approach is, preparation of medicated shampoos for dandruff. A medicated shampoo is required to have the following functions :

1. It should be clean both the hair and the scalp and should leave the hair manageable.
2. It should not irritate sebaceous glands, and contain and anti-microbial to prevent growth of increased incidence of microbes.
3. The active material used should not sensitise the scalp.

4. It should reduce the degree of itching and scaling.

The component used for treatment of dandruff are : Thymol, 1,2 Bithionol, Pyrithione Zinc, Resorcinol, Selenium Sulphide, Prepared Coal tar, Quaternary Ammonium compounds when used as shampoo base. Use of thymol, camphor and menthol has been examplified in formulae 12 and 13.

Formula 12

Constituents	*per cent*
Thymol	0.1
Camphor	0.1
Triethanolamine lauryl sulphate	60.0
Water	to make 100.0
Colour, Perfume and Preservative	q.s.

Formula 13

Constituents	*per cent*
Thymol	0.05
Camphor	0.1
Menthol	0.1
Triethanolamine lauryl sulphate	55.0
Water	to make 100.0
Colour, Perfume and Preservatives	q.s.

Thymol, menthol and camphor are dissolved in alcohol and incorporated in the formulation. Cationic surfactants with high molecular weight possess lower degree of bactericidal action. While selecting these compounds ensure that defatting of scalp and irritation do not occur after use for long time. Of these, quaternary ammonium compounds are of interest. Cetrimide, a mixture of dodecyl, tetradecyl and hexadecyl-trimethyl ammonium bromides is non-irritant and non-toxic in dilutions which are generally used. Other quaternary ammonium compounds are benzalkonium chloride and stearyl dimethyl benzyl ammonium chloride. Though stearyl dimethyl benzylammonim chloride is less bacterio-static than centrimide or benzalkomium chloride, but its use improves appearance of hair. Centrimide is soluble in two parts of water but alcohol is used so that clarity is maintained during storage. In shampoos based on centrimide-diethylphthalate is also added to increase the viscosity. Formula 14 is an example of such a formulation. A cream shampoo can be prepared by adding cetyl alcohol as given in formula 15.

Formula 14

Constituents	*per cent*
Centrimide	15.0
Alcohol	10.0
Diethylphthalate	2.0
Water	to make 100.0

Formula 15

Constituents	*per cent*
Centrimide	15.0
Cetyl alcohol	12.0
Water	to make 100.0

Conditioning Shampoos

The two terms "conditioning shampoos" and "shampoo conditioners" appear to mean the same thing. Their applications are same. The prime function of conditioning shampoo is cleaning . Also it improves manageability, feel and appearance of air. Whereas conditioner untangle wet hair and to improve manageability of both wet and dry hair.

Quaternary ammonium compounds have conditioning and bactericidal properties. Conditioning properties in quaternary ammonium compounds are imparted by the relatively large complex cation which is substantive to protein. The static charge is removed due to absorption of quaternary ammonium compounds on to the hair fibre. This reduces friction between individual hair strands. Thus hair become more manageable. Satisfactory products can be prepared using stearyl dimethyl benzyl ammonium chloride. Formulae 16 and 17 illustrate use of stearyl dimethyl benzyl ammonium chloride.

Formula 16

Constituents	*per cent*
Stearyl dimethyl benzyl ammonium chloride	5.5
Ethylene glycol monostearate	2.0
Cetyl alcohol	2.5
Water	to make 100.0
Perfume and Preservatives	q.s.

Formula 17

Constituents	*per cent*
Stearyl dimethyl benzyl ammoniumchloride	4.0
Cetyl alcohol	3.0
Mineral oil	0.5
Water	to make 100.0
Perfume and Preservatives	q.s.

MANUFACTURE OF SHAMPOOS

Manufacture of Liquid/Cream Shampoos

Clear liquid shampoos can be made from preformulated concentrated solutions which are many a time available from detergent manufacturer. These are to be diluted, coloured and perfumed. The dilution can be done in a stainless steel tank with a low speed stirrer.

There is a general method, if an alkanolamide is being used. Alkanolamide should be dissolved in about half the total amount of the detergent with gentle heating. Then the remaining detergent solution is added slowly. Perfume is dissolved in cold concentrated detergent. Colour and preservative(s) and dissolved separately in water and are added to the mix. The remaining water is added with slow stirring finally to make up the volume. Rapid stirring will cause froth and will incorporate air bubbles. The mixing operations are usually carried out in stainless steel tanks with a stirrer having speed regulator.

Viscosity of solutions of lauryl alcohol ether sulphates is usually controlled by adding a solution of sodium chloride (1 part sodium chloride and 3 parts water) to the shampoo in small proportions. The shampoo is stirred well after each addition. With the addition of salt solution viscosity increase and reaches a maximum.

In case of cream shampoos where glycol stearates are used as opecifiers, glycol stearates are heated gently with a part of detergent to dissolve them. To this solution are then added detergents and other additives. In a cram shampoo where waxes are to be incorporated, the following procedure can be used.

First in a steam or water jacked vessel detergent is heated to 80°C. Then melted wax is added with stirring. Cool the mixture to 40-45°C and add perfume, colour, preservative with stirring. The product is filled into containers while it is still warm.

Chapter - 15

NAIL AND MANICURE PRODUCTS

INTRODUCTION

The top surfaces of the end joint of each finger and toe and protected by translucent plates, composed of hard keratin are called as nails. Each lies upon a *nail bed,* to which it appears to be fused, except at the far or distal end where there is a free margin. At the near or *proxima*l end a paler *lumina* is visible, and the posterior margin is slightly overlapped by a narrow extension of the horny layer of the epidermis which is known as the *cuticle.*

Many variety of cosmetic preparations related with the cleansing and decoration is complete manicure treatment. The discussion is followed on those treatments.

CUTICLE REMOVER

When the free edge of the nail has been shaped, by mechanical means such as cutting or filling, the next problem is to shape the base of the nail. Where the skin adjoins the nail it becomes cornified and the dead cells, together with sebum, form an irregular appendage which grows thick and ragged and partially obscures the 'halfmoon' or lunule. Some improvement can be effected by mechanically loosening and pushing back the cuticle, but removal of excess cuticle by cutting is unsatisfactory and cuticle removers are used.

Cuticle removers are basically alkaline materials in liquid or cream form. To 2-5% of aqueous or alcoholic solution of potassium hydroxide add 10-20% of glycerine or propylene glycol. The humectant added serve to counteract the irritation potential of alkali hydroxides and also to retard evaporation and increase viscosity. The latter effects can also be achieved by the use of suitable water-soluble gums or hydrocolloids.

Formulation is given in formula 1 :

Formula 1

Constituents	*per cent*
Trisodium phosphate	8.0
Glycerine	12.0
Water	80.0
Perfume	q.s.

The milder products incorporate 8-10 per cent of monoethanolamine or isopropanolamine or 10-12 per cent of triethanolamine. Formula 2 gives a basic formula suggested for such a preparation :

Formula 2

Constituents	*per cent*
Sorbitan monopalmitate	2.0
Polyoxyalkylene sorbitan monopalmitate	2.0
Mineral oil	15.0
Water	81.0
Cuticle remover	q.s.

The process to prepare cuticle remover is heat first three items at 65°C. The emulsify using water without using cuticle remover. Now mix them when cold. The special emulsions prepared has following composition :

Formula 3

Constituents	*per cent*
Cetyl alcohol	2.5
Myristyl alcohol	3.5
Polyoxyethylene (5) lauryl ether	1.0
Glycerine	4.0
Potassium hydroxide	1.6
Water	87.4

NAIL BLEACH

Nail bleaches are solutions or creams used for the removal of ink or tobacco stains, vegetable stains, etc., from the nails due to oxidation or reduction. Oxidation may be achieved by the use of hydrogen peroxide, either at 20 vols or diluted to about 1 : 4, by chlorine compounds such as the hypochlorites and the cyanurates and by sodium perborate and zinc peroxide (the latter two substances decompose in aqueous solution). Use of sulphites with dilute acid is probably the easiest method for achieving reduction in such preparations. A good quality nail bleaching lotion has the following composition :

Formula 4

Constituents	*per cent*
Hydrogen peroxide (10 vols – 3% w/w)	73.5
Ammonia (SG 0.93)	0.5
rose water	25.0
Preservative	1.0

NAIL CREAM

At the beginning the relief of brittle nails was obtained by massaging them with olive oil after having bathed in warm water. Emollient cream is practical solution which contains a suitable humectant. The base of emollient creams is lanolin or beeswax-borax emulsion. These creams should be applied after soaking the hands in warm soapy water and thoroughly drying them, just before retiring for the night. This treatment should be carried out at least once and preferably 2-3 times per week (that is, on alternate nights) depending upon the condition of the nails. Wearing fingerstalls or gloves may assist the treatment.

It is found that cholesterol, appear to assist in maintaining the natural elasticity of the nail. The requisite degree of moisture in the keratin is maintained due to water in oil emulsion of cholesterol. It would appear that the use of a nail cream containing oils in an emulsified form with water (and possibly incorporating a mild antiseptic) would be of immense value. The inclusion of a little lanolin or emollient or sufficient humectant to cold, vanishing, foundation or all purpose cream will result into nail cream.

NAIL STRENGTHENER

The appearance of nails is affected due to splitting and breaking which makes manicuring difficult and painful. This had led to the development of various products. For strengthening brittle nails and for eliminating brittleness and dryness the following composition is suggested (Formula 5) :

Formula 5

Constituents	*per cent*
Potash alum	3.00
Glycerine	10.00
Formaldehyde	0.01
Menthol	0.001
Water	to 100.00

NAIL WHITE

Nail whites are preparations used to produce an even white edge to the nails. They are based on an inert white pigment such as zinc oxide titanium dioxide, kaolin, talc or colloidal silica, of which the first two are the best. The pigment forms 20-30 per cent by weight of the preparations, which is generally presented as a stiff paste. For general purposes a fatty base is preferable. The 38% of titanium dioxide along with 62% of petroleum jelly is best example.

It is readily produced by milling the titanium dioxide into the melted petroleum jelly. Various mixtures of suitable fats and waxes may replace the petroleum jelly as desired.

Nail white pencils have largely replaced nail white creams. They are easier to apply, are less messy in use, and simply require moistening with water before application to the under-surface of the nail free edge. The pencil then being recapped. A wax may be used as a base formula 6 :

Formula 6

Constituents	*per cent*
Beeswax	55.0
Hydrogenated cottonseed oil	9.0
Cocoa butter	9.0
Castor oil	8.0
Lanolin base	9.0
titaniumdioxide	10.0

Such a base is ready for use and is not wetted before application. The usual type, which requires preliminary damping is prepared by massing casein or gum arabic with the inert pigment, or by suspending it in sodium stearate base.

NAIL POLISH

A distinction is drawn between those polishes which by abrasive action bestow a gloss on the nail surface, and a nail varnish. The former, by reason of the friction set up in the buffing process, draw the blood to the numerous capillaries of the nail bed and, by increasing the blood supply, may exert some slight stimulating effect upon the growth of the nail. The latter, which depend upon the deposition of a thin film of highly lustrous cellulose lacquer upon the nail plate, have increased enormously in popularity and have largley replaced the abrasive type, although abrasive polish may also be used between two successive coats of varnish to enhance the lustre, in the manner of the French polisher.

Abrassive polishes consist of a suitably fine abrasive powder which is applied to the nail and then polished with a shaped chamois leather pad. The principal constituents of such powders are stannic oxide, talc, silica, kaolin, precipitated chalk, etc., the first being an excellent abrasive but rather more expensive than the others listed. The composition of a abrasive is given in formula 7 :

Formula 7

Constituents	*per cent*
Stannic oxide	90.0
Powdered silica	8.0
Butyl stearate	2.0
Pigment, perfume	q.s.

Butyl stearate render the product less gritty. It may be replaced, by oleic acid. The method of preparation is by simple trituration in a mortar or revolving mill. The liquid or paste or pencil form may be prepared by addition of methyl cellulose or tragacanth with glycerine or glycol ethers.

Wax polishing pencils embodying a large proportion of abrasive powder replaced the older powder and block type. They were effective and could be carried and used without the danger of split contents. The formation is shown in formula 8 :

Formula 8

Constituents	*per cent*
Hardened palm kernel oil	22.0
Synthetic wax (high melting point)	7.0
Stannic oxide	71.0

A softer stick may be obtained by omitting the synthetic wax and making a simple mixture of abrasive powder with the hardened oil. Alternatively, a base of rosin, beeswax, ceresin and petroleum jelly, or other suitable combination of waxes, may be employed. Nail polish should be easy to apply, giving a good cover of the nail with two coats, and should not steak or apply unevenly. The polish should dry quickly to the touch and leave a high-shine finish film that will not stain the nail when removed. The polish is mostly dispensed from a bottle with a brush applicator Fig.31.1.

NAIL LACQUER (NAIL VARNISH)

The largest and most important group of manicur preparations is that of nail varnish or lacquer. A nail lacquer should fulfill the following properties :

1. It should be innocuous to the skin, nails and stable on storage.
2. It should be easy and convenient to apply and give a film with satisfactory characteristics.

The characteristics of a satisfactory film are :

(i) Even thickness; (ii) Uniform colour; (iii) Good gloss; (iv) Good adhesion; (v) Sufficient flexibility (vi) Hard, non-tacky surface; (vii) Satisfactory drying properties; and (viii) The film should maintain these propeties for approximately 1 week.

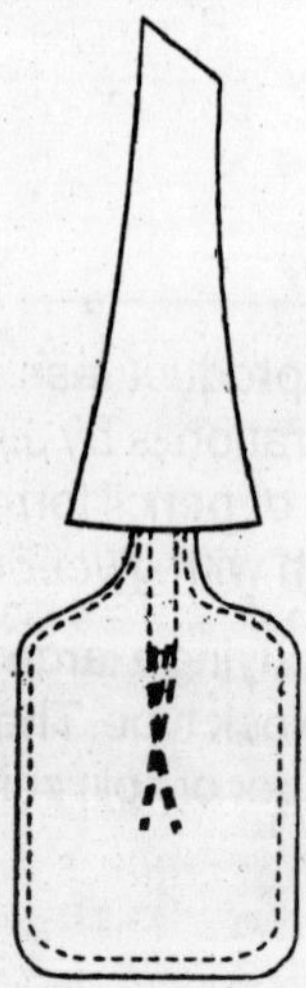

Fig. 31.1. Nail polish bottle.

Ingredients of Nail Lacquer

The main essentials for the manufacture of nail lacquer are a lacquer base with suspending properties and a colouring system. These two components can be broken down into necessary constituents, and these are described before manufacture of the product is considered.

Film-Formers

The basic film-forming material in nail lacquers is nitrocellulose. A cellulose nitrate obtained by the reaction of mixtures of nitric acid and sulphuric acid with cotton. film formed are waterproof, hard , tough and resist abrasion.

Resins

The resins are used to impart adhesion and to improve gloss. With a dry nitrocellulose resin ratio of 2:1, the moisture permeability of a film has been reduced to about half of that of an unmodified nitrocellulose film of the same thickness. these resins are moderately stable to light and soluble in the majority of lacquer solvents and diluents.

Plasticisers

Plasticisers alongwith nitrocellulose are included in nail lacquer formulations. this ensures adhesion of a film on the nails after evaporation. the film is flexible and does not flake off. The film becomes pliable due to high boiling point of plasticisers. Plasticisers, even at low concentration, will furthermore enhance the gloss of resultant films and will also improve the flow properties of lacquers.

Solvents

It will be seen from the list of desirable film properties that the properties of the solvent, particularly the evaporation characteristics, are of the utmost importance. It is common practice to rank solvents by their boiling points, which also appear to correlate with the viscosities of the resultant nitrocellulose solutions and hence with the spreading characteristics.

Diluents

Diluents are organic solvents miscible with nitrocelluose. They are used as solvents for modifying resins used in lacquers, since true nitrocellulose solvents are expensive. They also help to stabilise the viscosity of lacquers. Their use reduces the overall cost of formulations.

Colours

Insoluble lakes with titanium dioxide are incorporated in the majority of nail lacquers to produce a suitable shade, opacity and creaminess and to produce pastel shades.

Soluble dyestuffs such as erythrosine, carmoisine and rhodamine, which were used at one time in nail lacquers, were found to stain the surrounding skin and the use of such dyestuffs has been virtually abandoned.

Pearlescent (Nacreous) Pigments

In addition to the conventional pigments, nail lacquers can incorporate iridescent materials guanine (2-amino-6-hydroxy purine), a crystalline substance from the scales and body of various fish, has been one of the most frequently suggested. In its pure form it is non-toxic, but there have been references to this material being the cause of dermatitis arising from nail lacquers.

Suspension

The modern trend towards highly pigmented and pearlescent nail lacquers has led to a critical assessment of the ability fo traditional nail lacquer formulae to suspend materials at high concentration. The suspension properties are objatined by creating a thixotropic system with the use of pretreated colloidal clays such as benzyl dimethyl hydrogenated tallow annonium montmorilonite, dimethyl dioctadecyl ammonium bentonite, or dimethy l dioctadecyl ammonium hectorite. The clays increase the viscosity of the system to such an extent that the heavy oxide pigments remain in suspension.

Formulation

The flow characteristics of formulations were ascertained by finding out rate of drying of lacquer films, their appearance, hardness, adhesion and resistance of soap, deterfents. Tests should also be carried out on the flow and evenness of application of lacquer films, their hardness and gloss. Any drag observed on the applicator brush should also be recorded. Formulation of base nail lacquers can be illustrated by the following formulae 9 and 10.

Formula 9 (Typical nail lacquer base)

Constituents	*per cent*
Nitrocellulose (about 1/2-second viscosity)	10.0
Resin	10.0
Plasticiser	5.0
Alcohol	5.0
Ethyl acetate	20.0
Butyl acetate	15.0
Toluene	35.0

Formula 10

Constituents	*per cent*
Nitrocellulose (1/2-second)	18.28
Santolite (resin)	6.43
Dibutyl phthalate (plasticiser)	2.15
Camphor (plasticiser)	1.88
Ethyl acetate (solvent)	6.45
Butyl acetate (solvent)	25.42
Toluene (diluent)	29.56
Isopropanol(diluent)	9.83

Resins consisting of polymerisation products of acrylic acid and its derivatives may be used in nitrocellulose compositions. It overcomes inherent diadvantages of nail varnishes like shrinkage during drying, peeling at the edge of the nail, discoloration, thickening of the enamel by evaporation of volatile ingredients when stored in poorly stoppered containers, and failure to achieve proper gloss and durability. A typical formula cited is the following formula 11 :

Formula 11

Constituents	*per cent*
Cellulose nitrate	3.2
Denatured alcohol	1.4
Butyl acetate	19.3
Ethyl alcohol	19.3
Toluene	19.3
Propyl methacrylate resin	15.0
Plasticiser	3.2

Both high-boiling and low-boiling solvents are said to be eliminated in the above formula and the enamel produced is said to afford excellent adhesion and to be remarkably resistant to soapy water, alkali, marking and scratching. An interesting formula containing a chlorinated biphenol plasticiser is given in formula 12 :

Formula 12

Constituents	*per cent*
Polyvinylchloride-acetate copolymer	10.7
Polymethylmethacrylate	7.0
Methyl ethyl ketone	21.5
Sorbitol	20.0
arochlor	15.0
Tricresyl phosphate	8.0
Ethyl acetate	22.3
Colours	0.5

Manufacture of Nail Lacquer

In practice it is more usual to buy a base lacquer which incorporates the particular requirements for plasticiser, resin, etc., and mix with it pearlescent materiasl and pigments, etc. The specialist approach is needed to handle and process nitrocellulose and bentone. Hence, most cosmetic manufacturers handle nail lacquer production along these lines. Many just fill the finished product as supplied to them from specialist contract manufacturer, although they themselves may well have developed the shades, etc. An outline of all the manufacturing procedures involved in nail lacquer production is given in Fig. 31.2.

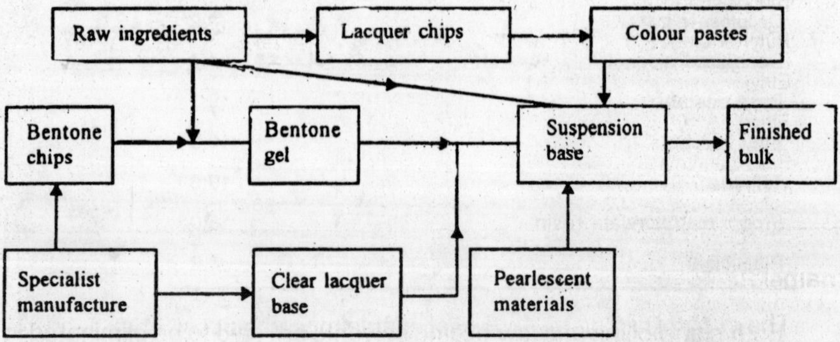

Fig. 31.2. Manufacturing routes for nail lacquer production.

Base COATS and Top COATS

The chipping of the nitrocellulose film is prevented by base coat. Here the film is formed on the nail is to which nitrocellulose film adheres closely.

Phenol-formaldehyde resins, sulfonamide-formaldehyde resins, alkyd resins and methacrylate are used for this purpose.

A larger amount of resin is used in base coat for increased adhesion. They dry more rapidly and give a harder film that the normal lacquer film. Films built on a base coat are far less liable to crack than ordinary nail enamels. Clear and pigmented base coat formulations are available with a lower solid content and lower viscosity than normal lacquer formulations.

Top coats are usually clear lacquer films. They are applied over the pigmented lacquer film in order to increase film thickness and thus resistance to abrasion and wear, and also to improve gloss. Top coats have a higher nitrocellulose and plasticiser content and a lower resin content than normal nail enamel. They also have a relatively high diluent content and tend to dry rapidly. Three formulae for a base coat, a clear lacquer and a top coat are given in formulae 13–15 :

Formulae	13	14	15
Constituents	*Base coat per cent*	*Clear lacquer per cent*	*Top coat per cent*
Nitrocellulose	10	15	16
Santolite resin	10	7.5	4
Dibutyl phthalate	2	3.75	5
Butyl acetate	-	29.35	10
Ethyl acetate	34	-	10
Ethyl alcohol	5	6.4	10
Butyl alcohol	-	1.1	-
Toluene	39	36.9	45

Enamel Remover

The enamel removers consist of simple mixtures of solvents, such as acetone, amyl acetate or ethyl acetate, which may contain small amounts of fatty material to counteract any excessive drying action of the solvents on the nails. Originally castor oil was used, but now-a-days esters such as butyl stearate or dibutyl phthalate, fatty alcohols or soaps may be used for the same purpose. An example of an enamel remover is provided by the following formula :

Formula 16

Constituents	*per cent*
Butyl stearate	5.0
Diethylene glycol monoethyl ether	10.0
Acetone	85.0

Cream Nail Enamel Removers

A number of creamy nail enamel removers have been introduced. These consist of a fairly high-boiling solvent for the lacquer, introduced into a cream having lanolin or other emollient material. Alternatively they may be composed of a lacquer solvent solidified by means of a suitable wax. The different composition of enamel remover is shown in formulae 17, 18 and 19.

Formula 17

Constituents	*per cent*
Paraffin or beeswax	11.5
Lanolin	4.0
Sodium or potassium linoleate	2.6
Methyl ethyl ketone	to 100.0

Formula 18

Constituents	*per cent*
Sulphonated olive oil	10.0
Sodium hydroxide (10%)	1.0
Benzyl acetate	15.0
Acetone	15.0
Titanium dioxide	0.5
Bentonite	2.0
Water	56.5

Formula 19

Constituents	*per cent*
Stearic acid	9.5
Triethanolamine	3.5
Mineral oil	10.0

(Cont'd)

butyl acetate	50.0
Butyl stearate	5.0
Carbitol	5.0
Water	17.0

Nail Drier

Nail driers are aerosol formulations. It makes use of the rapid evaporation of a propellant to speed up the drying of freshly enamelled nails, by drawing off the solvent present in the nail varnish. The drying is also combined with the deposition of a transparent film of oil over the freshly applied enamel. This reduces tackiness and prevents it from smearing if touched.

PLASTIC FINGERNAILS AND ELONGATORS

For improving the cosmetic appearance of damaged or short stubby nails plastic fingernails and elongator are used. They are produced by the polymerisation or copolymerisation promoter. A plasticiser, an opacifier, a pigment and a filler may also be included.

The most frequently employed monomer has been methyl methacrylate while poly (methyl methacrylate), polystyrene, polyisobutylene and cellulose acetate have been used as the polymer. If methyl methacrylate is copolymerised with a crosslinking agent such as ethylene dimethacrylate, more brittle polymers with improved solvent resistance are produced. The crosslinking agent polymer is usually employed in amounts ranging between 2 and 10 per cent by weight of the monomer. The actual level at which it is used largely determines the hardness and brittleness of the product. Compounds of improved flexibility may be produced by forming a copolymer containing 5-20 per cent by weigth of a higher- molecular-weigth ester of acrylic or methacrylic acid such as lauryl methacrylate. Triphenyl or tricresyl phosphate, dimethyl, diethyl or dibutyl phthalates (1-10%) may be used as plasticiser.

Polymerisation of methyl methacrylate is a free radical-catalysed reaction entailing the dissociation of the catalyst to free radicals which initiate polymerisation. The catalysts which are preferred in the production of nail elongators are benzoyl peroxide or lauroyl peroxide, and they may be used in amounts of up to 3 per cent by weight of the solid constituent of the preparation; usually, however, 1 per cent of the catalyst on the weight of monomer will be adequate. A polymerisation promoter is also usually present ot induce free radical release and to allow polymerisation of component monomers to take place at room temperatures, that is at temperatures appreciably lower than those at which polymerisation usually takes place.

Among fillers, silica and aluminium silicate, mica and metallic oxides (25%) have been used. Pigments and opacifiers (0.1%) are generally used.

Prepare the surface of the nail by removing any excess cuticle and traces of old lacquer. This makes nail ready for applying nail elongator. it also ensure good adhesion between the nail surface and the plastic material applied. The skin surrounding the nail is protectd from polymerisation taking place on its surface by applying to the skin a material with little adhesion for the plastic,usually a water-soluble resin easily removable with water.

The procedure used to form a nail elongator *in situ* entails successive applications, first of the liquid monomer and then of the powder containing the catalyst. This is repeated until the nail has been adequatedly lengthened. Once the tip of the anil has been strengthened, the nail is then built up from the centre of the nail to the outer edge. The polymerisation of methyl methacrylate and vinyl monomers is inhibited by addition of hydroquinone. The amount of catalyst and promotor is also kept under control. The composition of solid and liquid comjponents, the following formulation given in gormula 20 :

Formula 20

Constituents	*per cent*
Solid component	
Poly(methyl methacrylate) (granules)	75
Aluminium silicate	23
Benzoyl peroxide	2
Liquid component	
Methyl methacrylate (monomer)	83
Lauryl methacrylate (crosslinking agent)	15
Diethyl aniline (promoter)	2

The artificial nails are produced *in situ* by rapid polymerisation or copolymerisation of a constituent monomer at room temperature in the presence of a polymer and a redox catalyst system.

They are formed from two components, one of which is a primer. It contains a mixture of poly(methyl methacrylate), a copolymer of vinyl chloride vinyl acetate, and the oxidising component of a redox catalyst system. This component is used to form coatings on the exposed nail bed and the surrounding skin and protects them from irritation by the monomer contained in the second composition. The film-forming solids content of the primer composition should not exceed 25 per cent.

The second composition contains most of the resins for the artificial nails. It consists of a solution of a poly(methyl mehacrylate). It also contains the reducing component of the redox catalyst. both compositions are stable as long as they are stored separately, but when they are combined the monomer begins to polymerise.

NAIL MENDING COMPOSITIONS

Mending compositions are basically mixtures of an adhesive, a fibre reinforcing material and a solvent. The first two components produce a film which forms a strong Bond between the broken parts of the damaged fingernail, improving its appearance and preventing further damage. Whereas the solvent will quickly evaporate and allow the reinforced adhesive film to set and to mend the damaged fingernail. These preparations are preferably applied in four coats. Each coat is applied before drying the next coat in a direction perpendicular to the previous one. The nail polish is applied about one hour after the application of teh final coat of the mending preparation, to allow all the coats to dry thoroughly.

The nitrocellulose is preferred organic film-forming material of the mending composition. An aryl sulphonamide formaldehyde is also included to make the film produced by the composition more adherent, flexible and tough. A plasticiser may be added to make the film flexible. Short rayon fibres (1.5 mm long) and of small diameter (1.5-5 denier) are used as reinforcing agent. Other fibres may also be used if they are not soluble in the mending composition. A gelling agent (preferably silica) is also present, to ensure that the fibres used remain suspended within the adhesive. Solvents are ethyl acetate, butyl acetate and toluene used in a combination of 30-50 per cent, 5-20 per cent and 20-30 per cent respectively. Pigments or dyes may also be included to confer the desired colour. The compositions just described are illustrated by formula 21. It has been claimed that nail polish can be applied to and removed from such mended nails without difficulty and without disturbing the 'repair'.

Formula 21

Constituents	*per cent*
Nitrocellulose	10.3
Aryl sulphonamide formaldehyde resin	4.1
Silica	2.0
Dibutyl phthalate	0.5
Rayon fibres	0.5
Ethyl acetate	46.2
Butyl acetate	5.1
Toluene	31.3

Chapter - 16

HAIR SETTING LOTIONS AND CONDITIONERS

INTRODUCTION

The hair setting is required for men and women, to improve the control and manageability of hair, to impart some lustre, and to maintain a hairstyle and despite the various environment conditions to which hair is submitted (wind, humidity, dryness, cold, heat, sun, etc.).

The relative importance of these factors varies from one country to another, from age to age, and according to the state of the hair. It also differs notably between male and female users : men generally consider adequate control as the prime requisite for a hair dressing, with gloss as secondary, and as such men's products have been classically based on the use of oleaginous materials. Women first look for products that give a pleasing appearance to the hair, but at the same time they require good hold; they do not want product which render hair heavy and which tend to make it lank or greasy.

The trend in women's fashions for softer and freer styles. The increasing use of the brushing technique have led to an increase in the demand for products. These products enhance disentangling and a greater need for products that protect, strengthen and /or improve the condition of the hair. This has occurred at the same time as the extraordinary development of conditioners.

HAIR SETTING

All the methods attempt to form a film or coating on the hair for maintenance. The methods that could be used are :

1. A film on the hair is obtained on evaporation of water from water soluble materials like gums, protein derivatives, water soluble synthetic polymers.
2. A film/coating of anhydrous materials can be achieved by purely physical means. This method is applicable to fats of vegetable,

mineral or animal origin. However, the film/coating is quite greasy. This problem has been overcome by availability of some fatty esters.

3. Emulsions can form film or coating with much more ease. Dilution of any phase can be accomplished in a w/o or o/w type emulsion.
4. Another method that can be utilised is to make a solutionof water insoluble materials in volatile solvents like alcohol and apply to the hair. Volatile solvent(s) evaporate(s) leaving behind a film on the hair.
5. Using adsorption process film can be deposited on hair. Properly formed films made by this method resist rinsing, handling and sometimes even washing. Such a phenomenon is exhibited by cationic substances.

It may also be noted that sometimes the effect can be achieved with lower concentrations and increase in the concentrations dissipates the effect. The points of concern in such preparations are firmness of dispersion of material(s), freedom from irritation or sensitisation.

Formulation

Wave-Sets

The former formulations of wave-sets were based on natural gums like gum karaya, acacia, tragacanth and quince seed. These natural products have varying physical properties according to climate, soil, method of collection. In addition to this, they yield dull and brittle films which may crumble and may become sticky in humid weather. Formula 1 is given as an example of such products.

Formula 1

Constituents	*per cent*
Gum karaya	1.5
Sodium alginate	0.5
Glycerine	5.0
Ethanol	5.0
Water	to make 100.0
Perfume, Colour and Preservatives	q.s.

Synthetic polymers soluble in water-alcohol mixture have replaced natural gum. These products can be formulated with a film forming material, plasticiser, solvent (water-alcohol), perfume and colour. Formulae 2 and 3 are examples of such products.

Formulae	2	3
Constituents	*per cent*	*per cent*
Polyvinyl pyrolidone(PVP)	3.5	1.0
Propylene glycol	2.5	2.0
Triethanolamine	-	1.0
Ethanol	40.0	-
Carboxyvinyl polymer	-	1.5
Water	to make 100.0	to make 100.0
Perfume and Colour	q.s.	q.s.

Later on hair setting or styling gels became popular. Hair setting lotions due to low solid content cannot form gels. Thickening agents like carboxy polymethylene resins (Carbopols-Goodrich) have been extensively used for making gels. Propylene glycol and phthalates (e.g., di-methyl phthalate) are used as plasticisers. See formulae 4 and 5 :

Formula 4

Constituents	*per cent*
Carbopol	0.25
PVP	3.00
Di-isopropanolamine	0.25
Di-methyl phthalate	0.50
Ethyl alcohol	10.00
Water	to make 100.0
Preservatives, Perfume and Colour	q.s.

Formula 5

Constituents	per cent
PVP/VA (50 : 50)	5.0
Carbopol 940	0.3
Propylne glycol	3.5
Di-isopropanolamine	0.5
Water	to make 100.0
Preservatives, Perfume and Colour	q.s.

Hair Rinses

Since centuries vinegar and lemon juice have been used to remove lime soap after shampooing. Subsequently, solutions of polybasic acids like citric acid, tartaric acid were used. These were marketed in solid formulations with instructions to make solutions for rinse. Single application package were also available. These also contained colour and were called temporary colour rinses.

The products made with quaternary ammonium compounds are available as emulsions or creams. The earliest quaternary ammonium compounds that were used are alkyldimethyl benzyl ammonium chloride. A simple cream rinse can be prepared with alkyl dimethyl benzyl ammonium chloride and glyceryl monostearate. This cream rinse should be diluted to about 15 times before use. While selecting quaternary ammonium compounds their skin irritancy should be taken into consideration. Usually concentrations of 0.1% lose their irritancy and are still effective in their action on hair shaft. Formula 6 is an example of cream rinse.

Formula 6

Constituents	*per cent*
Alkyl dimethyl benzyl ammonium chloride	2.5
Glyceryl monostearate	2.5
Water	to make 100.0
Colour, Perfume	q.s.

HAIR-GROOMING PREPARATIONS

The groups of hair dressing are : brilliantines; alcoholic solutions; two layer systems; hair tonics; gum-base hair dressings; oil-in-water emulsions; and water-in-oil emulsions.

Formulation

Brilliantines

Brilliantines overcome dull appearance of hair. The main function of a brilliantine is to impart a measure of grooming and sheen to the hair. There are two types of brilliantines, liquids and solids. The mineral oil with small quantity of colour and perfume is liquid brilliantines. Another liquid constitute mineral oil (75%) and deodorised kerosene (25%).

The coupling agents may be added to keep the product clear on storage. Materials like vegetable oils, fatty alcohols/esters, non-ionic surfactants can solubilise perfume oils.

Vegetable oils are liable to become rancid, therefore, use of anti-oxidants in hair oils containing vegetable oils is necessary. Formulae 7 and 8 are examples of hair oils containing vegetable oils.

Formulae	*7*	*8*
Constituents	*per cent*	*per cent*
Castor oil	20.0	60.0
Deodorised kerosene	to make 100.0	-
Colour, Perfume and Preservatives	q.s.	q.s.
Almond oil	-	40.0

Formula 9 is related to hair oils based on mixtures of mineral oil and vegetable oil(s) have also been formulated as :

Formula 9

Constituents	*per cent*
Mineral oil	70.0
Peanut oil	30.0
Colour, Perfume and Preservatives	q.s.

Solid brilliantines are used for unruly or kinky hair where greater grooming is required. These products are invariably opaque. Opacity of these products increases with increasing proportion of waxes. Formula 10 is an example of typical solid brilliantine.

Formula 10

Constituents	*per cent*
Mineral oil	75.0
Stearic acid	25.0
Colour, Perfume	q.s.

Formulae 11 and 12 are examples of solid brilliantines having vegetable oils in them.

Formulae	11	12
Constituents	*per cent*	*per cent*
Castor oil	40.0	77.0
Cocoa butter	10.0	-
Petroleum jelly	50.0	-
Ceresin	-	23.0
Colour, Perfume and Preservatives	q.s.	q.s.

Alcoholic Solutions

Alcoholic lotions as hair dressing can be prepared diluting viscous oils with alcohol. It is possible to get wetting action first and deposition of thin layer of oil next after evaporation of alcohol. Castor oil is soluble in alcohol in all proportions and therefore, enjoys the unique place amongst fixed oils. Formulae 13 and 14 are examples of alcoholic lotions.

Formulae	13	14
Constituents	*per cent*	*per cent*
Castor oil	30.0	20.0
Glycerine	10.0	-
Ethanol	60.0	78.0
Tincture benzoin	-	2.0
Colour, Perfume	q.s.	q.s.

Oil-in-water Emulsions

Good pouring, spreading and attractive cream like properties made oil-in-water (o/w) emulsion immediately acceptable. It does not give greasy feeling and can be easily removed by shampooing. Since emulsions are vulnerable to microbial growth, preservatives soluble in oil phase and soluble in water phase should be added. Desired grooming can be achieved using mineral oil of low or medium viscosity is generally used. Other materials like petroleum jelly, waxes are added to increase the body of the emulsion. Gums have also been used to increase fixative properties, viscosity and stability of emulsions. A simple formulation (Formula 15) of this type comprises of oil and water with a suitable emulsifier.

Formula 15

Constituents	*per cent*
Mineral oil	45.0
Stearic acid	5.0
Triethanolamine	1.0
Water	to make 100.0
Perfume, Colour and Preservatives	q.s.

Method of Preparation

Separately heat mineral oil, stearic acid and preservative (oil and water soluble), water ethanolamine to about 70°C. Add aqueous solution to oil with slow stirring . Continue stirring and allow to cool to about 45°C. Add perfume and colour and blend thoroughly. The inclusion of lanolin, lanolin esters, fatty acids/esters for emollience, glycerine, propylene glycol gives humectancy, gums to increase stability and fixative properties.

Water-in-oil Emulsions

Inspite of difficulty to prepare water-in-oil emulsion hair dressing of this type are popular among men and women. These products are smooth lustrous creams which give excellent grooming and high sheen to the hair. The film deposited on hair is water resistant and this makes this type of hairdressing useful to swimmers. W/O emulsions have greasier feel but not as pronounced as in the case of brilliantines.

Several types of emulsifying agents have been used to prepare w/o hair dressings, polyvalent soaps being the oldest of them. Calcium stearate and oleates were used earlier but subsequently it was found out that magnesium is that more stable. A combination of emulsifiers has been found more useful than any single emulsifier. Zinc and aluminium stearates have been used in combination with other emulsifiers. Vegetable oils, waxes lanolin can be added for desired attributes in the product. Formula 16 can be considered as an example.

Formula 16

Constituents	*per cent*
Mineral oil	38.0
Petroleum jelly	20.0
Beeswax	18.0
Oleic acid	0.6
Lanolin absorption base	1.0
Sodium hydroxide	0.4
Magnesium sulphate	1.0
Borax	0.5
Water	to make 100.0
Perfume and Preservatives	q.s.

Manufacture of Hair Grooming Preparations

Brilliantines

Liquid brilliantines or hair oils are manufactured by mixing of miscible ingredients in suitable mixing tank. However, when liquid brilliantine is based entirely on low viscosity mineral oil, solubility of perfume may be a problem. Therefore, solubility of the perfume should be pre-determined. Perfume can be made oil soluble by using deodorised kerosene or isopropyl myristate. Before adding perfume, it is first dissolved in deodorised kerosene or isopropylmyrisate. Then added to the bulk. Similarly colour (oil soluble colour) is first dissolved in a part of oil and added to the bulk. Perfume and colour are thoroughly blended. For bright and crystal-clear appearance the bulk finished product may be filtered. These products should be processed either in stainless steel or high density polymer vessel. Anti-oxidants (oil soluble) should be mixed in a part of oil and should be added to the mix with stirring.

Solid brilliantines and pomades are prepared by melting and mixing all the ingredients except perfume, colour and preservatives (anti-oxidants) mixed with a stirrer. The heating is carried out in a water jacketted vessel. Colour and anti-oxidants are mixed in warm oil which will not cause solidification of the bulk. This mixture and perfume is added, as the cooling occurs but well before solidification in mixing vessel. Materials should not be worked when partially solidified, otherwise, air bubbles will be permanently incorporated. The product, while hot is run into warmed jars and these filled containers are allowed to cool slowly in a warm room.

Alcoholic Solutions

Alcoholic solutions of fatty materials, are manufactured by process of mixing. However the equipment should be such that would not permit evaporation of significant amount of alcohol.

PERMANENT HAIR WAVING PREPARATIONS AND HAIR STRAIGHTENERS

People having curly hair desire to have straight hair and vice-versa. This has resulted into generation of hair straighteners.

Heat Waving Preparations

General

As the name suggests these preparations are used when waving effect is achieved by heat. The hair are wound, moistened with heat waving preparations and are heated to about 93 to 104°C electrically or by means of heating pads. Scalp is protected from heat by so called "spacers" which are generally made of felt. The residual alkali is removed after heat treatment from hair by rinsing with water, or dilute acid or oxidising agent which are called as neutraliser.

Formulation

To protect the hair from drying and damage, non-volatile alkalies were replaced with volatile alkalies like ammonia, ammonium carbonate, morpholine etc. These alkalies initially provide pH 9-11 but being volatile during heating is dropped. Thus the chance of overwaving or partial hydrolysis of hair protein are minimised. These have disadvantage of ammonia odour and their premature loss from solution. The addition alkanolamines control premature loss of alkali. The use of sulphites in the heat wave preparations occurred about the same time as the use of volatile bases. Addition of a surface active agent helps in wetting of the hair. Formula 17 is an example of such a formulation. A similar formulation can be incorporated in absorption base to make a creamy preparation.

Formula 17

Constituents	*per cent*
Ammonium Carbonate	3.5
Potassium Carbonate	2.0
Borax	0.5
Potassium sulphate	2.0
Monoethanolamine	5.0
Sulphonated Castor oil	1.0
Water	to make 100.0

Cold Waving Preparations

General

In the cold waving process, external heat is not applied to the hair. The process is performed at room temperature. First, the hair are shampooed. Then moistened with waving lotion and wound on to curlers. After winding, the hair is left for 10-40 minutes. The wound curls are rinsed with oxidising solution (neutralisers) afterwards. The curls are unwound and usually a further rinse with neutraliser. The hair is finally rinsed with water and is set into the desired style.

Formulation

Most of the cold wave preparations are based on thioglycollic acid. Lotions are prepared with different concentrations of thioglycollic acid. The product is meant for professional use has 10% thioglycollic acid by the hair dresser. Formula 18 is an example of liquid cold waving preparations.

Formula 18

Constituents	*per cent*
Calcium thioglycollate	80
Ammonium chloride and/or	47-65
Ammonium formate	55-77

Creams containing thioglycollates can also be prepared. They have been used for hair straightening rather than hair waving. A typical product is shown in formula 19 :

Formula 19

Constituents	*per cent*
Modified & Stabilised polyglycerol	
monostearate emulsifier	21.0
Polyglycerol monostearate	18.0
Stearyl amide	2.1
Thioglycollic acid (38%)	13.0
Ammonia (26%)	1.0-2.0
Ammonium sulphite	1.0
Sodium lauryl sulphate	1.0
Water	to make 100.0

HAIR TONICS AND CONDITIONERS

Conditioners are the result of women's need for attractive and healthy looking hair. Conditioners should give to the hair many characteristics, life, spring, softness, volume, body, sheen, a silky touch, fly-away control and ease of styling. The hair look dull after various treatments like bleaching, permanent waving, frequent shampooing, handling abuse and weathering. The hair may also become porous and brittle. Conditioners take care of such hair. The base of conditioning is the concept of substaintivity. i.e., sorption of adequate ingredients to modify the surface properties of the hair. Keratin is anionic in nature and therefore, shows preference for cationic substances. Some treatments like bleaching enhance anionic nature by creating strongly anionic sulphonic acid sites. Though to less extent, long exposure to sun and environmental atmosphere also enhance anionic feature of keratin.

Formulation

Medicated Products

Excessive scaling and proliferation of micro-organisms are associated with dandruff, an anti-microbial agent and a keratolytic agent are included. Some anti-microbial agents which have been used are : quaternary ammonium compounds; chlorophenols; PVP - iodine complexes; quinolines.

The keratolytic agents are: colloidal sulphur; resorcinol; salicylic acid; selenium disulphide.

Derivatives of 2-pyridine-thiol-N-Oxide have strong anti microbial activity. According to Kligman, these derivatives besides anti- microbial activity exert cytostatic activity also. Cytostatic activity results in reduction in turnover rate of epidermal cells and induction of more complete keratinisation.

Anti-dandruff formulations can be prepared in aqueous alcoholic-base or in a rinse or setting lotion (formulae 20 and 21).

Formula 20

Constituents	*per cent*
Bis (2-pyridyl-1-oxide) disulphide soluble complex	0.15
Camphor	0.75
Menthol	0.05
Isopropyl alcohol	51.0
Water	to make 100.0

Formula 21

Constituents	*per cent*
Stearyl dimethyl benzyl ammonium chloride	5.0
Cetyl trimethyl ammonium chloride	0.2
Cocoamido propylamine oxide	2.0
Propylene glycol	5.0
Hydroxypropyl methyl cellulose	0.5
Water	to make 100.0

Conditioners

These were based on cationic surfactant, cetyl-trimethyl ammonium chloride. Subsequently, other cationics, alkyl dimethyl benzyl ammonium halides, alkyl isoquinolinium and alkyl pyridinium halides were used. Longer chain alkyl compounds of exhibited best conditioning properties. Important cationic surfactants introduced in the conditioners are : ethoxylated quaternary ammonium phosphates (SP); quaternised fatty acid amino-amides; N-acyl colaminoformyl-methyl pyridinium derivatives.

The high substantivity of cationic polymers resulted into excessive build-up. Another group of compounds that has been used is partially or totally hydrolysed proteins. Use of some of the compounds have been illustrated in formulae 22 and 24.

Formula 22

Constituents	*per cent*
Stearyl dimethyl benzyl ammonium chloride	5.0
Cetyl trimethyl ammonium chloride	0.2
Cocoamido propylamine oxide	2.0
Propylene glycol	5.0
Hydroxypropyl methyl cellulose	0.5
Water	to make 100.0

Formula 23

Constituents	*per cent*
PVA - VA Copolymer	1.0
Cetyl dimethyl (hydroxyethyl) ammonium chloride	0.5
Di-methyicone	0.2
Ethyl alcohol	23.3
Water	to make 100.0

Formula 24

Constituents	*per cent*
Stearyl amidopropyl-dimethylamine	1.5
Cetyl alcohol	2.5
Stearyl stearate	0.5
Hydrolysed protein	2.0
Lactic acid	0.5
Sodium chloride	0.5
Water	to make 100.0
Preservatives, Perfume and Colour	q.s.

Anti-Seborrhic Preparations

After shampooing hair become greasy quickly due to excess secretion of sebum from sebaceous glands. Bunches are formed and dust deposites on them. Greasy uptake by the hair can be reduced by applying an oil repellent treatment. Perfluorinated compounds such as CF_3 (CF_2) X (CH_2) X (CH_2) y Z (where Z is water-or oil-solubilising group) have been used. These compounds are used in concentration of about 0.05% to 0.2%. Formula 25 substantially retards the oil uptake by the hair.

Formula 25

Constituents	*per cent*
Perfluorononanoic acid	0.1
Polyoxyethylene polymetnyl siloxane	0.2
Alcohol	30.0
Water	to make 100.0
Perfume	q.s.

Oil adsorbing materials have also been used. A number of compounds have been recommended for seborrhea and hair growth. But classes of compounds which seemingly have more selective activity include thio-ether or sulphoxide derivatives of cysteine, cysteamine, glutathione, pyridoxine and hydroxy aminothiols; thiolanediol derivatives; poly-unsaturated acids.

Manufacture of Hair Tonics & Conditioners

Most of the hair tonics are hydroalcoholic solutions. Hair conditioners are either dispersions or emulsious. The following manufacturing conditions need specific mention as these will greatly affect the conditioners. These are :

1. In case of hair products, if oils or fats are heated to a too high temperature, they tend to form poor film and also lose their sparkle and become dull. Therefore, temperature should be only as high as is consistent with achieving a proper emulsification.
2. Better results are obtained if a cream conditioner is to be manufactured with fats like petroleum jelly, lanolin and emulsifying agents like Span 60, Tween 60, by adding water phase to oil phase slowly.
3. Viscosity, stability and shelf-life are greatly affected by rate and manner of agitation used. Reader may refer to the reference given in the foot note.

4. Where dispersion is of importance, colloid mill should be used because smaller the particle size, better the dispersion. Superior covering film can be achieved with smaller amount of product.
5. In case of creams, rate of cooling and length of cooling time are important factors.

Chapter - 17

HAIR COLOURANTS

INTRODUCTION

Since origin of man one of the way to beautify hair is colouring. The quest for a change of external appearance has found expression in various ways in all civilisations. The main reasons for colouring the hair are the following : to change the natural colour, to colour the white hairs which begin to appear with age, or to change the colour of the hair temporarily on a particular occasion. It is necessary to use a range of colourants with varying composition and behaviour for colouring. The various hair colouring systems, the characteristics of an ideal hair colourant and the various practical hair colouring processes are described in this chapter.

HAIR COLOURING SYSTEMS

The hair colouring is divided into three classes on the basis of duration.

1. The fugitive colours applied on hair have short duration hence, easily removed by shampooing. In this category the commercial products commonly designated 'colour rinses'. These products utilise colours of a high molecular weight which are in effect deposited on the surface of the hair without being able to penetrate into the cortex.

2. Semi-permanent Colouring : These colours are removed after several shampooings (three to six), but whose fastness is poorer than that of permanent colours. The colours used are direct dyes of low molecular weight, having a good affinity for hair keratin. Hence, they are capable of penetrating the cortex.

3. Permanent Colouring : This category provides effectively permanent colouration, resistant to shampooing and other external factors such as brushing, friction, light, etc. this is the process most widely used and represents at least 80 per cent of the total colourings effected.

In this system, uncoloured intermediates undergo series of chemical reactions produce the desired colour *in situ* in hair. The process is one of oxidation (almost always effected by hydrogen peroxide), followed by coupling and further oxidations.

Characteristics of an Ideal Hair Colourant

The ideal hair colourant should possess the following properties :

1. *Harmlessness :* It should colour the hair without impairing the natural texture and gloss and be non-injurious to the hair shaft. It should produce no toxic effect non-irritant with the skin and should not be a non-determatitic agent.
2. *Adequate Physical and Chemical Stability on the hair :* The stability of dye used for hair should be good to air, sunlight, friction and sweat.
3. *Compatibility with other Hair Treatments :* It should not change colour, nor bleach out, on the application brilliantines, setting lotions, hair lacquers, hair waving preparations, soaps or shampoos.
4. *Stability in Solution :* The stability of colour and formulated products in aqueous solution should be good.
5. *Selectivity :* Because it is always necessary to use a mixture of dyestuffs. The problem of selectivity plays a most important part. The dyestuff belonging to same chemical class has similar physico-chemical behaviour, hence they should be avoided.
6. *Affinity for Hair Keratin :* The physico-chemical characteristics of affinity, in conjunction with the penetration of the dyestuff into the hair shaft, can be seen to be very important when account is taken of the technical limitations controlling the dyeing of hair, such as : temperature not greater than 40°C; short time of contact of hair with the dye, up to say 40 minutes; very weak dye solutions, etc.

THE PROCESS OF HAIR COLOURING

The range of commercial hair colourants gives various shades and tints to hair. It ranges very light blonde to black, passing through a rang of tones : golden, ash, reddish, mahogany, violets, etc. There are more than sixty shades. The factors influencing process colouring hair are :

1. *Commercial Products are Mixtures :* Each particular colour is the overall result of the superposition of individual colourations (red, yellow, violet, blue, etc.) supplied by each of the dyestuffs in the commercial mixture.

2. *Concentrations of Dyestuffs :* The total quantity of all the dyestuffs used to obtain a shade is between 0.01 and 5 per cent by weight of the tinting medium applied to the head. The concentration is a function both of a dyestuffs used and of the procedure involved.

3. *Duration of Colouring Process :* The time of contact of the dyeing solution with the scalp and the hair is of the order of 5 to 40 minutes.

4. *Quantity of Solution applied :* The amount of dyeing solution applied to a female head varies between 15 and 100 ml.

5. *Frequency of Application :* For temporary colourants, this is of the order of once a week. On the other hand, for more permanent colourants, it is about once a month. In fact this is controlled by the regrowth rate of hair, which is about 1 cm per month.

6. *Treatment after Colouration :* Colourants must be conceived and formulated so as to avoid to the maximum extent the staining of the scalp. It is necessary to rinse with abundant of water and shampooing once or twice. This will remove the dye which is not adsorbent on the hair.

7. *Uptake of Dyestuff by the Scalp :* In order to achieve the desired colour, it is sufficient to place on the head a maximum of about 60 g of dye solution. This quantity is spread over a total surface of 700 to 1000 cm^2 of scalp and about 50,000 cm^2 representing the surface of the hair.

Permanent Colours (Oxidation)

It concerns the first stage of about 10 to 15 minutes, during which half the quantity of product is applied to the roots of the hair, the first 2 cm, close to the scalp, before applying the remainder to the rest of the hair and leaving in contact for a further 15 minutes.

TEMPORARY HAIR DYES

Dyestuffs

The dyestuffs used are basic dyes, acid dyes, disperse dyes, pigments or metallised dyes. The chemical class is azo, anthraquinone, triphenylmethane, phenazinic, xanthenic or benzoquinoneimine dyes. Table 35.1 lists dyestuffs with colour index number according to category.

Table 35.1

Dyestuffs used in temporary hair dyes

Chemical class	*Colour*	*Colour Index Number*
Acid Dyes		
Azo	Yellow	13065
	Yellow	19140
	Red	14720
	Red	15620
	Red	16185
	Red	16250
	Red	17200
	Orange	15575
	Orange	16230
	Brown	14805
Triphenylmethane	Green 22	42170
	Violet acid 49	42640
	Acid blue	42735
Xanthene	Acid violet	45190
Azine	Nigrosines(violet)	50420
Anthraquinone	Acid violet 43	60730
	Blue 62	62045
Basic Dyes		
Azo	Yellow 57	12719
	Orange	11270
	Orange	11320
	Red 76	12245
	Brown 16	12250
Triphenylmethane	Basic blue 5	42140
	Violet 14	42510
	Violet 3	42555
Azine	Red	50240
Indoaniline	L'Oreal 14-22	
Indophenol	L'Oreal 23-25	
Indamine	L'Oreal 26-32	
Disperse Dyes		

(Cont'd)

Azo	Yellow	11885
	Orange solvent 45	11700
	Orange solvent 9	11005
	Disperse Red 17	11210
Anthraquinone	Orange 11	60700
	Red 15	60710
	Violet	60725
	Blue 3	61505
	Blue	60500
	Black acetoquinone	-
	Black celliton	-
Methallised Dyes		
Azo	Cibalane blue F.B.N.	-
	Solvent yellow 90	-
	Solvent brown 43 etc.	-

Types of Commercial Temporary Product and their Formulation

Rinses and Coloured setting lotions are two main types of temporary hair colouring product. In rinses the dyestuffs are used in the form of simple aqueous or aqueous-alcoholic solutions. In order to increase the substantivity to hair, organic acids, special solvents are added or the hair may be pretreated with cationic compounds to increase the substantivity to hair. It should be noted that such tinting solutions may be sold as ready for use or alternatively be prepared by the user from concentrated products by simple dilution in water.

Crayons have been used from time to time for temporary colouring, and are employed like mascara–either rubbed direct on to the wet hair or transferred to the hair with a brush. They can be formulated with soaps and waxes, so as to give a product rather like a lipstick in formula 1 :

Formula 1

Constituents	*per cent*
Stearic acid	15.0
Triethanlolamine	7.5
Glyceryl monostearate	4.0
Beeswax	46.0
Paraffin wax	10.0

(Cont'd)

Microcrystalline wax	10.0
Coconut diethanolamide	7.5
Colour	q.s

SEMI-PERMANENT COLOURANTS

Dystuffs

These dyes occupy an important place in formulation practice. It is because their presence is often indispensable in the formulation of the permanent colours, the oxidation dyes. The three main classes are :

(i) Nitrophenylenediamines; (ii)Nitroaminophenols;

(iii) Aminoanthraquinones.

Various Dyes

Reactive Dyes

The use of reactive dyes has been a relatively new approach in the field of textile dyeing. These include materials such as dichlorotriazines (for example Procion dyes ex ICI), monochlorotriazines (for example Procion dyes ex ICI and Cibacron dyes ex Ciba) and trichloropyrimidines (Reactone dyes ex Geigy, Drimaren dyes ex Sandoz). These dyes work by actually reacting with the fibre and thus the dye part of the molecule is firmly held by the fibre.

It is now believed that conventional oxidation dyes such as *p*-phenylenediamine develop their final colour by interacting with reactive sites in the hair. Oxidation dyestuffs may thus be regarded as being a particular type of reactive dyestuff.

Metallised dyes

The preparation of such dyes may be based on the formulation of complexes in situ in the hair by means of nickel or cobalt ions and various complexing agents.

Azo dyes obtained by coupling on the hair

Diazonium salts, together with various coupling agents, may be applied to the hair.

The various dyes used as auxiliaries to modify the shade are : heterocyclid azo-derivatives, also derivatives of diazamerocyanines and quarternary derivatives of aminophenoxazinium.

Commercial Semi-Permanent Products and Their Formulation

Semi-permanent colourants can be presented either in the form of foaming lotions (anionic, cationic or non-ionic) or as anionic or cationic shampoos. According to the type of medium chosen and the product performance sought, various approaches to formulation have been developed, all having the goal of promoting the penetration of the dyes into the hair.

PERMANENT HAIR DYES

Permanent hair dyes are based almost exclusively on the use of reactive dyes, the so-called para-dyes. These are substances that are colourless at the time of their application to the head (the precursors) and are transformed into a coloured material *in situ* on the hair as a consequence of chemical reactions.

The precursors can be classified into two categories : the compounds called oxidation bases or primary intermediates and those called couplers or modifiers.

The chemical reactions in the formation of dyes are oxidation reactions and couplings or condensations. These are effected at alkaline pH (essentially due to the presence of ammonia) by the action of hydrogen peroxide or one of its solid derivatives–urea peroxide or melamine peroxide. The hydrogen peroxide is selected because its ability to promote the simultaneous decolouration of the hair to be tinted.

The bleaching which occurs simultaneously with but independent of the dyeing, results in the hair being rendered lighter. It permits to give new shades with the help of the new pigments. Thus it can thus be seen this system of colouration is unique and irreplaceable; this explains its widespread use and its name of colour lightening ('teinture eclaircissante').

Bases

The bases are benzene derivatives, substituted by at least two electron donor groups, such as NH_2 and/or OH. This confers the property of easy oxidation due to para or ortho position. The most important compounds of this class are thus p-phenylenediamine and p-aminophenol, and o-minophenol, to which one could add the p-and o-dihydroxybenzenes.

Couplers or Modifiers

Couplers or modifiers are benzene derivatives, substituted by the groups ($-NH_2$ and –OH) in *meta* position to each other. In this position it should be noted that the couplers do not have the property of easy oxidation by H_2O_2. The most usual couplers are among the following . (i) *m* phenylenediamine;

(ii) 2, 4-diaminoanisole; (iii) resorcinol; (iv) *m*-chlororesorcinol; (v) *m*-aminophenol; (vi) 1,5-dihydroxynaphthalene; (vii)6- methyl-3-aminophenol; and (viii) 2-methylresorcinol

Formation of Colours in the Hair

A very large amount of work has been devoted to elucidating the merchanism of oxidation dyeing and to the structure of the dyes. But all is not yet clear.

In fact, the number of parameters affecting the overall process is very great. For example, consider the influence of pH on the speed of reaction, the presence of the hair keratin itself which can affect the orientation of reactions, the complexity of the reaction mixtures (it is not unusual to use up to 10 couplers and bases), the possible hydrolyses of intermediate products, etc. All these variables make it practically impossible to specify exactly all the compounds which could potentially be formed. Thus empiricism in formulation still plays a very important part in the technology of oxidation dyeing, and no mean effort is required to arrive in practice at a formula that gives commercially reproducible performance.

FORMULATION OF PERMANENT HAIR DYES

For developing suitable formulation or note the following factors must be considered.

1. The formulation base-solution, emulsion, gel, shampoo or powder.
2. The selection of the dye components - the oxidation base, the coupling agent or the addition of a direct colourant.
3. The selection of an alkali - ammonia is usually used.
4. Antioxidants - usually a sulphite or ammonium thioglycollate is used to prevent oxidation of the dye before the product is to be used.
5. The pack - required to be attractive and convenient in use.

The most convenient medium for colouring the hair is a shampoo. The system consists of a solution of the dye precursors together with an ammonium oleate soap or other surfactant, to which is added at the time of use another solution of stabilised hydrogen peroxide contained in a separate vessel. This mixture is applied direct to the hair and left in contact for 20 to 40 minutes. Afterwards the hair is rinsed with water and then washed again.

By use of fatty alcohol sulphates, fatty acid dialkanolamides, non-ionic or amphoteric surfactants, fatty alcohols, amine oxides, fatty amines and cationic surfactants, a whole range of emulsions can be formulated in order to produce the dyes in the form of creams, gels, shampoos, etc.

Sodium sulphite or thioglycollic acid with or without hydroquinone can be used as antioxidant. The use of ascorbic acid has also been recommended as has that of pyrazolones. The hydrogen peroxide, can be used in various procedures.

The modern version of this process is that combined bleach and dye, in which oxidation dyes are used in the presence of enough hydrogen peroxide to bleach the hair while the dyes are penetrating. In this way, dark mousy hair can be dyed to a warm blonde colour several shades lighter than the original colour, yet not apparently bleached. The difficulties found with early formulae have been overcome and suitable products are now available for both home and professional use.

The formulae which may be used are similar to those used for conventional oxidation dyeing, except that more alkali and hydrogen peroxide are used. The degree of lightening depends on the concentration of hydrogen peroxide and ammonia. Thus, for example, if 15 per cent ammonia and 20 per cent hydrogen peroxide are used a lightening of one shade may be achieved (say from black to brown), while if 15 per cent ammonia and 30 per cent hydrogen peroxide (20vol) are used, then much greater effects can be produced (for example, dark auburn to blonde). The two end points on formulation are :

1. The improvement of essential dyeing properties can be obtained by better storage stability, ease of application, shortening of time of application , increased covering power and penetration, fixation in the hair, reduction in potential for skin damage and protection against eventual hair damage.
2. The conferring of new properties on the hair colourant are protection of hair structure, improvement of aesthetic quality of the hair, brightness, bulk, combability, general appearance, addition of antiseptics, antidandruff agents, antiseborrhea agents for the scalp, dyeing , for example, film-formers, etc.

OTHER DYES FOR HAIR

Vegetable hair Dyes

Henna

Of the vegetable hair dyes, only henna is of any real importance today. It consists of the dried powdered leaves of *Lawsonia alba, Lawsonia spinosa* and *Lawsonia inemis*, which are removed from the plants prior to flowering.

Henna owes its hair-dyeing properties to the presence of 2-hydroxy-1, 4-naphthaquinone, often termed *lawsone*, which is soluble in hot water and is, in acid solution, a substantive dye for keratin. In dyeing hair with henna, a paste of the powdered henna and hot water, slightly acidified with citric, adipic or other suitable acids to an optimum pH of about 5.5, is applied to the washed hair.

This 'henna pack', which is kept in place by means of a towel, is allowed to remain on the head for the required time, which may vary from five to sixty minutes. Then hair is thoroughly shampooed, rinsed and dried.

Henna Reng

Henna rengs produces blue-black shades. The addition of other substances to henna other than auburn i..e misture of indigo leaves and henna.

Chamomile

Of the various species of chamomile, only *Anthemis nobilis* and *Matricaria chamomillae* have a cosmetic use; they appear to be equally useful in tinting hair. The active ingredient in these flowers is 1,3,4-trithydroxyflavone, known also as apigenin. Either an aqueous extract or a paste of the ground flower heads may be used. To lighten the hair, a paste consisting of 2 parts chamomile and 1-2 parts kaolin mixed to a thin cream with hot water is applied to the head for a period varying from 15 minutes to 60 minutes depending on the shade required. Chamomile is also used as a constituent of hair-brightening rinses and shampoos.

Metallic Hair Dyes

In metallic dyes, compounds of lead are the most frequently used; compounds of silver, copper, iron, nickel and cobalt are sometimes employed, and less frequently salts of bismuth.

The colours produced by such compounds re due to sulphides formed by a reaction between the sulphur in the keratin and the metallic salts, or to metallic oxides formed by the keratin reducing the metal salts is not clear. It is possible that both reactions occur to some extent. Whatever the mode of action, the result obtained is the deposition of a coloured film along the hair shaft. This eventually, gives the hair a characteristic dull metallic appearance, renders the hair brittle and diminishes the efficiency of a subsequent permanent wave.

Lead Dyes

Lead acetate precipitated sulphur, glycerine and water are active ingredients. Example 2 is a typical formula. Sodium thiosulphate may be incorporated in place of precipitated sulphur. Such preparations have poor stability.

Formula 2

Constituents	*per cent*
Precipitated sulphur	1.3
Lead acetate	1.6
Glycerine	9.6
Rose-water	87.5

The action of lead dyes is slow and progressive. The shades produced in grey hair usually pass from yellow through brown to black. The shades achieved depend upon the concentration of lead salts in the preparation, the number of applications, the original colour of the hair and the time during which the colour has been allowed to develop.

Lead dyes interact with skin proteins. Hence, lead solutions are relatively non-toxic under normal conditions of use. However, it must be remembered that these preparations are usually sold for home use and systemic effects may follow if lead remains on the hands and contaminates food. The ingestion by children might be fatal and preparations containing lead should carry adequate precautionary notices.

Other Metallic Dyes

Other metallic hair dyes, such as bismuth, silver, copper, nickel and cobalt salts, have been proposed, however, due to toxicity it requires precautions.

HAIR DYE REMOVERS

Sometimes user may have a lighter shade, hence removal of hair dye is necessary. In the case of metallic dyes it is usually dangerous to remove the dye by chemical means since the metals catalyse many reactions and may cause a violent production of heat which will probably damage both hair and scalp. The only remedy for an unwanted metallic dye is to let the hair grow.

Oxidation dyes can be removed by treating the hair with reducing agents such as sodium hydrosulphite or sodium formaldehyde, sulphoxylate, usually at a concentration of 5 per cent. The use of formamidine sulphinic acid has also been described. A formula for hair remover is shown below :

Formula 3

Constituents	*per cent*
Formamidine sulphinic acid	1.5
Polyvinylpyrrolidone	5.0
Ethylene glycol monobutyl ether	5.0
Ammonium carbonate	1.0
Ammonia (25%)	0.5
Carboxymethyl cellulose	2.5
Water	to 100.0

Semi-permanent dyes can often be removed by vigorous washing with shampoos containing little ammonia. Some dyestuffs, however, prove very resistant and a mixture of shampoo, reducing agent and bleach in the proportions 1 : 1 : 2 has been recommended for such cases.

BLEACHING AND LIGHTENING

Blonde shades are obtained by bleaching the hair in the usual manner to the palest possible shade of blonde with ammonia and hydrogen peroxide. The hair is afterwards given a rinse with a blue rinse containing about 1 : 100 000 of methylene blue (Ext.D&C Blue No. 1), or other suitable blue certified colour. The addition of the blue colour is necessary since the human eye considers a substrate which is very slightly blue in colour as whiter than white.

Bleaching of the hair must be thorough or the combination of a deep yellow hair shaft and a blue rinse may give the hair a distinctly greenish appearance.

Powder products obtain better control in the application of peroxide to the hair and extend the bleaching time. These powders kaolin or magnesium carbonate, used with peroxide and ammonia. There are powders which themselves provide ammonia and some form, of active oxygen, when wetted with water or hydrogen peroxide. Typical early formulae contained up to one-third of sodium perborate or percarbonate, the balance being kaolin and or magnesium carbonate. More complex formulations are given in formulae 4 and 5.

Professional hair dressers use above preparations hence the degree of skill and care is required to get good colour.

Formula	4	5
Constituents	*per cent*	*per cent*
Ammonium persulphate	3.0	-
Potassium persulphate	-	8.0
Potassium hydrogen tartrate	3.0	-
Potassium hydrogen oxalate	-	8.0
Sodium carbonate	3.0	13.0
Surfactant	1.0	1.0
Thickener	5.0	-
Mangesium hydroxide and/or aluminium hydroxide	to 100.0	to 100.0

For home use, products are fomulated on much more simple lines. A suitable two-bottle pack would be :

Formula 6

	Constituents	per cent
A	Hydrogen peroxide 20 vol	98.6
	Tartaric acid	0.8
	Sodium stannate	0.6
B	Ammonia	4.5
	Surfactant, e.g., ammonium soap	3.0
	Water	92.5

Chapter - 18

ORAL HYGIENE PREPARATIONS

INTRODUCTION

The substantial progress has been made by oral products in therapeutic or biological activity. It has strong influence on oral care products. The number of oral care products are growing in the market. Stain free teeth, prevention of diseases and freshness is achieved by oral hygiene products. The current dental science has limited success with maintenance of a healthy dentition. It is the driving force in dental research on over the counter (OTC) oral care products.

The two major arenas of preventive self-applied dental formulations have been reduction of dental caries and prevention of gum diseases. Dental carries affected as much as 95% of people in industrialised populations. Periodontal diseases are still rampant in all populations, but this must be put into perspective.

There are many types and stages of periodontal diseases. If the disease is categorised in terms of disease which threatens tooth loss or the need for major surgical measures, the incidence is relatively low in industrialised societies. If all conditions which cause mild inflammation or irritation are considered to be periodontal disease, the incidence is considerably higher.

The incidence and seventy of caries, periodontal and other dental diseases are reduced on proper oral hygiene. The application of OTC and practice of dental products for healthy mouth is discussed in this product. Certainly, a clean dentition is a first, necessary step towards a healthy dentition.

THE HUMAN DENTITION AND ITS ENVIRONMENT

Teeth and Associated Oral Structures

Oral hygiene practices are designed to maintain the crown enamel, dentin (if exposed) and gingiva in healthy states. Maintenance of these structures is expected to result in the general health of the dentition, including other hard and soft tissues and the supporting bony structure. Humans have a complement of 20 teeth, which grow from 6 months of age (lower central incisors) to 20–24 months (second molars). Adults normally have a complement of 32 teeth, erupting from 6–7 years of age (first molars, central incisors) to 17–21 years (third molars). The teeth are supported by a bony structure. The principle diseases causing loss of teeth are dental caries and periodontal diseases. Good oral hygiene and dietary habits are effective preventive measures. If left undisturbed, the carious lesion will penetrate to the pulp and expand to destroy the crown. Similarly unless tended to, periodontal disease will result in inflammation and destruction of the soft tissue surrounding the tooth, and eventual loss of the tooth.

Saliva and Crevicular Fluid

Saliva is a mixture of the secretions of the parotid, submaxillary, sublingual and accessory salivary glands, occasionally along with the crevicular fluid.

Saliva performs two functions : (i) it is involved in protection of the oral cavity through several factors related to the bacterial population of the oral cavity; and (ii) it is involved in the initial process of food digestion. It is suggested that saliva could be anti-cariogenic by : (a) increasing the rate of carbohydrate clearance; (b) reducing acid production by fermentative pathways; (c) buffering the drop in pH caused by acid production in plaque; (d) increasing the rate of glycolysis in plaque, thereby reducing the time the plaque is below a critical pH for attack on enamel; (e) increasing enamel resistance to demineralisation by acid; (f) increasing the degree of saturation of plaque fluid with respect to hydroxyapatite or fluorapatite; (g) promoting remineralisation of initial subsurface carious lesions; (h) increasing bacterial clearance from the oral cavity; and (i) increasing the protection possibly afforded by the dental pellicle that selectively deposits from saliva immediately following cleaning of the teeth. Calcium ions present in saliva appear ;to play an important role in microbiological processes involved in both protection and destruction of the tooth by oral bacteria.

Crevicular fluid is introduced into the saliva through the gingival crevice. It is not noticeable in a healthy dentition or the absence of teeth and can be an indicator of the extent of periodontal disease; more is exuded as the condition worsens. Crevicular fluid exhibits enzyme activity that changes with condition. Knowledge of crevicular fluid is still far from complete.

ORAL ACCRETIONS AND CONDITIONS

Dental Pellicle

Dental pellicle, a film from saliva, covers the tooth after cleaning the tooth. The bacterial mass (dental plaque) adheres and stains of exposed to chromogenic materials to this film. Dental plaque can be removed without removing pellicle. Substantive tooth stains, however, are removed only with removal of pellicle. Tooth brushing alone is inadequate to remove pellicle and must be used in conjunction with an abrasive. Chemical removal is possible, but only at the risk of damaging the underlying enamel.

Dental pellicle consists of glycoproteins selectively absorbed from saliva. The amount of pellicle formed following brushing with an abrasive (pumice) increases for about 1.5 hour, then levels off. Pellicle may hinder penetration of substances from plaque into enamel.

Dental Plaque

Dental plaque is primarily a bacterial accumulation. It occurs supragingivally (above the gum line) and subgingivally (below the gum line).

A relation between dental plaque, periodontal disease and caries known. Freedom from dental disease is usually a consequence of the absence of plaque.

A mass of oral bacteria, which initially accumulates around the teeth at the cervical margin and then grows apically is dental plaque. Dental plaque contains leucocytes, desquamated cells, and other oral debris. It undergoes maturation, which involves changes in the microbial flora, possibly including calcification and loss of viability of some of the bacteria. It can be removed only by mechanical means on maturation. This definition acknowledges that plaque is a dynamic system and that quantitative measurements must be reported only in the context of that dynamism. A corollary would be that only a totally plaque-free tooth can confidently be expected to be disease-free. Inadequate control of plaque can lead to either or both of two serious disease conditions, periodontal disease and dental caries.

The relationship between dental plaque and caries is clear. Dental plaque generates acid from carbohydrate, and this acid attacks the tooth enamel and initiates formation of the carious lesion.

Dental Calculus (Tartar)

There are two types of dental calculus, supragingival and subgingival. The former is explained as a hard, mineralised dental plaque and/or materia alba permeated with crystals of various calcium phosphates covered with a layer of 'vital, non-mineralised plaque. Subgingival calculus is defined as an organic structure of micro-organisms and intermicrobial matrix, containing major amounts of crystalline calcium phosphates, in different amount and distribution from those of supragingival calculus. A major impetus for the study of dental calculus was the belief that this hard, rough accumulation, (or the plaque concentrated on it), in direct contact with the gum tissue, was an irritant leading to periodontal disease.

The nucleation of calcium phosphate occurs at salivary gland where saliva secretes which results into supragingival. The calcium phosphate crystals in both supra – and subgingival calculus consist of octacalcium phosphate, brushite, whitlockite and hydroxyapatite. Subgingival calculus has a major amount of whitlockite and amount of brushite. The contents of the periodontal pocket are apparently able to fulfil the conditions necessary for nucleation and subsequent crystal growth.

Periodontal Diseases

The marketers of oral hygiene products has more research interest in periodental disease. On the one hand, dental caries has to all intents and purposes been conquered with OTC fluoride toothpaste and rinses used in conjunction with water fluoridation and other fluoride treatments. On the other hand, OTC products offering the same degree of protection against tooth-threatening periodontal diseases as fluoride does against caries are not yet available.

The bacterial plaque formed spreads at the gingival margin. It generate toxins that inflame the soft gum tissue, which becomes soft, puffy and red, and bleeds easily. A periodontal pocket (a pathologically deepened gingival sulcus) may form in susceptible individuals, without destruction of tissue. Then the inflammatory process is aggravated : the pockets become enlarged and form the receptacles for subgingival plaque bacteria, debris and exudates. The surrounding connective tissue degenerates. The pockets continue to deepen, and the teeth start to loosen by the bacterial mass. Subsequently, the gums recede from the tooth crowns. Finally, microbial, plaque toxins and other materials in the pockets intensify the inflammatory process, supporting bone tissue is destroyed, and the teeth loosen and eventually fall out or are extracted. The relation between dental plaque and periodontal disease are :

1. Removal of supragingival plaque once every 24–48 hours is adequate to preserve gingival health.
2. There is a close relationship between the subgingival location of the advancing bacterial front and the level of connective tissue attachment. The bacteria produce an inflammatory reaction apically/laterally to the junctional epithelium.
3. Periodontal disease may proceed by bursts of increased inflammatory activity. Dental plaque, gingival redness and bleeding on probing, and initial pocket depth probing do not relate to the occurrence of probing attachment loss. The incidence of periodontal disease sites in untreated patients is low.
4. The level of oral hygiene correlates with the severity of periodontal disease.

Dental Stain

The tooth stains accumulated by a significant number of individuals are extrinsic in nature and result from discolouration of pellicle and/or plaque. The extrinsic staining has three steps : (i) Chromagenic bacterial produce colour substances in plaque; (ii) Dietary factors (berries, tea, coffee) or smoking retains colour and (iii) Chemical transformation of pellicle component produce colour products tea, wine, tobacco, pellicle reactive colour, oral use of antimicrobial agent produce stains.

Oral Malodour

Bacteria from virtually all sources in the oral cavity have been implicated. 'Morning breath' has been attributed to the overnight putrefaction of food deposits, salivary deposits, desquamated epithelial cells, and other types of oral accumulation and debris. Malodour of other than bacterial origin (for example due the intake of odouriferous foods or to diseases which cause the exhalation of odouriferous metabolic products) cannot be eliminated by oral hygiene measures.

The main cause of oral malodour is probably the putrefaction of sulphurcontaining protein substrates, predominantly by gram-negative bacteria. The process is not limited to specific bacterial populations, Micro-organisms indiginous to dental plaque, saliva, gingival crevice and tongue can participate, and mixed bacterial populations are most capable of odour production. The fermentation process releases hydrogen sulphide and methyl mercaptan (which together account for 90% of the volatile compounds generated), and dimethyl disulphide. The mouth air also contains aliphatic and aromatic alcohols, and indole. Mouth air and putrefying saliva from persons with periodontal disease show higher than normal levels of sulphur compounds.

The vigorous oral hygiene controls mouth malodour and can be considerably reduced by tongue brushing, toothbrushing, food ingestion and use of an oral rinse that reduces oral bacterial populations.

ORAL–CARE PRODUCTS

Product Categories

Oral-care products can be divided broadly into mechanical devices and chemical formulations.

Tooth Brush

The tooth brush is a mechanical device. It is the most important part of the oral hygiene regimen. Toothbrushing alone, without toothpaste can maintain a reasonable state of oral health. Toothpaste enhances its value as it removes stain, freshen the breath and accomplish specific functions. Other mechanical devices include dental floss, water irrigators and pics of various designs.

Toothpaste

Toothpaste is a preferred vehicle to apply special active substances to the dentition. It enhances the role of toothbrushing in oral care. Toothpastes are now being marketed with special active agents to combat dental caries, reduce the formation of dental calculus, combat gum disease and reduce tooth hypersensitivity. Wide acceptance of toothpaste has made it the vehicle of choice for applying therapeutic or special cosmetic additives to the dentition. Toothpaste brands are proliferating as new health benefit additives are discovered, and older concepts of toothpaste formulation are no longer applicable. Oral-care products have been categorised as cosmetic or therapeutic, depending on whether or not they contain a health benefit agent.

Oral Hygiene Preparations

Toothpaste and tooth powder essentially contain abrasives, moisturisers, bonding and foaming agents, surfactants, sweeteners, preservatives, pigments, aromas, and special active ingredients. Tooth powders differ from toothpastes in their lack of moisturising agents such as glycerine, sorbitol and water, which the abrasive content can reach 90% of their total volume.

Abrasives

The abrasives found in tooth care preparations are usually insoluble, inorganic materials present in toothpastes in concentrations of between 15 and 60%. An average size of 15 μm (micrometers) is preferred. In general, the abrasives chosen for tooth care preparations must accomplish a maximum amount of cleaning and a minimum amount of damaging erosion.

The most widely used abrasives are aluminum hydroxide ($AL(OH)_3$), calcium carbonate ($CaCO_3$), calcium hydrogen phosphate ($CaHPO_4$), calcium hydrogen phosphate-dihydrate ($CaHPO_4.2H_2O$), silicic acid ($SiO_2.H_2O$), sodium aluminum silicate with, for example, zeolite structure ($Na_{12}(AlO_2)_{12}(SiO_2)_{12}.27H_2O$), insoluble sodium metaphosphate ($(NaPO_3)n$) and hydroxylapatite ($Ca_5(PO_4)_3OH$).

Some toothpastes also contain water-soluble sodium hydrogen carbonate ($NaHCO_3$) as an abrasive, usually in combination with calcium carbonate. The commonly coarse-grained, soft sodium hydrogen carbonate is only a temporary abrasive, as is slowly dissolves during brushing in the saliva. Polymethyl methacrylate is also used as an insoluble, organic abrasive in an extremely fine-grained form.

Chapter - 19

DENTIFRICES
(Tooth Paste & Tooth Powders)

INTRODUCTION

The primary function of a dentifrice is to remove adherent soiling matter from a hard surface with minimal damage to that surface. This is done by using mild abrasive powder containing surface active agent. The foam produced also has a psychological effect in making tooth cleaning more pleasurable.

This cleaning function must be achieved in a short time – two minutes – and at body temperature. The paste, however, is convenient in packaging and use. The liquids having humectant properties is used to prevent the toothpaste drying out at the tube nozzle. The gelling agent is added to maintain a high solids suspension in a stable viscous form.

Finally it is necessary to add flavours and possibly preservatives, colours and active ingredients, and all these components must be non-toxic and non-irritant under the conditions of use.

The total product should maintain its consistency over a temperature range from 0°C to 37°C (that is, it should have a relatively flat viscosity-temperature curve). It should be stable when stored without physical or chemical change over the same temperature range. Most large manufacturers have international sales and may have to take into account local conditions in many countries.

BASIC REQUIREMENTS OF A DENTIFRICE

The minimum requirements are listed below :

1. An efficient toothbrush should remove food debris, plaque and stains and clean if used properly.
2. It should leave the mouth with a fresh, clean sensation.
3. Its cost should be reasonable for frequent use by all.

4. It should be harmless, pleasant and convenient to use.
5. It should be stable in storage during its commercial shelf-life.
6. It should confirm to accepted standards in terms of its abrasivity to enamel and dentine.
7. If prophylactic claims are made, these should be substantiated by properly conducted clinical trials.

TOOTHPASTES

Ingredients

A balanced formula can only be achieved by considering all the ingredients together since many of them may have a dual function or may interact with one another. Cost and availability as well as local laws, regulations and even local habits may cause formulations to vary from country to country.

Abrasives

The most commonly used abrasives are precipitated calcium carbonate and dicalcium phosphate dihydrate. Other materials include tricalcium phosphate, calcium pyrophosphate, insoluble sodium metaphosphate, various types of alumina, silica and silicates. Particles of plastics may also be used.

The abrasive used in a toothpaste must always be a compromise between the ability to clean the surface and the necessity to avoid damage to the tooth surface :

Calcium Carbonate

Chalk, or as it is normally purchased, precipitated calcium carbonate, is available in a number of grades varying in crvstalline form, particle size and surface area.

By varying the conditions of precipitation, precipitated chalks of different densities and crystal habit may be obtained. The two common crystal types are aragonite (orthorhombic) and calcite (rhombohedral) and particle sizes in the range 2-20 mm are normally used.

Chalk is an efficient cleaner but does not produce good lustre on teeth. Probably the best compromise is to use a small proportion of chalk with a larger proportion of one of the less abrasive phosphates.

Waterworks chalk has been employed in toothpastes but quality is not always uniform and the higher level of water-soluble calcium may cause problems in some formulations.

All chalks give an alkaline reaction to toothpastes and it may be necessary to protect aluminium tubes from corrosion by adding sodium silicate.

Calcium Phosphates

The varieties of calcium phosphates used in dentifrices are :

1. Dicalcium phosphate $CaHPO_4.2H_2O$.
2. Dicalcium phosphate anhydrous $CaHPO_4$.
3. Tricalcium phosphate $Ca_3(PO_4)_2$.
4. Calcium pyrophosphate $Ca_2P_4O_7$.

Dicalcium Phosphate Dihydrate

Dicalcium phosphate dihydrate (DCP) is most commonly used in dentifrices. The pH value of a toothpaste made with DCP is normally in the range 6-8. The taste of DCP-based toothpastes is normally better than that of chalk-based products and the flavour stability is improved.

DCP is in the metastable state and reverts to the anhydrous form with consequent hardening of the paste. This change is accelerated by the presence of fluoride ions. The DCP normally supplied is stabilised to delay or prevent this change. Trimagnesium phosphate, tetrasodium pyrophosphate and calcium sodium pyrophosphate are common stabilisers.

Anhydrous Dicalcium Phosphate (DCP)

It is more abrasive than the dihydrate it should be used in smaller quantities. It is less soluble than the dihydrate which is an advantage in fluoride-containing pastes

Tricalcium Phosphate

Tricalcium phosphate (TCP) is not used to a large extent. It too is less soluble than DCP.

Calcium Pyrophosphate

Calcium pyrophosphate (CCP) was originally developed as the abrasive of choice for products containing sodium or stannous fluoride. It is claimed that the low availability of soluble calcium ions contributes to the stability of the fluoride.

Insoluble Sodium Metaphosphate

Insoluble sodium metaphosphate (IMP) is a particularly useful abrasive for fluoride-containing dentifrices since it contains no calcium ions.

Other Abrasives

There have been a number of developments in abrasive systems. These have arisen because of particular demands :

The fluoride stability is increased by the use of hydrated alumina and synthetic plastics. The transparent dentrifices are obtained using silica in the form of hydrated xerogel and sodium aluminium silicates.Zirconium silicates are used to impart luster to the teeth.

Detergents

Tooth cleaning is essentially a detergent process surface-active agent is incorporated. Soap was the earliest detergent used, but the obvious disadvantages (high pH, taste and incompatibility with other components) has led to its replacement by synthetic detergents.

The detergent must of course be tasteless, non-irritant to the oral mucosa. The foaming qualities are important since they have a significant influence on the subjective assessment of toothpaste performance.

Some surface-active agents may have intrinsic prophylactic or therapeutic properties.

Sodium Lauryl Sulphate

Sodium lauryl sulphate (SLS) is probably the most widely used detergent for oral products and satisfies almost all requirements. In this context 'lauryl; denotes that the alkyl radical R in $ROSO_3Na$ is derived from a narrow cut alcohol predominantly C_{12} but with some C_{14}. The original sources are palm kernel or coconut oil fatty acids. Various grades are available from manufacturers and particular attention should be paid to taste. This is influenced by the free alcohol content. A low content of inorganic salts is also desirable. Recrystallised grades are excellent in quality but are expensive.

Sodium N-lauryl Sarcosinate

Sodium N-lauryl Sarcosinate ($R.CO.N(Me)CH_2COONa$) has been widely used in accordance with a Colgate patent which claims prophylactic effects as a consequence of its anti-enzyme properties. It is particularly useful in oral products because of its high solubility. Sodium ricinoleate (Castor oil soap) is highly soluble hence, used in dentifrices but is vulnerable (as are all soaps) to the presence of calcium ions. Sodium sulphoricinoleate (Turkey Red Oil) has also been used.

Other Detergents

Sodium lauryl ether sulphate ($R(OC_2H_4)_nOSO_3Na$), coco monoglyceride sulphate, alkane sulphonates and alkyl polyether carboxylates have all been proposed as surface-active agents for dentifrices.

Humectants

The humectant is required to prevent a dentifrice from drying out. This is most likely to happen if the cap is left off the tube.

More recently glycerine has been partly or wholly replaced by 70 per cent sorbitol syrup which has similar properties and is usually less expensive. It is available in crystallising and non-crystallising grades.

Propylene glycol has also been used as a third component of the humectant system.

Gelling agents

Gelling or binding agent is necessary to maintain a high-solids suspension in a stable form. It also modifies the dispersibilitiy, foam character and 'feel' in the mouth. Gelling agents used in toothpastes are hydrophilic colloids which disperse in aqueous media. These include natural gums such as Irish moss and gum tragacanth, synthetic cellulosic products and silica.

Gum Tragacanth

This gum is extensively used at one time and satisfactory pastes can be made with it. The final product may be variable because of the natural origin of the gum.

Cellulose Derivatives

They are used as gelling agents for toothpaste. They can be tailored to suit any requirement in terms of solubility, gel strength, etc. They are non-coloured, non-toxic and relatively tasteless.

Carboxymethyl Cellulose

Carboxymethyl cellulose (CMC) or, more strictly, sodium carboxymethyl cellulose (SCMC) is prepared by the action of sodium chloracetate on alkali cellulose. The physical properties may be controlled by adjusting the degree of breakdown of the cellulose before substitution and by the degree of substitution.

SCMC gels are anionic and sensitive to pH values outside the range 5.5–9.5. They are reasonably stable in the presence of electrolytes and calcium ions and in general are suitable for most toothpaste formulations. SCMC is used gelling agent for toothpastes.

Anionic SCMC is not suitable for toothpastes containing cationic agents such as certain antibacterials. Hence, a non-ionic cellulose derivative must be used.

One minor disadvantage of SCMC is its possible breakdown if toothpaste is infected with the organism *Penicillium citrinum* but this is a rare occurrence.

Cellulose Ethers

Cellulose ethers are generally the methyl or hydroxyethyl ethers of cellulose. These ethers can be tailor-made to give prescribed properties by varying the degree of substitution. They are of course non-ionic and are stable over wide pH ranges and unaffected by metal cations. They are most valuable in formulations that contain antibacterials which are cationic.

Methylcellulose is more soluble in cold water which is advantage. Methylcellulose is somewhat incompatible with glycerine and this can be a drawback.

Hydroxyethylcellulose (HEC) has the general characteristics of the cellulose ethers. Toothpastes made with HEC are slower to disperse than those made with SCMC so that foam and flavour are slower to develop. Nevertheless HEC is probably nearest to the ideal binding agent for toothpastes, particularly products that contain cations.

Miscellaneous gelling Agents

Starch ethers have been used in toothpaste and are satisfactory. Two synthetic resins, an ethylene oxide polymer and a carboxy-vinyl polymer have also been suggested for use in toothpastes.

Flavours

The flavour of a toothpaste is one of the most important characteristics influencing consumer acceptance. They have usually been based on the oils of spearmint and peppermint. These are often fortified with a trace of menthol to give a cooling effect. They are also modified with clove (or eugenol) wintergreen (or methyl salicylate), eucalyptus, aniseed, etc.

The nature of the foam and the dispersibility of the paste also affect the flavour impact in the mouth.

Other Ingredients

Preservatives

The preservatives are added to a toothpaste to protect it from micro-organisms. Formalin and sodium benzoate and *p*-hydroxy benzoates were commonly used for this purpose.

Sodium benzoate is not effective at neutral and higher pH values. Flavour components themselves have some anti-bacterial action.

In case the product manufactured is sterile, preservatives are not added.

Corrosion Inhibitors

Sodium silicate is often added to high pH chalk-based toothpastes to prevent attack on aluminium tubes. Some phosphates also reduce the corrosion risk with alumina-based toothpastes.

Increasing the glycerine level in the water phase will often reduce the risk of this type of corrosion.

Colours

Colours are sometimes added to toothpastes. These must be chosen with care as colour fading, particularly at the nozzle, is not uncommon.

Bleaches

To enhance the whitening effect of toothpastes and powders and to assist in the removal of stains, oxidising agents are often added to the product. These included sodium perborate, magnesium peroxide, hydrogen peroxide-urea compounds, stabilised hydrogen peroxide compounds, etc.

Formulation of Toothpastes

A standard toothpaste constitute, gelling agent 1%, humectant 10–30% and abrasive, 15–50%. The various formulations of toothpaste are given in formulae 1 to 8.

Formula 1 (Peppermint flavour)

Constituent	*per cent*
Peppermint oil	ca. 60
Menthol from peppermint oil	10-15
Anis oil, fennel oil	10-15
Eucalyptus oil	5-10
Spice oils	2-5
Nuances (flower and citrus oils)	0.5-10

Formula 2

Constituents	*per cent*
Spearmint oil	ca. 30-40
Peppermint oil	20-30
Menthol from peppermint oil	10-15

(Cont'd)

Anis oil, fennel oil	10-15
Spice oils	0.5-3
Nuances	0.1-5

Formula 3 Anticaries Toothpaste (base : calcium carbonate, sodium monofluorophosphate)

Constituents	*per cent*
Sodium carboxymethyl cellulose	1.30
Sorbitol (70%)	20.00
Water (demineralised)	37.54
Sodium saccharin	0.15
Sodium monofluorophosphate	0.76
Aroma	1.00
PHB methyl ester	0.20
PHB propyl ester	0.05
Calcium carbonate	35.00
Silicon dioxide (highly dispersed)	2.50
Sodium lauryl sulphate	1.50
	100.00

Formula 4 Anticaries Toothpaste (base : calcium hydrogen phosphate sodium monofluorophosphate)

Constituents	*per cent*
Sodium carboxymethyl cellulose	1.10
Glycerine (86%)	10.00
Sorbitol (70%)	15.00
Water (demineralised)	35.76
Sodium saccharin	0.05
Sodium cyclamate	0.10
Sodium monofluorophosphate	1.14
Benzoic acid	0.20
PHB methyl ester	0.15
Aroma	1.00
Calcium hydrogen phosphate (dihydrate)	25.00
Calcium hydrogen phosphate (non-aqueous)	7.00
Silicon dioxide (highly dispersed)	2.00
Sodium lauryl sarcosinate	1.5
	100.0

Formula 5 Anticaries Toothpaste (base : silicate acid/sodium fluoride)

Constituents	*per cent*
Hydroxyethyl cellulose	1.40
Sorbitol (70%)	28.00
Xylitol	5.00
Water (demineralised)	43.37
Acesulfam K	43.37
Sodium fluoride	0.25
PHB methyl ester	0.24
PHB propyl ester	0.18
Aroma	0.06
Abrasive silicic acid	1.00
Thickening silicic acid	11.00
Sodiumlauryl sulphate	2.00
Fatty acid tauride	0.50
	100.00

Formula 6 Gel Toothpaste (Base : silicic acid/ sodium fluoride)

Constituents	*per cent*
Sodium carboxymethyl cellulose	0.40
Sorbitol (70%)	72.00
Polyethylene glycol 1500	3.00
Water (demineralised)	4.64
Sodium saccharin	0.07
Sodium fluoride	0.24
PHB ethyl ester	0.15
Aroma	1.10
Abrasive silicic acid	11.00
Thickening silicic acid	6.00
Sodium lauryl sulphate	1.40
	100.00

Formula 7 (base : Calcium carbonate/carbamide)

Toothpaste for Gum Protection-I

Constituents	*per cent*
Methyl cellulose	1.10
Sorbitol (70%)	15.00
Water	31.00
Sodium saccharin	0.05
Carbamide	5.00
Sodium benzoate	0.20
a-bisabolol	1.10
Sage extract	0.50
Aroma	1.10
PHB methyl ester	0.15
Calcium carbonate	45.00
Soap (medical)	0.80
	100.00

Formula 8 (base : silicic acid/pyridyl carbinol/tartaric acid)

Toothpaste for Gum Protection-II

Constituents	*per cent*
Sodium carboxymethyl cellulose	1.00
Sorbitol (70%)	50.00
Water	25.72
Sodium saccharin	0.10
Sodium benzoate	0.15
Tartaric acid	0.12
B-pyridylcarbinol tartrate	0.15
Allantoin	0.30
Aroma	1.05
Silicic acid, xerogel	7.00
Siiicic acid, aerogel	13.00
Red dye (C.I. 16255)	0.01
Sodium lauryl sulphate	1.40
	100.00

The addition of fluorides (sodium or stannous) or sodium monofluorophosphate to a toothpaste presents problems. For example, if free fluoride ions are present in a calcium carbonate formula they will quickly be precipitated as calcium fluoride and the cariostatic activity will be lost. In these cases the abrasive must be chosen with care to prevent or reduce this effect.

Insoluble sodium metaphosphate (IMP) and special grades of calcium pyrophosphate (CPP) are usually used with compounds releasing fluoride ions (for example SnF2, NaF). sodium monofluorophosphate is less of a problem since the ion is FPO_3^{2-} and not F^-. In this case DCP and even precipitated calcium carbonate may be used. Great care must be used in all fluoride formulations to ensure that the fluoride activity remains at a high level throughout the life of the product.

The level of fluoride ingredient used has conventionally been such that there is 1000 ppm of fluorine in the final product. This corresponds to 0.2 per cent of NaF, 0.4 per cent of SnF_2 and 0.76 per cent of Na_2FPO_3.

Manufacture of Toothpastes

The processes involved in toothpaste manufacture are : the hydration of the gelling agent and the dispersion of the abrasive in the gel. The hydration of the gel is done by adding the solid gelling agent and water to the glycerine with vigorous agitation. It is not necessary to heat the mixture if CMC is used, but heating to 60°C is usual with Viscarin-type gelling agents. Overstirring of CMC gels results in an irreversible diminution of viscosity and should be avoided. Toothpaste manufacturing process is outlined in Fig. 38.1.

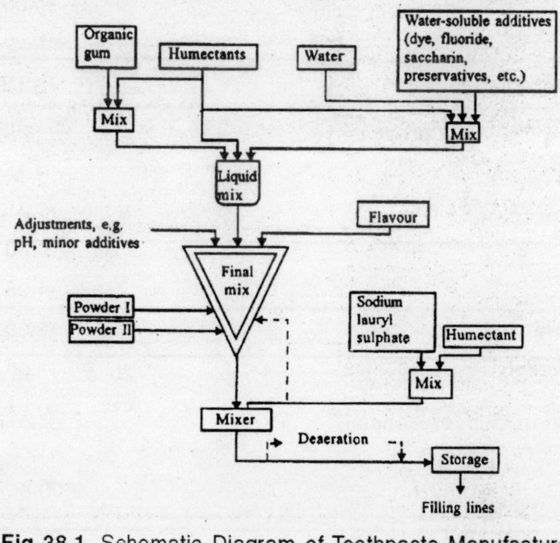

Fig 38.1. Schematic Diagram of Toothpaste Manufacture

Gel hydration can be continuous by means of an ejector (supplied by Hercules) in which the gel powder is introduced gradually into a stream of cold water which is then forced through a nozzle. The vigorous agitation produced gives a smooth uniform gel.

The heavy-duty mixing vesels like, Petzholdt, Fryma and Unimix are used for powder addition. The product is deaerated by mixing under vacuum. It is usual practice to add the active ingredients (if present) late in the mixing cycle and to add the surface-active agent and the flavour last of all. This is done to avoid excessive foaming and to reduce loss of flavour during evacuation.

The degree to which de-aeration is complete can be checked by density measurement. For a general formula such as that described above, a density of 1.55 – 1.60 would be expected.

TOOTH POWDERS

Toothpowders are the original, the simplest and the cheapest compounded forms of dentifrice. They are replaced largely by the more convenient pastes. Fluorides and oxidising agents are likely to retain their effective concentration longer than they would do in a paste formulation.

The problems in formulation are likely to be concerned with physical characteristics. The preparation of ingredients of fairly uniform size to prevent separation on shaking, and in ensuring that the product does not cake on storage. Typical formulations are given in formulae 9-12 :

Formula 9

Constituents	*per cent*
Precipitated Calcium Carbonate	95.0
Sodium palmitate	5.0
Flavour, sweetener	q.s.

Formula 10

Constituents	*per cent*
Dicalcium phosphate dihydrate	79.0
Precipitated calcium carbonate	20.0
Sodium lauryl sulphate	1.0
Flavouring, sweetener	q.s.

Formula 11 (Oxygenated powder)

Constituents	*per cent*
Precipitated calcium carbonate	96.0
Sodium lauryl sulphate	2.0
Magnesium peroxide	2.0
Flavouring, sweetener	q.s.

Formula 12 (Fluoride powder)

Constituents	*per cent*
Dicalcium phosphate dihydrate	75.0
Precipitate calcium carbonated	23.0
Sodium lauryl sulphate	1.0
Sodium monofluorophosphate	0.8
Flavouring, sweetener	*q.s.*

Manufacture of Toothpowders

The manufacture of powders is very simple. The sweeteners, abrasive powder flavour, together with a little alcohol are mixed with the rest of the powders in a conventional powder mixer.

SOLID DENTIFRICE

Solid dentifrice is essentially a soap in which the abrasive powder is mixed. The proportion of soap varies from 10 to 30 per cent depending on the glycerine content of the finished product and the hardness desired. A higher proportion of flavour is added than in paste dentifrices. The product is usually coloured. Solid dentifrices, like toothpowders, have largely been replaced by toothpastes. A typical formula would be :

Formula 13

Constituents	*per cent*
Dental soap	18.0
Precipitated calcium carbonate	79.0
Glycerine	3.0
Colour, flavour, sweetener	*q.s*

A plastic mass is obtained by milling soap, abrasive material with glycerin and water. Then plodded by adding colour and flavour and extruded in a conventional soap plodder, cut into billets and stamped.

The abrasive nature of the product demands specially fabricated plodders and cutters.

PERFORMANCE TESTS

In recent years performance of dentrifices has significantly improved. The ready availability of human & animal teeth has made easy to carry out experiment of teeth *in situ* in the mouth to the performance of oral products.Chemists, physicists and dentists have all contributed to the performance of oral products.

Abrasive Action

The nature and quantity of abrasive influences the cleaning properties of dentrifice. The design of toothbrush and detergent play significant part. During cleaning, food debris, plaque, acquired pellicle, stains and calculus should be removed from the tooth surface, if possible without damage to the underlying enamel. Dentifrice abrasives are a compromise between the desire for perfect cleaning and the desire to avoid enamel wear.

The most obvious methods of measuring abrasion should be by weight loss, but this requires excessive abrasion and would lead to wear far in excess of that met with in a real life situation. The method for the measurement of the abrasive quality of toothpastes include the shadowgraph method, the surface profile method, interference microscopy replication techniques radio-tracer method.

In fact almost all conventional toothpastes fall comfortably within this standard; abrasivity ratings of 50-100 against dentine and 50-120 against enamel would probably cover most commercial toothpastes. There is no evidence to show that any conventional dentifrice, when properly used, has caused excessive wear of enamel or dentine. Cervical erosion, that is, erosion at the neck of tooth following gum recession, which occurs in older subjects, is due to bad brushing technique. The amount of material lost by abrasion with a relatively abrasive paste has been calculated as 1.2×10^{-8} g per brush stroke from enamel and 98×10^{-8} g per brush stroke from dentine.

It is possible to assess the relative wear rates of different particle sizes of different abrasives by radio-tracer technique. Within the fairly narrow limits of conventional toothpaste formulations there is an almost linear relationship between: (i) particle size and wear rate and (ii) percentage concentration of abrasive and wear rate.

Hardness, crystallinity of particles and particle shape all play some part in determining wear rate. It is now possible to pre-set the abrasivity of a toothpaste within fairly narrow limits. Probably the best compromise would be to have a relatively high proportion of a large soft particles (e.g. DCP 5 - 10 mm in size) and a small proportion of small hard particles (e.g., zirconium silicate or silica 1 mm in size). The large soft particles should remove most of the adherent soiling matter from teeth and the small particles should give some degree of polish without visible scratching.

DENTURE CLEANSERS

Denture cleansers are either in powder or tablet form or as liquids. They comprise essentially an oxidising agent, an electrolyte and an alkali.

The oxidising agent used is normally sodium perborate or sodium percarbonate, though hypochlorites, trichlorisocyanuric acid and its salts and persulphates.

Sodium percarbonate is more soluble in water than sodium perborate, but is not quiet so stable, though in the solid form its stability is adequate. Sodium perborate is available in two forms.

1. *Sodium perborate tetrahydrate* : usually written as $NaBO_3.4H_2O$ but more properly $NaBO_2.H_2O.3H_2O$, has an active oxygen content of 10.38 per cent and is sold on the basis of 10 per cent active oxygen.

2. *Sodium perborate monohydrate* : usually written as $NaBO_3.H_2O$ but more properly $NaBO_2.H_2O_2$, has an active oxygen content of 16 per cent and is sold on a basis of 15 per cent active oxygen.

   The purpose of a denture cleanser is to loosen debris, which consists of saliva and food particles, to remove stains and to sterilise the denture.

Solid products are normally dissolved in water to form a solution in which the denture is immersed. Bubbles of oxygen formed helps mechanically to loosen food debris which is itself partly solubilised by the alkali present. Electrolytes have some solubilsing action or mucous deposits. The combined effect is to loosen the debris so that, after a suitable period of soaking, it is easily brushed away.

In addition the denture is sterilised and stains are removed. Regular use of denture cleansers will also prevent the build-up of calculus on the denture surface. The amount of sodium perborate or percarbonate used is usually in the range 20-25 per cent.

The electrolyte used is invariably sodium chloride and the alkali is most commonly anhydrous trisodium phosphate, though sodium carbonate or bicarbonate and other alkalies may be used. Typical formulations are given in formulae 14 and 15 :

Formula 14

Constituents	*per cent*
Sodium perborate	40.0
Sodium chloride	30.0
Trisodium phosphate	30.0
Flavour, colour	q.s.

Formula 15

Constituents	*per cent*
Sodium percarbonate	40.0
Sodium chloride	40.0
Sodium carbonate	20.0

Tables can also be prepared, either from conventional mixtures as in formulae 14 and 15, or as, for instance, in formula 16 :

Formula 16

constituents	*per cent*
Sodium percarbonate	88.0
Sodium chloride	10.0
Sodium silicate and/or other binders	2.0
Flavour, colour	q.s.

Liquid products are normally dilute solutions of sodium hypochlorite with sodium chloride. Such solutions of course lose some of their available chlorine over time.

The promotion of effervescence generated by carbonate acid mixture of copper salt helps in the break-up and dissolution of tablets and promotes the concept of activity. In the latter case great care should be exercised in checking the stability of the finished product. The inclusion of proteolytic and amylolytic enzymes in denture cleansers has been proposed. It is vital to keep moisture out of the product and to protect it from atmospheric humidity. The powder products must not cake on storage and solid products should dissolve quickly to give a clear solution.

The quality testing is performed on packed products. A performance of product under use should be monitored.

Chapter - 20

PERMANENT WAVING, HAIR STRENGTHENERS AND STRAIGHTENERS

INTRODUCTION

In permanent waving the normal anatomy of the hair is seriously disrupted. The keratin fibre of the hair are attacked by chemicals present in waving lotions. Here permanent waves break fewer bonds and then re-form them. Since not all of the broken bonds are restored by the setting agents, repeated use of permanents makes the hair weaker and much more brittle.

There are four steps involved in permanent waving. First, detergents strip away the chemically resistant sebum and expose the cuticle (outer layer of cells). Secondly, swelling agents then enlarge and open up the hair shaft, thus enabling chemicals to reach the keratin in the cortex (inner core of fibres), the backbone of the hair. Thirdly, the bond-breaking agents (usually the same chemical found in depilatories) enter the shaft and break the hair's "cross-linking" bonds. In the final step, a bond-forming agent (called a "neutraliser" or "oxidiser") enters to re-form the bonds in a new configuration, which gives the hair a permanent curl. These new bonds hold the hair in the curled position until it grows out, is cut off, or until extremely harsh chemicals are applied again.

Various types of hair respond differently to the waving process. A thin hair will not have as many fibres or as great a distance between cross-linked strands of keratin. Thus, when it is bent, there is not as great a stretching difference between the inside and outside strands of keratin as in a thick hair. The resulting curl will not be as small or tight. To offset this, stronger solutions or longer times are used to break as many bonds as possible. This increases the danger to the user. Special caution must be used when giving children permanents; their hair is usually fine, and the waving chemicals must be very strong to do the job. The original condition of hair can not be obtained although reforming of bonds may occur. As the cuticle is permanently eroded by waving temporarily some hair rinse and sprays patch the hair.

The most extensive damage can be found near the ends of permanent waved hair since that part of the hair is the oldest and has been waved the most. The cracking and eroding of the cuticle will split the ends and make the hair look drab, dull, and frizzy. For permanent wave or reshape hair there are three methods :

1. In cold waving powerful chemicals break the cross-linking bonds. The bonds are re-formed by "oxidising" or "neutralisting" chemicals.
2. Heat waving, which is based on Nessler's original method and uses both heat and water in the presence of bond-breaking chemicals to curl hair.
3. In tepid waving, which combines hot and cold processes to allow lower waving temperatures than heat waving and lower concentrations of dangerous chemicals than cold waving.

HOW COLD-WAVING PREPARATIONS WORK

Cold waving requires tow separate applications of chemicals. First, a waving lotions strips, softens, swells, and breaks the bonds in the hair. Second, a neutralising lotion reverses the effects of the powerful waving lotion by re-forming the bonds in a curled position. Normally, hair is first washed to remove the sebum, placed in curlers, and the waving lotion is applied to each curler. After about ten minutes, a control curl is taken to determine if enough bonds have been broken to leave the hair contoured around the curler. If the curl tends to return to its original state, the waving lotion is left on the hair for several minutes more to break additional bonds. Once enough bonds are broken, the waving lotion is rinsed out and neutralising lotion is applied. The longer the chemicals left tight curl results whereas shorter length yield soft curl. Principal ingredients of cold-waving lotions and their functions are shown in table 36.1.

Table 36.1.

Principle Ingredients of cold-waving lotions and their functions

Class of Ingredients (concentration)	*Function*	*Ingredients Names (as they appear on product labels)*
bond-breaking agents (4.6%-8.3%)	disrupt the structures that give hair its shape	calcium thioglycolate ammonium thioglycolate
antioxidants	prevent waxing lotion from reacting with air before it reaches the hair	sodium hydrosulphite

(Cont'd)

Sequestering agents	prevent trace metals dissolved in tap water from reacting with the thioglycolates	tetrasodium EDTA tetrasodium pyrophosphate
pH adjusters (10%)	hold the pH around 9.3 so the thioglycolates will work properly	Calcium hydroxide ammonium carbonate triethanolamine (TEA) monoethanolamine (MEA) ammonium hydroxide
emollients	replace some of the oils stripped off the hair by the strong surfactants and caustic chemicals in the waving lotion	lanolin, cetyl alcohol, synthetic spermaceti, mineral oil, propylene glycol
emulsifiers	keep the emollients dissolved in water	sodium lauryl sulphate sorbitan palmitate polysorbates
surfactants	remove sebum from hair	TEA & sodium lauryl sulphates
conditioners	cover some of the damage done to the hair by harsh chemicals and surfactants in the waving lotion	hydrolysed animal protein quaternium-40 potassium hydrolysed animal protein quaternium-19 acrylic copolymer

Waving Lotions

It is tricky to formulate safe and pleasant waving lotions. The chemicals present in depilators are similar to waving lotions, the little change in composition will result into destroying rather than waving hair. The bond-breaking agent in waving lotion is usually calcium thioglycolate or ammonium thioglycolate; both are highly alkaline, caustic chemicals that can burn or corrode the skin. In order for the bond-breaking agent to work properly in a cold-wave lotion, the pH must be around 9.3. This is ideal pH, as above 9.3 hairs are removed and below 9.3 bonds are not broken. Calcium hydroxide, ammonium carbonate, ammonia, or triethanolamine are commonly used as pH adjusters. These chemicals can harm the user.

Other less serious problems are involved in formulating a waving lotion. The main ingredient, calcium thioglycolate, smells like vinegar and develops a rotten-egg odour if it is left standing. This odour also arises when the lotion reacts with the hair. Moreover, wave preparations normally contain ammonia or other compounds, all of which have distinctive unattractive odours. Masking these odours is difficult. Usually a fresh cologne smell of higher value must be used. Lotion cosmetics form similar, but longer-lasting emulsions because emulsifiers hold the drops of oil in the water. Otherwise, the oil and water would quickly separate into distinct layers. Cloudy lotion-type waving liquid does not guarantee is gentle, soft, or more exotic formulation than a clear one. It means that it is costlier and cloudier.

Waving lotions also include surfactants (detergents) which remove sebum from the hair. The harsher surfactants are commonly found in permanent-wave preparations. Most waving lotions also contain emollients, which replace some of the oil stripped off the hair by the strong surfactants and caustic chemicals. Hair conditioners are now incorporated into some waving lotions. A combination of emollients and conditioners can patch damaged hair due to permanent waving.

Neutralisers

Once the hair's cross-linking bonds have been broken, they must be re-formed. The derivatives of citric acid tartaric acid and lactic acid neutralise the waving lotions, hence neutraliser.

They also contain a bond forming agent to speed up the work of the oxygen generated by H_2O_2 in air, which forms bonds naturally, but too slowly. Peroxide can bleach hair, but not very easily in acid solutions. Powder preparations must be mixed with water at home, may contain powerful, flammable toxic chemicals such as sodium or calcium bromate. If these bromates are used, flame retarders such as urea are added. Sodium perborate or ammonium persulphate are less flammable can be used. Principal ingredients are shown in Table 36.2.

Table 36.2.

Principal Ingredients of Permanent-wave Neutralisers and Their Functions

Ingredient Name	*Function*
Citric acid	neutralise the alkalanity of the waving lotion,
Acetic acid	usually around 0.1%-0.2%
Tartaric acid	
Lactic acid	
Phosphoric acid	
Hydrogen peroxide	re-form broken hair bonds 3%-6%
Sodium bromate	

(Cont'd)

Calcium bromate	
Sodium perborate	
Ammonium persulphate	
Urea	flame retardant
Methylparaben	preservative
Ammonium lauryl sulphate	detergents (remove excess oil and
Polysorbate 20	help hold waving lotion on the hair)
Polysorbate 40	

Some home permanent kits rely on self-neutralisation. The oxygen in the air reacts with the calcium with the calcium thioglycolate once it is placed on the hair. This method is too slow to be used in beauty parlours. However, it can be used at home with some advantages Self-neutralisation controls the overwaving of the hair that may occur if the user gets distracted and does not apply a neutralising liquid at the proper time. Unfortunately, self-neutralising products can make the hair frizzy.

HOW HEAT AND TEPID-WAVING PREPARATIONS WORK

The effect of the heat-waving process is also breaking and reforming of hair. The most important difference between steam heat and cold waving is that, heat is used instead of thioglycolate for bond breaking and reformed by cooling rather than neutraliser. Since steam, like water, can break only about 70 per cent of the cross-linking bonds, some chemicals must still be used to achieve a permanent heat-wave. Accelerators- alkaline compounds such as ammonia and monoethanolamine-increase the used speed with which water breaks the cross-linking bonds.

Sodium bisulphite, initiator, increases speed of the bond breaking. These chemicals can create consumer problems, however, as ammonia and monoethenolamine are both toxic, and ammonia has the added drawback of giving the hair a reddish tint.

But the greatest danger to the user is the risk of hair and scalp burns. Because of the high temperatures (200°F) involved. Tepid waves, in which heat is applied at a lower temperature along with the same chemicals used in cold waves. The advantage of tepid waving is that heat speeds chemical reactions. Thus lower concentrations of toxic chemicals can be used without increasing the total time needed to wave the hair. The ingredients for a tepid wave product will be similar to the chemicals in a cold wave but will occur in lower concentrations.

Permanent-Wave Pretreatments

People who have permanently waved, bleached, or dyed their hair or have exposed it to excessive sunlight or to extremely strong shampoos probably have damaged hair. Such weakened hair absorbs the powerful waving chemicals much more quickly and in much greater quantities than normal hair. It is thus particularly susceptible to further harm.Pretreatments can decrease the amount of damage the waving products will do to the hair.

Pretreatments work in one of two ways. They can cause more bonds to form in the hair, thus increasing the number of bonds that the waving product must break . Or they can contain an "arresting agent" that will remain on the hair and limit the action of the thioglycolates by reacting directly with these bond-breaking agents. Ammonium persulphate is a common waving-action limiter. Of the bond-forming agents, glutaral and glyoxal are the most common. These chemicals can be sensitising to the scalp. If your scalp becomes sore or irritated after repeated use of a product which contains one of these ingredients, try switching to a pretreatment which uses an arresting agent.

Health and Safety

Permanent-waving components are extremely toxic and corrosive to the skin. These chemicals in combination may be more dangerous than the individual chemicals . They can be fatal in small quantities also. They can damage fabrics and metals, as well as skin and hair. Beauticians are warned to protect their hands against the corrosive action of thioglycolate waving lotions. Home users, too, are cautioned not to apply waving products if their scalp or skin is "sensitive, sore, scratched or tender," and they are advised to wear rubber gloves.

The use of surfactants (detergents) in the waving solutions may enhance the skin-penetrating abilities and toxic effects of the thioglycolates. All cold-waving lotions with a pH of 9.0 or higher may cause a "sensitisation after prolonged contact and may result in hair damage as well."

Ammonia and thioglycolate are corrosive and can cause blindness in case of contact with eye. However, surfactants (detergents) – particularly the non-ionics and amides–have an anesthetic effect on the eyes, which numbs them to sensations of burning. Thus, users are less likely to be aware of eye damage and to take appropriate remedies immediately.

Many of the active ingredients in permanent-waving products are caustic and can damage skin. Some alkalies have additional toxic effects. The pH adjusters triethanolamine (TEA), diethanolamine (DEA), and monoethanolamien (MEA) should be avoided. Nitrosamines, proven cancer-causing substances in animals, are sometimes found in TEA and may be found in the waving lotions penetrate the skin. The bromates found in neutralisers may also cause problems. They are extremely flammable in the dry form and are poisonous if swallowed or if they enter the skin through cuts or abrasions on the scalp or hands.

HAIR STRENGTHENING PREPARATIONS

Weakened hair, which may result from sensitisation due to hair treatment or over-processing or from environmental or internal causes, usually lacks bulk, tensile strength, lubricity, sheen, body and a barrier to penetration. It is often stringly, oversensitive to moisture, or even flimsy and, as a result, difficult to handle. The prevailing factor in the weakening of hair is the breaking of too many disulphide links, as may be the case with hair that is too frequently and excessively waved, bleached or dyed.

A process for improving the strength and elascity of weakened hair, which entailed treatment of the hair with solutions or dispersions of dimethylol user or dimethlol thiourea for 15 minutes at a temperature of 30° - 40°C in the presence of a glycerophosphoric acid in an organic or aqueous medium at a pH between 1.5 and 6.0. The free amino groups of hair keratin, producing cross-links between the hair fibres, and polymerise in the presence of the acid catalyst to form a resin within the hair fibres. The resin strengthens the hair making it virtually insoluble in water and various organic solvents.

The commercial use of free formaldehyde and such compounds is banned in many countries. The release of free formaldehyde has subsequently been shown to be efficiently reduced by the inclusion of stabilising compounds such as urea, dicyandiamide, melamine or ethylene urea in the methylol compositions. The improved compositions for strengthening damaged or weakened hair contain, more specifically, monomethylol dicyandiamide and its methyl ether, methylolethylenethiourea, and methylolated melamines and 'methylols'.

Further compositions for strengthening degraded hair, which comprise at least one alkylated compound, to be so stable that virtually no formaldehyde was released during application. The methylol ether compounds proposed include mono-and dialkoxymethylureas or ethyleneureas and corresponding thioureas, tris (alkoxymethyl) melamines, N-alkoxymethyl carbamates or adipamides.

Other stable, easily obtainable yet more water-soluble compounds are condensation products of the former linear or cyclic methylolated substances with secondary amines such as N,N'-bis-(morpholinomethyl) urea or N,N'-bis-(ureidomethyl) piperazine and methylol derivatives of glyoxalurea or thiourea condensation products.

Lastly, addition of fairly small quantities of sulphites to any of the previous compounds prevents occurrence of free formaldehyde.

The 4 - 12% of methylocated compound is used in strengthening preparation. The concentration depends on product used, water solubility, type of hair to be treated. Hydroxylated acids, acetic , phosphoric and hydrochloric acids (or salts there of, such as acid phosphates) may be used as polymerisation catalyst. The reduction in solubility of hair in alkali indicate that remarkable strength is resulted by above composition.

Many new compounds have been proposed to enrich hair, enhance its protection against subsequent hair treatment, impart more body and bulk, eliminate a slimy feel on wetting and add lubricity, at the same time restoring it. Particularly interesting are, on the one hand, cationic resins with methylol groups and, on the other hand, methylolated compounds or derivatives with functional groups that may be transferred into the hair or onto its surface so as to modify its sensitivity to chemicals. The above-mentioned functional groups are disulphides– such as in. N,N'- bis-(hydroxymethyl) dithiodiglycolamide and 2,2'-dithiodiethyl-bis-(morpholinomethylurea); tertiary amines– such as in diethylaminoethylurea and methylimino-bis-(3-propylurea) methylols; and quaternary ammonium compounds–such as in alkyldimethylammonium acetamide chloride and diethyl (ureido ethyl) ammonium acetamide chloride methylols. Dicarbonyl compounds such as glyoxal, glutaraldehyde, quinone, etc. And amino-dialdehydes have also been claimed to have strengthening properties.

HAIR STRAIGHTENERS

Many consumers need hair straighteners, particularly curly hair one. The idea held at one time that curly or kinky hair is eliptical in cross- section whereas straight hair is circular is now completely discarded. There are several types of hair straightening preparation : (i) Hot comb-pressing oil methods; (ii) Caustic emulsion and (iii) Chemical reducing agents.

1. *Hot Comb Method.* In the hot comb method, hair is straightened by the use of petroleum jelly and a hot metal comb. This is called as 'hot pressing'. Alternatively a mixture of petrolatum and paraffin may be used. The petrolatum, major component acts as a heat transfer agent between the comb and hair, lubricating the latter to allow the comb to slide through it without drag. The hair is washed and dried before the pressing oil is applied and the heated metallic comb is used to straighten the hair.

2. *Caustic Emulsions.* Caustic emulsions are in cream form. The use of caustic lye involves risks such as irritation of the scalp and even accidental eye damage.

A typical composition is given in formula 1. This paste is applied by combing and allowed to remain on the hair for 30 minutes at 40°C. The hair is then washed well with water to remove all the paste.

Formula 1

	Constituents	*parts by weight*
A	Gum tragacanth	2
	Boric acid	1
	Water	40
B	Sodium carbonate	1
	Potassium hydroxide	1
	Glycerine	2
	Water	8

Formula 2

Constituents	*grams*
Hydroxyethylcellulose WP 4400	4.0
Lithium hydroxide	2.0
Sodium chloride	17.5
Water	to 100.0

The simple lye straighteners described above are mainly designed for people who want their hair straightened, not styled.

The multi-component lye straighteners conform to a general pattern of five components are also available. They have :

(i) A soft pomade based on mineral oil-jelly-wax applied to the scalp as a protective pretreatment.

(ii) The 'relaxer', which consists of an oil-in-water emulsion containing about 3 per cent caustic soda and about 40 per cent fatty material.

(iii) A cream shampoo which is used to follow the relaxer constitute 12 per cent alkyl sulphate, 2 per cent fatty acid diethanolamide and unspecified emulsified fatty material.

(iv) A dilute oil-in-water emulsion containing about 2 per cent fatty esters and a cationic wetting agent referred to as the 'neutraliser', preferably slightly acid.

(v) A stiffer pomade containing petroleum jelly, fatty ester and lanolin to provide the final set and dressing.

It has also been recommended to follow the alkaline treatment. When calcium as in quicklime reacts to form chelate with keratin. This firmly set in the new hair shape. Keratin may then be released from the chelates by means of a complexing agent (EDTA) and a surfactant.

Straightening and colouring consist of alkali at pH 12-13.8, dyestuffs together with shading agents in a vehicle containing cetyl stearyl alcohol, sodium lauryl sulphate and a carboxyl vinylic polymer.

3. *Chemical Hair Reducing Agents* :Hair straightening preparations contain a chemical keratin-reducing agent as the 'relaxer'. It effects the softening and straightening of the hair. The active agents are frequently thioglycollates at a slightly lower concentration.

In hair straightening the hair is free and kept in shape while combing by virtue of the high viscosity of the product. As a result, a cream-like formulation is no longer a disadvantage but becomes highly desirable, so that the majority of the preparations are oil-in-water emulsions, gels or thickened liquids.

This type of straightener is sold in two containers, one holding the 'relaxer', the other the 'neutraliser'.

Relaxer

The relaxer is an ammoniacal thioglycollate at pH 9.0-9.5. Organic bases such as monoethanolamine and an alkali carbonate of an amino acid may partly replace ammonia. Cream products are based on glycerol, glycol stearates, or on cetyl and cetyl stearylic alcohols emulsified in water by polyoxyethylated (usually 20 to 25 ethylene oxide) cetyl or oleyl alcohols. Gels or viscous liquids are obtained by means of carboxyvinyl polymer or copolymers. In formula 3, imidazoline is included with the aim of speeding up straightening.

Formula 3

Constituents *Emulsion base :*	*per cent*
Demineralised water	to 100.0
Cetyl alcohol emulsified by oxyethylated cetyl alcohol	22.0
Demineralised water	30.0
Sodium carbonate glycinate	5.0
Ammonium thioglycollate or thiolactate (50% aqueous soln)	12.0

(Cont'd)

EDTA (disodium salt)	0.3
Sodium p-hydroxybenzoate methyl ester	0.05
Monoethanolamine	2.0
Imidazoline	0.2
Perfume	0.2

Neutraliser

Neutralisers are the usual materials, either sodium perborate or hydrogen peroxide. It is important to remember that hair which has already been damaged during hot combing treatment or by the use of lye straighteners should not be subjected to a thioglycollate straightener after several weeks have elapsed. The thioglycollate cream is applied liberally to the hair, which is then combed rapidly until the hair no longer has a tendency to curl. When the hair is sufficiently straight the cream is rinsed off and the neutraliser is applied to give a permanent set. Care should be taken to ensure complete neutralisation so as to avoid hair damage. Again a cream-like composition is preferentially used to weight down the hair and improve the maintenance of a straightened shape. The formulation is given in formula 4 :

Formula 4

Constituents	*per cent*
Ammonium carbonate	4.5
Sodium bisulphite	2.2
Sodiumlauryl sulphate	4.2
Tallow soap	5.6
Oleic acid	1.0
Water	to make 100.0

The process of straightening is delicate hence require great care to avoid dryness, degradation and breaking of hair.

The addition of natural polymers promotes the setting of the straightened shape. They include soluble proteins, corn or rice starch, fruit galactomannan. More recently, the application of vinyl polymers used for wave sets has been claimed. An oxidation, chemical straightening process by alkaline monopersulphates changes the shape of natural hair.

Chapter - 21

MOUTHWASHES

INTRODUCTiON

For medication of the mouth, gums or teeths the application in any form is referred as mouthwash. These mouthwashes are antibacterial. They are expected to give healthier, fresher mouth and good breath odour.

The use of antibiotics, for example, might destroy normal bacteria and thus permit the growth of undesirable organisms such as *Candida albicans*. It is possible to reduce and maintain the bacterial population due to adsorption of antibacterials. The Buccal Ephitheliast test of *Vinson* and Bennet can serve as a standard technique. The total effect exerted is a combination of three factors : (1) the mechanical effect of rinsing food debris from the mouth; (2) the effect of the antibacterial agent on the oral flora; and (3) the effect of the flavour present. Since many flavouring substances have an antibacterial effect, there may be synergism between (2) and (3).

Mouthwashes used for general oral hygiene should nevertheless be rigorously tested for nontoxic and irritant properties. Prophylactic and therapeutic claims would require even more stringent clinical tests.

Choice of Antibacterial Agent

The antibacterial agents usually employed in mouthwashes include phenols, thymol, salol, tannic acid, chlorinated thymols, hexachlorophene and quaternary ammonium compounds.

Chlorinated Phenols

Parachlormetacresol and *parachlormetaxylenol* are both suitable for use in mouthwashes due to their antibacterial properties and their flavour. They are not very soluble in water but may be solubilised with terpineol (or other suitable solubiliser) and soap to give a 1 per cent solution of active material. Such solutions, for example liquid chloroxylenol, are used at 10-20 per cent dilution.

Soap-Based Mouthwashes

For cleaning and freshening mouth soap based mouthwashes without antibacterial properties used is given in formula 1.

Formula 1

Constituents	*per cent*
Powdered soap	2.0
Glycerine	15.0
Alcohol	20.0
Water	63.0
Flavour	q.s.

Non-irritant synthetic detergents for extra foaming standard antibacterials may be added above basic formula.

Thymol (Isopropyl Metacresol)

Thymol is soluble in suitable alcohols. An aqueous solution with borax is diluted to between 5 and 20 per cent concentration (Formula 2)

Formula 2

Constituents	*per cent*
Thymol	0.03
Alcohol	3.00
Borax	2.00
Sodium bicarbonate	1.00
Glycerine	10.00
Flavour	q.s.
Water	to 100.00

Hydrogen Peroxide

Hydrogen peroxide is an excellent non-toxic antibacterial agent for use in mouthwashes. It can be used for cleansing ulcers and abscesses in the mouth, etc. A solution of one part hydrogen peroxide (10 vol.) diluted with 8 parts of water is useful as a mouthwash, or twice the strength can be used for septic cavities. Because of its instability it is not normally used in proprietary mouthwashes.

The dissolution of sodium perborate water gives an alkaline solution of hydrogen peroxide. Dissolve 17 g of sodium perborate and 6 g of citric acid in 80 ml of water which gives 10 volume strength. It is further diluted to 1 : 8 for use. Such products should be used only sparingly and to combat specific conditions, since the citrate present could lead to decalcification of the teeth.

Hexachlorophene

Hexachlorophene is substantive to the mucous membrane and is an effective antibacterial agent. The suggested concentration is 0.02 per cent in a 25 per cent alcohol-water mix.

Quaternaries

The use of quaternaries is now well established in mouthwashes. These compounds combine antibacterial and substantive properties. Many of them are non-toxic and non-irritant at the concentrations normally used. They are effective against plaque e.g. Benzethonium chloride. Probably the most effective antibacterials are of the chlorohexidine type. Unfortunately chlorohexidine, in common with most cationics, can produce a brown stain on teeth with continued use which is easily removed with good toothbrushing. A product of this type has been presented in the form of a gel, which, though intended for brushing onto the teeth, is really a mouthwash rather than a toothpaste since it contains no abrasive.

Other Mouthwash Components

Tannic acid, alum and zinc salts are used in mouthwashes because of their astringent properties. Which have antibleeding effects on the gums. A dilute solution of sodium hypochlorite is also used.

Flavouring of Mouthwashes

To generate freshness of the mouth after use flavour is used in mouthwash. Peppermint, menthol, eugenol, etc. are used flavours. Chlorinated phenols always have a characteristic flavour which, though not unpleasant, is difficult to cover. Cationics normally are slightly bitter and must be covered. For selecting unique flavour small manufacturers can use services of flavour house.

Aerosol Mouth Fresheners

Aerosol mouth fresheners are recommended for freshenign the breath after eating, drinking or smoking. They contain only flavouring agents, though antibacterials could be added. Aerosol mouth fresheners are an alternative to chewing gum than as mouthwashes.

Chapter - 22

HERBAL COSMETICS

HEALING WITH HERBS

Beauty and health are, two sides of the same coin. If nature has the qualities of a cosmetologist, its therapeutic treasure is equally vast and abundant. Unfortunately, till recently, ayurveda was never considered a mainstream method of healing. The reason, of course, is that the emphasis has been more on symptomatic healing than curing the disease from its roots.

A time when herbal cosmetics are taking over the cosmetic market, it seems that herbal medicines still have to make a noticeable impact. And that can happen only if you are prepared to see the same doctor again when he prescribes Dashmolarishta intead of Vitamin C for you.

HERBAL OR PLANT MATERIALS

Some of the herbal ingredients which are being commonly used in cosmetics are given below.

Almond

Fixed oil obtained form almonds is emollient in nature. It has extensive applications in cosmetics. A white milk used in cleansers and astringents is obtained by soaking ground almonds in milk or water and then by milling. Ground almonds are used in facial and body scrubs.

Apricot

Apricots contain highly nourishing oil and rich in vitamin A. It is believed to improve condition and elasticity of skin. The pulp of both fresh and dry fruit is used in face masks. Finely ground shell and kernel of the stone is used in facial and body scrubs.

Avocado

Oil of Avocado is rich in vitamin A. Its uses are similar to apricot oil.

Azadirachta (Neem)

Neem leaves are antiseptic. Neem fruits yield an oil called neem oil. Nimbidin is the chief bitter principle of Neem oil. Neem oil is used in soaps. Extract of leaves can be used in toothpastes and skin care products.

Cabbage

Cabbage is chiefly valuable for its high mineral and vitamin contents. It has wonderful cleansing and reducing properties. Its juice can used in skin care products.

Camomile

Camomile flower contains a dye hence used with henna in herbal hair dye. Infusion of flowers can also be used for astringency in cleansers, conditioners and hair rinses.

Carrots

Carrots are rich source of vitamin A. These are good for irritated or sunburnt skin. The raw grated vegetables and juice make excellent cleanser. Carrot juice can be used in masks and tonics.

Comfrey

Decoction of root and infusion of comfrey leaves have antiseptic and healing properties. These can be used in creams and lotions.

Common Basil (Tulsi)

Flowers and leaves of tulsi yield an essential oil which is considered antiseptic. Juice of its leaves can be used in skin creams and lotions.

Cornflower

Infusion of flowers can be used in skin tonics and freshners.

Cucumber

Cucumber juice is used in cosmetics. Cucumber juice is soothing healing and slightly astringent. It can be used in masks, cleansers and toners

Dandelion

Infusion of dandelion flowers can be used in masks, cleansers. Sap from the stem can be used in bleaching creams.

E. Alba (Bhringaraja)

It is a source of black stain and is used in hair preparations.

Elderflower

Infusion of flowers are mildly bleaching and therefore can be used in skin cleansers, conditioners and creams. Decoction of leaves of elderflower is healing and can be used for sun-burnt or wind-burnt skin.

Eucalyptus

Decoction of leaves of eucalyptus is antiseptic and invigorating. Decoction can be used in skin care products.

Fennel

Infusion of chopped leaves is soothing and stimulating. Infusion can be used in masks, cleansers and toners.

Funegreek

Funegreek (Methi) is a traditional, component of hair care products. It is used for its Cleansing and softening activity. It promoters scape health. It can be used in hair care, skin care products.

Garlic

Garlic juice is considered antiseptic. Its juice can be used in antiseptic and smoothing creams.

Geranium

Geranium yields an essential oil which is used in perfumery. Geranium leaves and flowers can be used for healing or rejuvenating. Alternatively, geranium oil can be added in healing and cleansing creams.

Henna

Henna leaves contain a dye. Henna leaves are used in herbal hair dyes. Henna can be used with camomile flowers for dyeing the hair. Leaves and flowers yield an essential oil.

Indian Gooseberry (Amla)

Fruits, bark and leaves of India Gooseberry are rich in tannins. Fruits are used in herbal hair dyes, particularly with henna. Dried fruits are also used for washing the hair.

Indian Nard (Jatamansi)

Indian nard yields an oil, called spikenard oil. Oil is considered to improve hair growth and is also believed to darken hair. Spikenard oil can be used in hair preparations.

Jasmine

Flowers of jasmine yield an essential oil, called jasmine oil. Jasmine oil is used in traditional hair oils.

Lady's Mantle

Juice of leaves of lady's mantle has healing and mild bleaching properties. Its juice can be added to tonics for oily skin or to the creams for dry skin.

Lavender

Flowers and leaves of lavender yield an essential oil called lavender oil. Infusion of leaves and flower is considered antiseptic. Infusion can be used in skin creams and toners.

Lemon

Peel of lemon yields an essential oil which is used in perfumery and soaps. Infusion of leaves of lemon has soothing and mild astringent properties which can be used in skin tonics and cleansers.

Lime

Infusion of flowers and young leaves can be used in healing and moisturising creams and lotions.

Marigold

sInfusion and decoction of flowers and leaves can be used in skin creams and lotions. These can also be used for hair lightening rinses.

Marsh Mallow

Infusion of flower of marsh mallow and decoction of its roots have antiseptic properties. These can be used in skin creams and cleansers.

Nutmeg

Nutmeg butter or fat obtained from nutmegs is used as external stimulant in hair lotions. Nutmeg oil is also used in spicy perfumes in soaps.

Orange Blossom

Its essential oil is soothing and can be used in creams to soothe dry skin.

Parsley

Crushed leaves or juice of parsley can be used in poultices. Juice or infusion of leaves can be used in skin creams, lotions or cleansers. Also has antidandruff and deodorising properties. It can therefore be used in hair preparations also.

Peach

The pulp of fresh peach is used in face masks, cleansers and moisturisers. Peach nut oil is fragrant and rich and is used in nourishing cream.

Rose

Rose petals yield an essential oil, called rose oil. Infusion of petals can be used in skin toners, cleansers moisturisers and colognes.

Rosemary

Flowers and leaves of rosemary have antiseptic and anti-dandruff properties. Infusions of flowers and leaves can be used in skin cream and lotions. Herbal oil made from leaves can be used for the hair.

Safflower

Flower heads are a source of red and yellow dye called safflower. This dye is used in rouges.

Sage

Infusion of flowers and leaves of sage is healing and mild stringent. The intrusion can be used in skin tonics and cleansers.

Sandal

Sandalwood oil is extracted from heart-wood of sandal tree. Sandalwood oil is used in perfumes.

S. Racemosa (Lodhra)

Decoction of lodhra is used to prevent bleeding of gums.

Thyme

Leaves of thyme make astringent infusion. Leaves also make strongly perfumed herbal hair oil. Thyme also has deodorising anti-dandruff properties.

Turmeric

Turmeric has been long used in poultices and scrubs in India. Its water extract has antiseptic properties. It can be used in skin creams.

Wheatgerm

It is rich in vitamins and minerals. It is extremely beneficial in face masks and body scrubs. Wheatgerm oil is rich in vitamin E which is considered good for skin.

Witch Hazel

Steam distillate of bark is astringent and antiseptic and can be used in skin creams, lotions and toners.

HOW TO USE HERBS

In earlier times, herbs were used for both medicinal purposes as well as for beautification. They have been used in fresh form and dried form. These can be used by mashing and directly applying to the body with or without using other ingredients. In fact, in earlier times these were used this way. But now-a-days, their extracts, decoctions, infusions, tinctures, steam distillates etc., are used rather than herbs themselves. Whenever these are prepared, preservatives should be added to them as these are perishable.

Infusions

Infusions are basically strong teas of herb(s) and can be prepared either in china clay pots or stainless steel vessels. Aluminium vessels should not be used as these can taint the infusions. The process of preparation is as follows :

Pour freshly boiled water in the vessel containing herb (coarse powder). Cover and leave for at least three hours. Strain and filter. The quantity of herb and solvent (water) may vary depending on whether herb is fresh or dried. Usually, for 100 gm of fresh herb or 50 gm of dried herb 575 ml of water can be used.

Decoctions

Decoctions are prepared by boiling the herb with water. The following is the process :

Place the herb (coarse powder) in stainless steel or enamel pan, add sufficient water and cover the pan. Gently boil and continue boiling on gentle heat till the water is reduced to one quarter. This may require boiling for about 2-3 hours. Strain and filter. The same proportions of herb and water can be used as recommended in case of infusions.

Extracts and Tinctures

Extracts are generally prepared with hydro-alcoholic solvents and tinctures are prepared with either alcohol or hydro-alcoholic solvent with high percentage of alcohol. The following method can be used for preparing extracts and tinctures :

Place in a macerator crushed herbs or flowers. Add alcohol or alcohol-water mixture to cover the herb. Close the macerator tightly with lid and leave overnight. Add more solvent and further macerate for 2-3 days. Sometimes maceration may be as long as a week. Strain the mixture firmly with a strainer and filter the extract/tincture. Depending upon the constituents this extract/tincture could be used or it could be used as solvent for maceration of fresh herb. The recommended proportions are 100 gm of fresh herb or flowers and 575 ml. Extracts/tinctures should be stored in tightly closed containers.

Flower Waters

Flower waters are made in the same way as infusions. The same proportions of herbs and water can be used. However, the difference in infusion and flower waters is that solvent is allowed to remain in contact with flowers overnight in case of flower waters. Flower waters can also be prepared by using flower essence (essential oil) and purified water.

Oil Soluble Extracts

Oil soluble extracts are prepared by extracting herbs with petroleum ether. The herb (coarse powder) is left in contact with water overnight. More water is added next day. This herb-water mixture is placed with oil in a vessel and the vessel is heated till all the water has been removed. The oil is allowed to cool and is then filtered. In this way oil soluble principle of herb go into oil.

Some herbal extracts are available commercially. Balsara Herbal Products (Pvt.) Ltd. are making herbal extracts under the trade name Folicon. Some of the extracts are oil extracts and some are aqueous-glycol extracts. A list of these extract and the products in which these can be used is given below in table 41.1.

Table 41.1.

Folicon Herbal Extracts (Cosmetic grade)

Application	*Type*	*Code*	
AMLA	Aqueoust extract	C 3101	Hair Care
AMLA	Oil extract	C 3101	Hair Care
ALOE	Aqueoust extract	C 3102	Skin & Hair Care
BHRINGRAJ/MAKA	Aqueoust extract	C 3103	Hair Care
BHRINGRAJ/MAKA	Oil Extract	C 3103	Hair Care
BRAHMI	Aqueoust extract	C 3104	Hair Care

(Cont'd)

BRAHMI	Oil extract	C 3104	Hair Care
HENNA/MEHENDI	Aqueoust extract	C 3105	Hair Care
HALDI/TURMERIC	Aqueoust extract	C 3106	Hair Care
HIBISCUS	Aqueoust extract	C 3107	Skin & Hair Care
KHUS	Aqueoust extract	C 3108	Skin & Hair Care
LEMON PEEL	Aqueoust extract	C 3109	Skin & Hair Care
METHI/FENUGREEK	Aqueoust extract	C 3110	Skin & Hair Care
NEEM	Aqueoust extract	C 3111	Skin & Hair Care
ROSE PETAL	Aqueoust extract	C 3112	Skin & Hair Care
SHIKAKAI	Aqueoust extract	C 3113	Hair Care
SANDALWOOD	Aqueoust extract	C 3114	Hair Care
TULSI	Aqueoust extract	C 3115	Hair Care

Recommended concentration in different preparations are shown in table 41.2

Table 41.2.

Folicon herbalextracts cosmetic products guidelines (use levels).

FOLICON Hair oil Herbal Extracts	*Anti Perspi- -rants*	*Cleansers, Freshners, and masks*		*Lotions, Creams*	*Hair Condi- tioners*	*Medicated shampoo sun-cream*	*Creams*
	%	%	%	%	%	%	%
Amla	-	5-10	5-10	5-10	-	1.5	-
5-10							
Aloe	5-10	5-10	5-10	5-10	10-15	1-5	-
Bhringraj/Maka	-	-	-	-	-	-	-
5-10							
Brahmi 5-10	-	-	-	-	10-15	1-5	-
Henna/Mehendi	-	-	-	5-10	-	1-5	-
Haldi/Turmeric	-	5-10	-	-	5-10	-	-
Hibiscus	-	-	-	-	-	1-5	-
Khus	5-10	1-5	-	-	-	-	1-5
Lemon peel	1-5	-	1-5	-	1-5	-	-
Methi/Fenugreek	-	-	-	1-5	-	1-5	-
Neem	5-10	-	-	-	5-10	-	-
Rose petal	-	1-5	-	-	-	-	-

(Cont'd)

Shikakai	-	-	-	5-10	-	-	-
Sandalwood	5	-	1-5	-	-	-	10
Tulsi	1-5	-	-	-	5-10	-	5

HERBAL COSMETICS FOR THE SKIN

Creams and emulsions are all basically mixtures of water, oils, waxes and fragrances perfumery products in varying proportions. A slight change in the quantities in the preparations changes the character of the preparation and one should be careful when measuring the ingredients. When measuring the following rough equivalents should be kept in mind while formulating the product.

1 Teaspoon + 60 drops = 5 ml.

3 Teaspoon = 1 Tablespoon = 15 ml.

2 Tablespoons =1/8 cup = 10 ml.

4 Tablespoons = 1/4 cup = 20 ml.

8 Tablespoons = 1/2 cup = 40 ml.

16 Tablespoons = 1 cup = 80 ml.

15 4 grains = gm.

28 3 gms = 1 oz.

16 oz = 1 lb. = 454 gms.

1 kg. = 2.202 lbs.

Equipment Used for Herbal Preparations

(i) Enamel or pyrex bowls; (ii) One large frying pan; (iii) Measuring spoons; (iv) Measuring cups; (v) Electric heater or manual heater; (vi) A good strong sieve; (vii) A pipette or eye dropper; (viii) A wool of tissue paper for wiping jars, spoons, hands etc; (ix) Jars and Bottles and (x) Printed/plain labels.

Cleansing Creams

Cleansing creams are used to lift the dust. Also to remove stale make up. Soap can not remove waxy base of make-up thus, cleansing cream is used. The cleanser is generally applied with an upward movement and kept on the skin for about half a minute os as to dissolve the make up. Then it is removed with a tissue or damp cotton wool. The dirt and grime not only dogs the pores of the skin causing block heads but also coarsens the skin. A few formulations of cleansing creams are given below :

Formulation

Beeswax	1/2 Tablespoon
Emulsifying Wax (Petroleum)	1 Tablespoon
Baby oil	4 Tablespoons
Coconut oil	2 Tablespoons
Water	2 Tablespoons
Borax	1/4 Teaspoon
Witch Hazel	1 Tablespoon
Perfume	3-5 drops

Note : Witch hazel is made from twigs of hamamelis or alderbush.

Process of Manufacture

Melt the mixture of waxes and oil by transfering from enamel bowl to pan of boiling water. Prepare solution of borax in water in another bowl, add witch-hazel and heat it to dissolve. Mix solutions of both bowl in water with stirring cool to form, add perfume. It begins to thicken as it cools and beatens.

Rose Water Cleansing Cream

Formulation

Beeswax or white Paraffin Wax	1 1/2 Tablespoons
Emulsifying Wax (Petrolatum)	1 Tablespoon
Mineral oil	4 Tablespoons
Rose water	6 Tablespoons
Borax	1/2 Teaspoon
Perfume	3-5 drops

Cucumber Cleansing Cream

Formulation

Beeswax	3 Teaspoon
Coconut Oil	4 Teaspoons
Mineral oil or Olive oil	4 Teaspoons
Cucumber Juice	4 Tablespoons
Glycerine	1 Teaspoon
Borax	1 Pinch
Green Colouring	1 Drop

Violet Cleansing Cream

Formulation

Lanolin	1/2 Tablespoon
Petroleum Jelly	1 Tablespoon
Mineral oil	4 Tablespoons
Water	10 Tablespoons
Violet extract	5 drops

Masks

Masks have been used for beauty treatment of the face. They are applied and kept on the face, left on the same for ten to twenty minutes and then washed off. They have nourishing, healing, cleansing and an astringent effect. These masks whip up the circulation and temporarily iron out wrinkles. They freshen the skin and leave it glowing. A few formulations of simple home made face masks are given as under :

Milk Mask

This is one of the cheapest and simplest masks. Cotton wool is soaked in milk and rubbed on the face and left to dry for 10-15 minutes and then the face is washed.

Cleansing Mask

Formulation

Powdered Brewers yeast	1 Table spoon
Yogurt	1/2 Table spoon
Lemon Juice	1 Tea spoon
Orange Juice	1 Tea spoon
Carrot Juice	1 Tea spoon
Olive Oil	1 Tea spoon

Procedure

Make a paste by mixing above ingredients, then apply and keep on face for 15 mins. If the skin is very dry more oil is added and discarded if the skin is oily. The brewer's yeast stimulates the flow of blood to the skin and gives the complexion a healthy glow. The yogurt cleanses the skin and the fruit juices provide vitamins and minerals.

Butter Milk Mask

A cup of butter milk is heated and three tablespoons of elderflower blossoms are put into it. The mixture is simmered on a very low heat for about 30 mins. And then allowed to cool. It helps in bleaching and cleansing large pores.

Meal Mask

A paste of barley meal, pea flower and rose water is applied and left on the skin for several hours to make the skin soft and supple. One tablespoon each of finely ground oatmeal and milk along with a few drops of almond oil are allowed to form paste. The paste is applied and left on the skin for 15 mins. And then rinsed off.

Carrot and Turnip Mask

A paste is prepared by boiling carrot and turnip. It is applied for 10-15 minutes and then rinsed off with milk. This make leaves the skin feeling fresh and clean.

Oatmeal Mask

Formulation of Oatmeal mask is given below :

Dried orange peel	2 Tablespoons
Oatmeal	2 Teaspoons
Cold cream	2 Tablespoons

The above ingredients are mixed into a paste and then applied generously all over the face and neck. After 10 to 15 minutes when it is dry the same is rubbed off using an upward circular motion. This leaves the skin smooth and shining.

Potato Mask

Formulation of potato mask is given below :

Potato juice	1 Tablespoon
Fuller's earth	1 Tablespoon

The above ingredients are mixed to form a paste and applied on the face. Potatoes contain Vit-C and clear the skin of blemishes. Fuller's earth absorbs all the dirt and grease from the skin.

Paw Paw Mask

This is also known as Papaya Mask. Two tablespoons of ripe papaya flesh can be used as mask. Face is washed with water after applying mask.

Luxurious Cleansing Mask

Three strawberries are mashed into a paste and applied as a mask and then left on for 10 minutes and then washed off with rose water. Strawberries have slightly acidic properties and contain vitamin C, which cleanses the skin leaving it sparkingly clean. Another luxurious formulation consists of mashing and sieving the flesh of half a peach and then mixing it with a tablespoon of brandy.

Bath Salts

Two cups of ordinary washing soda are taken and two tablespoons of potassium carbonate is added to the same. A drop of an aromatic essential oil such as lavender or pine are added to the mixture and the mixture homogenised.

Bath Oils

Bath oil can be prepared by adding any vegetable oil such as almond, olive or sunflower to the bath water. Baby oil or mineral oil is not suitable as it cannot be absorbed by the skin and only remains on the skin surface. These basic oils can also be mixed with some of the herb oils or aromatic oil.

Bath Oil

Formulation

Eggs	2 Nos.
Almond Oil	1/4 Cup
Sunflower oil or Corn oil	1/4 Cup
Safflower oil or Olive oil	1/2 Cup
Honey	1 Teaspoon
Washing Detergent	2 Teaspoons
Vodka	1/4 Cup
Milk	1/4 Cups
Perfume	3-5 drops.

Procedure

The thick emulsified mixture is prepared by adding eggs, honey, oil and detergent. Continue beating with addition of Vodka slowly, also add milk and perfume.

Massage Preparations

This is a special recipe for brides to be used daily at the time of bath for ten days before marriage. The following ingredients are mixed to a paste and rubbed vigorously. They cleanse and stimulate the skin leaving it soft, supple and shiny.

Formulation

Dried, ground and sieved orange peel	1 Tablespoon
Dried, ground and sieved lemon peel	1 Tablespoon
Ground Almond	2 Tablespoons
Salt	1 pinch
Ground Thyme	1 Tablespoon
Ground all spice	1 pinch
Almond Oil	Sufficient to make a paste
Jasmine Oil (Perfume)	3-5 drops

Massage Paste

This consists of wheat flour or oatmeal mixed into a paste with double cream. The paste has a deep cleansing effect on the skin and removes dead cells and dirt.

Massage Oil

The oils are heated and then the heated water is slowly added along with a tablespoon of winter green or camphor oil to make a really invigorating massage cream.

Formulations

Almond Oil	1/2 Cup
Castor Oil	1/2 Cup
Camphor Oil	1 Teaspoon

Body Lotions

Mix three tablespoons of rose water, one tablespoon of glycerine and two tablespoons lime juice. This mixture is used after the bath if you suffer from dry skin. The proportion of this lotions is to suit this type of skin. The lotion no longer feels sticky and mixed into the skin easily. It has to be stored in a refrigerator.

Blue Ratin Body Lotion

Formulation

Soap flakes	3 Tablespoons
Glycerine	1 Teaspoon
Witch Hazel	1 Teaspoon
Olive Oil	4 Teaspoons
Water	5 Teaspoons
Blue Colouring	3-5 drops
Perfume	3-5 drops

Procedure

First soap flakes are dissolved in water with heating in a saucepan. Add glycerine, olive oil and witch hazel. Continue stirring until it cools, add blue colour and perfume. A lovely thin creamy blue mixture thus made is an ideal non-greasy, after-bath lotion which leaves the skin glowing like satin.

Lavender Body Lotion

Dissolve 1 teaspoon of borax in 1 cup of rose water and then add 2 tablespoons warmed olive oil with continuous beating. When all the oil has been added to the water and an emulsion has been formed the lavender water is added. The lavender water is made by infusing a handful of lavender flowers in 2 cups of boiling water. The above mixture is allowed to stand for an hour and then strained for use.

Almond body Lotion

The formulation of almond body lotion is given below :

Formulation

Lanolin	3 Teaspoons
Almond Oil	1 Teaspoon
Petroleum Jelly	1 Teaspoon
Vegetable Lard	1 Teaspoon
Glycerine	2 Teaspoons
Water	10 Tablespoons
Soap Flakes	1 Teaspoon
Cornflower	1 Teaspoon
Perfume or Almond Essence	*q.s.*

Moisturising Creams

Almond Oil Moisturising Cream

Melt two and one teaspoon of beeswax and emulsifying wax heating with water in a bowl and add five teaspoon almond oil. Now add hot water in melted mixture with stirring. Stop heating after sometime, cool and add lavender oil.

Herb Cream (Comfrey Cream)

A lanolin, white emulsifying wax and beeswax (1, 2 and 6 tablespoon) is melted. Add herb lotion or almond oil or infusion (6 tablespoon). This mixture is comfrey cream. Comfrey is a healing herb which is ideal for the sensitive skin or for skin having irritations or spots. A handful of comfrey is taken, liquidised and then strained. The comfrey residue need not be thrown away. A teaspoon honey may be added to tablespoon of this residue to form a paste and this can be used as a face mask.

Avocado Almond Cream

The formulation of avocado almond cream is given below :

Beeswax	3 Teaspoons
Emulsifying Wax (Petroleum Wax)	3 Teaspoons
Almond Oil	1/2 Cup
Avocado Oil	1/4 Cup
Rose Water	3 Tablespoons

Sun flower Cream

The process to prepare sunflower cream is as follows. The waxes, oil and lanolin are heated over a water bath till they melt. The water, glycerine and borax are heated separately till the borax gets completely dissolved. While the melted oils and waxes are still on the heat, the water is added drop-by-drop with continuous beating with a wooden spoon till a whitish thick and creamy textured rich cream is formed. This is a good moisturising cream leaving the skin looking soft and moist.

Jasmine Moisturising Cream

The composition of jasmine moisturising cream is given below :

Emulsifying Wax (Petroleum)	2 Tablespoons
Almond or Sunflower Oil	2 Tablespoons
Lanolin	1 Teaspoon

(Cont'd)

Borax	1/2 Teaspoon
Witch Hazel	1 Teaspoon
Glycerine	1 1/2 Teaspoons
Water	8 Tablespoons
Jasmine Oil	3-5 drops

Nourishing Creams

Preparations of this type include all skin nutrients whether they are oil based or of the moisturising type. They may be light and immediately absorbed or heavy and sticky requiring to be managed into the skin. The nourishing creams comprise of Hormone creams and lotions, vitamin products, screen ampoules, antiwrinkle creams and lotions, and biologically active preparations. A few formulations of nourishing creams are given as under :

Cocoa Butter	2 Table spoons
Emulsifying Wax (Petroleum Wax)	2 Table spoons
Beeswax	1 Table spoons
Sesame Oil	4 Table spoons
Almond Oil	1 Table spoons

Elderflower Cream

The process to prepare elderflower cream include mixing of almond oil, elder flower blossoms and lanoline (3, 4 and 1 tablespoon) in a bowl over a water bath and allowed to simmer together for an hour. It is then strained and then warm water is added slowly with constant stirring.

Wheat Germ Cream

The composition of wheat germ cream is given below :

Beeswax	1 Teaspoon
Emulsifying Wax (Petrolatum)	1 Teaspoon
Lanolin	5 Table spoons
Sesame Oil	3 Table spoons
Wheat Germ Oil	2 Tablespoons
Water	5 Table spoons
Witch Hazel	1 Tablespoon
Borax	½ Teaspoon
Perfume	3-5 drops

Honey Cream

Honey is a very useful ingredient creams used for dry, coarse and sensitive skin. For a nourishing cream for sallow skin melt lanolin, honey, lectithin (3, 0.5, 1, tablespoon) in a bowl with heating. Add slowly warm water (4 tablespoons) with beating and cool it.

Vitamin Cream

The composition of vitamin cream is given below :

Beeswax	1 Tablespoon
Emulsifying Wax	1 Tablespoon
Lanolin	1 Tablespoon
Wheat Germ Oil (or vitamin - E Capsules 2 No)	3 Tablespoons
Carrot Oil (or Vit-A Capsules -2 Nos)	3 Tablespoons
Borax	½ Teaspoons
Distilled Water	6 Tablespoons
Tincture of Benzoin	2 drops
Orange Flower Oil	3-5 drops

Mixed Vegetable Cream

Beeswax	2 Tablespoons
Emulsifying Wax (Petrolatum)	4 Tablespoons
Lanolin	3 Teaspoons
Almond Oil	4 Tablespoons
Sesame Oil	4 Tablespoons
Avocado Oil	2 Tablespoons
Safflower Oil	2 Tablespoons
Sun flower Oil	2 Tablespoons
Water	5 Tablespoons
Borax	½ Teaspoon
Amber Oil	3-5 drops

Water-in-Oil Emulsions

These are grooming preparations hence more popular. The emulsifiers like polyvalent soaps, bees wax and borax haven been used. The other emulsifiers for the water-in-oil emulsions which are used are calcium oleate, calcium stearate, zinc stearate, aluminium stearate. The composition of hair grooming preparation is given below, 1 to 5.

No. 1	*per cent*
Mineral oil	65.55
Beeswax white	2.5
Water	34.8
Borax	0.15
Perfume	q.s.

Formulations (Emulsified Hair Grooming Preparation)

	per cent			
Ingredients	*2*	*3*	*4*	*5*
Oleic acid	12	20	1.0	-
Beeswax	2	1	1.5	2.5
Mineral Oil	45	-	41.7	48
Lanolin	2	0.5	-	-
Lime Water	19	33.5	53.8	-
Saccharated lime water	20	5	-	-
Olive Oil	-	40	-	-
Magnesium sulphate(25%)	-	-	2.0	-
Stearic acid	-	-	-	1.5
Absorption base	-	-	-	5.0
Petrolatum	-	-	-	12.5
Magnesium oleate	-	-	-	2.5
Water	-	-	-	28
Perfume and Preservative	q.s.	q.s.	q.s.	q.s.

HERBAL COSMETICS FOR THE HAIR

The cosmetics having ayurvedic base with some medicinal compound yielding desired properties are implied as herbal cosmetics. The preparations like herbal hair oil, herbal shampoos are best examples. Hair Care products and cures comprising of herbal Hair Rinses, Hair tonics, Shampoos, Henna powders, are designed to restore beauty and health to the hair. They contain extracts known for their qualities of stimulating hair growth, improving hair texture and colour. The range of Market Products are :

Herbal Hair Conditioners

This is a powerful combination of invaluable herbal ingredients like Amla, sandalwood, Brahmi, Lichens and other precious herbs. It makes the hair strong, healthy and lustrous. Prevents hair loss and acts as a scalp deep cleanser while maintaining the natural moisture balance. It provides body to dull lifeless hair.

Herbal Hair Oil

This is an effective combination of Arnica, Henna, Shikakai and other herbal extracts, especially created to prevent hair loss and promote luxurious hair growth.

Herbal Henna

The preparation of herbal henna include combination of pure henna leaves and various herbal ingredients. They make the hair lustrous, manageable and silky. It also works as a powerful treatment for scalp disorders and gives a mild natural colour and sheen to the hair.

Herbal Hair Tonic

This preparation is for controlling hair loss/dandruff/greying hair. It stimulates hair growth and thickness. It is a specialised tonic treatment for revitalising the hair and generating a natural lustroics glow. It serves well for texturising rough brittle hair and split ends.

Herbal Henna Shampoo (for normal to oily hair)

This preparation is to cleanse the scalp and controls excessive secretion of scalp oils and imparts sheen to dull hair making it tangle free.

Herbal Amla Shampoo (for normal to dry hair)

This preparation is made from extracts of Amla, Dater and Arnica and Other rare herbs. This shampoo makes the hair lustrous, healthier and manageable and cleanses the scalp while retaining and stimulating its natural oil.

Hair Treatment Cream

This preparation is an effective, medicated antiseptic ointment for the treatment of dandruff scalp disorders, seborrhoea and sealy skin conditions and is used for the treatment of dandruff and falling hair.

Herbal Mint/Hair Gloss conditioner

It is used as a hair sheen and can be used just before shampoo for providing texture and conditioning to the hair.

Herbal Hair Rinse

This is a combination of mint, brahmi and other herbal extracts and is an effective control for dandruff and scalp disorders and promoters hair growth.

Herbal Hair Oils (Medicated)

Medicated herbal oils are also used as scenting material for the hair. The base oil may be a mineral oil such as coconut oil, groundnut oil, castor oil, neem oil etc. To make an oil ayurvedic or a herbal product certain essential oils are added which provide certain specific characteristics of the individual used in the formulation

Base Formulation For Herbal hair Oil

Til Oil	91 ml
Mollha Kankola	0.3 ml
whees Charrila	0.3 ml
Sailag Nagar	0.03 ml
Chander	0.04 ml
Long Dalchini	0.03 ml
Ratanjot	0.02 ml
Kapur Kachuri	0.05 ml
Satabar	0.02 ml
Tejpal	0.03 gms
Howber	0.03 gms
Balhere	0.06 gms
Amla	0.06 gms
Harral	0.03 gms
Chanpa	0.03 gms
Keora (keya)	0.06 gms
Gulabphul	0.03 gms
Alaichi (Big)	0.02 gms
Pudhina	0.4 gms
Perfume	0.3-15 gms
Quatah water	1.5 kg
Menthol	0.2

There is no unique formulations for herbal hair oil. The formulations of the manufacturers are trade secrets. However, the above formulation can be taken as a standard base and it can be changed according to requirements.

Herbal Shampoos

These products are more suitable in hard-water areas. *Quillaja saponania* is one of a whole class of Saponias widely distributed in nature. Commercially saponin is extracted with water and alcohol from the *Quillaja* bark or from the soap root. Preparations of saponin are generally intended to cleanse the scalp and to reduce scaliness. These are generally compounded with rosemary or celandine and in addition to its use in shampoos saponin has found some use in bubble baths. Some formulations for Herbal Shampoos are given as under :

	Ingredients	*per cent*
(i)	Quilaja bark, powdered	5.0
	Ammonium carbonate	1.0
	Borax	1.0
	Bay leaf oil	0.1
	Water	92.9
(ii)	Sodium carbonate anhydrous	19.4
	Powdered soap	79.0
	Saponin	1.6
	Perfume	q.s.
(iii)	Borax	20.0
	Sodium, sesquicarbonate	40.0
	Powdered soap	35.0
	Saponin	5.0
	Perfume	q.s.

Hair Dye

Henna is the only important vegetable dye. The presence of 2- hydroxy-1, 4-naphthaquinone gives henna a dyeing properties. It consists of the dried powdered leaves of Lawsonia alba, Lawsonia spinosa and Lawsonia inemis, which are removed from the plants prior to flowering. It is soluble in hot water and is, in acid solution, a substantive dye for Keratine. The powdered henna is mixed with hot water. Citric or adipic or other suitable acid is added to adjust pH 5-8. Then hair is dyed using this paste and kept for five to sixty minutes, then shampooed, rinsed and dried. The "Henna Pack" is kept in place by means of a towel and is allowed to remain on the head for the required time varying from five to sixty minutes after which the hair is thoroughly shampooed, rinsed and dried

Henna

The henna plant is shrub, *Lawsonia alba lans* of bears small, fragrant, greenish-white flowers, but as the only plant utilised for dye are the leaves and stems, the plants are frequently at back. For infusions, used as raises the leaves are usually left whole, but is the more common commercial form of henna, the leaves and stems are ground to a powder, about the colour of dark unstand and with characteristic earthy odour.

The principal advantage offered by henna as a modern hair dye is that it is harmless to the system and causes no irritations on the skin. A few applications impart a slight amount of colour to the entire hair shift and depending on the original colour of the hair, a whole range of reddish pure vegetable shades - tomato, beet, egg plant - can be produced. If it is plied often enough, therefore, hair of any and all original shades can be brought to the same characteristics orangered.

Applications of Henna

Despite the intense dark red shade of solutions of henna, the active dyeing principle, is only about 1% of it. This dye is used mostly in beauty shops, as a rinse or as a pack.

Henna Rinse

For slight change of colour, bring out highlights on dark hair, henna levels are steeped in boiling water until all the dye is extracted. This solution is then poured several times over freshly shampooed hair. Commercial preparations of a henna rinse should be acidified with 1 to 2% of some mild organic acid viz adipic acid, citric acid, tartaric.

Henna Pack

For a more decided, or more lasting, change in shade, powdered henna leaves are made into a paste with boiling water. This is applied to all the hair, which is allowed to remain covered and undisturbed until test on a single strand shows that the desired shade has been attained. The subsequnet treatment, the colour can be kept uniform by applying the paste to only the new growth of hair.

To prepare henna powder, the fresh leaves are ground extremely fine. Fresh powder is dark brownish-green, as it ages bearing yellowish red. It is usually packed in waxed paper in cans or boxes that can be tightly sealed.

Henna Mixtures

To modify the often unpleasing reddish shades that are the only ones possible with henna alone, this plant was long ago mixed with indigo. The dried and powdered leaves of indigo origin are either mixed with ground henna or applied alternatively with henna, to produce a good black. Shades from light brings to black can be produced by varying the proportions of henna and indigo.

Camomile

Camomile is another plants used for colouring the hair. Sveral varieties of related plants are found in U.K., Western Europe, and the U.S.A., of which only two - camomile and German or Hungarian camomile - are used to any extent. The essential oil distilled from camomile flowers in pale blue, due to the presence of some hydrocarbon azulien. Like henna, camomile can be used as rinse, a pack, or a shampoo.

Camomile Pack

Camomile pack is prepared by mixing 2 parts of its powder with Kaolin or 1 part of fullers. Boiler water is then added to make paste. The shade produced depends on the original shade of the hair and the time of contact, and the change in color lasts considerably longer than the glints produced by a rinse. As with the henna pack the paste must be kept hot during the entire application, and the operation should be completed as quickly as possible.

Camomile Shampoo

German camomile is usually prepared because it produces a slightly better colour and because it is considerably cheaper than Roman variety. Camomile shampoos are marketed as powders and as liquids. It constitutes : Camomile German Powdered (10%); Mild organic acid (5%); Sodium sulphate (85%); Oil of camomile (q.s. (for perfume).

A liquid shampoo is most effective when freshly prepared. Hence it may be made in concentrated form. It constitutes : Camomile infusion (10%); Sodium laurge sulphate (30-40%); Water (50-60%).

Camomile-Henna Mixtures

Pack of this type may be prepared to very good effect to produce a fair range of colours on hair of different basic shades as shown below.

Formulations for Camomile-Henna Mixture

Ingredients	*1*	*2*	*3*
Camomile	75	50	25
Henna	25	50	75
Orininal Colour	Shade Produced		
Blond	Golden-blond		
	Red - Gold		
	Gloden - Red		
Light brown	Light auburn		
	Auburn		
	Bright auburn		
	Chest Nut		
Dark Brown	Reddish - Brown		
	Dark auburn		

Henna Reng Dye

It is possible to produce other shades instead auburn. The blue black shade shade is obtained by the mixture of powered indigo and henna. It is known as henna renges.

Camomile Herbar Dye

Of the various species of camomile, only 'Anthemis nobilis' (Roma Camomile) and Matricaria camomile (German camomile) have been used in cosmetics and are useful in tinting the hair. The active ingredient of these flowers in 1, 3, 4-trihydronyflavore, known as apigenin. Either an aqueous extract or a paste of the ground flower heads are generally used. To lighten the hair a paste consisting of 2 parts camomile and 1-2 parts Kaolin mixed to a thin cream with hot water is applied to the head for a period varying from 15 minutes to 60 minutes depending upon the shade required. While making a formulation it is essential that at least 5% camomile or its equivalent in extract, must be present to produce any effect at all and the azulene also present in camomile contributes to the brightening effect.

Fresh Soap-Wort Shampoo

When water is added to soap-wort foam is produced due to saponina. All parts of the plant produce a gentle cleansing lather that does not sting the eyes or make the hair brittle. It can be combined with other herbs that suit particular types of hair and colour.

Formulation No. 1

Leafy Soapwort stems 6-8 long	10 Nos.
Water	500 ml.
Strong Herb or flower infusion	3 Tablespoon

For making an infusion use the following amounts. To each ½ litre of boiling bottled spring water add.

Dried Herbs :	14 gms for weak infusion
	28 gms for normal strength
	56 gms for strong infusion
Fresh Herbs :	1 1/2 handfuls for weak infusion
	3 handfuls for normal strength
	6 handfuls for strong infusion

Dried herbs of any of the flowers given below can be used.

– Camomile, Lime flower, yarrow.

– Rosemary, sage, comfrey, henna (powder).

– Marigold flowers.

– Lavender, peppermint, white, dead nettle.

– Marsh mallow, comfrey

– Southerriwood, stinging nettle.

– Elder flower, Uiyme, rosemary.

Procedure

The stems are cut into short lengths and put into an enamel saucepan. Then bruised lightly with a wooden spoon and water is added. The mixture is boiled and then covered and allowed to simmer for 15 minutes with continuous stirring, till cool Then the contents are strained and bottled for future use. A flower infusion is prepared and 3 tablespoon of strong herb or flower is added. The shampoo is covered and then allowed to cool and then strained. The whole of the above liquid is used for one hair wash.

Dried Soap-Wort

The process of preparation of dried soap wort root shampoo include soaking of dried soap-wort in a boiling water for 12 hours or overnight. Transfer it to enamel and, boil and simmered for 15 minutes. The dried herbs or flowers are then added, strirred, covered and left to cool. The mixture is then stirred into a fug and used for one hair wash.

Nettle Rinse and Conditioner

Nettle is an excellent hair conditioner. it is an acidic plant and promotes a healthy gloss. it is prepared by first cutting nettles, thenput it saucepan and add cold water and boil. Simmer for 15 minutes by covering it. Strain the mixture into a jug and allow it to cool.

Lotion for Unruly Hair

Formulation No. 2

– Herb or flower infusion of normal strength	– 8 Tablespoons
– Eau de cologne	– 1 Tablespoon
– Glycerien	– 1Tablespoon

Horsetail Hair Rinse and Tonic

Herba hair tonics and conditioners help restore the scalps natural acidity and strengthen the circulation giving a healthy shine to the hair. Horsetail Contains saponins which create lather, flavour-glycosides which act on the scalps tiny blood vessels to stimulate the circulation and silica which provides body to the hair. The horsetail stems (long) are bruised with a spoon before adding the boiling water to make an infusion. They are then covered and left until lukewarm and then strained. After shampooing and rinsing, the infusion is poured on the hair and massaged on the scalp. Blot the mixture with towel and the hair is combed. Before dry hair cover the head with warm towel and wait for 10 mins.

Tonic Shampoo

Put 135 gms each of dried reetha, shikakai and amla into one litre water. Keep it for 24 hours. Boil and then allow to cool. Filter the mixture and use as a shampoo.

Herb Shampoo

Soak overnight in an iron pot 210 gms of dried olives and shikakai in cold water. Then boil for 10-15 minutes and strain liquidige the flesh that remains and use the paste to wash your hair. This shampoo leaves your hair soft and shining.

Chapter - 23

SKIN LIGHTENERS OR BLEACHES

INTRODUCTION

Some knowledge of the physiology and biochemistry of skin colour and particularly of the pigmentation processes is essential for an appreciation of the mode of action of skin lightening agents.

SKIN LIGHTENING AGENTS AND FORMULATIONS

Opaque Covering Agents

In a wider sense, normal make-up with a higher than average content of white or plae pigments such as titanium dioxide, zinc oxide, talc, kaolin and bismuth pigments may be used.

Oxidising Agents

The use of hydrogen peroxide has limited use as a skin bleaches.

Mercury Compounds

Red mercuric oxide and mercurous chloride have been used, but mercuric chloride and ammoniated mercury give the most effective preparations.

When mercuric chloride used in lotion reacts with skin generates hydrochloric acid. This causes sloughing of the epidermis. Ammoniated mercury $-NH_2.HgCL$ – does not cause the same degree of exfoliation of the skin.

In a modern context, ammoniated mercury can scarcely be considered to be a suitable material for use in a cosmetic product which will be applied regularly, day-by-day, depsite its existence in pharmacopoeial formulae.

Hydroquinone

The most favoured material for use in skin bleach preparations is hydroquinone which is to be effective at 1½-2 per cent in a vanishing cream in producing a temporary lightening of skin colour.

Hydroquinone has been 'found to be safe and effective (for skin lightening) by a Food and Drug Administration.

Hydroquinone is a white crystalline material, melting point 170 - 171°C, soluble in water (1 : 14), freely soluble in alcohol and ether. Solutions become brown on exposure to air as a result of oxidation and must be stabilised. The oxidation is very rapid if the solution is alkaline.

In formulation, the usual stabilisers are sodium sulphite or metabisulphite, often with the addition of a little ascorbic acid. Compositions should preferably be slightly acid (pH 4-6). Manufacturing equipment must be stainless steel or glass-lined to avoid discolouration,and contact with air minimised. Formualtion is given in formulae 1 and 2 :

Formula 1 (Hydroquinon bleach cream)

Constituents	*per cent*
Lexemul	15.0
Lexate	6.0
Stearyl alcohol	3.0
Silicone oil	1.0
Propyl paraben	0.1
Water, deionised	67.8
Propylene glycol	5.0
Hydroquinone	2.0
Sodium metabisulphite	0.05
Asccorbic acid	0.05

Formula 2 (Hydroquinone lotion)

Constituents	*per cent*
Lexemul	5.0
Mineral oil light	2.5
Isopropyl myristate	2.5
Cetyl alcohol	1.0
Brij	0.9
Deionised water	79.85
Propylene glycol	5.0
Sodium lauryl sulphate 30%	0.9
Sodium metabisulphite	0.15
Ascorbic acid	0.1
Hydroquinone	2.0
Citric acid	0.1

The process involves addition of the oil phase to the water phase at 75°-80°C with high shear mixing. When a smooth emulsion has been formed, transfer to low shear mixing. Cool with stirring and at 55° – 50°C add, in order, sodium metabisulphite, ascorbic acid, hydroquinone and citric acid perfume at 40°C.

The following formula for a medium viscosity lotion which will function as a sunscreen lotion as well as lightening and evening out skin tone is given in formula 3 :

Formula 3 (Oil-in-water toning lotion for black skin)

Constituents	*per cent*
Veegum	1.5
Titanium dioxide	0.2
Cetyl alcohol	1.8
Polychol	0.6
Glycerine	5.0
Uvinul	1.0
Sodium myristyl sulphate	1.0
Hydroquinone	3.0
Perfume	1.0
Sodium metabisulphite	0.2
Aluminium chlorhydroxyallantoinate	0.2
Water	to 100.0

A soft cream with a dry emollience may be formulated as given in formula 4 :

Formula 4 (Skin lightening cream)

	Constituents	*per cent*
A	Arlacel 165	8.0
	Crodamol CSP	8.0
	Liquid base CB.3929	4.0
	Crodalan IPL	2.0
	Polychol 15	3.0
	Cetyl alcohol	1.0
	Nipasol M	0.05

(Cont'd)

B	Propylene glycol	5.0
	Kelzan	2.0
	Nipagin M	0.15
	Deionised water	64.4
C	Sodium metabisulphite	0.1
	Ascorbic	0.1
	Hydroquinone	2.0
	Perfume	0.2 or q.s.

The preparation include heating A to 72°C; disperse the Kelzan in B and heat to 70°C. Add A to B with stirring until emulsified. Cool with stirring, adding the sodium metabisulphite, ascorbic acid and then the hydroquinone at 55° - 50° C. Add the perfume at about 40°C. Adjust the pH value if necessary to 5.0 - 5.5 with citric acid. The clinical experiences with the cream shown in formulae 5 and 6 :

Formula 5

Constituents	*per cent*
Tretinoin	0.1
Hydroquinone	5.0
Dexamethasone	0.1
Hydrophillic ointment	to 100.0

Formula 6

Constituents	*per cent*
Hydroquinone	5.0
Hydrocortisone I.P	1.0
Retinoic acid	0.1
Butylated hydroxytoluene	0.05
Polyethylene glycol 300	47.0
Methylated Spirit 74 o.p.	to 100.0

Ascorbic Acid and Its Derivatives

Ascorbic acid is an active constituent of skin bleaching preparations. Scientists have reported on the successful use of creams containing 3 and 5 per cent ascorbyl oleate for bleaching freckles in human skin, resulting also in a marked improvement in the condition of the skin, which became softer and more supple.

By reviewing the chemistry of a number of esters of ascorbic acid and the stability of a few when incorporated into cosmetic creams. One in particular, the magnesium salt of ascorbic acid-3 phosphate, had shown to have a bleaching effect on pigmentation in human skin and to be useful in clinical practice.

The Natural Way

Limited skin lightening effects can be achieved with natural materials which have been used for centuries and which are useful for bleaching out fading suntan and freckles. Among the materials used are cucumber juice, lemon and lime juice, buttermilk, crushed strawberries and fresh horseradish.

Chapter - 24

QUALITY CONTROL OF COSMETICS

INTRODUCTION

Quality is the totality of features and characteristics of a product or service that bear on its ability to satisfy a given need ! Thus, quality is seen not as a single factor, but as a concept made up of several criteria.

Quality is the sum of all factors which contribute directly or indirectly to the safety, effectiveness and acceptability of the product !

Quality means conformance to requirements. Quality department personnel cannot be concerned with the various mystical aspects of quality – beauty, elegance, value for money, or even fitness for purpose (unless this means conformance to a defined purpose). The emphsis on conformance throws the responsibility on the marketing and technical departments to define the requirement and the product, such that a product specification is produced. This specification should define the environmental and reliability characteristics that the product must have, the workmanship standards that are applicable, and so on. The quality department are responssible for checking conformance to this specification.

The traditional view of quality requires modification, and that a new philosophy of quality is needed. The terms quality and productivity are not only to be related to the production of goods but also to process. For this reason, these concepts of quality must encompass every level of a business organisation – from administration,sales, to financing and marketing. The new concept of quality "built in" instead of 'tested for' emphasises prevention in all phases of the production cycle and beyond that in every work process within a business, rather than verification or post-improvement procedures. In this chapter, we discuss this new conception of quality.

The Analytical Laborator – Its Significance for Raw Materials/Active Ingrdientws and the Finished Preparation

All the raw materials and ingreients needed for cosmetic preparations are tested for usability in an analytical laboratory.The finished cosmetic preparations are also tested here.

The prerequisites for optimal chemical control (optimal is used here to signify the lowest expenditure that provides the highest degree of protection) are the msot modern technical aids, such as IR, Uv, AAS spectrometers as well as gas chromatography and personal computers. Qualified and experienced technical personnel are also indispensable.

The Microbiological Laboratory – Assurance of Purity and Hygiene

It is the task of microbiological laboratory to control mould or bacteria in cosmetic preparations. During production of a cosmetic preparation it must already be known which micro-organisms the preparation is exposed to; the germs discovered must be analysed and tested to ensure that a precisely fixed germ count is not exceeded.

Sterile working conditions are not required for cosmetic preparations, buy hygiene regulations must be observed during the production process. The Good Manufacturing Practice (GMP) and Good Laboratory Practice (GLP) guidelines are generally regarded as the applicable regulations. Cleaning and disinfecting are just as essential as the provision of hygiene education to personnel. Only informed employees can gurantee that all regulations are adhered to. Disinfecting machines and machine components is normally cost and time-intensive. The "clean in place" system is an example of innovative attempts in this area, which no business can ignore.

"Clean in place" refers to washing, cleaning and disinfecting machines by an installed system of pipes, without having to take apart machine components or pumps.

Raw Material Inspection

The inspection of cosmetic ingredients is based on specifications. It takes into consideration the specific requirements of the company as well as legal guidelines. Each detail of the specification must be coordinated with the producer of the raw materials. An inspection certificate which is given to the user with each delivery makes it easier for laboratory administrators to decide which properties of the specification need to be sujected to chemical analysis. It is not necessary to analyse every property of each delivery. The decision regarding how often to test is dependent upon the frequency of delivery, coordination of all specification properties between supplier and buyer, the inspection certificate accompanying each deliery, the histroy of the raw material in question, the degree of trust between buyer, supplier, and the complete documentation of all data. A sensory test of smell, colour and/or appearance, together with an IR spectrum is often sufficient to identify a delivery accurately. The decision as to whether a full analysis of all specific values needs to be carried out on every third, fourth or fifth delivery is made by the laboratory administration. It is also absolutely necessary to store allanalytical data in a personal computer. An evaluation of the raw material or supplier can be made at any time with the help of this data.

Inspection of the Finished Product

Specific manufacturing instructions are essential for the production of the finished preparation. Instructions regarding temperature, mixing speed, instruments or the order in which ingredients are incorporated make it easier to keep to the specification. here too an in-process control which registers the actual values (temperature, mixing speed, etc.), in relation to the specified values should be adopted.

A particular risk can be bound up with the weighing of the individual raw materials. However great the inspection expenditures are (for example, the additional presence of a psecialist from the analytical laboratory while weighing in active ingredients), mistakes by personnel cannot be excluded. For example, too much of an active ingredient (such as a preservative) could cause fatal effects. For this reason active ingredients are often inspected again by the analytical laboratory as to their proportion in the final preparation. This doubled or tripled safe guarding is cost-intensive and hence not justifiable according to modern conceptions of quality. In the search for preventative test characteristics, the use of computerised weighing controls has therefore become prominent. A preparation manufactured under these conditons will generally meet the prescribed standards.

Inspection of Containers and Packaging Materials

It would not be possible to inspect each of bottles delivered for packaging purposes. Yet it must be guaranteed that they are all in flawless condition. Breakage and structural faults which would lead to leakage or glass splinters must be totally excluded. it is impossible to compromise on this issue. the problem can be resolved with the help of statistics. Probability statements regarding the specific quality of a delivery can be made through the use of spot tests and fault evaluation methods that practically eliminate error. The results of tests on a small representative sample of a total delivery are used to decide whether an entire delivery of an item should be acepted or rejected. In terms of cost-benefit analysis, this is the only practicable system for inspecting large lot quantities, from the view point of both buyers and manufacturers of packaging materials.

Skip Lot Inspection

The cosmetics industry also makes use of packaging materials which are relatively simple to produce. They have therefore retained consistently good quality over the years, but each delivery must nevertheles be thoroughly inspected. If the history of the packaging component has remained unchanged, it is sufficient to tinspect every third, fourth, or fifth delivery (hence the term skip lot). Precise knowledge of the packaging components and the supplier are however essential prerequisites for using this method of inspection. For deliveries which are not inspected, an identity check (appearance, potential transport damage, code number and so on) will sufice.

Source Inspection

Packaging materials that are produced in large quantities and ordered in partial lots also do not require comprehensive inspection of each delivery. This is especially important when using the just-in-time inventroy method, where small quantities of the material are ordered with greater frequency. Source inspection requires that the total amount be statistically checked once by the producer. An identity check is then sufficient for all deliveries of partial lots. In this case too, cooperation beteween supplier and buyer is necessary, especially regarding the lot size per order.

Vendor Certification

There are suppliers whose preparations have proved themselves over the years to be of exceptional quality. Packaging components supplied by them do not need to be routinely checked with every deliver, since the risk remains small. A control can be made via skip lot or source inspection methods at any time.

Computer-Assisted Delivery Testing

An exact record and evaluation of all available data is an essential prerequisite of the above mentioned tests employed in less frequent quality inspection methods. A computerised system of measurement at the packaging delivery point makes this possible. Such a system is organised so that it contains all the basic data regarding a supplier and a component, and the data from every further test procedure, regardless of whether it is a skip lot or routine test method, is fed into its memory. The results of attributive tests (of appearace, colour and so on), are entered manually. The analysis of a number of these tests shows immediately whether there is a tendency towards deviation from the norm, or whether the values remain constant within the specifiction. The computer is "queried" every time goods arrive. It provides the decision on whether to test that particular delivery. This system has proved its reliability in practice and can therefore be recommended for use in every business.

In-Process Control

Prevention is the only possible means of recognising and correcting errors, and cutting costs. In-process controls are preventative technical-operational procedures which monitor the work process by means of measurement devices intergrated into that process. An example of this is the computerised weighing control of ingredients. In this system, the quantity of an ingredient which is given in the formulation instructions is stored in memory and automatically compared with the actual amount weighed. Each deviation is communicated immediately by a signal or a print-out. The sum of the individual weitht readings must correspond exactly to the quantity of the formulation. Projections of the actual amount of a basic ingredient used in relation to the target amount with reference to the amount in stock provides additional security.

Integrated Inspection Processes in the Manufacture of the Finished Product

Different companies offer memory-programmed management and ispection systems. Their purpose is to automate a mixing process with computer assistance according to predetermined specifications. This optimises effective time management of a facility and consistent reproducibility of the finsihed preparation, as well as the storage of formulation data. Control systems continually monitor temperature, mixing speed and process duration.

These systmes also help in prevention, or advance inspection (in-process control procedures). The check weigher belongs to this group of systems, for example. This is a weighing system which is intergrated into the production line and automatically checks the weight of each individual preparation. A computer evaluates the measurement results. In production facilities which cannot implement check weigher, weight inspection takes place during the production process by means of spot checks (computer assisted inspection of fill quantities). The evalutaion and projection of individual results at a central point provides certainty that the proper fill quantities are always contained. Torque measurement, an ongoing check for container leakage, and inspection of the finished product with automatic removal of faulty items - those with missing labels or lot codes, empty containers, containers without lids, or insufficiently filled containers - are also possible in this way.

Finished Goods Control

The systematic prevention of error encompasses errors related to machines on the one hand and to human error on the other. In production of the finished product, this is especiall important because it is the last opportunity to spot and rectify errors before the product is released. Specifications features for the packaged preparation are prescribed by the Cosmetics Decree, the Finished Package Decree, and the Guidelines for

Aerosols, as well as by the specifications. The "in-process controls" are employed as a rule in this inspections. The manufacturer msut estblish the extent of inspection activities in such a way that every preparation which reaches the consumer fully meets all legal requirements.

Good Laboratory Practice (GLP) and Good Manufacturing Practice (GMP)

Good Laboratory Practce (GLP) and Good Manufacturing Practice (GMP) are used widely for the production of cosmetic preparations.GLP offers guidelines for laboratory investigations of chemical substances in terms of their characteristics and/or safety. The guidelines cover the direction of laboratory tests, the responsibilities of the laboratory administration, and quality assurance .Similarly, GMP provides fundamental advice concerning hygienic production practices in the cosmetics industry, including recommendations concerning raw materials and packaging materials, disinfection, microbiological quality control, personnel and preservation.

Environmental Protection

In accordance with regulations regarding waste products, tariffs are levied on companies in proportion to the burden they place on the waste disposal system.

The determination of disposable substances and of the chemical oxygen demand (COD) should be part of the routine of a laboratory concerned with environmental protection. Expenditure on such controls is justifiable and inspection can be restricted to 2 or 3 times per year once values have been standardised. The biological oxygen demand (BOD) must as a rule be determined by an independent body. The quality of the air should also be known, at least for the prodution facility. With the help of this kind of data, a company can have an influence on air and waste water quality and thus keep these costs under control.

Quality promotion

Improvement of quality is an attitude which every level of a company needs to adopt, because the goal of improvement demands that every work procedure, every service and product meets the norms of quality every time. The process of improving quality and productivity is an ongoing process which has in view nothing less than the approach and the engagement of all co-workers. This approach requires a philosophy of quality whose goal is to encourage employees in the direction of improving quality within the framework of the company's strategy.

The following plan is based on bringing the classic works proposal system together with an innovative quality team.

Works Proposal System

The works proposal system, which is usually regulated by agreements between managment and the works committee, is an instrument of the employees for voluntarily improving current conditions.

A transitional stage from the works proposal system to quality team is offered by the group proposal. The regulation stipulates that "suggestions for improvement may be prepared and submitted by individual workers (individaul proposals), or by a group of workers (group proposals)." Employees are thus motivated to develop new ideas and initiatives that lie outside of their immediate assignment areas.

It may seem strange to intergrate the classic works proposal system into the general category of "quality assurance." However, a modern conception of quality must concern itself with systems of improvement that ultimately secure success through implementation of quality standards.

Chapter - 25

TESTING OF COSMETICS

INTRODUCTION

Cosmetic analysis is both specialised and diversified. The range of tests covered in this chapter reveals that it utilises the full gamut of modern analytical chemistry to identify and determine inorganic and organic components in extremely complex mixtures. However, as is often the case techniques developed by cosmetic chemists to solve their particular problems also have great utilitarian value in other areas of analytical chemistry.

A cosmetic is considered to be adulterated if it contains a poisonous or deleterious substance which may cause it to be injurious to users under customary conditions of use or if it is contaminated in a manner which may render it harmful to health. It is misbranded if its labeling is false or misleading, if it does not bear the required labeling information, or if it is not truthfully packaged.

The composition of cosmetic raw materials themselves requires increasing scrutiny by the analytical chemist for the support of safety testing programmes for ingredients and for the establishment of precise standards and specifications for such ingredients.

This chapter provides both specific procedures and general methods for approaching the analysis of cosmetics, toiletries, in a logical and systematic manner. The analyst must supplement this information with laboratory experience gained in the actual analysis of products. The chemist should have a good understanding of spectrophotometry and chromatography. It is hoped that the experienced cosmetic chemist will find this text a source of new ideas from which to increase the range and scope of his investigations.

SPECTROSCOPY IN COSMETIC ANALYSIS

Ultraviolet and visible, fluorometric, infra-red, mass, and nuclear magnetic resonance spectroscopy plays vital role in cosmetic analysis.

Ultraviolet and Visible Spectroscopy

Ultraviolet (uv) spectrophotometry plays an important role in cosmetic analysis for identifying and determining compounds which, through electronic transitions, absorb radiation in the region from 200 to 380 nm. Primarily this technique applies to aromatic compounds, although uv spectra are useful for characterising some aliphatic substances such as compounds with conjugated double bonds, ketones, and mercaptans.

Constituents that Absorb in the Ultra-Violet

The following partial listing of cosmetic raw materials which absorb in the ultra-violet :

Alkyl aryl polyether alcohols, Alkyl aryl sulphonates, Aminobenzoates, Aminophenols, Arylamines, Aryl sulphonamide-formaldehyle resin, Benzoyl peroxide. Camphor, Cinnamates, Coumarins, Dichlorophene, Furocoumarins, Hexachlorophene, *p*-Hydroxybenzoates, Nitroarylamines, Phenosulphonates, Phthalates, Quaternaries containing aryl groups, Salicylates, Silicons containing phenyl groups, Tricresyl phosphates.

For several cosmetic ingredients, e.g., sunscreens, preservatives, and arylamine oxidation hair dye intermediates, uv spectrophotometry is an invaluable analytical technique.

Visible spectrophotometry (colourimetry) is based on the same principles as uv spectrophotometry, except that the absorption range of interest extends from 380 to 800 nm. The substances to be determined appear coloured to the human eye. Many coloured inorganic and organic cosmetic materials have been investigated. For example, ethanol can be measured through its reaction with potassium dichromate; a coloured chromic complex is determined. The coloured Schiffs derivatives of citral and citronellal have been evaluated. Poloyvinyl pyrrolidone and its copolymers form a coloured complex with a red dye which enables their determination down to 0.1 ppm. As a final example, the amount of tartar emetic in certain toilet waters can be measured through its coloured iodonatimonous acid complex.

Infrared Spectroscopy

The infrared (IR) region of the spectrum most frequently studied by the analytical chemist lies between 4000 and 660 cm^{-1} (2.5 and 15 μm). Organic molecules selectively absorb energy at specific wavelengths within that region. A plot of the wavelengths where absorption occurs vs. their intensities provides an IR spectrum which can be useful for characterising or identifying a cosmetic ingredient.

Sample Preparation

Analysis of a cosmetic may be initiated by obtaining an IR spectrum of the non-volatile portion of the sample. Almost all preparations containing water (which absorbs IR radiation), such as creams, lotions, antiperspirants, depilatories, shampoos, and hair dyes, can be dehydrated by heating them on a steam bath or at 105°C in an oven.The IR spectrum of the liquid or solid residue may be obtained by placing the sample between salt plates either as a neat film or in mulls made with mineral and/or halocarbon oil. A neat film is deposited on a plate by evaporation of a volatile solvent, such as alcohol or acetone, containing the dispersed or soluble residue. Solids with low melting points may be placed on the plate, heated to the liquid state, and resolidified by cooling into thin glassy films. Alternatively, about 2 mg of a solid sample can be mixed with approximately 200 mg of KBr powder and pressed into a pellet in a die at 20,000–50,000 psi pressure.

IR spectra of solutions and gases are generated with the aid of sealed cells of various pathlengths. Spectra of volatile solvents in nail lacquers are obtained by dissolving a sample aliquot in carbon disulphide, a solvent which is transparent to most IR radiation, and adding the solution to a selected liquid cell. Gases, such as propellant mixtures in aerosol products, are allowed to flow into a previously evacuated gas cell. (If the concentration of gas in the cell is too great, it can conveniently be reduced by using a pipet to which a rubber bulb is attached to withdraw some of the gas.)

Characteristic Absorbances

A cosmetic sample IR spectrum should first be examined in the 2–9 μm region, where absorption peaks at specific wavelengths can be associated with given functional groups. Such a study can frequently provide a quick indication of the presence or absence of alcohols, amines, acids, esters, ethers, amides, soaps, nitriles, mercapto compounds, nitro compounds, alikyl sulphates, sulphonates, and sulphonamides. Frequently, closely related ingredients can be differentiated by comparison of the "fingerprint" region (9–15 μm) of the spectrum where secondary information may be provided. The relationship among the observed absorbances at the various wavelengths is studied for an estimation of the relative amount of each ingredient.

Structural Elucidation

Infrared spectrophotometry is a helpful too for structural elucidation of previously uncharacterised compounds which may be encoutered in many of the complex raw materials used in cosmetic formulation. When IR spectra of pure substances differ to only a minor degree, the substances are very similar chemically. On occasion, the absence of a key absorption peak can provide important in formation which may be used to reduce the number of suspected compounds.

Fluorometry

When selected excitation wavelengths of uv light impinge upon certain types of chemical substances, characteristic light emissions occur at longer ultravioler or visible wavelengths. Usually, an excitation wavelength which elicits a maximum emission response is chosen for a given compound in order to achieve the greatest sensitivity. The most appropriate emission wavelength is the one with the greatest intensity whose maximum is well removed from that of the excitation band. Fluorometric sensitivity is very good; it is common to measure microgram levels of material with ease.

The application of the fluorometry technique is greatly expanded by conversion of non-fluorescing compounds into fluorescent derivatives. For example, formaldehyde, a cosmetic preservative, is determined through quantitative conversion to its fluorescent lutidine derivative. Aluminum can be determined qualitatively and quantitatively in deodorants and antiperspirants through the fluorescent aluminium salt of 8-hydroxy- quinoline.

Mass Spectrometry

Submicrogram sample of pure compounds may be identified readily by mass spectrometry. A sample is introduced into a highly evacuated chamber (ca 10^{-10} atmospheres) and bombarded with a beam of electrons powerful enough to strip away one or more electrons from its molecular orbitals. These collisions produce a number of positively charged molecular fragments along with a frequently occurring positively charged species of the same molecular weight as the sample molecule. These species are separated electromagnetically by various instrumental techniques into discrete particle types represented by different relative mass-to-charge ratios. A plot of particle mass vs. relative abundance is obtained which represents the mass spectrum of the sample. Some samples may be identified by comparison with standard reference mass spectra but the structural elucidation of unknowns requires skilled interpretation. The positively charged molecular fragments form spectral peak patterns which are characteristic of certain structural features. The molecular weight of the unknown compound may be determined if its corresponding parent ion peak is present in the spectrum.

Mass spectral analysis has been used for the verification of suspected structures of derivatives of cosmetic compounds. Various alkanolamines in hair sprays must be acetylated prior to their determination by gas chromatography. Some contain several – OH groups as well as a – NH group. Mass spectral analysis determines whether or not the – NH group was acetylated and the number of – OH groups converted to acetates.

Nuclear Magnetic Resonance

Many spinning atomic nuclei, such as those of hydrogen (protons), boron, fluorine, and phosphorus, possess angular momentum and a magnetic moment. Because of the most widely studied of the nuclei are protons, the description of their nuclear magnetic resonance (NMR) behaviour is emphasised. When organic molecules containing protons are placed in a large magnetic field of known fixed strength and this field is swept with small known magnetic fields at right angles to the sample, certain of the applied frequencies (or small magnetic fields) interact with the magnetic moments of the protons, causing the protons to "flip" from their orientation with the large magnetic field to an orientation against it. Energy absorbed during this "flip" is considered to be "nuclear magnetic resonance" energy. The amount of absorbed energy required to cause a proton to flip depends upon its structural location in the molecule, because the electronic envelope surrounding a proton has a significant influence on its magnetic properties. An NMR plot of the radio frequency energy absorbed by a molecule vs. the changing magnetic field strength can yield valuable information about the various types and numbers of hydrogen atoms in the molecule. Thus ;nuclear magnetic resonance is an important tool for the structural elucidation of many complex molecules.

Nuclear magnetic resonance reference spectra are useful for verifying the identities of many compounds; however, it should be emphasised that no single spectral technique should be relied upon for proof of structure. Confirmation is best obtained by a number of mutually supportive instrumental and chemical approaches. As a case in point, the structure of β1-cadinene (now known as α– cadinene), a sesquiterpene hydrocarbon isolated from olibanum oil, could not be varified by comparison with any available standard reference spectra (infrared or nuclear magnetic resonance). Through a process of elimination with a combination of chemical and spectral techniques, the number of possibilities was narrowed down to two alternative cadinene isomers, δ_1 and β_1 (now known as α). The NMR spectrum provided confirmatory evidence that the unknown is the δ1 isomer, based on the number of olefinic protons.

CHROMATOGRAPHIC TECHNIQUES IN COSMETIC ANALYSIS

Adsorption Column chromatography

Adsorption column chromatography is a useful technique for separating mixtures of organic compounds possessing varying degrees of polarities.

In principle, the more polar the compound the more strongly it is held by the adsorbent. In applying this technique, a solution or slurry of the sample in a solvent of relatively low polarity is introduced into a chromatography column containing a porous bed of finely divided adsorbent such as silica, alumina, Florisil (magnesium silicate), or magnesia. The components of a mixture are separated through the successive use of eluting solvent of increasing polarity. Even though a practical knowledge of the relative polar strengths of various solvents or mixtures may be gained from experience, some information on this subject has been published and may be used by the analyst in establishing an experimental design for his intended purpose.

Column Preparation, Sample Application and Elution

The preferred method for preparing the column is to prepare a wet slurry of the adsorbent using the least polar solvent of the proposed solvent system. This slurry is then added in increments to the column containing some of this least polar solvent, and each increment is "packed" into the column with the aid of 5–6 psig of air pressure. To prevent channeling, the liquid level should not be allowed to fall below the top of the adsorbent bed within the column, either during its preparation or during use.

The sample is dissolved or dispersed in a small amount of the initial eluting solvent with gentle warming if necessary to increase the solubility of the sample. This sample solution is then added to the column and a constant flow rate is maintained by gravity or by the application of air pressure. The column is then eluted successively with solvents of increasing polarity. Uniform aliquots are collected and the chromatographic procedure is continued until all components of interest have been collected.

Qualitative and Quantitative Analysis

Components in the eluted aliquots may be determined by gravimetric or volumetric analysis or such instrumental techniques as infrared (IR), ultraviolet uv, nuclear magnetic resonance, and mass spectrometry. Other helpful techniques are thin layer chromatography (TLC), refractometry, fluorometry, and polarimetry.

Variables and Efficiency

Reproducibility and efficiency of separation are dependent on certain variables, most of which can be controlled by the analyst. For example, the selection of a smaller mesh size adsorbent offers a correspondingly larger surface area for adsorption which favours improved separations. Other factors affecting accuracy, reproducibility, and efficiency of adsorption chromatographic procedures include proper selection of solvent polarity, viscosity, and compatibility of successive solvents; packing procedure; method of sample application; and flow rate. Although ambient temperature is satisfactory in most cases, the temperature of the column can affect the separation process.

Application to Cosmetic Analysis

The cosmetic analyst is frequently confronted with the problem of separating complex mixtures of cosmetic ingredients with polarities ranging from non-polar aliphatic bydrocarbons to such highly polar compounds as polyols. The selective elution of components of increasing polarities can be demonstrated by the analysis of a commercial grade of glyceryl monostearate. The order of elution is aliphatic hydrocarbons, triglycerides, fatty acids, diglycerides, monoglycerides, and finally glycerol.

Partition Column Chromatography

The partition column chromatography is generally a glass tube packed with a solid support which has been coated with a stationary or immobile phase, one of two immiscible, equilibrated liquids. The sample is introduced at the top of the column and the column is then developed by introduction of a moving or mobile phase, the other liquid of this immiscible pair of liquids. As the mobile phase, moves down the column, the sample component of interest (solute) will move in the system at a rate which depends on its relative solubilities in the two phases. This is expressed as the partition coefficient and is defined as the concentration of the solute in the mobile phase divided by its concentration in the immobile phase under equilibrium conditions. This value is constant for any given solute in a specific system. Usually, development of the column is continued until all solutes of interest. have been eluted from the column. These eluates are collected in uniform aliquots and reserved for analysis by chemical or instrumental techniques.

In conventional practice, the more polar liquid of the solvent pair is used as the immobile phase. This is referred to as normal partition chromatography. In reverse phase partition chromatography the less polar solvent is the immobile phase.

Partition chromatography is generally used for the separation of chemically similar compounds that have some solubility in both liquid phases and different partition coefficients. Adsorption chromatography is primarily useful for the separation of compounds into different chemical classes.

Solid Support

The ideal solid support consists of small, uniform inert particles with high permeability and large surface areas. Of the materials commonly used as solid supports, diatomaceous earths such as Celite or Filter-Cel most closely fulfill these requirements. Other materials that have been used as solid supports include cellulose powder, potato starch, modified cellulose, polyamides, and silica gel.

Commercial grades of diatomaceous earth require sieving to the desired mesh range followed by washing with HCl, distilled water, and finally methanol or ethanol to remove impurities. After drying at 120°C, the support is suitable for preparing columns. Analytical grades of diatomaceous earth do not require further treatment. If the support is to be used for reverse phase partition chromatography, it must be silanised with a preparation such as dimethyldichlorosilane by exposing the support to vapours of the silanising reagent in a closed container or by treating the support with a toluene solution of the silanising reagent. If non-silanised support is used to prepare a reverse phase partition column, the polar mobile phase will wet the support, displace the immobile phase, and render the column useless.

Selection of the Liquid Phase

The first step in the design of an analytical partition chromatography columns is to determine the composition of the mobile and immobile liquid phases. The analyst first selects two partially immiscible solvents in which the component to be separated is soluble. Typically, this may involve a solvent pair such as hexane and methanol. Usually a third and possibly a fourth solvent is introduced into the system to modify the partitioning of the solute between the two phases. Chloroform, for example, may be introduced to increase solubility in the non-polar phase. Water can be used to increase immiscibility of the two phases as well as to change the solute solubility in the polar phase. Equal volumes of the two liquids selected as the mobile and immobile phases are added to a separatory funnel along with several milligrams of the compound to be determined. The system is then mixed thoroughly by shaking to establish equilibrium. After the liquid phases have separated, the amount of solute in each phase is determined. The partition coefficient should be approximately 0.01. If it is not, other solvents are introduced to adjust the partition coefficient to the desired value. The phase in which the solute has the highest concentration is always used as the immobile phase.

Preparation of Column

After a suitable solvent system has been selected, the appropriate amount of each component of the solvent system is added to a separatory funnel and mixed thoroughly. The equilibrated phases are then separated and stored in stoppered flasks until used. Silanised support is used for reverse phase and non-silanised support for normal partition chromatography.

For analytical columns a glass chromatographic tube approximately 2 cm id is usually used. There are several methods for packing the column. For example, the support is coated by mixing with a calculated amount of immobile phase. Until uniform, and then is added to the column in increments, with tamping, until the column beck is the desired height. Alternatively, the uncoated support is packed into the empty tube and then washed with immobile phase. Mobile phase is then added and allowed to flow through the column until no immobile phase is observed in the eluate. Other methods of column packing are variations of the above techniques. After the column has been prepared, approximately 10 mg of the sample to be analysed is added to the column in one of the following ways :

1. The sample is dissolved in the immobile phase, mixed with a small portion of the support and packed on the top of the prepared column.
2. The sample is dissolved in a minimum amount of mobile phase and added to the column.
3. When neither of the above methods is applicable, the sample is dissolved in a volatile solvent and mixed with a small amount of support. The solvent is then removed and the dried mixture is added to the column.

After the column has been prepared and the sample added, the column is developed with the mobile phase. During development, the level of mobile phase should not be allowed to fall below the level of the coated support. Ideally, the flow rate should be about 8 $ml/hr/cm^2$ obtained either by gravity or applied air pressure. Development is continued until the components of interest have been eluted. If the components are coloured or can be rendered visible under uv light, each resolved band is collected separately. If components are not visible, a series of uniform aliquots are collected for analysis to determine composition.

Application to Cosmetic Analysis

Many active ingredients in sunscreen preparations, such as *p*-hydroxybenzoates, cinnamates, and aminobenzoates, are successfully separated by partition chromatography and determined by uv spectrometry. Sixteen cosmetic preservatives have also been separated and determined in different cosmetic products.

Ion Exchange Chromatography

Organic or inorganic compounds containing ionic functional groups can be separated from other ionic or non-ionic compounds by ion exchange chromatography. The ion exchanger is normally a solid, finely divided, insoluble material containing ionic sites which are available for the attraction of oppositely charged ions in solution. Although naturally occurring materials such as the alkaline aluminosilicates (zeolites) have served in this capacity, synthetic organic polymers (resins) containing various functional groups are nearly always used for analytical purposes. The separation is usually carried out in a glass column containing the ion exchange resin selected to perform a specific separation. The sample is introduced onto the column in the appropriate solvent and the column is then usually washed with a solvent to elute all non-ionic compounds.

After sample introduction and removal of non-ionic components, the column is developed by displacement chromatography or elution chromatography. Displacement chromatography is carried out by forcing the sample component of interest (solute) from the resin by adding a solution (eluant) containing an excess of an ionic solute that is more strongly attached to the ionic sites on the resin than is the sample solute. In elution chromatography, the eluant contains an ionic solute that is less strongly attracted to the ionic sites on the resin. The sample solute is equilibrated between the resin and the eluant. As the eluant flows each solute moves down the column at a rate dependent upon pH and ionic concentration of the eluant and the ionic attraction between the solutes and ionic sites on the resin.

Column Preparation, Sample Addition and Elution

For most analytical purposes, a 1 x 20–25 cm chromatographic tube is filled with 10–15 ml of pretreated resin. In order to ensure column uniformity, the resin is added in increments as a thick slurry to a tube already one-third filled with liquid, which is gradually drained as the addition proceeds. Each successive addition should be made before the resin has completely settled. Ion exchange resins in acid or base form are packed in columns containing distilled water or a non-aqueous solvent, while those in the "salt" form are added to the appropriate salt or buffer solution. After the column is packed, the resin in the column is washed with the same liquid used for packing until the pH of the effluent is the same as that of the liquid added [illegible] top. The resin in the column should always have liquid above it.

After the level of liquid in the column is adjusted to just cover the top of the ion exchange resin, the sample is added as a solution in the appropriate solvent, i.e., distilled water or organic solvent if the resin is in acid or base form, or buffer if the resin is in "salt" form. The sample solution is added slowly to the top of the column and allowed to percolate [illegible] resin bed at the same flow rate that will be used during the chromato-graphy step. The walls should be rinsed several times with the selected solvent and the rinse solution allowed to settle into the resin bed. Uniform aliquots are collected continuously until development is complete.

The amount of sample added to the column depends on the total ion exchange capacity of the resin and the type of chromatography used. The total "sample load" in the elution procedure should not exceed 1% of the total ion exchange capacity of the resin in the column for analytical purposes or 5-10% for preparative work. Sample load in displacement chromatography may range from 25 to 50% of the total ion exchange capacity of the resin.

A flow rate of 0.005–0.05 ml of solution/ml of resin/minute is suitable in analytical determinations for particle sizes of 0.15–0.5 mm but in any case it should not exceed 0.05 ml/minute.

After eluates have been collected they can be analysed by IR or uv spectrometry or any other applicable chemical or instrumental technique.

Applications to Cosmetic Analysis

Alkanolamine salts of various acid polymers are used in some hair spray formulations. The alkanolamine can be separated from the acid polymer by a strongly acid ion exchange resin, Type I. The polymer is eluted with 75% ethanol. The amine is displaced from the resin with HCl (1 +1) and determined by gas-liquid chromatography (GLC). Triethanolamine lauryl sulphate is separated into its acidic and basic components by chromatography on the strongly basic ion exchange resin, Amberlite CG–400. The triethanolamine is eluted with water and determined by GLC.

Amberlite CG–400 is also used to remove interfering surfactants from solution prior to TLC identification of hexachlorophene. These surfactants, if not removed, frequently alter the R_f of hexachlorophene, making its identification more difficult.

Alkanolamines may interfere with the GLC determination of glycerol in cosmetic creams. Alkanolamines and glycerol remain in the aqueous phase when the sample is extracted from an acidified solution of methanol-water with $CHCl_3$ or petroleum ether. Glycerol may be separated and recovered by elution with wagter in a column which contains pretreated, strongly acidic resin. The alkanolamine is retained by the resin.

Boric acid in certain deodorant preparations can be accurately determined after removal of interfering zinc or aluminum ions with the cationic exchange resin Amberlite.

Alkanolamindes and/or soap can be separated from shampoos containing alkyl sulphates and/or sulphonates. A weakly basic anion exchange resin. Amberlite, is suitable for this separation. It must, however, be throughly pretreated by being washed with all of the same solvents to be used during the separation. Acidified ethanol elutes the alkanolamide and/ or soap from the column, and the sulphate-sulphonate mixture retained by the resin is then isolated by elution with a basic (ammonium carbonate) methanol solution.

Thin Layer Chromatography

Over the past decade TLC has become an increasingly popular analytical tool for the analysis of cosmetic raw materials and products. The principles of adsorption TLC are based on those previously discussed in the section on adsorption chromatography. The principal differences are : A smaller mesh size adsorbent is supported as a thin layer with the aid of a binder, such as calcium sulphate, on a plastic sheet or a glass plate, and the mobile liquid phase (developer) separates but does not remove the sample components from the TLC adsorbent layer. Silica Gel and aluminum oxide are the adsorbents most frequently used. Although adsorption TLC is the most common type, TL C separations may also be achieved with partition or ion exchange coating materials according to the principles of ion exchange and partition chromatography discussed previously.

General Techniques

The sample is spotted on the plate near one edge (origin) and the plate is placed in an almost vertical position in an enclosed chamber containing developer previously added to a height of 1.0 cm. The origin should be above the developer after the plate is in place. As the developer rises through the adsorbent layer by capillary action, the components of the sample are separated. After the developer reaches a predesignated height (solvent front), the plate is removed from the chamber and allowed to dry. Each component may appear as a circular or elliptical spot somewhere between the origin and the solvent front. If the spot is not visible, chemical or other pretreatment may be required for its detection.

The use of several developments (multiple development) is often helpful in achieving a separation. After an initial development, the plate is removed from the chamber and allowed to dry, and one of its edges is immersed in the same or a different developer. If the same edge is immersed, the second development occurs in the same direction, but if the plate is rotated 90^0 it is developed perpendicular to the original direction. This technique is referred to as two-dimensional thin layer chromato- graphy.

Each separated component can be isolated by preparative TLC, performed with the use of thicker adsorbent layers (500 μm) than those used for analytical purposes (250µm). The adsorbent is lightly scored around the area containing the component. All of the material within the scored area is removed from the plate, and the component is separated from the adsorbent by extraction with a suitable solvent. Any chemical or instrumental procedure previously described may then be applied to its identification and/or determination. Components may also be determined without their removal from the plate (*in situ*) by visible, uv, or fluorometric spectral scaning with a densitometer.

Variables

Many factors influence the reproducibility of R_f values as well as separation of components. In adsorption TLC, separations are influenced by variation in the composition, purity, particle size, uniformity, layer thickness, and moisture content (activity) of the adsorbent, as well as the composition of the developing solvent, degree of vapour saturation and shape of the developing chamber, temperature, development technique, and sample composition.

Application to Cosmetic Analysis

Citral and citronellal are identified and determined in various essential oils. After their separation on Silica Gel, the plate is sprayed with a modified Schiff's reagent to produce distinctively coloured derivatives which are removed from the plate and determined spectrophotometrically.

Mixtures of naturally occurring coumarins and psoralens (furanocoumarins) in certain citrus oils are separated on Silica Gel and each compound is tentatively identified through its R_f and its fluorescent colour when viewed under uv radiation. Their isolation by the preparative TLC technique provides sufficient material for further investigations. Bergapten, a psoralen with the potential for causing a phototoxic reaction on human skin, occurs naturally in certain essential oils. It is identified in fragrance products through comparison of its fluorescent colour and spatial relationship with those of a standard. It is also determined at levels as low as 0.001% by weight by comparison with various amounts of standard. Separation is achieved by using two-dimensional multiple development with two different solvent systems.

Natural resins can sometimes be differentiated by the respective patterns of their acidic constituents on TLC plate. The components are visualised with the acid indicator spray, bromocresol green.

Thirty different hair dye intermediates used in commercial products are detected through two-dimensional development of the sample with accompanying standards in two different solvent systems. Although some of the compounds or their oxidation products are naturally coloured, others are identified only after the application of various chemical sprays. Their spatial relationship and colours are compared to those of the standards. Some of these intermediates can be detected in commercial hair dyes at levels as low as 0.02%. TLC is helpful in the identification and determination of the products formed by the oxidation of one of the above intermediates, *p*-phenylenediamine in alkaline solution.

The identification of preservatives in cosmetic products is facilitated by TLC on plates coated with Silica Gel impregnated with fluorescent additives. The uv-absorbing compounds show up as redish brown spots under short wave uv light, which is useful as a preliminary identification step.

High Pressure Liquid Chromatography

High pressure liquid chromatography (HPLC) is merely an extension of adsorption, partition, and ion exchange column chromatography. All theoretical and practical considerations that apply to these forms of chromatography apply to HPLC as well. Although efficiency and resolution can be significantly increased by reducing column diameter, support or adsobent particle size, and sample size, practical considerations limit the steps that can be taken in this direction. Instrumentation is now available which overcomes these limitations and significantly shortens analysis time. The high inlet pressure available in HPLC systems allow the use of narrow diameter columns and small uniform particles of packing materials. High efficiency chromatographic separations also require systems of low dead volume, a problem effectively handled by the use of micro detectors and capillary tubing.

HPLC systems usually employ : (a) inlet pressures of 500–5000 psig; (b) column lengths of 10–100 cm; (c) column diameters of 1–6 mm id (average, 2 mm); and (d) eluant flow rates of 10 to several hundred ml/ hour. Many HPLC systems are also equipped with gradient elution devices which can change the composition of the eluant continuously during the course of an analysis. The detectors most commonly used are uv/visible of fixed or variable wavelength. Refractive index (RI) detectors are also used. The uv detectors are sensitive but are limited to the detection of aromatic and other compounds that are strong uv-absorbers. The RI detector is universal but is relatively insensitive and different to use with gradient elution.

GAS CHROMATOGRAPHY IN COSMETIC ANALYSIS

Gas chromatography has become an increasingly important analytical tool for separating, identifying, quantifying, and isolating ingredients from a wide variety of complex cosmetic formulations. Individual components may be separated rapidly by this technique (usually in less than one hour) and in many cases identified and determined at very low levels.

Gas chromatography actually comprises two alternative separation modes, one based on adsorption (gas-solid chromatography, GSC) and the other based on partition (gas-liquid chromatography, GLC) interactions.

Gas Liquid Chromatography

In GLC, a light inert carrier gas such as helium or nitrogen serves as the "mobile phase." This mobile phase flows continuously through a copper, glass, or stainless steel column packed with a relatively non-volatile film of "stationary liquid," which is coated either on a large number of small, inert, solid particles ("solid support") contained therein or directly on the inside column walls. Such "packed column" will be emphasised because of their high frequency of use in current cosmetic analysis and their dual utility for analytical and preparative functions. Narrow bore capillary columns (0.04–0.05" id), which have the stationary liquid phase coated directly on their inner walls, are used almost exclusively for analytical purposes because of the very limited amounts of sample they can handle successfully. Either column is supported in a thermostatically controlled oven in the gas chromatograph so that is may be maintained at a preselected temperature or range of temperatures.

A sample in the solid, liquid, or gaseous state is introduced into the chromatograph via an "injection port," which is usually maintained at an elevated temperature to aid in volatilisation. (Lower injection port temperatures are sufficient for sample constituents with higher vapour pressures, such as gases and low boiling liquids.) In some cases, a chemical derivative of the sample may have to be prepared to form a product volatile enough so that it can be separated by GLC. No decomposition or destruction of components should occur at the temperatures required for volatilisation. The solid support coated with stationary phase should be readily permeable to the carrier gas flow. Vapour pressure of the stationary liquid phase should be minimal or non-existent at the operating temperature of the column.

The separation of volatilised components is influenced by a number of factors as the mixture is swept through the column by a flow of carrier gas. At the head of the column, each component of the vapourised mixture partitions itself in an equilibrium between the carrier gas and the stationary liquid phase. These multiple equilibria are continually established as the carrier gas sweeps the solutes through the column. The degree of interaction of each of the solutes with the liquid phase depends upon combinations of various electronic forces which selectively retard each component until it exists from the column as a separate entity. Separation is therefore based on the continuing competition between the liquid and gas phases for the volatilised solutes. The velocities of the solutes differ at a rate reflected mathematically by the partition coefficient, *K*, which is a measure of the degree that each component is retained by the liquid phase. For a given solute *A*,

K = Concentration of solute *A* in stationary phase/concentration of solute *A* in mobile phase.

Preparation of Packed Columns

Selection and Preparation of Tubing

Stainless steel copper, aluminum, and glass are all common materials from which tubing for columns may be manufactured. Some chemical entities in the sample or the stationary phase may be catalytically converted by the composition of these metallic tubes. Glass is the least likely material to contribute to such adverse activity, and it has the added bonus of furnishing a clever view of the progress made during the column packing procedure. However, glass tubes are fragile and expensive, and they usually must be ordered specially to fit a given gas chromatograph. Packed columns may serve in an analytical (1/8–1/4" od) or preparative (3/8–1/2" od) capacity. In order to fit in the oven, tubes must be either U-shaped or, more, often, coiled. After the tubes are coiled, they are cleaned with solvents, filled with packing material (solid support coated with stationary phase), and connected to the chromatograph with Swagelok fittings.

The tubes are cleaned with solvents prior to packing to remove industrial contaminants used in their manufacture. Usually a cacuum is applied to one end and a detergent solution and/or a series of organic solvents is introduced at the opposite end. Each successive organise solvent should have a higher polarity, the final one being the same as the solvent used for coating the liquid phase onto the solid support–eg., pentane,chloroform, acetone, and the liquid phase solvent.

Preparation of Solid Support

The support should be sieved in order to select the appropriate narrow range of particle (mesh) sizes required for efficient column performance, as previously discussed. Most of the fines should be removed; if they are created by sieving an easily fractured support, the support should instead be added to water and the fines eliminated by decantation. Many solid supports are commercially available in the required mesh range and are adequate for use as is.

Packing the Column

A well packed column should have a uniform distribution of closely packed solid particles (not crushed or fractured) to keep the pressure drop of carrier gas between the column's inlet and outlet at a minimum. One end of the clean, previously shaped tube is plugged with a gas-permeable material such as silanised glass wool or a thin metal fritted disk so that the packing material will remain in the tube. As the packing material is poured through a funnel temporarily attached to the open end, a full vacuum is applied to the plugged end while the column is tapped lightly and/or vibrated to facilitate proper settling. When no more material can be transferred into the column, it is assumed to be full and properly packed. Alternatively, 40–50 psig of inert gas or air can be applied to a specially designed reservoir (commercially available) containing the packing material. The reservoir is attached to the open end of the column, and the column is tapped or vibrated mildly until no more material is transferred into the column. Care should be taken not to disconnect any part of the apparatus until after the pressure is turned off and enough time has elapsed for the pressure to equilibrate to ambient conditions.

After the column has been packed, the open end is plugged with silanised glass wool or a fritted metal disk, and nuts and ferrules are attached to both ends (if they have not been attached previously) to provide for connection of the column to the instrument. (Special plasticised ferrules are available for glass columns).

Specialised details must be observed in packing certain types of supports. For example, only gently tapping or minimal vibration should be used for easily fractured solids; packed porous polymer beads, because of their shrinkage, should be conditioned in an oven for at least two hours at 25–50°C below the maximum recommended operating temperature with a slow carrier gas flow, followed by column removal and further packing.

Column Conditioning

After packing, all freshly prepared columns should be conditioned, primarily to eliminate various volatile impurities introduced by the coating and packing procedure or previously present in the liquid phase or solid support. Common impurities include water, unpolymerised monomeric species from which the liquid phase was synthesised, and solvents. Conditioning may also aid in achieving a more even distribution of the liquid phase throughout the packing material.

One end of the column, usually the one to which the packing was added, is attached to the inlet portion of the chromatograph while the other end is left unconnected in order not to contaminate or damage the detector.

Generally, the column, under low carrier gas flow, is heated gradually to 10–20°C above the expected operating temperature. The column is conditioned overnight at this temperature.

Certain liquid phases, require specialised treatment; for example, they may be conditioned initially for various time periods at specified temperatures with no carrier gas flow. To obtain accurate quantitative results, it is frequently necessary that certain other highly specialised and unique steps be taken. Several examples are presented below under determination.

Sample Preparation

One or more physical and/or chemical steps frequently must be taken in order to separate and isolate the components to be measured in the sample from the rest of the ingredients that may interfere with the analysis. It is also useful to concentrate the sample, especially when handling small quantities.

Reduced or ambient pressure distillation is helpful for the isolation or removal of volatile materials. The higher boiling sesquiterpene hydrocarbon portions, frequently present in small amounts in essential oils used in fragrance compositions, may be isolated along with other higher boiling compounds as the residue remaining after distillation of the more abundant, volatile terpene hydrocarbons. Such a residue is then separated further on alumina into sesquiterpene hydrocarbon fractions by liquid column chromatography. Azeotropic distillation is also useful. In this process, a liquid immiscible with the sample is added and the temperature is raised to the boiling point. The components of interest are quantitatively distilled over along with the immiscible liquid. This procedure is useful for the separation and isolation of propylene glycol from a variety of cosmetic products. In this case, iso-octane is the immiscible liquid of choice since one of the prerequisites for its selection is that only a minimum amount is required for quantitative transfer for the component of interest, propylene glycol.

Extraction with immiscible solvent systems is effective when selectivity is achieved for the ingredients of interest. Hexachlorophene is extracted from whole blood with an ether-alcohol (18 + 7) solution in a study of the extent of its penetration through mammalian skin. Glycerol is separated from most other ingredients in cosmetic creams through the addition of water (in which it is soluble) followed by extraction (and separation) of most other organic ingredients in the cream with chloroform or petroleum ether. Most cosmetic ingredients, except for highly polar water-soluble compounds such as glycerol, are soluble in these organic solvents. Glycerol is isolated from toothpastes or gums by extraction with 2-methoxyethanol, in which it is soluble. Any insoluble materials are separated by filtration of the extract.

The preparative liquid column chromatographic methods are also useful tools for separation and isolation. As indicated above, an alumina column is useful for fractionating various sesquiterpene hydrocarbon mixtures; a silica gel column is helpful for removing interfering hydrocarbons from fatty acid esters and alcohols determined in lipsticks.

The chemical reactivity of any functional group of a cosmetic ingredient may be useful for its retrieval from a mixture. The acidic (phenolic) nature of hexachlorophene, for example, facilitates its alkaline extraction from whole blood.

In headspace analysis, vapours of solutions of sufficiently volatile ingredients may be injected directly into the gas chromatograph without any need for elaborate sample clean-up or separation procedures. The sample is placed in an enclosed system so that an equilibrium of the component(s) is established between the gaseous and liquid phases. An aliquot of the vapour is then withdrawn through a septum or membrane covering and injected into the chromatograph. Cosmetics containing methanol, ethanol, or isopropanol, as well as chloroform in toothpastes, are easily handled by this technique. These ingredients can be identified and also determined by headspace analysis. A number of propellants and solvents found in aerosol hair spray formulations may also be identified.

In practice, the solute molecules not only partition between the two phases but may also be adsorbed by the so called "inert" solid support. Such an adverse effect may be significant even after the support has been "deactivated". The tendency toward adsorption on the active sites of the support is directly proportional to solute polarity, i.e., acids are adsorbed most readily, followed by phenols and amines. Adsorption, manifested in peak tailing, leads to incomplete separations and, in turn, to inaccurate qualitative and quantitative results. If such highly polar compounds are quantitatively converted to less polar derivatives not able to form hydrogen bonds with the stationary liquid phase and/or support, this problem can be minimised or eliminated. For example, phenols or alcohols are treated with acid anhydrides or azomethanes to form ester or ether derivatives, respectively. In addition, alkanoloamines, used as neutralisers for acidic polymer resins added to various aerosol hair spray formulations, are converted to their corresponding difunctional amide and acetate derivatives with acetic anhydride-pyridine (2 + 1) reagent (if the amine is tertiary, only an acetate is formed).

Because high molecular weight compounds may have inordinately long retention times, it may be necessary to convert them, by chemical means, to lower molecular weight products which are more volatile and therefore more amenable to GLC. In some cases, these products may also have the potential, because of their high polarity, for being easily adsorbed on the support. Both problems are eliminated in an analysis of castor oil in lipsticks by the following technique : Castor oil, the relatively non-volatile triglyceride of ricinoleic acid, is converted by transesterification with a methanolbenzene-sulphuric acid solution (300 + 100 + 3.7) to glycerol and the methyl ester of ricinoleic acid. The amount of castor oil present is then determined by a GLC analysis for methyl ricinoleate. Multiple products from reactions such as this one also afford further confirmatory evidence for identification by the accumulation of additional retention time data. Mixtures of certain higher molecular weight isomeric fatty acid esters of fatty alcohols are difficult to separate; however, after transesterification with methanol, they become readily separable mixtures of fatty alcohols and methyl esters of fatty acids. The alcohols can be verified by acetylation. The alcohol peaks then disappear and retention times for the corresponding acetate peaks are obtained.

Detectors

In selecting a detector, points to consider are (1) sensitivity, (2) signal-to-noise ratio, (3) linearity, (4) stability, (5) specificity (range of application), and (6) destructive effect on the effluent (reactivity with the sample molecules). Thermal conductivity, flame ionisation, and electron capture detectors are used more frequently than other types in the GLC analysis of cosmetics.

Most common is the thermal conductivity detector in which a metallic filament, heated by the passage of a constant electrical potential, exhibits a given resistance which is subject to change when a corresponding change is induced in its environmental temperature. An inert carrier gas is diverted over two such heated filaments that are part of a Wheatstone bridge assembly. The heat loss from both filaments, maintained through a block set at constant temperature, is equal until a component is swept over one of them. At this point, the heat conductance away from this filament is affected, along with its temperature and resistance. The bridge circuit measures the difference in the electrical signal generated between the two filaments because of their difference in resistance and emits a signal which restores balance and indicates the presence of the solute. In order to achieve optimum sensitivity and wide linearly of response, the carrier gas should have a low molecular weight, high thermal conductivity and low viscocity. Helium is ideal in all these respects and is usually employed as the carrier gas when using a thermal conductivity detector. The thermal conductivity detector performs best with a high bridge current and low block temperature, and its performance may be adversely affected by carrier gas flow fluctuations or ambient temperature effects. This detector is less sensitive (about 1 x 10^{-9} g/second) than those discussed below.

In the flame ionisation detector, the organic vapour of the solute enters a flame supported by hydrogen and air, and it is converted to cationic species and free electrons. A gap between two electrodes with a difference in applied potential is oriented so as to monitor the current increase over that generated from background. This detector is destructive to the compounds measured and relatively insensitive to inorganic compounds such as water, hydrogen sulphide, carbon disulphide, and carbon dioxide; however, it is more sensitive to organic compounds (about 3 x 10^{-12} g/second) than the thermal conductivity detector. The presence of inorganic compounds may decrease the sensitivity of the flame ionisation detector to organic compounds. This detector has a wide linear response. Either nitrogen or belium may be used with it as a carrier gas because both (i) have small background conductivity–necessary for the detection of proportionately large currents produced by sample components; (ii) have minimal viscosity and (iii) are inert. Optimum sensitivity is dependent on carrier gas and combustion gas (hydrogen and air) flow rates.

The election capture detector is also dependent upon ionisation of the sample but, unlike the flame ionisation detector, it does not destroy the compounds measured. Certain types of vapour molecules, when bombarded with electrons, accept or "capture" them and become negatively charged. These highly energised electrons are emitted from a radioactive source, usually ^{63}Ni. The negatively charged molecules produced enter a gap between oppositely charged electrodes where a current has previously been established by ionisation of the carrier gas. When the negatively charged, slower moving components enter this gap, the current is diminished and the sample is detected accordingly. This detector is much more selective than those discussed above, since it detects only electron-accepting molecules containing halogen, sulphur, organo-metallic, phosphorus, or polyaromatic substituents. It is also the most sensitive of the three at about 3 x 10^{-14} g/second. Although nitrogen has been used as a carrier gas with electron capture detectors, it may foster other ionic mechanisms that may erroneously be attributed to electron capture. In order to avoid such effects, argon containing 5–10% (v/v) methane (sometimes butane) is used as carrier gas, and pulsed electrical waves are applied across the electrode gap.

Table 44.1 lists the range of operating temperatures chosen for each type of detector with corresponding injector and column temperature ranges selected from a cross-section dealing with the gas chromatographic analysis of cosmetic products and raw materials.

Table - 44.1

Operating temperature ranges (°C) for various types of detectors with accompanying injector and column temperatures[a].

	Thermal Conductivity	*Flame Ionisation*	*Electron Capture*
Detector[b]	240–320	190–300	300
Injector[b]	240–320	200–-310	270–275
Column[c]	65–250	70–270	125–250

a Based on methods developed for the analysis of cosmetics and cosmetic raw materials.

b A selected isothermal temperature is chosen for any given analysis.

c Most temperatures are selected for isothermal runs within this range; some are a programmed span of temperatures from this range for a given analysis.

Identification

The time between injection of a sample onto the column and elution of a component represented by its peak on a chromatogram is known as the "retention time" of that component. Its reproduction is difficult because of many inherent variables associated with GLC. However, reproducible relative retention times may be calculated by adding a known compound, called an internal standard, to the sample and comparing the time it takes for emergence of this compound to that required for the unknown. Relative retention times are frequently expressed in terms of Kovats indices or McReynolds constants.

Many of the raw materials used in cosmetic products are complex mixtures of ingredients. A distinctive GLC peak pattern (fingerprint) may emerge based on the relative retention times of the various components. Comparison of these relative retention times with those of standard materials can be very helpful in identifying unknown constituents. For example, the sesquiterpene hydrocarbon fractions of many essential oils used in fragrance compositions contain characteristic identifiable combinations of specific sesquiterpene hydrocarbons which generate peaks that are representative of or unique for a given oil. Comparison is made of their peaks with those peaks from a similar fraction obtained from a standard oil.

Mere knowledge of the retention time of an ingredient does not provide confirmatory evidence of its identity. The pure unknown compound may be isolated by trapping as it elutes from the column and then subjected to various "wet" chemical or instrumental techniques to confirm its identity or elucidate its structure. Instrumental techniques frequently used for this purpose include ultraviolet and infrared spectrophotometry, fluorometry, nuclear magnetic resonance spectroscopy, mass spectromety, refractometry, and optical rotation (polarimetry and circular dichroism). Melting point and boiling point measurements are also useful. With mass spectrometry and, less often, infrared spectrophotometry, it is possible, and indeed common, to connect the instrument directly in series to the exit port of the GLC column via an interface which oviates trapping or handling of the compound.

Determination

The internal standard method is the preferred approach for GLC analysis of cosmetics because :

1. Errors which could arise from non-linear detector response are minimised.
2. Identical aliquots of the standard and sample solutions are not required for injection.
3. Identical concentrations of the sample and standard are not required. The standard is a volumertrically prepared solution consisting of a known concentration of a purified compound that is identical in structure to that to be determined in the sample. The internal standard is a compound different from the one being determined and should meet the following criteria : absent from the sample, miscible with the component to be determined in the chosen solvent system, pure, non-reactive with any chemical in the sample or solvent, and chemically and chemically and thermodynamically stable. The internal standard should also generate a symmetrical peak on the recorder with a retention time close to but not identical with that of the compound to be determined or any other constituent of the sample solution.

In applying the internal standard technique, a suitable volume of a known concentration of the internal standard is added to the sample solution containing all of the unknown constituent such that the peak heights generated by both in the resulting chromatogram are similar (within 10--25%). Increasing accuracy is usually assured as the ratio of peak heights approaches unity. Although each peak should be no less than 50% full scale on the recorder, 75–95% is preferred.

An identical (or similar) amount of internal standard is then added to a separate vessel into which an experimentally determined amount of the compound of interest from a standard solution containing only that compound has been added such that the peak height ratio of unknown to internal standard is similar to that in the sample solution. The total solution volume is adjusted so that it is similar to that of the sample solution containing the internal standard. The above criteria for peak heights and ratios also apply here.

Aliquots of each solution should be injected alternately at least twice so that all peak heights for the unknown in all chromatograms vary by less than ± 10%. An average value is obtained for the peak height ratios for each solution. Values which vary by more than 10% from this average should be rejected.

The percentage by weight of unknown in the sample may be calculated as follows :

% Unknown = [$R_u R_s$) x weight unknown in standard x

(weight internal standard in sample/weight internal standard in

standard)/weight of sample] x 100

Where R_s = average peak height ratio of sample solution (peak height unknown in sample/peak height internal standard in sample of several injetions), and R_s = average peak height ratio of standard solution (peak height unknown in standard/peak height internal standard in standard of several injections).

If possible, all determinations should be made on the same day in order to minimise instrumental errors resulting from carrier gas flow rate change, temperature deviations, detector response variables, etc. It is also best to work at the same attenuation and range settings of the instrument for both sample and standard solutions throughout the determination.

Two examples of potential errors that may arise in internal standard analyses are illustrated : In the headspace determination of chloroform in toothpaste, the difference in absorption by the rubber dam and smaller concentration (10%) of the 1, 1, 1-trichloroethane internal standard compared to the choloroform necessitates that all measurements be made over a short time span before peak ratios change drastically, Second, the peak response for ethanol may vary because of the dependence of this response on the time between emergence of the internal standard from the previous injection and the injection of the current ethanol sample. This phenomenon, caused by support adsorption, requires injection of all ethanol samples at a preset time differential.

ANALYSIS OF CREAMS AND LOTIONS

Three types of ingredients are essential in the formulation of cosmetic emulsions. One ingredient is water. Another is "fatty" or water-insoluble material such as beeswax, spermaceti, hydrocarbons, lanolin, fatty acids, alcohols of high molecular weight, glycerides, isopropyl myrisate, etc. The third essential ingredient is a surface active agent that emulsifies the water and "fatty" material. Some common emulsifiers are soaps, glyceryl monostearate, alkyl sulphates, lanolin, quaternary ammonium salts, and polyoxyethylene compounds.

Because these products are either water-in-oil or oil-in-water types of emulsions, they can, in most cases, be analysed in a similar manner.

GENERAL ANALYSIS

Net Contents

1. If the product is a cream, weigh the intact container at the beginning of the analysis. After the analysis is completed, remove any remaining sample and weigh the empty container. Calculate the weight of the product by difference.
2. If the product is a lotion, mark the outside of the bottle at the surface level of the liquid before beginning the analysis. Upon completing the analysis, empty the bottle and note the volume of water required to fill it to the mark.
3. For aerosol products in metallic containers, weigh the intact container, chill in a dry ice chest for 2 hours, and punch out the top of the chilled container with a cold chisel and hammer.
   (a) If contents are liquid, pour out the contents and weigh the parts of the container together. Calculate the contents by difference.
   (b) If contents are solid, place the opened can with the frozen material in a 4 L beaker and let it warm to room temperature. Decant the liquefied contents and proceed as in above.

Description of Product

Note colour, odour, and other physical characteristics of the product.

Type of Emulsion

1. Smear a thin film of the product, ca 1" square by about 1/16" thick, on a watch glass. Sprinkle small amounts of a finely ground oil-soluble dye and a water-soluble dye on separate areas of the film. Spreading of the oil-soluble dye indicates a water-in-oil emulsion; spreading of the water-soluble dye indicates an oil-in-water emulsion.
2. As an alternative procedure, determine the type of emulsion by noting whether a portion of the product readily mixes with mineral oil (w/o emulsion) or water (o/w emulsion).
3. Another procedure involves electrical conductivity, as follows :

"Equipment for this may be easily constructed by wiring in series a 30,000 ohm 1/2-watt resistor, electric contacts for the test sample, a resistorless neon lamp (1/4-watt 104 to 120 v.), and a push-button switch. The sample is placed across the test contacts and the circuit is closed. If the neon lamp glows, the emulsion is o/w; if it does not, the emulsion is w/o. There are occasions when the lamp will glow dimly or will start to glow upon continued application of the electric current. This usually indicates either a dual emulsion or a gradual inversion of the emulsion. The presence of electrolytes, particularly at high levels, may result in conductivity even though the emulsion is essentially w/o."

pH of Emulsion

1. For o/w cream emulsions, mix 1 g of cream with 9 ml of water and determine the pH of the resulting mixture with a glass electrode instrument. Report the pH (1 part cream plus 9 parts water).
2. For o/w lotion emulsions, determine the pH directly on the liquid.
3. Alternatively, determine the approximate pH of (a) and/or (b) with short range pH test paper.

Ashing at 600°C

Weigh about 5 g of the product in a flat-bottom platinum dish and heat on the steam bath under a jet of air for 1 hour. Remove the dish and add 1 g of ashless cellulose powder, then mix with a glass stirring rod. Wipe any adhering material from the stirring rod with a piece of filter paper and add the paper to the dish. Heat the dish under an infrared (IR) heating lamp until the sample is charred. Complete ashing at 600°C in a muffle oven.

Examination of Ash

1. *Borates* – Mix a portion of ash with a few drops of H_2SO_4 in a platinum dish, add several ml of methanol, stir well, place in a darkened hood; and ignite. A green flame indicates the presence of boron.
2. *Carbonates* – Mix a portion of ash with a drop of HCl. An odourless effervescence indicates the presence of carbonates.
3. *Other water-soluble salts*–Dissolve the remainder of the ash in water or dilute HNO_3, filter off any insoluble material, and test aliquots of the filtrate for chlorides with $AgNO_3$, for sulphates with $BaCl_2$, and for phosphates with ammonium molybdate. Also check for Na and K by platinum wire flame tests.
4. *Water-insoluble ash* (Commonly TiO_2, ZnO, or talc) – ignite the ash in a platinum crucible. The appearance of a yellow colour that

fades on cooling indicates the possible presence of ZnO. Dissolve the ZnO in acid and precipitate as ZnS for confirmatory test.

Solubilise TiO_2 by heating in a covered porcelain crucible with 8 ml of H_2SO_4 and 4 g of Na_2SO_4. Cool and carefully pour the solution into 50 ml of ice-cold water. Test for titanium colorimetrically with H_2O_2.

Fuse talc with a 1 + 10 mixture of Na_2CO_3 and K_2CO_3 and test for magnesium and silica.

5. *Infrared spectrum of ash* – Prepare a mineral oil mull or KBr disk of the ash and obtain its infrared spectrum. This spectrum is helpful in identifying the nature of the ash.

6. *X-ray fluorescence spectroscopy* – Elements with atomic numbers equal to or greater than that of aluminum can readily be identified by X-ray fluorescence spectroscopy.

Non-volatile Matter at 105°C

Weigh about 1 g of the product into a large weighing bottle and heat on a steam bath under a jet of air for 30 minutes. Continue heating at 105°C in an oven for 2 hours. Cool in a desiccator, weigh, and report as non-volatile matter (2 hours at 105°C).

Infrared Examinations of Non-volatile Matter

Smear a film of the non-volatile matter on a salt crystal and obtain the IR spectrum of the film. Examine this spectrum carefully for clues to the composition of the sample. The positions of the absorbance peaks indicate the identity of the ingredients present; the absorbance values indicate the relative amounts of the various components present.

In particular, look for the presence of esters, hydrocarbons, alcohol polyhydroxy compounds, polyoxyethylene compounds, amides, soaps fatty acids, and alkanolamines.

Chloroform-Extractable Matter

This extraction is applicable to soap emulsions such as the beeswax-borax, alkanolamine, glyceryl monostearate, and alkali metal types. The emulsification of the $CHCl_3$ may preclude its use with creams emulsified by other surface active agents.

1. Transfer about 3 g of sample to a separatory funnel with 50 ml of water, strongly acidify with HCl, and extract with four 35 ml portions of $CHCl_3$. Combine the $CHCl_3$ extracts wash with 10 ml of water, and add the washing to the reserved extracted aqueous solution. Filter the $CHCl_3$ extracts through a cotton plug into a tared 250 ml

beaker, evaporate the solvent on a steam bath under a jet of air, and dry the residue at 105°C in an oven for 15 minutes. Cool in a desiccator and weigh as $CHCl_3$-extractable matter.

2. Test $CHCl_3$-extractable matter for lanolin or sterols, or both, by the Liebermann-Burchard reaction :

   Dissolve a small portion of the material in 10 ml of $CHCl_{3}$, add 5 ml of acetic anhydride and follow with 5–10 drops of H_2SO_4. Stir well. The appearance of a characteristic green colour indicates the presence of lanolin or sterols.

3. Obtain an IR spectrum of a film of the $CHCl_3$-extractable matter and examine the spectrum to ascertain what material may be present.

Material Not Extractable by Chloroform from Acid Aqueous Solution

1. *Total non-extractable matter*– Dilute the reserved extracted aqueous solution from above to 100 ml with water in a volumetric flask. Pipet out a 40 ml aliquot into a tared 100 ml beaker and evaporate the water on a steam bath under a jet of air. Dry the residue at 105°C in an oven for 10 minutes, cool in a desiccator, and weigh as non-extractable matter.

   (a) Obtain an IR spectrum of a film of the material and note whether a polyhydroxy compound or an alkanolamine hydrochloride (usually triethanolamine) or both may be present.

   (b) As an additional test for alkanolamine, add excess *n*-propyl alcohol to the residue in a beaker, boil to a small volume, chill, scratch the sides of the beaker with a glass rod to induce crystallisation, filter off the crystals, and dry. Determine the melting point of the crystals of alkanolamine hydrochloride or obtain an IR film spectrum of a mineral oil mull of the crystals.

2. *Chemical test for glycerol*– Neutralise a 10 ml aliquot of the extracted aqueous solution, (a), to methyl red with CO_2-free 0.1*N* NaOh, making the final adjustment with 0.02*N* NaOH and leaving the solution just barely yellow. Add 30 ml of 0.02*M* KIO_4 and stir well. If the red colour of methyl red appears immediately, glycerol, is probably present.

   (c) *Additional chemical test for glycerol*– place 3 ml of the aqueous solution containing glycerol in a large test tube. Add 3 ml of freshly prepared 10% catechol solution, then 6 ml of H_2SO_4. Heat in boiling water for 30 minutes. An orange-red colour indicates the presence of glycerol.

Saponification of Chloroform-Extractable Matter

1. Reflux the $CHCl_3$-extractable matter for 2 hours with 25 ml of 95% alcohol, 1 g of KOH, and 50 ml of benzene. Transfer the saponified mixture to a separatory funnel (with Teflon or ungreased glass stopcock), add 50 ml of hot water, shake well, and draw off the aqueous layer. Continue the extraction with two additional 50 ml portions of hot benzene. Reserve the extracted aqueous solution. Combine the benzene extracts, and wash with three 30 ml portions of 30% alcohol, shaking very gently with the first washing and more vigorously with the other two. Add the washings to the reserved extracted aqueous solution. Filter the washed benzene extract through a cotton plug into a 250 ml tared beaker, evaporate the benezene on the steam bath, and dry the residue at 105°C in an oven for 15 minutes. Cool and weigh as unsaponifiable matter. Obtain its IR Spectrum.

2. Acidify the reserved aqueous solution (a) with HCl and extract with three 30 ml of portions of $CHCl_3$. Reserve the extracted aqueous solution and use it to test for combined glycerol and a polyxyethylene compound. Wash the combined $CHCl_3$ extracts with water. Filter the washed $CHCl_3$ extract through a cotton plug into a tared 250 ml beaker, evaporate the $CHCl_3$ on the steam bath under a jet of air, dry the residue at 105°C in an oven for 15 minutes, cool, and weigh as fatty acids.

Examination of the Saponifiable Matter

1. Equivalent weight of fatty acids – Dissolve saponifiable matter in 50 ml of alcohol that has been neutralised to phenolphthalein with 0.1 *N* alkali. Titrate with 0.1 *N* NaOH to a phenolphthalein end point. Calculate the equivalent weight of fatty acids.

2. Hanus iodine absorption number.

Hydrocarbons and Alcohols in Unsaponifiable Matter

Dissolve the unsaponifiable matter in 50 ml of boiling heptane and cool the solution to room temperature with stirring.

1. If there is any precipitated matter, filter the resulting mixture through filter paper, wash the residue well with petroleum ether and reserve the filtrate. Dissolve the residue by pouring hot $CHCl_3$ through the filter paper, and evaporate the $CHCl_3$ on the steam bath. Dry at 105°C in an oven for 10 minutes, cool in a desiccator let stand in air 10 minutes, and weigh as alcohols insoluble in heptane-petroleum ether.

Evaporate the reserved heptane-petroleum ether solution on the steam bath and take up the residue in 50 ml of warm petroleum ether (b.p., 30–75°C). Transfer the solution, with the aid of 25 ml of petroleum ether, to a glass chromatographic tube holding a 9 x 3/4" activated alumina column (Alcoa grade F–20, 80–200 mesh), and let the solution flow through the column at a rate of 3–5 ml/minute, collecting the petroleum ether eluates in a 400 ml beaker. Follow this solution with 175 ml of petroleum ether. Reserve the petroleum ether eluate.

Remove the petroleum ether from the column by passing 50 ml of 95% alcohol through the column under air pressure. Then, again using air pressure, force 125 ml of boiling alcohol through the column at a rapid rate (4–7 minutes for 125 ml). Collect these two eluates in a tared 250 ml beaker labelled *First Hot Alcohol Fraction*. Pass another 50 ml of boiling alcohol through the column and collect it in a tared 250 ml beaker labelled *Second* Evaporate each of the hot alcohol fractions to dryness on the steam bath under a jet of air, redissolve the residue in 10 ml of $CHCl_3$, and evaporate to dryness again. Dry the residue at 105°C in an oven for 10 minutes, cool and weigh as alcohols soluble in heptane-petroleum ether.

Evaporate the reserved petroleum ether eluate to about 50 ml on the steam bath under a jet of air, transfer to a tared 250 ml of beaker with 50 ml of petroleum ether, and evaporate the solvent on the steam bath. The residue will be hydrocarbons. Dry at 105°C in an oven for 10 minutes, cool, and weigh. Obtain an IR film spectrum of the hydrocarbons.

(b) If there is no precipitated matter, evaporate the heptane solution on the steam bath and proceed as in (a), beginning "take up the residue in 50 ml of warm petroleum ether...."

Examination of Alcohols in Unsaponifiable Matter

(a) Obtain the IR spectra of the alcohols.

(b) Combine all alcohol fractions and determine the solubility of the combined fractions in cold methanol to aid in identifying the wax.

Weigh a sample not exceeding 0.5 g into a 150 ml beaker, add 80 ml of methanol, cover the beaker with a watch glass, and heat on a hot plate until solution is complete. Transfer the beaker to an ice bath and stir the solution vigorously with a thermometer until the temperature is 5°C. Pour the resulting mixture through a 4" Buchner funnel containing an 11 cm No. 595 S & S filter paper, with 1/2" of the edge turned up, wetted with methanol. Filter by gravity or gentle suction. Do not allow the material on the filter to dry or cake. Wash the residue with 20 ml of ice-chilled methanol and drain it dry with suction. Transfer the filtrate to a tared beaker with the aid of $CHCl_3$, evaporate to dryness on the steam bath, heat at 100°C in an oven for 10 minutes, cool in a desiccator, and weigh. Repeat the drying in the oven until the weight is constant to 1–2 mg. Table 44.2 gives the results obtained with beeswax alcohols.

Table 44.2

Solubility of beeswax alcohols in cold methanol[a]

Sample, g	Soluble Alcohols, g	Insoluble Alcohols, g (By Difference)
0.1	0.027	0.073
0.2	0.040	0.160
0.3	0.045	0.255
0.4	0.054	0.346
0.5	0.062	0.438

a A 0.500 g sample of spermaceti alcohols contains a maximum of 0.008 g of insoluble alcohols (10).

Composition of Chloroform-Extractable Matter

1. *Hydrocarbons* – For direct and easy identification of hydrocarbons, determine their IR spectra.

2. *Fatty acids* – If the IR spectrum of the $CHCl_3$- extractable material indicates only fatty acids, no further analysis is necessary and the IR spectrum of the non-volatile matter will probably have the characteristic absorption maximum of soap at about 6.5 µm.

   The presence of saponifiable matter but no unsaponifiable matter suggests several possibilities. The fatty acids may have originally been present as a triglyceride, a monoglyceride, the ester of some other polyhydroxy compound, or the ester of a water-soluble alcohol such as isopropyl alcohol.

3. *Waxes* – Some of the more common waxes such as spermaceti, beeswax, and lanolin contain roughly equal amounts of saponifiable and unsaponifiable matter. If the IR spectrum of the $CHCl_3$-extractable matter indicates that only esters and possibly hydrocarbons are present, and if the amounts of fatty alcohols and acids are approximately equal, it may be assumed that the waxes are equal to the sum of the alcohols and fatty acids.

Some indications as to the types of waxes may be obtained from the IR spectra, the equivalent weight of the fatty acids, the solubility of the alcohols in methanol, and a test for lanolin.

4. *Waxes plus other materials* – If both saponifiable fatty acids and unsaponifiable alcohols are present in unequal amounts, there are several possibilities. If the alcohols greatly exceed the acids, multiply the weight of the acids by two and calculate the resulting value as waxes. Subtract the weight of acids from the weight of alcohols and calculate the remaining value as free alcohols. (It is assumed that the IR spectrum of the material before saponification indicates esters and alcohols.) Conversely, if the fatty acids exceed the alcohols, multiply the weight of alcohols by two to obtain a value for waxes. Calculate the unassigned fatty acids as free fatty acids, soap, or some fatty acid compound which has no unsaponifiable matter. (Again, reliance is placed on the IR spectra and chemical tests).

5. *Charts* – A diagrammatic summary of the analysis of mixtures of hydrocarbons, beeswax, and spermaceti is presented in Figs. 44.1, 44.2 and 44.3. With suitable modifications this scheme is applicable to the analysis of most "fatty materials" or their mixtures.

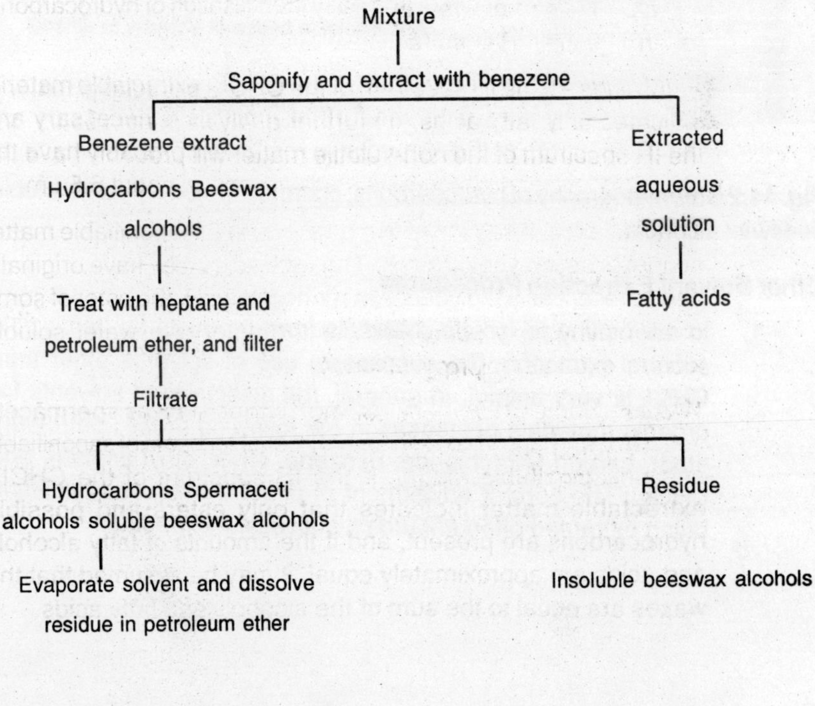

Fig. 44.1 Preparation of a mixture of hydrocarbons, beeswax, and spermaceti for chromatography.

Chromatographic petroleum ether solution of hydrocarbons, spermaceti alcohols, and soluble beeswax alcohols on an activated alumina column

Petroleum ether eluate

Hydrocarbons

Absorbed on activated alumina

Soluble beeswax alcohols spermaceti alcohols

Elute with hot ethanol

Hot ethanol eluate

Soluble beeswax alcohols spermaceti alcohols

Add insoluble beeswax alcohols to ethanol

eluate and evaporate solvent

Fig. 44.2 Chromatography of hydrocarbons, spermaceti alcohols, and soluble beeswax alcohols.

Other Solvent Extraction Procedures

1. In attempting to isolate materials from products by immiscible solvent extraction, the successive use of solvents other than $CHCl_3$ is very helpful. In general, the selectivity of solvents for organic materials decreases in the following order : petroleum ether, carbon tetrachloride, benzene, ether, ethyl acetate, and $CHCl_3$. The correct adjustment of pH of the aqueous solution being extracted often ensures a successful extraction.

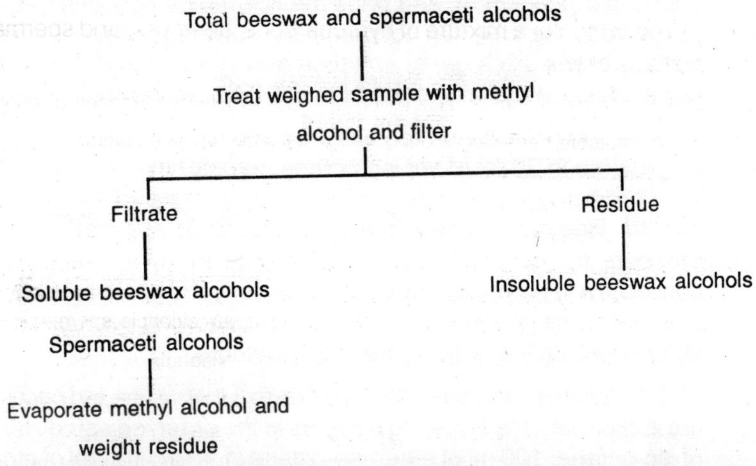

Fig. 44.3 Solubility of combined total beeswax and spermaceti alcohols in cold methyl alcohol.

2. The system petroleum ether – 80% methanol separates organic compounds on the basis of polarity.
3. Ethyl ether does not extract fatty acids from a 25% alcohol solution containing 1% KOH. In washing such ether extracts with 25% alcohol to remove alkali, shake with the dilute alcohol very gently for first washing to avoid emulsification.
4. Non-volatile matter may often be directly extracted by solvents.
5. A useful procedure is partition chromatography with a silicon-coated Celite; heptane and aqueous alcohol solutions are used as the immiscible solvents.

Adsorption Chromatography on silica Gel in Analysis of Isolated Fatty Materials

Mixtures consisting of extracted organic compounds are often best separated by adsorption chromatography on silica gel using eluants of increasing polarity. This technique, employing solvents ranging in polarity from iso-octane to methanol, is usually applicable to mixtures of materials increasing in polarity from aliphatic hydrocarbons to highly ethoxylated compounds or polyols.

1. *Preparation of silica gel column* – Insert a small glass wool plug into the bottom of a 24 x 1/2" id glass chromatographic tube, stopper the bottom of the tube with a rubber policeman, and fill with 20–30 ml of iso-octane. Slurry 10 g of silica gel with 30 ml of iso-octane, pour ca half of the slurry into the chromatographic tube, remove

the rubber policeman, and pack the column by applying 5–6 psi pressure to the tube. Do not permit the solvent to drain below the surface of the silica gel at any time during the analysis. Add the remainder of the slurry to the tube and pack as before.

2. *Sample addition*– Accurately weigh ca 200 mg of material, dissolve or disperse in 20 ml of hot iso-octane, transfer the hot solution to the chromatographic tube, and elute at the rate of 1/2 to 1 ml/minute. Regulate all flow rates by gravity or application of air pressure to the tube. Collect all eluates in 20 ml fractions in consecutively numbered, tared 50 ml beakers. Rinse sample beaker with two 10 ml portions of hot iso-octane, allowing each rinsing to elute separately at a flow rate of 2 ml/minute.

3. *Column elution*– Increase the flow rate to 3 ml/minute and continue the elution with the following solvents in the order indicated : 80 ml of iso-octane; 100 ml of ether-iso-octane (1 + 19); 100 ml of ether-iso-octane (1 + 9); 100 ml of ether-iso-octane (1 + 3); 200 ml of ether-iso-octane (1 + 1); 200 ml of ether; and 100 ml of methanol.

4. *Analysis of eluates* – Evaporate the eluates on the steam bath under a jet of air and heat the residues at 105°C for 10 minutes in a drying oven. Cool and weigh the residues.

   Plot as a bar graph the weight of the residues as the ordinate against the corresponding eluate numbers as abscissa. Indicate on the bar graph the eluant for each residue.

   The plot will consist of $\geq$ 1 peak. Choose the largest residue in each peak and obtain its infrared film spectrum. Use the IR spectra to characterise the residues.

   It is worth noting that the interpretation of the IR spectra by visual inspection could occasionally be in error. For this reason it may sometimes be necessary to compare the eluting pattern of the isolated component to that of the suspected raw material.

Determination of Water by Toluene Distillation

Transfer a 10–20 g sample to a 250 ml Erlenmeyer flask and add 50 ml of toluene and a few glass beads. Connect the flask to a Dean & Stark distilling tube receiver, and distill until no more water collects in the receiver. Cool read the volume of water under the toluene at room temperature, and from this volume calculated the percentage of water.

Examination of Aqueous Fraction from Toluene Distillation

1. *Specific gravity or density*– Determine with a small specific gravity bottle, or pipet 2 ml into a weighing bottle and weigh.

2. *Propylene glycol*

(a) Transfer 3 ml of an aqueous solution of propylene glycol to a large test tube, and add 3 ml of freshly prepared 10% catechol solution and then 6 ml of H_2SO_4. Heat in boiling water for 30 minutes. If the solution turns red and a precipitate forms, propylene glycol is present.

(b) To several ml of solution add 5 ml of 0.02*M* KIO_4. After 1 minute add an excess of 5% alkali followed by 0.1*N* I_2 solution. If a precipitate of iodoform forms immediately, propylene glycol is present.

Silicons in Creams

The IR spectra of silicons are very characteristic, but often the silicons are present in such small percentages that they are easily overlooked in the IR spectra of the product. Some selective separation is necessary. The extraction procedures used in the course of the analysis may concentrate the silicon enough so that it can be recognised. One of a number of special procedures for silicons is as follows :

Shake the emulsion with twice its volume of (1 + 1) dioxane-toluene mixture, centrifuge, and draw off the top layer, which is mostly toluene containing the silicon plus a small amount of organic material. Evaporate the toluene. Examine the IR film spectrum of the residue for the presence of a silicon.

Determination of Esters of *p*-Hydroxybenzoic Acid

Esters of *p*-hydroxybenzoic acid can be isolated from emulsion products by partition chromatography and determined by ultraviolet uv spectrophotometry. The *p*-hydroxybenzoates are quantitatively eluted by the acidified 10% alcohol eluate and are determined as combined esters of *p*-hydroxybenzoic acid.

Emulsifiers

1. *Beeswax-borax w/o cream* gives positive tests for boron and sodium in ash; it contains less than 35% water.
2. *Beeswax-borax o/w cream* gives positive tests for boron and sodium in ash; the pH of a mixture of 1 part cream plus 9 parts water is usually between 8 and 9.
3. *Soap o/w cream* has the following characteristics : the pH of a mixture of 1 part cream plus 9 parts water is usually between 8 and 9; a Na_2CO_3 ash is obtained; the water content is over 70%;

the IR absorption maximum of the soap may be discerned at about 6.5 μm in the spectrum of the non-volatile matter; and glycerol or other polyhydroxy compounds are probably present.

4. *Triethanolamine-soap o/w cream* yields no ash; the pH of a mixture of 1 part cream plus 9 parts water is usually between 7 and 8; the water content is over 70%; the IR absorption maximum of soap may be observed at about 6.5 μm in the spectrum of the non-volatile matter; glycerol or other polyhydroxy compounds are likely to be present; and triethanolamine will be found in the acid aqueous solution after extraction by $CHCl_3$.

5. *Glyceryl monostearate-soap o/w cream* gives a positive test for combined glycerol; more than 60% water is present; and glyceryl monostearate may be detected in the IR spectrum of the $CHCl_3$-extractable matter.

It may be possible to isolate some of the glyceryl monostearate by dissolving the $CHCl_3$- extractable matter in hot heptane and chilling the solution in an ice bath. Remove any precipitated glyceryl monostearate and identify by an IR film spectrum.

AEROSOL PRODUCTS

1. Analyse the product that emerges from the pressurised can. The propellant dissipates almost immediately and is not available for analysis.

2. To identify a halogenated propellant, spray a small amount of product into a suction flask and immediately stopper the top of the flask. Allow the gases emerging from the side arm of the flask to flow into a cell suitable for determination of spectra of gases. Obtain the IR spectrum of propellant, and identify. If the concentration of propellant in the gas cell is too great, remove the excess with a pipet fitted with a rubber bulb.

(If too much of the product is released into the suction flask, the flask becomes chilled, and only the more volatile constituent of the propellant vapourises).

ANALYSIS OF LIPSTICKS

A lipstick generally consists of a moulded, solid fatty base containing dissolved coal-tar dyes and suspended pigments. The base is usually composed of waxes, oils, and fatty material; typical ingredients might include carnauba wax, candelilla wax, beeswax, hydrocarbons, castor oil oleyl alcohol, butyl stearate, polyethylene glycols, Propylene glycol, lanolin, and cocoa butter.

The characteristics and quantity of the waxes present in the lipstick determine the gloss and hardness of the product. The oils are selected primarily on the basis of their solvent effects on the fluorescein dyes. Oils may account for more than half the total weight of the lipstick. The fatty material gives the lipstick film more body, softens the skin of the lips, and promotes the dispersion of insoluble pigments.

Dyes, including the fluoresceins, are used predominantly to stain the lips; lakes and other pigments are used for their brightening and covering effects. A typical product may contain as much as 10% lakes and other pigments and only 2-3% pure dyes in a fatty base. The use of colour additives in lipsticks is regulated by the Food and Drug Administration.

Because of the tendency of all oil-fat-wax mixtures to decompose rapidly, antioxidants and preservatives are added to lipsticks to prevent rancidity and deterioration. Flavours are also added to camouflage any unpleasant fatty taste and odours of the base.

General Analysis

Determine net content, non-volatile matter, ash and infrared spectra as described earlier. Note: colour, odour and other physical characteristics of the lipstick.

Lakes and Fillers

Accurately weigh 0.25-0.30 g of lipstick into a 100 ml beaker. Add 10 ml of trichloroethylene, cover with a watch glass, and heat on the steam bath to dissolve hydrocarbons, waxes etc. Filter the warm mixture under vacuum into a 250 ml suction flask through a tared. Gooch crucible containing double glass fibre filter disks for extra fine precipitates. To prevent contamination of the solvent by rubber fittings, wrap the Gooch crucible with a piece of Al foil so that the foil projects slightly below the bottom of the crucible. Wash the beaker and Gooch crucible with five 5 ml portions of trichloroethylene, followed by 5 ml portions of acetone until the washings are colourless or nearly colourless. Reserve the filtrate for determination by 5.7. Dry the crucible in an oven at 105°C for 2 hours, cool in a desiccator, let stand in air for 10 minutes, and weigh as lakes and tillers.

Trichloroethylene-Acetone Solubles

Transfer the reserved filtrate in the suction flask from above into a tared 100 ml beaker, using two 5 ml portions of trichloroethylene and two 5 ml portions of acetone. Evaporate the solvents on the steam bath under a gentle jet of air. Add 10-15 ml of $CHCl_3$ to the beaker, cover with a watch glass, and reflux on the steam bath until the sides of the beaker are free of any adhering material. Remove the watch glass and evaporate to dryness on the steam bath under a gentle jet of air. Dry the beaker in an oven at 105°C for 15 minutes, cool in a desiccator, let stand in air for 10 minutes, and weigh as trichloroethylene-acetone solubles. This fraction contains all of the ingredient of the lipstick except lakes, fillers, and volatile materials. Reserve for determination of trichloro ethylene - acetene soluble and lenolin or sterols.

Chromatographic Analysis of Trichloroethylene-Acetone Solubles

Prepare silica gel column, introduce the sample and carry out elution as per the process described earlier.

Treatment of eluates–Evaporate the eluates on the steam bath under a jet of air and heat the residues in an oven at 105°C for 10 minutes. Cool in a desiccator and weigh the residues. Obtain an IR spectrum of each residue, using the smallest amount possible to obtain the spectrum. Use the spectra to characterise the residues as containing aliphatic hydrocarbons, liquid or solid alcohols, castor oil, and esters, including isopropyl esters, acetates, etc. Reserve the residues.

Gas-Liquid Chromatographic (GLC) Determination of Castor Oil

1. *Apparatus*

   (a) Gas chromatograph–with hydrogen flame detector. Operating conditions: temperatures (°C) – detector 235, injection port 300, column 235; helium carrier gas flow rate, 85 ml/minute.

   (b) GLC column –6' x 4 mm id glass tube backed with 100-120 mesh Chromosorb W HP coated with 5% SP- 2100. Coated the support with the liquid phase by the funnel coating procedure. Condition the column overnight at 250°C with a helium flow rate of ca 10 ml/minute.

   (c) Refluxing apparatus – All glass, with T24/40 joints, consisting of 100 ml round-bottom flask and water-cooled refluxing condenser, heated with an electric heating mantle.

2. *Reagents*

   (a) Transesterification mixture – Menthol-benzene-sulphuric acid (3+1+0.037). Prepare fresh every 2 or 3 days.

   (b) Dicyclohexyl phthalate internal standard solution–20 mg/ml. Accurately weigh ca 1 g of dicyclohexyl phthalate in a 50 ml volumetric flask, and dilute to volume with toluene.

   (c) Methyl ricinoleate standard solution – 209 mg/ml. Purify ether-extractable methyl ricionleate by adsorption chromatography as follows: Tamp a small glass wool plug into the bottom of a 24 x 1/4" id glass chromatographic tube. Fill the tube with ca 100 ml of $CHCl_3$. Slurry 40g of silica gel in 100 ml of $CHCl_3$ and pack half of the slurry in the tube under 5-6 psi of air pressure. In this and subsequent steps, do not let the solvent drain below the surface of the silica gel. Pack the remainder of the slurry as before. Dissolve the ether extract of the methyl ricinoleate in 40 ml of hot $CHCl_3$ and add to the chromatographic column. Rinse the beaker with two 20 ml portions of hot $CHCl_3$ and add to the column after eluting the initial solution. Continue eluting the column with 120 ml of $CHCl_3$ and 200 ml of $CHCl_3$-ether (9+1). Discard the $CHCl_3$ eluate and collect the $CHCl_3$-ether (9+1) eluate in 25 ml portions in tared 50 ml beakers. Evaporate the eluates on the steam bath under a gentle jet of air, and dry the residues in an oven at 105°C for 5 minutes. Cool and weigh the residues. Combine the 4 largest residues and rechromatography as before. Again combine the 4 largest residues and reserve. Accurately weigh ca 1 g of residue in a 50 ml volumetric flask, and dilute to volume with toluene.

3. *Transesterification* – Accurately weigh a 200-300 mg lipstick sample into a tared 100 ml round-bottom boiling flask. Add 20 ml of transesterification mixture and 3 glass beads to the flask.Connect the flask to water-jacketed reflux condenser with a 24/40 male joint. Attach a heating mantle and adjust the voltage on the power source so that the solution in the flask boils gently. Reflux the solution for 2½ hours. Cool the condenser and rinse with 10 ml of water. Transfer the transesterification mixture and rinse into a 125 ml separatory funnel. Rinse the condenser and boiling flask with an additional 10 ml of water and add to the seperatory funnel. Rinse the condenser and flask with 25 ml of ether, transfer the rinsing to the funnel, and shake well. Draw off the lower aqueous layer into a second 125 ml separatory funnel and extract with 20 ml of ether. Discard the water layer. Combine the two ether extracts, rinse the second 125 ml separatory funnel with a small amount of ether, and add to the ether extracts. Wash the combined ether extracts with three 5 ml portions of water and discard the wash each time. Filter the ether extracts through a cotton plug washed with 20 ml of ether into a 125 ml Erlenmeyer flask. Rinse the separator with two 5 ml portions of ether, and filter the rinsings through the cotton plug. Wash the plug with 20 ml of ether. Reduce the volume of ether to 30-40 ml by evaporating under a gentle jet of air, and reserve the remainder for (4)

4. *Determination* – Add 1 ml of dicyclohexyl phthalate internal standard solution to the reserved ether extract from (c). Inject 2-5 µl of sample

solution into the gas chromatograph. Adjust the operating conditions to elute the methyl ricinoleate peak in ca 8-10 minutes. Compare the peak heights of the sample and internal standard, and, if necessary, add 1.0 ml aliquots of dicyclohexyl phthalate internal standard solution until the ratio of sample peak height most nearly approaches 1.

Prepare a standard solution containing 6.0 ml of dicyclohexyl phthalate internal standard solution and 4.0 ml of methyl ricinoleate standard solution, and inject 2-5 μl into the gas chromatograph. Compare the peak heights and, if necessary, add 1.0 ml aliquots of standard solution or internal standard solution so that the ratio of peak heights most nearly approaches that obtained before for the sample (ca 1).

Inject a 2-5 μl aliquot of standard solution and adjust the range and attenuation to keep the peaks from 60 to 95% of full scale. Under the conditions determined previously, alternately inject 2-5 μl aliquots of the standard and sample solutions, making a minimum of 2 injections of each.

Calculate the peak height rations at follows :

R_u = peak height of sample methyl ricinoleate/peak height of dicyclohexyl phthalate

R_s = peak height of standard methyl ricinoleate/peak height of dicyclohexyl phthalate

Neither R_u nor R_s values from each set of injections should differ by > 5%. Determine average values of R_u and R_s, and calculate the amount of methyl ricinoleate in the sample as follows :

Methyl ricinoleate, mg

$= (R_u/R_s) \times M \times (I_s/I')$,

Where M= mg methyl ricinoleate in standard, I_s = mg internal standard in sample, and I' = mg internal standard in standard.

The castor oil content of the lipstick can be estimated by dividing the methyl ricinoleate content by a factor of 0.9.

ANALYSIS OF SHAMPOOS

Every shampoo contains one or more surface active agents. In commercial preparations the two most widely used surfactants are soaps and alkyl sulphates. They may be salts of either alkali metals or alkanolamines. The vehicle for the surface active agent is ordinarily water. Many other materials are used in conjunction with the surfactant to sequester cations, control the viscosity of a liquid product, and alter the characteristics of the foam; or to serve as hair conditioners, bacteriostats, opacifiers, etc.

Some of these materials are lanolin, the Versenes, water-soluble gums, hexachlorophene, fatty acid-alkanolamine condensates, polyoxyethylene compounds, alcohols of high molecular weight, hydrocarbons, and inorganic salts.

General Analysis

Net Contents

1 At the begining of the examination, mark the outside of bottle at the surface level of the liquid. At the end of the examination, empty the bottle and note the volume of water required to fill it to the mark.

2. Determine net content, pH, ash at 600°C, distillation examination of ash, non-volatile matter and water by toluene using the procedure described earlier.

Description of Shampoo

Infrared Examination of Non-volatile Matter

1. Obtain an infrared (IR) film spectrum of the non-volatile matter on a salt crystal.

It may be necessary to prepare the sample by slurrying the non-volatile matter with alcohol, placing a film of the mixture on a salt crystal, and drying at 105°C in an oven for 5 minutes.

2. Examine the spectrum for the possible presence of soap, alkyl sulphates, alkanolamines, fatty acid-alkanolamine condensates, polyoxyethylene compounds, polyhydroxy compounds, and quaternary ammonium compounds.

Test for Ammonia

1. Make a portion of the shampoo strongly alkaline with 30% NaOH, and note whether the odour of ammonia can be detected.

2. Alternatively, hold a piece of moistened red litmus paper over the shampoo which has been made strongly alkaline. If the paper turns blue, ammonia is present.

Test for Basic Nitrogen Compounds Including Ammonia

Mix about 1 g of shampoo with 8 g of anhydrous Na_2CO_3 in a large Pyrex test tube, cover with another 2 g of Na_2CO_3, and heat the mixture strongly over a gas flame. If a moistened red litmus paper turns blue when it is held in the vapours, ammonia or some other basic nitrogen compound is present.

Lanolin and/or Sterols

The extract from any method of extraction that removes the fatty material will contain the lanolin and/or sterols. Test a portion of such an extract by the Liebesrmann-Burchard colorimetric test.

Water-soluble Gums

1. *Preparation of water-repellent glass plate on which film is formed* – Wash a 4" square of window pane glass thoroughly with soap and water, and dry it with a towel. Dip a solid glass stirring rod in a bottle of Desicote and streak and adhering liquid across the top of the plate. Repeat the streaking process several times. Rub the plate with lens paper to distribute the Desicote evenly, and then rub it with clean lens paper to remove any excess Desicote. The plate is now ready for use. The coated plate may be used for two or three films provided it is washed with cold water and dried with a towel after each use. The plate can be recoated by repeating the described procedure.
2. *Preparation of gum solution* – Precipitate any water-soluble gums by adding alcohol to the shampoo. Centrifuge to concentrate the gum, decant, and discard the supernatant liquid. Redisperse the gum in a minimum amount of water, reprecipitate with alcohol, centrifuge, and decant as before. Dissolve the residue in 10 - 25 ml of water.
3. *Preparation and identification of gum film* – Place the water- repellent glass plate over an open 2" aperture in the steam bath. Pour the aqueous gum solution on the plate so that a circle of liquid about 2" in diameter is formed (about 10 ml is required). Heat the plate on the steam bath until all the liquid has evaporated. Remove the film with forceps (if the film is stuck to the plate it can usually be removed by scraping with a razor blade). Transfer the film to a beaker and dry at 105°C for an hour. Place a piece of dried film between two salt plates and obtain the IR spectrum. To identify the gum, compare the spectrum with spectra of known gums.

ANALYSIS OF NAIL LACQUERS

Most nail lacquers are solutions of nitrocellulsoe , Plasticisers, and resins in mixed volatile organic solvents. Colour and opacity are produced by pigments suspended in the lacquer.

In nail lacquers, n-butyl phthalate, camphor, and tricresyl phosphate are common platicisers; an aryl sulphonamide-formaldehyde polymer is a frequently used resin, and the pigments are likely to be organic lakes, guanine, and titanium dioxide. The solvents are usually mixtures of toluene, butyl acetate, ethyl acetate, ethanol, isopropanol, and butanol, and occasionally include acetone, xylenes, or methyl ethyl ketone.

A typical nail lacquer might contain 12% nitrocellulose, 5% n-butyl phthalate, 5% aryl sulphonamides-formaldehyde resin, 1-3% camphor, and 1-2% pigment. The solvent may approximate 35% toluene, 40% butyl acetate, 15% ethyl acetate, and 10% ethanol. Ethanol is sometimes present as the packing solvent for the nitrocellulose.

General Analysis

Net Contents

Remove the brush and cap from the bottle and mark the height of the liquid on the outside of the bottle. When analysis has been completed, empty the bottle, rinse it with acetone, and fill it with water to the previously inscribed mark; then empty the water into a graduated cylinder and record the volume of liquid.

Description of Nail Lacquer

Note colour, odour, opacity, and other physical characteristics of the nail lacquer.

Infrared Film Spectrum of the Nail Lacquer

1. Prepare a sample by coating a salt crystal with a thin film of the lacquer and drying at 105°C in an oven for 5 minutes.

2. Observe whether the infrared (IR) spectrum can be interpreted as a mixture of nitrocellulose, n-butyl phthalate, and aryl sulphonamide-formaldehyde resin.

Non-volatile Matter at 105°C

After discarding the brush from the bottle top, weigh the closed bottle of nail lacquer. Pour ca 1.0-1.2 g into a tared weighing bottle 65 mm high and 45 mm in diameter, and weigh the nail lacquer bottle again. The difference in weight is the sample weight. With the top removed, manipulate the weighing bottle so that the lacquer covers the entire inside surface of the bottle as a thin film. Then heat the lacquer at 105°C in an oven for 2 hours. Cool and weigh the residue as non-volatic matter.

Determination of Non-volatile Constituents

The overwhelming majority of commercial nail lacquers contain these non-volatile components: nitrocellulose, organic lakes, inorganic pigments such as TiO2, n-butyl phthalate, and an aryl sulphonamide-formaldehyde resin. The following is a method of analysis (Fig. 44.4) for these nail lacquer ingredients :

(a) Dilute a 4-6 g sample with 5 ml of acetone, add 20 ml of benzene, and pour slowly with stirring into a 400 ml beaker containing 150 ml of hot benzene. Rinse the sample container with 5 ml of acetone and add the rinsings to the benzene. Evaporate the benzene on the steam bath under a gentle jet of air to about 80 ml, dilute with 90 ml of benzene, and cool to room temperature. Pour the mixture into a 250 ml centrifuge tube, rinse the precipitation beaker with 10 ml of benzene, and add the rinsings to the centrifuge tube. Reserve the precipitation beaker and any precipitate that adhered to the sides. After centrifuging, decant the supernatant liquid into a 250 ml beaker labelled no. 1 and set it aside.

(b) Dissolve the residue in the precipitation beaker and the centrifuge tube from (a) with 15, 10, and 10 ml portions of acetone, and pour the combined acetone solutions into a 100 ml beaker. Evaporate the acetone on the steam bath, redissolve the residue in 10 ml of acetone, add 20 ml of benzene, and repeat the precipitation and centrifuging procedure described in (a) Decant the supernatant liquid into a beaker labelled no. 2. Reserve the precipitation beaker and the centrifuge tube containing the residues.

(c) Filter the decanted liquids in beakers No. 1, (a) and No.2 (b) through the same 12.5 cm filter paper into two tared beakers labelled I and II. Reserve the filter paper and beakers Nos. 1 and 2.

(d) Evaporate the filtrates in beakers I and II, (c) on the steam bath under jets of air, and dry the residues in an oven at 105°C for 10 minutes. Cool and weigh I and II as combined resin and plasticiser.

(e) Rinse the reserved beakers Nos. 1 and 2 (c) with two 30 ml portions of hot methyl ethyl ketone and pour the rinsings through the reserved filter paper, (c) into a tared beaker. Discard the filter paper, evaporate the filtrate on the steam bath under a jet of air, dry the residue in an oven at 105°C for 20 minutes, cool, and weigh as a mixture consisting essentially of nitrocellulose and pigments.

Obtain an IR film spectrum of the residue from a film prepared in the following manner : Dissolve a little of the material in acetone, pour some of the solution on a salt crystal, let the acetone evaporate in air, dry the film on the crystal in an oven at 105°C for 5 minutes, and cool to room temperature.

(f) Dissolve the residues in the reserved precipitation beaker and the centrifuge tube, (b) in acetone and transfer the acetone solutions to a tared 250 ml beaker. Evaporate the acetone on the steam bath, redissolve the residue in 5 ml of acetone, and add 75 ml of alcohol-ether solution (1+2) followed by 10 ml of water. Evaporate the solvent on the steam bath under a gentle jet of air and dry the residue in an oven at 105°C for 1 1/2 hours. Cool, and weigh as nitrocellulose plus pigments.

Obtain an IR film spectrum of the residue as described in (e)

(g) Use 32 ml of methanol to dissolve and transfer the resin and plasticiser residues in beakers I and II (d) into a 250 ml separatory funnel. Add 8 ml of water and extract with four 40 ml portions of petroleum ether. Reserve the extracted methanol solution. Set the separatory funnels aside for rinsing later.

(h) Filter the combined petroleum ether extracts (g) through a 12.5 cm filter paper into a tared 250 ml beaker. Follow with an additional 40 ml of petroleum ether wash through the filter paper. Reserve the filter paper. Evaporate the filtrate on the steam bath under a jet of air, dry the residue in an oven at 105°C for 10 minutes, cool and weigh as butyl phthalate.

Obtain an IR film spectrum of the material from a liquid film spread on a salt crystal. Also obtain the ultraviolet uv spectrum of an alcohol solution of the phthalate.

(i) Transfer the reserved extracted methanol solution, (g) to a 500 ml separatory funnel, add 50 ml of $CHCl_3$, dilute with 200 ml of water, and acidify with a little HCl. Shake the mixture well and draw off the $CHCl_3$ layer. Continue the extraction with additional 50, 50 and 30 ml portions of $CHCl_3$. Reserve the extracted aqueous solution. Set the separatory funnel aside for rinsing later.

(j) Filter the combined $CHCl_3$ extracts, (i), through the reserved filter paper, (h), and follow with an additional 40 ml wash with $CHCl_3$. Reserve the filter paper. Evaporate the filtrate on the steam bath under a jet of air, dry the residue in an oven at 105°C for 10 minutes, cool, and weigh as aryl sulphonamide- formaldehyde resin.

Obtain an IR film spectrum of the resin as described in (e) Also obtain a uv spectrum of an alcohol solution of the material.

(k) Filter the extracted aqueous solution, (i), through the reserved filter paper, (j), Discard the filtrate. Rinse all the separatory funnels used in the extractions, (g) and (i), with two 30 ml portions of acetone, and filter the acetone solutions through the filter paper into a tared 250 ml beaker. Discard the filter paper. Evaporate the filtrate on the steam bath, dry the residue in an oven at 105°C for 10 minutes, cool, and weigh as a mixture of resin and nitrocellulose.

Obtain an IR film spectrum of the material as in (e).

Separation of Nitrocellulose from Pigments

1. *Guanine*–The mother-of-pearl appearance of some nail lacquers arises from the presence of guanine. To analyse such a product, dilute a weighed sample with acetone, centrifuge, and decant the acetone. Identify the guanine residue from the infrared spectrum of a mineral oil mull or from a film prepared by rubbing the guanine between two salt crystals with a drop of acetone. Separate the crystals and evaporate the acetone at 105°C in an oven.
2. *Opaque coloured nail lacquers* – The opaque coloured effect is achieved through the dispersion of finely divided organic lakes and inorganic pigments such as TiO_2. The nitrocellulose may be separated from the colouring agents by the following procedure (3) :

Dissolve, disperse, and transfer the residues of precipitated nitrocellulose and pigments, from steps of the non-volatile estimation process into a 50 ml heavy-duty centrifuge tube with the aid of 25 ml of hot methyl ethyl ketone. Add 4 drops of water and 50 mg of silicic acid (Mallinckrodt's chromatographic grade) to the solutions. Centrifuge at high speed for one hour and decant the supernatant liquid into a 250 ml separator. Treat the residue in the centrifuge tube with successive 15 and 10 ml portions of methyl ethyl ketone, centrifuging 15 minutes each time and decanting as before into the separator. Discard the residue in the centrifuge tube.

Add 1 ml of HCl to the separator, shake 2-3 minutes, and extract with 50 ml of water saturated with methyl ethyl ketone. Discard the extract. Make the methyl ethyl ketone solution slightly basic with ammonia, and extract with 50 ml of an aqueous solution which is weakly ammonical and saturated with the ketone and which contains 0.5% ammonium chloride. Continue the alkaline extracts until no further colour is extracted (three extractions usually suffice). Discard the extracts, re-acidify the ketone solution with HCl, and wash with two 25 ml portions of water that is weakly acid with HCl and saturated with the ketone. Discard the washings.

Filter the extracted methyl ethyl ketone solution through an 11 cm filter paper into a 250 ml tared beaker. Wash the separator and the filter paper with two 25 ml portions of hot methyl ethyl ketone, collecting the washings in the tared beaker.

Evaporate the volatile solvent on the steam bath under a gentle jet of air Redissolve the residue in 5 ml of acetone and add 75 ml of alcohol-ether solution (1+2) followed by 10 ml of water. Again evaporate the solvent on the steam bath under a gentle jet of air and dry at 105°C in an oven for 1 1/2 hours. Cool, and weigh as nitrocellulose.

In separating the nitrocellulose and the pigments from the nail lacquers, traces of pigment may adhere to the sides of the glassware or on the filter paper. These traces can be dissolved by alcohol strongly acidified with HCl.

Tricresyl Phosphate in Nail Lacquers

When tricresyl phosphate is used with n-butyl phthalate as the plasticiser, the two substances are isolated together. The IR spectra of these two materials differ sufficiently so that each can be identified in the presence of the other. If it is necessary to determine the amount of each component, the uv spectra differ enough so that the methods for the analysis of two-component mixtures can be applied.

Acrylonitrile-Butadiene Polymer

An acrylonitrile-butadiene polymer may be detected in the infrared spectrum of the non-volatile matter. The CN absorbance peak is at 4.45 µm.

When the polymer is present as an additional ingredient in a nail lacquer, it is isolated by precipitation with methanol. The methanol solution may be used for the usual nail lacquer analysis.

Base Coats

1. Base coats are preparations which are applied prior to the nail lacquer. They are usually solutions of polymeric substances. The polymers are most readily recognised by examination of the IR spectrum of the non-volatile matter. Ultra-violet spectra, sometimes of films on a quartz surface, are also helpful if the polymers have aromatic constituents. When a base coat contains two or more polymers, it is good practice to separate them, e.g., by extraction.
2. Acrylonitrile-butadiene and phenol-formaldehyde-polymers are among those used in base coats.

Infrared Spectrophotometric Analysis

Description and Interpretation of Spectra

A commercial colourless nail lacquer, known to contain nitrocelllulose, n-butyl phthalate and aryl sulphonamide-formaldehyde resin as non- volatile ingredients, was analysed. The IR spectra of the following fractions were examined.

1. *Non-volatile matter*

(a) The presence of nitrocellulose is immediately apparent from the absorption maximum just beyond 6 µm and the one at 12 µm.

(b) Although there is no positive identification for n-butyl phthalate, the indication of carbonyl absorption at 5.85 µm suggests that it might very well be a constituent of the product. Likewise the absorption at 8.6 µm may arise from an aryl sulphonamide-formaldehyde resin.

2. *Nitrocellulose*

(a) The principal absorption maxima at 6.05 and 7.8 µm are characteristic of the covalent nitrate groups. The strong absorption at 11.9 µm is also associated with the nitrate group and that at 9.4 µm with the cellulose ring. Note the broad but weak OH bond absorption just before 3 µm and the weak C–H absorption just before 3.5 µm . The minor absorption maxima also aid in identifying nitrocellulose.

(b) In the analysis of coloured opaque nail lacquers containing suspended pigments, the precipitation of the nitrocellulose entrains the pigments. However, it is difficult to differentiate the infrared film spectrum of the contaminated nitrocellulose from that of pure nitrocellulose. In part this is due to the small amount of pigment, 1-2%, ordinarily present in nail lacquers.

3. *n-Butyl phthalate*

(a) The characteristic strong absorption maxima of phthalats are the carbonyl ester absorption at 5.8 µm and the maxima at 7.8, 8.9, and 9.3 µm The weak doublet centred around 6.3 µm always appears in phthalates. The other absorption peaks are also helpful for identification.

(b) The intensity of the C–H absorption in the 3.5 µm region is indicative of the length of the alkyl carbon chain of the ester.

4. *Aryl sulphonamide-formaldehyde resin* – is the spectrum of a commercial sample of the resin.

(a) The major absorption maxima attributable to sulphonamides appear at 7.5 and 8.6 µm. The weak C-H bond absorption in the 3.5 µm region as well as the relatively strong absorption between 12 and 15 µm indicates the aromatic nature of the material. The weak but sharp absorption peak just before 3 µm suggests N - H linkages. The absorption at other wave lenghts aids in uniquely identifying the resin.

(b) There is some difference in absorption between the commercial and isolated resins in the 13.5 μm region. The resin may be slightly altered chemically, in the course of the analysis, or else some component of the resin may be lost in the extraction procedure.

Infrared Spectra of Guanine and Tricresyl Phosphate

1. *Guanine from commercial Nail Lacquer* - Spectra of known sample of guanine obtained by heating the hydrochloride to 200°C. Guanine has many identifying absorption maxima. Two readily recognisable linkages are the N-H absorption between 2.9 and 3.5 μm and carbonyl absorption below 6 μm.

2. *Tricresyl phosphate* - Technical grade (80% para and 20% meta isomers). The spectrum of an n-butyl phthalate-trcresyl phosphate mixture spectrum can easily be interpreted as a composite of the widely differing individual spectra of the phthalate and phosphate.

The weak C-H absorption maximum at 3.5 μm, the absorption between 6 and 7 μm and that beyond 12 μm strongly suggest the aromatic character of tricresyl phosphate. The strongest absorption maximum, however, occurs between 10 and 11 μm and is attributed to the phosphate radical.

Gas-Liquid Chromatorgraphy

Gas-Liquid Chromatographic (GLC) Determination of Solvent and Camphor (Plasticiser)

1. *Apparatus and Reagents* - (1) Gas chromatograph - F& M Model 810, or equivalent, equipped with a thermal conductivity detector capable of operating in a rapid program mode after an initial isothermal period. Operating temperatures (°C) : injection port 260; detector 250; column initially 118 until solvents elute (ca 20 minutes), then programmed to 240 at 60/minute, held isothermal until camphor elutes (ca 7 minutes), and returned to the starting temperature, Helium carrier gas flow rate: 80ml/minute.

   (a) GLC column -Copper tubing, 20' x 1/4" outer diameter packed with 70-80 mesh Gas-Chrom R coated with 10% PEG 20M.

   (b) *Stock solutions* - Accurately weigh ca 5 g each of isopropanol, ethyl acetate, toluene, butyl acetate, butanol, camphor (dl), and propyl acetate (internal standard) into separate 25 ml volumetric flasks and dilute each to volume with iso-octane (distilled in glass).

2. *Preparations of samples* - Accurately weigh ca 1 g of nail lacquer into a tared 25 ml glass-stoppered Erlenmeyer flask. Slowly add, with stirring, 10-15 ml of iso-octane. Pulverise the resulting precipitate with

a stirring rod. Add 1.0 ml of n-propyl acetate internal standard solution.Stir the mixture and let it settle for 4-5 minutes before analysis.

3. *Preparation of standard solution* – Prepare a standard solution containing the following amounts of the stock solutions from (a): 2.0 ml of ethyl acetate (ca 400 mg), 3.0 ml of propyl acetate internal standard (ca 600 mg), 4.0 ml of toluene (ca 1200 mg), 4.0 ml of butyl acetate (ca 800 mg), 6.0 ml of butanol (ca 1200 mg), and 2.0 ml of camphor (ca 400 mg).

4. *GLC determination* – Inject 10-15 µl of sample onto the column, using the operating temperatures given in (a). Adjust the sample volume and / or attenuation to bring each peak to ca 50-90% of full scale deflection (do not adjust the iso-octane peak). The sample volume should not exceed 15 µl. In a similar manner, inject the standard solution and a determine the correct injection volume and attenuations. Identify the solvents in the sample by comparing their retention times with those of the components of the standard solution. After determining the correct operating conditions, alternatively inject the sample and standard ≥ 3 times each.

5. *Calculations* - Calculate the amount of each solvent or plasticiser in the sample as follows :

% Solvent or plasticiser = $(R_u / R_s) \times K_s \times (IS_u/IS_s) \times (100/W)$,

Where R_u = peak height of solvent in sample x attenuation /peak height of internal standard in sample x attenuation, R_s = peak height of standard solvent in standard solution x attenuation/peak height of internal standard in standard solution x attenuation , K_s = mg of standard solvent in standard solution, IS_u =mg of internal standard in sample solution IS_s = mg of internal standard in standard solution, and W = mg of sample.

Gas-Liquid Chromatographic Determination of Acetone, Xylene, and Methyl Ethyl Ketone

Acetone, xylene, and methyl ethyl ketone may also be determined by GLC with a minor temperature adjustment (1-2°C) for methyl ethyl ketone and a longer initial isothermal operating period for xylene. If either ethanol or isopropanol is present by itself, the alcohol can be identified by its retention time. Mixtures of these alcohols cannot be resolved under the conditions described. The shape of the curve indicates the presence of a mixture and some estimate can be made of the relative amounts of each. It should be noted that mixtures of alcohols may also be determined by headspace analysis.

ANALYSIS OF SUNSCREEN PRODUCTS

Sunscreens are incorporated into cosmetic preparations for the selective absorption of potentially harmful burning radiation between 290 and 320 nm while permitting the transmission of longer wavelenghts that permit tanning. A variety of chemical compounds, mostly aromatic, are available for incorporation into creams, lotions and solutions as sunscreens. These preparations can be roughly classified according to the vehicle or base in which the sunscreen is incorporated, e.g., hydrocarbons, vegetable oils, alcohols and oil-in-water or water-in-oil emulsions.

Determine net contents, description of product, non-volatile matter at 105°C, ash content and pH as per the procedure described earlier.

Infrared Examination of Non-volatile Matter

Examine the infrared (IR) spectrum for possible identification of sunscreens as well as other materials.

Determination of Sunscreen

1. *In an alcohol base* – Dilute a known amount of the product to a definite volume with alcohol Identify and determine the sunscreen from the ultra-violet uv spectrum of the resulting solution. Make dilutions as necessary.
2. *In an emulsion base* – It is generally necessary to isolate the sunscreen from the emulsion before its determination. The method for the isolation and determination of amyl p-dimethylaminobenzoate described in Official Methods of Analysis, (AOAC), with some modifications, is also applicable to the determination of certain other sunscreens. For example, elute 2-ethoxyethyl *p*-methoxycinnamate with acidified 50% alcohol and homomenthylsalicylate with acidified 70% alcohol. Before eluting with eluants of high alcohol concentration, wash the eluant with 2-3 ml of the immobile solvent, *n*-heptane-CCl_4 (1+1). Determine these sunscreens in acid solution by uv spectrophot- ometry.

3. In a hydrocarbon or vegetable oil base

(a) Dilute the preparation with spectrophotometric grade iso-octane. Identify the determine the sunscreen from the uv spectrum of the isooctane solution.

(b) Alternatively, it may be neccessary to isolate the sunscreen from the hydrocarbon or vegetable oil base by partition chromato-graphy before the determinative step. If so, chromatography the preparation directly without prior solvent extraction, and then proceed as in (2).

Analysis of Sunscreen Vehicle

1. *Alcohol base* - See determination of sunscreen.

2. *Hydrocarbon or vegetable oil base* - An examination of the IR spectrum of the non-volatile matter should be sufficient for the characterisation of these base ingredients.

3. *Emulsions* - These preparations are normally mixtures of several ingredients. The base ingredients can generally be determined by methods used for creams and lotions. (Fig. 44.4),

SKIN SENSITISATION AND SENSITIVITY TESTING

A variety of substances are used in the manufacture of cosmetics. Therefore , finished cosmetics when used on human body have potential for several type of adverse reactions. The adverse effects that may be caused include skin irritation and allergic sensitisation, contact urticaria, stinging, phototoxicity and photoallergy. Skin irritation and allergic sensitisation is the most frequently encountered adverse effect. With growing consumer awareness and enforcement of consumer protection act, it is necessary for cosmetic manufacturer to assess the potential of adverse effects of his product. Safety considerations are not only relevant to consumers but also to factory workers who handle cosmetic raw materials in large quantities.

The substances that induce inflammation are known as irritants. Inflammation may be caused by use either immediately or through prolonged use or on repeated use. Irritants may be classified as primary irritants and secondary irritants. Primary irritants cause inflammation on the first contact (the duration of contact may be of several hours). Secondary irritants are harmless on first contact but cause inflammation on repeated contact and inflammation becomes more severe with progressive contacts.

In view of the potential of the of the cosmetic for harmful effects mentioned above, some tests have been designed to predict the potential of substances to induce irritation or sensitisation.

Sensitivity Testing

For detection of potential primary irritation, Draize test or its slight modification is used. In this test, Albino rabbits are clipped and the substance to be tested is applied to : intact skin, abraded skin, or lightly scarified skin.

All of them are covered with a patch for 24 hours. The sites of applications are examined at intervals and changes are assessed and recorded. The skin of rabbit is more susceptible than man. However, this method of testing can lead to false positive and false negative. It is advisable to compare results of test substance with the result of known harmless substance. Bureau of India Standards 4011 - 1982 (6.1 - Test for Irritant Potential) recommends that if there is no reaction in any of the animals, the

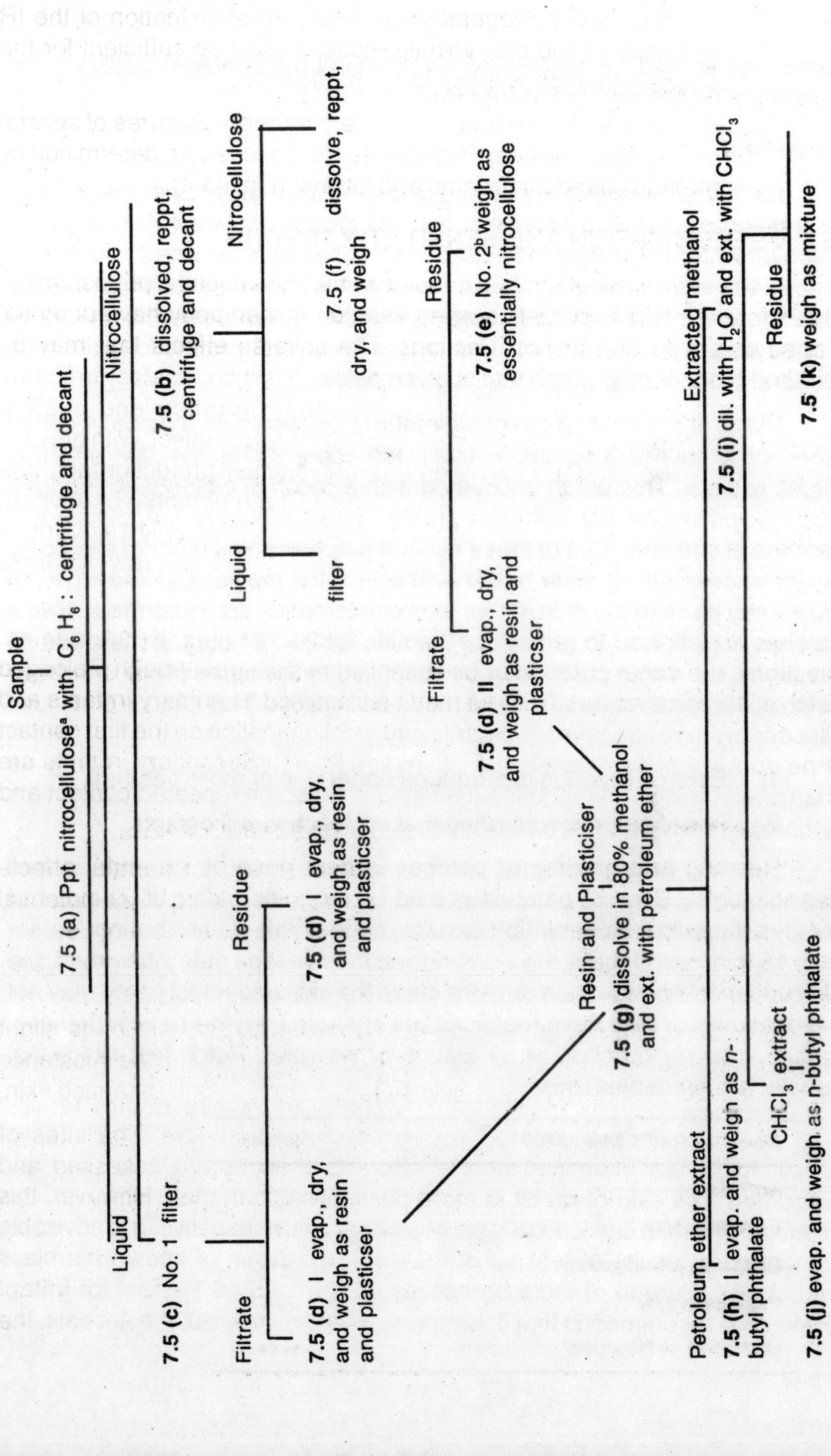

Fig. 44.4 Diagrammatic scheme for nail lacquer analysis.

same test should be performed on 10 human volunteers applying the substance on the skin of the forearm.

Patch Test

On humans, sensitivity testing of cosmetics may be performed either as a diagnostic or as a prophetic test. By diagnostic test if is intended to discover whether the cosmetic used has caused dermitis and if cosmetic is known, the ingredient which has caused it. It is known as diagnostic patch test. Prophetic test is done to assess whether a new cosmetic should be placed on the market or not. This test is known as prophetic patch test. General procedure of patch test is given below.

Place about 0.1-0.3 gm of cosmetic to be tested on a piece of cotton fabric or flannel (2-3 sq.cm. in size) and apply this to the skin of arms, thighs or back. This patch is covered with a patch of cellophane (about 5 sq.cm.) and sealed with adhesive plaster (about 40 sq.cm.). Apply several patches at one time. Out of these several patches some of them should be of similar cosmetic of other brand available in the market and known not to cause any harm to the skin. Other similar cosmetics act as controls. These patches are allowed to remain on the skin for 24-72 hours. If there are no reactions, the same patch may be reapplied to the same place or a fresh patch of the same material may be made and applied. This may be continued till :

1. Either a reaction is produced under one or more patches, or
2. Investigator is confirmed that no reaction will occur.

Reading and grading of patches is best done by an experienced dermatologist. Sites of patches should be examined after 30 minutes of removal or patch. Observation can be made a little earlier but not earlier than 15 minutes. Usually the skin under adhesive tape gets inflammed, the skin under cellophane tape remains clear, the skin under test patch may not have reaction or may have reactions like erythema, erythema with papules, papulo-vascular reaction or ulceration or neurosis. Patch test reactions, usually, are graded as under :

Description of Observation	*Symbol*
No reaction	–
Erythema only	+
Erythema with papules	++
Papulovascular	+++
Ulceration of Neurosis	++++

Open Patch Test

In case of cosmetics containing higher percentage of potential irritants like hair dyes, shampoos, hair tonics, patches should not be sealed. These should be used as open patches. Open patch test is performed on sensitive part of skin, e.g., bend of elbow, popliteal space of the skin behind the ears. The site of patch is inspected after 24 hours. If there is no reaction, the test is repeated once more on the same site. If still no reaction is there, the test is repeated a third time. If no reaction is observed on third application, the person may be taken as not hypersensitive.

Prophetic Patch Test

Before a programme of prophetic skin test is undertaken, the investigator should perform test on himself to as certain that the material is not primary irritant. After satisfying himself, the investigator can select ten subjects. He should get signed from each of the subjects a waiver for any damage. The amount of money to be paid should also be got agreed upon. If the results of the test are favourable, the investigator may use more subjects. For full scale prophetic patch test, 200 normal subjects are used. The cosmetic to be used is placed on the skin of the subjects for one to five days depending upon the nature of the cosmetic and judgement of investigator. The purpose of this application is inducing or establishing sensitivity and also detecting the presence of any primary irritant the patch sites are examined and observations are made. Subjects are observed for three more days for development of any late reactions. After 7 -10 days, patches are again applied to the same area of those subjects who did not show reaction to the test. One or more similar cosmetics known to have been used for years without complaints are used as controls. If there are no reactions or one or two reactions out of 200, new product can be placed on trial sale in small community of about 10,000 persons.

Prophetic patch test may be covered or open. Many a time, question is asked what is percentage of hypersensitive persons that is allowable. Schwartz suggests that incidence more than one in 10,000 may not result in safe cosmetics.

Repeated Insult Test

The prophetic patch test has certain shortcomings, to name :

1. Quick absorption of potential skin irritant through skin.
2. Rapid evaporation of volatile skin irritant from the patch.
3. Small amount of cosmetic in patch in comparison to large amount in actual use.

4. Small area of skin used in comparison with skin surface area used in actual use of cosmetic.

5. Short exposure of skin to cosmetic than the exposure actual in use.

To overcome some of the shortcomings of prophetic patch test, its modification in the form of repeated insult technique has been suggested. Draize described this technique as under.

The repeated insult technique consists in applying the finished cosmetic, or if the test substance is an ingredient of the cosmetic, it is applied in the same concentration as is found in the finished formulation incorporated in a bland base. The bland base must necessarily vary according to the nature and solubility of the test substance. Therefore, the diluting bland base may vary from physiologic saline to such nonirritating , nonsensitising organic solvent as dimethyl phthalate. Ordinarily 0.5 gram or 0.5 ml. of the test sample is applied by usual patch test procedure. The skin of the back or upper arm is used, such areas as are ordinarily covered by wearing apparel. The test material is maintained in situ for 24 hours. Allowing 15 to 20 minutes after the removal of the patches, readings are made and the reactions recorded. The test subject is allowed 24 hours of rest and the second test patch is applied to a different test site, otherwise the procedure is identical to that of the first application. Each individual is thus subjected to a series of 10 such consecutive exposures, exclusive of Sundays and nonwork days. Following the 10 individual exposures the subject is given 10 to 14 days rest after which item a "retest application" is made similar to one of the original 10 applications. A comparison of the reaction following "retest" with the average reading of the 10 original applications permits an appraisal of the sensitising propensities of the test substance Preferably the test subjects should be equally divided as to sex and cover as wide an age range as practicable.

To be comprehensive, a panel of 200 test subjects should be employed. Two hundred subjects represent an auspicious number and smaller groups possibly should be used at first, gradually building up to 200 subjects. It would be unwise to use a large number if it were possible to demonstrate on a smaller panel, 25 or 50 individuals that the substance is a potent sensitiser and unfit for its intended use.

Another modification of patch test for volatile substances has been described in BIS : 4011 in section 5.3.1 reader may refer to the same.

In BIS: 4011 - 1982 it has been suggested that this test should first be performed on 10 laboratory animals and if there is no reaction in any of the animals, it should be performed on 10 human volunteers.

Photopatch Test

Certain substances are not harmful by themselves but they become harmful when exposed to sunlight. It has also been mentioned earlier that substances that absorb light wave lengths between 300-800 nm have potential of phototoxicity. In case, a substance is considered phototoxic, photopatch test may be performed. To perform this test, the substance to be tested is applied in duplicate patches in the same manner as for standard patch test. After 24 hours, one of the patches in the pair is exposed to sunlight for 30 minutes. Alternatively the patch can also be exposed to ultraviolet light. The light exposed patch is covered again. One additional site in the adjoining area of the skin is exposed to sunlight or ultraviolet light as has been done in case of one patch of the pair. The time of exposure is also same as for the exposed patch. This site acts as control. After further 24 hours the patches are opened and examined. If the patch not exposed to light and the skin area exposed to light do not show reaction but the patch site which has been exposed to light shows reaction, the test indicates that substance is phototoxic. If no reactions are observed on patch sites and control skin site, the substance may be taken as non-phototoxic.

Test for Sensitising Potential

An individual is not likely to be allergic to a substance, if he is exposed to it for the first time. In immunological terms, it can be said that lymphocytes of that individual acquire capability to recognise and elicit immunological response. Thus next exposure of that individual to the substance has chance of sensitising him. With the number of exposure his chances of developing hyper-sensitivity increase.

Test for sensitising potential has been described in BIS : 4011. It has been recommended that standard patch tests with same chemical or cosmetic are repeated in the same 200 volunteers after an interval of 10-14 days. The number of persons who will show positive reaction will represent the sensitising potential of the substance or cosmetic which has been tested.

Provocative Patch Test

Weak sensitising agents, generally, do not sensitise a person with first exposure. Repeated exposures, however, to even weak sensitising agent may make a person hyper-sensitive. This can be indicated by provocative patch test. In this test, 10-15 applications of a substance or cosmetic are made on alternative days on the same spot of skin in 10 volunteers. Standard patch test is perfomed after 10 days of the last application. The test will show, how many persons have been sensitised. It has also been recommended in the Indian Standard that in case of unknown chemicals, the test should be first performed on animals like guineapigs or rabbits.

Use Test

In use test, the cosmetic to be tested is actually used and its adverse effects, if any, are observed. BIS : 4011 suggests that 15 volunteers should be asked to use the cosmetic and they should make 15 applications of it. If there is no adverse reaction, cosmetic can be released for trial.

Skin Testing with some Specific Cosmetics

Creams

Dermatitis, usually with cleansing and emollient type creams, is not frequent. Dermatitis may occur with creams containing substances like mercurials, salicylic acid, deodorant creams containing salts of aluminium, bleaching creams containing oxidising agents and vanishing creams (because of alkalinity). Another important ingredients in creams is perfume which may cause dermatitis. Allergy has also been reported because of lanolin. Hydroxy fatty acids in lanolin are said to be allergic in nature.

To carry out diagnostic test, rub cream into an unaffected suitable part of the body (e.g., forearm) for five days. However, if positive reaction occurs before five days, rubbing of cream may not be continued. While carrying out prophetic patch test, the patch may be covered. A similar cream available in market for long time without any adverse effects may be chosen as control. The best test remains the user test.

Deodorants and Antiperspirants

Dermatitis from deodorants is infrequent. However, some phenolic antimicrobials can cause dermatitis. Perfumes of deodorants can cause dermatitis in hyper-sensitive persons.

Deodorants in powder and cream form can be tested using diagnostic patch test. In these forms the patches can be covered. But perfumes in solution should not be sealed in patch test. Perfume should be sprayed on the skin and the skin should be kept open.

On the other hand, dermatitis from antiperspirant is not uncommon. Aluminium chloride in antiperspirant is more irritant that aluminium sulphate. Often modern antiperspirant preparations are buffered to minimise irritation. Both diagnostic and prophetic patch tests can be employed for these cosmetics.

Depilatories

Depilatories (chemical) contain sulphides of alkali (e.g., NaS), alkaline earth (BaS) or thio-glycolic acid. These substance are reducing agents and disrupt cystine linkages of hair protein and thereby act as depilatories. These are capable of acting a primary irritants. Often some degree of erytherma is associated with depilatories. Intensity will depend upon concentration, pH and time of exposure. Therefore losed patch tests for diagnostic purposes are not recommended.

In case of testing of new depilatory, actual user test should be employed with well established depilatory in market as control. However, before undertaking actual user test, irritant properties of new depilatory may be assessed by carrying out prophetic test on 10 subjects with well established depilatory as control. The following procedure could be followed for the prophetic patch test.

Prepare inactive base of depilatory. Prepare dilutions given below of the well established depilatory and depilatory to be tested:

one part depilatory + one part base

one part depilatory + two parts base

one part depilatory + three parts base

one part depilatory + four parts base

+

One part depilatory + n part base

Place patches of well established depilatory dilutions on one thigh and patches of depilatory dilutions to be tested on other thigh of the subject. Examine the patches on two thighs after appropriate time. This time could be 24-48 hours.

Hair Dyes

If prophetic patch test is to be carried out on new hair dye, its composition should be ascertained. Because it may contain primary irritant, e.g., ammonia (more than 1% ammonia is primary irritant). Prophetic patch should not be closed, if the dye contains primary irritant.

Normally hair dye is applied to grey hair and is allowed to remain in contact with hair for about 1-1 1/2 hour. Excess of unconsumed hair dye is washed with shampoo. Hair dye is applied every four to six weeks to colour emerging roots of hair. In view of this open prophetic patch test should be used in case of hair dyes. The test could be carried out as follows :

Prepare hair dye for application and paint one square inch skin on the forearm or behind the ear. Repeat it every day for three days (application should not be washed off during this period). On the other forearm run a control with well established hair dye available in market. Repeat the procedure after seven to fourteen days. Reaction of the dye to be tested should not be more than the reaction with control dye.

If the new hair dye passes this test, it should be tried on 1000 subjects twice. When found satisfactory on trial, it may be placed on the market.

Cold Wave Lotion

Thioglycollates are used in permanent waving lotions. Thioglycollates in higher pH on long exposure can cause dermatitis. However, dermatitis from cold wave lotions is not frequent. Closed prophetic patch test can be performed with long established cold wave lotion. The following procedure could be followed :

Place 0.2 ml of new preparation on a piece of flannel (3 sq.cm. in are). Place this patch on forearm, cover it with uncoated cellophane (about 9 sq.cm. in area) and cover this with adhesive plaster (about 18 sq. cm. in area). A similar patch of control waving lotion is placed on the other forearm. Remove the patches after 24 hours and examine the patch sites after 15 - 30 minutes of removal of patches. Reaction should not be more than the reaction with control. The test is repeated after 7-10 days for finding out sensitisation potential. This test should be perfomed on 100 female subjects. This Test is more stringent than actual user test as in practice cold wave lotion does not come in contact with scalp and even if it comes in contact, the contact time is not more than 3 hours. Another factor for stringency is that in practice, cold wave lotion treatment is given once in a few months while the second patch test is followed with in 7 -10 days.

Lipsticks

Before introduction of indelible type lipstick cheilitis was rare. Cheilitis occurred frequently with the use of bromofluorescein type dyes in lipstick formula. This adverse effect was caused by photosensitising effect of fluorescent dyes. However, the fluorescent dyes being used in modern cosmetics are less photo-sensitive than earlier ones. Addition of pigment lakes which act opacifiers reduce photo-sensitisation.

Closed prophetic test can be performed on lipsticks. After removing the patch, the patch site should be exposed to bright sunlight for several hours to observe the tendency of the lipstick to photosensitisation A well-established lipstick in market should be used as control. At least 200 subjects should be taken for this test. Along with patch test, they should also use the lipstick under test and should continue to use for at least one month. If results of patch test and actual user test are favourable, an extensive user test on additional 800 subjects should be carried out before the lipstick is put on the market.

Nail Polish

With use of nail polish fingers have been rarely affected. However dermatitis may be caused at those places which are frequently and habitually touched, stroked or scratched by finger nails. Solvents of nail Polish evaporate quickly. As such, causative factors could be resins, colour and pigments.

Earlier actual loss of nail occurred due to phenolic type of resin and synthetic rubber. Their use has been discontinued since then. Splitting of nails on long usage of nail polish has been observed.

In case of nail polishes, open prophetic patch test is carried out. The following procedure could be used :

Apply new nail polish about 1 sq. inch in area on forearm. A well-known and established nail polish should similarly be applied to the other forearm. Do not cover the patch. Apply test nail polish on nails of hand which has patch of test nail polish. Similarly apply control nail polish on the nails of forearm which has patch of control nail polish. Remove patches after 48 hours and after 7 - 10 days repeat the test on same subjects. Continue the use of nail polishes for two months. In performing this test take 200 subjects. Compare the results of test nail polish and control nail polish. Reactions with test nail polish should not be greater than the control nail polish. If new nail polish passes this test, user test on additional 800 subjects should be carried out before nail polish is put on the market.

Testing of hair & bath preparations for eye irritation properties

Eyes can be accidentally exposed to shampoos, other hair preparations and bath preparations. Draize and Kelly designed test on eye mucosa of albino rabbit. Such tests can be conducted as follows :

Instill 0.1 ml of test substance in conjunctival sac of one eye nine albino rabbits (the other eye works as control). Divide rabbits in three groups comprising of three rabbits each.

Group - 1 Leave the eyes of this group unwashed.

Group - 2 Wash the treated eyes with 20 ml of lukewarm water after 2 seconds of instillation of test substance.

Group - 3 Wash the treated eyes after 4 seconds of instillation of test substance with 20 ml of lukewarm water.

Read the occular reactions with hand slit lamp for seven days or till any residual injury persists.

Any preparation, which leaves corneal or iris lesions for more than 7 days, is considered severe eye irritant. Eye irritant effect of combination of synthetic detergents is greater than produced singly by them. All synthetic detergents preparations used on hair or during bath should be assessed for their eye irritating effect.

Efficacy Testing

The majority of skin-care products are sold to improve the appearance and feel of the skin, and are broadly classified as moisturisers. The condition and appearance of the skin is a function of its softness and flexibility, which is adversely affected by loss of water. Tests for moisture content and moisture transmission, as well as the viscoelastic response, ultrasound techniques, and electrical properties of skin have been the subject of much study, with the development of increasingly sophisticated instrumentation to show the condition of the skin and its water content. Most of these new methods have evolved to help evaluate the potential performance of products, and are very useful in screening formulations, levels of ingredients and other stepwise formula variables.

Cell Turnover Testing

A very useful test to determine cell turnover rate utilises the dansyl chloride test, in which dansyl chloride, which fluoresces under a long-wave uv or woods lamp, is applied to the skin. This material penetrates the stratum corneum to a uniform depth. The cell turnover rate, or transit time, is determined by disappearance of the stain compared to a non-treatment site.

Instrumental Tests

The instrumental test is proving to be of great value is profilometry, which is especially useful in the assessment of the changes to the skin's surface caused by the anti-ageing effect of retinoid therapy on sun damaged skin. Two primary methods are used inprofilometry. One method employs replicas and the other uses photographs. Fully hydrated skin has altered surface characteristics, as measured by both lower peaks and greater distance between peaks. This is also the case with skin that has fewer lines and wrinkles due to effects other than hydration. In evaluation with a replica, an instrument with a stylus produces a tracing of the topography of the skin, based on a replica produced by dental impression material. With two-dimensional photographs, computerised image analysis techniques are used to review the image.

The gas-bearing electrodynamometer (GBE), has been widely used to evaluate the viscoelastic properties of the stratum corneum, both in vivo and in vitro. More recently computer handling of data generated by this device has improved its utility. The Twistometre device measures resistance to torsion of the skin, as applied by a rotating disc inside an external ring, which acts as a stator. This device is used to evaluate the skin's softness and suppleness. There has been a long history of the measurement of not only the water content of skin, but also the flow of moisture from the skin, which is known as the moisture vapour transmission rate (MVTR) or the moisture/water loss or transepidermal moisture loss (TEML). MVTR is a technique that has shown continual refinement. Progress has continued to the more recent development of a well-accepted instrument, the Servo-Med evaporimeter. Most of the work on the direct measurement of water content in skin has utilised an infrared (IR) spectrophotometer.

Testing For Moisturisers

The tests consist of the flow of moisture through a barrier, which is often a synthetic film with a transmission rate similar to that of skin. This technique (MVTR) combined with a water-holding technique to measure hydration or the ability of the formulate or test material to maintain humectancy is very useful in evaluating or predicting potential in vivo results.

Test methods other than MVTR and water-holding capacity include scanning colourimetric techniques, scanning electron microscopy (SEM) and biomechanical properties of skin under various in vitro conditions. *In vitro* test methods can be instructive when their correlation to in vivo performance has been established. In the author's experience, a battery of tests and an excellent history of correlation are necessary for the test to be of predictive clinical value. The problem is that, when *in vitro* tests are used with excised skin or a synthetic membrane, unlike the human skin, there is a lack of the biological underpinnings of the epidermis, which is anything but an inert, static or dead layer.

Test For Sebum

This device (Sebutape) is a film that visualises and traps sebum. The tape can then be analysed, and total relative sebum amount computed using image analysis. If quantification is not the only requirement, the sebum can be solvent-extracted, gravimetrically analysed and broken down into component parts. This can be a very useful technique for assessing the instant removal of sebum by cleansers, or the effect on sebum production of various treatments.

Test for Cleanser Mildness

A wide variety of cleansers are available on the market and will be covered within this chapter. Tests for cleansers have focused primarily on testing soap or detergent formulations for mildness. In this test, dilute solutions of soaps or test solutions are maintained in a cup held against the skin of human volunteers. The skin is then evaluated for redness, scaling , and fissuring, often against high irritancy (non-fatted soap bar) and low irritancy (fatted sodium cocoisethionate bar) controls. A more recent modification of this method calls for a shorter test, and measures the increase in MVTR by a Servo-Med evaporimeter. This has shown close correlation with the longer duration visual assessment technique. These methods differs from the Soap Chamber Test in that the Forearm Test adjusts frequency for humidity, while the Flex Test is reported to be unaffected by humidity. For evaluation of facial cleansers of all types for mildness and drying potential, the method outlined by Frosch utilisers half-face testing with realistic use conditions. In order to obtain suitable dryness scores, this test is best run during periods of low relative humidity. Cleanser tests for efficacy, evaluating soil and make-up removal, as well as esthetic properties and after-cleansing skin-feel must also be done to obtain a complete picture.

A combination of all these test methods, together with adequate clinical and consumer trial and observation, should enable one to have a great insight not only into the performance of products but, more importantly, as to how and why products work, and how variations in formula affect performance. The is necessary for the enlightened formulator.

Stability Testing

Stability testing is done to ensure that a developed product will be fit for use during its expected life. Stability testing should be done early in the development cycle to remedy any problems before final testing. A well-run stability trial can provide much information about a product in a relatively short period of time. Prototype products in packaging representing the ultimate trade package material, can be placed at ambient, and elevated (e.g., 37°C and 45°C) temperatures, refrigerated and cycled through freeze/thaw cycles and placed in high humidity chambers. During these trials, testing should focus on attributes most important to the products performance, or on the integrity of any active ingredients. In addition, there should be physical testing, for example pH and viscosity, chemical content of active ingredients, water content, etc. The formulator must not overlook attributes relating to consumer perception, such as fragrance, colour, rub-in characteristics and appearance. Two or three months of successful elevated temperature testing and three of four freeze/thaw cycles will usually indicate that products will have an adequate shelf-life. It is important, however, to continue testing for longer periods at ambient temperature, to obtain an understanding of the product's ultimate shelf-life. Further testing whenever changes are made to the supply of raw materials or to the formulation is essential.

Chapter 26

PLANT ECONOMICS ON HERBAL COSMETICS

Rated Plant Capacity = 305.00 Kgs/Day

LAND & BUILDING (Land 2000 sq.mt.) = Rs. 26,50,000.00

PLANT & MACHINERY

1. Stainless Steel Tank with agitator
2. Stainless Steel Tank (closed top)
3. Tray Dryer
4. Pulveriser
5. Crusher
6. Filter Press
7. Homogeniser
8. Percolator
9. Grinding machine
10. Sterilization unit
11. Storage Tank (SS)
12. Bottle filling & sealing machine
13. Automatic filling & sealing machine
14. Laboratory and testing equipments
15. Miscellaneous viz weighing balance, screen etc.

FIXED CAPITAL

1.	Land & Building	Rs.	26,50,000.00
2.	Plant & Machinery	Rs.	12,35,000.00
3.	Other Fixed Assets	Rs.	3,20,000.00
	TOTAL	Rs.	42,05,000.00

RAW MATERIALS

1. Til Oil
2. Motha, Kankol
3. Thus, Charrila
4. (Sailag) Nagar
5. Chandar
6. Long, Dalchine
7. Ratanjot
8. Kapur Kachure
9. Sat bar
10. Tejpal
11. How bar
12. Bahara
13. Amla Oil
14. Harral
15. Clampa
16. Keora (Keya)
18. Alachi,
19. Pudeena
20. Perfume
21. Menthol
22. Ouotl water
23. Ouillaya bark powder
24. Ammonium Carbonate
25. Borax
26. Bay leaf oil
27. Heena powder
28. Sodium Carbonate
29. Potassium Carbonate
30. Soap powder
31. Perfume
32. Calcium Carbonate
33. Sodium Carboxy Methyl Cellulose
34. Glycerin
35. Preservative
36. Soda Lauryl Sulphate
37. Herbal Extract (Flower)
38. Annar ke phul (Pomegranate flamer)
39. Annar ke chilke (Pomegranate skin)
40. Bhuna Huwa suhaya (Roasted Borax)
42. Bhuna Huwa Fitkari (Roasted alum)

43. Akarkara
44. Majuphal (Gall Nut),
45. Rume Martage
46. Samendra Thag
47. Supari Bhuni Huwi (Roasted tal Nut)
48. Lanolin
49. Emulsifying wax
50. Beer wax
51. Almond
52. Herblotion
53. Powdered Mehandi leaves
54. Powdered Caanill flamer
55. Walnut bark
56. Kohl Powder
57. Indigo Leaves

TOTAL WORKING CAPITAL/MONTH

1.	Raw Material	Rs.	4,60,644.45
2.	Salary & Wages	Rs.	63,000.00
3.	Utilities & Overheads	Rs.	41,500.00
	TOTAL	Rs.	5,65,144.45

TOTAL CAPITAL INVESTMENT

Total Fixed Capital	Rs.	42,05,000.00
Total Working Capital for 3 Months	Rs.	16,95,433.35
TOTAL	Rs.	59,00,433.35

TURN OVER/ANNUM

Herbal Hair Oil 15,000 litres
Herbal Hair Shampoo 30000 litre
Herbal Tooth Paste 15000 kgs
Herbal Tooth Powder 1500 kgs
Herbal cleansing cream 1500 kgs
Herbal Henna 15000 kg

TOTAL Rs. 1,08,75,000.00

PROFIT SALES RATIO = 23.47 %
RATE OF RETURN = 43.25 %
BREAK EVEN POINT (B.E.P) = 44.46 %

Chapter 27

PLANT ECONOMICS ON MODERN COSMETICS

Rated Plant Capacity =

120000 kgs. Shampoos
120000 kgs. of Talcum Powder
Hair removing cream 90000 kgs.
All purpose cream 150000 kgs.
Liquid make ups 90000 kgs.
Compacts 60000 kgs.
Mascara 90000 kgs.
Liquid eyeliner 60000 kgs.
Lipstick 90000 kgs.
Nail Polish 90000 kgs.
Nail Polish Remover 60000 kgs./Year

LAND & BUILDING (Land 2000 sq.mt.) = Rs. 75,25,000.00

PLANT & MACHINERY

1. SHAMPOO UNIT: Storage tank
2. Reaction vessel
3. S.S. Homogeniser or emulsifier
4. Bottle washing, cleaning & drying weighing
5. Filling, Sealing unit
6. Pumps & Accessories
7. Piping and Instrumentation
8. Heating and other miscellaneous Electrical appliance
9. Automatic sachet filling sealing machine

10. TALCUM POWDER UNIT: Sieving screens, shifter
11. Mixer (Ribbon Blender)
12. Powder weighing filling and capping unit
13. M.S. Storage tank
14. Misc. Equipment such as blowers tools & accessories.
15. SPRAY PERFUME UNIT: S.S. storage tanks Cap.100 lit. (10 nos.) with sight glass & closetop
16. Mixing vessel arrangement with stirrer, jacketed vessel, conical bottom
17. Propellant (gas) filling unit
18. Bottle washing cleaning drying unit
19. Liquid filling sealing
20. Labeling machine
21. Misc. equipment and accessories & lab testing equipments
22. CREAM: Mixing vessel
23. Various tanks (S.S.)
24. Tripple Roll
25. Vacuum Deacrator
26. Paste,weighing, filling and sealing
27. Lipstick moulds
28. Mould Chilling unit,with cold water circular
29. Filter/strainer
30. Double can seamer
31. Carton Sealing machine
32. Marking/stamping Machine
33. Pad printing machine
34. Conveyer belts, bucket elevators
35. Water Storage tank, pumps valves and others
36. Instrumentation and process control equipment
37. Laboratory testing equipment
38. Miscellaneous equipments

FIXED CAPITAL

1.	Land & Building	Rs.	75,25,000.00
2.	Plant & Machinery	Rs.	1,06,35,000.00
3.	Other Fixed Assets	Rs.	54,00,000.00
	TOTAL	Rs.	2,35,60,000.00

RAW MATERIALS

Sodium lauryl sulphate
Coconut Diethanolamide
Glycol Stearate
Methyl p-hydroxy Benzoate
Formaldehyde
Sodium Benzoate
Phosphoric acid
Sodium Chloride
Dye
Perfume
Egg Powder
Misc. Chemicals and packaging materials
Zinc Stearate
Zinc Oxide
Light Calcium Carbonate
Talc
Essence or perfume
Misc. Chemical & packaging cost
Perfumery compounds
Alcohol
Freon gas (propellant)
Isopropyl myristate
Dipropylene glycol
Aerosol container
Calcium thioglycollate trihydrate
Cetyl alcohol
Sodium lauryl sulphate
Glycerin
Nitrocellulose
Santolite
Dibutyl phthalate
Butyl Acetate
Ethyl Alcohol
Butyl Alcohol
Toluene
Spenrmaceti

Tincture of Benzoin
Bees wax
Borax etc.

TOTAL WORKING CAPITAL/MONTH

1.	Raw Material	Rs.	74,69,145.50
2.	Salary & Wages	Rs.	5,82,250.00
3.	Utilities & Overheads	Rs.	8,50,000.00
	TOTAL	Rs.	89,01,395.50

TOTAL CAPITAL INVESTMENT

Total Fixed Capital	Rs.	2,35,60,000.00
Total Working Capital for 3 Months	Rs.	2,67,04,186.50
TOTAL	Rs.	5,02,64,186.50

TURN OVER/ANNUM

120000 kgs. Shampoos
120000 kgs. of Talcum Powder
Hair removing cream 90000 kgs.
All purpose cream 150000 kgs.
Liquid make ups 90000 kgs.
Compacts 60000 kgs.
Mascara 90000 kgs.
Liquid eyeliner 60000 kgs.
Lipstick 90000 kgs.
Nail Polish 90000 kgs.
Nail Polish Remover 60000 kgs./Year

TOTAL Rs. 16,05,00,000.00

PROFIT SALES RATIO = 25.75 %
RATE OF RETURN = 82.23 %
BREAK EVEN POINT (B.E.P) = 31.75 %

Chapter 28

PLANT ECONOMICS ON COSMETICS AND PLASTIC PACKAGING MATERIALS MFG.

Rated Plant Capacity = SHAMPOO = 50 Kgs../Day

TALCUM POWDER = 50 Kgs./Day

CREAM = 50 Kgs./Day

PERFUME = 5 Kgs./Day

LAND & BUILDING = Rs. 16,08,200.00

(Land Area 350 sq.mt)

PLANT & MACHINERY

1. Stainless steel vessel with stirrer
2. Filling tank
3. Steel tank
4. Pipes, Pumps, valves, etc.
5. Gas burner with cylinder
6. Sieving screen
7. Ribbon blender
8. Weighing machine
9. Perfume blending tank
10. Perfume Filling machine
11. Injection moulding machine
12. Injection blow moulding machine
13. Mould sets
14. Cooling Tower
15. Compressor
16. Tools, tackles and others

FIXED CAPITAL

1.	Land & Building	Rs.	16,08,200.00
2.	Plant & Machinery	Rs.	7,87,500.00
3.	Other Fixed Assets	Rs.	2,35,000.00
	TOTAL	Rs.	26,30,700.00

RAW MATERIALS

Colour, perfume and additives.
Talc, zinc oxide, perfume & Additive
Stearic acid, essential oils, diluents and others
Plastic granules Corrugated boxes, labels, adhesive tapes etc.

TOTAL WORKING CAPITAL/MONTH

1.	Raw Material	Rs.	3,52,500.00
2.	Salary & Wages	Rs.	85,785.00
3.	Utilities & Overheads	Rs.	51,200.00
	TOTAL	Rs.	4,89,485.00

TOTAL CAPITAL INVESTMENT

Total Fixed Capital	Rs.	26,30,700.00
Total Working Capital for 3 Months	Rs.	14,68,455.00
TOTAL	Rs.	40,99,155.00

TURN OVER/ANNUM

Sale of Shampoos 15,000 kgs.
Sale of Talcum powder 15,000 kgs.
Sale of Cream (various types) 15,000 kgs.
Sale of Perfumes (aerosol) 1500 kgs.
Sale of Plastic containers 15,000 kgs

TOTAL Rs. 82,50,000.00

PROFIT SALES RATIO = 17.57 %
RATE OF RETURN = 35.35 %
BREAK EVEN POINT (B.E.P) = 52.23 %

Chapter 29

PLANT ECONOMICS ON HERBAL SHAMPOO AND CREAMS

Rated Plant Capacity = 750.00 Bottles/Day

1.250 Bottles SHAMPOO/Day (100 ML. PACK)

500 Bottles SKIN TONING CREAM/Day (50 gms PACK

LAND & BUILDING (Land required 500 Sq.mt.) = Rs. 16,40,000.00

PLANT & MACHINERY

1. Storage tank
2. Reaction vessel
3. S.S. Homogeniser
4. Bottle washing, cleaning & drying.
5. Filtering unit
6. Pumps & accessories.
7. Heating & other miscellaneous electrical appliance.
8. Lab testing equipment.
9. Mixing tank
10. Filling Machine
11. General Equipments piping & instrumentation.
12. Lab testing equipment.
13. Weighing machine equipment.
14. Other miscellaneous tools etc.
15. Pumps, fans, blowers, etc.

FIXED CAPITAL

1.	Land & Building	Rs.	16,40,000.00
2.	Plant & Machinery	Rs.	4,50,000.00
3.	Other Fixed Assets	Rs.	1,10,000.00
	TOTAL	Rs.	22,00,000.00

RAW MATERIALS

1. Sodium lauryl sulphate
2. Coconut diethanolamide
3. Glycol stearate
4. Methyl p-hydroxy benzoate
5. Formaldehyde
6. Sodium benzoate.
7. Phosphoric acid.
8. Sodium chloride
9. Yellow dye
10. Perfume
11. Egg powder
12. Gainda flower
13. Motir flower petals
14. Anarpeel
15. Pudina
16. Potato meal
17. Kheera
18. Orange peel
19. Tulsi
20. Nimboo peels
21. Chandan powder
22. Neem leaves
23. Chironji
24. Shakti chur
25. Multani mitti
26. Glycerine
27. Methyl-p-hydroxy benzoate

TOTAL WORKING CAPITAL/MONTH

1.	Raw Material	Rs.	69,600.00
2.	Salary & Wages	Rs.	69,520.00
3.	Utilities & Overheads	Rs.	59,000.00
	TOTAL	Rs.	1,98,120.00

TOTAL CAPITAL INVESTMENT

Total Fixed Capital	Rs.	22,00,000.01
Total Working Capital for 3 Months	Rs.	5,94,360.00
TOTAL	Rs.	27,94,360.01

TURN OVER/ANNUM

Sale of 75000 Nos. of shampoo bottles (100 ml pack)

Sale of skin toning cream 15000 bottles

TOTAL Rs. 44,25,000.00

PROFIT SALES RATIO = 34.75 %

RATE OF RETURN = 55.03 %

BREAK EVEN POINT (B.E.P) = 42.29 %

Chapter 30

PLANT ECONOMICS OF CAR SHAMPOO

Rated Plant Capacity = 100.00 Ltr./Day

LAND & BUILDING (Land reqd. 500 sq. mts.) = Rs. 7,00,000.00

PLANT & MACHINERY

1. Reaction vessel (SS)
2. S.S. Homogenizer or Emulsifier
3. Bottle washing cleaning & drying
4. Filling and Sealing machine
5. Storage tanks
6. Pump & Accessories.
7. Piping & Instrumentation
8. Heating & other miscellaneous
9. Miscellaneous.

FIXED CAPITAL

1.	Land & Building	Rs.	7,00,000.00
2.	Plant & Machinery	Rs.	3,92,000.00
3.	Other Fixed Assets	Rs.	1,00,000.00
	TOTAL	Rs.	11,92,000.00

RAW MATERIALS

1. Polyethylene Glycol
2. Ethylene Glycol monostearate
3. Propylene Glycol

4. Ammonium Lauryl Sulphate
5. Distilled water
6. Packing Material
7. Dyes, preservative colours and perfumes

TOTAL WORKING CAPITAL/MONTH

1.	Raw Material	Rs.	3,16,873.50
2.	Salary & Wages	Rs.	40,875.00
3.	Utilities & Overheads	Rs.	25,950.00
	TOTAL	Rs.	3,83,698.50

TOTAL CAPITAL INVESTMENT

Total Fixed Capital	Rs.	11,92,000.00
Total Working Capital for 3 Months	Rs.	11,51,095.50
TOTAL	Rs.	23,43,095.50

TURN OVER/ANNUM

By sale of 30,000 Ltrs. Car Shampoc	Rs.	60,00.000.00

PROFIT SALES RATIO = 13.92 %
RATE OF RETURN = 35.64 %
BREAK EVEN POINT (B.E.P) = 51.34 %

Chapter 31

PLANT ECONOMICS OF SHAMPOO

Rated Plant Capacity	=	400.00 Lts/Day
LAND & BUILDING (Land 500 sq. mts.)	=	Rs. 13,12,500.00

PLANT & MACHINERY

1. Storage tank
2. Reaction vessel
3. S.S. Homogeniser or emulsifier
4. Bottle washing, cleaning and drying weighing
5. Filling and Sealing unit
6. Pumps & Accessories
7. Piping and Instrumentation
8. Heating and other miscellaneous electrical appliance.
9. Automatic sachet filling and sealing machine.

FIXED CAPITAL

1.	Land & Building	Rs.	13,12,500.00
2.	Plant & Machinery	Rs.	16,30,000.00
3.	Other Fixed Assets	Rs.	5,80,000.00
	TOTAL	Rs.	35,22,500.00

RAW MATERIALS

1. Sodium lauryl sulphate
2. Coconut Diethanolamide
3. Glycol Stearate
4. Methyl p-hydroxy Benzoate

5. Formaldehyde
6. Sodium Benzoate
7. Phosphoric acid
8. Sodium Chloride
9. Dye
10. Perfume
11. Egg Powder
12. Misc. Chemicals and packaging materials

TOTAL WORKING CAPITAL/MONTH

1.	Raw Material	Rs.	8,77,798.00
2.	Salary & Wages	Rs.	56,500.00
3.	Utilities & Overheads	Rs.	1,49,250.00
	TOTAL	Rs.	10,83,548.00

TOTAL CAPITAL INVESTMENT

Total Fixed Capital	Rs.	35,22,500.00
Total Working Capital for 3 Months	Rs.	32,50,644.00
TOTAL	Rs.	67,73,144.00

TURN OVER/ANNUM

By sale 120000 ltrs. shampoos	Rs.	1,80,00,000.00

PROFIT SALES RATIO = 18.12 %
RATE OF RETURN = 48.16 %
BREAK EVEN POINT (B.E.P) = 45.50 %

Chapter 32

PLANT ECONOMICS OF TOILET SOAP AND HERBAL SOAP

Rated Plant Capacity	=	500.00 Kgs/Day
LAND & BUILDING	=	Rs. 42,50,000.00

(Land required 1000 sq.mt.)

PLANT & MACHINERY

1. Boiling Kettle
2. Mixing & Kneading Machine
3. Chilling rolls
4. Dryer
5. Plodder Machine
6. Cutting machine
7. Semi-automatic stamping press
8. Miscellaneous like pipe fitting, conveying system etc.
9. Complete Plant for Manufacturing of Herbal Toilet Soap with Cosmetics Products

FIXED CAPITAL

1.	Land & Building	Rs.	42,50,000.00
2.	Plant & Machinery	Rs.	7,52,500.00
3.	Other Fixed Assets	Rs.	27,500.00
	TOTAL	Rs.	50,30,000.00

RAW MATERIALS

1. Neem Oil, Castor Oil, Soap Noodles, Common Salt etc. for Herbal Soap
2. Coconut oil

3. Castor oil
4. Caustic Soda lye
5. Carbolic acid
6. Colour
7. Palm Rosa oil and other perfume

TOTAL WORKING CAPITAL/MONTH

1.	Raw Material	Rs.	5,71,225.00
2.	Salary & Wages	Rs.	51,750.00
3.	Utilities & Overheads	Rs.	73,850.00
	TOTAL	Rs.	6,96,825.00

TOTAL CAPITAL INVESTMENT

Total Fixed Capital	Rs.	50,30,000.00
Total Working Capital for 3 Months	Rs.	20,90,475.00
TOTAL	Rs.	71,20,475.00

TURN OVER/ANNUM

By sale of 1,50,000 Kg. of Toilet Soap and Herbal Soap	Rs.	1,09,50,000.00

PROFIT SALES RATIO = 13.34 %
RATE OF RETURN = 20.51 %
BREAK EVEN POINT (B.E.P) = 54.24 %

Chapter 33

PLANT ECONOMICS OF HERBAL HAIR OIL (AYURVEDIC)

Rated Plant Capacity = 14700.00 Bottles/Day

LAND & BUILDING = Rs. 12,75,000.00
(Land required 3000 Sq.Mtrs.)

PLANT & MACHINERY

1. Stainless steel kettle
2. Pulverizing
3. S.S. Vessel fitted with agitator
4. M.S. Tanks
5. Mixer
6. Filter
7. Packing machine
8. Til oil storage tank
9. Lab equipments.

FIXED CAPITAL

1.	Land & Building	Rs.	12,75,000.00
2.	Plant & Machinery	Rs.	9,30,000.00
3.	Other Fixed Assets	Rs.	2,23,000.00
	TOTAL	Rs.	24,28,000.00

RAW MATERIALS

1. Hartago (harar) fruit
2. Bahera fruit
3. Til oil
4. Manjisht twigs

5. Turmeric (haldi)
6. Kapur (camphor)
7. Amla oil
8. Lawanga (clove oil ext.)
9. Chandan (sandal wood oil)
10. Kewara ext.
11. Jatamansi oil ext.
12. Pudina salts
13. Almond oil
14. Packaging material

TOTAL WORKING CAPITAL/MONTH

1.	Raw Material	Rs.	53,43,609.90
2.	Salary & Wages	Rs.	77,750.00
3.	Utilities & Overheads	Rs.	67,000.00
	TOTAL	Rs.	54,88,359.90

TOTAL CAPITAL INVESTMENT

Total Fixed Capital	Rs.	24,28,000.00
Total Working Capital for 3 Months	Rs.	1,64,65,079.70
TOTAL	Rs.	1,88,93,079.70

TURN OVER/ANNUM

By sale of 44,10,000 bottles(100 ml each) of herbal oils (ayurvedic) like banphool oil	Rs.	7,93,80,000.00

PROFIT SALES RATIO = 12.35 %
RATE OF RETURN = 51.90 %
BREAK EVEN POINT (B.E.P) = 31.01 %

Chapter 34

PLANT ECONOMICS OF ANTISEPTIC CREAM

Rated Plant Capacity	=	200.00 Kgs/Day
LAND & BUILDING	=	Rs. 15,25,000.00
(Land 750 sq. mts.)		

PLANT & MACHINERY

1. Stainless Steel Jacketted Vessel
2. Stainless steel tank
3. S.S. filling tank
4. Automatic weighing filling, tube sealing machine
5. Conveyor
6. Cardboard Pack, filling sealing machine
7. Electronic weighing balance
8. Electronic balance small
9. Carton sealing machine
10. Laboratory Equipments

FIXED CAPITAL

1.	Land & Building	Rs.	15,25,000.00
2.	Plant & Machinery	Rs.	35,95,000.00
3.	Other Fixed Assets	Rs.	8,20,000.00
	TOTAL	Rs.	59,40,000.00

RAW MATERIALS

1. Extract of Calendula
2. Extract of Chandan
3. Extract of Ushir

4. Extract of Ghritkumar
5. Extract of Tulsi
6. Extract of Jatamansi
7. Extract of Saussurea Lappa
8. Extract of Aguru
9. Extract of Daruharidra
10. Zinc Oxide
11. Absolute Alcohol
12. White petroleum jelly
13. Lanoline
14. Mineral Oil
15. Packaging Tubes, Printed cardboard packs, cartons etc.

TOTAL WORKING CAPITAL/MONTH

1.	Raw Material	Rs.	6,61,725.00
2.	Salary & Wages	Rs.	1,09,500.00
3.	Utilities & Overheads	Rs.	1,65,500.00
	TOTAL	Rs.	9,36,725.00

TOTAL CAPITAL INVESTMENT

Total Fixed Capital	Rs.	59,40,000.00
Total Working Capital for 3 Months	Rs.	28,10,175.00
TOTAL	Rs.	87,50,175.00

TURN OVER/ANNUM

By sale of 30,00,000 Packs of Antiseptic cream in 20 gms size packs (60000 kgs. total cream)	Rs.	1,80,00,000.00

PROFIT SALES RATIO = 22.85 %
RATE OF RETURN = 47.01 %
BREAK EVEN POINT (B.E.P) = 49.09 %

Chapter 35

PLANT ECONOMICS OF NAIL ENAMEL

Rated Plant Capacity = 4000.00 Nos/Day

LAND & BUILDING = Rs. 3,25,000.00
(Land Required 500 sq. mts.)

PLANT & MACHINERY

1. Mixer with agitator
2. Centrifuge
3. Storage Tank
4. Values, Weighing scalers, pipe, pumps.
5. Liquid filling machine

FIXED CAPITAL

1.	Land & Building	Rs.	3,25,000.00
2.	Plant & Machinery	Rs.	1,84,000.00
3.	Other Fixed Assets	Rs.	1,05,000.00
	TOTAL	Rs.	6,14,000.00

RAW MATERIALS

1. Nitro cellulose
2. Santilite
3. Dibutyl phthalate
4. Butyl Acetate
5. Ethyl alcohol
6. Butyl alcohol
7. Toluene

TOTAL WORKING CAPITAL/MONTH

1.	Raw Material	Rs.	46,775.00
2.	Salary & Wages	Rs.	22,680.00
3.	Utilities & Overheads	Rs.	1,57,200.00
	TOTAL	Rs.	2,26,655.00

TOTAL CAPITAL INVESTMENT

Total Fixed Capital	Rs.	6,14,000.00
Total Working Capital for 3 Months	Rs.	6,79,965.00
TOTAL	Rs.	12,93,965.00

TURN OVER/ANNUM

Revenue by sales of 12,00,000 Nail Enamel containers of each containing 10cc of enamel	Rs.	48,00,000.00

PROFIT SALES RATIO = 37.54 %

RATE OF RETURN = 139.26 %

BREAK EVEN POINT (B.E.P) = 38.78 %

Chapter 36

PLANT ECONOMICS OF NAIL POLISH & NAIL POLISH REMOVER

Rated Plant Capacity = 300.00 Kg./Day

200 Kg./Day NAIL POLISH

100 Kg./Day NAIL POLISH REMOVER

LAND & BUILDING (Land 500 sq.mts) = Rs.13,50,000.00

PLANT & MACHINERY

1. Lacquer mixer
2. Centrifuge
3. Mixing tank for nail polish remover
4. Storage tank
5. Nail Polish Filling & Sealing Machine
6. Laboratory Testing Equipment
7. Pipes, Pumps, Fittings, Structures Electrical Fitting etc.

FIXED CAPITAL

1.	Land & Building	Rs.	13,50,000.00
2.	Plant & Machinery	Rs.	18,65,000.00
3.	Other Fixed Assets	Rs.	3,40,000.00
	TOTAL	Rs.	35,55,000.00

RAW MATERIALS

1. Nitrocellulose
2. Santolite
3. Dibutyl phthalate
4. Ethyl alcohol

5. Butyl acetate
6. Toluene
7. Butyl alcohol
8. Pigment
9. Packing materials
10. Butyl stearate
11. Ethyl acetate
12. Acetone

TOTAL WORKING CAPITAL/MONTH

1. Raw Material		Rs.	7,79,625.00
2. Salary & Wages		Rs.	89,110.00
3. Utilities & Overheads		Rs.	1,07,400.00
	TOTAL	Rs.	9,76,135.00

TOTAL CAPITAL INVESTMENT

Total Fixed Capital		Rs.	35,55,000.00
Total Working Capital for 3 Months		Rs.	29,28,405.00
	TOTAL	Rs.	64,83,405.00

TURN OVER/ANNUM

1. By sale of Nail Polish 60000 kgs			
2. By sale of nail polish remover			
	TOTAL	Rs.	1,80,00,000.00

PROFIT SALES RATIO = 26.70 %

RATE OF RETURN = 74.12 %

BREAK EVEN POINT (B.E.P) = 33.53 %

Chapter 37

PLANT ECONOMICS OF TALCUM POWDER

Rated Plant Capacity	=	1.00 Ton/Day
LAND & BUILDING (Land required 500 sq.mt.)	=	Rs. 3,52,500.00

PLANT & MACHINERY

1. Mixer
2. Powder filling & packing machine
3. Storage tank powder
4. Miscellaneous

FIXED CAPITAL

1.	Land & Building	Rs.	3,52,500.00
2.	Plant & Machinery	Rs.	2,50,000.00
3.	Other Fixed Assets	Rs.	1,25,000.00
	TOTAL	Rs.	7,27,500.00

RAW MATERIALS

1. Zinc Stearate
2. Zinc oxide
3. Light calcium carbonate
4. Talc
5. Essence (cosmetics)
6. Packing material

TOTAL WORKING CAPITAL/MONTH

1.	Raw Material	Rs.	3,69,000.00
2.	Salary & Wages	Rs.	12,750.00
3.	Utilities & Overheads	Rs.	16,500.00
	TOTAL	Rs.	3,98,250.00

TOTAL CAPITAL INVESTMENT

Total Fixed Capital	Rs.	7,27,500.00
Total Working Capital for 3 Months	Rs.	11,94,750.00
TOTAL	Rs.	19,22,250.00

TURN OVER/ANNUM

By selling of 300 tons of Talcum Powder	Rs.	60,00,000.00

PROFIT SALES RATIO = 11.88 %

RATE OF RETURN = 37.08 %

BREAK EVEN POINT (B.E.P) = 47.65 %

Chapter 38

PLANT ECONOMICS OF TOOTH PASTE [GEL TYPE]

Rated Plant Capacity	=	500.00 Kgs/Day
LAND & BUILDING (Land area 500 sq.mts)	=	Rs. 15,42,500.00

PLANT & MACHINERY

1. Closed jacketed mixing reaction vessel
2. Storage vessels
3. Homogenizer of paste
4. Laboratory test and quality control equipments.
5. Automatic paste weighing, tube filling and sealing machine.
6. Cartoons packing and sealing machine.
7. Weighing Balance (digital & manual)
8. Generator
9. Piping, fitting & valves, slurry pumps and motors etc.
10. Miscellaneous, material handling equipments, etc.

FIXED CAPITAL

1.	Land & Building	Rs.	15,42,500.00
2.	Plant & Machinery	Rs.	18,25,000.00
3.	Other Fixed Assets	Rs.	2,50,000.00
	TOTAL	Rs.	36,17,500.00

RAW MATERIALS

1. Glycerine
2. Carbopol
3. Sodium saccharine

4. Dupenol c (sodium Lauryl sulphate)
5. Sodium hydroxide (10% solution)
6. Peppermint oil
7. Miscellaneous materials,(flavouring compounds, perfumery compound, colouring matter.)
8. Collapsible tubes plastic
9. Corrugated boxes and other packing materials

TOTAL WORKING CAPITAL/MONTH

1.	Raw Material	Rs.	12,37,750.00
2.	Salary & Wages	Rs.	71,875.00
3.	Utilities & Overheads	Rs.	37,500.00
	TOTAL	Rs.	13,47,125.00

TOTAL CAPITAL INVESTMENT

Total Fixed Capital	Rs.	36,17,500.00
Total Working Capital for 3 Months	Rs.	40,41,375.00
TOTAL	Rs.	76,58,875.00

TURN OVER/ANNUM

By sale Gel Type Tooth Paste Nos. 30,00,000 (50 gm each tube)	Rs.	1,95,00,000.00

PROFIT SALES RATIO = 7.80 %
RATE OF RETURN = 19.85 %
BREAK EVEN POINT (B.E.P) = 60.60 %

Chapter 39

PLANT ECONOMICS OF AFTER SHAVE LOTION

Rated Plant Capacity = 380.00 Ltrs./Day

LAND & BUILDING = Rs. 11,00,000.00
(Land required 500 sq.mts)

PLANT & MACHINERY

1. Soap Crutcher
2. Mixing Tank with Agitator
3. Storage tank
4. Semi Automatic Bottle filling and labelling machine
5. Baby Boiler oil fired
6. Laboratory equipment
7. Miscellaneous Equipments pumps, motors, pipes etc.

FIXED CAPITAL

1.	Land & Building	Rs.	11,00,000.00
2.	Plant & Machinery	Rs.	8,40,000.00
3.	Other Fixed Assets	Rs.	3,90,000.00
	TOTAL	Rs.	23,30,000.00

RAW MATERIALS

1. Chloroxylenol
2. Terpinol
3. Alcohol
4. Caustic Soda
5. Castor oil/fatty Acid

6. Miscellaneous chemicals perfumes
7. Packaging charges Bottles of 100ml. and 200 ml., Cartons, Labels, tapes

TOTAL WORKING CAPITAL/MONTH

1.	Raw Material	Rs.	7,85,500.00
2.	Salary & Wages	Rs.	47,824.00
3.	Utilities & Overheads	Rs.	1,60,500.00
	TOTAL	Rs.	9,93,824.00

TOTAL CAPITAL INVESTMENT

Total Fixed Capital	Rs.	23,30,000.00
Total Working Capital for 3 Months	Rs.	29,81,472.00
TOTAL	Rs.	53,11,472.00

TURN OVER/ANNUM

Receipt by sale of 1,14,000 - litre of Antiseptic Solution in 100 ml. & 200 ml. bottles Rs. 1,71,00,000.00

PROFIT SALES RATIO = 25.15 %
RATE OF RETURN = 80.96 %
BREAK EVEN POINT (B.E.P) = 30.35 %

Chapter 40

PLANT ECONOMICS OF LIPSTICKS

Rated Plant Capacity	=	1000.00 Pcs./Day
LAND & BUILDING (Land area 500 sq.mts.)	=	Rs. 6,05,000.00

PLANT & MACHINERY

1. Mixer
2. Grinder
3. Moulds and moulding equipments
4. Packaging machines etc.

FIXED CAPITAL

1.	Land & Building	Rs.	6,05,000.00
2.	Plant & Machinery	Rs.	85,000.00
3.	Other Fixed Assets	Rs.	50,000.00
	TOTAL	Rs.	7,40,000.00

RAW MATERIALS

1. Beeswax
2. Castor Oil
3. Cetyl alcohol
4. Perfumes, colours etc.

TOTAL WORKING CAPITAL/MONTH

1.	Raw Material	Rs.	54,480.00
2.	Salary & Wages	Rs.	17,000.00
3.	Utilities & Overheads	Rs.	17,650.00
	TOTAL	Rs.	89,130.00

TOTAL CAPITAL INVESTMENT

Total Fixed Capital	Rs.	7,40,000.00
Total Working Capital for 3 Months	Rs.	2,67,390.00
TOTAL	Rs.	10,07,390.00

TURN OVER/ANNUM

By sale of 3,00,000 pieces of lipsticks	Rs.	18,00,000.00

PROFIT SALES RATIO = 27.77 %

RATE OF RETURN = 49.61 %

BREAK EVEN POINT (B.E.P) = 44.27 %

Chapter 41

PLANT ECONOMICS OF KESH KALA TEL

Rated Plant Capacity = 5000.00 Bottles/Day
100 gm each bottle

LAND & BUILDING (Land area 500 Sq.Mts.) = Rs. 12,50,000.00

PLANT & MACHINERY

1. Mixing vessel (S.S.) with stirrer
2. Reaction vessel
3. Baby boiler
4. Automatic bottle filling, sealing & weighing machines.
5. Lab equipments.

FIXED CAPITAL

1.	Land & Building	Rs.	12,50,000.00
2.	Plant & Machinery	Rs.	18,95,000.00
3.	Other Fixed Assets	Rs.	6,70,000.00
	TOTAL	Rs.	38,15,000.00

RAW MATERIALS

1. Paraffin oil
2. Triethanolamine
3. Glyceryl monolaurate
4. Gum tragacanth
5. Stearic acid
6. PPD dye

7. Methyl parahydroxv benzoate
8. Water (distilled)
9. Perfumes
10. Packaging material
11. Card board boxes
12. Miscellaneous packaging materials viz. cartons etc.

TOTAL WORKING CAPITAL/MONTH

1.	Raw Material	Rs.	8,93,775.00
2.	Salary & Wages	Rs.	64,625.00
3.	Utilities & Overheads	Rs.	76,000.00
	TOTAL	Rs.	10,34,400.00

TOTAL CAPITAL INVESTMENT

Total Fixed Capital	Rs.	38,15,000.00
Total Working Capital for 3 Months	Rs.	31,03,200.00
TOTAL	Rs.	69,18,200.00

TURN OVER/ANNUM

Sale of 15,00,000 bottles of Kesh Kala Tel (100 gm. each bottle)	Rs.	1,87,50,000.00

PROFIT SALES RATIO = 24.26 %
RATE OF RETURN = 65.76 %
BREAK EVEN POINT (B.E.P) = 35.12 %

Chapter 42

PLANT ECONOMICS OF KALI MEHANDI

Rated Plant Capacity	=	20.00 Kgs./Day
LAND & BUILDING	=	Rs. 1,79,500.00
(Land required 150 sq.mts)		

PLANT & MACHINERY

1. Pulverizer-cum -mixer
2. Storage vessel
3. Mixing vessel
4. Homogeniser
5. Drier
6. Grinding machine
7. Bottle filling machine
8. Powder packaging machine
9. Lab-Equipments
10. Baby boiler
11. Screening Machine
12. Weighing Machine
13. Generator
14. Erection and others

FIXED CAPITAL

1.	Land & Building	Rs.	1,79,500.00
2.	Plant & Machinery	Rs.	2,29,000.00
3.	Other Fixed Assets	Rs.	80,000.00
	TOTAL	Rs.	4,88,500.00

RAW MATERIALS

1. Mehandi Powder
2. Lecithin
3. E.D.T.A.(Ethylene diamine tetracetic acid tetrasodium salt)
4. Water
5. Sodium sulfite
6. Ammonium hydroxide
7. Isopropanol
8. Para-phenylenediamine
9. Para amino phenol
10. 2-Hydroxy 1:4 naphthaquinoze
11. Pyrogallol
12. Hydroquinone
13. Perfume

TOTAL WORKING CAPITAL/MONTH

1.	Raw Material	Rs.	1,46,425.00
2.	Salary & Wages	Rs.	11,125.00
3.	Utilities & Overheads	Rs.	9,950.00
	TOTAL	Rs.	1,67,500.00

TOTAL CAPITAL INVESTMENT

Total Fixed Capital	Rs.	4,88,500.00
Total Working Capital for 3 Months	Rs.	5,02,500.00
TOTAL	Rs.	9,91,000.00

TURN OVER/ANNUM

Receipt By sale 6000 kg in packed Kali Mehandi powder	Rs.	29,10,000.00

PROFIT SALES RATIO = 20.77 %
RATE OF RETURN = 61.00 %
BREAK EVEN POINT (B.E.P) = 39.62 %

Chapter 43

PLANT ECONOMICS ON HAIR OIL AND FORMULATION

Rated Plant Capacity = 60.00 Kgs./Day

LAND & BUILDING (Land Required 200 sq.mt.) = Rs. 3,00,000.00

PLANT & MACHINERY

1. Stainless steel tank with stirrer
2. Filling machine manually operated
3. Sealing machine
4. Bottle washing machine pump, motors etc.,
5. Bottle dryer
6. Filter press
7. Laboratory equipments

FIXED CAPITAL

1.	Land & Building	Rs.	3,00,000.00
2.	Plant & Machinery	Rs.	1,62,000.00
3.	Other Fixed Assets	Rs.	62,000.00
	TOTAL	Rs.	5,24,000.00

RAW MATERIALS

1. Castor oil (Deodorised)
2. Colour
3. Tincture cantheridine
4. Oil rosemary
5. English lavender
6. Heiko Tuberose

7. Coconut oil
8. Amla oil
9. Benzoic Acid
10. Oil colour
11. Lemon oil
12. Bergamout oil
13. Rosemary oil
14. Nerole oil
15. Lavender oil
16. Bela (Jasmine) oil
17. Refined coconut oil
18. Alkanet root
19. Oil lavender
20. Oil geranium rose
21. Clores oil
22. Oil cinnamon
23. Oil bergmol

TOTAL WORKING CAPITAL/MONTH

1.	Raw Material	Rs.	1,05,706.55
2.	Salary & Wages	Rs.	12,878.75
3.	Utilities & Overheads	Rs.	11,460.00
	TOTAL	Rs.	1,30,045.30

TOTAL CAPITAL INVESTMENT

Total Fixed Capital	Rs.	5,24,000.00
Total Working Capital for 3 Months	Rs.	3,90,135.90
TOTAL	Rs.	9,14,135.90

TURN OVER/ANNUM

Sale of Amla oil 6000 kgs.
Sale of Jasmine oil 6000 kgs
Sale of catheridine oil 6000 kgs.

TOTAL Rs. 24,30,000.00

PROFIT SALES RATIO = 27.21 %
RATE OF RETURN = 72.32 %
BREAK EVEN POINT (B.E.P) = 32.97 %

Chapter 44

PLANT ECONOMICS OF BABY OIL

Rated Plant Capacity	=	500.00 Kgs./Day
		2500 Bottles/Day OF 100 ML
		1250 Bottles/Day OF 200 ML

LAND & BUILDING	=	Rs. 14,00,000.00
(Land Area 500 sq.mt)		

PLANT & MACHINERY

1. Mixer (M.S)
2. Filter
3. Storage Tanks
4. Boiler
5. Bottle filling & scaling machine
6. Laboratory Testing Equipment
7. Misc. pipe & pipe fitting, tools etc.

FIXED CAPITAL

1.	Land & Building	Rs.	14,00,000.00
2.	Plant & Machinery	Rs.	5,00,000.00
3.	Other Fixed Assets	Rs.	1,00,000.00
	TOTAL	Rs.	20,00,000.00

RAW MATERIALS

1. Mineral oil light
2. Olive Oil
3. Hexachlorophene

4. Antioxidant(tocopherol)
5. Perfume
6. Packaging Materials (Glass/Plastic/PET Bottle) Labels & other Misc. Consumables (L.S)

TOTAL WORKING CAPITAL/MONTH

1.	Raw Material	Rs.	10,94,995.00
2.	Salary & Wages	Rs.	1,00,415.00
3.	Utilities & Overheads	Rs.	53,550.00
	TOTAL	Rs.	12,48,960.00

TOTAL CAPITAL INVESTMENT

Total Fixed Capital	Rs.	20,00,000.00
Total Working Capital for 3 Months	Rs.	37,46,880.00
TOTAL	Rs.	57,46,880.00

TURN OVER/ANNUM

Sale of Baby Oil	Rs.	2,06,25,000.00

PROFIT SALES RATIO = 21.79 %
RATE OF RETURN = 78.19 %
BREAK EVEN POINT (B.E.P) = 29.53 %

Chapter 45

DETAILS OF PLANT, MACHINERY & EQUIPMENTS

MIXER:

With all contact parts made our of mixing S.S-304 quality with two mechanical seal ends to prevent outside lubricants from entering into mixing chamber. The paddles on the shaft are so arranged as to give thorough and uniform mixing. The unit is supplied with dust proof stainless steel cover, tilting and safety device to prevent any accident. Complete with motor, gear box and starter etc.

MULTIMILL

The Multimill is useful for various purposes like granulation, shredding, pulverizating etc. The unit consists of vertically mounted 3 HP motor which drives the shaft through bearing housing. The motor has Nos. swinging type type knife blades and 2 Nos. scrapper blades. All contact parts are made out of S.S. complete with motor, DOL starter with reversible switch and one No. stainless steel sieve.

HERBS GRINDER

The unit is suitable to reduce the size of the herbs as per your requirement. All contact parts of body made of stainless steel. The S.S. body is fitted with 1 HP single phase motor D.P. switch for ON/OFF, with provision for affixing mesh of different sizes as per the nature of the material to be grinded, supplied with different sizes perforated sieves.

HOT AIR OVEN/TRAY DRYER

Complete in all respect with electrically heated drying chamber, suitable for drying granules, with double wall body, housing heavy fibre glass wool insulation, with special U type heaters, air circulation fan, thermostat, panel box etc. Machine duly painted and finished inside with heat resistant aluminium paint complete body made out of m.s. sheet of 16 swg thickness. The unit is with aluminium trays of 18 swg sheet material.

PORTABLE MECHANICAL SHIFTER

Machine complete in all respects, will all contact part of SS-304, suitable for bolting of free-flowing powders and granules, with flanged type motor, flywheel mechanism giving gyratory vibrations, with one S.S.-304 screen/sieve of given mesh, discharge chute, screen loading channel and hoisting clamps etc. fitted with heavy duty castors, machine duty castors, machine duly painted and finished etc.

OSCILLATING GRANULATOR

Machine complete in all respects, with all contact parts of SS-304, horizontal type, suitable type, suitable for wet and dry granulation process, complete with suitable electric motor, reduction gear box, quick opening and locking arrangement for changing the sieves, machine duly painted and finished.

SEMI AUTOMATIC-2-TRACK STRIP PACKING MACHINE

Complete with one set of change parts, feeding Fibre Disc, Chute Rollers, complete with batch printing attachment, with 0.5 HP Electronic motor stainless contact part etc.

AUTOMATIC 4 TRACK STRIP PACKING MACHINE

Complete with vibrator, S.S. feeding disc, Set of Rollers, chute, cutter etc. with batch printing attachment complete with 0.5 HP Motor, starter etc.

PACKING CONVEYOR BELT

Compete in all respects, designed for packaging /transportation operations of the inspected strips, cartons packs, etc. with 9-inch width superior quality, P.V.C. coated belt at the center having 12-inch width sunmica top working table on both sides of the conveyor belt, with HP/3 phase electric Motor reduction gear DOL starter and roller, with MS pipe legs, height adjustable between 30" to 36" standard 10-ft. length machine.

DOUBLE CONE BLENDER

Double cone blenders are useful for mixing dry powders or granules and are especially useful for small portion of One Product Mix with larger Portion of other. The blender is made of stainless steel and is mounted on mild steel stand. Unit is driven by a motor, through a gearbox with sliding angular blades for efficient mixing complete in all respects.

FOIL SEALER/TAGGER SEALING MACHINE

The machine is complete in all respect, all covered with stainless steel, with thermostatically controlled heaters of 1 KW enclosed in a heating plate. The heater works on single phase. The machine can seal lid size of various plastic PET & PVC container of dia-1 inch to 5 inch.

BATCH PRINTING MACHINE (MOTORISED)

This is small printing unit and is most suitable for over printing labels, cartons, etc. for printing details like mfg. Date batch no. Expiry date, retail price etc. The unit is supplied with composing block, set of words, ink, roller, L.N. Key etc. and Motor of 1/4 HP.

PULVERIZER S.S.

The unit is to reduce the size of the herbs, medicines powder etc. All contact parts of made of stainless steel 304 quality. The S.S. body is fitted with 2 HP/3 phase motor, the size of main body is 6" dia.

The unit is provided with provision for affixing mesh of different size as per requirement and nature of matérial to be pulverized.

PULVERIZER M.S

With contact parts of milk steel.

-capacity 50 Kg/hr./3HP/3 phase Motor

-capacity 75 Kg/hr./3 phase Motor

LABEL GUMMING MACHINE MOTORISED

Fitted with Crompton motors, Base Plate of stainless steel with Gum pot fitted on wooden mica Board, Cord and Plug, Roller size 6" with 3 brass label lifter.

DEHUMIDIFIER

The unit is a versatile, wherever excess humidity must be removed from the air. One ton hermetically sealed compressor of **'Kirloskar'** mini starter etc. suitable etc. suitable for approx. 2000 cu. ft. area with 3/4 occupants. The unit is fully mobile indegendently without attendant.

PLATE FORM BALANCE

This is a versatile and general weighing machine. It is strictly manufactured according to weights and measures, specifications and rules.

Capacity Steel yard graduation Plate form size

200 Kg. 10 Kg x 100 gms. 370 mm x 550 mm

300 Kg. 10 kg x 100 gms. 500 mm x 625 mm

S.S.SIEVE

Fitted in S.S. frame size 22" x 18" complete with one sieve fitted with out bolt system.

S.S.SIEVES: MOUNTED IN NON FRIABLE WOODEN FRAME

Stainless steel sieve of different meshes size 24" x 18" all mounted in teak wood friable wooden frame.

STAINLESS STEEL SCOOPS S.S 304 QUALITY

With handles highly polished

-Small sizes 300 gm.

-Medium size 700 gm.

-Bigger size 1200 gm.

-Extra bigger size 2 kg.

BOTTLE WASHING MACHINE

Complete in all respects with ss-304 brushing heads, 1/2 HP electric Motor, with suitable covering, duly painted & finished etc.

BOTTLE DRYING OVEN

Complete in all respects with 8 M.S. crates to hold 240 bottles/lb., size/per loading with 1 HP/3 phase electric Motor, uniform heat distribution fan, starter, indicators, thermostat, 6kw special tubular heaters,complete body made out of m.s. sheet of 16 swg thick and its double wall housing heavy fibre best quality glass wool insulation, machine duly painted and finished with inner chamber given heat. resistant aluminium paint.

AUTOMATIC VOLUMETRIC LIQUID FILLING MACHINE

Complete in all respect with all contact parts and suitable covering of ss-304, double head filling system with filling capacity of 15-125 ml on one side and 90-260 ml on the other side, with adjustable nozzle 1 HP/3 phase electric Motor, starter, suitable reduction gear box, quantly adjustment device, and no-bottle-no fill device, etc. with attached ss-belt chain conveyor of 7-ft. length. The conveyor belt is driven by a separate 1 HP/3 phase electric Motor coupld to a sturdy reduction box and starter, etc. Output 26-30 bottles per minute.

SEMI AUTOMATIC VOLUMETRIC LIQUID FILLING MACHINE

Complete in all respects with two filling heads and all contact parts of ss-304, with filling capacity of 15-125 ml on one side and 90-260 ml on the other side, with adjustable nozzle, 1 HP/3 phase electric Motor, starter, suitable reduction geat box and quantity adjustment device etc. with filling speed 26-30 bottles per minute/single stroke. Standard Table Model machine.

SEMI AUTOMATIC ALL-PURPOSE FILLING MACHINE (SINGLE HEAD)

For filling liquids, semisolids etc. in filling range of 15 ml/gm to 125 ml/gm, with ss-304 hopper of 22 kg kg/Lt. capacity and all contact part of ss-304, 1/2 Hp standard electric Motor suitable reduction gear box, one filling nozzle etc. machine all covered with ss-top and heavy duty castors, etc. with filling speed of 16 to 20 counts per minute/single stroke.

FOOT/HAND OPERATED ALL PURPOSE FILLING MACHINE

With all contact parts and 15 Lt/Kg capacity hopper of ss-304, liquid valve, m.s. angle frame stand, ss-304 filling nozzle & culinder, etc. suitable for filling 5 ml/gm to 50 ml/gm range in all types of liquid/semi-solids, creams pasts, inks in tubes, jars cans and bottles etc.

BOTTLE INSPECTION TABLE (SIZE 18"X36")

With flourescent tube and shaded background, provision for attachment of conveyor at any later stage

HIGH SPEED DISSOLVER & STIRRER MACHINE

Self balancing type with 3 variable speed complete in all respects with all contact parts of ss-304 mechanical height adjustment system, suitable electric Motor, heavy m.s. base & pipe stand complete with motor starter etc.

STAINLESS STEEL MIXING/STORAGE TANKS

These vessels are fabricated out of imported stainless steel sheet of 304 quality with M.S. frame legs mounted on wheels. Wheels provided are special type, with two ball bearing for effciently working especially rounded from circumference for easy rotation. Vessels are with removable type lid at the top having hinge lever arrangement, so that during mixing. The unit is also provided 'Internal Marking' in liters at various levels, complete with ball valve for solution removal. The vessels are given mirror finished polish.

PRIMARY SYRUP VESSELS

Stainless steel primary syrup vessels with 16 SWG 304 quality body-14 SWG base with handle bars on both sides, complete with removable type lid.

- Capacity : 50 ltrs.
- Capacity : 100 ltrs.
- Capacity : 200 ltrs.

P.P.CAP SEALING MACHINE (FLOOR MODEL)

For pilfer proof capping, capacity to seal 900 to 1200 cap/hr. depending upon the efficiency of the operator, complete with bottle resting tray and dies of 22,25 & 28mm, easy & adjustable, according to requirement

STAINLESS STEEL CHAIN CONVEYER MACHINE (10 FT. LENGTH)

Complete in all respects, with 1HP/3 Phase electric Motor, suitable reduction gear box, starter and height adjustable between 28" to 34" from the floor level, with suitable s.s.covering etc.

PACKING CONVEYER BELT MACHINE

Complete in all respects, designed for packaging/transportation the inspected bottles, carton packs, etc, with 9-inch width superior quality pvc coated belt at the centre having 12-inch width Sunmica top working table on both sides of the conveyer belt, with 1HP/3 Phase electric Motor, to a sturdy reduction gear box, DOL starter, tension idler and roller, with coupled m.s.pipe legs, height adjustable with between 28" to 34" from the floor level with the help of guided screws, machine duly painted and finished (standard 10-ft length).

EMUILSIFIER/HOMOGENISER WITH LIFTING SYSTEM

Complete in all respect with all contact parts of s.s-304, mounted on heavy m.s. angle Frame hanger, arrangement for height adjustment, with impeller of specially design to suit the HP of the drive, motor protected with four studs, rotor encaged with four studs, rotor encaged with four bars, complete with motor, starter and one classifying screen of any desired mesh.

-100 lt. Mixing capacity, with 1 HP/3 Phase motor

-200 lt. Mixing capacity, with 2 HP/3 Phase motor

-300 lt. Mixing capacity, with 3 HP/3 Phase motor

-500 lt. Mixing capacity, with 5 HP/3 Phase motor

HORIZONTAL PLATE FILTER PRESS MACHINE

Complete in all respects with all contact parts of s.s-304, with 8" dia, transfer gear pump of s.s-304, 1HP/3 Phase electrict. motor, 6-Plate (7-Filter pad) model machine, with s.s.-filter holder, Plates assembled in a cartridge with interlocking kin cups, mounted on m.s. pipe trolley with s.s-top portable unit.

WATER DEIONISER PLANT

To produce Deionised water output depends on the PPM of the total hardness of in-feed Raw Water. The unit is complete with Anion & Cation column, conductivity meter, cell, etc.

H.D. PURIFIED WATER STORAGE TANK

Vertical high density polyethylene, made, purified water storage tank, wide mouth complete with removable type lid.

DOUBLE CONE BLENDER

Double cone blenders are useful for mixing dry powders or granules and are especially useful for small portion of One Product Mix with Portion of other. The blender is made of stainless steel and is mounted on mild steel stand. Unit is driven by a motor, through a gearbox with sliding angular blades for efficient mixing complete in all respects.

PORTABLE MECHANICAL SHIFTER

Machine complete in all respects, with allcontact parts of S.S-304, suitable for bolting and sifting of h free-flowing powders and granules, with flanged type motor, flywheel mechanism giving gyratory vibrations, with one S.S-304 screen/sieve of given mesh, discharge chute, screen loading channel and hoisting clamps etc. fitted with heavy duty costors, machine duly painted and finished etc.

DEHUMIDIFIER

The unit is a versatile wherever excess humidity must be removed from the air. One ton hermatically sealed compressor of 'Kirloskar' refrigeration type to operate on 230 volts, single phase, complete with trolley, water collecting tank, mini starter etc. suitable for approx. 2000 cu. ft area with 3/4 occupants. The unit is fully mobile works independently without attendent.

THREE SPEED PLANETARY MIXER

Complete in all respects with all contact parts of ss-304 suitable for mixing, kneading and emulsifying creams, ointments, pastes, powders, wet mass, chavanaprash, gums and duplicating inks, etc. with ss-bowl, suitable locking plug for fixing the bowl to the machine, with specially designed slow speed beater rotating planetarly ensuring effecient and uniform mixing, with specially designed slow speed beater rotating planetarly ensuring efficient and uniform mixing, driven by an electric motor coupled to a 3-speed gear box with belt and pulley arrangement, hand operated mechanical up & down lifting device etc. Planetary movement speed-18,27 & 36 r.p.m. Beater movement speed 54,8 and 108 r.p.m. approx.

DOUBLE SPEED PLANETARY MIXER (SPECIAL TYPE) MACHINE

Complete in all respects with all contact parts of ss-304, with double speed (960/1440 rpm) TEFC motor for most efficient working, with suitable reduction gear box, panel box and DOL changing switch and starter, etc. with a fully jacketed bowl of ss-304 housing, thermostatically controlled suitable capacity heaters for cooling/heating of material, with hand operated mechanical up and down lifting devices.

DOUBLE SPEED PLANETARY MIXER (SPECIAL TYPE/HEAVY DUTY) MACHINE WITH MOTORISED LIFTING.

Complete in all respects, with all contact parts of ss-304, fully jacketed bowl of ss-304 with thermostatically controlled suitable capacity heaters for cooling/heating of materials, with two electric Motor, one dual speed (960/1440 rpm) TEFC motor with suitable reduction gear box coupled through belt and pulley arrangement for driving the agitation assembly and the other single speed (1440 rpm) motor with suitable reduction gear box, belt and pulley arrangement, for lifting the drive assembly for up and down, height adjustment of the drive assembly.

VACUUM PLANETARY MIXER MACHINE

Complete in all respect with all contact parts of ss-304, with a fully jacketed bowl of ss-304 housing thermostatically controlled suitable capacity heaters for cooling/heating of materials, suitable for products where air entrapment is problem, machine complete with dual speed (960/1440 rpm) TEFC motor, suitable reduction gear box belt and pulley arrangement for driving the main agitation assembly, flexible pipe for vacuum application through suitable vacuum pump and provided with a light & light & sight glass, etc. with hand operated mechanical up and down lifting device.

SEMI AUTOMATIC ALL-PURPOSE FILLING MACHINE (SINGLE HEAD)

For filling liquids, semisolids etc. in the filling range of 15 ml/gm to 125 ml/gm, with ss-304 hopper of 22 kg kg/Lt. capacity and all contact parts of ss-304, 1/2 Hp standard electric Motor suitable reduction gear box, one filling nozzle etc. machine all covered with ss-top and heavy duty castors, etc. with filling speed of 16 to 20 counts per minute/single stroke.

FOOT/HAND OPERATED ALL PURPOSE FILLING MACHINE

With all contact parts and 15 Lt./Kg capacity hopper of ss-304, liquid valve, m.s. angle frame stand, ss-304 filling nozzle & cylinder, etc. suitable for filling 5 ml/gm to 50 ml/gm range in all types of liquids/semi-solids, creams pasts, inks in tubes, jars can and bottles etc.

HOMOGENIZER

Complete in all respects, specially designed to grid the mixture of ointment, pastes, suspensions, ink, etc. up to the required fitness through regulation of emulsion head, hardened rotor etc. with 1 HP/3 phase electric Motor, starter and suitable reduction gear box, suitable for 15-25 kg/hr. capacity output.

LABORATORY EQUIPMENTS

HOT AIR OVEN:

Outer body is made of M.S. finished in hammerton spray stoving white enamel paint, with superior quality glass wool insulation in a gap of 65 mm, between the two walls. Heating elements are placed in ribs at the bottom and sides, adjustable air ventilator at top, built in horizontal L shaped thermometer 0 to 250 C, supplied complete with two pilot lamps, thermostate, perforated shelves adjusted at any level to work on 220/230 volts. A.C.main.

VACUUM OVEN

Double walled vacuum chamber made of Al/stainless steel, top lid of thick aluminium sheet with glass window and rubber gasket, vacuum gauge nozzles for suction release valves. Thermometer pocket at top, tempr. from C to 150 C accuracy + 2 C for 220 volts 50 cycles A.C. main. Outer body mild steel with stoving enamel paints wool insulation, complete with perforated aluminum/stainless steel, but without VACUUM PUMP.

STAINLESS STEEL WATER DISTILLATION APPARATUS

Wall type electrically operated on 220/230 volts, AC main complete.

AUTOCLAVE VERTICAL

Inner chamber made of SS outer of M.S. top lid of GUN METAL fitted with pressure gauge safety valve, steam release cock, pressure adjustable upto 35 lb sq. inch, complete with Al/stainless steel basket for sterilizing culture media, glass ware, utensils, instruments etc. In steam under pressure. Also with plug and cable to work on 220 volts AC main. Single rod-locking device with cladding.

FRIABILITY TEST APPARATUS

Used to determine the durability of tablets from the production to the time of use. Acrylic plastic drum has plastic handles, which carries the tablet along with it up to a predetermined height. The rotation period is determined by a timer to work on 230/220 volts, complete with wire & plug.

HERBS GRINDER

The unit is suitable to reduce the size of the herbs as per your requirement. All contact parts of the body made of stainless steel. The S.S. body is fitted with 1 HP single phase motor D.P. switch for ON/OFF, with provision for affixing mesh of different sizes as per the nature of the material to be grinded, supplied with different sizes perforated sieves.

HOT AIR OVEN/TRAY DRYER

Complete in all respect with electrically heated drying chamber, suitable for drying granules, with double wall body, housing heavy fibre glass wool insulation, with special U type heaters, air circulation fan, thermostat, panel box etc. Machine duly painted and finished inside with heat resistant aluminium paint complete body made out of m.s. sheet of 16 swg thickness. The unit is with aluminium trays of 18 swg sheet material.

PORTABLE MECHANICAL SHIFTER

Machine complete in all respects, with all contact parts of SS-304, suitable for bolting and sifting of free-flowing powders and granules, with flanged type motor, flywheel mechanism giving gyratory vibrations, with one S.S-304 screen/sieve of given mesh, discharge chute, screen loading channel and hoisting clamps etc. fitted duty castors, machine duly painted and finished etc.

DOUBLE CONE BLENDER

Double cone blenders are useful for mixing dry powders or granules and are especially useful for small portion of One Product Mix and larger Portion of other. The blender is made of stainless steel and is mounted on mild steel stand. Unit is driven by a motor, through a gearbox with sliding angular blades for efficient mixing complete in all respects.

PULVERIZER S.S.

With all contact parts of stainless steel.

The unit is to reduce the size of the herbs, medicines powder etc. All contact parts of the made of stainless steel 304 quality. The S.S. body is fitted with 2 HP/3 phase motor, the size of main body is 6" dia.

The unit is provided with provision for affixing mesh of different size as per requirement and nature of material to be pulverized.

PULVERIZER M.S.

With contact parts of mild steel.

The unit is for size reduction of herbs, medicinal powders etc. with all parts made of mild steel (M.S) all mounted on M.S. stand with extra heavy duty cyclone type.

POWDER & MASS MIXER :

All contact parts of stainless steel. Capacity : 25 Kg to 200 Kg. with motor, gear box, starter etc.

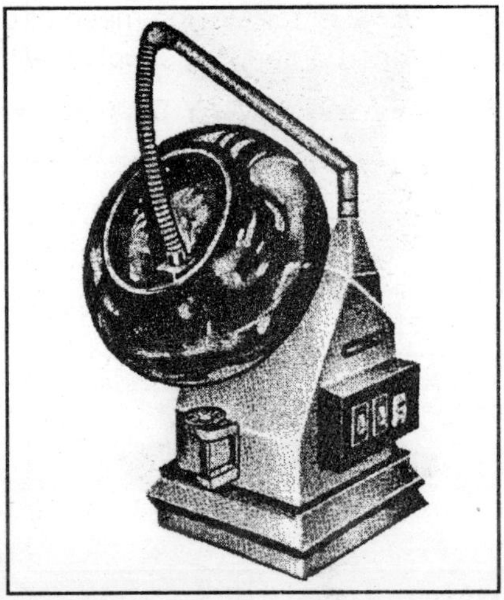

COATING PAN MACHINE :

Pan Dia 12", 36" & 42" with motor, hot Air Blower etc.

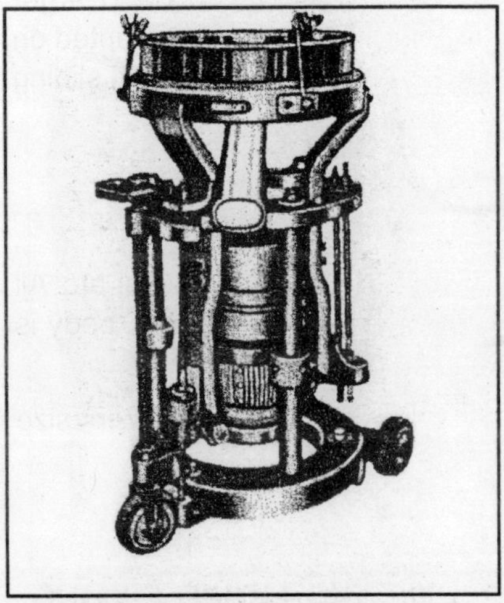

PORTABLE MECHANICAL SHIFTER

All contact part of S.S. with motor of 1.5 H.P. Size of sieve 22" dia. Unit is with one sieve

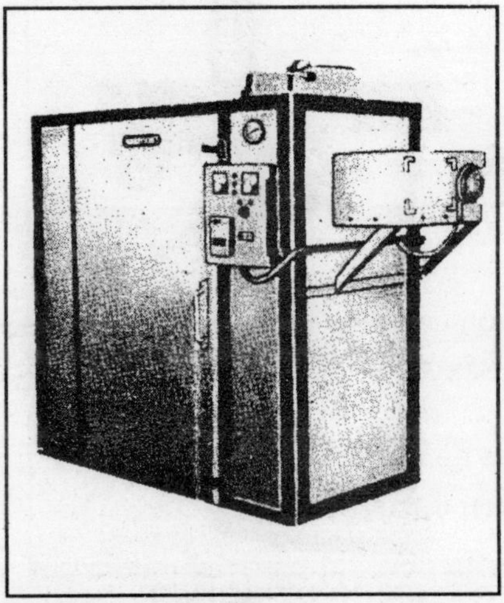

POWDER DRYER :

Model for 12, 24, 48 trays. size of tray 16" x 32" x 1¼"

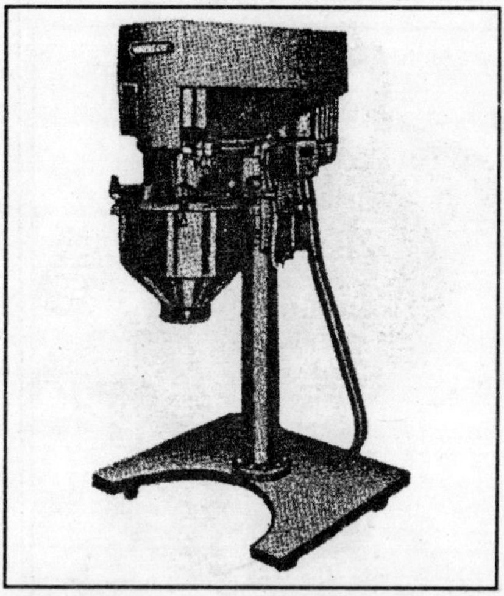

MULTIMILL :

For granulation and pulverization of dry & wet material.
All contact parts of S.S. with motor of 3 H.P./3 Phase.

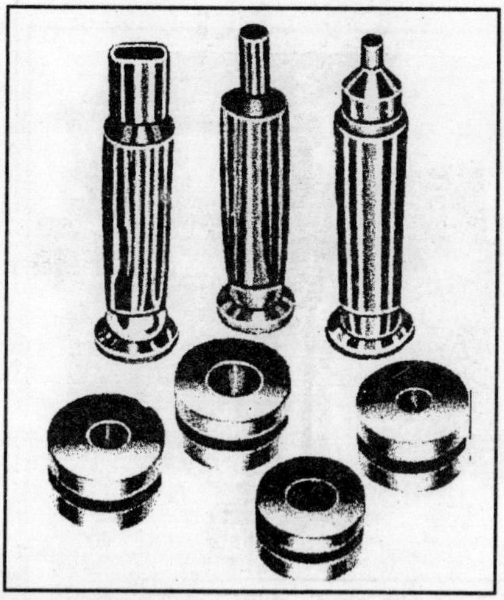

DIE PUNCH :

For all sizes and shapes for type of tablet compression machine

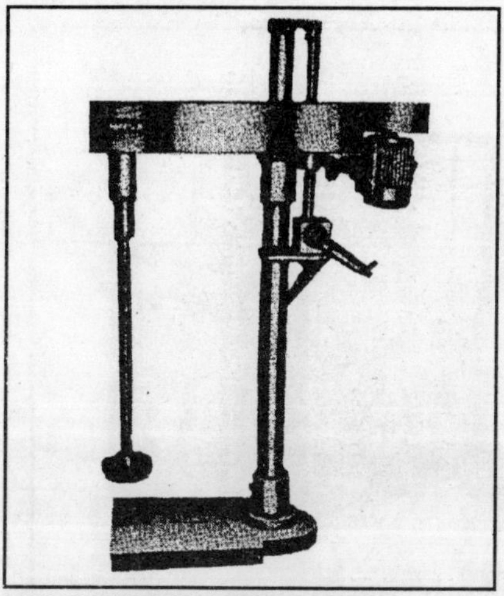

HIGH SPEED DISSOLVER :

With three variable speed and mechanical arrangement for increase and decrease in height.

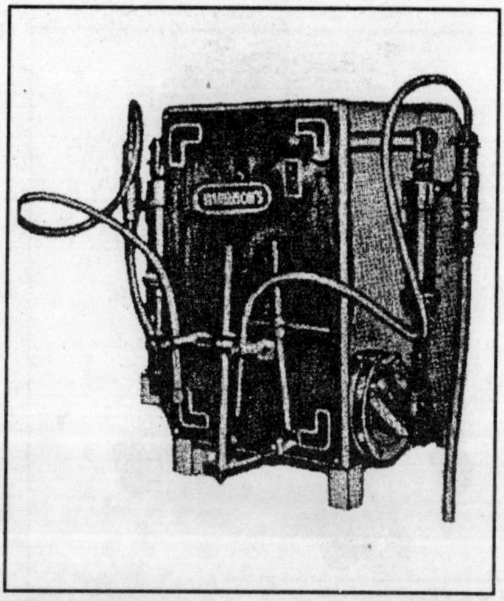

VOLUMETRIC LIQUID FILLING MACHINE :

All contact parts of stainless steel.
Filling Range 2 CC to 540CC filling accuracy ± 1%
Capacity 1200 bottle/hr

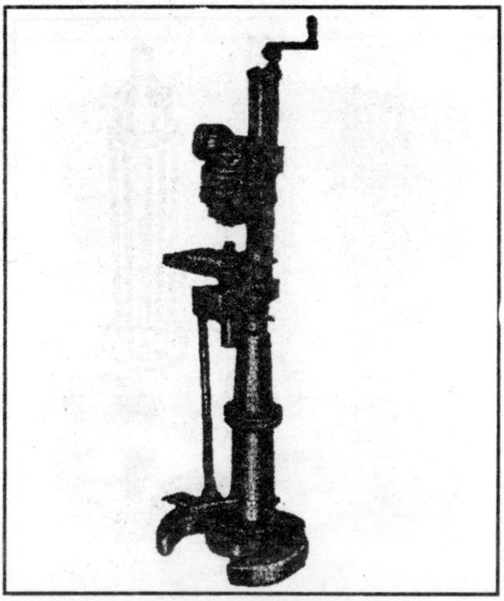

P.P. CAP SEALING MACHINE :

With bottle resting tray and dies of 22, 25 & 28 mm. size.

BATCH PRINTING MACHINE :

(Hand operated & motorised)

for over printing mfg. date batch No, etc. with composing block, set of words, Ink, Roller complete.

STAINLESS STEEL MIXING/ STORAGE TANK :

Fabricated out of S.S. sheet, with hinge lever lid, INTERNAL MARKING, ball valve capacity 50 ltr. to 2000 ltr

WATER DEMINERALISER :

To remove minerals from the raw water available in various capacity.

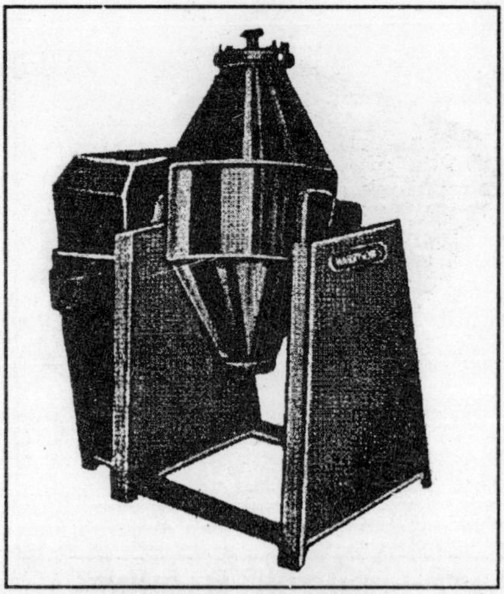

DOUBLE CONE BLENDER :

Contact parts of stainless steel. Capacity : 25 Kg. to 200 Kg./batch size

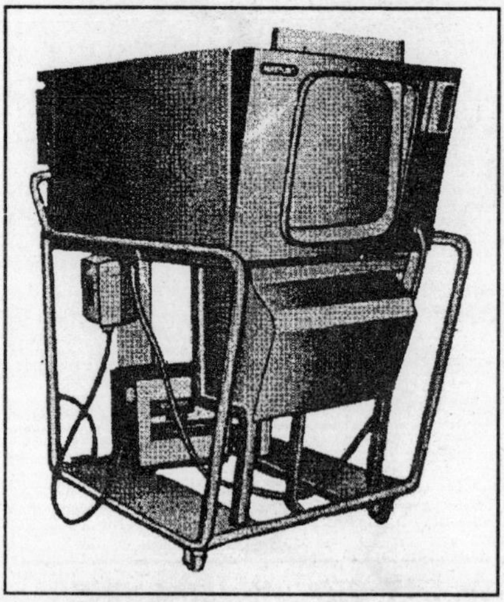

DEHUMIDIFIER :

Refrigeration type with Hermatically sealed compressor, motor fan, Voltage stabilizer, trolley through humidistate etc.

DISINTEGRATION TEST APPARATUS :

As per I.P/B.P/U.S.P. specification Frequency 30/32 cycles/min. with six glass tubes, disc beaker etc.

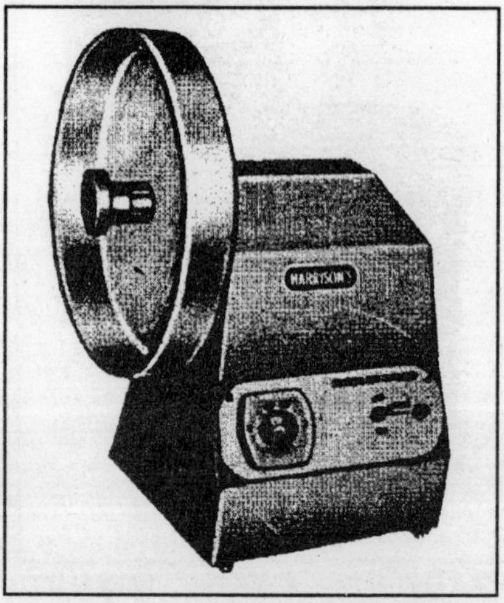

FRIABILITY TEST APPARATUS :

With transparent plastic drum, timer, wire & plug.

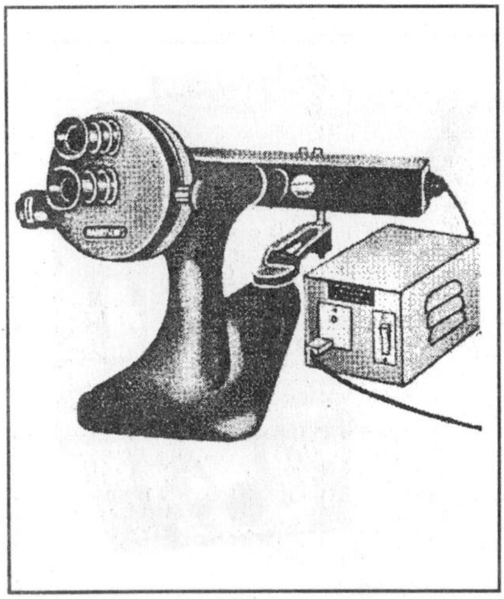

POLARIMETER :

Complete with sodium lamp assembly

Both angular & sugar scale.

Range:On ISS scale from -30⁰ to +130⁰

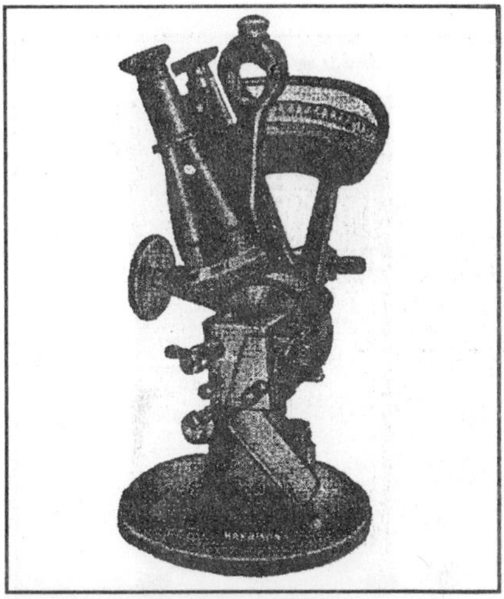

REFRACTROMETER ABBE TYPE :

Accuracy 0.001 by direct reading and 0.0001 by estimation.

With refractive and sugar index.

AUTOCLAVE : (Horizontal/Vertical)

Suitable for rapid sterilization of culture media, utensils, glass ware etc.

Avaliable in various sizes.

INFRARED MOISTURE BALANCE :

Capacity from 5 gms. to 25 gms.

Accuracy 0.2% by direct reading & 0.1% by estimation.

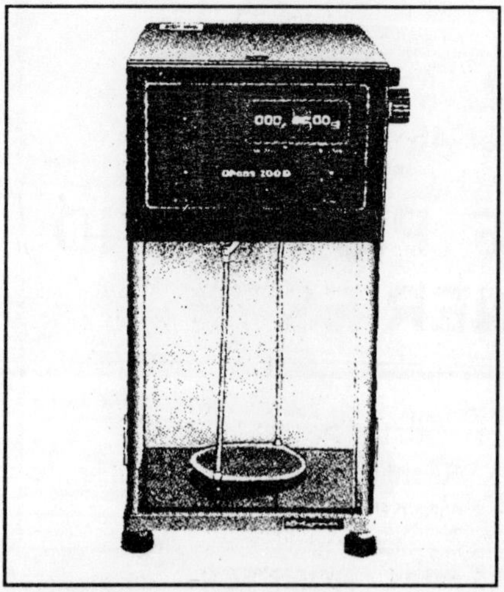

SINGLE PAN BALANCE :

Weighing range 100 gm, 160 gm and 200 gm. electrical operated

RECTANGULAR MUFFLE FURANCE :

Max. Tempr. 1000^{0}C working tempr. 900^{0}C Available in various sizes.

OVEN UNIVERSAL :
(Mammert Type)

outer body of M.S. and inner chamber of Al/S.S.
Available in various sizes

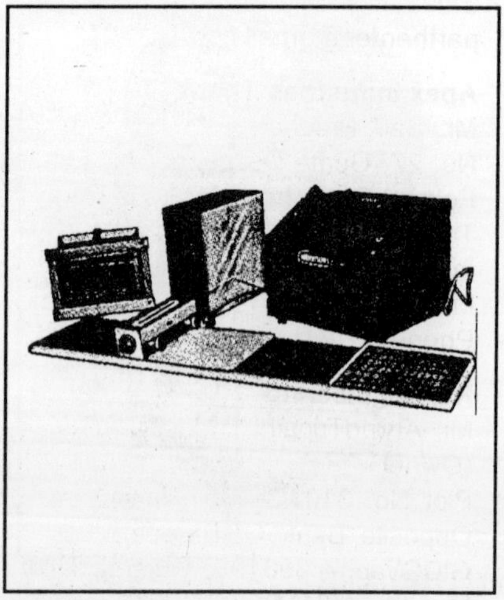

THIN LAYER CHROMATOGRAPHY KIT :

With applicator spreading board, rack, Micropipette & ultra violet lamp assembly.

Chapter 46

SUPPLIERS OF PLANT AND MACHINERIES

SUPPLIERS OF MACHINERY

Parth Enterprise
Mr. Roopesh Dave (Proprietor)
3, JivanVihar Society,
Opp. Bank of Bikaner & Jaipur,
Maninagar (East),
Ahmedabad - 380008,
Gujarat, India
Mobile: +(91)-9909018406
Email: roopesh_dave2000@yahoo.com
parthenter@gmail.com

Apex Industries Thane
Mr. Salil Pradhan
No. 27, Gupta Despande Indl Estate,
Pokran Road No. 1, Upavan
Thane - 400 606, Maharashtra,
India
Mobile: +(91)-9892522986
Phone: +(91)-(22)-25856039

Raj Engineering
Mr. ArvindTripathi / Mr. BabluTripathi (Owner)
Plot No. 3103/3, 4th Phase,
Opposite Bank Of Baroda,
GIDCVapi - 396195, Gujarat, India
Mobile: +(91)-9998242011
+(91)-9173521303
+(91)-9974889361
+(91)-9662734333

Kashi Machine Tools
Mr. Kashi Ram Sharma
C - 131, Sector - 10
Noida - 201 301, U.P., India
Mobile: +(91)-9312223649
Phone: +(91)-(120)-4346836

BLENDERS

Prism Pharma Machinery
Plot No. 3713, Ph. 4, G. I. D. C.,
Vatva, Ahmedabad - 382445,
Gujarat, India
Phone: 08376805843

Shiv Shakti Process Equipment Private Limited
Shiv Shakti, No. 407, Shivam Chambers,
S. V. Road, Goregoan West,
Mumbai - 400104,
Maharashtra, India
Website:www.shivshaktiequip.in

Hexamide Agro Tech LLP
Plot No.-11, Aditya Industrial Estate,
At Post Kumbiwali, TalukaKhalapur,
District- Raigad, Navi Mumbai - 410210,
Maharashtra, India
Phone: 08447556832
Web: www.usedchemicalreactor.com

Namdhari Industrial Works
D - 26, Focal Point,
Khanna - 141 401, Punjab, India
Phone: 08377804783

FILTER PRESS

Mech Static Hydraulics
No. 43/A, Srinivasa Nagar,
Third Street, Uppilipalayam,
Coimbatore - 641015,
Tamil Nadu, India
Phone: 08588874078

The Adarsh Engineering Works
Ghat Road, Near Union Bank,
Nagpur - 440018,
Maharashtra, India
Phone: 08447569191
Web: www.theadarshengineering.com

Energy Equipment
No. 9 - A, Zackaria Colony,
Main Road,
Choolaimedu, Chennai - 600094,
Tamil Nadu, India
Phone: 08447507985
Website: www.aquaflex.in

Charul Polymer Products
Plot No. 3235/3236, GIDC,
Phase- 3, T A, Kalol, Chhatral,
Gandhinagar, Ahmedabad - 382729,
Gujarat, India
Phone: 09953358163

BDS Hydro Treat Consultants Private Limited
G - 42, Ground Floor,
Dilshad Colony, New Delhi - 110095, India
Phone: 08376808134

DRYERS AND DRYING OVENS

Richard Engineering Bom P. Limited
First Floor, Brij Complex, K. B. Rd,
Railway Flyover Junction,
Ambarnath (W),
Thane - 421 501,
Maharashtra, India
Phone: 08447558651
Website:
www.chemicalpharmaequipment.com

Krishna Scientific Works
D - 23, Site - C,
Surajpur Industrial Area,
Dadri Road, Gr Noida - 201306,
Uttar Pradesh, India
Phone: 08377805857

Ahlada Industries Private Limited
Sy. No. 66- 68, Bahadurpally,
QutbullapurMandal,
Ranga Reddy District,
Hyderabad - 500043, Andhra Pradesh, India
Phone: 08376808108
Website: www.ahladaindustries.net

Biomate India Pvt Ltd
436, Shahabad Daulatpur, Near Sec -17,
Rohini, New Delhi - 110042,
Delhi, India
Phone: 08376805941
Website: www.fermentor.co.in

Balaji Enterprises Krishna & Co.
Paper Box, Near Hotel White House,
Mahakali Caves Road,
Andheri East,
Mumbai - 400093,
Maharashtra, India
Phone: 09953362138

Shreeji Instruments
Shop No. 8/9 G, Karnavati Shopping Center,
Near Bhurhani Society, Behind SmrutiMandir,
Ghodasar, Opposite Pushpkunj Bungalows,
Ahmedabad - 380050,
Gujarat, India
Phone: 08377805971

Rajyog Industries
Plot No. 5209,
Near Seven Water Tank,
G. I. D. C., Ankleshwar - 393 002,
Gujarat, India
Phone: 09099021320

PLANETARY MIXERS

Gangaa Machines
No. 13/ 62 - C, Trichy Main Road,
ChinthamaniPudur Post,
Coimbatore - 641103,
Tamil Nadu, India
Phone: 08447501162
Web: www.gangaamachines.com

Haifa Engineering
5, BR NathPaiMarg, Pine Building,
Opp. Hajee Cassum Compound,
Mazgaon, Mumbai - 400010,
Maharashtra, India
Phone: 09953358657

Traxit Engineers Pvt. Ltd.
406, Solaris- 2, Opposite L & T
Gate No. 6
Saki Vihar Road, Powai,
Mumbai - 400072,
Maharashtra, India
Phone: 08377809843
Website: www.traxiteng.co.in

East India Trading Co.
No. 71/ B, NetajiSubhash Road,
2nd Floor,
Room No. 118, Gooptu Mansion,
Kolkata - 700001, West Bengal,
India
Phone: 09953360763

Prism Pharma Machinery
Plot No. 3713, Phase - 4
G. I. D. C., Vatva,
Ahmedabad - 382445,
Gujarat, India
Phone: 08376805843

Excel Plants & Equipment Pvt Ltd
Gat No. 611, MoujeKuruli,
Chakan M. I. D. C., Tal- Khed,
Pune - 410 501, Maharashtra,
India
Website: www.excelplants.com

Conveying Machines Manufg Co.
No. 106, Ashok Service Industrial
Estate,
L. B. S. Marg, Bhandup West,
Mumbai - 400 078,
Maharashtra, India
Phone: 08376806177

Sahyog Enterprise, Mumbai
No. 5, Tarun Plastic Industrial
Estate,
Mogra Village Road, Andheri East,
Off Nagardas Cross Road,
Mumbai - 400 069,
Maharashtra, India
Phone: 08373902911
Website: www.agitatorsindia.net

Imochem Engineers
411, Janabai House, Kurla West,
Mumbai - 400070, Maharashtra,
India
Phone: 08373903857
Web: www.imochemengineers.com

PASTE FILLING EQUIPMENTS

Om Chamunda Enterprises
123, Diamond Industrial Estate,
Near Tolnaka, Ketki Pada Road,
Dahisar East, Mumbai - 400068,
Maharashtra, India
Phone: 08447496851
Web: www.omchamundaindia.com

Ad Industries
No. 29, Dhanlaxmi Indl Estate
Near Police Commissioner Office,
Shahibuag,
Ahmedabad - 380004,
Gujarat, India
Phone: 08376805975
Web: www.adpackagingmachine.com

Manilal Pack Plast Private Limited
Chandanmani, Opposite Kalupur Chakla Post Office,
Tankshal Road, Kalupur,
Ahmedabad - 380001,
Gujarat, India
Phone: 08373902742
Web: www.manilalpackplast.com

S. S. Pharma Tech
PX 65, Azad Lane,
AmbhedkarChowk,
ITT Bhatti, West Express Highway,
Goregoan East, Mumbai - 400063,
Maharashtra, India
Web: www.creamfillingmachine.com

Komal Enterprises
Shop- 5, Opp NMC Mini Market,
Near Ambad Police Station,
Nashik - 422009,
Maharashtra, India
Phone: 08377806967

Indian Packaging Machineries
I - 15, Phase - 1,
D. L. F. Industrial Area,
Faridabad - 121 003,
Haryana, India
Web: www.packagingmachinary.com

CREAM GEL AND LOTION PLANT

Bectochem Consultants &Enggs Private Limited
Mr. Mayur S. Hedaoo (Manager)
Building 5, C /204, Mittal Estate,
Andheri - Kurla Road, Andheri
East, Mumbai - 400 059,
Maharashtra, India
Mobile: +(91)-9167390040
+(91)-9970922799
Phone: +(91)-(22)-28502400
+(91)-(22)-28500057
+(91)-(22)-28500008
Fax:+(91)-(22)-28506785
Email:mayur@bectochem.com,
sales@bectochem.com

Prism Pharma Machinery
Mr. DilipPatidar (Partner)
Plot No. 3713, Phase - 4,
G. I. D. C., Vatva
Ahmedabad - 382445,
Gujarat, India
Mobile: +(91)-9825044789
+(91)-9375044789
Phone: +(91)-(79)-29095204
Fax: +(91)-(79)-25841623
Email:
sales@prismpharmamachinery.com,
mkt@prismpharmamachinery.com

Yoga Industries
Mr. Rajesh B. Panchal
A - 1/1 & 2, G. I. D. C.,
National Highway,
District- Gandhi Nagar,
Kalol - 382725, Gujarat, India
Mobile: +(91)-9825712535
Phone: +(91)-(2764)-224261
Web: www.pharmamachineries.co.in

Chapter 47

SUPPLIERS OF RAW MATERIALS

Shankar Dyes & Chemicals
No. 1209, Shankar Building,
Gali No. 11, Sadar Bazar,
New Delhi - 110 006, Delhi, India
Phone: 08447498163
Website: www.shankardyes.com

Cosmetics Of India
Plot No - 221, Pocket-C, D sidc,
Sector-5, Bawana Industrial Area,
Delhi - 110039, Delhi, India
Phone: 09811230720

Dev International
No. 301, 3rd Floor, Solitaire Complex,
Opposite Bombay Garage, Shahibaug,
Ahmedabad - 380004, Gujarat, India
Phone: 08377800758

Chemical Corporation
No. 2, Rajputpara No. 4, Amardeep Complex,
Near Khodiyar Chamber,
Rajkot - 360 001,
Gujarat, India
Phone: 09427209556

Herbal Cosmetic Raw Materials
Vasavi India
No. 122, Varadhamuthiappan Street, Geroge Town,
Chennai - 600 001, Tamil Nadu, India
Phone: 09840123444

Indian Commercial Company Pvt. Ltd.
Oriental House, 5th Floor, No. 7,
Jamshedji Tata Road, Churchgate,
Mumbai - 400020,
Maharashtra, India
Phone: 08588802838

Kirpal Export Overseas
BP- 130, Shalimar Bagh West,
New Delhi - 110 088, Delhi, India
Phone: 08447557523
Website: www.henna-manufacturers.com

Hennex India
Unit- II, No. 489, Link Road, Delhi Gate,
Old Faridabad, Faridabad - 121002, Haryana, India
Phone: 08376807668

Chapter 48

COSMETICS PACKAGING MATERIALS

Silvertone Gravu Flex Pvt. Ltd.
No. 27, DLF Industrial Area,
Opposite Metro Pillar No. 311,
Moti Nagar,
New Delhi - 110015, Delhi, India
Phone: 08377801826

Ask Enterprises
Gate No. 63, Jyotiba Nagar,
SonawaneWasti, Talawade,
Pune - 412114, Maharashtra, India
Phone: 08376806769
Website: www.ask-pack.com

Star Industrial Corporation
No. 79 / 81, Bora Bazar Street,
NarayandasWadi Building, 1st Fl,
Fort, Mumbai - 400 001,
Maharashtra, India
Phone: 09953364077

Venkatesh Gifts, Indore
No. 207, Mamta Tower,
Manormaganj, Near Mayank
Hospital,
Indore - 452001, M.P., India
Phone: 08588874473

AyushFlexipack Private Limited
B - 5, Sector - 57, Noida - 201301,
Uttar Pradesh, India
Phone: 09953358609

COSMETIC BOTTLES

Hary Pack Pharma Pvt. Ltd.
No. 19, Prakash Estate,
Ritanagar Road, Vastral Road,
Near Rabari Colony, Charrasta,
Amraiwadi, Ahmedabad - 380026,
Gujarat, India
Phone: 09426511776

Master Pet Industries
K1 - 26/1, G.I.D.C. Kadi,
Near Somani Ceramic,
Kadi - 382 715, Gujarat, India
Phone: 08588873504

MedoshaPlast
No. 210, Hiranandani Indl Estate,
Opp Kanjurmarg Railway Station,
KanjurMarg W., Mumbai - 400 078,
Maharashtra, India
Phone: 09953362236

Plastopack Industries
No. 26 - 29, Sheetal Shagun
Industrial Estate, 1st Fl,
Sativali Road, Near Waliv Phata,
Opposite Mahindra Showroom,
Vasai East,
Mumbai - 401208,
Maharashtra, India
Phone: 08588802564

PAPS Electronics
W. Z. - 49, Khampur, West Patel Nagar,
New Delhi - 110 008, Delhi, India
Phone: 08588874520

PMD Enterprises
No. 4, Aban'sPravesh, Aban Park, Kolshet Road, Dhokali,
Thane - 400607,
Maharashtra, India
Phone: 08586982595

Sri Maruthy Marketing Company
No. 1596, New No. 26, 2nd Cross, Nagappa Block, Srirampuram,
Bengaluru - 560021,
Karnataka, India
Phone: 09953362747

EIRI PROCESS TECHNOLOGY BOOKS

CHEMICAL/ DYES/ PETROCHEMICALS/ LUBRICANT/ ELECTROPLATING

01 Small Medium & Large Chemical Industries
02 Industrial Chemicals Technology Hand Book
03 Modern Technology of Organic & Inorganic Chemicals
04 Hand Book of Electroplating Anodizing & Surface Finishing Technology
05 Hand Book of Agro Chemical Industries (Insecticides & Pesticides)
06 Technology of Synthetic Dyes, Pigments Intermediates
07 Petrochemicals, Lubricants, Greases & Petroleum Refining
08 Hand Book of Lubricants, Greases & Petrochemicals Technology

GUMS, ADHESIVES AND SEALANTS

01 Technology Of Gums, Adhesives & Sealants With Formulations
02 Hand Book Of Adhesives With Their Formulaes
03 Adhesives Technology & Formulations Hand Book (Hand Book of Adhesives)
04 Technology of Glue and Adhesives with Adhesives Bonding and Formulations

SMALL SCALE INDUSTRIES/ STATIONERY/PAPER/ INKS/ CANDLES & EXPORT BUSINESS

01 Start Your Own Export Business (How To Export)
02 Start Your Own Small Business And Industry
03 Candle Making Processes & Formulations Hand Book
04 Stationery, Paper Converting & Packaging Industries
05 Modern Inks Formulations & Manufacturing Industries
06 Profitable Businesses To Start For Entrepreneurs
07 Modern Small & Cottage Scale Industries
08 Profitable Small Cottage Tiny & Home Industries

BIO FUEL & BIOPROCESSING

01 Technology Of Bio-Fules (Ethanol & Biodiesel)
02 Modern Technology Of Bioprocessing

PRINTING, SCREEN PRINTING & PACKAGING

01 Hand Book of Printing Processes Technologies & Industries
02 Hand Book Of Printing Technology (Offset, Screen, Flexo, Gravure, Inkjet & Digital)
03 Hand Book Of Offset Printing Technology
04 Screen Printing With Processes & Tech.
05 Hand Book Of Prepress
06 Hand Book Of Packaging Technology
07 Modern Packaging Technology for Processed Food, Bakery, Snack Foods, Spices and Allied Food Products
08 Hand Book Of Food Packaging Technology
09 Modern Technology of Printing Inks

PAINT, VARNISH, SOLVENTS, COATING & LACQUERS, POWDER COATING

01 Paint Pigment Varnish & Lacquer Manufacturing
02 Paint Varnish Solvents & Coating Technology

EIRI PROCESS TECHNOLOGY BOOKS

20 Technology of Chicken Meat and Poultry Products
21 Agro Food Processing and Packaging Technology
22 Modern Technology of Tomato Processing and Dehydration (Ketchup, Juice, Paste, Puree, Soup and Drying)
23 Modern Technology of Agro Processing and Food Packaging Products with Project Profiles
24 Start Your Own Coffee and Coffee Processing

SOAPS & DETERGENTS

01 Household Soap. Toilet Soap & Other Soap
02 Profitable Small Scale Manufacture Of Soaps & Detergents
03 Synthetic Detergents With Formulations
04 Modern Technology of Acid Slurry, Surfactants, Soap and Detergents with Formulae

ORGANIC FARMING AND FOOD

01 Hand Book Of Organic Farming And Organic Foods With Vermi-Composting And Neem Products

FISH FARMING & FISHERY PRODUCTS

01 Hand Book Of Fish Farming And Fishery Products

COSMETIC (SYNTHETIC & HERBAL)

01 Cosmetics Processes & Formulations
02 Herbal Cosmetics & Beauty Products With Formulations
03 Profitable Small Scale Manufacture Of Cosmetics (Synthetic & Herbal)
04 Hand Book Of Synthetic & Herbal Cosmetics (How to Make Beauty Products)
05 Technology Of Herbal Cosmetics & Toiletries Products With Formulae

OIL AND FATS

01 Hand Book of Oils, Fats And Derivatives With Refining & Packaging Technology
02 Technology of Oilseeds Processing, Oils & Fats and Refining

ESSENTIAL OILS & AROMATIC

01 Essential Oils Manufacturing & Aromatic Plants
02 Modern Technology Of Essential Oils
03 Technology Of Perfumes, Flavours & Essential Oils
04 Essential Oils Processes & Formulations

PERFUMES AND FLAVOURS

01 Hand Book Of Flavours & Food Colourants Technology
02 Hand Book Of Perfumes & Flavours
03 Hand Book of Perfumes With Formulations
04 Technology Of Perfumes, Flavours & Essential Oils
05 Hand Book Of Flavours Technology

BUILDING MATERIALS & CHEMICALS

01 Technology Of Building Materials & Chemicals With Processes

EIRI PROCESS TECHNOLOGY BOOKS

TEXTILE, GARMENTS, DYEING

01 Modern Technology Of Bleaching, Dyeing, Printing & Finishing Of Textiles
02 Technology Of Textiles (Spinning & Weaving, Dyeing, Scouring, Drying, Printing And Bleaching)
03 Garments Manufacturing Technology

SPICES & COLD STORAGE

01 Spices & Packaging With Formulaes
02 Start Your Own Cold Storage Unit

PULP & PAPER TECHNOLOGY

01 Hand Book Of Pulp & Paper, Paper Board & Paper Based Technology

NON WOVEN TECHNOLOGY

01 Complete Technology of Nonwovens Fabrics, Carry Bags, Composite, Geotextiles, Medical Textiles, Fibres, Felts, Apparels, Spunlace and Absorbent Nonwoven

TEXTILE AUXILIARIES & CHEMICALS

01 Textile Auxiliaries And Chemicals With Processes And Formulations

PHARMACEUTICALS & DRUGS

01 Pharmaceuticals And Drugs Technology With Formulations

LEATHER & LEATHER PRODUCTS

01 Hand Book Of Leather & Leather Products Technology

BIOTECHNOLOGY

01 Hand Book Of Biotechnology

CERAMICS

01 Hand Book of Ceramics and Ceramics Processing Technology

TREE FARMING

01 Hand Book Of Tree Farming

MUSHROOM CULTIVATION/ PROCESS

01 Hand Book Of Mushroom Cultivation, Processing and Packaging

BIOFERTILIZERS & VERMICULTURE

01 Hand Book Of Biofertilizers & Vermiculture

MINERAL AND MINERALS

01 Hand Book Of Minerals And Minerals Based Industries

RUBBER CHEMICALS, COMPOUND & RUBBER INDUSTRIES

01 Rubber Chemicals & Processing Industries
02 Modern Rubber Chemicals, Compounds & Rubber Goods Technology
03 Technology Of Rubber & Rubber Goods Industries

AYURVEDIC MEDICINES

01 Ayurvedic & Herbal Medicines With Formulaes
02 Hand Book Of Ayurvedic Medicines With Formulations (A

PAINT, ENAMEL, SOLVENTS, THINNERS, INKS & VARNISH

MEDICINES, HOMOEOPATHIC MEDICINES, DISPOSABLE SYRINGE, DENTAL COLLEGE & FINE CHEMICALS ETC.

FACTORY-ORIGINAL
SPORTING MK2 ESCORTS

FACTORY-ORIGINAL
SPORTING MK2 ESCORTS

The originality guide to the sporting variants of the Ford Escort Mk2

By Dan Williamson
Photography by Simon Clay

Herridge & Sons

Acknowledgements

Sporting Ford Escorts are all about the thrill, the performance and the ownership experience. And it's thanks to the commitment of Escort owners worldwide that these remarkable cars are still alive, kicking the competition and stirring our senses.

Our thanks go to all the Escort custodians who made their machines available for photography, including Steve Ogle, Dave Robinson, Eddy Gaskell, Aled Hopwood, Chris Parkes and Keith Wilkinson. Not to mention all the folk whose cars we've seen, inspected, lusted over and snapped at shows nationwide.

Credit also goes to the clubs and internet forums that make being part of the sporting Escort community such a rewarding experience – namely the Rallye Sport Escorts website and all its helpful contributors, the RS Owners' Club, the Sporting Escort Owners' Club (mainly Geraldine Ridgewell) and the AVO Owners' Club.

Personally, I'd like to thank Dave Hill and John Nevill at Ford, Dan White at *Fast Ford* and my publisher Ed Herridge. I must also express everlasting gratitude to Richard Farrell (for decades of Escort assistance and all those half-hour Mk2 gearbox swaps), Dave Robinson (for insight into a lifetime's RS1800 experience, I'm truly indebted), Richard Moore (let's call the Mk2 Escort Ghia an honorary sporting Escort), Loyd Gerken (for RS Mexico facts and recollections), Jon Evans (for Aussie Escort info and mutual motoring mutterings), Stephen Roser (for more Aussie Escort info and photos), Tony Wade (for Harrier facts and build plate puzzling), Kevin Frost (YUE 477S RIP), Mum and Dad (for starting my Escort obsession and playing host to a rotting 1600 Sport for too long to mention), Sarah (for Macwork of this book's chassis plate illustrations and putting up with years of Escort excuses).

Photography credits

Simon Clay, Ford Motor Company, Dan Williamson, Stephen Roser.

Published in 2012 by
Herridge & Sons Ltd
Lower Forda, Shebbear
Devon EX21 5SY

Reprinted 2017, 2022

ISBN 978-1-906133-29-0
Printed in Great Britain by Short Run Press, Exeter, Devon

CONTENTS

INTRODUCTION

A pure factory-original sporting Mk2 Escort, this early 1600 Sport leads a queue of similar cars along the 1976 Saarlouis production line just before its stripes were applied. Stuck to its windscreen is probably the build sheet that determined its specification.

Does lightning ever strike twice? The motorsport world was bolted, jolted and blown away by the Mk1 Ford Escort, which stormed a thunderous path through rallying, circuit racing and virtually every other form of four-wheeled competition.

Its shockwaves of success rippled though to Ford's road cars, creating a legend that electrified driving enthusiasts across the globe. From GT to Twin Cam, RS1600 and Mexico, the Escort's immense impact brought sporting saloon cars to the eyes and ears of anyone even remotely interested in having a great time behind the wheel. And with the birth of the evocative Rallye Sport brand, fast Fords became objects of desire to blue-collar workers, landed gentry and everyone in between.

Who could ever guess the Mk1's replacement would make even more of an impact?

Launched on 19 March 1975, the Escort Mk2 scooped awards for its clean, simple design. It was Ford's family machine for the masses, newly revised for space, refinement and economy.

But underneath that fresh, boxy body, much of the Mk1 remained. Only now, with its enlarged glass area and secretly inferior aerodynamics, the Mk2 was a less lively performer.

For Ford's image-conscious bosses and motorsport managers, that simply wouldn't do. A new range of sporting Escorts was needed – and they had to be more dramatic than ever before.

A principal player in the new lineup was the Escort Sport, which was sold as an all-encompassing model to replace the outgoing Sport and Mexico, meanwhile adding consumer-friendly options like four-door bodywork and an automatic gearbox. Clearly, this wasn't the correct formula for building a world-beating competition machine, but it certainly laid some magnificent foundations.

So when Ford's Essex-based development team (the blokes from the defunct Advanced Vehicle Operations) got their hands on a few early Sports, the Mk1 suddenly became a distant memory. Using the RS1600's revolutionary 16-valve BDA powerplant, well-proven running gear and a few styling tweaks, the RS1800 was born – and with it the career of what's probably the most successful rally car of all time.

Like its predecessors, the RS1800 (and subsequent motor-sport-only derivative, simply named Escort RS) was evolved by a team of enthusiastic engineers and heroic wheelmen rather than pen-pushers and committees. Their only concerns were that it was faster than the opposition. Not build quality, not consistency, and certainly not recording notes on what parts were fitted to any particular vehicle.

Alongside the RS1800's inception was a foray into the young executive formula that proved so strong for the Mk1 RS2000. Again named RS2000, the Mk2 now boasted a funky slant-nosed front end and an even greater nudge towards cockpit comfort.

Although much of the car's design took place in Great Britain, Ford decided to manufacture the RS2000 – plus its lower-specced, flat-fronted, UK market-only brother, the RS Mexico – on mainstream production lines in Saarlouis, West Germany. So, did build quality improve? Did German efficiency ensure spreadsheets of chassis numbers and break-downs of every model's individual components?

Sadly not. Although Saarlouis Escorts were said to be slightly better, the panel gaps were imperfect, paintwork still received runs, specifications changed seemingly without notice, and there was no 100 per cent guarantee that any Escort would leave the factory with the trim outlined on its order sheet, never mind what the brochure said (which itself was often a contradiction of Ford's press information). And besides, with hundreds of accessories available from Rallye Sport dealers, owners were actively encouraged to improve and modify their cars before they'd even turned a wheel.

What's more, despite buying huge numbers of sporting Escorts when new, there's almost no following for these fast Fords among German car fans. So nothing at Saarlouis was saved for posterity – much like all the missing files from Ford's Halewood factory, where home-market Sports and Harriers were assembled.

If any records were taken, they're inaccessible to us mere mortals. Today, to work out the truth behind factory-original sporting Escorts, all we can go on are old photographs, Ford manuals, microfiche files, parts lists, the few remaining unre-stored Mk2s and the dedication of expert owners.

That's why this book isn't perfect – and why we'd always welcome reader comments and corrections. Indeed, this book isn't a restoration guide and it doesn't list the colours required to reproduce the coatings on every nut and bolt. What it is, though, is an attempt to record the ingredients mixed by a mainstream manufacturer to create a legendary machine, and our tribute to a car that truly deserves the title.

A left-hand-drive 1600 Sport on the 1976 Saarlouis production line, about to receive its engine and running gear. Just a tiny fragment of a legendary story.

ESCORT SPORT

It wasn't especially fast but who cared? The Escort Sport really looked the part – helped or hindered (you decide) by some rather funky colour combinations. Keith Wilkinson bought this June 1979-built 1600 Sport when it was just eight months old, after it had served time as a dealer demonstrator in Chelmsford, Essex. Its Roman Bronze and orange stripe scheme is original, as is much of the paintwork; Keith has simply added a few personal touches, as is the way for most sporting Escort owners.

History has been kind to the Mk2 Escort Sport. Today it's usually viewed with reverence reserved for RS models, yet it was never part of the Rallye Sport range. In fact, the Sport was integral to the regular Escort line-up, based on L spec levels and slotted hierarchically between GL and Ghia. Some might say it was a typically cynical Blue Oval marketing exercise to achieve an inflated price for a few sexy side stripes. Others would agree it was a handy stepping-stone to lever enthusiastic drivers into the world of fast Fords.

Whatever the reason, there's no denying the Sport was a key player in keeping the Escort atop sales charts and pulling punters into showrooms. It was essential to Ford's grand plan of ensuring a deep shine glowed across the Escort range from the halo effect of the Sport's rallying siblings.

For the Mk2 Escort's UK launch on 4 March 1975, 17,000 new-shape Escorts were made available to the public, and the Sport was part of the mainstream scheme to sell them all. Each of Ford's 570 dealerships displayed a Phoenix Orange 1600 Sport two-door, complete with optional black fabric trim, black vinyl roof, rear fog lamps and MW/LW radio. Under the bonnet of every car was a special PVC tag to highlight the GT engine's features.

As if that wasn't exciting enough, dealers were encouraged to proffer an 'Escort personality girl' by selecting their, "Most attractive receptionist/secretary and designating her 'Miss Thameside Motors' or whatever … with a distinctive uniform." Now, who said the 1970s was a decade of sloppy sexism?

By that point, of course, Escort Sport production was well

Originally half-an-inch lower than a standard Escort, the Sport's suspension settings were relatively tame. This example's slightly nose-up stance is a mild symptom of age.

Instantly recognisable from the front, a Sport wore circular halogen headlamps, driving lamps, quarter bumpers and over-riders. This car's lower fog lamps were a later addition, but similar Ford accessories were available from new.

under way. Assembly began during December 1974 at Ford's facility in Saarlouis (Germany), closely followed by cars from Halewood in Merseyside (England). Generally, right-hand-drive machines came from the British plant (with a vehicle number starting in BB) and left hookers were from the European factory (complete with GC on the chassis plate). That said, fluctuating order levels meant there was some crossover, and several Sports bound for Britain came with an unusual spec. All were built on regular production lines using standard Escort bodyshells, although overseas markets often gained a heavy-duty body.

Quite a change, then, from the specialised AVO Mk1 Mexico, which was the technical – if not spiritual – predecessor to the 1600 Sport. Both were powered by a Cortina GT-sourced 1598cc Kent Crossflow engine, although the Mk2's extra trim and additional weight took the edge off performance. The Sport also lacked the Mexico's rally-bred running gear, instead managing just fine with uprated versions of the ordinary Escort transmission and suspension. Almost all these components were shared with the 1300 Sport, which was a direct descendent of its Mk1 namesake.

Unusually for a motorsport-inspired model, Ford offered the Sport in four-door format, with even the option of an automatic gearbox on 1600 Sports. Overseas markets could also purchase a 1300 Sport with four doors, but it was never available to UK buyers. The first Halewood-built two-door Sport bore the chassis number BBATRC09618, while the initial four-door was BBAFRC09627.

From the outset, the 1300 and 1600 Sport came with a

The back of a Sport was a bit of a let down, with no rear spoiler or black panel to differentiate it from lower models.

half-decent specification, including twin-choke Weber carburettor, high-lift camshaft, close-ratio gearbox and sports wheels with low-profile tyres. The bodywork boasted bonnet and side tape stripes bearing Sport script, hazard flashers, heated rear window, circular halogen headlights, auxiliary driving lamps, front quarter bumpers and overriders. In the cabin was a black loop-pile carpet, vinyl seats with head rests, three-spoke steering wheel and rev counter.

A list of options offered metallic paintwork, tinted glass, a laminated windscreen, remote-control driver's door mirror, vinyl roof, cloth trim, recliners and a choice of radios. Plus, of course, that awful autobox.

If it wasn't for the racy stripes you'd easily overlook any Mk2 Escort Sport. Most examples came with black-painted sills, front panel and rear valance, but several shades – including the Roman Bronze seen here – went without.

Press reports of the Sport were mainly positive, with praise for the car's driveability, superb gearchange, lively performance and handling – even though test machines seemed to vary between understeer and oversteer, presumably depending on the setup of the individual car in question.

Yes, some scowled down on the Sport with derisory sneers from the bucket seats of their AVO-engineered Escorts. But many compared the Sport favourably with RS products, advising buyers to bag the cheaper car and save their cash for upgrades.

Which is exactly what Ford did to create the RS1800 – the initial batch started life as humble Sports, as did several Boreham-built rally monsters. There's a chance the very first RS Mexicos were Sport-based too. Ford even promoted the Sport with eligibility in the Mexico Challenge and subsequent one-model championships, including the celebrity Shell Sport series.

In July 1976 the 1600 Sport four-door was sadly discontinued, wearing chassis number BBAFSK47455. The date coincided with Ford dropping the two-door 1600 Ghia and deleting the Sport's automatic transmission availability (thank heavens).

In August 1976, cloth Cadiz (informally known as deck chair) trim became standard, while 1977 brought badge and suspension changes.

By the following year the Sport was considered such an effective sales tool for Ford that it was pretty much responsible for killing the RS Mexico. To drive nails further into its superior's coffin, the Sport had a September trim upgrade. There was now new Chevron fabric on the seats, along with improved sound deadening.

A few final specification improvements followed in 1979, along with Warm Black cabin treatment across the Escort range. Meanwhile, the model gave rise to several special editions. The Australian market had an Escort Escapee with decals in red, yellow and matt black. Malaysia had the 1.3 GT Sport and 1.6 GT Sport in four-door form – little more than Ls with Sport stripes, rectangular driving lamps, front spoiler and a Weber 32DGV carb. Most important of all, the British market benefited from the Sport-based Escort Harrier, released in December 1979 and worthy of its own chapter in this book.

Eventually, the rear-wheel-drive Escort was forced to die, but the Sport sold in vast quantities until the axe fell. It was discontinued in July 1980 with the official final chassis number BBATAD87545, although the author's own 1600 Sport says otherwise, bearing the tag BBATAD87550.

No individual production figures were recorded for the Sport, but with 960,007 Mk2 Escorts built in the UK alone, you can bet it was many times more plentiful than the most common RS. And that can't be a bad thing – the Sport was fast, fun, cheap and chuckable. It was the very essence of a sporting Escort.

Business as usual – the ever-faithful Kent Crossflow was put to good use in both varieties of Escort Sport, offering a humble 69bhp from the 1300 version and 83bhp from its bigger brother. Still, it felt lively enough for a mainstream motor.

Enormous numbers of Sports were sold worldwide, generally with a similar specification to British examples. This left-hand-drive Sport's engine bay shows the flipped-across brake servo, battery tray and fuse box.

Engine – Block, Head and Sump

On paper, the Mk2 Escort Sport's performance was nothing to get excited about. Even in 1975, the 1300's 69bhp at 5,500rpm (68lb.ft torque at 4,000rpm) was a bit puny – especially since it was a drop from the outgoing model's 72bhp. Likewise, the 1600 Sport's 83bhp at 5,500rpm (92lb.ft at 3,500rpm) didn't match the Mk1 Mexico's 86bhp.

With the Mk2's added bulk (the 1300 Sport weighed 857kg, with its fatter brother now tipping the scales at 868kg) and reduced aerodynamic efficiency, top speed was down to 94mph for the smaller engine and 101mph for the 1600 version. Acceleration was quoted at a dawdling 0-to-60mph in 13.9 (1300 Sport) or 11.1 seconds (1600 Sport).

Still, very little had changed under the bonnet. As before, the familiar overhead-valve, chain-driven, GT-specification Kent Crossflow came in 1297cc or 1599cc sizes, referred to in Ford code as J3 and L3 respectively. Regardless of capacity, the cylinder block was a metric 711M finished in semi-gloss black. External differences between the two were down to height (the 1600 block was 7/16in taller, seen in the gap between water pump and head) and casting number – 1300cc units had 711M6015AA cast in raised digits on the side of the crankcase near the starter motor, whereas the 1600 read 711M6015BA.

Like earlier Kent engines, Mk2 blocks wore a T-number

Rare official underbonnet photo of a 1979 1600 Sport. Note the original stickers on the radiator, battery and air pan, along with white printed lettering on the brake servo. The zinc-passivated suspension tops were found on most (if not all) Halewood-built Mk2s, as were the brightly-coloured paint splashes.

cast high up on the exhaust side and behind the engine mount on the intake side; modern myths suggest higher numbers (between 12 and 20) denoted stiffer cylinder walls but there's no evidence to back this up. Each engine had a unique number hand-stamped into the top of the cylinder block, found between the first pair of exhaust manifold ports; it began with a two-digit date code, followed by a series of unique digits that corresponded to the car's chassis number.

As for the so-called GT spec, well that was mainly due to the Escort Sport's mildly hotter-than-standard camshaft. Similar to (if a little softer than) a Mk1 cam, it boasted 272-degree duration, as opposed to the standard Mk2's 265 degrees. The 1300 Sport camshaft had 50-degree overlap and part number 771M6250CA, while 1600 models had a 771M6250BA with 54-degree overlap; the latter was an identical profile to the regular Cortina Mk3 1600HC (high-compression) component. Intricate identification was difficult, although the 1300GT cam had a red/white paint ring and the 1.6 wore red; a regular 1300HC's was yellow. Of course, GT camshaft-equipped Escorts revved more happily than their breathless counterparts too.

Internally, Mk2 GT Kent powerplants were otherwise identical to regular 1300HC or 1600HC lumps, including the crankshaft, pistons (all the same, whether for a 1.3 or 1.6) and connecting rods. Naturally, all compression ratios were 9.0:1, although Ford literature often quoted the 9.2:1 of early Mk1 1300GT engines.

What's more, it wasn't unheard of for some 1300 Sports to receive 1300HC engines from the factory, including standard camshaft and flywheel.

Sport cylinder heads were virtually stock HC parts, simply carried over from the Mk1 (although part numbers changed). All were cast iron in semi-gloss black, with four inlet ports on the right-hand side and four exhaust ports on the left. Characters corresponding to the engine code were stamped into the head near the top rearmost exhaust manifold stud – so a 1300 Sport's head said J3, (a regular 1300HC read J2) and a 1600 Sport's was L3. All Sport cylinder heads regardless of size also featured a number 37 cast under the rocker shaft, visible only with the rocker cover removed.

The only differences between 1300 and 1600 heads were the valve cutouts, which were larger on the bigger engine – the 1300 Sport's valve head diameters were 38mm inlet and 31mm exhaust, whereas the 1600's were 39mm and 34mm respectively. It's thought that some very late-model 1300 Sports were fitted with front-wheel-drive-type cylinder heads with extra drillings to fit into Fiestas.

Above the head sat a semi-gloss black rocker cover like you'd find on any other metric Kent engine, complete with ignition wire separator. From 1977 the angled oil filler spout was made shorter, while in November 1977 the filler cap changed too – it swapped from smooth to textured, bigger and sturdier black plastic, with bolder lettering and a pair of oblong breather slots underneath rather than multiple holes. By and large, Mk2 Crossflows never had an engine size identifier on the rocker cover, but initial 1600 Sport press cars wore a red-on-silver 1600GT sticker, so it's possible some early customer cars did too.

A bare alloy standard Crossflow dipstick was slotted inside a Mk1 GT tube and bracket. It reached down into a run-of-the-mill Escort sump – the 1300's was the same as a Mk1 part, while the 1600's looked very similar but was deeper at the back. Neither model gained a big-wing sump like the Mk1 Mexico.

All Sports kept the late-spec Mk1 Escort 35-to-40psi oil pump (generally painted black), screw-on cartridge filter and small breather arrangement, complete with internal plunger.

Other than the minor alterations mentioned, there were no changes to Sport motors throughout production. Even so, Ford's quoted performance figures improved continually. In September 1978 the 1300 Sport had managed to slash its 0-to-60mph run to 13.1 seconds, while the 1600 Sport was down to 10.4 seconds along with a 102mph top speed.

By June 1979 the 1300 Sport's Crossflow was rated at 74bhp at 6,000rpm, giving a 0-to-60mph time of 12 seconds flat and a top speed that had jumped to 97mph. Meanwhile, the 1600 Sport was now hitting the magic 60 in 10.1 seconds and hauling an impressive 103mph top end, from an increase to 86bhp at 6,000rpm.

Was it a miracle, was it thanks to a series of fuelling and timing tweaks, or was it more closely related to a little creative marketing in the face of incoming hot hatchback competition?

Cooling System

Small and straightforward, the 1300 Sport's entire 8.7-pint cooling system was the same as a standard 1300cc Escort's, including a 12-fins-per-inch radiator with a semi-matt-black top and black fins, AC 13psi radiator cap and yellow or beige seven-blade fan surrounded by a black plastic cowling. A black (or, rarely, bare aluminium) water pump was bolted to the front of the engine, plus an 88-degree C wax thermostat inside a black-painted housing (again, some early versions may have been bare).

The 1600 Sport featured a similar setup but with an ivory or clear seven-blade fan and a bigger radiator providing 9.5-pint coolant capacity. It was physically comparable in size to the Mk2 RS radiator but had a straight top coolant outlet and an overflow exit normally pointing to the nearside, extended down the side in a black (or green in Germany) plastic tube. A black sticker bearing the part number in white digits was often seen positioned to one or the other side of the cap, not always neatly.

Both 1300 and 1600 Sport used the same regular Crossflow black rubber coolant hoses as found on Mk1 Escorts, complete with wire hose clips rather than Jubilee types.

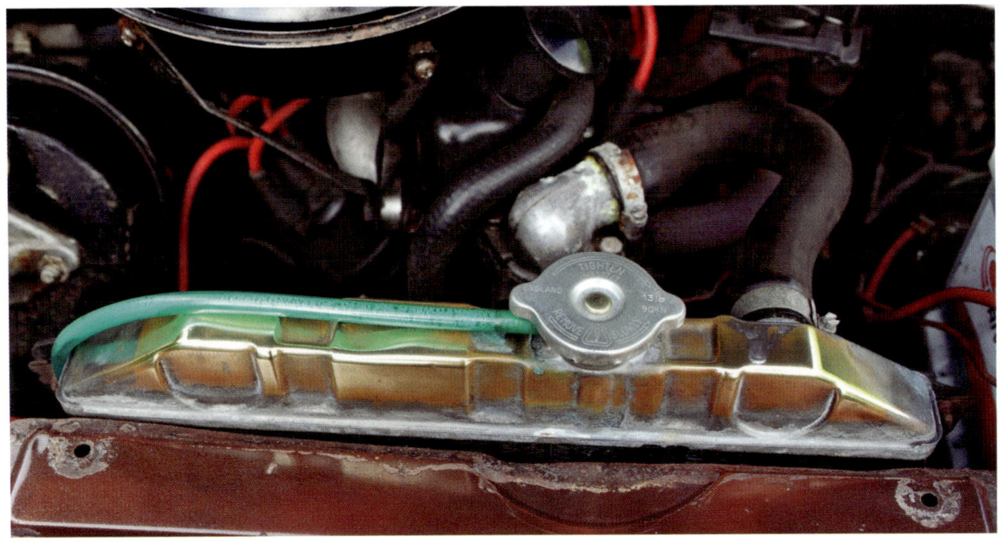

Keeping a 1600 Sport cool was the job for a bigger radiator than its 1300cc-engined counterparts. Usually the header tank was painted black.

Changes occurred in August 1978, when the thermostat was swapped for a 92-degree C part, then again in April 1979 when almost all Mk2s (1.1 Populars were excluded) gained a viscous-coupled fan – often yellow or beige on 1300 models, usually beige on 1600cc engines. The water pump was altered to suit, now bearing the code 8591ABA (rather than the 8591EBA of before).

Fuel System

True to its evocative name, the Escort Sport continued fast Ford tradition of squirting in fuel through a twin-choke Weber carburettor. In the 1300 Sport's case it was a familiar downdraught 32/36 DGV, while its bigger brother used a downdraught DGAV with automatic choke and anti-stall device. Each carburettor featured a metal tag attached to one of the float chamber screws plus a code on the flange at the inlet manifold; carbs were also stamped as made in Italy.

Over the years, Sport carburettor part numbers changed (in June 1975 and again a year later) but the type remained the same. The only alterations were to jet sizes, intended to provide a leaner mixture. The ploy worked so well that for the 1979 model year an anti-dieseling kit with solenoid assembly was added to the offside inner wing, which helped to avert problems of running on.

The same alloy inlet manifold was used on both Sport models, taken from the late-spec Mk1 Escort 1300GT engine, complete with casting for a two-bolt throttle linkage. Although the bracket was unique to Weber-equipped engines, a regular Escort Mk2 throttle cable worked just fine on all right-hand-drive Sports.

Early 1300 Sports were fitted with the round metal air cleaner setup from the Mk1 Escort Sport and 1300E. It featured a Ford oval, two-stud top fixing and adjustable intake tube, complete with rubber ring; unlike previous cars,

As Ford's exhaust emission controls were tightened up, Escorts were encouraged to run leaner than ever. Eventually, for 1979 this clumsy-looking anti-dieseling solenoid kit was added to the Sport's offside inner wing.

the Mk2's airbox was supposed to be painted black (but several early cars had blue).

From May 1975 the 1300 Sport gained the 751F-9600-DC air pan found on all 1600 Sports. This type was a large, black, circular part with two-stud fixing and square-section intake pipe. The lid was plain other than a Ford oval readable from the front of the car, although European-built Sports wore an almost-identical 751F-9600-CC airbox, which had the part number and oval readable from the nearside wing. All used a disposal paper filter element.

Sport fuel lines were typical black braided Ford parts, connected to a Motorcraft UFO-type fuel strainer and AC mechanical fuel pump, which lived at the right-hand rear of the engine, underneath the inlet manifold. As usual, it came in a bare silver finish.

Exhaust System

A new tubular four-branch exhaust manifold was designed for the Escort Sport (and Ghia), complete with integral upper adaptor for the air cleaner assembly; it was found on all Sports except 1300s built before May 1975, which featured the Mk1 GT setup.

The manifold was a four-into-two-into-one design that served as a downpipe with swan neck, connecting to the exhaust system alongside the gearbox. For rigidity, the manifold had a bracket that linked it to the engine through two block-to-bellhousing bolts.

Sport exhaust systems were larger-bore than standard Escort kit, and differed slightly from 1300 to 1600 – mainly in that the 1600's front pipe was extended where it curved up to meet the manifold (allowing for the 1600cc engine's extra height). Each system featured an oval centre silencer and unique round back box, dangled from a single rear hanger. The entire system from manifold to tailpipe was so-called aluminiumised mild steel, in a silver-coloured finish; Ford's economy replacement systems weren't offered for the Sport. No changes were made throughout Mk2 production.

Mk2 Sport exhaust manifold followed the familiar four-into-two-into-one pattern for better torque, adding a plate for warm-air ducting to the airbox.

Slightly larger than standard bore, the Sport's tailpipe was fed by a free-flowing exhaust system.

A Capri Mk2-type cover was used on Mk2 Escorts, which served to disguise the Mk1 fuse box. All the wiring was now hidden underneath.

Much like the Mk1 Escort RS, the Mk2 Sport had a relay screwed to the nearside inner wing, here for the standard auxiliary driving lamps.

Ignition and Electrical System

The Sport's status as a mainstream Escort model meant most of its engine ancillaries and electrical accessories were shared with standard Kent-powered Mk2s. Minor alterations were made during the Sport's lifespan, the majority of which were due to assembly plant and supply differences.

The 1300 Sport used a Mk1 1300GT-sourced Motorcraft distributor until May 1975, when it was replaced by a 761F12100NA with a blue or red-and-blue paint splash (on later, low-emission, engines swapped for a JA-suffixed part). Meanwhile, British-built 1600 Sports had a Motorcraft 751F12100BA distributor with purple paint splash, or beige on very late cars. All had a black plastic Motorcraft cap. That was, of course, unless the car was a German-sourced Sport, which would most likely have a Bosch distributor with terracotta-coloured cap.

Motorcraft plug leads were in black siliconised rubber with black rubber ends; they were printed with white lettering and a Ford logo, and were numbered with black-on-white stickers. All 1300cc Mk2s used the same leads taken from 1.3-engined Mk1s, but the leads of 1600 Sport models were slightly longer. They were all kept tidy in a black rubber separator squeezed into a bracket on top of the rocker cover. The original Motorcraft or Autolite AGR22 spark plugs were generally replaced by Ford dealers with AGR12s for better running; the AGR12s became standard-fit on 1600s.

Sport ignition coils were always nine-volt ballasted units with round terminals, and were generally coloured black (plus a sticker bearing the Ford logo) within a bare alloy bracket. But there were no hard and fast rules about what was used – because German-built cars were usually fitted with Bosch coils, while Merseyside-made machines had a variety of brands including Motorcraft, Lucas, Femsa and Zelmot.

Similarly, a selection of suppliers stocked Halewood's shelves with starter motors. Ford's intended unit for the UK Sport was a Lucas M35J, with the option of a Lucas 5M90 pre-engaged device, particularly for cold climates; due to supply issues between August and October 1977 some British cars were fitted with Femsa or Nippondenso starters instead. German-made Sports received a pre-engaged Bosch 0.7PS but most British Escorts had inertia starter motors with a solenoid mounted on the nearside inner wing underneath the washer fluid reservoir.

Meanwhile, Sport alternators indulged in a game of musical chairs, being found in a variety of forms. Until May 1975 British Sports came with a Lucas 15 ACR 28-amp alternator but on 1600s and many later 1300s a 35-amp Lucas 17 ACR was present. That said, Ford also used the 43-amp Lucas 18 ACR, Femsa ALD 12-32 or 33 (32-amp), Bosch K1-35A (35-amp) or K1-55A (55-amp). Generally, export-spec and German 1600s, and all cars equipped with automatic gearboxes had higher-rated alternators, with the option of 55-amp parts. Lucas alternators had an integral voltage regulator, but all the others were separate. To confuse matters even further, it's reckoned that some British Sports produced between August and October 1977 were fitted with Motorola alternators instead.

Very early 1600 Sports (until May 1975) were supplied with a triangular Mk1 Mexico-type (Cortina Mk3) alternator mounting bracket and fan belt; by 1976 they'd reverted to a normal two-prong Crossflow bracket.

Needless to say, a selection of square-post batteries could be found under the bonnet against the passenger-side inner wing – usually a 38Ah Motorcraft unit in UK Sports, but 44Ah or 55Ah parts for Germany, overseas markets and cars with autoboxes; the smaller battery used a long, narrow clamp, while the bigger batteries were squeezed into the tray with a shorter, fatter clamp – all were black but some clamps had a securing cutout that was absent on others. Right-hand-drive leads were always the same (negative in black and positive in red, each wearing a blue sticker with white Ford logo) but the battery-to-starter motor cable's length was altered in February 1978. On very early cars there was a black plastic cover over the battery's positive terminal but it soon disappeared.

All Sports were fitted with a bulkhead top-mounted fuse box, connected internally and containing seven continental fuses. It was topped with a Mk1-type clear plastic lid plus broad black plastic Capri cover above. Halewood-built Sports had fuse boxes with English writing, while Saarlouis machines featured German.

In-line fuses were also found under the heated rear window and radio, plus a separate fused relay for the standard auxiliary driving lamps, mounted in the traditional sporting Escort position on the nearside inner wing top – on early cars a Mixo relay was used, later swapped for a square, metal-bodied part with clear plastic cap.

The Sport wiring loom differed depending on the car's specification, intended market and year of build, and was pretty much the same as an RS Mexico's. It was wrapped in the usual grey loom tape at first, switching to black during 1976 – probably around August.

A single-tone (low-pitch) horn was fitted behind the Sport's grille, unlike the Ghia, which had a high-pitch horn as well. An optional air horn kit was available throughout production, with high- and low-pitch horns plus compressed air tank.

Transmission

Stepping away from its hardcore Mk1 Mexico predecessor, the Mk2 Sport was equipped with an essentially standard Escort transmission, complete with cable-operated clutch.

The 1300 Sport used the same flywheel and clutch setup previously seen on the Mk1 GT, with slim 16lb lightweight flywheel (taken from the 1100cc Escort) and 7.5in diaphragm-spring single dry plate clutch. The 1600 Sport featured a heavier flywheel (from the 1300HC Escort estate, van and Cortina Mk3), along with the same 7.5in clutch – supplied by Borg and Beck on British Sports or Laycock on German versions. The clutch cable was the regular Crossflow item.

The normal-ish gearbox was the familiar Escort Type 2 in GT-spec close-ratio guise, strengthened for the 1975 Sport with shot-peened gears and beefier gear cluster bearings. As such, this exact type wasn't used in any other Escorts (except other GT-spec Mk2s like the Ghia), Cortinas or Capris. But it did use the bigger cars' single-rail all-alloy tail housing (rather than the usual alloy and steel) to accept the Sport's heavy-duty layshaft. Otherwise, the casing and bellhousing looked identical to those on normal Mk2 Escorts –originally all in black or black with an alloy back.

Internally, the ratios were taken from the Mk1 GT, with first 3.337:1, second 1.995:1, third 1.418:1, fourth 1:1 and reverse 3.867:1. The only change between 1300 and 1600 Sport was the final drive ratio, with a heavy-duty 4.125:1 differential (pinion/crown wheel number of teeth: 8/33) on the smaller engine (or a 4.444:1 option for left-hand-drive cars) and a heavy-duty RS-type 3.54:1 on the 1600 Sport (pinion/crown wheel number of teeth: 11/39).

For the British market the Sport's bolt-on differential was sited within a black Timken one-piece axle. German-built Mk2s were different, though, with 1300 Sports featuring a lightweight Salisbury axle casing, containing differential mounted inside the axle housing. All 1600 Sports had the Timken axle; all Sports had rear anti-roll bar links.

Propshafts were always two-piece parts, all in black, with rubber-mounted centre bearing on 1300 Sports; different props were used on Timken and Salisbury axles, but they served the same purpose. The 1600 version (regardless of origin) was similar but used a central CV joint. Although a comparable design, it wasn't the same as the prop found on RS Mexicos and RS2000s.

Oh yes, and you can of course ignore most of that information as far as the short-lived, little-sold 1600 Sport automatic was concerned. Instead of the slick four-speed manual 'box, its transmission tunnel housed a sluggish Bordeaux C3 three-speed autobox, complete with oil cooler built into the bottom of the engine radiator. Although unresponsive by modern standards, the C3 had a rod linkage and used a vacuum system to control upshifts according to engine load, which made it much more refined than the Mk1 Escort's cable-operated Borg Warner 35 gearbox. Incidentally, its propshaft was the same as the part found on the Mk2 Escort RS.

The automatic Sport option was dropped in July 1976 (hopefully from a great height) and it's unlikely there are any survivors.

Steering and Suspension

Sport by name and relatively sporty by nature, the budget Escort's underpinnings were closer to Rallye Sport specification than some folk would have you believe. So close, in fact, that RS2000 and RS Mexico multi-leaf rear springs were taken directly from the early Escort Sport.

Like most of its underpinnings, the Mk2 Sport's chassis was a straightforward development of the late-model Escort Mk1. That meant Macpherson front struts with coil springs, front and rear anti-roll bars, plus telescopic dampers and leaf springs at the back.

The first Sports were fitted with struts of two types: standard (the same as basic German-built Mk2 saloon parts) or heavy-duty versions, which were identical those on Italian-spec Mk2s. All were satin black, with integral Armstrong shock absorbers and metric cast-in steering arms (unlike RS models, which were detachable and imperial-sized). At the top were large (post-'73 Mk1 RS waisted-type) black or galvanised strut mounts with black collars and brightly-coloured paint dabs (on the damper inserts and top mount retaining bolts) to confirm they'd been torqued to specified settings.

Sport front suspension was basically standard Escort kit, with top mounts swapped for these smaller zinc-passivated versions in February 1977. Chassis number was stamped around the aperture.

The front springs were black-coated 109lb coils, wrapped with black plastic tubing at the top and bottom. Normally, they were half-an-inch lower than standard (at 294mm in length) with red, yellow and orange paint splashes, but optional heavy-duty springs were 279mm with a red, yellow and blue code.

There was a front anti-roll bar that measured 22mm diameter until August 1975, after which it was swapped for a 20mm bar. In February 1977 the top mountings were exchanged for smaller offset mounts, while in October 1977 the struts were replaced with revised versions, again in regular or heavy-duty form but now unique to the Sport. Spring rates remained the same.

Sports were fitted with a normal Escort front crossmember, plus standard oblong Mk1 engine mounts on the 1300 model. The earliest 1600 Sports (until around August 1975) also wore the basic mounts; they were soon replaced with round rubber insulators, which raised the engine enough to provide the deep sump with additional clearance of the crossmember whenever the car's gearbox was removed. Most 1975 Sports were retrofitted with round mounts by dealers.

Sport steering was primarily regular Mk2 Escort, including metric-threaded 17.9:1 ratio rack, Mk1-type control arms and metric-tapered track rod ends, with revised gaiters from August 1978. The steering column lock was changed in mid-1976, while the whole assembly was swapped in May to July 1978, depending on whether German or British built. Most notably, the Sport shared a steering gear shaft joint with the RS Mexico and RS2000.

At the back, the Mk2 Sport retained a standard Escort layout with rear anti-roll bar rather than the radius arms found on its RS brothers.

The pre-October 1977 Sport featured 116lb, 60mm-wide, multi-leaf springs, which made the car sit half an inch lower than standard. With a red, lilac and white colour code, they were the same as springs used on Mk2 RS models. Sports were also offered a heavy-duty multi-leaf option, with orange-and-white code (as found on the heavy-duty Mk2 estate).

From October 1977 the Sport switched to single-leaf rear springs and new U-bolts. Regular Sport springs wore a red paint code, while heavy-duty parts were yellow – and were again identical to uprated estate offerings.

At the same time, the rear anti-roll bar diameter was reduced from 14mm to 12mm and the black Girling telescopic rear dampers (the same as shocks seen on heavy-duty saloons and standard on all Italian-market cars) were recalibrated to provide a softer ride.

Late-spec Sports were fitted with this Girling brake servo and master cylinder, which from October 1978 featured a sensor for the dashboard-mounted brake fluid level warning switch.

Brakes

Mainstream Mk2 Escorts were praised for the inclusion of hefty servo-assisted front disc brakes on all but the weediest versions. Of course, the Sport was no exception, wearing Girling 247.5mm solid front discs (as found on RS models) and M16 callipers (usually in pale silver finish but sometimes black or light gold) with 54mm pistons, which were standard-fit for all disc-braked Mk2s (and Mk1 RS models before them). The discs were backed by black dust shields.

All GT-engined Escorts (including the Sport) received uprated brake pads from Ferodo. British Sports kept these parts throughout production, but German callipers weren't Girling until May 1978; before then they were Bendix.

Sports wore drum brakes at the back, which were usually identical to those on RS Mk2 Escorts, sized 9x1.75in. The exceptions were 1300 Sports built between December 1975 and February 1976 (in Britain) or June 1976 (in Germany), which had 8x1.5in drums. All were black-painted cast iron, with self-adjusting shoes; from August 1978 the back plates featured a brake shoe inspection aperture, complete with blanking plug.

Rear wheel cylinder sizes varied somewhat, being 17.8mm on all 1600 Sports and some 1300 versions – namely those made until September 1975 in the UK or December 1975 in Germany; later cars gained 19mm cylinders.

All Sports featured a dual-line braking system, with mild steel brake pipes in Bundy tubing; their ribbed flexible brake hoses were revised throughout production, and were generally retrofitted to earlier cars by dealers. The only significant difference between Sport and RS was the latter's bigger brake servo, but even then some parts were shared – such as the in-line servo bracket.

Sport servo and master cylinder changes occurred in March 1977, when German Crossflow-powered cars generally ran a Teves setup and British Sports wore a revised Girling system. The tandem master cylinder (19.05mm on cars built until February 1976 Britain and June '76 Germany; 20.64mm thereafter) originally featured two lines out and a pair of screws holding the reservoir at the back of a rounded, clear plastic bottle, which had a red cap and large circular disc between cap and reservoir.

Later Girling master cylinders had three outlets and a flat, square design of reservoir, which was a push-fit into the two rubbers atop the cylinder. It had a clear plastic cap that, from October 1978, was equipped with a brake fluid level warning indicator switch linked to a test button inside the car. Later master cylinders wore a plastic yellow hoop; there was a matching horizontal yellow stripe on the servo drum's vacuum hose, and often white-printed lettering on the drum.

Wheels and Tyres

Rolling along on regular Escort Mk2 sculptured sports steel 13in wheels, the Sport almost looked the part – especially with satin black-painted inset detailing in the silver finish to provide a spoke effect, as seen on the Mk1 Escort Sport. The only drawback was the rim width of 5in, which was narrower than RS models.

Still, the appearance was improved in August 1978, when the wheel offset was increased to provide a wider look and increased track. All types came with black wheel nuts and black plastic caps with twin silver circles around their centres.

Despite the presence of alloy wheels on many of today's remaining Escort Sports, they were not a factory option until autumn 1979. Even then, rather than sexy four-spoke RS rims, the Sport was allowed 5.5x13in late-model Ghia-type eight-spoke alloys. Of course, alloy wheels were always available for the Sport as official Ford dealer accessories.

Sports were equipped with 175/70SR13 radial tyres, generally Michelin MXLs or Uniroyal Rallyes (especially on later cars). Dunlop SP68 and Goodyear G800S rubber were also approved fitments.

Sport steel road wheels were 5x13in, and identical to the rims worn by lesser Escorts. Black detailing was to provide a pretend spoke effect.

Bodywork

Racy looks were the Sport's obvious selling point – and it's amazing to see what was achieved with little more than a few stickers and a chopped-up front bumper. There were no wide wheelarches, no special strengthening, and there weren't even any spoilers offered as factory optional extras.

Indeed, the Sport was essentially a standard Mk2 Escort bodyshell, made in two-door form throughout production and sometimes as a four-door – in the UK only as a 1600 Sport until July 1976, and in export territories with a 1300cc or 1600cc engine depending on country. Overseas buyers were often treated to a heavy-duty bodyshell, which included RS-type uprated front suspension turrets and rear spring hangers; British Sports never had this setup.

All Sport body panels were standard Mk2 kit, including wings, bonnet, doors and boot lid. The most noticeable additions were the front quarter bumpers, which continued the Mk1 RS and Lotus Cortina tradition. Unlike the van-sourced parts found on previous cars, for the Mk2 Escort they were unique to the Sport, Harrier, RS Mexico and RS1800. Finished in satin black heat-set epoxy, Sport bumpers were also fitted with satin black overriders front and rear (specific for cars with driving lamps); on very early cars the overriders were chromed before being painted black, and featured sculptured ridges at each side; later overriders were smooth.

Beneath the front bumpers was a standard Escort front panel, with the lower bib painted satin black – a theme that extended to the sills, rear valance and underside of the spare wheel well. There were, as usual, exceptions to this rule – in particular, Sports with special-order black bodywork, or those finished in Midnight Blue or Roman Bronze built from late 1977 onwards.

British Sports never left the factory with a front spoiler, but some cars in overseas markets wore RS-type accessories,

A very early Sport in Vista Orange, shot by Ford in 1974. Note the early grille, chrome windscreen surround, drip rail, front wing badges and door handles.

Signal Yellow Sport, wearing standard black-painted sills, air dam and rear valance.

It was 1977, but this Sport was still wearing a grille with silver highlights (along with Ford oval), black badges on its front wings and a chrome remote driver's door mirror, with matching fixed part for the passenger side.

Satin black door handles were first added to the Sport in August 1975, before when they were chrome. Lock barrels matched throughout the car.

often finished in matt black.

A rear spoiler was never standard, nor was the satin black back panel found on many RS Mk2s.

Like other Escorts, the Sport's front grille went through a few facelifts. The first cars featured a matt-black plastic grille with bright silver FORD lettering in the middle, along with centre bar and grille surround picked out in silver paint. In August 1977 a blue oval logo ousted the FORD block capitals, while a new all-black grille came along in September 1978 for all Escorts (except the Ghia). Behind the grille, the front panel was painted satin black between and around the headlamps.

Badging was fitted to the lower front wings until August 1977, which designated engine size. The Sport wore tall, chrome 1.3 or 1.6 digits until July 1975 (or August 1976 in Germany), when they were swapped for black plastic. These early cars featured a simple Escort badge on the boot lid's nearside, along with individual FORD letters beneath the boot lock. The very first Sports wore chrome badges, but from July 1975 they were painted matt black.

In August 1977 the black Escort badge was made wider, while the FORD boot lettering was dropped in favour of a blue oval on the offside. Engine identifiers were then added to the boot lid, slightly distanced from the Escort badge – they read 1.3 or 1.6 but never gained the capital S seen on other Sport models in Ford's line-up.

A fixed, satin black door mirror was standard on the passenger side of every Sport – unless the Sport in question was an early model with optional remote-controlled driver's door mirror, which had matching chrome on each side.

Most Sports were equipped with a body-coloured petrol cap, but in the days of siphoning, a locking fuel filler was a popular accessory.

Many Sports were equipped with a factory-fitted radio, accompanied by retractable chrome aerial mounted in the offside front wing.

Incidentally, the colour of a Sport's boot lock was not dependant on its badges – British-built cars had a chrome lock assembly, but German-sourced machines gained a satin black version in October 1977.

Sport exterior door handles and locks were chrome until August 1975, when they were replaced with black. A pair of satin black door mirrors was fitted as standard, with the option of a remote control version on the driver's door. Until August 1975 remote mirrors were only available with a chrome finish, so Ford fitted Sports with a chrome non-remote passenger door mirror to match; after August 1975 all Sport door mirrors were supposed to be satin black but it's possible the chrome tradition continued for years to come. A handful of the earliest press cars had only a chrome remote driver's mirror, with nothing on the nearside.

All Sports featured black-painted B-pillars, door frames and window surrounds, although the drip rails were only finished in matt black heat-set epoxy from early 1976 (probably around March), before which they were chrome. Early windscreen rubbers wore chrome beading, which was swapped for black during 1976 – also most likely around March.

The windscreen wipers were matt black with a two-speed motor, which gained intermittent facility as standard in August 1976. The blades were standard Ford types but could be swapped for Super SR accessories. They laid against a Triplex (or Sekurit in Germany) zone-toughened windscreen,

If it wasn't for the racy stripes you'd easily overlook any Mk2 Escort Sport. Most examples came with black-painted sills, front panel and spare wheel well, but several shades – including the Roman Bronze seen here – went without.

A Diamond White 1600 Sport press shot from 1979, displaying its blue decals, black boot badges, chrome boot lock and body-coloured fuel cap.

with a laminated version available as an extra until autumn 1979, when it became standard. Opening front quarter vents were also optional, with revised internal handles in August 1977. A heated rear windscreen was always standard Sport kit. Usually it was plain Escort glass, although all-round tints were an optional extra; green was the theme until August 1978, when bronze tints took over. Tinted glass was offered irrespective of whether the windscreen was toughened or laminated.

Sports were often seen fitted with vinyl roofs, which were available at extra cost throughout production. A black vinyl top was usually offered, although on later models it was dependent on interior colour, believe it or not. From September 1978 the Sport's black vinyl roof was joined by a tobacco version, which had already been seen on other Escorts. On the Sport it was used exclusively with Solar Gold, Sable Brown, Diamond White, Cordoba Beige or Terracotta body colours when equipped with Chocolate/Indian Red interior trim.

Occasionally, Sports would be dealer-fitted with roof-mounted aerials, but when a radio was specified as a factory

Sport coachlines ended abruptly at the front wings, with their tops positioned just millimetres from the body swage line.

Sport coachlines were identical to those on the RS Mexico, mating up to the large 1600 Sport (or 1300 Sport) logo on each back wing. But unlike the Mex, the Sport's stripes were offered in a wide variety of colours.

Rare today but pretty popular when new, the 1300 Sport was an appealing, if underpowered, machine.

option there was a retractable chrome Ford-stamped aerial mounted on the offside front wing; although RS2000 aerials were black after July 1979, it's unlikely they made it onto any British-built cars as standard. An automatic aerial kit could be added as an official accessory.

As for those in-your-face decals, the Sport sticker kit comprised tape along the body sides and bonnet top. It was identical to that of the RS Mexico, albeit reading 1300 Sport or 1600 Sport on the flanks (the end section was a separate piece). Sport decals were available in a variety of different colours depending on build date, location and interior trim. Generally they were colour-keyed to the first trim colour; for example, a Sport with Jupiter Red paintwork wore silver or gold stripes depending on whether the seats were black with grey or tan highlights respectively.

A few export markets used variations of the decal kit; for example, the Philippines, where the Sport had RS2000-type stickers, with a broad stripe along the sides at bumper level and Sport 1600 on the back wings in RS-type lettering. The chart below refers to the coachlines found on European 1300 Sports and 1600 Sports.

Sport side windows wore satin black surrounds, painted into the swage lines in alignment with the rubbers.

Stripe colour	Introduced	Discontinued
Black	Dec 1974	Jul 1980
White	Dec 1974	Aug 1976
Gold	Dec 1974	Aug 1977
Red	Dec 1974	Dec 1975 (Aug 1975 in Germany)
	Aug 1978	Jul 1980
Silver	Aug 1977	Jul 1980
Blue	Aug 1978	Jul 1980
Brown	Aug 1978	Jul 1980
Orange	Aug 1978	Jul 1980

Underbonnet

Under the bonnet, a Sport revealed its true identity – that of a humble Mk2 Escort. There were no strengthened suspension tops, and there was only a well-loved Kent motor in the engine bay. It was very much business as usual.

Like all Mk2s, the Sport had its chassis number stamped into the right-hand suspension top of the inner wings, along with a VIN plate and colour tag on the slam panel; from January 1980 onwards (November 1979 in Saarlouis) the VIN plate was moved to the offside inner wing. Well, that was the theory; in practice the changes were more gradual.

During February 1977 the mounting holes for the suspension tops were reduced from 105mm to 85mm diameter, along with revised Macpherson struts. The Sport's windscreen washer fluid reservoir was screwed into a black bracket attached to the nearside suspension tower. In white plastic with matching top, the same bottle was always fitted to British Sports, although German-built machines were listed with a 78AG171618AA part. The bracket assembly changed in September 1979 (or March 1979 in Germany), while the standard-fit electric washer pump was updated in April 1976 – some were plain black, while other washer motors were pale gold coloured, with a printed black Ford oval logo. Clear plastic tubing led to a white plastic T-piece and copper nozzles that fed through the scuttle panel.

Across the top of the bulkhead of the first 1975 press cars was an engine compartment cowl, made from a sandwiched foam material and identical to the insulator found on the Ghia – but customer Sports did not have one. The bulkhead metalwork was altered in February 1977, swapping from

Technically, the Escort 1.6 boot badges should be black on all Sports made after July 1975. Ford being Ford, of course, it's possible some cars were different.

Like all mainstream Mk2s, the Sport had a windscreen washer reservoir screwed into a black bracket on the nearside suspension tower, complete with electric washer pump as standard.

five dimples beneath the scuttle panel to seven; a bonnet rubber sat in the central recess.

The Sport always had its battery on a tray at the passenger-side front corner of the engine bay, with its brake servo on the opposite side. On the inner wing beside the battery sat an Italamec 004 16-amp relay for the auxiliary driving lamps, fed by a multi-plug from the main loom in black- (or grey-) taped wiring, along with a short brown earth cable fastened on a ring connector under one of the self-tapping screws. Initially a cylindrical Mixo part, it was later swapped for a square metal relay with white cap.

At the opposite side, screwed to the inner wing at an angle, was a Ford-labelled anti-dieseling solenoid, fitted for the 1979 model year.

The Sport's galvanised bonnet prop hinged from the offside front corner of its engine bay, clipped into a white plastic retaining clip on the nearside of the slam panel. The bonnet release cable was black plastic-coated, and ran from a handle under the driver's-side dashboard to the release mechanism within the slam panel; the handle's securing pin was enlarged on British-built cars in September 1978 to match German machines.

Mk2 engine bays weren't crammed with stickers like their predecessors, although the Sport had an E11 lighting decal on the slam panel to the left of the bonnet release mechanism or just behind the auxiliary lighting relay on the inner wing. On early cars it was a pale grey square, while later models (from 1976) had a wider purple version. Many early cars also wore a Mk1-type black-on-white engine coolant decal on the offside inner wing.

The back lights were standard, but a rear fog lamp was a Ford factory or dealer option; many owners simply fitted an aftermarket version instead.

Lighting

Following fast Escort tradition, the Sport was fortunately equipped with halogen headlamps as standard – in 7in circular H4 60/55W semi-sealed beam guise. Early Sports tended to have flat Lucas lights, with Lucas written on the glass plus a blue H4 emblem in the middle; but from August 1978 Carello flat lamps were commonly fitted, made with a Ford oval in the centre of the glass above the word halogen, plus the Carello logo off to one side. German Sports were also available with headlamp washers, complete with pump and motor assembly.

Between the headlamps, the Sport was equipped with a pair of 5.5in circular auxiliary halogen long-range driving lamps on black metal brackets, which were attached to the panel behind the front quarter bumpers. The lamps were 55W halogens with a Ford oval logo in the centre of each lens; they illuminated as part of the main beam circuit. Early cars' lamps featured chrome rims and black backs, but from October 1979 the lens surrounds were satin black too.

Everything else about the Sport was stock Escort saloon. The orange front indicators were the same (albeit mounted in quarter bumpers) Vega parts (okay, German-built machines had Altissimo) and hazard warning flashers were standard fit.

At the back was a pair of regular Escort rear lights (made in England by Butlers on Halewood Sports or Altissimo on German cars) with integral reversing lamps, plus one black Altissimo number plate light mounted in the middle of the rear bumper; from around August 1976 a pair was fitted instead. A single Altissimo (Ford branded) rear fog lamp dangling from the offside rear valance was a popular optional extra (it was also available as a dealer accessory) until it was made standard in August 1979.

Inside the Sport was a normal Escort interior light – at first a thin, all-white Mk1-type but swapped in November 1975 for a chunkier courtesy lamp with black override switch. It was triggered by a pair of black plastic door control switches set into the A-pillars.

Interior

Think of an Escort Sport's cockpit, and you'd be forgiven for picturing seats with deck chair patterns in gaudy colours. While, yes, the Sport did spend a couple of years looking like a reject from Skegness sea front, many more were supplied with relatively sedate cabins.

The first Escort Sports were kitted out with a lowly L-specification interior, albeit adding head rests to the front seats. But they were simply covered in vinyl, complete with unevenly-spaced vertical double-stitch lines. Two-door models had tipping backrests, but in four-door Sports they were fixed; reclining front seats were an optional extra, using an eight-spoke handwheel on the base. Plain Beta cloth trim was optional too, independently of the reclining mechanism; when fitted it used the L-pattern vertical stitching, rather than the GL-type's equidistant lines.

Early Sports were offered with a variety of seat trim shades, depending on external bodywork colour – often black but also Light Tan, Saddle Brown 74 (browny-red), Marquis/Medium Blue 74 or Chocolate 76, which took over from Saddle during December 1975.

Fabric seat covers were made standard in August 1976, along with reclining backrests. That was when those infamous deck chairs appeared – otherwise known as Cadiz upholstery.

Cadiz came in black cloth with a selection of coloured stripes, including black with green, tan, grey or orange. The back seat was trimmed to match, but the head rests remained

It didn't take much to add a sporty touch to what was essentially an Escort L interior. Just fancy seat trim, head rests and a nicer steering wheel, yet the Sport's cockpit was an engaging place to sit. This car's centre console and toggle switches were fitted by the owner.

Sport cabin trim changed throughout the years but the seat frames remained very similar, complete with vinyl head rests. Here the upholstery is Chevron fabric in chocolate and orange flavour.

Vinyl-trimmed head rests on single chrome posts were found in the front of every Sport – even early models with L-type non-reclining vinyl seats.

A pre-launch (1974) Sport interior, complete with optional black Beta cloth upholstery and crossed-flag steering wheel centre.

black vinyl with a central chrome pillar.

September 1978 saw the deck chairs binned in favour of Chevron-patterned fabric upholstery in the following colour schemes: black and grey (black main/side panels, white stripes and grey centres), black and red (black main/side panels, red stripes and grey centres), black and blue (black main/side panels, blue stripes and grey centres) or chocolate and orange (chocolate main/side panels, orange stripes and grey centres).

From August 1979, Chevron options were chocolate and red (chocolate main/side panels, red stripes and grey centres), chocolate and Indian red (chocolate main/side panels, terracotta stripes and grey centres), chocolate and tan (chocolate main/side panels, tan stripes and grey centres) or chocolate and blue (chocolate main/side panels, blue stripes and grey centres). At this point, all the plastics around the seats swapped shade to Warm Black (a dark brown officially called Warm Black 80).

The September 1978 trim upgrades also lifted the Sport up a notch, now featuring GL-levels of sound insulation. Perhaps it was Ford's way of repositioning the Sport to replace the recently-axed RS Mexico.

Even so, the Sport kept its lowly little-padded rear bench seat cushion (unless it was a foreign-market machine, some of which contained padded affairs). Its door cards were basic L-type too (with vertical double stitch lines) throughout production, revealing painted body-colour door tops rather than the full-height door cards found on GLs. Until August

The Sport's deck chair (AKA Cadiz) cockpit in all its style-free Seventies' glory. This one's black with orange stripes, found inside a 1978 Signal Amber Sport.

1976 they were vinyl, coloured to match the seats, in black, Light Tan, Saddle Brown, Marquis or Chocolate. With the change to Cadiz upholstery the door cards were always black vinyl, until becoming Warm Black in August 1979.

Attached to the panels were small vinyl armrests in matching-colour vinyl, the usual Mk2 Escort chrome window winders with black plastic inserts and plastic knobs,

Stolen from Blackpool beach? Commonly called deck chair cloth, Cadiz fabric was a fast Ford favourite in the Seventies. It was found on Escort Sports from August 1976 till September 1978.

Chevron cloth seats came in black or chocolate with a selection of coloured stripes. Here a Diamond White Sport contains a black and blue interior.

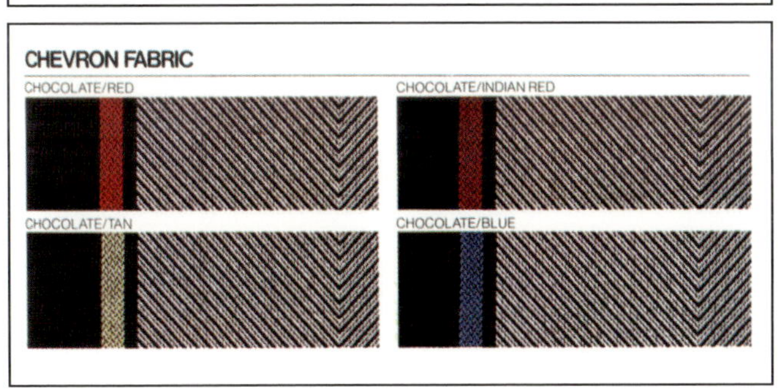

Chevron upholstery was seen inside Escort Sports from September 1978 onwards. Several colour schemes were available. All were chocolate-coated from September 1979 (lower illustration).

Mk2 handbrake and seat belt stalks were carried over from the late Mk1, while this car's centre console was an aftermarket addition. None was normally fitted, but late-spec Sports received a Ghia-type console.

A basic Escort back seat was found in the Sport, complete with upholstery to match the fronts. This car's rear seat belts are a later addition, but Ford versions were a period option.

Standard Mk2 black rear-view mirror; the Sport had a cream plastic cover where it fastened to the roof.

Sport sun visors and headlining were perforated, putty-coloured vinyl, with a darker shade on the flip side of each visor. Passenger grab handle was alone.

along with plain black plastic internal door handles and frames. The door inner push buttons were simple black plastic pins, with late Mk1-type wider flared tops until a slimmer version was introduced in August 1977. If an optional remote-control driver's door mirror was fitted, there was a chrome knob within a chrome or black escutcheon and black spacer in the door card; after May 1977 the knob and escutcheon were generally black.

In the back, the rear quarter trim panels were L-spec, with body-painted metal above and small, revolving, black plastic ashtrays. The panels were coloured to match the seats until Cadiz came along in August 1976, after which they were black; all then became Warm Black in August 1979.

Similarly, the Sport's front plastic kick panels started out in a selection of colours to match the seats – including black, Light Tan or Chocolate – until August 1976, when black became permanent, followed by Warm Black in August 1979. They overlapped a simple black, one-piece loop-pile carpet (rarely Chocolate or Light Tan, depending on trim), which tended not to become Warm Black alongside the plastics. Floor mats were commonly-fitted by dealers from new; they were black or grey rubber, in a grid or honeycomb pattern.

The carpet tucked under ribbed aluminium scuff plates along the inner sills, which also overlapped the door rubbers. Although Ford officially swapped to Warm Black rubbers in August 1979, Sports seemed to stick with regular black.

The Sport fascia comprised a basic Escort satin black metal dashboard panel, with padded vinyl dashboard top – in black until August 1979 and Warm Black thereafter (although the metal section stayed black). Some export markets wore a 'Sport' impressed GL-type padded passenger crash pad but no UK cars had anything of the kind. Under the dashboard, each side had a black cardboard parcel shelf with padded vinyl edging. There was no glovebox.

In the middle of the dashboard were the illuminated heater controls, containing two-speed heater/demister switch, temperature sliders and foil indicator panel. The foil was altered in October 1976 when the positions for hot and cold were reversed (hot swapped from right to left), presumably when the metal Mk1-type heater box was replaced with a quieter, two-piece plastic, Mk2-specific unit. The heater control bezel in British Sports was always black plastic with a silver rim, making no change to Warm Black in August 1979. Eyeball vents fed air into the cabin from both sides of the dashboard; they stayed black throughout production, complete with silver rim around each fitting.

Beneath the heater controls sat a lower fascia panel in black plastic (until Warm Black arrived in August 1979) containing a push-round ashtray flanked by rocker switches; from left to right they were a blanking plate for a brake low pressure switch (made standard in October 1978), hazard flasher switch, circular blank for a cigarette lighter (optional until September 1979, when it became standard), heated rear window switch (with warning lamp), blank for (optional) fog lamp switch. Further to the right, on the steering column shroud, sat the choke control knob on 1300 Sports, or a round blanking plug on 1600 Sports (which in August 1979 changed for, you guessed it: Warm Black).

The switches received minor updates along the way: British cars got a new hazard warning switch in August 1976 (the inverted warning triangle now pointed upwards), although German cars remained the same. Meanwhile, the heated rear window switch was updated with a less fussy diagram. Where fitted, switches for the rear fog lamps and long-range lamps were updated during August 1976 in Britain, where the warning lamps were red; one year later in Germany, where they were green.

Sport instruments were a halfway house between basic Escort and RS model, having fewer auxiliary gauges than even its sporty Mk1 predecessor. On the left was a large 7,000rpm rev counter (with no red line), while a 120mph speedometer was on the right, containing trip and mileage recorders. Between them was a smaller circular dial housing vertical gauges for fuel level and water temperature. All the gauges had white needles. Beneath was a row of five warning lights, from left to right: left-hand indicator, oil pressure, main beam, ignition, right-hand indicator.

Some early Sports had a silver rim around the outside of the instrument binnacle, but this was dropped during 1976.

A bigger change was applied to the instrument cluster in October 1977, when the font on each dial became rounder, the needles were swapped from white to orange and the speedometer lost its 10mph increments; a year later it rose to a 140mph maximum.

Three-spoke steering wheel was identical to what kept RS models in a straight line (or sideways, of course). The spokes were originally sprayed satin black, swapping to Warm Black in August 1979.

Mid-way between proper RS and pure poverty-spec, the Sport's instrument cluster housed 7,000rpm rev counter, 140mph speedometer, fuel and water temperature gauges

Well-worn heater controls were illuminated and outlined with silver rim. Lower fascia panel housed ashtray and rocker switches – here (from left to right) for brake warning, hazard flashers, fog lights and heated rear window. Note the round blanking plug, showing where the Sport lacked a fag lighter.

Sport door cards were always base-spec vinyl trims that exposed the upper metalwork, complete with small armrests. The speakers on this car were added by its owner.

The Sport steering wheel was a Mk2 RS-type flat three-spoke item (the Mk2 shaft was a different diameter from the Mk1 and Capri) in matt black with leather-grained plastic rim (although early press cars had real leather) and satin black metal spokes. In the centre was a crossed-flag motif, as seen on the Mk2 Capri. The badge was swapped in February 1977 for a Ford blue oval.

In August 1979 the entire steering wheel was switched for an almost identical version in Warm Black, along with the centre boss and steering column shrouds.

The Sport had a set of three column stalks with two-speed wash/wipe controls on the right-hand side, updated for intermittent wiper function in August 1976. A shorter stalk was behind it to control the headlights and sidelights. On the left-hand side was a single stalk for the indicators, horn and headlamp dip/flash.

All Mk2 Escorts had the same basic pedal box assemblies, including satin black brake and clutch levers with rubber pads taken from the Mk1 Escort, featuring a horizontal line pattern. The accelerator pedal was the same as a very late Mk1's, having a cranked silver lever with black plastic pad, also in a horizontal line pattern.

The gearstick found in a Mk2 Sport was chrome until December 1976, when black became the norm. Most Sports had a normal Escort round, black gearknob, but it was replaced in September 1979 with a chunky Capri/RS-type sports gearshift knob. The gearstick gaiter was black.

The Sport's gearstick was often seen surrounded by a centre console, but it wasn't made standard until September 1979, when a Warm Black Ghia-type unit was used, complete with quartz clock, Warm Black gearstick gaiter and radio aperture. Before then, similar consoles were available (mainly as dealer accessories) in black vinyl designed for use with or without a clock, radio, speaker or radio/cassette player – complete with storage space for cassettes.

A massive variety of radios was offered to the Sport buyer from Ford's factory options list. Cheapest was a Ford-branded M21 manual-tune radio, with a Ford P21 MW/LW push-button radio (with pre-selection for six stations) the next step up. You could also specify a manual-tune multi-band M32 (with MW/LW/SW/VHF), a multi-wave push-button P32 or a high-performance P42 (each boasting pre-selection for six stations) if your wallet was big enough.

The P21 was fitted as standard to the Sport from September 1978, while the better versions remained optional (other than the M32, which was dropped in January 1978). A cassette player was never available from the factory, even though you could listen to your favourite tapes in a lowly Fiesta if you ticked the right box on your order sheet.

Radios were occasionally slotted into the aforementioned centre console but usually in a specific holder mounted underneath the fascia/switch panel. A speaker would usually be installed in the dashboard top, although dealers could fit them in the doors or cowl side trim too.

The Sport's centre console stopped short of its handbrake lever, which was black with a black push button and black gaiter. Behind it on the transmission tunnel was a pair of black plastic-coated seat belt stalks identical to those found on very late Mk1 Escorts, with gold-and-red release buttons. The inertia-reels were supplied (at extra cost in the early days), bolted to the B-pillars. These belts (referred to in Ford terms as Type A) were used until March 1980, when they were occasionally (very rarely on UK cars) replaced by Securon (Type B) versions.

Static rear seat lap belts were optional, with an upgrade to lap/diagonal inertia-reels from August 1977 (anchorage points were built into the floorpan and C-pillars of standard Mk2 bodyshells). The inertia-reel rear seat belt guides were plastic rectangles, which slotted into the back parcel shelf at each corner, while the reels lived in the boot below. In the

Mk2 door latches were the same as those found on late Mk1s. Black door rubber on this car wasn't intended to match the brown interior.

early Sport the parcel shelf matched the interior trim, staying black from August 1976 and Warm Black three years later.

Sports had a vinyl C-pillar covering to match the headlining – which was putty coloured (called Pastel Parchment 70) and more heavily perforated than the similar Mk1 roof lining. There was no vinyl trim on the Sport's B-pillars.

A pair of padded sun visors was also trimmed to match the headlining, in Pastel Parchment and black (on the flipside) until August 1979, then Pastel Parchment and Warm Black. There was no vanity mirror on the passenger-side visor (nor driver's, of course) throughout production.

Between the sun visors was a black dipping rear-view mirror, with parchment-coloured plastic cover where it joined the roof lining. Some German-built cars for export markets had a dipping rear-view mirror bonded to the windscreen, which switched from black to Warm Black in August 1979.

The Sport started life with no roof-mounted grab handles, although the first press cars had one for each passenger. Customer cars (probably from August 1976) had one black grab handle above the front passenger seat, along with black coat hooks at the top of each B-pillar; the hooks stayed black when the handles went Warm Black in August 1979.

Inside Boot

Based on the L bodyshell, the Sport's boot lacked the Ghia's fancy carpet or even the GL's insulation.

In the offside wheel well was the Sport's nine-gallon petrol tank, which was identical to a late-spec Mk1 Escort's, and painted satin black. In the opposite corner was the Sport's vertically-mounted spare wheel – a 13in sports steel (the same as its road wheels but without the centre cap). It was strapped into place (normally face first, with its back showing silver paint). The black, woven retaining strap was the normal Mk2 Escort part (admittedly, there were different sizes for 12in and 13in wheels) but with a bracket inside the well rather than the RS's extra lug welded to the boot floor.

A basic tool kit was strapped beside the spare, comprising a blue (on early cars, until black took over) vertical jack and wheel brace inside a black canvas bag. Most Sports came with a boot lamp as standard – a small, round lamp fitted underneath the rear parcel shelf. There was a protective rubber cover on the latch inside the boot lid.

The floor itself was body-coloured, beneath a black Hardura rubber mat. A black cardboard partition was fitted against the rear bulkhead from June 1975 onwards.

There was nothing in here to differentiate the Sport from a lesser model. With space in the well for an upright spare wheel and a regular Escort mat, the luggage compartment was nothing but practical.

COLOUR SCHEMES AND INTERIOR TRIM

Colour	Colour code	Introduced	Discontinued	Interior colour	Coachline colour	Vinyl roof colour (optional)
Signal Orange '79	0	Sep 1978	Sep 1979	Black/grey or chocolate/orange (Chevron)	Black	Black (with black/grey) or tobacco (with chocolate/orange trim)
Signal Amber	0	Aug 1977	Aug 1978	Black/tan or black/orange (Cadiz)	Black	Black
Signal Red	0	Sep 1979	Jul 1980	Chocolate/Indian red or chocolate/tan (Chevron)	Black or brown	Black
Miami Blue	1	Launch	Aug 1977	Black or Marquis (plain vinyl/cloth) until Aug 1976; black/grey or black/tan (Cadiz)	Black	Black
Stardust	3	Launch	Dec 1975	Black or Marquis (plain vinyl/cloth)	Black	Black
Jupiter Red	3	Aug 1977	Sep 1979	Black/grey or black/tan (Cadiz); black/grey or black/red (Chevron)	Silver (with black/grey or black/red trim) or gold (with black/tan trim)	Black
Bermuda Blue	4	Sep 1976	Sep 1978	Black/grey (Cadiz)	Black	Black
Nova Green	4	Sep 1979	Jul 1980	Chocolate/tan (Chevron)	Black	Black
Green Jade	5	Launch	Aug 1977	Black or tan (plain vinyl/cloth) until Aug 1976; black/grey or black/green (Cadiz)	Black	Black
Cosmos Blue	5	Sep 1978	Jul 1980	Black/grey or black/blue (Chevron); chocolate/tan or chocolate/blue (Chevron)	Black, silver or blue	Black
Copper	7	Launch	Dec 1975	Black or Saddle (plain vinyl/cloth)	Black	Black
Velvet Red	7	Sep 1976	Aug 1977	Black/grey or black/tan (Cadiz)	Gold	Black
Nevada Beige	8	Sep 1976	Sep 1978	Black/grey or black/tan (Cadiz)	Black	Black
Signal Yellow	9	Sep 1976	Jul 1980	Black/grey or black/green (Cadiz); black/grey (Chevron); chocolate/tan (Chevron)	Black or brown	Black
Black	A	Launch	Jul 1980	Special order	Special order	Special order
Diamond White	B	Launch	Jul 1980	Black or Saddle (plain vinyl/cloth) until Dec 1975; black or tan (plain vinyl/cloth) until Aug 1976; black/tan or black/orange (Cadiz); black/red or black/blue (Chevron); chocolate/Indian red or chocolate/blue (Chevron)	Black until Aug 1978; black, blue or red (but usually black) after Aug 1978	Black or tobacco (Indian red trim only)
Sahara Beige	C	Launch	Sep 1976	Black or Saddle (plain vinyl/cloth) until Dec 1975; black or chocolate (plain vinyl/cloth) after Dec 1975	Black	Black
Oyster Gold	C	Aug 1977	Sep 1979	Black/tan or black/orange (Cadiz); black/grey or black/blue (Chevron); chocolate/orange (Chevron)	Black	Black or tobacco (with chocolate/orange trim)
Carnival Red	D	Launch	Sep 1976	Black or tan (plain vinyl/cloth)	Black	Black
Regency Green	D	Aug 1977	Sep 1978	Black/grey or black/green (Cadiz)	Black	Black
Terracotta	D	Sep 1979	Jul 1980	Chocolate/Indian red or chocolate/tan (Chevron)	Orange	Black or tobacco (with Indian red trim)
Olympic Blue	E	Launch	Sep 1976	Black or Marquis (plain vinyl/cloth)	Black	Black
Hawaiian Blue	E	Aug 1977	Aug 1978	Black/grey or black/tan (Cadiz)	Silver (with black/grey grey trim) or black (with black/tan trim)	Black
Java Green	E	Sep 1979	Jul 1980	Chocolate/tan (Chevron)	Black	Black
Purple Velvet	F	Launch	Sep 1976	Black or tan (plain vinyl/cloth)	White	Black
Solar Gold	F	Sep 1979	Jul 1980	Chocolate/Indian red or chocolate/tan (Chevron)	Black or brown	Black or tobacco (with Indian red trim)
Royal Blue	G	Launch	Spring 1978	Black or Marquis (plain vinyl/cloth) until Aug 1976; black/grey or black/tan (Cadiz)	Gold (until Aug 1977); gold (with black/tan Cadiz) or silver (with black/grey Cadiz) from Aug 1977	Black
Tuscan Beige	G	Sep 1978	Sep 1979	Black/grey or chocolate/orange (Chevron)	Black or brown	Black or tobacco (with chocolate/orange trim)
Signal Orange '77	H	Dec 1976	Aug 1977	Black/tan or black/orange (Cadiz)	Black	Black
Calypso Green	K	Sep 1978	Sep 1979	Black/grey (Chevron)	Black	Black

Colour	Colour code	Introduced	Discontinued	Interior colour	Coachline colour	Vinyl roof colour (optional)
Laurel Green	K	Dec 1975	Aug 1977	Black or tan (plain vinyl/cloth); black/grey or black/green (Cadiz)	Black until Dec 1976; gold from Dec 1976	Black
Signal Orange '76	L	Dec 1975	Dec 1976	Black or chocolate (plain vinyl/cloth)	Black	Black
Modena Green	M	Launch	Dec 1975	Black or tan (plain vinyl/cloth)	Black	Black
Sierra Beige	P	Sep 1978	Sep 1979	Black/red Chevron or chocolate/orange (Chevron)	Black or brown	Black or tobacco (with chocolate/orange trim)
Cordoba Beige	P	Sep 1979	Jul 1980	Chocolate/Indian red or chocolate/tan (Chevron)	Black or brown	Black or tobacco (with Indian red trim)
Signal Green	P	Sep 1976	Aug 1977	Black/grey or black/green (Cadiz)	Black	Black
Arizona Gold	Q	Launch	Aug 1977	Black or tan (plain vinyl/cloth) until Dec 1975; Black or chocolate (plain vinyl/cloth) until Aug 1976; black/tan or black/orange (Cadiz)	Black	Black
Venetian Red	R	Sep 1976	Jul 1980	Black/grey or black/tan (Cadiz); black/grey or black/red (Chevron); chocolate/tan or chocolate/red (Chevron)	Black or brown	Black
Roman Bronze	S	Dec 1975	Sep 1979	Black or tan (plain vinyl/cloth) until Aug 1976; black/tan or black/orange (Cadiz); black/grey or chocolate/orange (Chevron)	Gold until late 1977; silver or orange thereafter	Black or tobacco (with chocolate/orange trim)
Sable Brown	S	Sep 1979	Jul 1980	Chocolate/Indian red or chocolate/tan (Chevron)	Orange	Black or tobacco (with Indian red trim)
Daytona Yellow	T	Launch	Sep 1976	Black or Saddle (plain vinyl/cloth) until Dec 1975; black or chocolate (plain vinyl/cloth) after Dec 1975	Black	Black
Peppermint Green	T	Aug 1977	Sep 1978	Black/grey (Cadiz)	Black	Black
Riviera Blue	T	Sep 1978	Sep 1979	Black/grey or black/blue (Chevron)	Black, silver or blue	Black
Nordic Blue	T	Sep 1979	Jul 1980	Chocolate/Indian red or chocolate/blue (Chevron)	Black or blue	Black
Platinum Silver	U	Sep 1976	Aug 1977	Black/grey or black/orange (Cadiz)	Black	Black
Phoenix/ Vista Orange	V	Launch	Dec 1975	Black or Saddle (plain vinyl/cloth)	Black	Black
Strato Silver	V	Aug 1977	Jul 1980	Black/grey or black/orange (Cadiz), black/red or black/blue (Chevron); chocolate/blue or chocolate/red (Chevron)	Black or blue	Black
Midnight Blue	X	Spring 1978	Jul 1980	Black/grey or black/tan (Cadiz); black/red or black/blue (Chevron); chocolate/blue or chocolate/tan (Chevron)	Silver (with black/grey Cadiz trim) or gold (with black/tan Cadiz trim); silver (with Chevron trim)	Black

Four-door 1300 Sport, as seen in a brochure from Singapore, was never an option on UK shores, but we were offered a similarly over-endowed 1600 Sport until July 1976.

ESCORT RS1800

The rarest of the rare – unique Venetian Red RS1800 was one of only two non-white cars and is now the sole surviving example. A special order from the factory, this March 1977 RS1800 was delivered from new with steel-crank BDA and deleted side stripes. Since then it was used (and mildly abused) for 60-odd-thousand miles, rebuilt more than once (although never reshelled), modified, unmodified and eventually returned to standard. Bought by Dave Robinson in 1987, the RS1800 started winning shows before being stripped of every nut and bolt during 1991. One or two setbacks (and 15 years) later, it returned to the road in completely stock, concours condition. It's (quite rightfully) been scooping show prizes ever since.

Ford never wanted you to buy an Escort RS1800. Well, not a road-going version anyway. And, if truth be told, you had very little reason to need one. The RS1800 was overpriced, over-complicated, under-specced and deliberately underpowered. Why would anyone want all the aggro of a temperamental twin-cam engine when there was a whole range of hot Escorts to choose from?

The RS1800 looked like an RS Mexico yet was pricier than an RS2000 – which in real-world terms offered very similar performance. In the eyes of Ford's marketing department, even an Escort 1300 Sport would be more suitable to sell you than that troublesome RS1800.

And if you fought against all logical arguments to decide that yes, an RS1800 was for you, it was still a case of ordering one of the road-going rarities and waiting for it to leave the factory. So why not buy that already-in-stock Escort model instead?

If you had to ask, you were missing the point. The RS1800 was the closest you could get to Ford's fire-breathing, motor-sport-conquering competition Escorts. Under the bonnet was an all-alloy BDA (Belt Drive type A) 16-valve engine, complete with howling, high-revving soundtrack and immense performance potential.

Of course, that was a setup familiar to fans of the RS1800's

Think of an RS1800, and chances are (unless you've an irrational attraction to Ford Fiestas) you'll picture a white Mk2 with two-tone blue stripes. Even then, only just over 100 were made in this colour scheme – although you could probably quadruple that by counting all the fakes and replicas (which this car most definitely is not).

immediate predecessor, the Mk1 Escort RS1600. As Ford's marketing brochure pointed out, 'The RS1800 has been developed and built to carry on where the RS1600 left off – way out in front.'

You see, the RS1800 road car was little more than a bluff. A token gesture. A mere tool to meet motorsport rules. And even then, showing its photo in a catalogue was adequate to play the game – because Group Two homologation meant 1,000 examples needed to be built, and the boxes were already ticked by claiming the RS1800 was an evolution of the RS1600.

So at the start of 1975, Ford's Aveley engineers (yes, the heroes responsible for most sporting Mk1 Escorts) grabbed a few new Mk2 1600 Sports straight from the Halewood production line. They were taken to a special two-ramp workshop (not the carousel on which Advanced Vehicle Operations machines were constructed), where their engines, gearboxes, front struts and wheels were discarded. Their bodyshells were strengthened around the suspension mountings, and radius rods added to keep the back axle in check. The cars were then rebuilt as RS1800s, complete with a collection of go-faster goodies.

Most important was the magnificent BDA powerplant, which by then had already been accepted into competition use in alloy-block, 1.8-litre guise. For the RS1800 it was rated at 1,834cc but ran a compression ratio of 9:1 rather than the RS1600's 10:1. The same alloy head and cams were retained, yet Ford chose to fit a single twin-choke Weber downdraught carburettor rather than the side-draughts of old. Officially the idea was to provide better torque, fuel economy and refinement, although chances are it was a typical cost-cutting exercise.

Besides, Ford reckoned 115bhp and 112mph performance was quite enough for the road – although, as the catalogue boasted, it was 'capable of being boosted to push out approximately 250bhp.'

To cope with all the grunt, a new gearbox was concocted from bits of Mustang, Granada and RS2000 Type E four-speed manual. The now-traditional Capri front suspension was added, along with an uprated crossmember and bigger brake servo. The wheels were swapped for half-inch-wider steels – another throwback from the Mk1 RS.

Meanwhile, Ford stylists achieved what they did best – managing a thorough makeover on minimal budget. The decal kit was most obvious, in two shades of Ford Motorsport blue. At the front, below the Sport's quarter bumpers, was added an aerodynamic bib, while the tail received a functional lip spoiler (colour-coded on 33-or-so of the first cars).

RS1800s were offered only in Diamond White, although

Yes, they did make them this colour! Despite its passing resemblance to a Popular Plus, the stripeless RS1800 was an ultra-rare factory special. It's still ruggedly handsome, nevertheless.

two press machines were Carnival Red: JJN 100N (sadly now scrapped) and a left-hand-drive Escort built for the Geneva motor show, where it was displayed alongside white LHD RS1800s in road and rally guise; all three cars were Aveley-built. There was also a later customer car (photographed for this very book) in Venetian Red. No side stripes were fitted to two of the red cars, although the Geneva machine wore orange decals.

After three press cars left Ford's doors in March 1975, RS1800s were built in small batches bearing consecutive chassis numbers – usually only to order. May 1975 saw 20-or-so Sport-based cars produced, while a handful came out in November the same year; it's unclear whether these RS1800s used Halewood bodies or RS shells imported from Saarlouis (which seems most likely) – although all retained British chassis numbers and build plates. Officially, the RS1800 was available from Ford dealers on 10 June 1975, but normal punters couldn't get their hands on a car until the following year.

In 1976 came a change in RS1800 assembly. Now, the

Up front, there was nothing to distinguish the flat-front RS1800 from its RS Mexico sibling – aside from the lack of decals and the hint of silver (oil cooler) behind the grille.

It's like any early Mk2 RS2000 from this angle, with flexible rear spoiler and satin black panel. A stock RS1800 wouldn't disappear into the distance much quicker than its Pinto-powered counterpart either.

Diamond White paintwork with two-tone blue decals was the official Ford Motorsport colour scheme. And didn't it look perfect.

Aveley workshop took fully-trimmed examples of the newly-launched RS Mexico from Germany, including GCAT identity numbers. Their Pinto powerplants were sent back to Saarlouis, then the precious BDAs, better gearboxes and bits of trim were installed.

Production dribbled along until around September 1977. All the while, RS1800s were batch-built – including 30-ish in March '76, one-or-two in June and three during September that year. March 1977 brought four more, followed by up to 15 in April and 20-to-30 in May. Historians counted 109 UK registrations of RS1800s but it's rumoured there was one more supplied to Ireland and potentially others overseas. All RS1800s were British built.

By and large, most were pretty similar, although seven had black vinyl roofs, four-or- more (including a P-registration, wide-wheelarch-equipped press car) were left-hand drive, several lacked decals and about 20 received the optional Custom pack, including reclining roll-top seats, full-height door cards, centre console and passenger glovebox. The Custom was killed at the end 1976, although subsequent cars were offered with extras instead.

Today, it's reckoned that fewer than 70 genuine RS1800s survive, including a mere 27 with their original bodyshells and engines.

Reading the statistics in isolation, it sounds like the RS1800 was a complete flop for one of the world's biggest car manufacturers. It held little advantage over its RS2000 counterpart, and contemporary road tests said a 1600 Sport was equally good for everyday use.

But that's ignoring the most important point: in April 1977, the RS1800's motorsport equivalent was homologated with the name of Escort RS, allowing BDA-powered competition cars to be constructed from bare shells or pre- registered Sports (which explains why works cars had chassis numbers such as BBAT or BFAT). As such, the Mk2 Escort became one of the world's most prolific motorsport machines, taking championship titles around the globe.

It's to the RS1800's credit that even today, BDA-engined Mk2s are still phenomenally successful rally weapons. The car is nothing short of a legend.

It might look high by modern standards, but there are still very few cars that can match an RS1800's handling for foolproof fun.

An amazing engine in an incredible car. The magnificent (if somewhat temperamental) BDA was developed and homologated in the Mk1 Escort RS1600 before being tamed in the RS1800. Not that most cars stayed standard for very long.

Pale blue rocker cover was a modified part from the RS1600, while the mid-blue air pan was also found on 1600 Crossflow-powered Mk2 Escorts – before being reworked for the RS1800. The big-header radiator was taken from the RS1600.

Engine – Block, Head and Sump

Descended directly from the Mk1 Escort RS1600's 1.6-litre, 16-valve engine, the BDA bestowed upon the lucky RS1800 was more of the same but better. Thanks to homologation of an overbored 1.8-litre unit during the RS1600's rallying reign, the RS1800 was launched with an 1834cc version of the late-spec Mk1 bottom end, complete with aluminium-alloy Kent Crossflow-based cylinder block and steel liners. The bore was 86.75mm (in place of the RS1600's 80.97mm), and the stroke was the standard Kent's 77.62mm. Now, though, the compression ratio was dropped to 9.0:1, using special Cosworth pistons with valve clearance recesses in their crowns.

Like RS1600 motors, the BDAs in RS1800s came from a variety of sources (namely Hart and Holbay Racing Engines) using Ford-supplied components. The final 50-or-so RS1800s (built by Holbay during 1977) were lucky recipients of a steel billet crankshaft with 12-bolt flywheel fixing. The big end caps were machined for unique bearings but (despite claims to the contrary) the con rods remained standard Crossflow parts throughout production.

Externally the RS1800 BDA was identical to its predecessor, featuring a casting code on the left-hand side of the crankcase, which read H721F6010AA; there were also Ford oval logos under the inlet manifold and between the core plugs beneath the exhaust manifold.

Each engine had its own unique identity number, which never matched any code on the car's slam-panel-mounted chassis plate or logbook. Early RS1800s had numbers starting in 75 or 76 (with reference to the engine's year of production, meaning some 1976 RS1800s had 75-prefixed engine numbers), followed by three digits, numbered sequentially in manufacture. This code was found on the right-hand side of the cylinder block on a machined flat between the upper two engine mount holes.

Later RS1800 BDAs (fitted with steel cranks) were numbered from HRE7701 to HRE7750. The code was stamped into the left-hand side beneath the rearmost exhaust port, above the core plug. The cylinder blocks were otherwise unchanged, although the breather system was slightly altered.

Another unique code was stamped onto all RS1800 blocks during the machining process (by Essex firm Modern Precision) above the H721F digits; it was prefixed MP, followed by numbers in the five-to-six hundreds (not every sequence was used). The code was repeated several times around the bottom end, including a couple on the sump.

Atop the block was the terrific twin-cam, 16-valve, aluminium-alloy cylinder head first found on the RS1600. The Cosworth casting featured a pair of inlet ports (on the right-hand side) and two siamesed exhaust ports (on the left) for each cylinder. Inside were four valves per cylinder, with 30.9mm diameter inlet faces and 27.4mm exhaust faces. They lived within hardened seats.

The camshaft carrier housed a pair of cams with profiles unchanged from the RS1600's. They were turned by a rubber, single-row, 146-tooth belt connected to a two-section crankshaft pulley, which also fed the engine ancillaries. On top of it all was a rectangular cam cover, very similar to the part seen on BDA-powered Mk1s. That meant a pale blue hammered finish, with bare alloy FORD lettering embossed above each cam. The difference was its breather tube, which had been swapped from right- to left-hand side, plus a small aluminium blanking plug in the redundant (RS1600) position. As before, a stainless steel three-eared oil filler cap was found at the front of the cam cover (without the original Cortina Twin Cam's retaining wire, except on one or two press cars).

At the very front of the BDA was a black cam belt cover, as seen on the RS1600; early RS1800s had a single-fixing lower clamp, but later cars had two holes at the bottom.

Like its AVO-built predecessor, a 13-row oil cooler (with integral pipe connectors and printed-on ARO 9969 part number) was fitted as standard to the RS1800 – it was mounted upright in front of the water radiator, off-centre towards the nearside, attached through the radiator fittings plus a black bracket affixed to the bonnet slam panel via a hand-drilled hole. The pipework was fed underneath the offside headlamp, from an adaptor sandwiched between a large Motorcraft EFL90 oil filter and the 5.72-litres-per-minute oil pump, which was secured by three bolts on the right-hand side of the engine.

The RS1800 used the standard 751M Crossflow-powered Mk2 Escort steel sump, finished in semi-gloss black; steel-crank-equipped BDAs had the baffles beaten out by hand to prevent them being clipped by the crank webbing. The oil dipstick could trace lineage back to the Escort Twin Cam, with minimum marked slightly higher than a 1600cc Crossflow component.

Unique to the RS1800 (and not even fitted to the RS1600) was an oil gallery transfer pipe, which ran from offside to nearside galleries underneath the sump via large holes in the side of the crankcase.

As usual, the BDA sat askew in the RS1800's engine bay – and again it was fitted using round rubber engine mounts from AVO Mk1 Escorts. Likewise, the crossmember was reinforced – by hand on early cars, and a regular RS Mexico part on Saarlouis-sourced machines – with welded strengthening plates and repositioned TCA mountings.

Cooling System

Just like its Mk1 predecessor, the RS1800 contained a high-capacity (in this case 11.97-pint) cooling system with an oversized radiator featuring a big, semi-gloss black header tank. In fact, the RS1800's radiator was taken directly from the Mk1 Escort RS1600, complete with angled overflow spout pointing towards the offside front. On early Sport-based RS1800s the mounting brackets were hand-fitted at Aveley, but later models retained the usual RS Mexico arrangement.

The radiator was fitted with a 13psi AC cap and black rubber Ford hoses, which were similar to RS2000 parts. But, like the RS1600, the RS1800's upper coolant hose featured a horizontal red stripe; two types were used – an early wrapped hose with thick red stripe (identical to the RS1600's) and a

Orange eight-blade plastic fan was a cast-off from the RS1600.

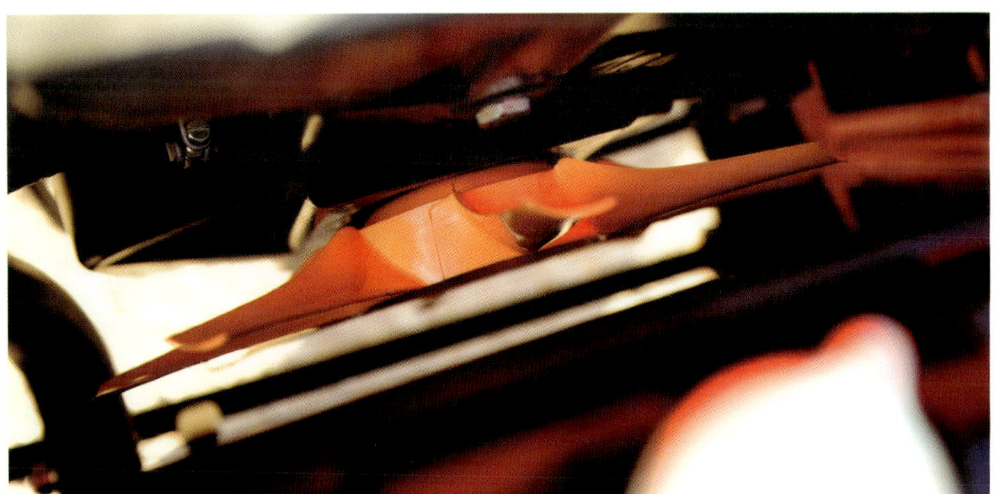

Alloy inlet manifold was unique to the downdraught-carb'd RS1800. Swapping to RS1600-style side-draughts transformed the RS1800's performance but reduced usability.

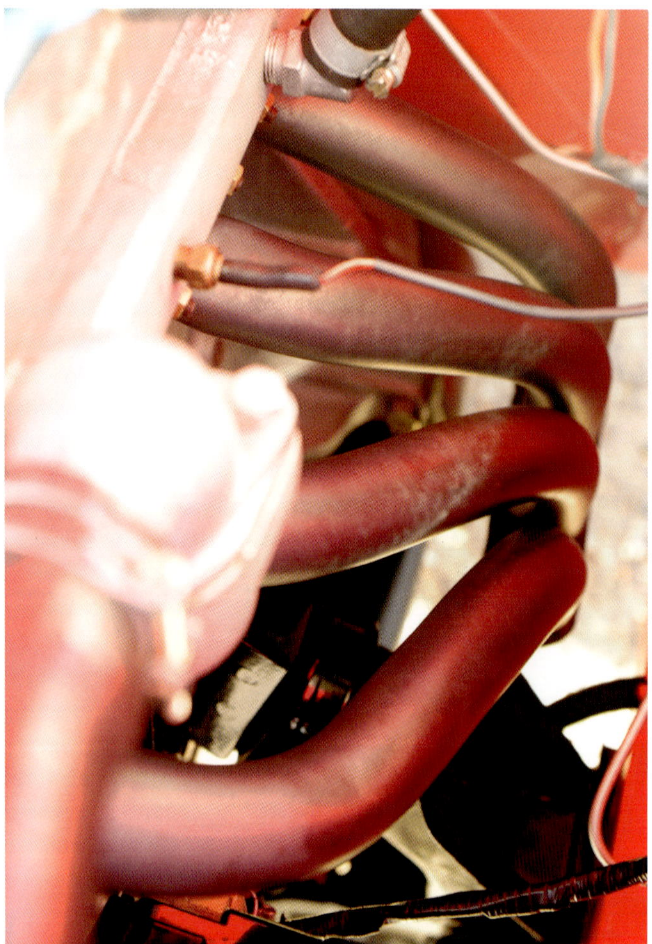

RS1800 exhaust manifold was the four-branch originally found fitted to left-hand-drive RS1600s.

rubber hose used in 1977, with thinner stripe. For 1977, RS1800s had their top hoses trimmed by 15mm at the radiator.

The hose's other end connected to an alloy thermostat housing on the top left-hand side of the cylinder head above the exhaust manifold. All hoses were fastened with wire clips.

The RS1800's fan was the orange eight-blade plastic part found on the BDA-powered Mk1; the water pump was a shallower version of the familiar Kent design, again previously seen on the RS1600.

Fuel System

Was the RS1800 deliberately detuned by Ford? And, if so, was the idea to cut costs rather than improve refinement and reliability? Officially, the extra cylinder capacity of the bigger BDA meant the RS1800 was quite fast enough thank you, kicking out 115bhp at 6,000rpm and 120lb.ft at 4,000rpm. In fact, that meant the RS1800 was slower than the RS1600 and barely lifted above RS2000 performance, so small matters of increased fuel economy and everyday usability possibly played a part.

More likely, though, Ford realised any RS1800s used in anger would automatically be swapped to bucket-sized carbs (or even fuel injection) by the purchaser, and it was unnecessary to spend money at the factory.

So, rather than fitting the RS1600's twin side-draught carburettors, the RS1800 was strangled with a single downdraught. The chosen part was a Weber 32/36 DGAV twin-choke in place of the preferable 40s, complete with autochoke mechanism. There was a metal tag attached to one of the screws plus a code on the carburettor body, describing carb type and calibration; original Webers were made in Italy, although some later replacements were sourced from Spain.

A unique alloy inlet manifold was designed for the RS1800, which bolted to the cylinder head on the right-hand side. Three different manifolds were fitted during production: press cars and the earliest consumer models had no bolt for the dipstick tube, whereas a tapped thread was added later in 1975. An extra breather was added to 1977 cars using a Y-piece from the airbox to the cam cover. On German-sourced cars a single black stabiliser bracket was connected to the front manifold stud to support what appeared to be a regular 1600 Crossflow-type oval metal air pan with two-bolt fixing and disposable paper filter; in fact, the RS1800's air pan (fitted to all cars) had been modified internally to include a small gauze filter fed by the breather hose, which entered underneath through a built-in metal fitting. The air pan was painted mid-blue gloss, including the intake neck's rubber joint. That said, a couple of press cars had black air pans, and some were even seen in metallic blue.

The RS1800's fuel pump was a mechanical diaphragm AC type, mounted on the right-hand side of the engine and operated by an auxiliary shaft.

Fuel lines on RS1800s followed the Crossflow route,

snapped into clips on the underbody. The earliest cars used the standard Escort Sport setup but RS Mexico-based machines came with clips on the opposite side, so the fuel pipes were rerouted with new clips into the standard chassis slots (they were already present on both sides), along with anti-chafing strips to prevent them from kinking.

Exhaust System

The RS1800's exhaust system differed slightly from the RS1600's in that the Mk2's tubular steel four-into-one manifold was taken directly from the left-hand-drive Mk1 – regardless of where the steering wheel was on an RS1800. It was generally left with a bare aluminiumised finish.

The rest of the system was large-bore mild steel, coated in an aluminiumised silver-grey colour; later Ford service parts were painted a dark bluey-grey. It was basically the same as an RS1600 exhaust, with round centre box and oval rear silencer, except the mounting hangers were unique to the RS1800, being chopped off and moved closer to the back of the car (after the spring hanger rather than before it). The underbody brackets were bolted on, with a figure-of-eight rubber rather than twin rings of other Mk2 RS models.

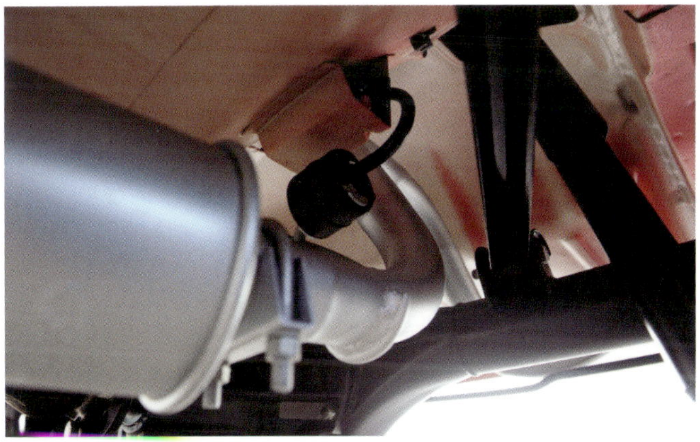

Unique exhaust hanger mated RS1600-derived system to RS Mexico shell.

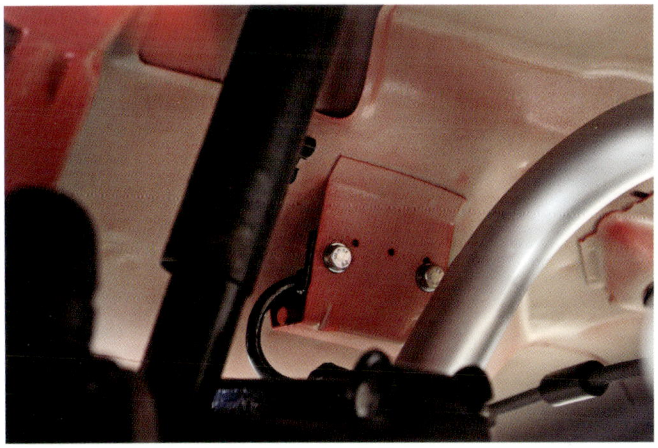

Regular Mk2 fuse box was found on the upper bulkhead, possibly always inset within an RS2000-type insulation pad..

Ignition and Electrical System

Thanks to its mixed heritage, the RS1800's electrical system was a combination of British and German components – with an emphasis on British thanks to where the BDA powerplant was built and the Essex location of final finishing.

Up front was a square-post 55Ah Motorcraft battery in the nearside corner of the engine bay, mounted on a regular Escort tray with black clamp. Its leads were the usual Mk2 parts in black and red (negative and positive respectively), each wrapped with a blue-and-white Ford sticker.

Charging the battery was a silver-coloured Lucas 18 ACR 43-amp alternator, fitted onto the lower left-hand side of the engine with a black Mk1 RS1600-sourced two-piece steel bracket, which had rubber-bushed mountings and a white nylon adjustment arm (aimed at calming vibrations caused by the BDA). A short, separate wiring loom ran from alternator to cylinder block as an earth.

The RS1800's wiring loom (a mildly revised Sport pattern) was wrapped in grey tape until late 1976, when it was swapped for black. The fuse box and twin covers were standard Mk2 Escort parts, found atop the bulkhead – the clear inner cover had English text on early RS1800s and German on RS Mexico-based cars. Inside the box were the usual seven continental fuses. A single-tone (low-pitch) horn was fitted behind the radiator grille, although wiring was present for twin horns.

A common-or-garden Lucas M35J starter motor was entrusted with turning over the BDA engine, having a separate Lucas starter solenoid fitted onto the nearside inner wing beneath the windscreen washer bottle. A Motorcraft nine-volt ballasted ignition coil was used on early cars, with round terminals, red Ford sticker and bare alloy bracket attaching it to the inner wing; German (RS Mexico-based) RS1800s had Bosch coils instead, with a brown top, black body and Ford logo.

A unique but remarkably normal-looking Motorcraft distributor found its way onto the RS1800, which had mechanical and vacuum advance mechanisms. The cap was a regular black push-on Motorcraft part, while the plug leads were black siliconised rubber with black ends, black divider and each numbered with a white tag. The spark plugs were Motorcraft AGR12s.

Transmission

Unique to the RS1800 was its German Type E gearbox, which was modified specifically for the BDA-powered Mk2 Escort.

In essence it was an RS2000- (or RS Mexico-) type single-rail transmission but featuring closer ratios (first 3.36:1, second 1.81:1, third 1.26:1, fourth: 1:1, reverse 3.37:1) and a longer, heavier-duty mainshaft found in some 2.3 V6 Granadas and Mustangs. The cast iron casing looked like the RS2000's, with pressed top cover and aluminium-alloy extension and clutch housings. Similarly, there was a stubby lever with quickshift linkage (a raised pivot point for shorter throw) and the same gate; reverse was forward to the left.

Early gearboxes were similar to the 2000E, with three holes in tail housing and a bolt to secure the speedo cable.

Like Pinto-powered Mk2s, the RS1800 used a standard Escort gearbox mounting but with alloy spacer blocks to drop the back of the 'box by half an inch.

The transmission tunnel was tapped out for clearance on early cars around the reversing light switch, and some gearboxes reportedly had a rear lug ground off to make them fit. On RS Mexico-based cars, the regular modified RS tunnel was used, featuring a specially plated-over gearstick aperture, which moved the hole 71mm further back along the tunnel; early cars had a plate welded in by hand.

A cable-operated, heavy-duty, single-plate, diaphragm-sprung 8.5in Borg and Beck clutch was used, along with a standard 1600 Crossflow flywheel – even the final 50 cars with 12-bolt flywheel fitting on the crank used the Crossflow part, simply held on with six bolts... The input shaft did change, though – on early cars it was from the RS1600, but HRE-engined machines used a mixture of Escort and Cortina components. Fortunately, the clutch cable was the usual 1600 Sport part.

In the transmission tunnel was a regular black RS Mexico two-piece propshaft with rubber-mounted central CV joint. It connected to a black Timken one-piece axle with removable differential and radius rod brackets rather than anti-roll-bar mounts; it's a fair possibility that Escort Sport-based RS1800s used the standard back axle but with hastily welded-on radius rod brackets. Like the 1600 Sport and subsequent RS Mexico around which they were built, RS1800s had a 3.45:1 final drive ratio with tooth-count on the pinion and crown wheel of 11 and 39 respectively.

Of course, the RS1800 was a proper Rallye Sport product, meaning countless extras were available from new – including a wide range of ratios (3.11:1 to 5.14:1), complete Atlas axle with limited-slip differential and even a ZF five-speed gearbox. But although one or two RS1800 road cars were equipped with such goodies, they weren't fitted on the production line.

Early suspension tops were slightly larger than post-February 1977 parts; note original chassis number stamped into the strengthening plate.

Small strut tops were a feature of all Escorts from February 1977. Chassis number was stamped into the offside suspension reinforcing plate, left masked in grey primer.

Suspension and Steering

RS1800s were praised for their handling during contemporary road tests, with progressive understeer-to-oversteer ability thanks to racing drivers' influence on the Mk1 Escort RS2000.

That said, RS1800 press cars exhibited different traits – presumably due to the suspension fitted by the chaps at Aveley. While one was equipped with Bilstein gas rear shock absorbers and Bilstein front damper inserts, another used Armstrong competition-spec struts and Girling gas-filled shockers at the back.

Customer cars received a version of the latter setup, as found fitted to the RS Mexicos on which they were based. That meant Fichtel and Sachs oil-filled shocks up front, inside black Capri/Mk1 Escort RS suspension legs with black dust covers over the rods. Around them were 277mm, 130lb front springs, which were also black (with brown/grey colour code) and featured plastic protectors at each coil end.

The strut tops were from the late-spec Mk1, in semi-gloss black with waisted middles, black collars and the usual brightly-coloured paint dabs made at the factory during the tightening sequence. From February 1977 they were replaced with smaller, offset top mounts, again in black.

Like the Mk1 RS, the RS1800 had struts with imperial-sized detachable steering arms. The usual Escort Mk2 metric steering rack was used, with 17.9:1 ratio and metric-threaded track rod ends with imperial tapers. There was a standard Sport steering gear shaft joint and steering column lock, with an updated coupling in mid-1976. A high-ratio quick-rack was optional but perhaps never factory-fitted.

The RS1800's front anti-roll bar was the usual Mk2 RS 22mm version, complete with revised mountings for improved castor and lowered brackets. The Sport's rear anti-roll bar was binned (it's unknown whether early cars retained the mounts) in favour of twin radius rods to locate the rear axle – they were the stock RS Mexico bits on German-sourced cars but on Sport-based RS1800s the axle and underbody mounts were probably welded on by hand at Aveley.

There was also a pair of Sport 116lb multi-leaf rear springs of 60mm width, with a red, lilac and white colour code. They were held on U-bolts over the back axle, with a metal saddle and moulded rubber pad. Bolted to the bottom plates were upright Girling rear dampers, or Boge on later cars. Everything (aside from the nuts and bolts) was finished in satin black.

Of course, there were plenty of Rallye Sport options from new, including those gas-filled Bilstein shock absorbers and single-leaf rear springs – but it's unknown whether many RS1800 road cars received these bits before being sent to customers.

Sport-spec rear leaf springs were attached to a Timken rear axle – which differed from standard thanks to radius rod links rather than a rear anti-roll bar.

Brakes

Although the Mk1 Escort RS had a beefed-up braking system, much of that setup was carried over onto mainstream Mk2s – so there was no point changing the RS1800 very much from its 1600 Sport starting point.

It featured a dual-line braking system, Girling 247.5mm solid front discs, Ferodo 2445 pads and Girling M16 callipers with 54mm pistons – usually finished in a galvanised silver/gold coating.

On the back was a pair of self-adjusting 9x1.75in drums, with 17.8mm wheel cylinders (19mm on German-built cars) and Ferodo shoes but without the brake shoe inspection aperture found on later Escorts. RS1800 brake lines were the usual

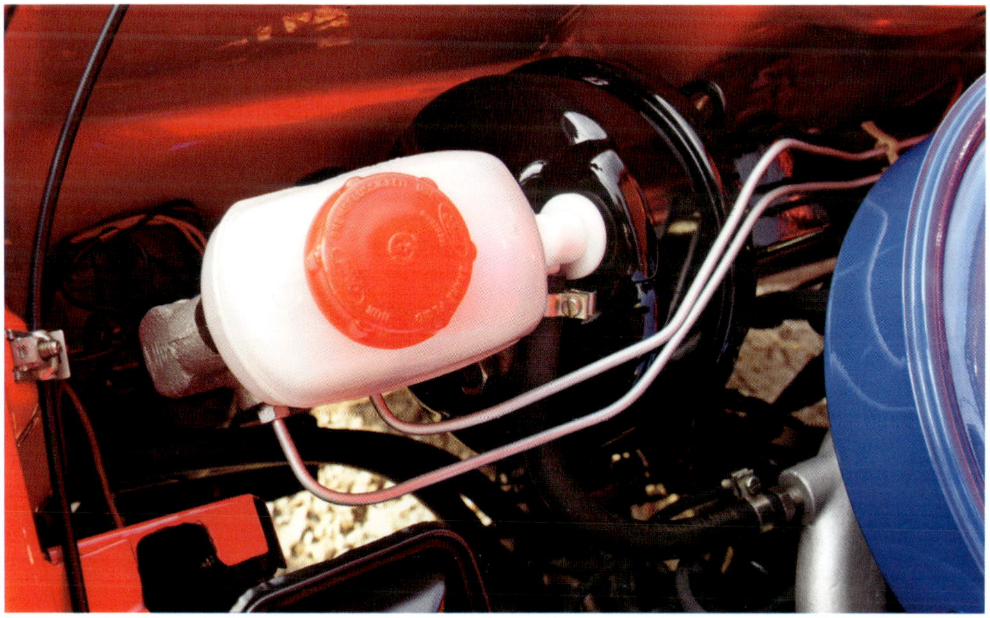

Girling Hydrovac 7in brake servo was a handy boost above the standard Escort's 6in unit. The same setup was seen on all early Mk2 RS models.

mix of silver/zinc-coloured Bundy mild steel tubing and black Girling flexible hoses.

The main change was the RS1800 brake servo, which was a Girling Hydrovac 7in booster rather than the Crossflow-powered car's 6in unit. It was mounted on the regular in-line bracket attached to the offside inner wing. Like other early (pre-1978) Mk2 RSs, the RS1800 had a setup similar to late-model AVO MK1s, with 20.6mm master cylinder and white plastic reservoir with red cap. The servo body was black, and there was a red plastic band around the master cylinder (itself usually zinc coloured, but black on some 1977 cars). A white plastic clip above the servo tower kept the brake lines neat and tidy.

Wheels and Tyres

Despite its hefty price tag compared to the contemporary RS2000, the RS1800 lacked its sibling's four-spoke RS alloy wheels. Instead, it kept the Capri-type 5.5x13in sculptured steel rims found on its AVO-built predecessors, always finished in Silver Fox paint.

Early cars used the Mk1 wheels, which had solid bands around the backs where the faces were welded to the rims. Later RS1800s (probably from some time in 1976) swapped to very similar (although lighter-weight) versions – the most noticeable change was a set of four cutouts where the rims attached to the backs, which were barely visible when viewed from the faces. They also had stampings between the bolt holes, including size, part number and Ford oval logo. Some early rims had a Ford logo stamped on their reverse sides.

RS1800 centre caps were black metal with dished middles, and wore a silver entwined RS logo. The wheel nuts were metric M12x1.5s in black with rounded heads. Road-going RS1800 customer cars were usually equipped with 175/70SR13 or 175/70HR13 Pirelli CN36 Cinturato tyres.

Needless to say, Ford and Rallye Sport dealers offered a choice of alloy wheels (up to 7.5x13in), although the regular four-spoke RS alloys (with 175/70HR13 Pirellis) were the only factory-fitted options. And, even then, they only made it onto a handful of RS1800s from new.

There's reason to believe one or two early RS1800s were equipped with Mk1-type 5.5x13in four-spokes, which had plain spoke centres and chrome centre caps (pushed through from behind) with blue stickers featuring the Mk1 RS logo. Later alloy-wheeled RS1800s wore RS2000-type 6x13in four-spokes with polished rims, Dove Grey cutouts and black face-fitted centre caps with silver entwined RS motif.

Bodywork

Who needed a fancy droop-snoot nose cone, when international rally Escorts were flat-fronted? Indeed, because Ford's world-beating competition cars had the standard Mk2 front end (no point bashing up expensive polyurethane parts while hammering through forests), that's what was required for the road-going version rather than the posh RS2000's beak.

Still, the RS1800 wasn't quite all go and no show – it did boast a pair of spoilers and a few unique decals. Everything else was pure heavy-duty Escort Sport, including completely stock Mk2 exterior bodywork.

Underneath, of course, were a few alterations. As found on the donor RS Mexico shell, the RS1800 had uprated front suspension turrets, skidded rear chassis rails, mounting points for the rear radius rods and revised transmission tunnel with special gearstick aperture. From November 1975 there was also a redundant guide for keeping the speedometer cable clear of a Pinto engine's exhaust system, and Pinto-type fuel line clips on the nearside chassis rail

Sports steel wheels were a throwback to AVO Mk1 Escorts, although the design (seen on most RS1800s) was mildly revised for the sporty Mk2. All were finished in Silver Fox paint.

Wheel centre caps were black metal with silver RS logos. Wheel nuts were black M12x1.5s unless alloys were specified.

(rather than the offside rail of Crossflow-powered cars, including the early 1975 Sport-based RS1800s).

At the front of the RS1800 was a pair of satin black quarter bumpers, lacking only the Sport's overriders and spot lamp brackets (which were deliberately removed from the first RS1800s). The bumpers were mounted on a regular Escort Mk2 front panel (painted satin black around and between the headlamps), above an aerodynamically-designed bib spoiler (front-end lift was allegedly reduced by up to 25 per cent).

Very early RS1800s featured a fibreglass wrap-around spoiler, which was affixed on four nuts underneath, along with pop rivets through the inner wheelarch lips (one on each side). From mid-1976 the spoiler was swapped for a polyurethane part of almost identical design; the main visual difference was that it was screwed into each front corner, as well as the inner wheelarches. RS1800 front spoilers were the same as those worn by RS Mexicos, and were always colour-coded to the bodywork.

Similarly, the very first RS1800s (mainly press cars and dealer demonstrators) were fitted with a flexible, high-density foam boot spoiler, which displayed a raised Ford oval directly above the boot lock; most were body-coloured, but one car's was black. Six or seven RS1800s wore this rear spoiler, although it's likely that 33 were pro-

FORD-lettered grille was fitted to all RS1800s – as was the 13-row oil cooler mounted in front of the main radiator (visible behind the grille).

Blue boot decal was found on all RS1800s, even the two red machines that were otherwise sticker-free.

Escort badge on nearside of boot lid was always the smaller type, always painted black.

FORD badging was found on every RS1800 but the chrome boot lock and twin number pate lamps were only seen on later models.

Black heat-set epoxy rain gutters and satin black window surrounds were fitted to all but the very earliest RS1800s – which had the blacked-out surrounds but retained chrome drip rail trims.

A heated rear window was standard kit, even on the RS1800 base model. British-built RS1800s had Triplex glass but RS Mexico-sourced cars wore Sekurit.

Unlike early Sports, all RS1800s wore black door handles – presumably painted over chrome on the early press cars.

duced. All other RS1800s wore a normal matt-black rubber RS rear spoiler (with slightly different profile from the earlier part), which was said by Ford to reduce lift by up to 57 per cent.

Like the contemporary Mk2 RS2000, the RS1800 also boasted a satin black back panel, which wrapped around the rear lights and into the boot shut in alignment with the lid, giving the visual effect of a continuous straight line. Below it was a satin black back bumper (painted over chrome plating on the earliest cars), again minus the Sport's overriders.

The RS1800's only real distinctive feature was its decal kit, which comprised Ford Motorsport-themed two-tone blue stripes at bumper height along each side. A large blue RS1800 motif was placed on each rear wing at the same height as the back lights, along with a smaller version on the offside of the boot lid.

All RS1800s were supposed to wear the full sticker kit (possibly painted instead on the first prototypes) but it was specified as a delete option on four cars. Two Diamond White RS1800s plus two of the non-white machines (one a Carnival Red press car and the other a customer-specified Venetian Red example, pictured on these very pages) left the factory with no decals but for the (blue) boot lid logo. The red Geneva show prototype had orange stripes.

Badging on the RS1800 was mainly standard Sport stuff, with a small black ESCORT emblem on the nearside of the boot lid and black FORD lettering beneath the boot lock (which used the same key as the doors and ignition barrel); very early cars had a black boot lock, but German-based

Aerodynamic rear spoiler was said to reduce lift by up to 57 per cent. Mainly, though, it looked the part.

Late-model polyurethane RS1800 front spoiler showing under-arch fastenings

cars wore chrome.

A pair of black 1.8 badges was found on the lower front wings behind the wheelarches; on the very earliest cars (including those built in November 1975) they were created by welding an extra section of metal into the donor Sport's 1.6 badges; later cars used properly-made black plastic parts.

Meanwhile, the matt-black plastic front grille wore bright silver FORD lettering in the centre, with the surround and middle bar highlighted in silver.

Satin black paint treatment around the car echoed that of a standard white Sport, with black B-pillars, door frames and window surrounds (up to the drip rails and along the bottom in alignment with the window rubbers). On most RS1800s the sills and spare wheel well were body-coloured, but due to time constraints during production many later examples stayed in the satin black of RS Mexicos.

Until the end of 1975 the roof gutters had chrome trims, which were then swapped for matt black heat-set epoxy. Around the same time, the windscreen rubbers switched from chrome to black beading. RS1800 windscreen wipers were always black, with two speeds and electric screen wash plus the addition of an intermittent facility on German

Black plastic 1.8 emblem was unique to the RS1800; the first press cars had a bodged-up metal badge instead.

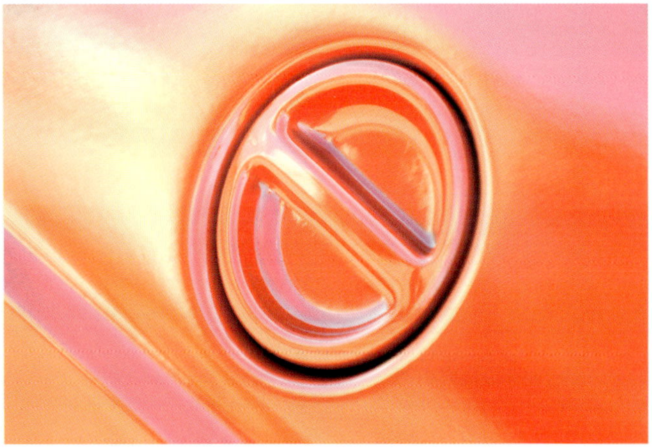

Fuel cap was the same pressed steel item found on other Mk2 Escorts. Many were ditched in favour of dealer-accessory locking caps.

RS1800 rear wing motif and matching stripes were standard on all but four machines.

Satin black back panel was painted into boot shut, angled at the edges.

The first half-dozen RS1800s wore a pre-production rear spoiler colour-keyed to the bodywork. The size and shape was subtly different from the later rubber spoiler.

Prototype rear spoiler had Ford oval in the middle. Black-painted boot locks were found on RS1800 press cars.

bodies. A black wind deflector (with H75AB part number) was fitted to the driver's-side wiper arm of press RS1800s and a few early customer cars.

RS1800 front 'screens were always laminated, a heated rear windscreen was standard and opening front quarter vents were available – although probably never fitted to an RS1800. Green tinted glass was an extra-cost option, found on a handful of cars. Windows were produced by Triplex on British-sourced shells (the earliest cars) or Sekurit for RS Mexico-based machines.

Unlike early Sports, RS1800 door handles and mirrors were always finished in satin black, although one or two of the earliest cars kept chrome door locks. A black remote-control driver's door mirror was listed as optional, although rarely seen on production cars.

Slightly more popular was the optional black vinyl roof, which found its way onto seven white RS1800s (including a now-demised press car). A couple of RS1800s received a dealer-fitted Webasto sunroof when new, while one car gained a full-size electric sunroof and black vinyl top after leaving the production line.

Many RS1800s had (optional) factory-fitted radios, accompanied by a retractable chrome Ford-stamped aerial on the offside front wing.

Of course, there were countless other options available from new – including the motorsport arches and even tow bar seen on an RS1800 press demonstrator – but they were fitted pre-delivery rather than by the factory.

Underbonnet

If you could tear your eyes (and ears) away from its splendid BDA powerplant, it was clear that under an RS1800's bonnet were one or two subtle differences from the basic Mk2 Escort.

Most noticeable were the strengthening plates around the suspension mounts (and underneath in the towers) – which were the same parts found on all other RS Mk2s and heavy-duty export-spec shells. The circular openings for each strut were reduced from 105mm to 85mm diameter in February 1977.

The car's chassis number was hand-stamped into the steel around the offside strut top, masked and left in primer grey to protect the surface. Its VIN tag and build plate were found on the bonnet slam panel, with a variety of stampings. The first RS1800s had a VIN plate describing an Escort 1600 Sport, with chassis number starting BBAT, an L3 in the engine code box (denoting 1.6-litre Crossflow) and A7 (for black cloth) in the trim section; these cars' build plates said ARTQML along the top line (Q meant Sport) and WHITE S RS 1800 across the bottom (except for the red car, of course). Early May 1975 machines received a random selection of numbers on the type section of their chassis plates, including ATR or ATB (instead of BATR), and one left- hand-drive car reading BZATRZ. Almost all 1975 RS1800s had an S in the version box. November 1975 RS1800s had a similar setup, but with an R in the engine code box of the VIN tag and AA in the trim section (relating to a black vinyl interior, of all things).

RS Mexico-based RS1800s (with Saarlouis-built shells – namely all from 1976 onwards) retained RS Mexico VIN plates, including a GCAT-prefixed chassis number, LE (1600cc Pinto) engine code and A7 trim; their build tags were the normal Saarlouis type, listing spec and options.

It's worth noting that the engine number on any RS1800's VIN plate was that of the donor Escort 1600 Sport or RS Mexico rather than its BDA identity.

Almost everything else under an RS1800's bonnet was pure Escort Sport. There was an opaque plastic windscreen washer fluid bottle screwed into a black bracket mounted on the nearside suspension tower, complete with plain black or pale gold-coloured electric washer pump featuring a printed black Ford oval logo. It fed clear plastic tubing, leading to a white plastic T-piece and copper nozzles that squirted through the scuttle panel. RS Mexico-based RS1800s also wore a hole on the offside inner wing where the reservoir previously sat.

Most – if not all – had the Ghia-type engine compartment cowl in place across the top of the bulkhead, in the usual black sandwiched foam with cutout for the fuse box on the passenger side. Until February 1977 the bulkhead featured five dimples directly beneath the scuttle panel, after which there were seven; theoretically, all RS1800s with small suspension tops had seven dimples, but in practice this wasn't the case.

Beneath the pad, the RS1800's bulkhead resembled the Mk1 RS1600's, complete with cut-and-turned-down lip to clear the back of the BDA's rocker box. The work was done by hand (supposedly using a hammer, welding and seam sealer, although 1977 cars lacked any welds), along with a little beating to clear the big gearbox's bellhousing – much more, in fact, than found on RS Mexicos or RS2000s. Some RS1800s had white paint roughly applied to any damage, including overspray on the bulkhead drain hose.

RS Mexico shells came with a bulkhead hole for an oil pressure pipe, but Sport-based cars had the choke cable aperture drilled out to 19mm to accept the pipe.

Like other Mk2 RSs, the RS1800's slam panel and radiator crossmember were revised to allow the big radiator to sit further forward. On early Sport-based RS1800s the box-section and mounting brackets were adapted by hand at Aveley, and even the three wiring loom tags were tacked

Windscreen washer bottle was mounted on the regular Escort side, rather than the opposite position on Pinto-powered RS models.

Radiator top hose with red stripe was another piece taken straight from the RS1600; later RS1800s had a different hose with thinner red stripe.

back into position. Later cars simply retained the RS Mexico's redesigned metalwork.

The RS1800's battery tray was in the normal position (the passenger-side front corner of the engine bay), with the brake servo on the driver's side. RS1800s lacked the Sport's lighting relay on the inner wing, so it's assumed early cars still had a pair of screw holes above the battery.

On the slam panel in the nearside corner was a white plastic retaining clip for the galvanised bonnet prop, which hinged from the offside front corner of the engine bay. The black plastic-coated bonnet release cable was fed under the offside inner wing drip rail; alongside its release mechanism in the slam panel was an E11 lighting emissions sticker – a pale grey square until 1976, when it was swapped for a wider rectangle, now in purple. Some early cars were also equipped with a black-on-white Mk1 Escort-type engine coolant decal on the offside inner wing top.

Most unusually, a couple of early RS1800 Customs were fitted with a large engine compartment lamp affixed to the bonnet's underside just above the fuse box, complete with pin-switch operation.

Lighting

Despite being such a limited-run machine, the RS1800 saw several changes to its lighting arrangement, mainly based on build date.

All RS1800s featured 7in Lucas H4 semi-sealed beam halogen headlamps with 60/55w bulbs, a blue H4 sticker in the middle and Lucas in raised letters on the glass. Early lamp units featured a pale blue-tinted outer ring, but it's probable that only Sport-based RS1800s received these parts. The white 1975 Geneva show car also boasted a headlamp wash/wipe system, complete with rocker switch on the ashtray panel.

Beneath the headlamps were the usual Escort front indicators, mounted in the bumpers. British-built RS1800s had Vega (built in England) lenses, while later cars wore the all-but identical Altissimo (made in Germany) versions. Hazard flashers were standard.

The earliest RS1800s – really just the press demonstrators – were also equipped with a pair of round, orange Carello side repeaters with chrome surrounds, which were very similar to Fiat parts. Such cars had a special section of wiring plugged

Halogen H4 headlamps and quarter bumpers were the same as you'd find on contemporary Mk2 Sport and RS Mexico. Note the late-spec front spoiler's lower fixing screw.

Two-up-two-down driving lamps weren't factory original, but they represented what the RS1800 was all about – rallying.

Early Lucas H4 headlamp with blue outer ring, as fitted to a handful of early cars.

Side repeaters were seen on press-destined RS1800s, but were any customer cars similarly equipped?

into the main loom. Although the vast majority of RS1800s lacked these repeaters in their front wings, many were retro-fitted by subsequent owners.

At the back, the RS1800 had the Mk2's standard setup, with the usual rear light clusters (Butlers-made on English-built RS1800s or Altissimo on RS Mexico-sourced cars) including integral reversing lamps. Some cars had their build date painted neatly on the backs of the clusters. Early RS1800s featured a single number plate light positioned in the middle of the back bumper, before switching to a pair during autumn 1976.

A Ford-branded Altissimo rear fog lamp was a factory optional extra, positioned on a bracket attached to the offside rear valance. Similarly, several RS1800s had a set of two-up-two-down front spot lamps fitted from new, but by dealers rather than the factory; such cars regained a relay attached to the nearside inner wing.

RS1800 interior lighting was just the same as other Escorts, using an all-white Mk1-type courtesy light above the rear-view mirror until 1976, when a bigger unit was fitted, complete with black override switch. A pair of black plastic door control buttons were mounted in the A-pillars.

Interior

Ford's marketing men were keen to promote the RS1800 as an executive express, with the brochure proclaiming, 'If you are going to win, you might as well win in comfort.'

Two types of RS1800 were available from the outset – with standard or Custom trim – but the range was reduced to just the regular RS1800 at the end of 1976. By then, only about 20 RS1800 Customs had been built. So much for all that comfort!

While the standard car's trim was much like an Escort Sport's, the Custom pack added RS2000-ish reclining seats with head rests, full-height door cards and rear three-quarter panels, centre console, glovebox, dashboard cubby-hole, loop-pile carpet, inertia-reel seat belts and carpeted luggage compartment.

So, what about those RS2000-ish seats? Well, the first RS1800s (all those built during 1975 except for the initial prototype, which wore black Sport seats) were fitted with Scheel recliners trimmed in black Beta cloth. They had chrome adjuster handles at the bottom of the back rests and vertical stitching running to the front of the seat squabs. In contrast, later RS1800s (all 1976-built cars, with GCAT chassis numbers) were equipped with the usual Mk2 RS2000-type seats – again in black Beta cloth, they were also made by Scheel but had deeper side bolsters, knurled black plastic adjuster wheels to recline their backs and vertical stitching that ended halfway down the squabs. It's worth noting that sometimes a cardboard tag (bearing a production date of a month or two before the car's manufacture) was secreted inside the seats.

Roll-top head rests were standard, trimmed in black Beta cloth with horizontal block pattern and Velcro fastening along their bottom edges.

The base-spec RS1800 was supposed to come with light-weight, low-back, non-reclining bucket seats (again in black Beta cloth) featuring harness slots and provision for roll-top headrests, but in fact they were a no-cost option and rarely seen on production cars.

Like its predecessors, the RS1800's cabin was a sombre setup, with black, black and a bit more black. On the floor was a black loop-pile carpet – the normal RS Mexico mat (identical to the standard Escort carpet but with a different gearstick aperture) unless Custom trim was specified, which added a plush cut-pile covering as found in contemporary

RS2000s, along with additional soundproofing. It was tucked into ribbed aluminium scuff plates on the inner sills, which also retained the black door rubbers. In each front footwell was a black plastic kick panel.

The RS1800's pedal box was just a stock Mk2 Escort setup, with satin black brake and clutch levers, Mk1 Escort-type rubber pads (with horizontal pattern) and cranked silver-coloured accelerator lever with matching black plastic pad.

Most RS1800s were equipped with a black vinyl-rimmed, three-spoke, 14in RS steering wheel with black metal spokes. It was much the same as the Sport part but featured a large black plastic centre cap with debossed, entwined RS emblem until late-spring 1977, when it was superseded by a cap wearing a regular blue oval. Early press cars apparently had leather-rimmed wheels.

The steering column shroud was the usual Escort black plastic part, with three stalks – one on the left for indicators, horn, headlamp dip and flash, one on the right for two-speed wipers with intermittent facility (from 1976), plus a smaller stalk for controlling the lights.

Immediately in front of the driver was a plain black instrument binnacle (without the silver highlight seen on some Mk2s) containing a 7,000rpm tachometer with no red line and a 120mph speedometer, which included trip and mileage recorders; 1975 RS1800s only read in miles per hour, but later cars featured smaller yellow digits for kilometres per hour too. Between them were three smaller circular dials for fuel, water temperature and oil pressure. All the gauges were black with white needles. Underneath was a strip of warning lights for left-hand indicators, main beam, ignition and right-hand indicators; an RS logo was in the middle of the

RS1800 Custom interior added creature comforts of fully-trimmed door cards, passenger glovebox, glove pocket, clock and centre console.

row, which did nothing other than remind the driver he was sitting in something quite special.

A regular black vinyl pad stretched across the top of the dashboard, above a satin black steel fascia panel. The dash was simply the standard Sport part unless Custom trim was specified – in which case there was a pressed cutout in front of the passenger, housing a plastic cubby box (called a glove pocket in Ford language) screwed into the recess; on its right-hand side was a Smiths clock featuring white digits, white Ford logo and red needle.

Custom packs also included a black plastic glovebox with fold-down lid, mounted under the passenger-side fascia. Base models made do with the usual Escort cardboard parcel shelf, featuring padded vinyl edging; all RS1800s had a cardboard shelf on the driver's side too.

In the centre of the dashboard were the RS1800's illuminated heater controls, comprising black plastic bezel with silver detailing, foil indicator diagram, black temperature sliders and two-speed heater/demister switch. During autumn 1976 the foil was replaced with an updated version, when hot and cold swapped places (red changed from right to left) and the metal heater box was replaced with a quieter plastic unit. A pair of black eyeball vents was mounted in the dashboard (one at each side), complete with silver rims around the housings.

A black plastic lower fascia panel was found beneath the heater controls, including central swivelling ashtray and a row of rocker switches. Depending on the individual car's specification they were (left to right): blanking plate, hazard flasher switch (updated in autumn 1976 with an upright rather than inverted warning triangle), cigarette lighter (standard fitment, swapped in April 1977 from deep-reach Mk1-type with silver sticker to smoother Mk2 part with white diagram printed on), heated rear window switch (with warning lamp and diagram updated during autumn 1976) and blank for (optional) fog lamp switch with red warning light. A circular blanking plug was on the steering column shroud in place of a choke control knob.

Custom-trimmed RS1800s were fitted with a deep centre console of the type found in contemporary RS2000s. It wrapped around (where fitted) the plastic under-dash mount for an optional MW/LW radio – a push-button Ford P21 with pre-selection for six stations or (only on 1975 cars) a vastly dearer manual-tune multi-band M32 (with MW/LW/SW/VHF). Either was accompanied by a speaker in the dashboard top.

The centre console surrounded the RS1800's black gear lever and gaiter, capped with a Capri sports gearknob complete with impressed selector gate featuring the usual Mk2 Escort pattern, having reverse to the left and towards the front. Non-Custom RS1800s had the same gearknob but no console.

A standard Escort handbrake lever was found on the trans-

Scheel reclining front seats were a delete-option, thus fitted to the vast majority of RS1800s. Note the Custom back seat, likewise trimmed in black Beta Plus fabric.

Handbrake and seat belt stalks were regular Mk2 kit but the gearknob was RS-specific (oh, okay, except for some Capris and late-model Escort Sports…). Seats were trimmed in black Beta Plus fabric.

Inertia-reel seat belts were optional unless you'd specified Custom trim. Stalks were the same throughout the range.

RS three-spoke steering wheel was similar to Sport part but boasted an impressed logo in the middle. The rim was a mock-leather stitched effect.

RS1800 had 120mph speedometer and 7,000rpm rev counter. A few engine modifications would see those figures easily exceeded.

Lower fascia panel contained ashtray, cigarette lighter and rocker switches – here for hazard flashers and heated rear window.

Most RS1800s were fitted with black Beta Plus cloth-trimmed L-spec back seat; rear quarter panels were only full-height on Custom pack cars.

mission tunnel, in black with black push button and black gaiter. A pair of black plastic-coated seat belt stalks were behind it, with gold-and-red release buttons. Static seat belts were standard, with inertia-reels optional or included as part of the Custom pack.

Custom-spec RS1800s boasted full-height door cards trimmed in black vinyl with carpeted lower sections; the cards also featured chrome upper beading and large, angled armrests, along with chrome frames around the door release handles.

Base-spec RS1800s contained the standard L-type Mk2 door cards in black vinyl, with vertical double stitch lines and body-coloured paintwork evident along the top. The release handles were again black, but with black plastic frames. The armrests were small black vinyl items.At least one of the prototypes and

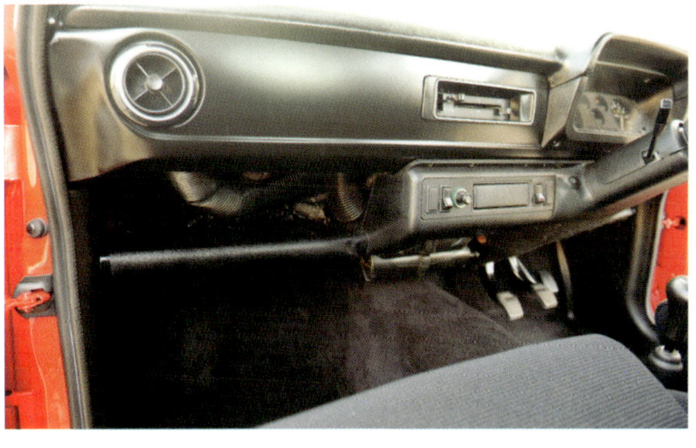

Base-spec dashboard lacked the passenger-side glove pocket and clock found on RS1800 Custom.

RS1800 rear-view mirror was black, with black inner cap where it met the roof lining.

All (or nearly all) RS1800s had black Mk1-type headlining with small dimples rather than late-spec RS2000 putty colour.

press cars had its metalwork above the door cards painted matt black instead of the regular Diamond White.

All doors used the standard Mk2 Escort chrome window winders with black plastic inserts and plastic knobs, plus black plastic internal lock buttons with flared tops.

The story continued in the back of an RS1800. Standard cars had regular black rear quarter panels with small, rotating plastic ashtrays but Customs had fully-trimmed rear quarters complete with bigger ashtrays and chrome beading strips. Meanwhile, the standard car's L-spec back seat (with dual stitch lines) was swapped for a comfier GL version, identifiable by its evenly spaced stitching.

At each side of the back seat was a black vinyl pad covering the inner wheelarch. Beyond it was a black cardboard parcel shelf, which was dusted with matt black paint beneath the slats. Curiously, under the floor, 1977 RS1800s lacked the normal Escort mounting points for rear seat belts.

No grab handles were fitted above the rear seat – there was a pair of black plastic coat hooks at the top of each B-pillar instead. The front-seat passenger was rewarded with a black grab handle plus a vanity mirror on the flipside of the sun visor. All RS1800s had sun visors trimmed to match the headlining, in black Mk1-type vinyl (with small dimples); that said, at least one pre-production car kept its Sport putty-colour vinyl. Above the headlining, the metal inner roof skin of black vinyl headlining-equipped, Sport-based RS1800s was painted matt black; Saarlouis-produced shells were body-coloured.

A black dipping rear-view mirror was mounted between the sun visors, complete with black plastic cover where it joined the roof lining.

Only the Custom came with a posh boot carpet – the regular RS1800 made do with this Hardura vinyl mat.

Most of the RS1800's roof pillars weren't trimmed internally – the A-pillars were painted satin black, while the B-pillars were covered in black vinyl only on British-built cars – the rest revealed body-coloured metal. Meanwhile, the C-pillars were trimmed in black vinyl like other RSs.

Inside Boot

Let's be honest: if you were buying a new RS1800, the last thing you cared about was the luggage compartment. Even so, Ford thought it a good idea to fit a tidy black Ghia-type carpet in the boot of Custom cars, replacing the standard Mk2 Escort Hardura mat of base models. Unlike later RS2000s and Ghias, though, the early carpet was the regular Escort shape, lacking a spare wheel cover.

RS1800 Customs also gained a boot lamp, which worked while the headlights were switched on; in the earliest cars it was a bulbous Mk1-type light affixed to the boot lock strengthener but later RS Mexico-based models received a regular, round Mk2 lamp under the parcel shelf.

Like other Mk2s, the RS1800's spare wheel was mounted upright in the nearside well. The spare always matched the road wheels – whether steel or alloy, but lacking a centre cap – and was strapped into place with a woven belt; the lower end of the belt was hooked over a small bracket spot-welded onto the boot floor above the rearmost chassis rail – most likely tack-welded less neatly on early Sport-based machines thanks to being fitted by hand.

Steel spare was supplied to match the road wheels. Note the strap's lower lug, visible through a slot in the boot mat.

In the opposite side of the luggage compartment was a satin black nine-gallon petrol tank (with flush, body-coloured cap externally); a couple of the November 1975-built RS1800s were found with a green 'OK' sticker on their tanks.

Like other Mk2s factory-equipped with a rear spoiler, the RS1800 had uprated boot spring tensioners.

Naturally, the RS1800's luggage compartment also had all the usual Mk2 contents, including a black cardboard partition fitted against the rear bulkhead, a black screw pillar jack and wheel brace inside a black canvas bag (strapped in with the spare wheel) and a protective rubber latch cover.

The only other difference was found in the first RS1800 press cars, which had their entire luggage compartments painted satin black, in what was referred to by Ford as 'Ghia treatment.'

Inside the boot, the RS1800 was much like any other Mk2 – here showing its black wiring loom tape, luggage compartment divider and paper inspection stickers.

COLOUR SCHEMES AND INTERIOR TRIM

Body colour	Interior colour	Stripe colour(s)
White	Black	Blue/blue (delete option)
Carnival Red	Black	–
Venetian Red	Black	–

ESCORT RS MEXICO

Pure Rallye Sport Escort – Steve and Martin Ogle's January 1976 RS Mexico is one of the oldest surviving examples, in one of the finest states of repair. That's thanks to a genuine mileage of 80,000 plus some sensitive restoration work, including new front wings, rear wheelarch, door skin and full respray in original Diamond White. Owned by the father and son team for a dozen years, this RS Mexico sports its standard steel wheels, Scheel reclining front seats and optional remote-control driver's door mirror.

The RS Mexico could have been perfect. It was, after all, everything you could want in a sporting Escort. Well, almost everything. The RS Mexico looked like a rally car, outdragged rivals' offerings and slid around the countryside with all the foolproof fun we'd grown to expect of a fast Ford.

And, like the Mk1 Mex, the Mk2 version got the formula just right. It had proper motorsport heritage and a funky decal kit – and the feel-good factor came free. Now, too, there was a healthy dose of refinement, impeccable manners and a helping of creature comforts.

But that was part of the problem. Whereas the early Mk1 Mexico was a cheap and cheerful way to emulate Roger Clark, the Mk2 (now with that all-important RS title added to its moniker) had become a mid-range model sitting above an essentially similar 1600 Sport – itself seen as a worthy Mex successor.

So, what was the RS Mexico? Officially released on 14 January 1976 alongside the high-profile Mk2 RS2000, the RS Mexico came as a bit of a surprise. It was originally intended to be an entry-level machine for all European markets, created somewhat reluctantly to provide Rallye Sport dealers with a two-model line-up. In the end, RS Mexicos were only made for UK shores – and only in right-hand drive (well, except for one or two pre-production cars).

So to keep British buyers happy without upsetting its own

With its spoilers, wide steel wheels and purposeful stance, a Diamond White RS Mexico looked ready for any form of motorsport action.

A plain, white, flat-front Mk2 really takes some beating; the front spoiler, quarter-bumpers and bonnet pinstriping enhanced its timeless appeal.

accountants, Ford built the RS Mexico by reworking the new RS2000 – all the while wearing a very cynical, very cost-conscious hat. With the mutual goals of saving money and attracting punters, the familiar tactics came into play. Existing parts bins were raided and little bits of trim were discarded, then the marketing men were let loose.

'To continue the successful formula that made the Mexico a household name,' they said, 'the new RS Mexico was conceived with the careful specification mix of performance, handling and originality.'

In reality, that equated to an RS2000 with a smaller engine and the expensive nose hacked off. Built on the same Saarlouis production line as its bigger brother, the RS Mexico also boasted a German-sourced powerplant and transmission system – again keeping costs to a minimum. Both models used a heavy-duty bodyshell, specially reinforced around the suspension points and reworked to house a beefy Type E four-speed gearbox.

Indeed, most of the cars' underpinnings were identical. The uprated suspension that received so much praise was simply made up of Mk1 Escort RS/Capri-type front struts plus Mk2 Escort Sport rear leaf springs and a pair of radius rods rather than the standard saloon's anti-roll bar. The stock 9.62in front discs and Girling callipers were fitted, boosted by a bigger servo on RS-badged machines.

Under the bonnet, the RS2000's two-litre Pinto had been swapped for a 1593cc version of that big, heavy lump using all the same mountings and ancillaries. Which meant that

The rubber rear spoiler was always in place but the RS Mexico lacked the RS2000's and RS1800's satin black back panel.

A few little changes went a long, long way – RS Mexico's rear spoiler and sticker kit turned the basic Mk2 shape into a properly sexy beast.

although the engine was just a run-of-the-mill Cortina or Capri 1600S unit, it gained an extra 7bhp in the Escort thanks to the RS exhaust manifold and system. On paper, it provided figures of 94bhp at 5,750rpm, 92lb.ft torque at 4,000rpm, a top speed of 106mph and 0-to-60mph time of 10.2 seconds. On the road, well, it certainly felt considerably slower than its bigger brother.

Still, the RS Mexico's bodywork really set it apart from the droop-snoot Escort, reflecting the bobble-hatted style of contemporary competition cars rather than the RS2000's urban cool. It was based very closely on the Mk2 Sport, retaining the front quarter bumpers, blacked-out brightwork and even the same side stripes, albeit bearing the Mexico legend across the rear wings. Adding to the motorsport appeal was a pair of functional spoilers first seen on the RS1800, including colour-coded front bib and flexible rubber at the back.

Even the RS Mexico's wheels looked like the Sport's; despite being the half-inch wider sculptured sports steels seen on late Mk1 RS models, they were at a glance inseparable from those of the cheaper Mk2. Still, the RS Mexico was at least offered with the option of the four-spoke alloys that were fitted as standard to the RS2000.

Inside, the RS Mexico was a combination of other models. Most of the basic Sport trim remained, except for RS2000 instruments, steering wheel and black headlining, plus Scheel front seats. No Custom trim was available.

RS Mexico assembly began in November 1975, with the first cars hitting British roads in January '76. All RS Mexicos were built in Germany, accompanied by a GCAT-prefixed chassis number.

Few changes were made during production, although August 1977 saw the front grille's FORD lettering replaced with a blue oval, some bodywork colours were altered and various bits of chromework were swapped for black along the way.

The final RS Mexicos were constructed in July 1978 and officially dropped from the range on 13 September 1978, by which time an estimated total of 2,290 had left the lines.

Eventually, even Ford agreed the model was too similar in appearance and apparent performance to the (much cheaper and recently upgraded) Escort 1600 Sport. And there's no doubt most buyers happily paid the little-bit extra to get their hands on an altogether better-equipped RS2000 – which in some respect was a re-run of how the Mk1 Mexico's sales plummeted when the original RS2000 was released. The RS Mexico simply had to die.

Yet that was a real shame, because the RS Mexico had great, untapped potential. Okay, it had no competition history (unlike the Sport, which had a real motorsport career) but the RS Mexico was homologated by Ford, and always offered with the option of Rallye Sport accessories to construct a Group One or Two machine. And let's not forget, it formed the basis for most road-going RS1800s, which were built from already-completed RS Mexicos.

So when the RS Mexico was ousted from Ford price lists in favour of a base-spec RS2000 it was the unfortunate, untimely end to an iconic Escort (we'll pretend the awful Mexico limited edition of 1995 was a bad dream). Would history have been different if Ford had dropped the two-litre Pinto into the RS Mexico instead? Possibly so. And then the RS Mexico really could have been perfect.

Big Pinto powerplant slotted very neatly into the RS Mexico's engine bay, needing very few revisions to the metalwork or even an electric cooling fan.

Engine – Block, Head and Sump

Thousands of Escorts were built with 1600cc engines, but the RS Mexico was the only small Ford to receive the 1593cc, belt-driven, single overhead cam Pinto rather than its similar-sized Crossflow counterpart.

Not that the 1.6 Pinto was anything unusual. Far from it, in fact – the exact-same powerplant (known as the TL16G in increased-performance GT guise) was found in numerous other machines, most notably the Cortina and Capri 1600S.

Of course, the unit's outwardly identical big brother (the two-litre Pinto) was a familiar sight in both generations of the Escort RS2000, and it was on these cars that the RS Mexico was very closely based.

Use of the Cologne-built Pinto made a perfect case for constructing RS Mk2s in the Saarlouis plant, and sharing so many components was even better for Ford's budget. Yes, it's fair to say fitting the larger-capacity (1993cc) lump into the RS Mexico would have cost exactly the same, but it was more a question of marketing than giving buyers what they wanted…

What they received was a normal cast iron Pinto LEC-type cylinder block, painted semi-gloss black. The crankcase's part number 70HM6015AA was cast into the lower right-hand (exhaust) side of the block just in front of the exhaust-side engine mount; it stayed the same throughout production, as did the identification code – a 16 (for 1.6-litre, of course) – above it.

Higher up, the engine's own unique number was stamped on a machined face under the exhaust manifold; its digits were reflected on the car's VIN plate and matched the last part of its chassis number.

Pinto blocks also featured a date code cast into an oval on the lower right-hand-side of the block, immediately behind the engine mount. Its first number was its day of manufacture, the next character its month (A for January, B for February etc) and the next two related to the year (75 meaning 1975 and so on).

Mk2 RS Pinto sump was taken from the Mk1 RS2000, complete with embossed FORD lettering and H73HF part number; from June 1976 there was a cast Ford oval logo instead

Part number was found atop the header tank of replacement Ford radiators, and sometimes on factory-direct machines.

With all those codes on the outside, it was pretty easy to work out what was inside – in the RS Mexico's case a regular 1600S with 9.2:1 compression ratio, flat-topped alloy pistons and cast iron, counterweighted, five-bearing crankshaft. Exactly the same as any Cortina engine from the Cologne production line.

Likewise, the RS Mexico's cylinder head was the usual lump of Pinto-flavoured cast iron in semi-gloss black, with four individual exhaust ports on the right-hand side and four square inlet ports on the left. With the cam cover removed it was possible to see a large part number, identity code (6) above the rear spark plug, and year of production (in date clock) cast onto the head; it was also where you'd find the standard Pinto single camshaft (with less lift than the RS2000's and corresponding white colour code), which was driven by a toothed rubber belt. The eight valves, too, were standard parts, with face diameters measuring 38.5mm (inlet) and 34.2mm (exhaust), along with single valve springs. Lifting eyes were attached using the exhaust manifold studs.

Above the head was a ribbed camshaft cover painted mid-blue; its colour matched the front cover, which shrouded a toothed rubber timing belt (and was slightly different from the part used on two-litre Pintos). Across the top of the belt cover was often a white, red and black 1600HC sticker, although many early cars had none. Later RS Mexicos also lacked a decal when, from June 1976, their cam and cam belt covers were painted gloss black instead of blue.

A black plastic oil filler cap plugged the spout in the cam cover; early models used a Mk1 Escort-type with thin outer rim and 71HF part number moulded above a central Ford oval; later RS Mexicos (from around November 1977) had a chunkier cap with 79TF part number around the bottom, along with a Ford logo in the middle.

The RS Mexico's oil pump was the usual Pinto component, located inside the sump with central pickup pipe. Talking of which, to fit over the Escort's crossmember, a self-coloured Mk1 RS2000-type aluminium sump was used, including big wing protrusion at the back and anti-surge baffling inside, plus cast FORD lettering and H73HF-prefixed part number visible underneath.

A slightly revised sump was used from June 1976, which had a cast Ford oval logo on the underside and H77HM part number. Again, the sump was unique to the Escort RS Mexico and RS2000, along with the sump plug and red-handled dipstick, which was found at the rear of the engine on the passenger side.

The oil filter was a disposable cartridge screwed into the left-hand side of the cylinder block; there was no oil cooler from the factory, but RS1800-type Rallye Sport parts were available from dealers.

Like the Mk2 RS2000, the RS Mexico's engine was fitted onto special alloy mounts rather than the Mk1's; a longer mount was fitted onto the nearside, with a shorter version below the exhaust manifold; there were cast part numbers pointing towards the front of the car.

As part of the Rallye Sport accessories range, a big-valve cylinder head and high-lift cam were readily available – but it's unlikely any RS Mexicos received such goodies on the production line.

Cooling System

A 10.15-pint cooling system was fitted to the RS Mexico, which shared its setup with the Mk2 RS2000.

Up front was a large-capacity radiator, which occasionally wore its part number (H75AB-8005AA) on the upper nearside of the header tank. Unlike a standard Escort rad, it featured an agled top outlet plus satin black tank, black fins and overflow outlet pointing towards the offside front, extended downwards in a green plastic tube. The cap was a normal Escort 13psi part and even the coolant hoses were mostly the same as its Mk1 predecessors' – again in black rubber with wire hose clips.

The RS Mexico used a regular Pinto water pump in bare alloy, which mounted on the front of the engine and carried the usual yellow, seven-blade, plastic fan; unlike the Mk1 RS2000 it was a mechanical rather than electric unit.

The fan matched the Mk2 RS2000's, as did the RS Mexico's wax thermostat, which lived in a unique bare-alloy Escort housing.

High-capacity coolant radiator was slotted into specially recessed slam panel; note brake servo hard pipe clipped in front.

Simple but it got the job done – RS Mexico's twin-choke Weber 32/36 DGAV was the same as several other sporty Fords', jetted to suit different models.

Weber carbs originally wore a metal dog tag to denote identity and application.

Fuel System

Sticking to the formula for a refined and reliable Rallye Sport range, the RS Mexico forwent twin carburettors in favour of a single Weber with automatic choke. Like the Mk2 RS2000 (and the Mk1 before it, and the 1600 Sport) the chosen carb was a twin-choke downdraught Weber 32/36 DGAV; of course, it was rejetted for the 1600cc Pinto (with 130/120 mains), thus requiring a different part number – but it was otherwise the same.

The carburettor originally came with a metal identity tag attached to a float chamber screw, along with a code on the side that displayed its model number and internal calibration; it was also stamped to say it was made in Italy.

The RS Mexico and RS2000 shared the same inlet manifold – a cast alloy Ford-made Pinto part – along with identical Granada/Consul (left-hand drive) throttle cable and Capri bracket rather than the Mk1 RS2000's.

Above the carb was a blue plastic air cleaner housing with moveable intake and disposable paper filter, as found on contemporary 1.6 and two-litre Capris. It was swapped in June 1976 for a bare black plastic airbox of the same design.

A regular Cortina-sourced AC mechanical diaphragm fuel pump was mounted on the left-hand side of the engine underneath the distributor; it had a bare metal finish and connected with black rubber pipework – which was unique to the Pinto-engined Mk2 Escort. So too was the routing for the RS Mexico's fuel lines, which were clipped to its nearside chassis rail, rather than the opposite side on Crossflow-powered cars.

Like the RS2000, the RS Mexico was offered with a host of extras through Rallye Sport dealers prior to registration; a pair of 44IDF Weber carburettors and Group One airbox were actively encouraged for the Mex.

Exhaust System

Pinto cylinder heads were designed with their breathing setup on the opposite side to the Kent Crossflow units found in most Escorts, so the RS Mexico (and RS2000) required a completely different exhaust system from the regular Mk2.

At the front was a special cast iron exhaust manifold, designed for better flow characteristics than the regular Pinto part and attributed by Ford to a 7bhp gain over the identically-engined Capri 1600S. Finished in dark grey, the manifold featured a raised RS logo (with entwined letters) rather than the visually-similar Group One Mk1 manifold's individual RS lettering. A small heat shield was fitted above it to protect the rear three spark plug leads.

The RS manifold fed a twin-tube mild steel downpipe, which then connected to a large-bore exhaust system – all finished in aluminiumised silver-grey colour. The system switched sides (offside to nearside) underneath the gearbox, leading into an oval centre silencer and oval back box.

Special exhaust manifold was designed for the Pinto-powered Mk2, complete with neat RS logo.

Exhaust centre silencer was an oval box dangling from a twin-rubber mounting welded to the floorpan underneath the back seat.

Oval exhaust backbox was supported on a normal-type hanger mounted further back on the chassis rail than the usual Mk2 Escort's.

Special welded bracket kept the speedometer cable away from the hot RS downpipe, which ran on the opposite side from Crossflow-powered cars.

The first of these hung on a twin-hook mounting from a bracket welded to the floorpan on a strengthener under the back seat, just in front of the rear axle and aligned with the passenger-side seat belt fixing. Meanwhile, the back box had a regular J-shaped hanger arrangement, connected to a rubber on a bracket bolted to the nearside chassis rail further back than on a Crossflow-powered car.

Ignition and Electrical System

German origins meant the RS Mexico used quite a few Bosch components, although British-market Lucas and Motorcraft parts were often found on official spec lists.

At the front of the car, in the nearside corner (of all but the few left-hand-drive Mexicos) was a square-post Motorcraft 55Ah battery, fixed onto the normal Mk2 tray with the usual chunky-type black clamp. Its red positive lead was similar to the standard Escort part (there were two different lengths, swapped in February 1978), complete with blue-and-white Ford labels; its black negative cable was the same on all right-hand-drive Escorts.

The rest of the wiring loom was essentially identical to the RS2000's (and 1600 Sport's, for that matter), but could vary depending on specification. It was wrapped in grey loom tape until around August 1976, when black tape took over.

The fuse box was identical throughout the Escort range, featuring seven continental fuses under a clear plastic cover (with raised German lettering) and a black cover above. It was mounted on top of the bulkhead on the passenger side.

RS Mexicos were listed with a variety of starter motors (including a pre-engaged Bosch 0.7 or Lucas 5M90, or even Nippondenso between August and October 1977) but most (if not all production cars) were fitted with a Lucas M35J plus Lucas solenoid mounted on the inner wing.

A Motorcraft nine-volt ballasted ignition coil was intended for UK shores, but a Bosch coil was generally fitted instead (especially from 1977), with black body, Ford oval logo and orangey-brown top. It sat inside a bare alloy bracket affixed to the inner wing.

Plug leads on the RS Mexico were the usual Pinto parts in black siliconised rubber, complete with printed white numbering, black end caps and coil separator. A set of Motorcraft BF22 spark plugs was screwed into the head.

At the other end of the leads was a Motorcraft distributor with black cap – although, again, Bosch was generally found on later cars. Essentially the RS Mexico used an RS2000 distributor, although it came with a slightly different part number and advance.

Charging duties were taken care of by a 45-amp alternator, found at the right-hand front of the engine. It was reckoned to be a Lucas 18 ACR but until August 1976 cars came with a 55-amp Bosch. Like the Mk2 RS2000, the RS Mexico had an otherwise-unique aluminium alloy alternator bracket with rubber bushings.

Until August 1976 there was an external voltage regulator box mounted on the RS Mexico's inner wing, with short section of wiring loom connecting it through the normal alternator plug.

RS Mexicos were fitted with 45-amp alternators made by either Lucas or Bosch.

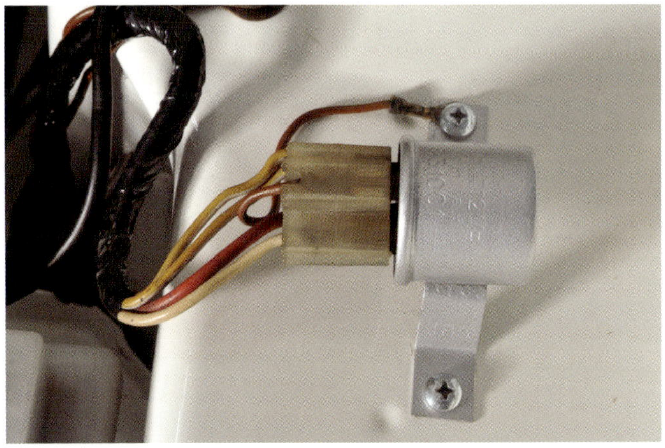

Where driving lamps were factory-fitted, the auxiliary lighting relay was screwed to the RS Mexico's nearside inner wing; on this car it wasn't standard.

Transmission

The RS Mexico shared its entire transmission system with the Mk2 RS2000, which itself was just a revision of the Mk1 and similar Pinto-powered, blue oval-badged machinery.

Principally, that meant a Type E four-speed manual gearbox – again German-made, meaning Saarlouis production of the UK-only RS Mexico almost made sense...

The Type E was a long, relatively bulky unit with black, cast iron casing, aluminium alloy tail housing and pressed alloy top cover – exactly what was found in thousands of contemporary 1.6 and two-litre Cortinas, Capris and Granadas. The difference was the Escort's bellhousing, which was an aluminium alloy component as used in the Mk1 RS2000, complete with H73AB part number and provision for left- or right-handed starter motor mounting; the unused hole contained a large blanking grommet.

Inside, the gear ratios were identical, with first 3.651:1, second 1.968:1, third 1.368:1, fourth 1:1 and reverse 3.66:1. Reverse was over to the left and forward towards the dash, while a quickshift mechanism was made specifically for the RS Escort using a modified gearstick (in black at first, then swapped for chrome on later cars) with raised pivot point and adapted Cortina rod-change mechanism.

Like the RS2000, the RS Mexico featured a cable-operated Borg and Beck 8.5in diaphragm spring clutch – reckoned by Ford to be heavy-duty but in reality the regular Pinto clutch plate and pressure plate (with 74BB part numbers), along with normal 70HM Cortina flywheel. The clutch cable was a left-hand-drive Crossflow component.

The gearbox was positioned within the usual Mk2 Escort transmission tunnel, albeit with one or two alterations. At the bulkhead end it was tapped back to clear the bellhousing. On top, the tunnel was revised to make room for the gearstick, which was found further back towards the rear seat; it was achieved by cutting a hole in the tunnel and spot-welding in a large plate with pressed gear lever aperture – always a neat, factory-fitted finish rather than the rough-and-ready effect of Mk1 RS2000s.

Standard Mk2 fuse box positioned within bulkhead pad cutout – where fitted, of course...

Similarly, though, the transmission tunnel stiffener was heavily cut back to make room for the hole. And to drop the back of the 'box enough for installation, a pair of spacer blocks was used between the normal Mk2 mounting brackets and gearbox crossmember; again like the Mk1 RS2000's but now in aluminium alloy.

Oh, and not forgetting, too, that spot-welded neatly to the offside floorpan, very close to the tunnel, was a small bracket designed to hold the RS Mexico's speedometer cable away from its exhaust manifold.

Transferring power to the back end was a two-piece propshaft with constant velocity joint and centre bearing. It mated to a Timken hypoid bevel rear axle featuring brackets for a pair of radius rods. The removable differential had a 3.545:1 final drive ratio, with 11 teeth on the pinion and 39 on the crown wheel.

Alternative ratios were readily available from Rallye Sport dealers (including 3.77:1 and 4.44:1) and Ford even offered an optional Salisbury limited-slip differential. By and large, though, most RS Mexicos came with the same standard spec.

RS Mexico front suspension was a mild development of the Mk1 RS. There was a 22mm anti-roll bar with lowered mounting brackets and metric Mk2 steering rack.

Front struts and brakes were Capri-type, as seen on the Mk1 RS. Sachs supplied the standard oil-filled dampers.

Suspension and Steering

The RS Mexico was always commended for its easy-going, well-balanced handling, but that was really no surprise. Its underpinnings were pure RS2000, which were simply a development of the circuit-bred Mk1.

Up front was essentially the same Capri-based suspension, featuring satin black Macpherson struts and integral oil-filled Fichtel and Sachs shock absorbers with black dust covers and blue-and-white colour code. They were accompanied by 277mm, 130lb front springs in satin black with brown-and-grey colour code and plastic protectors at the ends of each coil.

Late-spec Mk1 strut tops were used until February 1977, when they were replaced with smaller, offset versions. Both types were finished in semi-gloss black with black collars,

RS Mexico's Timken rear axle was identical to the RS2000's, complete with 3.545:1 differential and radius rod brackets.

Sport multi-leaf rear springs were good enough for the RS Mexico, only now the axle was held stable with a pair of radius rods rather than the lesser Escort's anti-roll bar arrangement.

and were dabbed with brightly- coloured paint around the securing bolts to confirm they'd been tightened to the correct torque settings.

At the bottom of each suspension leg was an imperial-sized, bolted-on steering arm; there was a standard, 17.9:1 ratio, metric Mk2 steering rack and metric-threaded track rod ends with imperial tapers. The steering column was regular Escort with Sport steering gear shaft joint, while May 1976 brought an updated coupling. A Rallye Sport option was a high-ratio quick rack.

Spanning the front suspension was an RS Mk2 22mm anti-roll bar, which came with lowered brackets. Meanwhile, the front crossmember was the same as the RS2000's, complete with repositioned track control arm mounts (they were raised by around 10mm) and strengthening plates – which were similar in purpose to the Mk1 RS2000's but welded with a factory finish. Sitting on the crossmember was a pair of alloy engine mounts.

At the back of an RS Mexico the suspension was remarkably normal. A live rear axle was connected on U-bolts to a pair of Escort Sport semi-elliptic, 116lb, three-leaf rear springs, which were 60mm wide and had a red, lilac (or yellow) and white colour code. Damping was taken care of by upright Boge telescopic shock absorbers. All the components were coated in shades of satin black.

Of course, on the RS Mexico the standard Mk2's rear anti-roll bar was ousted and replaced by a pair of radius arms, which coupled the axle to the car's floorpan in factory-welded brackets at each end.

Brakes

Although Ford was keen to shout about brakes that were 'designed to withstand the extra speed,' there was nothing particularly special about the RS Mexico's dual-line stopping system.

At the front was a pair of the usual Mk2 Escort silver/gold-coloured Girling M16 callipers with 54mm pistons, metric pipe fittings and Ferodo 2445 pads, which grabbed onto the regular Capri-derived Girling 247.5mm solid front discs.

The rears were also relatively normal, having black-painted, self-adjusting 9x1.75in drums, 19mm wheel cylinders and Ferodo shoes; the back plates lacked a shoe inspection slot. Like other Escorts, though, the RS Mexico's brake lines comprised black Girling flexible hoses and silver/zinc-coloured Bundy mild steel tubing.

The biggest alteration from a run-of-the-mill Mk2 stopping system was found in the RS Mexico's offside engine bay, where a bigger (7in) brake servo was fitted in place of the standard car's 6in booster. Like the Mk2 RS2000 – and very similar to the previous late-spec Mexico and RS2000 – the early RS Mexico featured a Girling Hydrovac setup with black servo drum, fitted on the usual satin black Mk2 in-line bracket on the inner wing.

RS Mexico inner wings always had heavy-duty strut tops with reinforcing plates; these large apertures were used until February 1977, when small strut tops were fitted instead.

There was a 19.05mm master cylinder (20.64mm from spring 1976), which was zinc-coloured until early 1977, when it became black. Above was a white plastic reservoir with red cap; a red plastic band wrapped around the master cylinder.

December 1977 saw a swap from the Girling to an ATE servo, which sported a black master cylinder, square-edged reservoir and black plastic cap. It mounted to the same black bracket on the inner wing. The black servo drum was equipped with a white-lettering-on-blue ATE sticker (in a sometimes random position).

The silver-zinc coloured brake vacuum pipe, which clipped to the slam panel behind the radiator, was now redesigned to access the ATE from below, rather than the Girling's top entry.

Girling 7in brake servo was found in the engine bay's offside front corner, complete with 20.6mm zinc-coloured master cylinder; on later cars it was black.

RS Mexicos were often specced with RS2000-type four-spoke alloys, as this press shot demonstrates; note the Dove Grey spoke centres.

Wheels and Tyres

Reverting to steel wheels rather than the new RS2000's standard alloys was an obvious way for Ford marketers to highlight pricing differences between the two cars – although RS four-spokes were often fitted from new.

Buyers who paid list price received Silver Fox-painted 5.5x13in sculptured sports steels similar to those found on many Capris and Mk1 AVO machines. Mk2 versions were slightly changed from their predecessors, though, featuring four cutout sections where the rear faces attached to the inner rims and a lighter overall weight. They were also stamped with their size, part number and a Ford oval logo between their bolt holes.

Steel wheels wore dished black metal centre caps with a silver RS logo in the typical Mk2 entwined design. They were fastened on with a set of black, metric M12x1.5 wheel nuts and were wrapped in Pirelli CN36 Cinturato 175/70SR13 radial tyres rather than the RS2000's H-rated rubber; sometimes, though, 175/70HR13s were fitted by Ford, and sometimes in Goodyear G800 guise.

Similar to several other Ford sculptured sports wheels, the stock RS Mexico 5.5x13in steels had a wide, flat rim; Silver Fox was the colour, with black caps and wheel nuts.

Standard 5.5x13in wheels closely resembled Mk1 AVO steels but with cutouts inside where the rims were welded to the faces.

When alloys were specified from the factory, the RS Mexico left Saarlouis wearing the same deep-dished 6x13in four-spokes found on the RS2000, including polished/bare alloy rims, Dove Grey spoke cutouts and black, face-mounted centre caps with the usual silver RS motif. The 13x6J size was cast onto one spoke, with another spoke wearing a pair of circles featuring month and year number identifiers – which were normally one or two months before the car's build date.

It's worth noting that these wheels looked similar to later Capri 6x13in alloys but featured thinner spoke webs plus flat seats for their chrome, metric nuts, which had integral flat (rather than tapered) washers.

As usual, Rallye Sport dealers were happy to supply a choice of optional wheels, and it's entirely plausible to suggest some RS Mexicos were fitted with alloys after manufacture but before registration – including RS four-spokes in 6x13in to 7.5x13in sizes; it's probable such rims came with H-rated tyres too.

Bodywork

Easily mistaken for a Mk2 Sport, the RS Mexico was in fact built around a greatly revised bodyshell. Still, why should such trivialities stop Ford from saving a few pennies here and there? The RS Mexico took most of its styling cues from its run-of-the-mill sibling, and even its stickers were all but identical to the Sport's.

Most of the changes were found beneath the skin: the RS Mexico featured strengthened front suspension towers with reinforced tops, reworked transmission tunnel, beefed-up rear chassis rails, radius rod mounting points, repositioned exhaust hangers and neat brackets for the speedometer cable and spare wheel strap.

But by far the most noticeable external alterations were the RS Mexico's functional front and rear spoilers, claimed by Ford to reduce front-end lift by up to 25 per cent and 57 per cent at the rear. On the back was a flexible rubber RS rear spoiler, in bare matt-black aside from the very first RS Mexico prototype, which was possibly RS1800-based and wore a colour-coded component. The nose featured a wrap around airdam painted in body colour. Until mid-1976 it was made from fibreglass, attached with pop rivets through the inner wheelarch lips (one on each side) and four nuts underneath; sometime during 1976 the fibreglass spoiler was binned in favour of an almost identical polyurethane version, which added a screwed fitting at each front corner.

The RS Mexico used a standard Escort MK2 front panel, complete with black-painted section behind the grille – which was always black plastic with silver-painted highlights on the surround and central bar. Bolted onto the front panel was a pair of satin black Sport quarter bumpers without overriders;

RS Mexicos had two-speed windscreen wipers plus intermittent control; very early cars wore chrome beading within the windscreen rubber.

Early cars had FORD lettering on the grille, along with silver-sprayed centre bar and surround. A blue oval was found on the grille from August 1977.

there was a matching black rear bumper, which also lost the Sport's overriders.

Unlike the RS1800 and RS2000, the RS Mexico wasn't equipped with a black back panel. It did, though, have the sporty models' satin black paintwork around the window surrounds, door frames and B-pillars, edged up to the rain gutters and aligned along the bottom with the window rubbers. Chrome trims were clipped onto the drip rails until spring 1976 (most likely around March), when they were replaced with heat-set black epoxy. The windscreen rubbers were also dressed with chrome beading until being replaced by black during spring 1976. Satin black windscreen wipers were fitted throughout production, with two speeds plus intermittent control (which, incidentally, was available only on RS models prior to August 1976) and electric screen washers as standard.

A laminated front windscreen was also factory equipment, along with a heated rear 'screen. Green tinted glass was available at extra cost, as were opening front quarter lights. RS Mexico windows were made by Sekurit rather than the Triplex-manufactured glass found on British Escorts (despite the probably-mocked-up 1976 Rallye Sport brochure car wearing Triplex).

A black vinyl roof was a fairly common RS Mexico optional extra, although some were fitted in the UK before registration rather than on the Saarlouis production line; likewise, a Webasto sliding sunroof was available from new but only through dealers.

Early RS Mexicos were supplied with chrome door handles and locks, but by spring 1976 (again, probably around March) they'd been swapped for a plated satin black finish; lock barrels always matched between the doors, ignition and boot. Talking of which, the RS Mexico's boot lock was chrome until October 1977, when black was usually (but not always) fitted instead.

A pair of satin black, fixed door mirrors came as standard, with a remote-control driver's mirror available at extra cost. Cars supplied with an optional factory-fitted radio were also equipped with a chrome Ford-branded retractable aerial in the offside front wing. An electric aerial kit was offered as a dealer accessory, while some dealers fitted roof-mounted aerials instead.

By and large, RS Mexicos had black-painted sills and spare wheel well, but a few early cars (probably only a couple of the 1975-built press machines) were finished in body colour.

As for the badging, RS Mexicos featured individual FORD lettering on the radiator grille until August 1977, when a Ford

RS Mexico coachlines were shared with the Escort Sport except for this big, bold motif on each rear wing. Decals were standard, with no factory delete option.

Although the Escort Sport was offered with a variety of stripe colours, the RS Mexico's decals were either black or silver – and there was no delete option.

RS Mexico pinstripes were based on the Sport's, ending abruptly on the front wings. Radiator grille protruded slightly from its recess.

Standard passenger-side door mirror was satin black and adjustable only from outside. No remote-control option was offered on the Mk2 Escort.

Chrome door handles were used on the RS Mexico until spring 1976, when the more usual satin black took over.

Chromed metal 1.6 badges were fitted to the lower front wings of early RS Mexicos. Black plastic 1.6 badges arrived in August 1976, until they were deleted a year later.

Black door handles were normally found on the RS Mexico; they'd become standard kit in early 1976.

Non-locking petrol cap was the normal Mk2 pressed steel part, painted body colour.

Like all sporty Mk2s, the RS Mexico's window surrounds were satin black; unlike most sporty Mk2s, early cars wore a chrome drip rail cover.

oval logo took the position. On the front wings behind each wheel was a 1.6 badge, which came in chrome metal until August 1976 when black plastic took over. From August 1977 the badges were dropped altogether in favour of an engine-size tag on the nearside of the boot lid. It was fitted to the right of a satin black Escort badge, which in August 1977 switched to a bigger, wider version. At the same time, satin black FORD letters beneath the boot lock were deleted and replaced with a blue Ford oval on the boot lid's offside.

Until then, an intertwined Mexico decal was found on the offside of the boot lid, but from August 1977 it appeared to the right of the 1.6 badge. A larger version of the Mexico graphic was found on the car's rear wings at the same height as its back lights. It wrapped into a mildly reworked version of the Sport's sticker kit, comprising pinstripe tape along the bonnet and body sides, wrapping slightly into the door shuts. Unlike the Sport, though, RS Mexico decals were restricted to just two colours – black or silver, the latter from December 1976 onwards.

Mexico legend was slapped proudly on the bootlid's offside; rear lights on German-sourced models were Altissimo rather than Butlers of British-built machines.

Almost an icon in its own right, the RS Mexico's rubber boot spoiler was the same part found on Mk2 RS2000s and most RS1800s.

A chrome boot lock was found on German-built Escorts until replaced by a black version in October 1977; FORD badging was generally black too.

Late-spec RS Mexico boot badge and boot sticker, as seen from August 1977 onwards.

Underbonnet

Rather neat and all very civilized – under the bonnet of an RS Mexico it wasn't immediately obvious that this was anything but a mainstream model. Okay, the 1.6-litre Cortina lump was pretty tall, but there was none of that hot-rod approach found on earlier AVO-built Escorts.

The battery was in the correct position (on the stock Mk2 tray in the nearside front corner of the engine bay), the brake servo was piped tidily into the opposite side, and even the radiator looked made to measure.

But that's not to say everything was identical to a Popular Plus. Far from it, in fact. That big rad was slotted into a specially redesigned cowling/slam panel with the middle cut out, allowing it to sit further forward than usual (giving room for the regular cooling fan); beneath it, the radiator cross-member box section was modified to suit.

Running along the cowling, and clipped to the back of the slam panel was the RS Mexico's black plastic-coated bonnet release cable, routed along the offside inner wing under the drip rail. The galvanised bonnet prop was hinged from the offside slam panel, and fastened into a white plastic clip on the opposite corner.

The RS Mexico's slam panel was also home to its VIN plate, found in front of the brake servo. All RS Mexicos had a vehicle identity number beginning with GCAT but many (pre-1977 cars) said BATR in the Type box; all others read GATR.

Between the chassis plate and bonnet release mechanism was a grey E11 lighting emissions sticker, which was swapped for a purple rectangular version during 1976. On the other side of the slam panel was the RS Mexico's build plate, which listed colour and specification details in Ford's Saarlouis (rather than Halewood) layout.

RS Mexico inner wings were the heavy-duty type with suspension top reinforcement plates. The round apertures for each strut were reduced in size during February 1977, switching from 105mm to 85mm diameter. All RS Mexicos had a GCAT-prefixed chassis number hand-stamped into the offside reinforcing plate, masked roughly into a rectangle and protected with primer-grey paint. Early cars were usually seen with a Mk1 Escort-type black-on-white engine coolant decal on the offside inner wing top, although this practice stopped during 1976.

Affixed to the same strut tower was the car's opaque plastic washer fluid reservoir, which attached via a black metal bracket bolted to the inner wing. It also contained an electric pump in plain black or gold with a printed black Ford oval logo; the pump squirted the car's windscreen via plastic tubing, a white plastic T-piece and copper nozzles pointing through the scuttle panel. Beneath it, like other Mk2s, the RS Mexico's bulkhead was pressed with five square dimples until February 1977, when seven were found there instead. A special hole for an oil pressure pipe was sited in front of the driver under the bulkhead drip rail, close to the heater hoses.

Sitting atop the bulkhead of the earliest RS Mexicos was a Ghia-spec Escort engine compartment cowl, in black foam with passenger-side fuse box cutout, screwed into the panel above the bulkhead drain tube. Although it was officially an RS Mexico part, few – if any – later cars were fitted with the pad.

The RS Mexico's bulkhead wasn't trimmed back like BDA-engined machines, but its transmission tunnel was often slightly bashed inwards to allow gearbox clearance where it met the bulkhead.

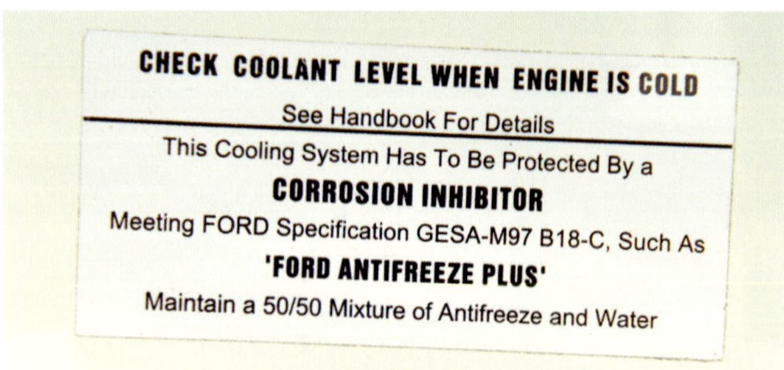

Mk1 Escort-type engine coolant decal was stuck onto the offside inner wing of early RS Mexicos.

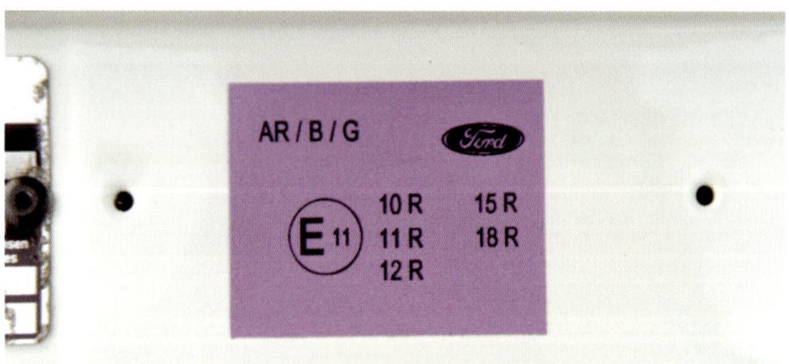

E11 lighting emissions sticker was found on halogen headlamp-equipped Mk2s; this is the wide purple rectangle used from 1976.

Red-handled dipstick was shared with the early Mk2 RS2000, as was the special alloy sump it read from.

Lighting

Proper Escort rally cars sported a pair of circular 7in headlamps, and the RS Mexico was no exception. Unlike its bigger brother the RS2000, here was the traditional fast Ford fitment in flat-lens, Lucas, semi-sealed beam halogen guise, complete with 60/55w H4 bulbs. Each lamp wore the word Lucas embossed on the glass and a blue H4 sticker in the centre.

Although the RS Mexico officially lacked them, it was readily available with the Escort Sport's long-range driving lamps, sold in pairs and fitted using black brackets; the lamps had chrome-plated backs, although Ford accessories swapped to black in November 1979. When factory-specified they were accompanied by a relay screwed into the nearside inner wing, complete with extra section of wiring loom.

Everything else about the lighting setup was standard Mk2 kit. In the front quarter bumpers was a pair of orange-lens Altissimo indicators, complete with hazard warning flashers.

The rear lamps were Altissimo-made clusters with integral reversing lights. Early RS Mexicos were fitted with a single number plate lamp in the centre of the back bumper, which was swapped for two during 1976 – probably around August.

A rear fog lamp was an option from the factory or dealer. Dangled from the offside rear valance, it was an Altissimo Ford-branded unit, which came with a suitable rocker switch (with red warning light) slotted into the car's fascia.

The RS Mexico was also available with an optional luggage compartment light under the rear parcel shelf, but the cockpit lighting was standard Escort. That meant a later-type Mk2 courtesy lamp above the rear-view mirror, complete with black override switch; the A-pillars contained a pair of black plastic door control buttons.

Interior

True to type, the RS Mexico followed the purest fast Escort tradition of sombre, stripped-out cockpit with only bucket seats, a sporty steering wheel and extra gauges to keep the driver committed to the task in hand.

Well that was the theory, although by the time of Mk2 production most owners demanded a little more than rubber matting on the floor.

Still, with only one trim level – always in black – and no offer of a Custom pack, the RS Mexico was fairly basic compared to the RS2000. A glovebox was never available, and even reclining seats weren't supposed to be standard – Ford intended the RS Mexico to boast a pair of 'tight-fitting competition' non-reclining, low-back buckets with harness slots, vertically-stitched black Beta cloth trim and provision for optional head rests (just plugged with caps instead). Some pre-production cars even wore basic Sport cloth seats with fixed backs, and some with no headrests.

In practice, the buckets became a no-cost option and most cars were supplied with RS2000-type Scheel high-back recliners, complete with curvy side bolsters; they also featured black Beta cloth trim with horizontal block pattern and vertical stitching that ended halfway down the squabs plus, at their bases, black plastic wheels to recline their backs. Inside the covers, some seats included a brown cardboard tag denoting a manufacturing date of a month or two before the car's production, and some were date-stamped underneath. The Scheels were topped with roll-top head rests as standard, again in black Beta cloth with horizontal block pattern and Velcro fasteners across their bottom edges.

In the back of an RS Mexico was a matching black Beta

Lucas H4 halogen headlamps and quarter bumpers matched the Escort Sport but on the RS Mexico spot lamps were deleted.

Blue H4 halogen decal was seen in the centre of RS Mexico headlamps, made for Ford by Lucas.

Pretty basic and very black – RS Mexico's cockpit offered little luxury but a perfect driving position. This car's dished steering wheel was a Rallye Sport accessory.

cloth-trimmed bench seat in Escort L specification with dual vertical stitching and horizontal block pattern, although to accompany the roll-top recliners some early cars (perhaps only until March 1976) had the extra-padded GL back seat with single vertical stitching. Black vinyl pads covered the inner wheelarches at each side.

Base-level door cards and rear quarter panels were always used, which revealed the car's painted body colour across the top. In the back they were black with small, swivelling black plastic ashtrays in each side. The fronts were black vinyl with vertical double stitch lines and small black vinyl armrests. The internal door release handles were black plastic with black frames, while the window winders were the regular chrome parts with black plastic knobs and inserts. The door lock pins were black plastic with flared heads, being ousted in favour of slimmer versions in August 1977.

Remote-control driver's door mirror was a relatively rare optional extra, always painted satin black; early cars had chrome lever and escutcheon.

When a remote-control driver's door mirror was specified, the internal control would be a chrome knob within a chrome escutcheon fitted into a specifically-made door card; all cars from May 1977 featured a black knob and escutcheon to accompany the remote mirror.

The RS Mexico's dashboard was little different from the Sport's, finished in satin black steel with a black vinyl pad across the top. There was no option of a pressed cutout for a Custom-type passenger-side cubby box. Nor was there a plastic glovebox under the dashboard – the RS Mexico made do with L-spec black cardboard parcel shelves with padded vinyl edging on driver's and passenger's sides.

At the centre of the dashboard was an illuminated heater control panel, which featured a black plastic bezel with silver-highlighted surround and foil indicator diagram, plus two-speed heater/demister switch and black plastic tempera-

RS2000-type Scheel seats tipped forward with a plastic lever and reclined using a handwheel at the base; their faces were Beta fabric-trimmed but the backs were black vinyl.

ture sliders. In October 1976 the diagram was swapped when the hot and cold positions changed places, along with the metal heater box being replaced by a quieter, two-piece plastic item. At each side of the dashboard was a rotating black plastic eyeball vent with silver-painted rim.

Under the heater controls was a black plastic fascia panel, which was home to the RS Mexico's rocker switches and swivelling ashtray in between. From left to right (depending on the car's specification) they were: blanking plate, hazard flasher switch (swapped in autumn 1976 for an upright instead of inverted warning triangle), cigar lighter (fitted as standard, and changed from long-neck/deep-reach Mk1 type with silver label to a more flush design with white-printed diagram during April 1977), heated rear window switch (with an updated diagram and warning lamp in autumn 1976) and blank for (optional) fog light switch with red warning lamp. A factory rocker switch was also used for long-range lamps, slotted into one of the blank spaces. On the far side (well, on the steering column shroud) was a circular blanking plug in place of a normal Mk2's choke control knob.

If an RS Mexico came with a factory-fitted (optional) radio, it was housed in a black plastic mount affixed to the underside of the fascia switch panel. The usual unit was a push-button Ford P21 MW/LW, although several other radios and cassette players were offered from Ford dealers prior to delivery – they included a manual-tune multi-band M32, multi-wave push-button P32, high-performance P42, or an RST-21 or 22 stereo tape player. None was ever fitted as standard to the RS Mexico, but factory-optional radios were accompanied by a chrome retractable aerial in the offside front wing plus speaker in the dashboard top.

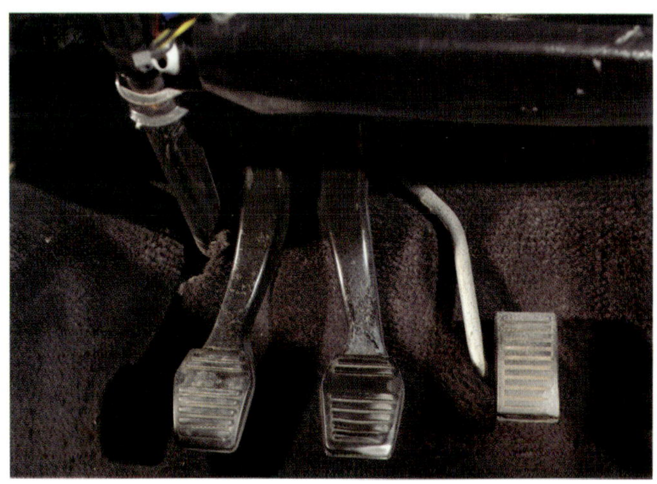

Like other Mk2s, the RS Mexico was fitted with a stock pedal box, including black plastic pad on the angled accelerator lever.

Rear-view mirror was the regular Mk2 part but with a black internal cover. Note this early car's chrome windscreen beading, which was ditched in early 1976.

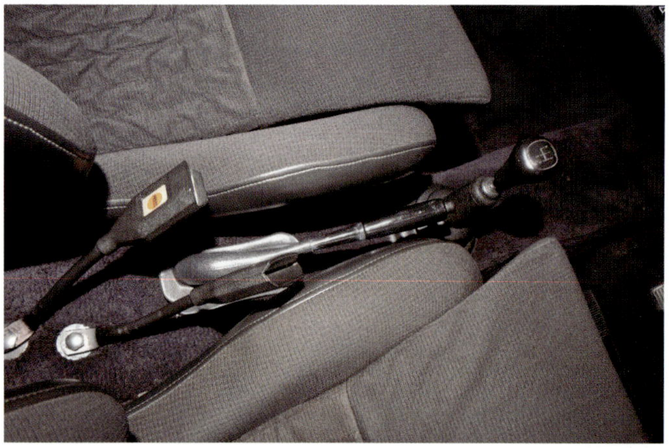

Handbrake lever and seat belt stalks were standard Mk2 equipment, but the gearknob was restricted to the Escort RS (oh, okay, and late-model Sport. And Harrier. And some Capris...).

RS instrument bezel boasted silver rim until it was phased out in 1976; just before production ended, the RS Mexico gained orange rather than white needles.

Early heater controls had this layout, swapping hot to the left-hand position in October 1976. Cigarette lighter came as standard, although early cars used a long-reach Mk1 part.

Likewise, the RS Mexico was not equipped with a centre console, but it wasn't unusual for owners to order one from a Ford dealer – possibly the RS2000 component but more likely what Ford described as an 'accessory type' (similar to the Ghia design) with clock, speaker or cassette box.

RS Mexico instruments were taken from the RS2000, comprising a black instrument binnacle (with silver rim until it was deleted during 1976) containing round rev counter (7,000rpm and no red line) on the left and 120mph speedometer on the right; both gauges were black with white digits and white needles; the speedo included trip and mileage displays, along with small, yellow kilometres-per-hour numbers. During mid 1978 (probably not long before RS Mexico production ceased) the dials were updated with slightly smaller numbers, orange needles and speedo with 140mph maximum and white KPH digits.

Between the two large dials were three small, circular dials for fuel (with markings for 0, 1/2 and 4/4, which were deleted around October 1977), water temperature and oil pressure, again with white lettering and white needles – until mid 1978, when orange needles took over. Beneath them was a strip of warning lights, which from left to right were: left-hand indicators, main beam, decorative RS logo, ignition, right-hand indicators.

That RS logo was repeated on the steering wheel, impressed into a black plastic centre cap. The rest of the wheel was a Sport-type 14in three-spoke with mock-leather covering and flat, black spokes. From February 1977 the centre cap was swapped for the standard Sport design with blue Ford oval logo.

Black headlining was the same material used in AVO-built Mk1 Escorts; passenger vanity mirror was standard in the RS Mexico.

RS Mexico was meant to come with base-spec seats, but this high-level GL type bench was found in the earliest examples.

Behind the wheel was a black plastic steering column shroud and three stalks; on the left was one for indicators, single low-pitch horn (wiring was present behind the radiator grille for dual-tone horns), headlamp dip and flash; on the right was a small headlight stalk plus a larger one for the two-speed windscreen wipers, which also boasted intermittent control.

The RS Mexico used a standard Mk2 pedal box. It included satin black brake and clutch levers with Mk1 Escort-type rubber pads (featuring horizontal pattern); the cranked accelerator lever was silver-coloured and had a matching black plastic pad.

Each front footwell contained a black plastic kick panel, overlapped by ribbed aluminium scuff plates on the inner sills (into which were tucked the black door rubbers) and one-piece black carpet. RS Mexicos built before August 1976 (and possibly some later cars too) contained RS2000-type luxury matting, although most RS Mexicos lost the cut-pile carpet; instead they included a standard Escort-type loop-pile affair but with the gearstick hole positioned further back.

Above the transmission tunnel was a black gear lever gaiter wrapping around a chrome gearstick (many were black during 1976) topped with a Capri-type knob, which had the usual Mk2 Escort pattern of reverse to the left and towards the front. Behind it was a standard, black Mk2 handbrake lever with black push button and gaiter, just in front of the black plastic-coated seat belt stalks with gold-and-red release buttons. The RS Mexico was supposedly equipped with static front seat belts as standard (albeit at extra cost), but most were supplied with optional inertia-reels. By 1977 the front inertia-reel seat belts were standard, with statics available for a reduced price.

Rear seat belts were also optional. The belts were static until August 1977, when inertia-reel lap/diagonals took over, complete with rectangular plastic guides in the rear parcel shelf and reels mounted in the boot; anchorage points were always standard in the C-pillars and underneath the back seat. The rear parcel shelf was black cardboard, with matt black paint beneath the slats.

L-spec door cards were part of the RS Mexico's grass-roots appeal, revealing body-coloured paintwork across the tops. Door pins are the early Mk2 type.

The RS Mexico's headlining was black vinyl with small dimples, as used in AVO Mk1 Escorts. The C-pillar trims were also black vinyl, but the RS Mexico lacked the RS2000's B-pillar coverings.

A pair of sun visors was trimmed in matching vinyl, including a vanity mirror on the passenger side. Between them was a black dipping rear-view mirror with black plastic cover over its fittings.

The front-seat passenger received a black plastic grab handle but rear seat occupants had none; instead there was a pair of black plastic coat hooks at the top of each B-pillar.

An RS Mexico's luggage compartment was virtually stock. The black boot mat was the same as a basic Escort's, albeit having a slit for the spare wheel strap bracket.

Spare wheel securing strap's special bracket was neatly welded to the boot floor alongside the well; it was found only on RS Mk2s and the limited-run Harrier.

Inside Boot

Move along – there's nothing to see here. Well, nothing much anyway. The RS Mexico's luggage compartment was really quite unremarkable, except for one tiny part – a small bracket spot-welded onto the boot floor alongside the spare wheel well. Its presence was to hold one end of the woven retaining strap over the RS's bigger-than-standard-Mk2 spare wheel; the spare was mounted upright in the well and always matched the car's road wheels, whether standard steels or optional alloys, but lacked a centre cap.

In the opposite (driver's-side) well was the RS Mexico's nine-gallon fuel tank, which was painted satin black and featured a flush, body-coloured cap on the offside

The RS Mexico's spare matched its road wheels, whether steel or alloy. Its securing strap hooked onto a special tag welded to the boot floor.

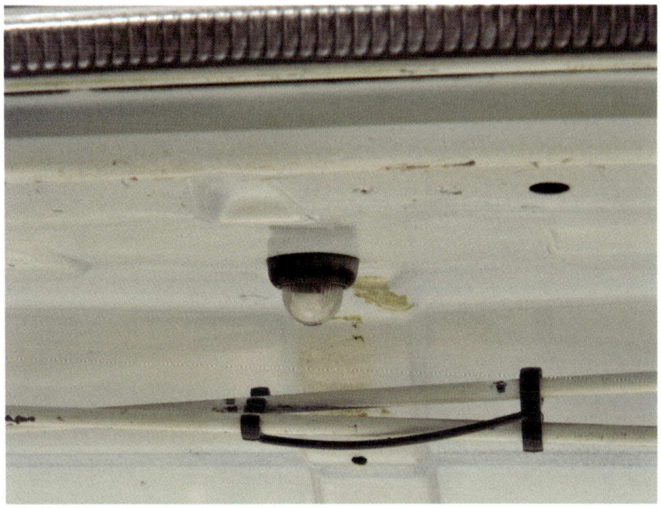

Small luggage compartment lamp was fitted underneath the parcel shelf; the boot spring tensioners were reportedly uprated to cope with the rear spoiler's extra weight.

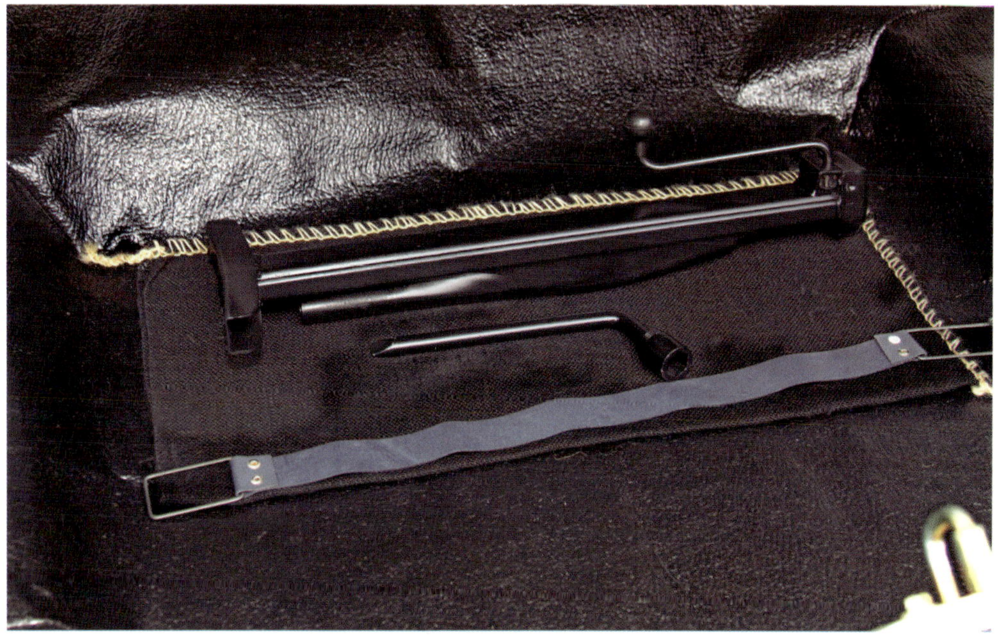

As usual, the tool kit was found inside a black bag; it included black jack and wheel brace.

rear wing.

Between the wells was a basic, black Hardura mat; no RS Mexico left the factory with Ghia-type carpeting or spare wheel cover. All, though, had uprated boot spring tensioners to cope with the weight of the rear spoiler. So, too, did they come with a black cardboard partition dividing the boot from the passenger compartment plus a protective rubber latch cover under the boot lid.

The regular Escort tool kit included a black bag, black screw pillar jack and wheel brace; the bag was stuffed between the spare wheel and its retaining strap. The RS Mexico wasn't fitted with a luggage compartment light as standard, although many cars received one from the factory, wired from the tail lamp loom.

RS MEXICO COLOUR SCHEMES AND INTERIOR TRIM

Colour	Colour code	Introduced	Discontinued	Interior colour	Decal colour	Vinyl roof (optional)
Signal Amber	0	Aug 1977	Jul 1978	Black	Black	Black
Signal Yellow	9	Dec 1976	Jul 1978	Black	Black	Black
Black (special order)	A	Dec 1976	Jul 1978	Black	Silver	Black
Diamond White	B	Launch	Jul 1978	Black	Black	Black
Carnival Red	D	Launch	Jun 1976	Black	Black	Black
Olympic Blue	E	Launch	Dec 1976	Black	Black	Black
Signal Orange 77	H	Dec 1976	Aug 1977	Black	Black	Black
Signal Green	J	Dec 1976	Aug 1977	Black	Black	Black
Signal Orange 76	L	Dec 1975	Dec 1976	Black	Black	Black
Venetian Red	R	Dec 1976	Jul 1978	Black	Black	Black
Daytona Yellow	T	Launch	Jun 1976	Black	Black	Black
Peppermint Green	T	Aug 1977	Jul 1978	Black	Black	Black
Non-standard	Y	Launch	Jul 1978	Black	Black or silver	Black

ESCORT RS2000

One of the oldest-surviving Mk2 RS2000s in captivity, Aled Hopwood's Carnival Red Escort was built in December 1975 and registered on the thirteenth of the following month. Although it's seen some restoration work – including a recently revamped engine bay – much of the car represents what the broadstripe buyer would have received from the Ford factory in 1976. Its black vinyl roof is a period extra that, along with a Janspeed single-box exhaust system and lowered suspension added by Aled, represent the tasteful modifications made by original RS2000 owners. Aled also fitted RS Mexico steel wheels for that authentic pre-production RS2000 look.

Iconic, inspirational and idolised by a generation of car nuts, the Mk2 RS2000 could rightfully be called the greatest Escort ever. It was the ultimate looker. A fabulous performer. And, in rear-wheel-drive Escort terms, the icing on a very tasty cake.

Okay, it wasn't the fastest, it wasn't the most expensive and it certainly wasn't the biggest motorsport champion. But the RS2000 was a true working-class hero – a star of road and television screens.

To this day, RS2000 is a well-loved household name, and with very good reason. In the mid-1970s it was an amazing attention-grabber – a top-selling rally reprobate that not only snapped necks with its ultra-modern styling but with its sportscar-thrashing performance too. Best of all, Saturday evenings in suburban households were spent watching a white RS2000 being slid around TV's streets by *The Professionals*. It was all just so perfect.

Yet despite outward appearances, the Mk2 RS2000 was little more than a reskin of the short-lived Mk1 model, with most of the mechanicals simply carried over to the brand-new body.

The engineering exercise was entrusted to the team behind AVO (Advanced Vehicle Operations), who built a slant-nosed prototype using an early Mk1 RS2000. It wasn't exactly a world-first (you could argue it was a direct copy of Vauxhall's droop-snoot Firenza), but the sloping front was a great

A real Seventies' rebel, the RS2000 was offered in a whole host of tasteful, eye-grabbing or downright drab colours. Make up your own mind about this car's Java Green paint scheme, but there's no denying it suits the slant-nosed Escort perfectly. Owned by serial Escort collector Eddy Gaskell (he's had 15 Mk2 RS2000s over the years), this stunning machine has been in his hands since 2003. Although it had a new nearside front wing and full respray in 1994, most of this car is resplendent in its unrestored glory, with around 69,000 miles on the clock. Other than the aftermarket 7x13in replica RS alloys and steering wheel centre cap, it's all pretty much as Ford intended. Today it's still driven and lusted-after wherever it goes – just like an RS2000 should be!

way for Ford to introduce aerodynamic design elements to the masses, as well as providing a fantastic talking point for the firm's ever-keen marketing men.

Sadly, plans to manufacture the finished product at the then-mothballed Aveley factory were quickly dashed; by this time, of course, AVO's bespoke-build ambitions had been binned, and the Mk2 RS2000 was to become something of a mainstream model. Besides, thanks to the use of an off-the-shelf German engine and four-speed Type E transmission, the only sensible option was to assemble every RS2000 on the efficient Saarlouis production line alongside the Escort Ghia.

Thanks to its predecessor's immense success, the Mk2 RS2000 stuck to the formula of a lightweight Escort body stuffed with a big, unstressed, two-litre Pinto powerplant and

Distinctive four-headlamp snout was a real marketing coup, bringing modern aerodynamics to the doorsteps of traditional Ford buyers.

If it's not broke, don't fix it – stylish slant-nose remained unchanged throughout production, except for the August 1977 swap to a blue oval badge in favour of previous FORD lettering.

Rubber rear spoiler and satin black back panel were easy ways to spot an RS2000 as it accelerated away; the black treatment was deleted on later base models.

Polyurethane droop-snoot nose lengthened the RS2000's Mk2 body by 165mm and considerably increased the front overhang, balancing out the back.

Even today, the RS2000 is an impressive, unmistakable shape from any angle. Rare Carnival Red really suits the angular lines.

matching gearbox. A couple of modifications were made, including an alloy sump, alloy bellhousing and short-throw gearshifter from the Mk1 RS2000. All new was a free-flowing exhaust setup that reckoned to gain ten horses, boosting power to 110bhp at 5,500rpm. And that was despite using an engine-driven cooling fan rather than the Mk1's electric item.

The Mk1 RS's Capri-based front suspension remained, as did the 3.54:1 differential, linked to a Mk2 Sport back end – albeit with RS radius rods instead of a rear anti-roll bar. Its braking system again used Capri-sized front discs (most lesser Mk2s were the same now, too), along with bigger-than-Mk1 back drums and an enlarged servo.

Most dramatically of all, the Escort's entire face had been redesigned, incorporating a deformable polyurethane nose that extended its overall length by 165mm. It featured a deep spoiler, impressive quad Cibie headlamps, longer bonnet and specially flanged front wings. Ford was keen to mention the new snout reduced the Mk2's drag factor from 0.444 to 0.386.

Of course, it looked very stylish as well. A functional, flexible boot spoiler perched over a satin black-painted back panel, which continued the theme set by blacked-out window surrounds and a broad stripe along each side at (wrap-around) bumper height. A bold, entwined RS2000 decal was positioned on each rear wing.

And the glamour didn't stop there: Ford's initial plans for lightweight and Custom versions were ousted in favour of the one model with four-spoke alloy wheels as standard. Meanwhile, the RS2000's cabin was crammed with enough goodies to excite its executive target market – a pair of Scheel reclining seats with roll-top head rests, centre console, glovebox and clock. A radio, tinted glass and remote-control driver's mirror were very popular optional extras.

Needless to say, the RS2000 was an immediate hit. After its announcement at the March 1975 Geneva show, it took until June for 20 prototypes to be built, 10 November 1975 for production to begin and 14 January 1976 for the RS2000 to go on sale. It rapidly became the best-selling Rallye Sport model to date, and widely recognised as the finest of all Escorts.

Yes, the RS1800 was marginally quicker but the RS2000 still hit 108mph and 0-to-60mph in 8.5 seconds. Plus it was easier on the wallet, simpler to maintain, offered far greater refinement and was available from stock. More to the point, to the average punter it just looked loads cooler.

Other than a few subtle badging alterations, RS2000 rear ends stayed pretty much the same from start to finish; twin number plate lamps were added in 1976.

It was the complete performance package, and even proved itself capable of what Escorts did best – competing in motorsport. Group One homologation was attained instantly, and scores of victories were achieved in rallying and circuit racing. Flat-fronted RS2000s were frequently used (for weight and cost of fixing), but European production cars never left the factory without the distinctive beak – instead, flat-fronts were permitted under regulations allowing for two-litre, standard-bodied Escorts built in Australia.

In summer 1976 the broad side stripes and big RS2000 graphics were replaced by a subtle double coachline, and during August 1977 the FORD front grille lettering was replaced by a blue oval badge.

The biggest change came on 13 September 1978, when a two-model RS2000 line-up was introduced. A new basic machine ousted the RS Mexico, slumming down with black cloth Sport-type front seats, poverty-level door cards and 5.5x13in steel wheels, meanwhile deleting the centre console, glove pockets and black rear panel.

In contrast, the Custom continued the existing RS2000's plush trim, now adding bronze tinted glass, a remote-control driver's door mirror and Recaro seats with fishnet headrests. For the very first time, an RS was offered from the factory with non-black interior trim – now available with an option of light-brown cloth seats and putty-coloured headlining.

August 1979 saw the last significant revisions, when Escort cockpits binned the black in favour of tan or chocolate-brown seats, along with dark brown carpets and plastics.

Few specials were built – but most notably there was one Roman Bronze three-speed automatic with polished Group One alloys and cream leather interior, created for Henry Ford II's 1976 UK visit.

Clean and uncluttered, the RS2000 had a classy side profile. Note the satin black sills, which were applied to most post-1976 cars.

RS2000 production ended in July 1980, by which point around 23,000 had been built (historians reckon a total of 25,638 Rallye Sport Mk2s of all kinds left the lines). More than 10,000 were sold in the UK alone, with late-model Customs outselling base-spec RS2000s by four to one.

With the RS2000's death came the end of an era and a stop to the tail-happy fun of rear-wheel-drive RS Escorts. No wonder the RS2000 still sold well in showrooms even after the less-pricey new Escort XR3 was released. And no wonder the Mk5 RS2000 of 1991 was little more than a shadow of its predecessor. The Mk2 RS2000 really did deserve its reputation as the king of Escorts.

Surely the most elegant of all Mk2s – an RS2000 still looks equally at home outside a fine country house as it does being thrashed through a forest rally stage.

Engine – Block, Head and Sump

It had all been seen before, but the two-litre Pinto never looked quite as comfy as when it was under the bonnet of a Mk2 Escort RS2000.

All but identical to the Mk1 RS2000's powerplant – not to mention hundreds of thousands of Cortinas and Capris – in this case it was a 1993cc, belt-driven, single overhead camshaft four cylinder. Referred to as a TL20H or NEE engine, it featured a semi-gloss black, Cologne-built, thin-wall, cast-iron cylinder block; its casting part number (70HM6015BA) was in raised characters on the lower right-hand-side of the block slightly forward of the exhaust-side engine mount. Above was a raised 20 (denoting two-litre capacity), beneath the unit's unique engine number, which was stamped into a machined flat face under the front core plug. The engine number's digits matched the last part of the car's chassis number and corresponding VIN plate attached to the slam panel.

As with all Pintos, the RS2000's block was also cast with a date code of slightly before the car was built – here in an oval shape on the right-hand side of the block, behind the engine mount; the code began with a number for its day of build, a letter for its month of manufacture (A equalled January, B was February and so on) and the next two for the year (with 75 representing 1975 and so on).

Inside the block were the standard two-litre Pinto internals, including flat-topped aluminium alloy pistons and cast iron,

Oversized Cortina powerplant looked remarkably at home when nestled under the RS2000's extended bonnet.

Late-spec RS2000 engine bay was subtly different from earlier type, including all-black covers and revised brake servo setup.

counterweighted, five-bearing crankshaft; the compression ratio was the usual 9.2:1.

Above the block was a stock Cortina or Capri cast-iron cylinder head in semi-gloss black, featuring four individual inlet ports on the left-hand side and four exhaust ports on the right. Inside was a belt-driven single camshaft in run-of-the-mill spec (albeit vaguely higher lift than the RS Mexico's) with yellow colour code. There were four inlet valves (with 42mm face diameters), four exhaust valves (with 35.8 to 36.2mm faces) and single valve springs.

The cylinder head had its own markings on top (visible beneath the camshaft), showing its part number, identity code (0) and year of build within a cast date clock.

Topping the lot was a ribbed camshaft cover, which was finished in mid-blue gloss with matching blue cam belt cover, which was slightly different from the RS Mexico's and protected a toothed rubber timing belt. There was often a long white, red and black 2000HC sticker across the cover. From June 1976 the camshaft and cambelt covers were swapped for gloss black instead of blue, meanwhile ditching the decal.

Inside the cam cover's oil filler spout was a black plastic cap, which at first was a Mk1 Escort type with slim outer rim and 71HF part number in raised characters above a Ford oval in the middle. From around November 1977 a chunkier filler cap was used instead, featuring a central Ford logo plus 79TF part number around the bottom.

At the left-hand-side rear of the engine was a red-handled dipstick, which delved into a special alloy sump that was unique to the RS2000 and RS Mexico, featuring anti-surge baffling and big-wing protrusion at the back. Early cars used a Mk1 RS2000 sump with raised FORD lettering and H73HF-prefixed part number cast underneath, but from June 1976 there was a revised version with H77HM part number and raised Ford oval logo. The sump plug was unique to Rallye Sport Mk2s.

Inside the sump was a regular Pinto oil pump and central pickup pipe. Outside, on the left-hand-side of the crankcase, was a stock disposable cartridge oil filter. No oil cooler was factory fitted, but an RS1800-type arrangement was a popular motorsport upgrade from Rallye Sport dealers.

To massage the big Pinto into the RS2000's engine bay, a special pair of alloy mounts was used, with a longer version on the nearside and raised part numbers pointing forwards. They were coupled up to a strengthened front crossmember with factory-welded reinforcing plates.

Although the Group One kit wasn't strictly speaking a factory-fitted setup, a wealth of options was offered to the RS2000 from new. They included a big-valve cylinder head (with 45mm inlet valves and 37mm exhausts) and high-lift camshaft. When accompanied by the Group One airbox above twin Weber 44IDF carburettors and free-flowing exhaust system, up to 145bhp was achievable without altering the standard 1993cc bottom end.

Coolant hoses wore these wire clips rather than aftermarket Jubilee types. Note the angled outlet to the top hose.

Cooling System

There was nothing particularly special about the RS2000's relaxed two-litre powerplant, so nothing unusual was required to keep it cool.

Even so, a big, 10.8-pint cooling system was used, incorporating a large-capacity radiator. With a satin black tank (sometimes decorated with a part number on a sticker across the top), angled top coolant outlet, black fins and overflow exit pointing towards the offside front (fed downwards in a green or black plastic tube), the whole rad was mounted further forward than a normal Mk2's within a specially cut out cowling/slam panel and crossmember.

A standard 13psi radiator cap was fitted, and the black rubber coolant hoses came mostly from the Escort Mk1, along with wire hose clips. Unlike the Mk1 RS2000, a regular bare-alloy Pinto water pump was used, mounted on the front of the engine and turning a yellow, seven-blade, plastic mechanical fan (just the normal Pinto part) rather than its predecessor's Kenlowe electric item. From April 1979 the mechanical fan was replaced with an orange viscous version.

Like the RS Mexico, the Mk2 RS2000 had a unique thermostat housing, finished in bare alloy and containing an off-the-shelf wax thermostat.

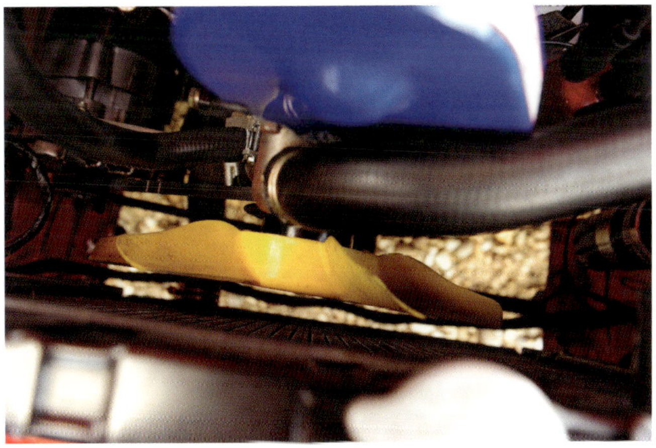

Yellow mechanical fan was found on the early Mk2 RS2000 in place of its predecessor's Kenlowe electric unit.

An off-the-shelf twin-choke Weber 32DGAV carb was ample for fuelling the RS2000's two-litre powerplant.

Fuel System

The RS2000's job was to be smooth, reliable, fast, practical and cost-effective. So for Blue Oval bean counters there was only one fuelling option – a single Weber downdraught carburettor.

The unit of choice was Ford's 1970s' favourite, the twin-choke 32DGAV with automatic choke facility. The same unit was used on a variety of contemporary Escorts, but the RS2000's jetting was unique, comprising 127/137 mains. Slight revisions were made in June 1976, but externally the carb was identical

As usual, the RS2000's Weber was supplied with an alloy identification tag on a float chamber screw and code on the side (where it met the inlet manifold), detailing its model number and internal calibration; Webers of the period were also stamped to say they were made in Italy rather than later models' Spanish origins.

The cast alloy Ford-built Pinto inlet manifold was fitted to the RS2000 (and RS Mexico, for that matter), as was a left-hand-drive-Granada/Consul-sourced throttle bracket and regular Capri cable. Left-hand-drive RS2000s used a normal Escort Crossflow cable instead.

The carburettor was topped with a wide, Capri 1.6/2.0 air cleaner housing in blue plastic, complete with moveable intake and disposable paper filter. In June 1976 it was swapped for an otherwise-identical bare black plastic airbox.

A Cortina AC mechanical diaphragm fuel pump (similar to the Mk1 RS2000 part) was mounted on the left-hand side of the engine beneath the distributor, featuring a bare metal finish. RS2000 fuel pipes were the same as those of the RS Mexico, but otherwise unique. All Pinto-powered Mk2 Escorts had their fuel lines routed along the nearside chassis rail in clips, rather than the other side used on Crossflow-engined cars.

As mentioned earlier, an essential part of the RS2000's Group One upgrade was a swap to twin 44IDF Weber carburettors on a special alloy inlet manifold, topped by a big, black airbox. It wasn't exactly factory-fitted kit, but it was actively encouraged by Ford and available from new courtesy of Rallye Sport dealers.

Exhaust System

While the Mk1 RS2000 was rated at 100bhp (and 108lb.ft at 3,500rpm), the Mk2 was reckoned to produce 110bhp at 5,500rpm and 119lb.ft at 4,000rpm. That was quite a jump, attributed by Ford to the redesigned airbox and – mainly – an all-new, free-flowing exhaust system.

Most importantly, a four-into-two, cast-iron manifold was bolted into place, based on the Mk1 RS2000 Group One part. Now featuring an entwined RS logo (rather than the Mk1's separate letters), it was coated in dark grey. Above it, a small heat shield protected the back three spark plug leads.

A twin-tube mild steel downpipe was connected to the manifold, with its lower end snuggling up to a large-bore exhaust system in aluminiumised silver-grey colour. It comprised one oval centre silencer and an oval back box, with pipework that swapped from offside to nearside beneath the gearbox.

The middle box was fitted on a twin-hook mounting (Crossflow Mk2s had a single hook) that hung from a spot-welded bracket to the nearside of the floorpan, before the car's rear axle and on a strengthener plate affixed below its back seat. The rear silencer was held on a normal-ish J-shaped hanger, rubber and bracket bolted to the nearside chassis rail, albeit further towards the back of the car than the normal Mk2 arrangement. The RS2000's entire exhaust system was shared with the RS Mexico.

Mk2 RS2000's free-flowing, cast-iron exhaust manifold and system was claimed to boost output by 10bhp. It came in dark grey, complete with legendary RS logo.

Neat black cover atop the Mk2 Escort bulkhead pad belied the old-fashioned Mk1 fuse box buried beneath.

Ignition and Electrical System

The mass-production Mk2 RS2000 was very much a German Ford machine, so it goes without saying that many of its electrical and ignition components came from local suppliers – in most cases Bosch. That said, Motorcraft and Lucas equipment sometimes made an appearance, often without explanation.

As an example, the UK-market Mk2 RS2000's distributor was supposedly a Motorcraft unit but Bosch parts were frequently found, especially from 1978 onwards. A set of white-Ford-logo-printed black siliconised rubber plug leads were just the normal Pinto parts, complete with printed white numbering, black end caps and coil separator. They reached from the RS2000's dizzy cap (Motorcraft caps were black, Bosch were terracotta-coloured) to a set of Motorcraft BF32 spark plugs, while a king lead connected to a nine-volt ballasted ignition coil positioned within a bare alloy bracket screwed to the inner wing. British RS2000s were specified with Motorcraft coils, but usually they were supplied with a black Bosch coil featuring a Ford oval logo and brown top.

All RS2000s had a battery at the passenger-side front of the car on a standard Mk2 tray, held in place with a fat, black clamp; normally it was a square-post Motorcraft 55Ah unit, although some early cars and foreign markets had a 57ah battery instead. Its leads were the normal Mk2 black negative and red positive cable (which changed length slightly in February 1978), complete with blue-and-white Ford labels.

The battery was charged by a Lucas or Bosch alternator in 45-amp or 55-amp size (generally a Bosch K1-55A in foreign markets and later cars), situated at the right-hand front of the engine on a special aluminium alloy bracket with rubber bushes – although very early cars were reckoned to have the cast iron RS2000 Mk1 part instead.

For the UK a 45-amp Lucas 18 ACR alternator was often fitted after August 1976; before then, RS2000s tended to come with a 55-amp Bosch and an external voltage regulator positioned on the inner wing, complete with short wiring loom linking it to the alternator through the normal plug. From around 1978 many were a normal-type Bosch.

Cranking over an early UK-market RS2000's engine was the job for a Lucas M35J starter with inner wing-mounted solenoid, but overseas cars wore a pre-engaged Bosch 0.7, Lucas 5M90, or Nippondenso (between August and October 1977); many later cars wore an inertia-type Bosch.

Although the RS2000 was equipped with a special RS wiring loom (to feed the headlamps and extra equipment), it was essentially similar to the stock Mk2 setup, wrapped in grey tape until around August 1976, when the grey was swapped for black. It was connected to a standard Escort fuse box atop the passenger-side bulkhead, containing seven continental fuses under two covers – a clear plastic shield with raised German lettering (like the Mk1 Escort cap) beneath a larger black cover (the type found on Mk2 Capris).

From 1978 the RS2000's wiring loom matched the Escort Ghia's (they were built on the same assembly lines, after all), although the luxury model's dual-tone horns weren't standard on the Rallye Sport machine. That said, some early cars and foreign models added the high-pitch horn to the normal low-pitch setup.

Transmission

The combination of Pinto power and a Saarlouis production line meant there was only one transmission suitable for the Mk2 RS2000 – the German-built Type E four-speed manual gearbox as seen in its Mk1 predecessor and RS Mexico stablemate. Not to mention millions of Cortinas, Capris, Consuls, Taunuses and Granadas...

The Type E was a big, oversized 'box with a black, cast iron casing, aluminium tail housing and pressed (not cast) alloy top cover. Unlike other Fords featuring this transmission, RS Escorts used Type Es with a unique aluminium alloy bellhousing, which was first seen in the Mk1 RS2000; it had apertures for left- or right-handed starter motor mounting and a large blanking grommet in the redundant hole.

Inside, there was a Borg and Beck 8.5in diaphragm spring

clutch, which was claimed by Ford to be heavy-duty but was actually exactly the same as the standard Pinto part; there was a Cortina clutch plate, pressure plate and run-of-the-mill flywheel too. The clutch was operated with a left-hand-drive Crossflow cable.

As before, the Mk2's ratios were: first 3.651:1, second 1.968:1, third 1.368:1, fourth 1:1 and reverse 3.66:1. The reverse position was found forward and over to the left, via a customised black stick that was swapped for chrome in 1976. Again, it included a makeshift quickshift, using a raised lever pivot point and modified Cortina rod change mechanism.

Thanks to its size, the Type E was a tight fit in the RS2000's standard Mk2 transmission tunnel, which was adapted in Saarlouis to suit. It was bashed a bit around the bulkhead to clear the bellhousing, then had the tunnel strengthener hacked away. This made space for a new gear-stick aperture, which needed to be fitted further back for the longer gearbox; metalwork atop the tunnel was cut out and a new plate with ready-pressed round hole was neatly spot-welded into place, providing a factory-fitted finish that was quite different from the Mk1 RS2000's hastily-reworked floorpan.

Like the Mk1, though, the Mk2 required a pair of spacer blocks to lower the back end of the 'box for installation. Squeezed between the gearbox crossmember and stock Mk2 tunnel mounting, the lowering blocks were now made from aluminium alloy.

The RS2000's tunnel area was also altered with the addition of a small bracket spot-welded to the offside floorpan, which kept the car's speedo cable clear of its exhaust manifold (which ran down the opposite side from a Crossflow Escort's, of course).

A two-piece propshaft with constant velocity joint and centre bearing transferred drive to a Timken hypoid bevel rear axle, which included a factory-mounted pair of forward-facing brackets for radius rods. Everything was finished in satin black.

Inside the axle was a removable differential, which featured a 3.545:1 final drive ratio, with 11 teeth on the pinion and 39 on the crown wheel.

Well, that was the standard setup. A range of rear axle ratios (usually geared for improved acceleration) was offered by Rallye Sport dealers, along with a Group One Salisbury limited-slip differential and even a close-ratio, four-speed Rocket gearbox and narrowed three-litre Capri back axle.

Early cars had a Girling Hydrovac servo and master cylinder. This car's Powerstop sticker isn't authentic but looks the part, at least.

Suspension and Steering

If you've got a great formula, you might as well stick to it – and that's exactly what Ford did when speccing the Mk2 RS2000's underpinnings. Following the success of tweaking the Mk1 RS2000's chassis with racing driver input, another circuit hero was borrowed to fine-tune the Mk2's handling – this time Tom Walkinshaw, who went on to become founder of top motorsport team TWR.

Naturally, his advice was spot on. Road testers reckoned all the AVO Escorts' rally-derived twitchiness was long gone, replaced by a refined ride and stable manner – yet with no loss of tail-sliding fun should the need arise.

So, what was done to broaden the RS2000's appeal? Surprisingly little. Indeed, much of the Mk1's Capri-derived front end remained, and even the Mk2 Sport rear springs stayed put.

At the nose, that meant oil-filled Fichtel and Sachs shock absorbers (some early cars apparently wore Armstrong) inside satin black Macpherson struts, bearing blue-and-white colour code, and black dust covers over the piston rods. Sitting on the enlarged (Capri-size) spring seats was a pair of satin black, 277mm, 130lb front coils, with brown-and-grey colour code and black plastic tubing at both ends of each spring.

Poking up through the inner wings were late-spec Mk1 strut tops in semi-gloss black with black collars, dabbed with brightly-coloured paint around their securing bolts to confirm their torque settings. In February 1977 they were swapped for smaller, offset strut tops through 85mm (rather than the previous 105mm) apertures.

Each strut had a bolt-on steering arm, rather than the standard Mk2's integral setup. But the steering rack was a normal metric Mk2 part, with regular 17.9:1 ratio, connected to metric-threaded track rod ends with imperial tapers. A Mk2 Sport steering column was used, with updated coupling from May 1976. The rack gaiters were revised in August 1978 too.

The RS2000's track control arm mounts were raised by around 10mm, with a redesigned Mk2 crossmember, featuring neat, factory-welded strengthening plates rather than the roughly-tacked Mk1 RS2000's component. The alloy engine mounts were unique to the Mk2 RS, as was the 22mm front anti-roll bar with lowered mounting brackets.

In contrast, the stock Mk2 rear anti-roll bar was thrown away in favour of anti-tramp bars, which connected to the axle at one end and factory-welded floorpan brackets beneath the car's back seat at the other.

Otherwise, the RS2000 was essentially the same as an early Mk2 Escort Sport, with live rear axle linked via U-bolts to semi-elliptic, 116lb, three-leaf Sport rear springs; each spring was 60mm wide and wore a red, lilac and white colour code. Boge telescopic shock absorbers were generally used (although it's said some early cars had Girling dampers), finished in satin black like the rest of the RS2000's running gear.

Needless to say, Rallye Sport dealers were keen to tailor the RS2000's chassis to each buyer. From new, a wide choice of upgrades was offered, including Group One high-ratio steering rack (with 2.5 turns lock-to-lock), single-leaf rear springs and uprated Bilstein dampers.

Brakes

Hauling up an RS2000 was the job of a relatively straightforward set of stoppers, which differed very little from its predecessors' brakes – or an Escort Sport's, for that matter.

Like the regular Mk2, the RS2000's front end wore a pair of silver/gold-coloured Girling M16 callipers with 54mm pistons and metric pipe fittings. They were kitted out with Ferodo 2445 pads and the usual Capri-type Girling 247.5mm solid front discs.

On the back was a pair of black-painted, self-adjusting 9x1.75in drums, which contained 19mm wheel cylinders and Ferodo shoes. From August 1978 they had inspection apertures in their back plates in line with the shoe leading edges and covered by a rubber blanking plug.

The dual-circuit system used silver/zinc-coloured Bundy mild steel tubing and black Girling flexible hoses throughout the car. Left-hand-drive RS2000s had a brake pressure differential valve fitted on the inner wing, but from 1978 all included a pressure control valve.

The RS2000's main change from a Sport's braking system was its inch-bigger brake servo (now 7in), which was found in the driver's-side front corner of the engine bay. On early cars it was a Girling Hydrovac similar to the part used on the Mk1 RS2000 but with a different-sized thread on one pipe fitting. It featured a black servo drum, and was mounted on the normal satin black Mk2 in-line bracket attached to the inner wing. Very early examples featured a square, white-on-black sticker on top and a 19.05mm master cylinder, although this was upgraded to 20.64mm from spring 1976. Until early 1977 the master cylinder was silver/zinc-coloured, before being swapped for black. A red plastic band wrapped around the master cylinder; it was topped with a white plastic reservoir and red cap.

The Girling was dropped during December 1977 in favour of an ATE (Teves) brake servo on the same mounting bracket. It included a black master cylinder, square-edged reservoir (with raised ATE logo) and black plastic cap, which swapped for a clear cap on later cars. From October 1978 the cap gained a three-wire electrical sensor for a now-standard brake warning light fitted into the dashboard switch panel.

When the RS2000's servo was updated, so too was its silver-zinc coloured hard pipe, which clipped to the slam panel behind the radiator – it now accessed the ATE from below, instead of entering the Girling from above.

As usual, Group One upgrades were popular from Rallye Sport dealers, though not from the production line. Most useful (and relatively popular) was a pair of ventilated front discs, along with DS11 brake pads and the option of a bias adjuster.

Wheels and Tyres

The first Escort to boast alloy wheels as standard kit, the Mk2 RS2000 was equipped with RS four-spokes from the start of production until the introduction of a base model in September 1978.

But that wasn't always intended to be the case. Some pre-production RS2000s wore 5.5x13in Capri-type sculptured sports steel wheels, which were initially destined for all customer cars. Painted Silver Fox, they were capped with black centres that wore silver stickers and black Mk1 RS logos – never getting beyond the prototype point.

So, what changed, and why weren't the steels standard? Who knows? But there's no denying the visual impact of RS

Girling brake servo was binned in favour of this ATE unit from December 1977; sensor for brake test switch was added during October 1978.

Steel wheels weren't standard until the introduction of September 1978's base model, but RS Mexico 5.5x13in rims were a cut-price option throughout the RS2000's lifespan.

alloys, which undoubtedly aided the RS2000's desirability and popularity.

A step up from the rims worn by many Mk1 RS2000s, Mk2s had a very similar four-spoke design but were half an inch wider, now measuring 6x13in. These Ford/GKN cast alloys featured polished/bare rims, Dove Grey spoke cutouts and black centre caps with the usual silver RS motif, which were clipped in from the front.

Their appearance was also similar to that of Capri Laser wheels, but RS2000 alloys had thinner spoke webs and were attached on flat nut seats using chrome, metric, nuts with integral flat washers; in contrast, Capri wheels had tapered seats and washers.

RS2000 rims also wore their 13x6J size cast onto one spoke, a Ford oval in another and a third spoke bearing a pair of circles with month and year number identifiers – which were normally one or two months before the car's build date.

To complicate matters, one or two pre-production RS2000s (and RS Mexicos, for that matter) were photographed wearing Capri RS3100-style alloys, with spokes right up to their front faces rather than the deep-dished production type. What's more, many RS2000s destined for Germany and Austria were equipped with 5.5x13in RS four-spoke wheels, featuring spokes flush to the faces.

And that's not to mention other overseas markets, some of which had 5.5x13in steels as standard, with alloys available as an optional extra. Oh, and not forgetting the UK, where RS2000s were always offered with RS Mexico steels for a price reduction; needless to say, it wasn't a popular option.

Wheels played a major part in September 1978's introduction of two RS2000 specification levels. From that date, base models received the silver-painted 5.5x13in sports steels while Customs were treated to the four-spokes. Just to confuse the issue, alloys were optional on base-spec RS2000s too…

Whatever wheel was ordered, there was one main tyre – the Pirelli Cinturato CN36 in 175/70HR13 guise – although other brands were available, including Goodyear G800s.

Of course, 6x13in wheels looked lost under a set of Series X wide arches, so Rallye Sport dealers offered a selection of upgrades, including RS four-spokes in 7x13in and 7.5x13in sizes.

Wider-than-standard 7x13in four-spokes set off the RS2000's stance. They're not original but are popular today because they look so damn good. Standard four-spokes were 6x13in.

Bodywork

Unique and unmissable, the RS2000's radical exterior was unquestionably a key element of its immense success.

At the heart (well, nose) of its design was an all-new front end, which bore an uncanny resemblance to Vauxhall's droop-snoot Firenza of 1973. Not that Ford cared about accusations of copying – a slanting snout was the firm's way of introducing modern styling to its rather conservative buyers, not to mention improving aerodynamics. The setup was wind-tunnel tested with fifth-scale models, dropping the regular Mk2's drag factor from 0.444 to 0.386. In so doing, Ford could happily boast about improvements in performance and fuel economy (3mpg was quoted) – even though some road testers reckoned the extra weight promoted understeer.

A complete new nose was designed for the car, made from deformable, energy-absorbing polyurethane plastic foam by German firm Phoenix. It incorporated a deep airdam, integral satin black bumper, satin black surrounds for quadruple headlamps and a satin black grille with chrome FORD lettering – which was swapped for a blue Ford oval badge in August 1977.

The snout was attached to a pair of RS2000-specific front wings, which were 100mm shorter and shaped at their

FORD grille was fitted onto the RS2000's beak until it was swapped for a blue oval in August 1977.

leading edges; it was held on with a steel flange plate, a selection of screws and expanding nuts. RS2000 inner wings were standard heavy-duty Mk2 but its bonnet was longer, at the front wrapping over its beak. The front wings wore tall, black 2.0 badges behind each front wheel until they were dropped altogether in August 1977.

All the other RS2000 body panels were stock Escort parts, with the addition of the common Mk2 RS upgrades, including modified transmission tunnel, speedometer cable bracket, uprated rear chassis rails, anti-tramp bar mounts, repositioned exhaust hangers, spot-welded spare wheel strap tag and those aforementioned inner wings with reinforced front suspension towers and strut tops.

The RS2000 was supplied with a laminated front windscreen as standard, along with heated rear window; all the glass was plain Sekurit, although green tints were an optional extra. So, too, were opening front quarter lights until part-way through 1980. From September 1978 the then-new Custom model was treated to standard all-round bronze tinted glass, which became an optional extra on base-spec cars.

Unlike mainstream pre-August 1976 Escorts, the RS2000 had two-speed windscreen wipers with intermittent control added as standard. Electric screen washers were always

Opening front quarter lights were fitted for foreign markets and optional on UK cars until 1980. Note this pre-Custom's lack of remote-control door mirror.

Remote-control driver's door mirror became standard kit from the start of the Custom trim level; it was optional on all others.

fitted, as were satin black wiper arms, which matched the all-black beading in the window rubbers.

One or two left-hand-drive RS2000 prototypes had the bright chrome rain gutter trims of other Mk2s but all production cars wore black epoxy-coated drip rail covers – which at the time of introduction were unique to the RS2000. On top, a black vinyl roof was optional on all RS2000s, trimmed from the stock Mk2 pattern by hand after the car was painted. Factory-fitted vinyl roofs were described on the car's build plate, but it was relatively common for them to be fitted by dealers before registration (likewise Webasto sliding sunroofs). Dealers were most likely the source of any tobacco-coloured vinyl roofs, which on the RS2000 weren't offered direct from the factory.

RS2000 side window surrounds were sprayed satin black, encompassing the door frames and B-pillars, meeting the rubbers along the bottom. Door handles and locks were always black-coated, as were the door mirrors; a pair of fixed mirrors were standard in the UK (it's possible some left-hand-drive RS2000s lacked the passenger-side part) and a remote-control driver's mirror was a popular option. From September 1978 the Custom specification gained the adjustable driver's mirror as factory kit, but it remained an extra-cost option on base models.

A chrome, Ford-branded retractable aerial was mounted in the offside front wing of cars equipped with an optional factory-fitted radio, although it was common for dealers to mount roof aerials when they supplied the sound system. Similarly, an electric aerial kit was offered as a dealer accessory. From July 1979 the retractable aerial was swapped for satin black instead of chrome.

Satin black paint treatment wasn't generally extended to the sills of early RS2000s, but from around August 1976 it was present unless the car's main bodywork was Midnight Blue or gloss black (or Series X arches were added by the supplying dealer). On cars with satin black sills, the underside of the spare wheel well was painted black to match.

Until September 1978 all RS2000s (other than black cars) were treated to a satin black rear panel, which followed a path around the back lights and into the boot shut in alignment with the lid, aiming to provide the effect of a continuous colour. From September 1978 only the Custom received the black back panel – base-model RS2000s were left in body colour.

Pre-August 1977 Escort badge was smaller than later versions and always black.

August 1977 brought a bold, black Escort badge with RS2000 decal to the right.

Above was an aerodynamically-developed, flexible, matt-black rubber RS spoiler, although – like early RS1800s – a couple of prototype RS2000s had body-coloured rear spoilers. There was a chrome boot lock until October 1977, when satin black was usually fitted instead.

Early cars wore a small, satin black Escort badge on the boot lid's nearside, individual FORD lettering beneath the boot lock and a black RS2000 decal at the offside; a silver sticker was available from December 1976 for black (and, later, Midnight Blue) cars. In August 1977 the Escort badge was swapped for a larger part (still in satin black), now accompanied by the RS2000 sticker. Meanwhile, the FORD lettering was replaced by a blue oval badge on the offside.

Like other Mk2s, the RS2000 was equipped with a colour-coded, pressed steel petrol cap recessed into the offside rear wing. A locking cap was a frequently-specified-from-new accessory, when the original part would generally be thrown into the car's luggage compartment.

A unique, narrower satin black bumper was fitted to the back of all RS2000s, complete with special ends to accept black polyurethane extensions that wrapped around the rear wings. No overriders were added.

Early cars – built until August 1976 – are often referred to as broadstripe RS2000s thanks to the wide black decals that ran from nose to tail at the same height as the front and rear bumpers. The stripes were accompanied by a bold, black RS2000 logo on each rear quarter in alignment with the back lights.

Strangely enough for a shouty sporting Escort, the RS2000's decals weren't widely liked, and many press reports bemoaned their appearance as ill befitting for an executive express. Which probably explained why it was possible to specify an early RS2000 with slimmer, so-called Sport-style coachlines instead.

Maybe that also justified Ford's decision to ditch the broad striping and RS2000 rear wing graphics during August 1976, opting instead for a twin black coachline 16.5mm below the swage and in alignment with the top of the black back panel. It was trimmed slightly short of all the panel gaps, and ended neatly in a bullet shape on the car's nose cone; Ford data said each front wing section was 1161mm, the doors were 1214mm and the rear quarters 1510mm. Silver graphics were fitted to black RS2000s from December 1976 onwards and subsequent Midnight Blue machines.

Broadstripe RS2000s also boasted big stickers on their rear quarters; the logos' August 1976 deletion was apparently to provide a more discreet appearance for executive drivers..

Broadstripe by nature, if not officially by name – the colloquial tag for early RS2000s came from the standard wide, black decals plastered along each side.

Coachlines continued onto the RS2000's nose, ending neatly in a bullet shape.

Double pinstripes lined up with the top of the RS2000's satin black panel, which wrapped around the back lights. The coachlines were standard from August 1976 onwards.

Three-piece wrap-around rear bumper was unique to the RS2000, and aimed to modernise the Escort's boxy appearance.

Rubber RS rear spoiler and satin black back panel continued throughout Custom production; only the base-model RS2000 dropped the black panel.

Unlike most other models, RS2000s never wore chrome door handles and locks – they were always black-coated; double coachlines didn't wrap into door shuts.

Boot lid Ford oval came in August 1977, displacing the previous RS2000 decal.

Underbonnet

Beneath the RS2000's extra-long bonnet was the big, well-known Pinto powerplant, squeezed into place like it was always meant to live within such tight confines.

Like all other Mk2s, the RS2000's battery was found on a normal Escort tray in the passenger-side front corner of the engine bay, grabbed firmly with a chunky, black clamp. The opposite side housed the RS2000's brake servo, complete with pipework routed behind the slam panel.

Talking of which, the back of the slam panel/radiator cowling was one of the few areas in which an RS2000's engine bay differed from a run-of-the-mill Mk2's. In fact, it was a new, reshaped part with cut-out middle section that allowed the radiator to be moved forward, which in turn made space for a cooling fan on the front of the big Pinto engine. At the bottom of the radiator, the RS2000's cross-member was also redesigned, with a new box section.

Surprisingly enough, the rest of the slam panel was just normal Mk2, albeit with a reshaped bonnet lock and spring mechanism. It connected to the usual black plastic-coated bonnet release cable, the other end of which reached a black handle under the dashboard at the driver's side; the cable itself was routed up the appropriate inner wing underneath its drip rail.

The RS2000's slam panel was also home to a galvanised bonnet prop, which was hinged from the offside, meanwhile fastening into a white plastic clip on the opposite corner.

To the right-hand-side (looking from the front of the car) of the bonnet release mechanism was the RS2000's Saarlouis-type build plate, listing the individual car's colour and

RS2000 slam panel differed from standard Mk2 to allow clearance for the mechanical fan; servo vacuum pipe was clipped into place.

RS2000 nose was grafted craftily onto standard Mk2 inner wings and redesigned outers.

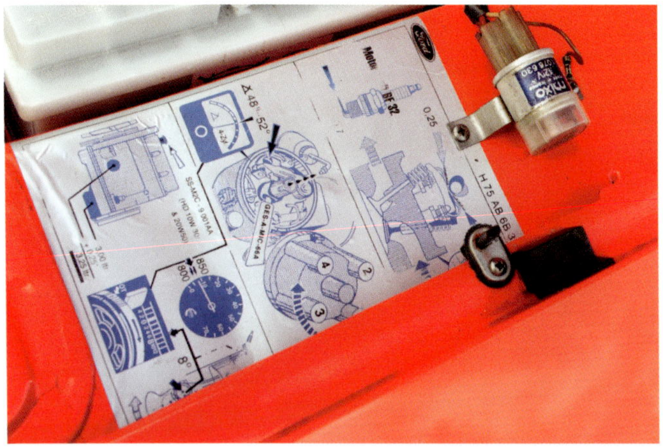

Lare, silver engine tuning sticker was found on some early RS2000s but was dropped during 1976; Mixo headlight relay was found on many halogen-equipped early Mk2s.

specification. Across on the left was a VIN plate, which sported a vehicle identity number beginning with GCAT; that said, although late (1977-onwards) RS2000s always had GATR in the Type box, many early cars read BATR. The last RS2000s (built from November 1979) had their VIN plates on their offside inner wings instead.

The chassis number was repeated on the offside suspension top, hand-stamped, masked and left in primer-grey paint. RS2000 inner wings were exactly the same as the RS Mexico's (and, for that matter, every other heavy-duty Escort), complete with spot-welded strengthening plates at each Macpherson strut mount. Their circular apertures were reduced in size during February 1977, dropping from 105mm to 85mm diameter.

Just in front of the nearside strut top was a Mixo lighting relay inside a bracket, screwed into the inner wing top and clipped into a multi-plug from an extension of the main wiring loom. The wiring was wrapped in grey tape (black from August 1976) and added a short brown earth cable under the screw. Later cars swapped to a square MAI relay with white cap.

Against the opposite (offside) suspension top was the RS2000's opaque plastic washer fluid reservoir, which was held onto a black metal bracket that bolted to the inner wing. It featured an electric washer pump that was generally plain black or zinc/gold in colour, with Ford oval printed on in black. It hooked up to plastic tubing and a white T-connector, which fed a pair of copper nozzles that poked through the car's scuttle panel.

All RS2000s wore a GL/Ghia-type thick rubber engine compartment insulator across the top of the bulkhead, which helped to deaden sound transmitted to the cabin; a screw and flat washer fastened it above the bulkhead drain tube. Beneath, the panelwork was mainly standard Escort but with a couple of differences – there was a 19mm hole for an oil pressure pipe drilled through the driver's side (close to the heater hoses) plus slight enlargement of the transmission tunnel where it met the bulkhead, which made room for the Type E gearbox.

Like other Escorts, until February 1977 the RS2000's bulkhead was pressed with five square dimples; later there were seven clearly-defined squares.

A variety of stickers were applied to the RS2000's engine bay, primarily depending on when it was built. All had an E11 lighting emissions sticker on the bonnet slam panel (between chassis plate and bonnet release mechanism), which changed from a grey square to a purple rectangle during 1976. Some early cars wore a black-on-white, Mk1 Escort-type engine coolant decal on the offside inner wing top (this ceased in 1976) and a few very, very early RS2000s had a large, silver engine tuning sticker on the nearside inner wing.

Large-hole strut tops were used until February 1977; chassis number was stamped on the offside RS reinforcing plate.

Small-hole strut tops were made standard during February 1977; chassis number remained stamped around the offside reinforcing plate.

Lighting

A real highlight of the RS2000's fresh front end was its quadruple headlamp setup, which was not only a bright idea for improving night driving but a brilliant marketing tool too.

Mounted into removable, satin black bezels within the new nose cone was a set of four Cibie 60/55W quartz-halogen, 155mm-diameter circular headlamps with convex lenses – including sidelight apertures on the outside pair. Each lamp had a separate chrome rim.

Beneath them, mounted into the front bumper was a pair of regular Mk2 indicators with orange Altissimo lenses and hazard warning flashers. One or two prototype RS2000s wore RS1800-type Carello side repeaters on their front wings but they never made it into production.

At the tail end of an RS2000 was the standard Mk2 lighting setup, featuring Altissimo rear clusters with integral reversing lights and single bumper-mounted number plate lamp, which was swapped for a pair during 1976 – probably around August.

An Altissimo rear fog lamp was a factory-fitted optional extra, which could also be specified from Ford dealers as an accessory. It was affixed on a bracket to the offside rear valance and was accompanied by a rocker switch in the cabin's fascia panel, complete with red warning light. The fog lamp became standard equipment around August 1979.

A luggage compartment lamp was standard on the early RS2000, as a small, round unit mounted under the parcel shelf; it continued into Custom trim but was dropped on the 1978-onwards base model.

All RS2000s had the standard later-type Mk2 interior courtesy light (except for the few pre-November 1975 cars, which had a Mk1 lamp), with black override switch and black plastic door control buttons fitted in the A-pillars.

Interior

A luxurious executive level was where the RS2000 was aimed, and its cabin was a perfect example of how Ford used a few carefully-selected extras to change a car's entire driving feel.

All pre-September 1978 RS2000s were furnished with a plush black-on-black cockpit featuring upmarket accessories, including centre console and gloveboxes. Well, all except Henry Ford II's 1976 special, which was kitted out in cream leather for the seats and matching Ghia door cards.

Although pre-production cars were fitted with RS1800 Custom- or Mk1 RS2000-type Scheel recliners, the standard seats in early Mk2 RS2000s were high-back Scheels with shapely side bolsters. They were trimmed in black Beta cloth with horizontal block pattern, stitched vertically; the stitching extended halfway up the squabs; the backs, sides and piping were black vinyl. Within the seat covers was often a brown cardboard tag, which detailed a manufacturing date of a month or two before the car's assembly.

A bright marketing idea – Cibie quad-headlamps were effective for aiding night driving and highlighting the RS2000's profile. They were mounted in removable satin black pods.

The seat bases featured black plastic handwheels to recline their backrests, rather than the chrome levers of earlier Scheels; the backrests were tipped forward using shaped, black levers on the sides. Atop each seat was a roll-top head rest, trimmed in black Beta cloth with horizontal block pattern, fastened across the bottom with Velcro.

As an optional fitment, Ford offered the black Beta cloth-trimmed, non-reclining, low-back buckets with harness slots that were originally earmarked for the RS Mexico. In the RS2000, though, they were available for a reduction from list price.

The Scheels and fixed-back buckets were ousted during September 1978 in favour of two new types of seat. Now, the Custom spec (which effectively replaced the standard RS2000) gained a pair of firm, Capri S-sourced Recaro high-

Differentiating the 14in RS wheel from the Escort Sport's was this chunky centre cap with entwined RS logo, which was replaced by the usual Ford oval in 1977.

Black was the only option for early RS2000 interiors, including these comfy Scheel reclining seats, affectionately known as roll-tops thanks to their chunky headrests.

Three-spoke RS steering wheel had plastic rim on all but the earliest press-tested RS2000s (which wore leather rims for journalists' delicate, Fairy-soft hands).

back recliners. Covered in traditional RS horizontal Beta cloth, the Recaros had vertical stitching, along with vinyl sides, piping and backs.

Most importantly, the Recaros were now nicknamed fishnets thanks to their new headrests, which featured vinyl surrounds with criss-cross mesh inserts in their middles.

Black was the usual colour but now there was an interloper – for the very first time on an Escort RS, brown upholstery was available when certain exterior paint colours were specified. Known as Chocolate 76, the fabric was mid-brown, coupled to dark-brown vinyl backs and sides.

Regardless of cloth colour, the Recaros had black plastic levers (including up arrows) in their sides to tip the backrests, and a black, eight-toothed handwheel on the base to operate the reclining mechanism.

Meanwhile, the September 1978-onwards base model (which took over from the laid-off RS Mexico) was downgraded with a pair of plain, Beta cloth-covered, Sport-type, low-back reclining seats, with vinyl sides and solid, vinyl-trimmed headrests. Again, they were offered with black or Chocolate 76 upholstery.

To complicate matters, the base model was available with fishnet Recaros as an optional extra, while the

Brown is the new black. Well it was in August 1979, when RS2000 cabins were switched to Warm Black (brown, in non-Fordspeak) plastics and tan or chocolate-coloured fabrics – this car's Bitter Chocolate 80 trim is several shades darker than the Chocolate 76 found on a small selection of 1978-to-1979 machines.

RS three-spoke steering wheel didn't escape the swap to Warm Black; it should wear a blue oval-badged centre cap rather than this car's RS emblem.

Custom was allowed poverty-spec seats for a reduced cost at 'special request'.

The final changes came during August 1979, when black interiors were banned from the RS2000. Instead, the seats – whether Custom or base-spec – were supplied in either dark brown (also known as Bitter Chocolate 80) or tan cloth (called Tan 79), complete with matching vinyl sides, head rests and so on. All seats now came with dark brown (AKA Warm Black 80) hard plastics.

RS2000 back seats came in two types, always trimmed to match the fronts. Early cars were treated to a GL-type rear bench, with extra padding between single vertical stitching, while Customs and base-spec RS2000s had the Escort L seat with twin vertical lines and less substance. At each side of the bench was a vinyl pad (in a matching colour) to cover the inner wheelarch.

The door cards and rear quarter panels in an RS2000 always corresponded to the seats in colour and trim level. So, early models and Customs were equipped with Ghia-type full-height door cards in appropriately-coloured vinyl and carpeted bottom sections, along with extended armrests and a chrome upper beading strip. Early cars had chrome frames around the black plastic door release handles but from

Base-model RS2000 from September 1978 lacked the luxury of RS2000 Custom, reverting to Sport-type recliners, L-level door cards and lack of centre console.

Pre-Custom door cards covered the entire door, complete with carpeted lower section and chrome beading.

August 1977 they were all black (and never dark brown).

Base models instead had L-type door cards, with less padding, smaller armrests and exposed, painted bodywork across the tops. These door cards were retained even if optional Recaros were specified.

All had the same, standard Mk2 window winders in chrome with black plastic knobs and inserts. All had black plastic door lock pins – with flared heads until August 1977, when slimmer versions took over.

When an early car or Custom was fitted with an optional remote-control driver's mirror, the door card wore a chrome escutcheon and lever (until May 1977 when it became black); but when specified on a base model there was always a black knob and escutcheon.

Padded GL-type back seat was trimmed in black Beta cloth with single vertical stitch lines.

As for the rear quarter panels, they matched the front door cards – full-height on early cars and Customs, complete with chrome beading strips and large, black plastic rotating ashtrays, which had a chrome rim until August 1977 and were plain thereafter. Shallower rear quarter panels were used on base models, which had smaller ashtrays and revealed body-coloured paintwork across the tops. Black was used until August 1979, when Warm Black or tan took over.

Early RS2000s and Customs were fitted with a unique (well, unique except for the 20-or-so RS1800 Customs) dashboard, using a satin black metal panel with a neatly pressed cutout in front of the passenger. Slotted in and affixed with cross-headed screws was an open-fronted plastic cubby box, which on its right-hand side contained a Smiths clock with white digits, white Ford logo and red needle.

In April 1978 the clock gained an orange needle instead of red, while in August 1979 the compartment was swapped for Warm Black plastic. Base models had a flat dashboard without an inset cubby box or factory-pressed cutout; the metalwork remained black throughout RS2000 production.

Across the top of the dash, all RS2000s wore the same padded vinyl pad, although Warm Black replaced the previous black in August 1979 (RS2000s with Chocolate 76 trim also had black plastics).

Heater controls lived in the middle of the dashboard, including black plastic bezel with illumination, foil indicator diagram, silver-rimmed surround, two-speed heater/demister switch and black plastic temperature sliders. Hot was originally on the right and cold was on the left, but their positions swapped in October 1976 when the Mk1-type metal heater box was replaced by a quieter two-piece plastic unit. In

Customs kept the full-height door cards and armrests of earlier models, but base-spec RS2000s reverted to Escort L trim levels.

Nothing at all to do with an Essex girl's stockings, the fishnet headrests found on RS2000 Recaros were designed as a safety aid for improved visibility. Still looked sexy though…

August 1979 the bezel was changed to Warm Black.

Each side of the dashboard had its own rotating plastic eyeball vent in black with silver-painted rim; the vents were never replaced with brown. Oh, and not forgetting the bold Custom decal, which was found immediately above the heater controls on RS2000 Customs (no surprises there, then).

A plastic fascia panel (in black until August 1979 and Warm Black thereafter) was mounted beneath the heater controls, which contained a centrally-positioned swivelling ashtray (in black plastic at first, then Warm Black in August 1979) and the RS2000's series of rocker switches. From left to right they were: blanking plate (until October 1978, when a brake low pressure switch became standard); hazard flasher switch (updated in autumn 1976 with an upright rather than inverted warning triangle); cigar lighter (included as standard on all RS2000s, and swapped from long-neck/deep-reach Mk1-style with silver label to a more modern-looking part with white-printed diagram during April 1977); heated rear window switch (swapped in autumn 1976 for an updated diagram and warning lamp); blank or fog light switch with red warning lamp (it was optional until August 1979, when it became standard kit).

Beneath the passenger side of the dashboard was a plastic, Ghia-type, fully-enclosed glovebox with fold-down lid; it was black until August 1979, when it was superseded by Warm Black. Base-model RS2000s were forced to manage without the glovebox, and instead came with a normal Mk2 Escort cardboard parcel shelf with padded vinyl edging; a similar shelf was used on the driver's side of all RS2000s. The parcel shelves were black until Warm Black appeared in August 1979.

In front of the driver was an impressive instrument binnacle, which was shared with the RS Mexico. Early cars featured a black surround with silver-coloured rim, but the silver was deleted during 1976; from August 1979 it was swapped for Warm Black.

Within the pod was a 7,000rpm rev counter (without a red line) on the left and 120mph speedometer on the right, each in black with white numbers and white needles. The speedometer included mileage and trip counters plus small, yellow kilometres-per-hour numbers beneath the miles-per-hour increments.

Between the two large dials were three smaller round gauges for water temperature, fuel (featuring markings for 0,

Bitter Chocolate Beta cloth back seat was L-style with double vertical stitching rather than padded GL-type.

White needles and 120mph speedo were found until 1978, when they were replaced by orange. Very early cars had silver-rimmed gauge pod.

Orange needles and 140mph speedometer were features of the 1978-onwards instrument panel. Dark brown plastics came in August 1979.

1/2 and 4/4, which were deleted during October 1977) and oil pressure, again with white lettering and white needles.

The instruments were updated during summer 1978, receiving orange needles, smaller digits and a 140mph speedo with white KPH digits.

A row of warning lights ran along the display beneath the dials, comprising (from left to right) left-hand indicators, main beam, decorative RS logo, ignition, right-hand indicators.

Taking pride of place was a 14in, three-spoke steering wheel with mock-leather rim and flat, black spokes. It wore a black plastic centre cap with impressed, entwined RS logo, which was ditched during February 1977 in favour of the Sport type centre with blue Ford oval badge. Then, in August 1979, the wheel and cap became Warm Black.

Similarly, the black plastic steering column shroud and lock bezel were replaced by Warm Black in August 1979, as did its circular choke control blanking plug. Three stalks sprouted from the column – one on the left for indicators, horn, head-lamp dip and flash; one on the right for the windscreen wipers (which came with intermittent facility) and a smaller stalk behind it for headlight control.

At the foot of the column was a stock Escort pedal box, comprising satin black brake and clutch levers with Mk1 Escort-type rubber pads (they had a horizontal block pattern) and cranked, silver-coloured accelerator lever with matching black plastic pad.

At the side of each front footwell was a black plastic kick panel; again, they were updated in August 1979 by switching to Warm Black. Their ends tucked into ribbed aluminium scuff plates on the inner sills, which overlapped the usual black door rubbers, which later swapped to Warm Black.

The kick panels also served to tidy up the edges of the

More a case of practicality than luxury, the posh RS2000 passenger was treated to a pair of gloveboxes and Smiths clock. Note the heater control layout, with red on the right.

August 1979 brought Warm Black plastics to the cabin, including these brown gloveboxes on Custom models; base-spec RS2000s lacked either. Heater control had red to the left from October 1976.

Black headlining was taken from the RS2000's AVO predecessors; it was eventually ousted in favour of a standard Mk2 putty colour.

Pastel Parchment headlining was found on all late-model RS2000s, bringing Rallye Sport machines into conformity with lesser Escorts

RS2000's one-piece black carpet. By and large, a luxurious cut-pile carpet was fitted, although a couple of early cars were seen with the standard Escort loop-pile mat; this carpet later became standard in the base-model RS2000, while the plush cut-pile remained in the Custom. Black carpets were ousted in August 1979 for Warm Black (basic), Bitter Chocolate (Custom) or Tan 79 to match the seats.

All early RS2000s and Customs were equipped with a deep centre console, which fitted around the plastic under-dash mount for an optional radio; needless to say, the console was swapped for Warm Black during August 1979. Base models were offered with a different console as an accessory, or just the fascia-mounted pod when a radio was specified.

A couple of radios were offered at extra cost from the factory – at first just the MW/LW push-button Ford P21, joined in late 1979 by the option of a multi-wave, push-button P32. Each was joined by a speaker in the dashboard top and aerial in the offside front wing. Many owners instead opted for a dealer-fitted radio or cassette player from a wider range of options – sometimes accompanied by a roof-mounted aerial and speakers in the doors or front footwells.

The centre console also wrapped around the RS2000's gearstick (usually black until late 1976, when it was swapped for chrome), with a black gaiter, which eventually became Warm Black. Atop the stick was a Capri sports gearknob with impressed pattern of reverse over to the left and towards the front.

A regular, black Mk2 handbrake lever with black push button and gaiter was further back along the tunnel, as was a pair of black plastic-coated seat belt stalks with gold-and-red release buttons. Most RS2000s left the factory with front inertia-reel seat belts – at extra cost at first, but standard for

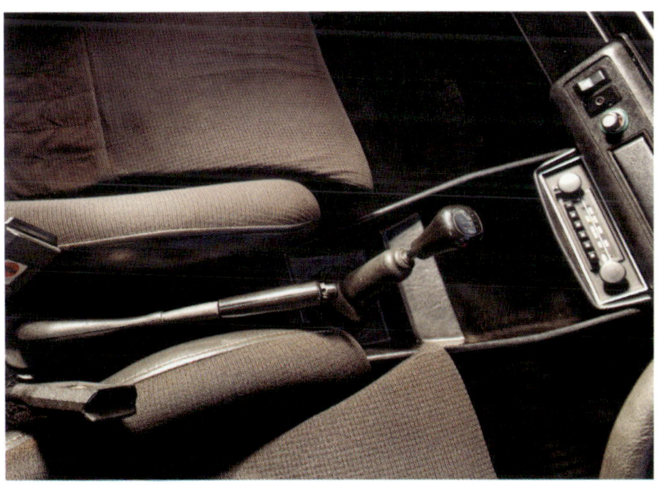

RS2000 handbrake was the standard Escort part, mounted above a modified transmission tunnel. Centre console was standard on all but post-September 1979 base models.

Custom decal reminded all the cockpit's occupants they were in something rather special. Even if the logo did look like the badge from the back of a Transit.

1977 onwards. Static seat belts were also offered – either for a lower price on early cars or a small reduction from 1977; they'd been dropped altogether by mid-1979. From March 1980 some RS2000s were fitted with Securon seat belts instead of the regular Mk2 design.

Rear seat belts were also available from the factory, as static lap belts until August 1977, when they were swapped for lap/diagonal inertia reels. As with virtually all Mk2s, the RS2000 bodyshell contained rear seat belt anchorage points built into the floorpan and C-pillars; when inertia reels were added, the reels were fitted in the boot and a pair of rectangular plastic guides were slotted into the rear parcel shelf. Speaking of which, the shelf was black cardboard until it was swapped for Warm Black in August 1979; beneath the slats was matt black paint.

Above the occupants' heads, all early RS2000s were kitted out like AVO Escorts, with the same black, small-dimpled roof lining. Matching vinyl trim was applied to the C-pillars and – unusually for a Mk2 – B-pillars; the A-posts were painted satin black. RS2000 sun visors were also black vinyl, complete with vanity mirror on the passenger side. In between the pair was a black dipping rear-view mirror with black plastic cover where it met the headlining. There was also a courtesy lamp, which had a black override switch.

That all changed in September 1978, when the headlining was swapped for a perforated version (the same as normal Escorts) in parchment colour, complete with matching C-pillar trims and mirror shroud. The sun visors were updated to match, now with black on the flip-down sides; Customs kept the vanity mirror but it was deleted from the base-spec RS2000. Finally, in August 1979, the sun visors were parchment coloured on one side and Warm Black on the reverse. Meanwhile, the B-pillar vinyls were swapped for Warm Black.

Early RS2000s had three grab handles (one above each passenger), including coat hooks for the back. August 1979 brought a change to Warm Black and reduction to a single coat hook.

Inside Boot

Ford's luxury theme extended to the RS2000's luggage compartment, where initial plans were to paint the inside of every boot in satin black (known as 'Ghia treatment'), presumably to give the impression of space.

But for whatever reason (price, probably), Ford opted out of the black hole feel for all but the earliest RS2000s; the rest were finished in body colour.

Still, that didn't mean the RS2000 owner had to feel like he was placing his sports holdall into the same place the Popular driver would drop his weekly shopping.

No, from August 1976 (if not before) the RS2000 received a plush, black Ghia boot carpet rather than the usual rubber mat; at first it was the normal Escort shape but it was improved during August 1977 with the addition of a matching carpeted cover for the spare wheel. September 1978's base-model RS2000s reverted to the Hardura mat of the Escort Sport, but Customs kept the carpets and wheel housing.

Not that there was anything to hide; far from it, in fact. The RS2000's boot always contained a spare that matched its road wheels – so underneath the cover was a 6x13in RS four-spoke alloy with 175/70x13 tyre and no centre cap; steel-wheeled models, of course, received a steel spare.

Like all RS Mk2s, the RS2000's wheel was held steady with

RS2000 Custom was treated to a luxurious luggage compartment, including cut-pile Ghia carpet, which in August 1977 added a spare wheel cover.

a woven strap and special bracket, which was spot-welded onto the boot floor above the rearmost chassis rail.

Stuffed between the spare wheel and its retaining strap was the usual Ford tool kit inside a black bag, comprising black screw pillar jack and wheel brace. At the opposite side was the RS2000's satin black, nine-gallon petrol tank.

Most RS2000s were fitted with a boot light as standard, which worked with the headlamps switched on. But there were always exceptions – some early test cars lacked the lamp, as did base-model machines.

All cars had a protective cover over the boot latch, and all had revised boot spring tensioners to cope with the rear spoiler's extra weight. An internal boot release device was available from dealers as an accessory.

Four-spoke alloy spare wheel and 175/70x13 tyre was found in the Custom's well, complete with strap attached to special spot-welded bracket.

RS2000 COLOUR SCHEMES AND INTERIOR TRIM

Colour	Colour code	Introduced	Discontinued	Interior colour	Coachline colour	Vinyl roof (optional)
Signal Amber	0	Aug 1977	Jul 1978	Black	Black	Black
Signal Orange '79	0	Aug 1978	Aug 1979	Black or chocolate	Black	Black
Signal Red '80	0	Aug 1979	Jul 1980	Chocolate	Black	Black
Signal Yellow	9	Dec 1976	Jul 1980	Black, chocolate or tan	Black	Black
Black	A	Dec 1976	Jul 1980	Black, chocolate or tan	Silver	Black
Diamond White	B	Aug 1975	Jul 1980	Black or chocolate	Black	Black
Carnival Red	D	Aug 1975	Jun 1976	Black	Black	Black
Terracotta	D	Aug 1979	Jul 1980	Chocolate or tan	Black	Black
Light Blue	E	Aug 1975	Dec 1976	Black	Black	Black
Java Green	E	Aug 1979	Jul 1980	Chocolate or tan	Black	Black
Tuscan Beige	G	Aug 1978	Aug 1979	Black or chocolate	Black	Black
Signal Orange '77	H	Dec 1976	Aug 1977	Black	Black	Black
Signal Green	J	Dec 1976	Aug 1977	Black	Black	Black
Calypso Green	K	Aug 1978	Aug 1979	Black	Black	Black
Signal Orange '76	L	Dec 1975	Dec 1976	Black	Black	Black
Sierra Beige '78	P	Aug 1978	Aug 1979	Black or chocolate	Black	Black
Cordoba Beige	P	Aug 1979	Jul 1980	Chocolate or tan	Black	Black
Venetian Red	R	Dec 1976	Jul 1980	Black, chocolate or tan	Black	Black
Daytona Yellow	T	Aug 1975	Jun 1976	Black	Black	Black
Peppermint Green	T	Aug 1977	Aug 1978	Black	Black	Black
Riviera Blue	T	Aug 1978	Aug 1979	Black	Black	Black
Nordic Blue	T	Aug 1979	Jul 1980	Chocolate or tan	Black	Black
Midnight Blue	X	Aug 1978	Jul 1980	Tan	Silver	Black
Non-standard	Y	Aug 197[illegible]	Jul 1980	Special order	Special order	Special order

ESCORT HARRIER

Possibly the prettiest Mk2 Escorts ever built, Harriers looked especially sexy in Strato Silver, a £35.83 optional extra. This December 1979 example is owned by Chris Parkes, who's a particular fan of these rare machines. "I'm yet to see one that's not been rebuilt," he jokes. Needless to say, Chris's 103,000-mile Harrier has received its share of attention, including reconditioned engine, gearbox, axle, brakes, suspension and steering rack. Countless parts were powder-coated, the Beta cloth seats were retrimmed, a new exhaust was sourced and a modified electronic distributor was fitted, which retains an authentic appearance. This Harrier's bodywork was also restored, featuring a new nearside rear quarter and sill, offside wheelarch, front panel, wings, slam panel and radiator crossmember. A non-standard RS Mexico spoiler makes a tasteful finishing touch.

What, in your eyes, were the essential ingredients of an RS Escort? Sexy side stripes? Four-spoke alloy wheels? Fishnet Recaro front seats? A big, rubber rear spoiler? A rally-bred reason to live? If they're your criteria, the Harrier got its recipe just right.

If not, you'll probably reckon the Harrier was a cynical promotional ploy, designed to flog an outgoing model using stockpiles of Escort Sports and an oversupply of go-faster goodies.

As usual, the truth was somewhere in between. The Harrier was neither conceived nor badged as an RS, yet it used a nicely-picked selection of Rallye Sport parts. It was also linked (in marketing terms, at least) to Ford's motorsport success, so its revered ranking in Escort history is pretty well deserved.

Launched in late December 1979 complete with TV campaign, the Harrier's advertising fanfare celebrated the Escort's amazing international rallying career. Ford had recently scooped the 1979 World Rally Championship manufacturers' title, meanwhile securing success in November 1979's British RAC rally – for the eighth consecutive year. Not to mention the countless victories that seemed to accompany Escorts in almost every form of motorsport.

"To commemorate these unique achievements," said Ford's brochure, "there's a special edition Escort, which combines rally-proven toughness and reliability, with the sports flair of a racing thoroughbred. The Escort Harrier."

You can't argue with that. The side profile shows why silver paint and four-spoke alloys suited the Harrier so well. Sills were painted black into the edges of the door steps.

With the simple, easy addition of an RS front spoiler, the Harrier's frontal stance is as tough as any Escort you care to mention.

To create the Harrier, Ford started with an Escort 1600 Sport in Diamond White or optional-at-extra-cost Strato Silver. The normal Sport decals were deleted in favour of new graphics in three shades of blue, plastered down each side of the car, along with smaller matching motifs on the bonnet and boot lid. The stock circular spot lamps and quarter bumpers stayed in place.

Bronze tinted glass was fitted as standard, along with a remote-control driver's door mirror. On the back was a rubber RS rear spoiler, while the eye-grabbing 6x13in polished alloy wheels were stolen from the RS2000; they were wrapped in 175/70SR13 tyres and bolted to regular 1600 Sport running gear.

Inside the Harrier the story continued. High-backed Recaro seats were also RS2000 cast-offs, complete with 'see-thru' head rests (christened fishnets by Ford fans – presumably more in tribute to ladies' hosiery than a Grimsby trawler's lower deck. Still, whatever takes your fancy...). Somewhat tellingly, the Harrier's cabin was completely trimmed in black, several months after other Mk2s went brown (or chocolate, or Warm Black, or whatever you want to call it). Sport instruments were in the dashboard (lacking the RS's oil pressure gauge) and a Sport centre console was found atop the regular transmission tunnel, rather than the deep RS compartment.

Almost everything else was pure 1600 Sport, albeit with a minor modification in the luggage compartment – an

This is why the Harrier amounted to that bit more than the sum of its parts – despite those parts being seen so many times before.

Rear spoiler was the same flexible rubber wing found on RS Mk2 Escorts. It massively added to the Harrier's appeal.

RS-type bracket for the spare wheel strap, required to accommodate a bulky 6x13in alloy. Other than that, the Harrier was a regular Escort from the Halewood production line, built only for the UK market, always in right-hand-drive format. That meant a chassis number beginning with BBAT; the first was reported to be BBATAB95400, but that's clearly incorrect because it's a January 1980 code – and we know for sure that many Harriers were built during December 1979.

Production continued in one stream during the start of 1980, with the final few possibly made in February. Some cars (definitely not every one) had the word HARRIER printed on the bottom of the colour tag riveted to the bonnet slam panel, and all were stamped with their colour – silver examples said PLATINUM (another name for Strato Silver) and Diamond White cars, of course, had WHITE. To make identification even trickier, many genuine Harriers were registered simply as 1600 Sports.

Ford quoted a total production run of 1,500 Harriers. It's reckoned that 1,000 of those cars were white, with the remainder in silver; it's entirely plausible that the real figures were slightly higher.

Even so, the Escort Harrier was a soaring success, grabbing the public's imagination and remaining today a very exclusive fast Ford. Never mind the reference to being a 'gas man's car' (thanks to the blue-and-white colour scheme resembling the livery of British Gas vans) or not-a-proper-RS comments. The Harrier looked, felt and drove every inch a true sporting Escort. What more could anyone want?

Engine – Block, Head and Sump

Despite its Escort Sport starting point, only one powerplant was available in the Harrier – the 1600 (well, 1599cc) Crossflow, producing 86bhp at 6,000rpm. That meant a top speed of 103mph, with 0-to-60mph acceleration in 10.1 seconds. By 1979 saloon car standards, it really wasn't too bad.

All Harriers were mechanically identical, housing a GT-spec, chain-driven, overhead-valve Kent engine (coded L3), built around a semi-gloss black metric 711M cylinder block. The part number 711M6015BA was cast onto the crankcase adjacent to the starter motor, while a raised T-number (usually between T12 and T20) was in raised characters on each side; despite popular opinion, it's unlikely this number related to a particular stiffness of the cylinder walls. The engine's unique identity number was stamped by hand into a machined flat on the cylinder block, between the first pair of exhaust manifold ports. All numbers began with a code for the car's build date (month and year), followed by the digits found in the numerical part of the car's VIN (vehicle identification number).

Inside the block was a standard 1600 crankshaft with matching pistons and connecting rods, providing 9.0:1 compression ratio. The supposed GT-specification camshaft was really just a mild, Cortina 1600HC-type component, with 771M6250BA part number, 272-degree duration, 54-degree overlap and red paint ring.

Bolted to the block was the usual high-compression Crossflow cast-iron cylinder head, as found in everything from Mk1 Escorts to Capris. Like the others, it was finished in semi-gloss black, and featured four inlet ports on the right-hand side, with four exhaust ports on the left. Unique to the 1600GT head (thus including the Harrier) were the big valves, featuring 39mm inlet and 34mm exhaust head diameters.

The 1600GT engine code (L3) was stamped into the head near the top rearmost exhaust manifold stud, while a number 37 was cast under the rocker shaft, only seen with the rocker cover removed. This cover was semi-gloss black, with tacked-on bracket for an ignition wire separator. All Harriers had a short, angled oil filler spout and chunky, black plastic filler cap with rough-textured finish, rectangular breather slots (on the underside), bold, raised part number and Ford oval logo. There were no stickers on the rocker cover.

Underneath the Harrier's block was a deep, black-painted sump, as found on other 1600cc Kent-engined Mk2 Escorts – nothing fancy like the Mk1 Mexico's big-wing version. A regular bare alloy Crossflow dipstick reached into the sump, down a GT-spec tube and bracket. The lubrication setup was the same as all Crossflow Mk2s, with black 35-to-40psi oil pump, screw-on cartridge filter and small breather.

It wasn't exciting but it got the job done. Harrier's 1600 Sport Crossflow powerplant was good for 86bhp and 103mph – which was reasonably hot in 1979.

Ford had swapped to viscous-coupled fans throughout most of the Escort range by the time of the Harrier's introduction; the plastic cowling fixed to the back of an enlarged radiator.

Cooling system

Identical to the 1600 Sport, the Escort Harrier featured a 9.5-pint cooling system. The centrepiece was a large, black radiator, with angular-topped header tank and overflow outlet pointing towards the passenger side, plus black plastic extension tube clipped down the side. Most radiators had a black sticker slapped on top (often to the offside of the cap), revealing the part number in white writing. A 13psi AC radiator cap was always fitted – usually in a pale gold finish.

The Harrier's cooling fan was a yellow (or, rarley, beige) viscous-coupled device, shrouded by a black plastic cowling. It was mated to a black (or bare aluminium in very few cases) water pump, which bolted to the front of the engine. On top of the cylinder head, a black-painted housing contained a 92-degree C thermostat.

Harrier coolant hoses were just the normal black rubber Kent parts, affixed with wire hose clips; sometimes (depending on supplier) they'd wear printed white part numbers or white stickers.

Fuel System

Feeding fuel to the Harrier's 1600cc Crossflow powerplant was a 32/36 DGAV twin-choke Weber carburettor, complete with automatic choke mechanism and anti-stall setup. The carb wore a metal identification tag attached using a float chamber screw, and was stamped as being made in Italy.

Jet sizes were the same as all late-model 1600 Sports (intended to run rather lean), meaning the Harrier was equipped with an anti-dieseling solenoid kit that was screwed into the offside inner wing.

The Harrier's Weber was attached to the normal metric Mk1 1300GT inlet manifold, with lugs for the two-bolt throttle linkage; a special bracket allowed the normal Escort Mk2 throttle cable to be used.

Atop the carburettor was the 1600 Sport's round metal airbox, painted black; it had a square-section intake pipe that connected to a bracket built into the four-branch exhaust manifold; the top cover featured a Ford oval logo and was held on with two studs. Inside the air pan was a disposal paper filter.

An AC mechanical fuel pump (in bare silver) was sited underneath the inlet manifold at the right-hand rear of the

Big, black radiator was standard-fit on all 1600cc Kent-powered Mk2s. Bonnet slam panel wore a purple E11 lighting sticker.

Starter motor solenoid was affixed to the nearside inner wing underneath the windscreen washer bottle. It accompanied a Lucas M35J starter.

engine. There was a Motorcraft UFO-type fuel strainer and black braided Ford fuel lines.

Exhaust System

Getting gases out of the Harrier's engine was a complete 1600 Sport exhaust system in aluminiumised mild steel – a silver-coloured finish. Up front was a tubular four-branch manifold complete with adaptor for seating the air cleaner intake pipe and a support bracket that stiffened the manifold by attaching it to the engine through two block-to-bellhousing bolts.

The manifold's four-into-two-into-one pipework had a swan neck where it reached downwards, before mating to the rest of the 1600 Sport system near the gearbox.

Constructed from bigger-than-standard-bore mild steel, the exhaust nevertheless looked pretty similar to the regular Crossflow-powered Escort setup, with oval middle box and round-section rear silencer, connected to the car with a single bolt-on hanger.

Exhaust manifold was the same four-branch big-bore found on the 1600 Sport. Windscreen washer pipework was clear plastic tubing.

Ignition and Electrical System

There was nothing special about the Harrier's engine ancillaries or electrical equipment. Predictably, everything came straight from the 1600 Sport, itself only mildly different from a standard Mk2 Escort.

In the nearside front corner of the engine bay sat a square-post Motorcraft 38A battery, bolted down with a chunky black clamp. The red (positive) and black (negative) battery cables wore blue stickers with white Ford logos.

Charging the battery was the job of a Lucas 17 ACR 35-amp alternator; that said, Ford fitted a massive variety of alternators to Mk2 Sports, and by the time of Harrier production may well have been using up stocks of whatever units were on the shelves – so Bosch or Femsa alternators were theoretically possible.

A Sport wiring loom, wrapped in black tape, was linked to the Harrier's fuse box, mounted on the nearside bulkhead. Inside, it housed seven continental fuses with connections made underneath. Like all Mk2s, the fuse box had a Mk1-type clear plastic lid (moulded with English writing) and a black plastic Capri Mk2 cover on top. The Harrier also featured in-line fuses for the heated rear

Black plastic fuse box top cover was the same as every other Mk2's. Wiring reached in from underneath.

Fly-on-the-wall view inside a Harrier engine bay, showing GT inlet manifold and non-standard distributor. Rocker cover was originally semi-gloss black – just like the thermostat housing and air box.

All Harriers had the late-model Mk2 Sport rear axle layout, with single-leaf springs and anti-roll bar. No radius rods were ever fitted.

window and radio, along with a bare metal Ford fused relay screwed to the nearside inner wing top, wired into the auxiliary driving lamp circuit.

The Harrier was cranked up using a Lucas M35J inertia starter motor, with solenoid mounted low down on the nearside inner wing. It had a black nine-volt ballasted ignition coil with round terminals, slotted into a bare alloy bracket screwed to the inner wing beneath the brake master cylinder. Motorcraft was the usual brand, although Ford at the time also fitted Lucas, Femsa and Zelmot coils.

A normal 1600 Sport distributor poked out from underneath the inlet manifold – a Motorcraft 751F12100BA part wearing a purple or beige paint splash and a black Motorcraft distributor cap. The black plugs leads were also Motorcraft, complete with white-printed Ford logo and lettering, plus black-on-white white numbering stickers. The leads were unique to the 1600cc Escort, and clipped into a black rubber separator attached to the rocker cover. Each lead clipped onto a Motorcraft AGR12 spark plug.

Like the Sport, the Harrier featured a single-tone (low-pitch) horn behind its grille. A two-tone air horn kit was available as an official accessory.

Harrier braking was assisted by the late-spec Girling servo, complete with warning switch sender in its cap.

Transmission

The Harrier's transmission was, of course, identical to the 1600 Sport's on which it was based. That meant a beefed-up Type 2 four-speed manual gearbox similar to what you'd find in almost any Crossflow-powered Escort. In the Sport's case it was a close-ratio unit, specially strengthened with shot-peened gears and uprated gear cluster bearings. The main casing was black, resembling the standard gearbox, but there was a big alloy tail housing designed to take a heavy-duty layshaft.

Harrier gearboxes housed Mk1 GT ratios, comprising first 3.337:1, second 1.995:1, third 1.418:1, fourth 1:1 and reverse 3.867:1. There was a heavy-duty differential with RS-type 3.54:1 final drive ratio (11 teeth on the pinion and 39 on the crown wheel).

The differential was bolted into a black Timken one-piece axle, featuring pick-up points for a rear anti-roll bar rather than RS-type radius rods. It was turned by a black two-piece propshaft complete with central CV joint.

Meanwhile, at the front of the gearbox was a Borg and Beck 7.5in diaphragm-spring single dry plate clutch, 1600 Sport flywheel (just a Cortina Mk3/Escort estate/van 1300HC flywheel) and regular Crossflow clutch cable.

Steering and Suspension

Sitting like an RS on its four-spoke alloys, the Harrier's suspension settings were actually unchanged from those of the 1600 Sport on which it was based.

At the front was a pair of Macpherson struts with coil springs and anti-roll bar. The Harrier's satin black suspension legs were the later Sport type, featuring mildly-uprated shock absorbers, integral steering arms (with metric tapers) and small, galvanised offset top mounts and black (or galvanised) collars. Paint splashes on the damper insert nut and top mount retaining bolts were in a random bright colour to confirm they'd been tightened to the correct settings.

The front springs were 109lb coils, finished in satin black with black plastic tubing at the end of each coil and red, yellow and orange paint splashes; the spring length was half-an-inch lower than a regular Mk2, at 294mm.

Tying the front end together was a satin black 20mm anti-roll bar. The engine crossmember was standard Escort Crossflow kit, including the usual 1600 Sport mounts with circular-shaped rubber insulators. Like the Sport, the Harrier's run-of-the-mill metric steering rack used Mk1-type track control arms and metric-tapered and threaded track rod ends; the steering gear shaft joint was the same as the RS2000's.

On the back of a Harrier was a regular Mk2 Escort suspension setup, featuring a 12mm anti-roll bar instead of RS-type radius rods, along with black telescopic rear dampers made by Fichtel and Sachs. There was a pair of 116lb, 60mm-wide, half-inch-lowered, single-leaf springs with red paint splashes too.

Polished rims revealed silver-painted M16 front brake callipers and RS-sized discs.

Four-spoke alloys were taken straight from the RS2000, with polished rims and Dove Grey spoke centres. This car's RS logos were an aftermarket addition to the plain black caps.

Brakes

Harrier stopping power was provided by a set of standard Escort Sport front discs and rear drums with dual circuit servo assistance.

The solid 247.5mm front discs were the same as RS Mk2s', as were the M16 callipers in silver/grey finish. They clamped onto the discs with GT-spec mildly-uprated Ferodo pads.

At the back of a Harrier was a pair of humble satin black-painted 9.0x1.75in brake drums with 17.8mm wheel cylinders, self-adjusting shoes and inspection slot bunged up using a blanking plug.

As usual, the dual-line braking system featured shiny mild steel brake pipes in Bundy tubing plus ribbed black flexible hoses. All Harriers had an in-line Girling brake servo with semi-gloss drum and bracket, which was attached to the offside inner wing. The clear, square plastic reservoir sat atop a silver- or gold-coloured Girling master cylinder, around which dangled a yellow plastic ring; similarly, a yellow plastic connector kept the brake lines tidy above the servo bracket, and a horizontal yellow stripe was seen on the black rubber vacuum hose. On the servo drum was sometimes found white-printed lettering.

The fluid reservoir was topped with a clear plastic cap that housed a sender for the Harrier's standard-fit brake fluid level warning indicator, linked to a test switch on the dashboard's lower fascia panel.

Wheels and Tyres

Call Harrier buyers superficial if you like, but there's no denying the model's sales and everlasting appeal were boosted by the presence of those sexy four spoke RS alloy road wheels.

Not that they were, strictly speaking, RS parts – whereas RS2000s wore RS-logoed centre caps, the Harrier bits were plain black plastic (like the caps found on Capri S or Laser alloys) pushed into place from the front.

Otherwise, though, they were the same Ford-produced 6x13in four-spokes seen on late-model RS2000s; in the recess of one spoke they were cast with 13x6Jx19 (relating to rim diameter, width and offset), in another there was a Ford oval,

Three-tone blue coachlines wrapped around the edges of each front wing, tucking neatly into the headlamp recess.

Satin black door handles were standard. Triple blue pinstripes were usually trimmed short of the door shuts.

a third had a casting number and the other wore a pair of circles featuring month and year identifiers – which were usually up to a few months before the car's build date.

Compared to other similar four-spoke alloys (such as those found on Capris), Harrier wheels had relatively thin spokes, with reasonably large cutouts beside them, along with flat seats for their chrome metric wheel nuts (which featured flat, built-in washers). All Harrier wheels had polished-and-lacquered rims and spoke edges, with Dove Grey paint inside the spokes and cutouts.

Wrapped around the alloys were Michelin ZX or MXL 175/70SR13 radial tyres, although it's possible some cars came with Uniroyal Rallyes.

There's no denying a Harrier at 100 paces - tri-shade graphics on rear quarters were big, bold and very blue.

Bodywork

It was all about the style – and the Harrier's fashion sense was bang on the money. Looking much like a funky flat-front RS2000 (which, let's face it, would've probably sold in massive numbers), almost everything about the Harrier's appearance was perfect for a sporting Escort. Okay, there was no RS1800-style front spoiler, but the rest was enough to excite any fast Ford enthusiast.

Built around a two-door 1600 Sport body (itself just a souped-up Escort L, with standard panelwork), the Hale-wood-produced Harrier lacked the RS shell's strengthening points. It's vaguely possible that a few Harriers were based on British heavy-duty export bodies (with inner wing supports and reinforced rear spring hangers but not the RS-type radius rod mounts), although there's no real reason to back this up.

Like the Sport, though, the Harrier did boast a pair of front quarter bumpers, coated in heat-set satin black epoxy and capped with late-spec (smooth) satin black overriders. Underneath the bumpers, the regular Mk2 front panel's lower airdam was sprayed satin black, which continued along the sills, rear valance and under the spare wheel well. Despite the omission of an RS front spoiler, many Harriers were fitted with a flexible polyurethane part as an aftermarket accessory – today, without an original receipt it's impossible to guarantee any cars were so equipped by dealers before first registration.

Still, there was always a genuine RS rubber rear spoiler (as found on the RS2000, RS Mexico and RS1800) supplied as standard on the Harrier's boot lid, which overlapped the back wings at each side and was fastened from underneath on four moulded studs.

Because the Harrier was basically a specced-up Sport,

Harrier motif on the bonnet's leading edge reflected the blue graphics found around the car.

Chrome locking petrol cap was a popular Ford accessory – normally the Harrier had a non-locking body-coloured part.

Remote-control driver's door mirror was standard in satin black; the passenger side stuck with a fixed mirror.

packed with optional extras as standard (possibly to clear some stockpiles) it was naturally fitted with Triplex bronze tinted glass, including laminated windscreen and heated rear 'screen. Opening front quarter vents weren't offered from the factory, nor was a sunroof or vinyl roof – although Ford dealers occasionally added them as extras to new cars.

Edging the roof was a pair of drip rail covers in satin black epoxy, beneath which the Harrier's door frames, window surrounds and B-pillars were painted satin black. The windscreen beading and wipers, exterior door handles and locks were all finished in satin black too.

The Sport options list provided the Harrier with its standard remote-control driver's door mirror, while the passenger

Also available in white – roughly two-thirds of the Harrier population were born Diamond White rather than Strato Silver. It's unusual today (although completely correct) to find a Harrier without an RS front spoiler

Harriers were built at Halewood between December 1979 and January/February 1980. All had their colour name (WHITE or PLATINUM) printed on the build tag, but not every car said HARRIER across the bottom.

Mounted against the nearside inner wing, the Harrier's windscreen fluid reservoir contained a recess for an electric washer pump.

Despite popular opinion, the Harrier wasn't based on an RS shell – so there were no suspension top mount reinforcing plates. Well, not unless the Harrier in question inadvertently received export-spec heavy-duty inner wings.

side made to with a regular fixed Mk2 item; both sides were finished in satin black. Meanwhile, all Harriers had a retractable Ford-stamped radio aerial – in chrome with black grommet – mounted in the offside front wing.

Harriers wore the usual late-model Mk2 front grille (all black, with Ford oval badge in the middle), behind which the front panel was sprayed satin black.

At the other end, the Harrier lacked the RS2000's black back panel, instead settling for a satin black Sport bumper with black overriders (again, the later, smoother shape) and twin number plate lamps. The boot lid wore a chrome lock (apparently, only German-built Escorts received the black part) and satin black-painted badges – which read Escort 1.6 (in the larger, late-spec font) on the nearside; the boot lid's offside bore a Ford oval.

Adjacent to the 1.6 badge was a small (ish) Harrier motif in three shades of blue. A matching decal was applied to the bonnet's offside leading edge. Big, bold versions were found on each side of the car, with three pinstripes beneath the body swage lines of the front wings and doors, which kicked up along the rear quarters in alignment with the wheelarches. The stripes wrapped around the edges of each front wing, but not into the door shuts; nor did they tuck underneath the rear spoiler. Nowhere did the decals say Harrier.

No extra-cost options were offered from the factory, other than metallic Strato Silver paintwork; around 500 Harriers were supplied in this scheme, with the other 1,000-or-so finished in Diamond White.

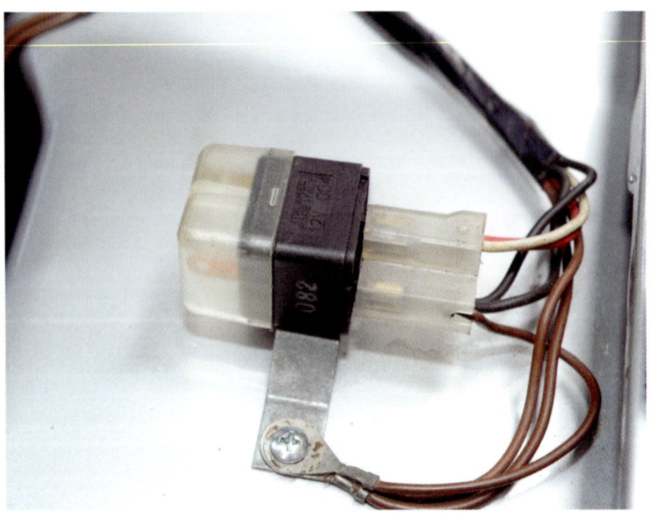

Auxiliary lighting relay was mounted on the nearside inner wing top, usually a bare metal Italamec 004 instead of this modern plastic equivalent, facing outwards rather than in.

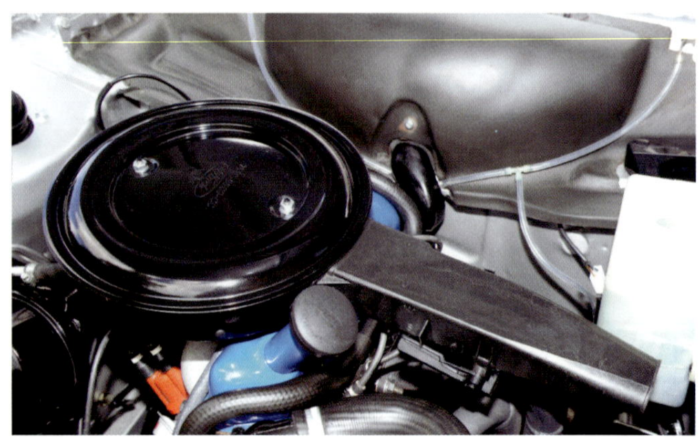

Harrier's black air pan was straight from the 1600 Sport; rocker box would have been black; oil cap is the chunky post-November 1977 type.

Underbonnet

Everything under the bonnet of a Harrier was what you'd find in a late-model Escort 1600 Sport – right down, in many cases, to the build plate on the bonnet slam panel; some were stamped across the bottom with the word Harrier but many others weren't. Incidentally, the Mk2 officially had its VIN tag moved from the slam panel to the offside inner wing from November 1979, but British cars waited until January 1980 for the change – so early Harriers had theirs in the original Escort position.

A handful of Harriers were allegedly built around heavy-duty export Escort bodyshells, which added RS-type inner wings with strengthening panels around the suspension top mounts, plates in the towers and fillets against the drip rails. There's no documented evidence to support this claim, though, so it's probably fair to say most Harriers seen today with RS reinforcements have been modified since leaving the factory.

So, what was definitely included? Well, the Harrier certainly always had later-type 85mm Mk2 strut top apertures, and on the nearside suspension turret was its windscreen washer fluid reservoir – an opaque plastic bottle with matching cap, which attached via a screwed-on black bracket. The electric washer motor was black with a printed white Ford oval logo or (possibly, rarely) pale gold with black writing. Washer pipework was clear plastic tubing with a white plastic T-connector and copper nozzles exiting through the scuttle panel.

Today, most surviving Harriers wear a Ghia-type sandwiched foam engine compartment cowl across the bulkhead top, but none were so equipped at the Halewood factory. It's also unlikely the pads were supplied by dealers before registration.

Screwed into the nearside inner wing top was a metal Italamec 004 16-amp relay for the Harrier's auxiliary driving lamps. It was connected to a multi-plug fed from the main loom in black-taped wiring, plus brown earth straps fastened on ring terminals under the forward-most self-tapping screw. On the opposite inner wing was the Sport's Ford-labelled anti-dieseling solenoid valve, screwed in at rather an aftermarket-looking angle.

Like other right-hand-drive Mk2s, the Harrier's bonnet release cable was coated in black plastic, and ran down the offside inner wing from a handle under the dashboard to a release mechanism in the slam panel. The galvanised bonnet prop also hinged from the offside front corner, resting in a white or black plastic clip on the slam panel when closed. Directly behind the clip was the Harrier's battery tray, with chunky black clamp.

As for underbonnet stickers, the Harrier didn't have many – mainly just a rectangular E11 lighting decal in pale purple, randomly affixed to the nearside inner wing in the vicinity of the spot-lamp relay or – occasionally – the bonnet slam panel.

When the Sport entered a phone box to change into its Superman costume, the Harrier came out with Clark Kent's extra eyewear – in this case a pair of black driving lamps.

Lighting

When the Sport underwent its Harrier transformation, all the regular equipment remained – including, of course, the twin auxiliary long-range driving lamps. In black metal with black surrounds, the Ford-branded 5.5in circular halogen units were wired into the main beam lighting circuit. They sat on black metal brackets affixed to the front panel behind the front quarter bumpers, just to the inside of the overriders.

Halogen headlamps were also standard, in this case 60/55W 7in circular semi-sealed beams made by Carello, complete with the Ford oval in the middle of the flat glass above the word 'halogen'. They lived above regular Escort (Vega-produced) indicators recessed into the bumpers, which came with hazard warning flashers as standard.

English Butlers-branded or – usually – Italian-made Altissimo rear light units were used at the back of the Harrier, along with a pair of Altissimo number plate lamps mounted in the bumper. Harriers also found themselves equipped with a factory-fitted Altissimo rear fog lamp from new, fixed onto the offside rear valance with two bolts poking into the boot.

Lighting a Harrier's cabin was a late-spec Mk2 courtesy lamp with black override switch, operated from black plastic A-pillar-mounted door control switches. A luggage compartment light was also standard, in the form of a circular lamp mounted under the parcel shelf.

By the time of the Harrier's December 1979 introduction, every other Escort had swapped to brown cabin colours. Yet the Harrier was offered only with black – because the trim suited the car's bodywork, or to use up stocks of seats?

Interior

One look inside the Harrier, and the RS theme was complete. All it took was a pair of Recaro front seats with fishnet headrests. Oh yes, and the regular refinements found in a late-spec Escort Sport.

But there was one crucial difference. Whereas the Sport and RS2000 swapped to Warm Black (that's brown to you and me) cabins in August 1979, the December 1979-onwards Harrier reverted to an all-black cockpit. Was it because Ford wanted a moody, monochrome appearance, or simply thanks to a stockroom somewhere stacked high with redundant high-backed Recaros? Who cares – the Harrier looked great, and it was a pleasure to sit in.

So yes, the seats were identical to those found in the

Ghia-sourced centre console contained a quartz clock and handy coin holder. Ford P21 radio was standard-fit, with the option of an M32 MW/LW/VHF for an extra £26.67.

There's no doubting the influence of Recaro recliners on the Harrier's desirability – with these fishnet headrests the finishing touch.

Black three-spoke sports steering wheel was much as you'd find in other sporty Mk2 Escorts; this Harrier's wearing the centre cap from an early Sport instead of the usual Ford oval.

RS2000 Custom from September 1978 until August 1979. Made by Recaro, they boasted reclining backrests controlled by an eight-toothed handwheel on the base; they also tipped forward using a black plastic lever (marked with an up arrow) in the side of the backrest. The seat faces were upholstered in black Beta Plus cloth with horizontal block pattern and vertical stitching; the sides, piping and backs were covered in black vinyl. Perhaps most recognisable were the fishnet headrests – trimmed in black vinyl, complete with mesh inserts in criss-cross pattern and supported on a pair of chrome legs.

Like the Recaro-equipped RS2000, the Harrier's L-spec Mk2 back seat was upholstered to match the fronts, in black Beta Plus cloth running horizontally, stitched vertically. At

Instruments were donated by the Sport and Ghia; all Harriers featured the 140mph speedo and orange needles.

Fascia was familiar to any Mk2 Escort owner, with illuminated heater controls and switch panel with ashtray. Factory-fitted cigar lighter wore a lit-cigarette emblem. Harrier also featured rocker switches for brake fluid level, hazards, heated rear window and rear fog lamp.

Back seat drivers made do with the usual Escort rear bench seat, trimmed in black Beta Plus cloth to match the Recaro fronts.

each side, the inner wheelarches were covered in black vinyl.

Harrier seat belts were the usual inertia reels, with black plastic-coated stalks on the transmission tunnel, featuring gold-and-red release buttons. The stock Escort belts were always present until March 1980, when Securon components were occasionally used instead – so it's highly probable they never made it onto a Harrier. Inertia reel lap/diagonal rear seat belts were a factory Harrier option, complete with rectangular plastic guides slotted into the black cardboard rear parcel shelf on each side, and reels in the boot.

Strangely, Ford didn't bother to fit the complementary Custom door cards – instead the Harrier made do with standard Escort panels in black vinyl, which revealed its body-colour painted door tops.

Up front, the cards had vertical mock double stitching, small armrests in black vinyl, plain black plastic release

All Mk2s wore a set of three column stalks, including this horn push and indicator controller on the left.

Dipping rear-view mirror was black, with parchment-coloured cover against the roof.

RS-type trim didn't extend to the door cards, which were lowly L-spec vinyl panels rather than full-height.

handles and frames, regular Mk2 chrome window winders (with black inserts and knobs), black knob and escutcheon for the remote control driver's door mirror control, along with black spacer (the door card was specially produced complete with hole); a few wore a chrome escutcheon. The inner lock buttons were slim black plastic pins. Meanwhile, Harrier rear quarter trims were L-spec in black, with plastic armrest recesses and small, black, swivelling ashtrays.

The Harrier's dashboard panel was the standard Mk2 satin black metal item, without the RS2000's clock pod. Above it, a padded black vinyl top reached across the car.

At each side of the dashboard was an eyeball vent for the heater/demister, in black plastic with silver rim. In the middle of the dash was the black heater control panel, with silver rim, two-speed flick switch, illumination, temperature sliders and foil showing hot to cold from left to right.

Both sides of the car received a black cardboard parcel shelf, finished at the front edges with black vinyl padding. There was no factory-fitted glovebox, but many Harriers had a Ghia/RS2000 part installed sometime in later life.

At the centre of the lower dashboard was the Harrier's black plastic fascia panel, which housed a row of rocker switches with a rotating ashtray in the middle. From left to right, the switches were brake low-pressure warning, hazard flashers, cigarette lighter (fitted as standard), heated rear window and rear fog lamp. Just over to the right, on the steering column shroud, was a blanking plug in place of a basic Mk2's choke control knob.

Beneath the fascia was a black vinyl Ghia-type centre console, which included a quartz clock and radio aperture, each with a silver rim. Slotted inside was a Ford radio –

Ford's press shot of the Harrier cockpit, with more than a hint of brown to those Beta Plus-trimmed Recaros. Was the original plan to use Chocolate trim, or was this merely a mock-up for the photos?

Inertia-reel front seat belts were standard. Rear belts were optional.

Seat belt clasps were these black stalks with silver-gold release button.

usually a P21 MW/LW push-button device with pre-selection for six stations, but the M32 MW/LW/VHF was a popular option; a choice of Ford radio and cassette players was also offered by dealers.

The console included a soft, black gaiter around the black gearstick, which was capped with a chunky, black RS/Capri-type sports gearshift knob. It didn't extend a far as the black handbrake lever, which featured a black gaiter and black push button.

In front of the driver was the usual Sport RS-type flat three-spoke sports steering wheel, with leather-grain-effect plastic rim and satin black metal spokes. In the centre was a black plastic cap with blue Ford oval badge.

The steering column shroud and associated plastics were all black, complete with three stalks – two-speed (plus intermittent) wash/wipe controls were on the right-hand side, a shorter stalk behind it operated the headlamps, and on the left was a stalk for indicators, horn and headlamp dip/flash.

Harrier instrumentation was lifted straight from the late-model Escort Sport, with orange needles and white writing on black dial faces. They comprised a 140mph speedometer on the right (which included mileage and trip recorders), 7,000rpm tachometer on the left and smaller circular gauge in between for water temperature and fuel level. Across the bottom of the instrument panel was a row of five warning lights for left-hand indicators, oil pressure, main beam, ignition and right-hand indicators.

At the driver's feet was the usual Escort pedal box, featuring satin black brake and clutch levers with rubber pads in a chunky horizontal pattern. The cranked silver accelerator lever wore a black plastic pad on its pedal. Harrier footwell kick panels were black plastic, and tucked into ribbed aluminium scuff plates that ran along the inner sills. The carpet was the usual single-piece, loop-pile rug rather than plush Ghia trim.

Harrier headlining was the Sport's standard Escort parchment colour, with large perforations. Matching vinyl C-pillar trims were fitted, but there were no covers on the B-pillars. The padded sun visors were the same parchment coloured material when tucked up to the roof, with black undersides when used to deflect light. No passenger-side vanity mirror was included.

A black, dipping rear-view mirror dangled from the Harrier's roof, complete with plastic cover in parchment-

Perforated parchment-coloured headlining had almost-matching sun visors, which flipped down to reveal black on the reverse.

Inside the Harrier's boot was much like any other Mk2, with one or two subtle alterations – in particular the 13in four-spoke spare wheel and special bracket to grab its retaining strap.

coloured plastic where it met the headlining.

Front-seat Harrier passengers had a black plastic grab handle, but people in the back had none – instead there was just a black coat hook at the top of each B-pillar.

Inside boot

Believe it or not, the boot of a Harrier was one of its most distinguishing features. Not because it was unique, but because it contained the only part that wasn't a simple bolt-on upgrade from the Sport on which it was based.

Yet it would be easy to miss the small bracket spot-welded by hand into place on the rearmost chassis rail top, alongside the spare wheel well. It was taken directly from the Escort RS, intended to hold one end of the woven wheel strap and necessitated by the Harrier's wide, four-spoke alloy wheels – of which there was a spare in the boot (without a centre cap, of course).

Theoretically, Harriers were supposed to benefit from an uprated boot spring tensioner to take the weight of the standard rear spoiler, but it's perhaps more likely that most machines had the torsion bars moved a notch instead.

Everything else about a Harrier's luggage compartment was the same as a standard Escort L, including satin black, nine-gallon petrol tank in the offside well, black cardboard partition behind the rear seat and black Hardura rubber mat over the body-coloured boot floor – complete with cutout in the mat for the aforementioned spare wheel bracket.

The Harrier was equipped with the usual circular Escort luggage compartment lamp (under the parcel shelf) and protective rubber latch cover, along with the standard tool kit strapped beside the spare wheel, which included a black vertical jack and wheel brace inside a black canvas bag.

Colour schemes and interior trim

Body colour	Interior colour	Stripe colour(s)
Diamond White	Black	Blue/blue/blue
Strato Silver	Black	Blue/blue/blue

AUSTRALIAN SPORTING ESCORTS

When anyone tells you about a 'genuine' flat-front RS2000, this is invariably the car they're referring to – an Australian 2.0 GS Rally Pack. It was used as the basis for international motorsport homologation of the snoutless two-litre Pinto-powered Escort in February 1978, passed as a styling evolution of the RS2000 despite countless differences under the skin.

Is the grass really greener on the opposite side of the globe? While British Ford fans bemoaned their inability to buy Australia's flat-fronted, two-litre Mk2 Escorts, their antipodean cousins longed for full-fat RS2000s with the power turned up to ten. While Great Britain wanted heavy-duty inner wings across the range, Australia asked for properly uprated suspension. While Brits begged for a Rallye Sport four-door, Aussies wished for proper RS four-spoke alloy wheels...

When the Australian Escort Mk2 was launched in late 1975, it was only available with a 1300cc Crossflow powerplant. It was soon supported by the option of a 1.6-litre version, which gained a twin-choke Weber carburettor in Ghia guise. Two-door, four-door or van bodystyles were available, with four-speed manual or three-speed C3 automatic transmissions. All very similar to Eurpoean offerings, albeit without an estate model.

But because Aussie Escorts were built at Sydney's Homebush plant, Ford Australia used a fair proportion of locally-sourced components and its own trim levels. Top of the tree were the XL and Ghia; the latter was a four-door only machine that was all but identical to its Saarlouis-built namesake, with plush velour seats, wooden dashboard cappings and vinyl roof. It really struck a chord with buyers

There's no such thing as a factory-built flat-front RS2000, but this is the closest you'll get. Note the standard GL badging rather than any fancy Rallye Sport moniker.

who'd previously seen such luxury in nothing smaller than huge Ford Fairlanes and LTDs.

In contrast, enthusiastic drivers generally picked the GS Rally Pack – a series of sporty options made popular on the Mk1 Escort Twin Cam, GT1600 and contemporary Ford Falcons. Although it was initially offered on top of Ghia trim, the Rally Pack found itself most at home when applied to the Escort 1.6XL, which from mid-1977 was renamed 1.6GL; it was sold in two- or four-door form and gained a Ghia-type centre console, meanwhile retaining the XL's full-height door cards (which looked like those found on European GLs, including curved chrome beading above and below the armrests instead of carpeted lower sections).

Included in the Mk2's GS Rally Pack was a selection of kit from hot European Escorts, including the Sport's black, epoxy-coated front quarter bumpers, overriders, long-range driving lamps, circular halogen headlamps, black back bumper, sculptured steel 5x13in wheels (with the black-painted spoke effect of UK cars), three-spoke steering wheel (including Mk1 Escort script-badge centre cap) and instruments with rev counter. It was available in bright colour schemes and also boasted a bold sticker set – the thick, black side decals found on German-built broadstripe RS2000s.

Underneath, everything else was stock Aus-spec Escort. That meant it was based on what the UK classed as an export bodyshell, with heavy-duty inner wings (featuring reinforced strut towers) and skidded rear chassis rails. Sydney-built Mk2s also came with side impact protection inside the doors from 1977, a redesigned rear bulkhead with cross-braced strengthening (for the compulsory rear seat belt mounts) and, from May 1977 a fuel filler hidden behind the rear number plate (which fed a 12-gallon petrol tank mounted beneath the

Australia's Rally Pack was a series of options applied to a regular Pinto-powered Escort in (detuned) 1.6 or 2.0 guise. This car's bright colour scheme and bold striping was standard but the wheels are aftermarket.

While European RS2000s kicked out around 110bhp, their Aussie counterparts kept a stock Cortina powerplant. Still, 94bhp was enough to gain a great following for this small Sydney-built car.

boot floor, complete with shielded fuel lines and crude, bolted-on blanking plate over the European filler hole).

There was an abundance of detail differences too. Australian cars carried high-backed front seats (the GL having recliners with perforated vinyl covers and built-in headrests), aerodynamic door mirrors, Olympic tyres, locally-sourced glass and rear-view mirror stuck to the windscreen rather than roof. Suspension settings remained standard, and even the sporty models lacked the close-ratio gearbox or high-performance tubular exhaust manifold of European GT machines.

To make matters worse, Ford's measures to appease DR27A emission control laws slashed 18bhp from the 1.6-litre engine, from July 1976 dropping the Ghia's twin-choke Weber in favour of Ford's so-called sonic idle carburettor (other 1.6 Escorts were already on single-barrel carbs). The biggest Crossflow instantly became a slug and its 1300cc counterpart was then deleted from the Escort lineup.

Any idea what car this could be? Nope, not a clue...

On the plus side, it was the perfect opportunity for Ford Australia to stuff a two-litre Cortina engine under the little car's bonnet.

Now, it wasn't the first time a Pinto-powered Escort had appeared in Aus. In June 1975, 25 Mk1 RS2000s were shipped over from England for motorsport use. Then in 1976, a batch of 25 consecutively-numbered droop-snoot Mk2 RS2000s were imported from Germany, again for the sole purpose of allowing Escorts to enter local rallying and touring car racing – especially the legendary Bathurst 1000 event, in which RS2000s won their class twice.

All were supplied in pretty much full European two-door, manual specification, including full Rallye Sport suspension and brakes (with Capri-type Sachs front struts and discs, rear radius arms and big Girling servo) and 110bhp Pinto power-plants that remained unaltered but for the addition of a charcoal canister.

The 25 cars were painted Diamond White, Carnival Red or Daytona Yellow, decked out with broadstripe decals, 5.5x13in sports steel wheels, Pirelli Cinturato CN36 175/70HR13 tyres and Ghia-type black velour front seats in place of the usual Scheels (although the black headlining and gloveboxes remained). They were also offered the option of high-power Group One engine goodies – although none were supplied with the kit from new.

Despite the RS2000's success, its specification wasn't reflected in Australia's February 1977-onwards home-built Escort 2.0. Instead, its overhead-cam two-litre lump was detuned for environmental legislation, strangled down to 94bhp in high-compression guise and a measly 85bhp as a low-compression unit. A special steel sump was developed, there was a single downdraft Weber 27/28 DCG carburettor with round air cleaner, a normal Cortina cast iron exhaust manifold and a Capri radiator, which was moved forward towards the slam panel in a similar fashion to the European RS2000 but featured a top hose coming straight out rather than at an angle.

The transmission incorporated a regular Aussie Escort gearbox, based on a Cortina Mk3 four-speed but with a removable iron bellhousing and different extension housing, which allowed the gearstick to poke through the standard Escort tunnel rather than the modified RS setup. The axle contained a 3.54:1 differential, with no radius rod mounts nor option of a limited-slip differential. In contrast, the two-litre (especially in Ghia form) was regularly supplied with a performance-killing C3 three-speed automatic gearbox. The suspension and brakes stayed as the standard Mk2 struts with non-removable steering arms, 9.6in front discs and 8x1.5in drums on the back.

By this point, two-litre Escorts were very much mainstream models, offered as a GL two-door saloon, GL four-door or even GL van; the Ghia was now only built with a 2.0 engine.

Luckily, the GS Rally Pack was given a revamp, available

on Escort 1.6L, 1.6GL or 2.0GL saloons – which (in 2.0 Rally Pack guise) formed the basis for February 1978's international homologation of the flat-nose Escort two-litre as a minor styling evolution of the European RS2000 (which itself was officially a revision of the Mk1).

Now the Rally Pack comprised the previous quarter bumpers, overriders, driving lamps, sports steering wheel and gauges plus intermittent windscreen wipers, black door mirrors, black RS1800-type front and rear spoilers and new decals (with thick, black side stripes featuring massive ESCORT lettering on the back wings and mirrored across the front bib spoiler; on the boot lid's offside was a huge 1.6-LITRE or 2-LITRE sticker).

The stock bodyside mouldings were deleted on the GS Rally Pack, but early cars still wore chrome trim to the windows, drip rails, door handles and badges – which said 1.6 or 2.0 behind the front wheelarches and Escort L or GL on the boot lid. Late 1978 brought Sport-style satin black paint treatment in place of the chrome, along with square headlamps. You win some, you lose some...

So-called sports handling suspension was an additional option on the two-litre Escort saloon, adding stiffer springs and shock absorbers, beefier front anti-roll bar plus a rear anti-roll bar. Globe Volante 5.5x13in alloy wheels shod with Uniroyal ZR tyres were offered at extra cost instead of the standard 5x13in sports steels.

Two-litre models were also available with air conditioning from August, including a compressor in place of the battery (which was relocated to the boot under a plastic cover where European cars kept their fuel tanks) and a panel under the dashboard containing two air outlets, switches and a Ford LTD digital clock. Cars with air conditioning also received tinted side glass (all Mk2s came with a tinted rear window as standard; the tinted sides were stock on Escort Ghias without air con).

From August 1979 the Rally Pack was replaced with the half-hearted Sports Pack. It ditched the front overriders, driving lamps, black decals and passenger mirror, meanwhile retaining the GL's chrome rubbing strips and offering gold-painted steel wheels.

Incidentally, the Escort GL saloon was also obtainable with a Fashion Pack, which added Cadiz upholstery from the European Sport plus colour-keyed bodyside stripes, chrome wheelnuts, 'styled' nearside door mirror, electric clock and vanity mirror on the passenger-side sun visor.

Two limited editions were worthy of mention as sporting Escorts – first, the Escapee of October 1976, which was a run of 400 cars built to coincide with RS1800s running in the Southern Cross Rally. Supplied in white with red and yellow stripes, black bonnet and white sports steel wheels, its paint scheme was a toned-down version of the livery worn by contemporary works machines. Underneath it was just a stock 1.6L but Ford grabbed GS bits out of the parts bin, including instrumentation, sports steering wheel, rear spoiler, quarter bumpers, spotlights, radial tyres and laminated windscreen. Its interior could be ordered in black, tan or dark blue.

In 1980 the Escort lineup was temporarily joined by the GL Sprint Pack, also known as the Colin Bond Special thanks to its promotion by Ford Australia works rally driver and team boss Colin Bond. In many ways a lesser version of the earlier GS Rally Pack, Bondy's Escort was a 1.6 or 2.0 two- or four-door painted Hermitage, Lemon Lime, Sno White or Silver Grey, complete with broad GS side stripes and rear spoiler. But there were full-width chrome bumpers, chrome wheel

Australian Escort model codes

Model code	Model	Production dates
11612	L two-door	Oct 1975 to Jun 1977
11616	XL two-door	Oct 1975 to Jun 1977
11636	XL four-door	Oct 1975 to Jun 1977
11638	Ghia four-door	Oct 1975 to Jun 1977
11712	1.6L two-door	Jun 1977 to Dec 1978
11716	1.6GL two-door	Jun 1977 to Dec 1978
11717	2.0GL two-door	Jun 1977 to Dec 1978
11736	1.6GL four-door	Jun 1977 to Dec 1978
11737	2.0GL four-door	Jun 1977 to Dec 1978
11739	2.0 Ghia four-door	Jun 1977 to Dec 1978
11912	1.6L two-door	Dec 1978 to Dec 1980
11916	1.6GL two-door	Dec 1978 to Dec 1980
11917	2.0GL two-door	Dec 1978 to Dec 1980
11918	RS2000 two-door	May 1979 to Dec 1980
11932	1.6L four-door	May 1978 to Dec 1980
11936	1.6GL four-door	May 1978 to Dec 1980
11937	2.0GL four-door	Dec 1978 to Dec 1980
11938	RS2000 four-door	May 1979 to Dec 1980
11939	2.0 Ghia four-door	Dec 1978 to Dec 1980
41682	L van	1975 to Jun 1977
41686	XL van	1975 to Jun 1977
41782	1.6L van	Jun 1977 to Dec 1978
41786	1.6GL van	Jun 1977 to Dec 1978
41787	2.0GL van	Jun 1977 to Dec 1978
41788	1.6GL Sundowner van	Dec 1977 to Dec 1978
41789	2.0GL Sundowner van	Dec 1977 to Dec 1978
41982	1.6L van	Dec 1978 to Dec 1980
41986	1.6GL van	Dec 1978 to Dec 1980
41987	2.0GL van	Dec 1978 to Dec 1980
41988	1.6GL Sundowner van	Dec 1978 to Dec 1980
41989	2.0GL Sundowner van	Dec 1978 to Dec 1980

It's worth noting that genuine RS2000s had the appropriate model code described on their VIN plates, along with a CK41-prefixed chassis number (two-door RS2000s) and CK42 for four-doors. GS Rally Packs and Sports Packs weren't identified by a special chassis code because they were merely options applied to existing models.

Four doors, flat front and two-litre Pinto power – you never found that happy combo on a Halewood production line.

trim rings, chrome window surrounds, beading, handles and badges. The standout feature was a unique interior with centre console clock and cloth-trimmed seats with see-through A-frame headrests and bold ESCORT logos repeated across the upholstery.

Oh, and let's not forget the Escort Sundowner of 1978 to 1981, which was a factory-finished custom van, sold as a lifestyle machine rather than utility vehicle. It came equipped with 1.6 or two-litre engine, manual or automatic gearbox and sporty bodywork including black-finished quarter bumpers with front overriders, driving lights, halogen headlamps (round, later swapped for square), blacked-out window surrounds, sports steel wheels with chrome trim rings, 254mm circular bubble side tinted windows, colour-coded sports door mirrors and huge side graphics in a variety of bright schemes.

The Sundowner's cabin was equally unusual, boasting sports instruments, reclining bucket seats in houndstooth or (later) striped beige cloth, three-spoke sports steering wheel, centre console, fluorescent roof light, loop-pile carpeted load space, vinyl spare wheel cover, internal rear door release and wooden extension behind the front seats designed for accepting a mattress. Air conditioning was optional, as were a laminated windscreen and Volante alloy wheels.

Fewer than 2,000 Sundowners were produced, from a total of around 45,000 Aussie-built Mk2s between 1977 and 1980, over half of which were two-litre GLs, Ghias and regular vans. Despite their underpowered Pinto lumps, most owners had never encountered a proper Escort RS, so the big-engined Escorts seemed to be lively performers. And besides, if they wanted a real enthusiasts' machine, the best Australian Escort was close at hand...

Behind that flip-down rear number plate is the Aussie Escort's petrol cap. Note the blanking plate over the redundant fuel filler.

Australian RS2000

Although the two-litre GS Rally Pack was a pretty handy performer, there was no getting away from the fact that it was a mere shadow of the Rallye Sport Escorts available in Europe. After all, Ford fans had been given a glimpse of the beak-nosed RS2000 when 25 broadstripes were imported for motorsport use during 1976.

So in May 1979 Ford Australia launched its very own RS2000, complete with slanting front end and RS cockpit. Okay, it wasn't quite the same as its Saarlouis-built namesake, but there were one or two tricks up its sleeve – not least its availability in two-door or four-door form, along with choice of manual or automatic transmission.

RS2000 production took place at Ford's Campbelltown, Victoria facility using a mixture of kit components from Germany and the locally-sourced components found on other Australian Mk2s.

Under the authentic RS2000 bonnet, quite a few European horses had escaped. Instead there was a stock 94bhp Pinto powerplant from the regular two-litre Escort, lacking the Saarlouis RS2000's alloy sump, alloy engine mounts and free-flowing exhaust. Instead there was the usual Aussie-spec configuration with steel sump, cast iron exhaust manifold, Capri radiator (again moved forward in the engine bay) and Weber 27/28 DCG carburettor below a round air cleaner. As with all Escorts, the RS2000's engine number matched its chassis number.

The standard Australian gearboxes stayed in place, in the guise of a four-cog manual or optional three-speed C3 auto within a stock transmission tunnel, which included a gear-stick aperture in the regular Escort position. There were no close ratios and no alloy bellhousing but there was, at least, a quickshift mechanism made from a small spacer attached to the bottom of the gearlever, along with a raised pivot point.

Needless to say, the RS2000's rear axle was the usual part found on other 2.0 Mk2s, complete with 3.54:1 diff. No LSD was offered.

Disappointingly, though, Ford opted to keep the entire Aussie Escort suspension and braking setup, albeit the sports handling upgrade from the GS Rally Pack. All that meant was uprated springs and dampers (still only the normal Mk2 struts with integral steering arms), increased-diameter front anti-roll bar plus an anti-roll bar at the back rather than European RS2000s' radius rods.

Yes, the handling was pretty good, but testers found there was less damping control than the Saarlouis RS2000 and the local car's tail end was rather skittish.

But none of that really mattered, nor even did the car's performance deficit (0-to-62mph was recorded on a calendar, in 11.5 seconds). Because behind its three-spoke sports steering wheel the RS2000 was an exciting car. Enthusiasts enjoyed its slick gearchange and loved the Scheel reclining seats, which were supplied as standard with black Beta Plus cloth covers. Their headrests were a different shape from the roll-tops found on German RS2000s, while only two-door models had tipping backrests – four-door cars lacked the levers on the sides.

A white headlining was fitted to all Aussie RS2000s (with three grab handles), as were a padded rear bench with standard-fit seat belts, black GL-type door cards (wearing curved chrome beading), Cortina Mk3 handbrake lever, standard Escort gearknob and GL centre console, which had a blanking plate where a clock could live. Still, an AM push-button radio was standard in the slot above.

The dashboard was plain satin black steel, with no cubby hole. But there was a plastic Ghia glovebox on the passenger side, and the driver benefited from full German orange-needle RS instrumentation with speedo, rev counter and three supplementary gauges.

A laminated, tinted-band front windscreen was an RS2000

On face value it looked like a European RS2000, but the Australian car wore a very different suspension setup. The 5.5x13in Volante alloy wheels were a factory optional extra.

Well worth waiting for – after importing two small batches of European RS2000s, Australia eventually built its own Rallye Sport Escort.

Similar to a UK-market RS2000 in all but detail, with Scheel recliners, GL door cards and European RS2000 instruments.

optional extra, as were Globe Volante 5.5x13in multi-spoke alloys with chrome or black centre caps (in place of the stock 5x13in steel wheels) within the standard Uniroyal ZR70S13 tyres. RS four-spokes were never offered in Aus.

Of course, the RS2000's visual appeal was its greatest selling point, thanks mainly to that stylish new nose. Identical to the polyurethane snout of European RS2000s, it was accompanied by the same German front wings and bonnet; the slam panel was standard Australian Mk2. Within the nose's black lamp pods were quad headlamps – Hella outers and Lucas inners, rather than the Cibies of German-built cars. All the RS2000's windows were locally-sourced, as were the colour-keyed sports door mirrors.

The rubber rear spoiler was the same throughout the Escort world but the Aussie RS2000 had a few more external detail differences, including chrome drip rail covers alongside blacked-out window surrounds and black handles. The rear bumper was Euro-spec RS2000, complete with corner extensions but no screw caps.

Its bodyshell was pure Australian-spec, including heavy-duty inner wings, uprated rear chassis rails and petrol tank under the boot floor, with fuel filler mounted behind the back number plate.

RS2000s were offered in five different colours: Sno White, Lemon Lime, Burnt Orange, Monza Red and Midnight, all with black sills. According to experts, five more were sprayed silver and a few others were painted Onyx Black. There was no vinyl roof option but big, broad multi-stripes at bumper height along each flank and RS2000 graphics on the rear quarters really set them apart from lesser models. Even if, as some suggested, the paintwork was poor and the snout was shoddily fitted.

Not that it really mattered. Yes, it was a compromise. A halfway house with the power turned down. But the RS2000 was the nearest thing to a proper RS, a fact reflected in healthy sales – apparently 2,444 until production ended in December 1980. Of that number, it's reckoned around 1,000 were RS2000 four-doors, and 250 (chiefly four-doors) came with autoboxes.

Escort Sundowner was offered with two-litre Pinto lump from the factory. The graphics, spot lamps and side window were stock too.

Paint codes

Code	Colour	Production dates
A	Polar White	Oct 1975 to Jun 1976
A	Blue Steel	Jun 1976 to Jun 1977
B	Onyx Black	Oct 1975 to Jun 1976
B	Artic Blue	Jan 1979 to Dec 1980
C	Antique Beige	Jun 1976 to Jun 1977
C	Midnight	Jan 1979 to Dec 1980
D	Mint Glaze	Jan 1979 to Dec 1980
E	Sandstone Beige	Oct 1975 to Jun 1976
E	Frosted Pine	Jun 1977 to Jan 1979
F	Frosted Lime	Oct 1975 to Jun 1976
F	Sweet Cream	Jun 1977 to Jan 1979
G	Banana Blush	Oct 1975 to Jun 1977
H	Tropic Gold	Oct 1975 to Jun 1976
H	Red Flame	Jun 1976 to Jan 1979
J	Blaze Blue	Oct 1975 to Jun 1977
K	Tango	Oct 1975 to Jun 1977
K	Monza Red	Jan 1979 to Dec 1980
L	Mushroom Blaze	Jun 1976 to Jun 1977
M	Yellow Blaze	Oct 1975 to Jun 1976
M	Satin Spruce	Jun 1977 to Jan 1979
O	Autumn Flame	Oct 1975 to Jun 1976
O	Modena Green	Jun 1977 to Jan 1979
O	Nutmeg	Jan 1979 to Dec 1980
P	Emerald Fire	Oct 1975 to Jun 1976
P	Pine & Lime	Jun 1976 to Jan 1979
Q	Yellow Fire	Oct 1975 to Jun 1976
Q	Coolmint	Jun 1976 to Jun 1977
R	Copper Bronze	Oct 1975 to Jun 1976
R	Raw Orange	Jun 1977 to Jan 1979
S	Brown Satin	Jun 1976 to Jan 1979
T	Outback Bronze	Jun 1976 to Jun 1977
T	Wedgewood	Jan 1979 to Dec 1980
W	Platinum Blue	Jun 1977 to Jan 1979
X	Red Pepper	Oct 1975 to Jun 1976
X	Stardust Silver	Jun 1976 to Jun 1977
X	Lemon Lime	Jan 1979 to Dec 1980
Y	Harvest Gold	Oct 1975 to Jun 1977
Z	Burnt Orange	Jan 1979 to Dec 1980
1	Peppermint Green	Oct 1975 to Jun 1977
3	Gold Dust	Jan 1979 to Dec 1980
4	Neptune Blue	Jun 1976 to Jan 1979
4	Silver Grey	Jan 1979 to Dec 1980
5	Deep Aqua	Oct 1975 to Jun 1976
5	Desert Haze	Jun 1976 to Jan 1979
7	Walnut Glow	Oct 1975 to Jun 1976
7	Ghost Gum	Jan 1979 to Dec 1980
9	Sno White	Jun 1976 to Dec 1980

Yes, this is the real thing – a beak-nosed RS2000 with four-door body. Even an automatic gearbox was a common optional extra.

Trim codes

Code	Colour	Production dates
B	Black	1975 to 1979
B2	Black/green Cadiz	1975 to 1978
B3	Black/orange Cadiz	1975 to 1978
B4	Black/tan Cadiz	1975 to 1978
E	Blue	1979-on
F	Red	1979-on
H	Chocolate	1975 to 1978
K	Tan	1979-on
L	Cloud	1975 to 1978
M	Light Marquis	1975 to 1978
N	Green	1975 to 1978
R	Orange	1975 to 1978
S	Saddle	1975 to 1978
T	Tan	1975 to 1978

Engine codes

Code	Engine	Production dates
D	1.6 Crossflow high compression	1975 to 1978
E	1.6 Crossflow low compression	1975 to 1980
J	2.0 Pinto high compression	1975 to 1980
L	1.3 Crossflow high compression	1975 to 1978
R	2.0 Pinto low compression	1975 to 1978

Transmission codes

Code	Gearbox	Production dates
V	Four-speed manual	1975 to 1980
Y	Three-speed automatic	1975 to 1980

South African RS2000s

Not to be outdone by its Australian counterpart, Ford South Africa produced its very own RS2000s from the end of 1978 to 1980. But rather than making do with a low-powered shadow of the Saarlouis RS2000, South African examples were built using Europe-supplied knock-down kits and the proper 110bhp Pinto, including full-fat Weber carb, exhaust manifold, alloy sump and bellhousing coupled to the familiar four-speed manual gearbox and a standard 3.77:1 final drive ratio.

South African two-door bodyshells were used, which automatically came with heavy-duty inner wings and rear chassis rails – along with numerous detail pressing differences from German Escorts. One notable omission was the South African RS's lack of radius rods to locate the back axle – instead sticking with a rear anti-roll bar and softer shock absorbers to cope with local road surfaces.

A Capri 55-litre fuel tank was fitted in the RS2000's boot – between its rear wheelarches and above the back axle. Everything else was almost identical to the RS2000s supplied in Great Britain, albeit with one or two trim differences. South African cars were equipped with 5.5x13 sports steel wheels from the factory, along with opening front quarter lights, a remote-control driver's door mirror and black Beta cloth-trimmed Scheel recliners with inertia-reel seat belts as standard. A host of go-faster goodies was available from dealers, including complete Group One mechanical upgrades.

South African RS2000s were offered in Diamond White, Venetian Red or Signal Yellow. It's not known how many were produced, but figures of over 1,000 seem realistic.

ACCESSORIES AND SERIES X

Motorsport was what built the sporting Escort legend, and motorsport was what's kept the cars roaring, blazing and winning well into the twenty-first century. Motorsport, too, was what allowed Ford to create a whole world of parts and accessories for international competition, weekend clubmen rally drivers and B-road blasters who simply wanted to look like Roger Clark.

Following the immense success of high-performance Mk1 Escorts, Ford wasted no time in developing components for its successor – even pushing complete, off-the-shelf Mk2 bodyshells to rebuild earlier machines into the more modern shape.

But unlike the bespoke days of old, where Advanced Vehicle Operations (AVO) and its special build facility could hand-craft a customer's ideal Escort from catalogues of extravagant extras, it was now down to the buyer to make the monster. Well, the buyer and his Rallye Sport dealer.

Now, of course, with the AVO plant mothballed and every Escort except the low-volume RS1800 a mainstream production machine, it made no financial sense for Ford to custom-build cars. Yes, it sounded like the big American manufacturer was starting to lose interest in its European enthusiasts, but that wasn't exactly true.

One of only a handful of official Series X cars converted by Ford, this brochure-starring RS2000 wore the full Zakspeed-style kit, complete with bonnet pins and 7.5x13in RS alloys.

In fact, it was abundantly clear that Escort fans would flock to the brand and modify their own motors, keeping the flag flying without incurring massive costs for Ford. All the manufacturer needed was to produce a great range of cars, make a mouth-watering selection of go-faster goodies available from dealers, and give buyers a little encouragement to put it all together.

By the time of the Mk2's 1975 launch, Ford's accessories catalogues were bulging at the seams, offering masses of useful everyday gizmos and fancy Rallye Sport parts.

And, just to nudge punters into parting with a little more cash, a special range of performance components was introduced for all the models in Ford's line-up (well, all bar the Granada), right down to the Fiesta Popular. Evocatively named Series X, the sexy new range (launched in August 1977) comprised a comprehensive, hand-picked collection of competition-derived parts, most of which were selected from rally-proven Group One kit.

Okay, even Series X (or X-pack, as it became informally known) cars were put together by Rallye Sport dealers rather than a top-secret Ford facility, but the championship-winning heritage was kept alive – after all, the bits people purchased for their Escorts were developed by the same blokes who brought us our favourite motorsport greats.

Were X-packs, Group One goodies or even official Ford aftermarket mud flaps factory-original? No, they weren't. But were they fitted to Mk2s from new, prior to registration? Yes, most definitely. And, as such, they surely deserve their places on authentic sporting Escorts.

Series X

Series X was marketed as a complete competition-based transformation, including promotional reports by rally ace Bjorn Waldegard, thrashing a fully kitted-out X-pack RS2000 through the pages of magazines.

But the complete Series X setup was in fact ineligible for most motorsport classes (Group One wouldn't allow bodywork modifications like the X-pack's Zakspeed-style wheelarches), and in the majority of cases was simply used as a catalogue of components to inspire buyers. They could specify as many parts as they liked for a brand new car or to

DIY-fit to their own second-hand Ford.

Although hundreds of Series X kits were supplied by Rallye Sport dealers, most mods were applied to hard-charging RS2000 road cars – and the vast majority made do with just the engine upgrades. Still, with around 145bhp offered from a hot Group One-spec Pinto (boasting twin 44IDF Weber carbs, high-lift cam and big-valve head but retaining its 1993cc capacity), you can certainly see why Series Xs gained legendary status.

Today, it's extremely difficult to identify an Escort that was upgraded with Series X gear from new. No special identification tags came with a Series X car, nor were there any unique characters on the build plate. Only period photos and receipts can prove an individual car's authenticity.

Series X Zakspeed-style fibreglass bodykits featured boxy square-arched extensions, complete with sealed-up, mock cooling slots for the brakes in the leading and tail edges of the rear wheelarches, and tail edges of the fronts. They were originally manufactured by Essex firm Fibresports (complete with small Ford oval logos moulded into the rear quarters and front wings), where kits continued to be produced for several decades after Mk2 manufacturing ended; it's said that contemporary parts used external mounting flanges, while later versions had an internal

Non-standard but fantastic to behold – these rounded Group Four-style wheelarch extensions (now confusingly, colloquially referred to as tarmac arches) are a bigger, wider version of what RS dealers offered as rally arches (now confusingly, colloquially referred to as forest arches...).

Broad front airdam was formed as part of full Series X RS2000 nosecone.

Series X rear wheelarch, as produced by Fibresports complete with Ford oval on the lower edge. The mock vents were always filled in.

Left-hand-drive Zakspeed RS2000, built in 1976 as a circuit car for the Monaco Grand Prix. Note the Ford logos on its wheelarch extensions.

flange. All were supplied in matt black.

To make matters just that little bit more complicated, different dealers had their own ways of attaching the bodykit (often riveted or bolted and bonded with fibreglass directly over whatever paintwork and decals were already in place) and it wasn't unusual for cracks to appear after several years' hard use.

According to experts, six RS2000s were decked out in X-pack trim by Ford's Aveley engineers. A similar conversion (including mechanical upgrades) was also offered by Ford of Germany, where Zakspeed produced its own RS2000 wide-arch kit; instead of the Fibresports version that included a complete nose section with flared corners, the German package contained extensions added to the Escort's original nose cone.

Series X sticker was an optional bit of the kit (just in case you'd not noticed the whopping wheelarches and deep-dished 7.5x13in alloys).

Zakspeed-style arches were, of course, available for flat-front Mk2 Escorts as well, but more popular were the rounded, forest rally-style wheelarch extensions (in fibreglass until 1978 and polyurethane thereafter). They're not generally referred to as X-pack parts, even though they were included in the range.

Series X catalogues also offered a host of handling upgrades, most of which were picked from the list of goodies homologated for Group One. They included an anti-dive kit for stability under heavy braking, high-ratio 'quick' steering rack (needing 2.5 rather than 3.5 turns from lock to lock), Bilstein gas-filled dampers, stiff springs and uprated brakes – deemed by Ford as only necessary when the Group One engine was used to its full potential.

Series X – the full works

- RS Racer Zakspeed-spec bodykit with wing extensions and front spoiler in fibreglass (RS2000 nose optional)
- Rally round-wheelarch bodykit in fibreglass or polyurethane (from 1978)
- Droop-snoot nose section (from 1979)
- Series X decals
- Hood locking kit (chrome bonnet retaining pins)
- Roll cage
- Fireproofing
- Reclining front seats with head restraints
- Three-spoke sports steering wheel
- Long-range (69-litre) fuel tank
- 6x13in RS four-spoke alloy wheels or 7.5x13in RS four-spoke alloys, black wheel nuts and silver centre caps
- 225/55x13 or 225/60x13 tyres
- Group One engine assembly with twin downdraught carburettors, big-valve head and high-lift cam
- Engine oil cooler kit
- Temperature control kit
- Group One air cleaner assembly
- Rocket ultra-close-ratio gear kit
- Short-shift gearchange kit
- Limited-slip differential and LSD mounting bolts
- Bilstein gas-filled front struts (Group One road/rally setting)
- Uprated, 1in lower front springs
- Bilstein gas-filled rear shock absorbers (Group One road/rally setting)
- Uprated single-leaf rear springs, rear spring spacers and spring pins
- Anti-dive kit
- High-ratio steering rack, bush and clamp
- Ventilated front brake disc kit
- Heavy-duty brake pads
- Heavy-duty brake shoes

Group One

Group One was an international FIA (Fédération Internationale de l'Automobile) motorsport class for touring cars entering into rallying and circuit racing. For eligibility, Group One machines had to adhere to regulations laid out by the FIA relating to production figures (a minimum of 5,000 cars was required for homologation) and specifications. The idea was to run Group One as a showroom category for standard cars (like its successor, Group N), but certain minor modifications were permitted – providing they were defined and accepted by FIA in advance.

Group Two and Group Four operated in much the same way, albeit allowing more modifications and fewer production vehicles (1,000 for Group Two and 400 for Group Four during the BDA-powered Mk2's reign).

Mk2 Escorts were homologated into all three categories, with Group Four being the domain of the world beating Escort RS and Group One at lower levels, often using RS2000s.

To encourage grass-roots Escort motorsport, Ford made its Group One parts freely available from Rallye Sport dealers, even including various components within the Series X range. All could be fitted to a Mk2 from new (although admittedly not on the assembly lines).

Group One homologation of the Mk2 RS2000 was achieved at the start of 1976 as a revised bodyshell of the previous model, along with updated instrument panel; existing modifications for the Mk1 RS2000 were therefore already acceptable.

On entering an RS2000 (or RS Mexico) into Group One, a competitor could specify his car with any or all of Ford's homologated gear. Here's a brief rundown of what was available.

A Group One RS2000 being driven in the 1976 Tour of Britain by the legendary Roger Clark.

Group One equipment

- Group One engine assembly, including big-valve (45mm inlet and 37mm exhaust) cylinder head, WR40 camshaft with drilled oilways, twin Weber 44IDF carburettors, inlet manifold, exhaust manifold, distributor, pumps, flywheel and clutch
- Group One air cleaner (satin black) and element (RS decal optional)
- High-efficiency radiator
- Rocket close-ratio gearbox
- 7.1kg flywheel
- Alternative axle ratios
- Limited slip differential
- Heavy-duty (World Cup) front crossmember
- High-ratio steering rack (2.7 turns lock to lock)
- Heavy-duty anti-roll bar
- Bilstein front struts with roller bearing top mounts
- Uprated (145lb) front springs, standard height or 1in lower
- Bilstein rear dampers
- Single-leaf rear springs (116lb or 146lb)
- Heavy-duty bushes
- Anti-dive kit
- Ventilated front brake disc kit
- 19.05mm rear wheel cylinders
- Adjustable brake bias bar
- Heavy-duty 6x13in RS four-spoke alloy wheels
- Long-range (60- or 69-litre) fuel tank
- Skid plates
- Bucket seats or recliners with runners

Rallye Sport dealer accessories

Engine

Although Group One upgrades gained great attention as official Rallye Sport accessories, Ford dealers could supply almost any model with an upgraded powerplant before it left the showroom.

For humble 1100cc Crossflow engines, the GT exhaust manifold and system was recommended, while 1300cc machines could also add the GT's camshaft, carburettor, inlet manifold and air filter.

Buyers of the Escort 1300 Sport had the option of a fast-road camshaft (valve lift: inlet 0.374in, exhaust 0.373in), for use with standard valve springs, as were 1600 Sport owners – although they needed to upgrade their carburettor jets too. A rally cam was the next stage (valve lift: inlet 0.376in, exhaust 0.374in), which needed to be accompanied by a large-bore exhaust (surprisingly, Ford didn't build a special system for the Crossflow-powered Mk2), twin sidedraught carburettors and a higher compression ratio.

Group One airbox was an optional – but very desirable – bit of the kit.

RS dealers also provided a variety of strengthened motorsport parts for the Mk2 Escort Sport, including steel main bearing caps, specially-selected con rods and bearings, single chrome silicon valve springs to deal with higher revs, a high-pressure oil pump, big-wing sump and pickup, 12-row oil cooler kit, high-efficiency radiator and a temperature control kit (a high-rate radiator cap and resistor for the temperature gauge wiring).

But although the Mk2 Sport was widely used in production-class competitions, Ford's emphasis was clearly now on supplying accessories for bigger-engined Escorts.

The Group One Pinto received special attention, with a complete 132bhp engine assembly available (containing big-valve cylinder head, cam, twin carburettors, inlet manifold, RS exhaust manifold, distributor, pumps, flywheel and clutch), an engine kit (including the carbs, inlet manifold, air cleaner,

Detail of the rare Group One airbox. You had to pay extra for the RS decal!

camshaft, valves and fittings) or all the parts separately.

So you could specify simply the standard-capacity bottom end, con rod bolts, big-valve cylinder head, 45mm inlet valves, 37mm exhaust valves, WR40 camshaft with drilled oilways, cam followers, front and rear Weber 44IDF carburettors (each was stamped 44IDF40 on the side; they had male and female linkages), inlet manifold, air cleaner assembly (two types were made, with an additional strengthener on top of later versions; an RS decal was optional), longer throttle cable, bracket, dipstick, extension tube, PCV breather setup and various fittings.

Pinto-powered Escorts were also offered a full big-bore exhaust system (different for right- or left-hand-drive cars), poly vee kit (to run a meaty Lucas 25 ACR alternator), high-pressure oil pump, 18-row oil cooler, high-efficiency radiator and a temperature control kit.

Of course, BDA engines weren't ignored, and Ford all but expected owners to upgrade them (as many did). Rallye Sport dealer parts included 1840 or 2000cc alloy blocks, steel bearings, con rods, Group Four cams, dry sump system (with boot-mounted oil tank), high-pressure oil pump, high-efficiency radiator, poly vee kit and Group Four exhaust with manifold. By that point, of course, even mechanical fuel injection was expected spec for a full-blown Escort RS.

Transmission

A new Escort could be equipped with a staggering amount of transmission options via the buyer's Rallye Sport dealer, from uprated clutch to ZF five-speed gearbox.

Heavy-duty clutches were offered for the Mk2 Sport, RS1800 and RS2000, as was the well-loved Rocket gearbox, with 170bhp capability and ultra-close-ratio cogs. Based on the Pinto's Type E four-speed, the Rocket's ratios were first: 2.54:1, second: 1.66:1, third: 1.255:1, fourth: 1.000:1. A gear kit was also available to upgrade the standard RS2000 or RS Mexico 'box. Meanwhile, a Sport could be persuaded to accept a Rocket by using a Rallye Sport fitting kit, complete with alloy bellhousing, heavy-duty clutch, propshaft, speedometer cable and so on. Bashing the transmission tunnel and relocating the gear lever hole further back was a job for whoever installed it all. A short-shift gear lever, gearknob and pivot spacer was also available for the Sport.

The RS1800's stock 'box could be equipped with a Group Two gear kit, with a choice of ratios – a setup Ford recommended as a straight swap in place of the RS2000, RS Mexico or Rocket gearbox. Better still was the ZF five-speed, available direct from your Rallye Sport dealer with BDA/Crossflow bellhousing. Again, floorpan modifications were required.

Similarly, Ford dealers were happy to supply and fit a narrow Atlas axle onto your Escort. Based on the Capri 3.0 part, the axle was strengthened, modified and narrowed to suit an Escort's standard-width body and brake drums, including thicker axle tubes and heat-treated halfshafts. Said to be suitable for Group One or Group Two Escorts, the narrow Atlas included a ZF limited-slip differential and final drive ratios ranging from 3.44:1 to 5.83:1. The ratios of 3.5:1, 3.75:1, 4.11:1 and 4.63:1 were all fine for Group One.

Group Four axles were also offered by dealers, along with a range of parts, fittings and rear brake callipers.

Limited-slip differentials and a range of final drive ratios were available for the more humble Escort axle, too, as were heavy-duty propshafts for Crossflow, Rocket or ZF gearboxes.

Suspension

Needless to say, Ford dealers were able to supply and fit your sporting Escort with a choice of suspension upgrades before it left the showroom.

Modifications were recommended in stages – the first to fit Bilstein gas-filled front struts and shock absorbers, then to add radius rods to a non-RS Escort, followed by shorter front springs and a rear lowering kit (which comprised 1in alloy spacer blocks and longer U-bolts).

For rally use, Ford also removed the rubber sandwich plates from between the car's rear axle and springs, added heavy-duty anti-roll bar bushes and rally springs. Uprated roller bearing top mounts were also required for Group One struts and beyond.

Even Group Four parts were readily available, including adjustable front suspension legs, rose joints, four-link kit and Panhard rod.

A chunky World Cup crossmember was suitable for all Mk2 models, as were Ford's hard rubber engine mounts. Similar heavy-duty bushes were available, too, for the Escort's gearbox crossmember, anti-roll bar, track control arms, radius arms, rear springs and steering rack mountings.

There was also a high-ratio steering rack (giving 2.5 turns lock-to-lock), a double-width front anti-roll bar mounting kit for RS models, and two anti-dive kits (road spec, for the Mk2 RS anti-roll bar or rally spec, using the Mk1 Twin Cam anti-roll bar to promote oversteer), which lowered the bar by two inches to help stability under braking.

Roller-bearing strut top mounts – essential when used with rally-spec Bilstein struts and high-ratio steering rack.

Front springs

Car	Spring	Spring rate	Ride height	Colour code	Free length
Sport	Road/rally/race	168lb	-1in	Silver/yellow/red	10in
RS2000/RS Mexico/RS1800	Race/tarmac	175lb	Standard	Yellow	11.5in
RS2000 Group One	Rally	145lb	+1in	Green/white	12.5in
Group Two/Group Four	Rally	190lb	Standard	Green/yellow	11.2in
Group Two/Group Four	Rally	190lb	Adjustable seat	Blue/white	13.4in

Rear springs

Car	Spring	Spring rate	Ride height	Leaves
Sport	Rally	115lb	+1in	4
RS2000/RS Mexico/RS1800	Race/tarmac	116lb	-1in	1
Mk2 with turret kit	Rally	115lb	+1in	4
RS2000 Group One/RS1800	Road/rally	116lb	Standard	1
RS2000/RS1800 Group Two	Rally	146lb	Standard	1
Group Four (four-link)	Rally	145lb	Standard	5

Official RS four-spoke 7.5x13in alloys were these silver, deep-dished delights, complete with H75EB-1007-AA part number within a spoke.

Brakes

Escort brakes were considered by Ford to be perfectly effective for road use, while heavy-duty pads and shoes were available as dealer upgrades.

Better still was the Group One ventilated front disc kit, complete with appropriate back plates and DS11 pads for their M16 callipers.

A brake bias adjuster (front to rear) was more suited to competition cars than road-going Mk2s, but it was again a popular dealer option – with cable-clutch pedal box for normal cars but hydraulic pedal box for Group Two/Four machines. Such advanced Escorts were also offered dealer-supplied upgrades including four-pot front callipers (again with DS11 pads), 10.2in ventilated front discs and 9in solid rear disc conversion.

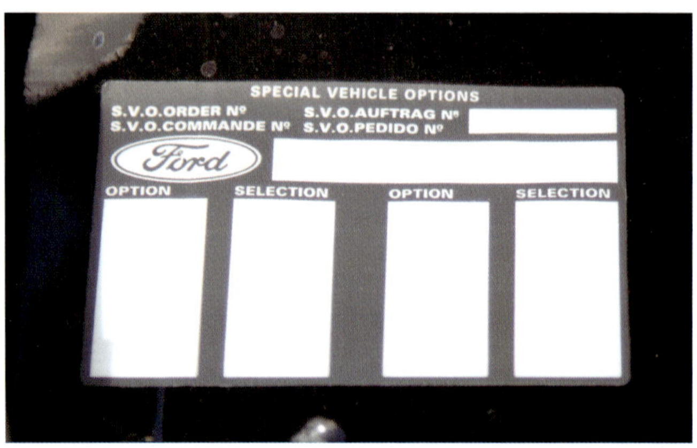

Black paintwork was a Ford optional extra that wasn't usually listed on colour charts. Thus this Special Vehicle Options sticker was found – blank, as pictured – on the inner wings of all factory-black Mk2 Escorts, from Popular to RS2000. The same SVO sticker was used when bodyside decals were deleted.

Wheels

There were several obvious choices for the new Escort owner seeking a wheel upgrade.

If his car came with standard steels, RS four-spoke 6x13in alloys were freely available – from dealers or as an extra from the factory on the RS Mexico, RS1800 or base-model RS2000; they were fitted using 19mm chrome nuts with 12mm threads and integral flat washers.

There was also the Rallye Sport dealer option of Group One-homologated, ATS-made 6x13in wheels, which looked almost identical to the RS four-spokes but featured deeper spokes (the wheel nuts sat further down their flat recesses – unlike the tapered nut seats of Capri wheels) with additional webbing on the backs for greater strength. Finished in metallic silver, they were cast with an H75AB part number inside one spoke recess.

Rallye Sport dealers also supplied silver-painted 7x13in Ronal four-spoke RS-type alloys, with Ronal and Ford RS logos cast onto the spokes. But they were never listed as available for Escorts (even though they fit perfectly), being suitable for Capris and wide-arch Fiestas instead.

Series X wheelarch-equipped Mk2 Escorts were recommended the ATS-built, deep-dished, 7.5x13in RS four-spoke alloy wheel. Each was finished in silver and wore castings within three spoke recesses, including the size and ET-19 offset, H75 EB-1007-AA part number and Ford oval. Again, they had flat nut seats; they were affixed with black nuts, again with integral flat washers.

For serious motorsport use, magnesium Minilite alloys were sold direct from Ford, generally in 6x13in, 7x13in or 7.5x13in sizes.

Body

As you'd expect, bodyshell strengthening was high on the agenda of any clubman rally driver, and Ford was keen to promote a host of tips to make his new Mk2 ready for the next event.

He was also able to spec his new Mk2 with a few bodywork upgrades directly from his Rallye Sport dealer, including steel sump guard, chrome bonnet pins, strut brace, RS front and rear spoilers (in rubber or polyurethane) and wheelarch extensions – in boxy Zakspeed style (tarmac spec), rounded rally design (fibreglass parts that were designed to be quickly attached using nuts and bolts) or larger Group Two polyurethane versions. Even the body adhesive to attach wide arches was available over the parts counter.

It goes without saying that single or two-up, two-down lighting brackets and Cibie (Super) Oscars were off-the-shelf accessories, along with RS-logo'd lamp covers. A bulky, black, long-range fuel tank was available too, which sat in the Escort's original boot-mounted position – in 60-litre form at first, soon followed by a 69-litre version.

Truly dedicated competitors could, of course, build themselves an Escort RS from scratch. Trimmed Sport or RS2000 (depending on whether you wanted a flat or slanting front) bodyshells were advertised as a basis for a brand new competition car, supplied in your choice of colour, complete with glass, instruments, lights and wiring loom.

Of course, Escort external modifications weren't restricted to hardcore motorsport goodies. Ford dealers were happy to fit a range of accessories to any Mk2 before delivery – including long-range driving lights, front and rear fog lamps, sports door mirrors, mud flaps, bumper overriders, locking fuel cap and even a shiny exhaust pipe trim.

Interior

Fixed-back bucket seats in black Beta cloth, complete with harness slots, were a direct upgrade from RS dealers; recliners were also offered for non-RS machines. Full harnesses were available too.

For cockpit safety, firewall panels were offered for the rear bulkhead, as was a 14-point race/rally roll cage finished in matt black epoxy resin, with removable diagonal, optional front section and matt black foam padding.

Meanwhile, a small, popular mod for upgraded Mk2s was a dished three-spoke steering wheel with leather rim rather than the standard RS 'wheel's pretend version; the same early Mk2 centre cap was used, though.

Don't forget, too, that a variety of practical accessories was offered for the road-going sporting Escort. From floor mats, head rests and map reading lamp to internal boot release mechanism, fire extinguisher and choice of centre consoles (with clock, cassette storage or speaker), it was all available to individualise a Mk2 Escort before leaving the showroom.

Finally, Ford dealers provided a wide range of radios – perhaps because factory-fitted options were rather restricted. They included the M21 manual-tune radio, P21 MW/LW push-button radio, manual-tune multi-band M32 (MW/LW/SW/VHF) until January 1978, multi-wave six-push-button P32 (MW/LW/VHF), high-performance six-push-button P42 (MW/LW/SW/VHF) or the Ford-branded stereo tape players: RST-21 (LW/MW), RST-22 (until January 1978), SRT-22 (from January 1978) or six-push-button SRT-32 (from January 1978). Fully-retractable, electric or roof-mounted aerials were all supplied and fitted by Ford dealers.

Sexy three-spoke dished steering wheel was a Rallye Sport accessory, complete with leather rim

BODYSHELLS

Forget about the Type 49 and AVO nomenclature of older Escorts, because all Mk2s were born equal. But some, of course, were more equal than others...

Escort bodies were built around the world, with European Mk2s pretty much identical whether created in Great Britain (at Merseyside's Halewood factory) or Germany (the Saarlouis plant). A few other territories (Australia, for example) produced mildly different pressings, which altered some inconsequential shaping (and sometimes moved the fuel tank) rather than added any strength.

Many export markets, though, received heavy-duty shells as standard. They were equipped with uprated inner wings – featuring reinforcement plates over the strut top mounts and stiffeners inside the turrets – and rear chassis rails. Occasionally, cars destined for the UK market (such as those destined for some government agencies) were constructed using export-spec shells but this was an exception rather than rule. Having said that, service shells (available primed or fully-painted to replace the bodies of damaged cars) were generally of the heavy-duty type.

From the beginning of production until the end, there were Mk2 Escorts in two-door saloon, four-door saloon, van and estate bodies. None were awarded any special designations, although each had its own reference letter on the car's build plate. The overwhelming majority of sporting Escorts were based on two-door shells.

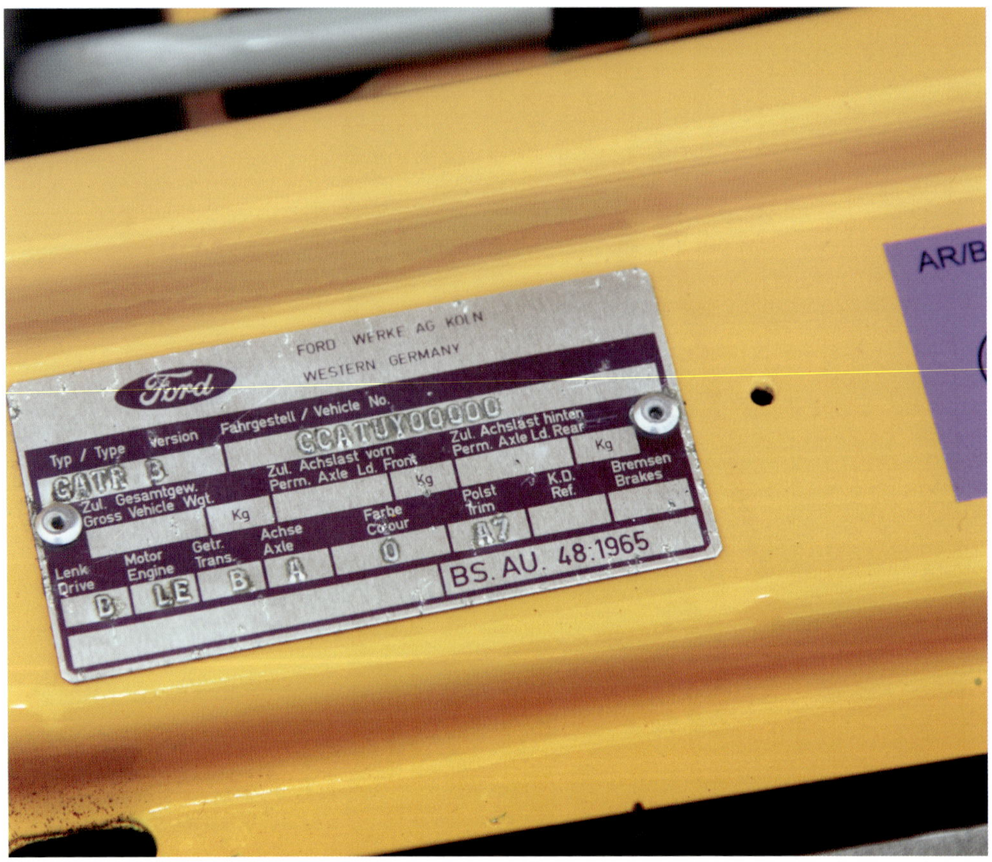

Most Mk2 Escorts had a chassis plate on the slam panel, to the left of the bonnet release mechanism (when looking from the front of the car).

Late Mk2s (generally from November 1979 in Saarlouis and January 1980 at Halewood) had their VIN tags moved to the offside inner wing. The redundant hole underneath the old-type chassis plate on UK cars was sometimes covered with a riveted, body-coloured, blank tag.

German-manufactured RS Mk2s (which they all were, other than the few hand-built RS1800s, the Australian RS2000 and South African cars assembled from knock-down kits) were based on the heavy-duty bodyshell. They also boasted a series of additions, including radius rod pick-up points on the chassis rails, repositioned gearstick aperture, different radiator housing and unique brackets for the spare wheel strap, speedometer cable and exhaust hangers.

Of course, the RS2000 also received new panelwork on its front end – but none of the internal structure was changed.

All European bodyshells underwent a few minor revisions over the years, most notably during February 1977 when the inner wings received smaller-diameter suspension top mounting points, along with subtly reshaped pressings at the bulkhead and slam panel.

This chapter looks at some of the distinguishing features between European Escort bodyshells and how they were finished from the factory. As usual, all Escort shells were cut from the same steel, painted using the same process and rolled along the same assembly lines (before being released into the world and prone to the same rusting tendencies). The only real changes occurred when all the special mechanical components were added…

All Mk2s wore a build plate on the slam panel, to the right of the bonnet release spring (viewed from the front of the car). This well-worn Halewood Sport's plate still wears its quality control tab, poking out from under the left-hand rivet.

Heavy-duty inner wings had these large (105mm) apertures until February 1977, when small strut tops were fitted instead. Factory chassis number was hand-stamped into the strengthening plate.

Small-hole strut tops were used from February 1977, now down to 85mm apertures. These spot welded reinforcing plates were still found on heavy-duty shells and all RS models.

Standard inner wings were found on all non-RS and most home-market European Escorts; here they have the larger pre-February 1977 strut top apertures. Note the original chassis number stamps, done by hand at the factory and left in grey primer for mild protection.

Small-hole stock inner wings received these smaller, 85mm strut top apertures from February 1977 onwards.

Early slam panels (until February 1977) had rounded edges where they overlapped the inner wings.

From February 1977, the slam panel's corners were square where they overlapped the inner wings.

Bulkhead of early Mk2 (until February 1977) had five square dimples where it met the scuttle panel.

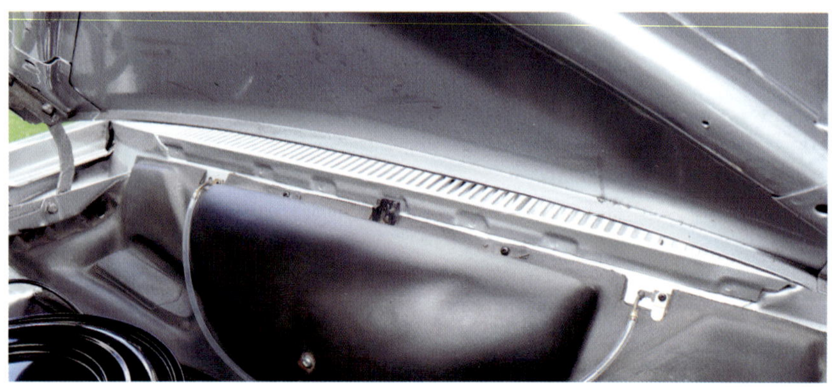

After February 1977, the Mk2's bulkhead featured seven square dimples where it joined the scuttle panel.

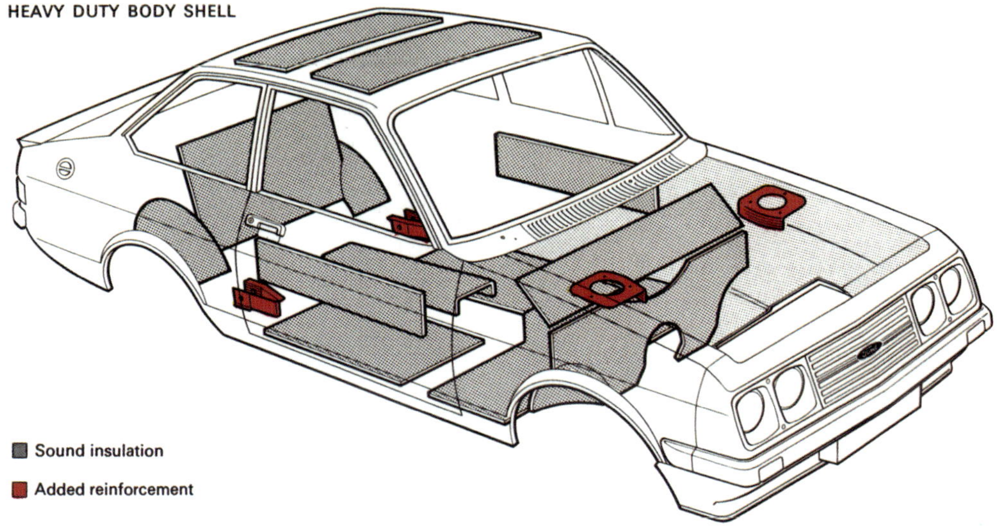

Heavy-duty inner wings featured stiffeners at the base of the front suspension turrets, visible from within the wheelarches. Higher up, there were strengthening fillets where the strut towers met the inner wing rails.

There was a little bit more to it than this… Ford's illustration of a heavy-duty bodyshell highlighted the two most obvious areas of reinforcement – strut tops and skidded rear chassis rails.

Besides the heavy-duty shell's skidded rear chassis rails, RS Mk2s also featured these pick-up points for the radius rods. They weren't found on any other Mk2 Escorts.

Spot-welded speedometer cable bracket was found only on the floorpan of RS models, keeping the cable clear of their Pinto exhaust downpipes.

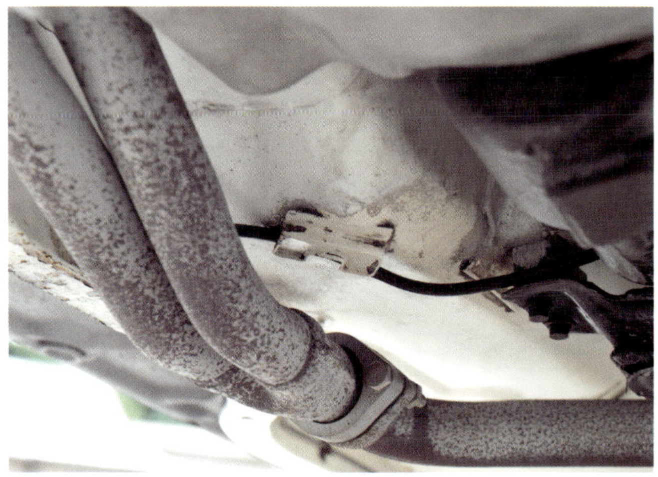

RS Mk2s and Harriers had this spare wheel securing strap bracket spot-welded to the boot floor alongside the well. Non-RS cars had a different bracket inside the well instead.

Passenger doorstep-mounted Ford oval badge was a throwback to the Mk1; it was seen only on Mk2s built until August 1977.

Door latches came directly from the late-spec Mk1 Escort. They remained unchanged throughout Mk2 production.

Vinyl roofs were a popular factory fitment on many Mk2s, but they were also often fitted by dealers before delivery to customers. All Mk2 vinyls used the same pattern (whether two- or four-door), so were trimmed by hand to fit the C-pillars.

Factory fuel cap on the Mk2 was this pressed steel part, painted in the car's body colour. It was heavier than the similar-looking Mk1 cap (which was riveted together on the back), and featured a flat rather than convex central bar.

Lockable petrol cap was an official Ford dealer accessory.

PDI (pre-delivery inspection) stickers were originally plastered randomly over Escorts from very late Mk1s onwards - mainly found haphazardly in the luggage compartment, inner wheelarches and underside of the boot lid, sometimes on the seat winders and pedal box.

Secreted in the luggage compartment was sometimes found a colour code sticker, giving the shade's name and international paint manufacturer reference.

RS Mk2's transmission tunnel was the same as a standard, Crossflow-powered Mk2's but had its gearstick aperture mounted further back towards the handbrake. To achieve the move, the Saarlouis factory cut a section out of the tunnel top, chopped back the tunnel strengthener underneath and spot-welded a large plate into position, complete with ready-pressed gearstick hole. The bulkhead end of the tunnel was generally tapped to make space for the big gearbox's alloy bellhousing.

RS dashboard panels were identical to the standard Mk2's unless a pre-September RS2000 or Custom, which featured a pressed cutout in the passenger side for this recessed plastic cubby box.

RS Mk2s had a unique J-shaped exhaust back box hanger, bolted to the nearside chassis rail further back than a Crossflow-powered car's.

Pinto exhaust downpipe was at the opposite side to the standard Crossflow setup, so RS Mk2s required new exhaust mountings – this central twin-hook bracket was welded to the floorpan, complete with strengthener under the back seat. Non-RS models had a single-hook mounting.

Fitting the big engine into a Mk2's bay meant moving the radiator forward into a new cowling with the middle cut out; beneath it, the radiator cross-member box section was also reshaped.

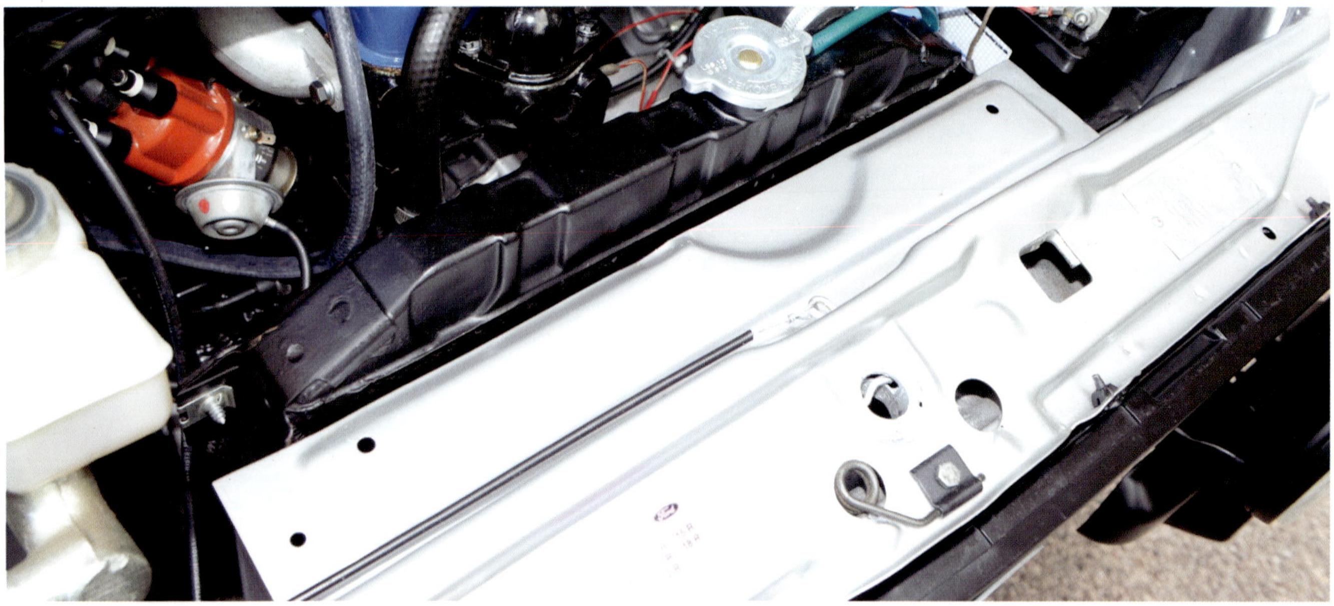

Stock Crossflow-powered Mk2's radiator was positioned further back than an RS model's, with uncut cowling.

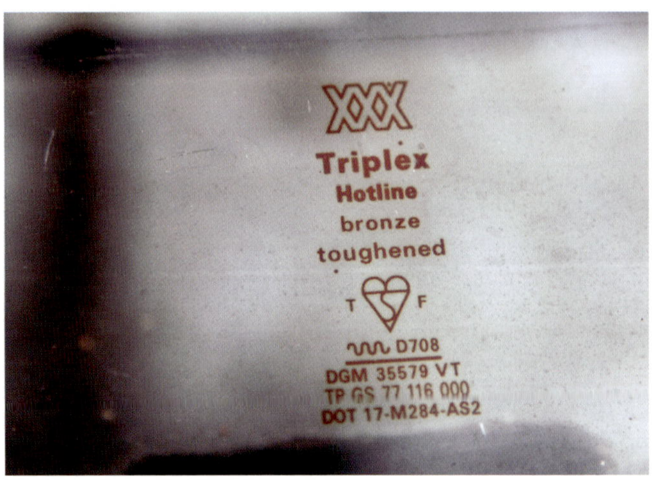

Triplex glass was fitted to Halewood-built Escorts, while their German counterparts received Sekurit. Triplex glass had an easy dating code, with dots over the 'Triplex' and under the 'toughened' lettering.

Sporting Mk2s' window surrounds were blacked out in alignment with the bottom of the rubbers, up to the C-pillar vent and rain gutters (some early models had chrome drip rail covers, but never RS2000s).

Saarlouis, 1976, and a pair of Carnival Red two-doors lead a gang of early Escorts along the assembly line. All Mk2s had satin black paintwork around their headlamps and behind the grille.

Saarlouis spray facility early in 1976, with a conveyor belt carrying shells through oscillating spray guns. Mk2 Escort panel gaps were never exactly perfect, and an orange peel effect came free. Runs were often buffed out by dealers before delivery to customers...

Halewood's spray booth in 1975. Grey primers were generally used, although early German metallics (in thermo plastic acrylic single-layer, rather than the base coat and clear lacquer used from 1976) were applied over black primer.

A Diamond White Sport on the Halewood production line in 1975 – note its satin black sills, black window surrounds and chrome door handles. Who knows this car's fate? Maybe it even became a pre-launch RS1800.

The birth of an Escort at Halewood, 1975. Look closely and you'll see its build plate was already attached to the slam panel – possibly the very first piece of a Mk2 jigsaw.

A late 1975 Daytona Yellow 1.3GL receiving its engine and front suspension assembly. Note the paint coverage, with zinc phosphate electrocoat primer plus PVC-type underseal (new to the Escort for the Mk2's introduction) within the wheelarches. The topcoat was applied as far as the chassis rails, with overspray wafted further under the floorpan.

Satin black paint was sprayed sparsely over areas of interior paintwork to disguise the body colour, including the back seat crossmember (pictured) and underneath the rear parcel shelf. Body-colour paintwork remained above the headlining on all Mk2s except for the first few RS1800s.

Skidded rear chassis rails were standard on the heavy-duty Mk2 bodyshell and all RS models.

Escort bodyshells were neatly spot-welded together, but there were no hard-and-fast rules about how many went where.

BUILD PLATES

Escort Mk2s were fitted with a pair of identity tags, both of which were found under the bonnet.

Most important of the two was the chassis (or VIN, standing for vehicle identification number) plate – a bare alloy tag that recorded basic details about the car, including build date, engine type, body colour and such like. More significantly, it noted the car's chassis number, which matched the characters on an Escort's offside strut top and engine number (on all but the RS1800).

The chassis plate was identical to the type found on post-August 1970 Mk1 Escorts, but on the vast majority of RS models read Ford Werke AG Koln Western Germany across the top rather than Ford Motor Co Ltd London, England.

The chassis plate was riveted to a Mk2 Escort's bonnet slam panel, just to the left of the bonnet release spring (when looking from the front of the car). That was until Ford switched to an all-new style of VIN plate, which conformed to 1979's International Organisation for Standardisation (IOS) guidelines. Designed to promote worldwide uniformity of vehicle identification, IOS required a revised layout and date coding system, resulting in Ford's year identifiers leaping from 1979's W to an A in 1980. Otherwise, the information provided was essentially the same as before.

The new plates were relocated to the Escort's offside inner wing, again riveted and now readable from the side of the car. The official changeover point was November 1979 in Saarlouis, followed up on Halewood-built cars from January 1980 – in short, they were found on all Mk2s manufactured from the start of 1980.

All Mk2s were also equipped with a body-coloured build plate, riveted to the slam panel on the right-hand side of the bonnet release mechanism (viewed from the front of the car). Reckoned to be stamped before any other part of an Escort was constructed, the tag was attached to the slam panel to tell factory workers exactly what to assemble. Thus the plate included codes relating to colour, trim, specification and options.

Two different types of build tag were used – one in Saarlouis and the other at Halewood. Ford officials refuse access to any records relating to the plates, so deciphering them today is fraught with problems – resulting in limited accurate information about German cars and very little for British machines.

As always, chassis plates and build tags were simply riveted to Mk2 Escorts, meaning they were easy to swap around. So only educated guesswork and documented evidence about an individual car can tell for sure whether the body and identity really do match up.

Chassis plate, January 1975 until November 1979/January 1980

Typ/Type

The first letter denoted the car's country of origin. However, most pre-1977 Mk2 Escort RS models said B rather than G (the G was found on all later RSs).
B = Ford Great Britain
C = Ford Netherlands
E = Ford Germany (affiliate assembly)
G = Ford Germany

The second letter related to the model range.
A = Escort

The third character referred to the body type.
T = two-door saloon
F = four-door saloon
D = estate
V = van

The fourth letter was the model homologation year (this would in many cases precede the car's year of build).
R = 1975
S = 1976
T = 1977
U = 1978
W = 1979

Version
This box wasn't always used.
S = base
D = L
P = GL
E = Ghia
Q = Sport/RS2000
C = Sport/RS2000
A = RS2000
B = RS Mexico

Fahrgestell/Vehicle No.
The car's serial number.

The first letter denoted the product source (the car's country of origin).
B = Ford Great Britain
C = Ford Great Britain (affiliate assembly)
N = Ford Netherlands
G = Ford of Germany

The second digit related to the car's assembly plant.
B = Halewood
C = Saarlouis
F = Aveley
K = Sydney
N = Amsterdam

The third character denoted the model range.
A = Escort

The fourth letter referred to the body type.
T = two-door saloon
F = four-door saloon
D = estate
V = van
The remaining figures were the car's own individual serial number, in order of

The fifth and six digits were the year and month of production respectively.

Year code	Year	Jan	Feb	Mar	Apr	May	Jun	Jul	Aug	Sep	Oct	Nov	Dec
P	1974	L	Y	S	T	J	U	M		B	R	A	G
R	1975	C	K	D	E	L	Y	S	T	J	U	M	P
S	1976	B	R	A	G	C	K	D	E	L	Y	S	T
T	1977	J	U	M	P	B	R	A	G	C	K	D	E
U	1978	L	Y	S	T	J	U	M	P	B	R	A	G
W	1979	C	K	D	E	L	Y	S	T	J	U	M	P

vehicles produced during the month. Numbering started at 10001 for all types during each month, rising to 99999.

Zul. Gesamtgew.
Gross Vehicle Wgt.
Gross vehicle weight in kilograms, used in Germany, France and Reunion territories only.

Zul. Achslast Vorn
Perm. Axle Ld. Front
Axle load, front, in kilograms used in Germany, France and Reunion territories only.

Zul. Achslast hinten
Perm. Axle Ld. Rear
Axle load, rear, in kilograms used in Germany, France and Reunion territories only.

Lenk Drive
1 or A = left-hand drive
2 or B = right-hand drive

Motor Engine
The first digit was the engine's size and the next its rating.

First digit
T = 950cc
G = 1100cc
J = 1300cc
L = 1600cc
N = 2000cc

Second digit
1 = Kent low-compression
2 = Kent high-compression
3 = Kent high-compression with increased performance
5 = Kent fuel economy type
E = OHC high-compression with increased performance

So...
G1 = 1098cc LC (low compression)
G2 = 1098cc HC (high compression)
J1 = 1298cc LC (low compression)
J2 = 1298cc HC (high compression)
J3 = 1298cc GT
L3 = 1598cc GT
LE = 1600cc RS Mexico
NE = 1998cc RS2000
RS1800s were built using already-plated Sport or RS Mexico shells, so had an engine code relating to that model (except for a few late 1975 cars, which had a letter R in the box).

Getr. Trans.
B = manual
D = automatic

Achse Axle
Rear axle ratio.
A = 3.54:1
Z = 3.54:1 heavy duty
B = 3.777:1
W = 3.777:1 heavy duty
C = 3.89:1
N = 4.11:1
D = 4.125:1
X = 4.125:1 heavy duty
E = 4.44:1

Farbe Colour
On British-built cars this was a two-character combination, with the first referring to the body paint code and the second the model year. German cars had just the single digit for paint code unless supplied in a non-standard finish or a vinyl roof was fitted, in which case the relevant letter was used instead of the model year designator.

First digit:
A = Black
B = Diamond White 73
C = Sahara Beige 74 or Oyster Gold 78 or Nova Green
D = Carnival Red 75 or Regency Green 78 or Terracotta
E = Olympic Blue/Light Blue 74 or Hawaiian Blue 78 or Java Green
F = Purple Velvet or Solar Gold
G = Royal Blue 75 or Tuscan Beige 79
H = Signal Orange 77
J = Signal Green 77
K = Signal Green 76 (GB) or Calypso Green 79
L = Signal Orange 76
M = Modena Green/Bitter Green 74
N = Saturn Gold 77
P = Signal Green 76 (Germany) or Tropic Green 77 or Sierra Beige 79 or Cordoba Beige
Q = Arizona Gold 75
R = Venetian Red 77
S = Roman Bronze 76 or Sable Brown
T = Daytona Yellow 72 or Peppermint Green 78 or Riviera Blue 79 or Nordic Blue
U = Platinum 76
V = Phoenix/Vista Orange or Strato Silver 77
X = Midnight Blue 78
Y = Non-standard
Z = primer
1 = Miami Blue 74 or Cosmos Blue 79
2 = Aquarius Green 77 or Apollo Green 79
3 = Stardust/Aero Silver 74 or Jupiter Red 77
4 = Bermuda Blue 77 or Nova Green
5 = Jade Green 75 or Cosmos Blue 79
6 = Neptune Blue 77 or Apollo Green 79
7 = Copper or Red Velvet 77
8 = Nevada Beige 77
9 = Signal Yellow 77
0 = Signal Amber 78 or Signal Orange 79 or Signal Red 80

Second digit:
1 = 1971
2 = 1972
3 = 1973
4 = 1974
5 = 1975
6 = 1976
7 = 1977
8 = 1978
9 = 1979
0 = 1980
A = black vinyl roof
M = tobacco vinyl roof
K or D = brown vinyl roof

Polst Trim (soft trim)
A two-digit combination comprising two characters. The first letter was for interior trim colour, the second denoted seat and trim material. Numbers in trim descriptions related to the model year in which the colour was first used by Ford.

First character (colour):
A = black
B = Tan 79 or bitter chocolate/tan stripes (Sport)
C = Cloud 74
E = Medium Blue 74
F = Blue 79 or bitter chocolate/blue stripes (Sport)
G = Blue 81
H = red or bitter chocolate/red stripes (Sport)
J = Chocolate 76
K = Light Tan 73
L = Saddle Brown 74
M = Green 77
N = Orange 77
P = Chocolate or bitter chocolate/Indian red stripes (Sport)
T = Saddle Brown 76
W = Light Tan 76
X = Black (Harrier)
Y = Non-standard

Second character (material):
1 = cloth/vinyl
3 = cloth
4 = cloth
5 = cloth
7 = cloth
8 = cloth
9 = cloth
A = vinyl
E = vinyl
G = vinyl
H = vinyl

K.D. Ref.
For export markets. Usually blank – denoted date of manufacture for cars supplied as knock-down kits for assembly in a different factory.

Bremsen Brakes
For export markets. Usually blank.

Chassis plate, November 1979/January 1980 onwards

Drive cond.
1 or A = left-hand drive
2 or B = right-hand drive

Next box
Type approval number, as required in some territories.

Engine Moteur
G1 = 1098cc LC (low compression)
G2 = 1098cc HC (high compression)
J1 = 1298cc LC (low compression)
J2 = 1298cc HC (high compression)
J3 = 1298cc GT
L3 = 1598cc GT
LE = 1600cc RS Mexico
NE = 1998cc RS2000

Next box
Vehicle identification number, starting with an asterisk, which was a legal requirement. The first letter denoted the car's country of origin.
B = Ford Great Britain
C = Ford Great Britain (affiliate assembly)
E = Ford Germany (affiliate assembly)
G = Ford Germany

The second digit related to the assembly plant.
B = Halewood
C = Saarlouis
F = Aveley
K = Sydney

The third character denoted the model.
A = Escort

The fourth letter referred to the body type.
T = two-door saloon
F = four-door saloon
D = estate
V = van

The fifth and six digits were the year and month of production respectively.

Year code	Year	Jan	Feb	Mar	Apr	May	June	July	Aug	Sep	Oct	Nov	Dec
W	1979	C	K	D	E	L	Y	S	T	J	U	M	P
A	1980	B	R	A	G	C	K	D	E	L	Y	S	T

The remaining figures were the car's own individual serial number, in order of vehicles produced during the month. Numbering started at 00001 for all types during each month, rising to 99999.

Trans trans.
B = Manual
D = Automatic

Axle PT. AR.
A = 3.54:1
Z = 3.54:1 heavy duty
B = 3.777:1
W = 3.777:1 heavy duty
C = 3.89:1
N = 4.11:1
D = 4.125:1
X = 4.125:1 heavy duty

Trim garn.
This was a two-digit combination comprising two characters. The first letter was for interior trim colour, the second character denoted seat and trim material. Numbers in trim descriptions related to the model year in which the colour was first used by Ford.

First digit (colour):
A = black
B = Tan 79 or Bitter Chocolate/Tan (Sport)
C = Cloud 74
E = Medium Blue 74
F = Blue 79 or bitter chocolate/blue (Sport)
G = Blue 81
H = red or bitter chocolate/red (Sport)
J = Chocolate 76
K = Light Tan 73
L = Saddle Brown 74
M = Green 77
N = Orange 77
P = chocolate or bitter chocolate/Indian red (Sport)
T = Saddle Brown 76
W = Light Tan 76
X = black (Harrier)
Y = non-standard
Second digit (material):

1 = cloth/vinyl
3 = cloth
4 = cloth
5 = cloth
7 = cloth
8 = cloth
9 = cloth
A = vinyl
E = vinyl
G = vinyl
H = vinyl

Type
The first letter denoted the car's country of origin.
B = Ford Great Britain
C = Ford Great Britain (affiliate assembly)
E = Ford Germany (affiliate assembly)
G = Ford Germany

The second letter related to the model.
A = Escort

The third character referred to the body type.
T = two-door saloon
F = four-door saloon
D = estate
V = van

The fourth letter was the year of the model's introduction.
R = 1975
S = 1976
T = 1977
U = 1978
W = 1979

The fifth digit was constant (RS2000 only).
A = RS2000

Version
Usually left blank.

Colour/Couleur
A two-character combination, usually with the first referring to the body paint code and the second the model year. That was except for German cars with a vinyl roof fitted, in which case the relevant letter was used instead of the model year designator.

First character:
A = Black
B = Diamond White 73
C = Sahara Beige 74 or Oyster Gold 78 or Nova Green
D = Carnival Red 75 or Regency Green 78 or Terracotta
E = Olympic Blue/Light Blue 74 or Hawaiian Blue 78 or Java Green
F = Purple Velvet or Solar Gold
G = Royal Blue 75 or Tuscan Beige 79
H = Signal Orange 77
J = Signal Green 77
K = Signal Green 76 (GB) or Calypso Green 79
L = Signal Orange 76
M = Modena Green/Bitter Green 74
N = Saturn Gold 77
P = Signal Green 76 (Germany) or Tropic Green 77 or Sierra Beige 79 or Cordoba Beige
Q = Arizona Gold 75
R = Venetian Red 77
S = Roman Bronze 76 or Sable Brown
T = Daytona Yellow 72 or Peppermint Green 78 or Riviera Blue 79 or Nordic Blue
U = Platinum 76
V= Phoenix/Vista Orange or Strato Silver 77
X = Midnight Blue 78
Y = Non-standard
Z = primer
1 = Miami Blue 74 or Cosmos Blue 79
2 = Aquarius Green 77 or Apollo Green 79
3 = Stardust/Aero Silver 74 or Jupiter Red 77
4 = Bermuda Blue 77 or Nova Green
5 = Jade Green 75 or Cosmos Blue 79
6 = Neptune Blue 77 or Apollo Green 79
7 = Copper or Red Velvet 77
8 = Nevada Beige 77
9 = Signal Yellow 77
0 = Signal Amber 78 or Signal Orange 79 or Signal Red 80

Second character:
5 = 1975
6 = 1976
7 = 1977
8 = 1978
9 = 1979
0 = 1980
A = black vinyl roof
M = tobacco vinyl roof
K or D = brown vinyl roof

Exh. Emiss.
Not used. Left blank.

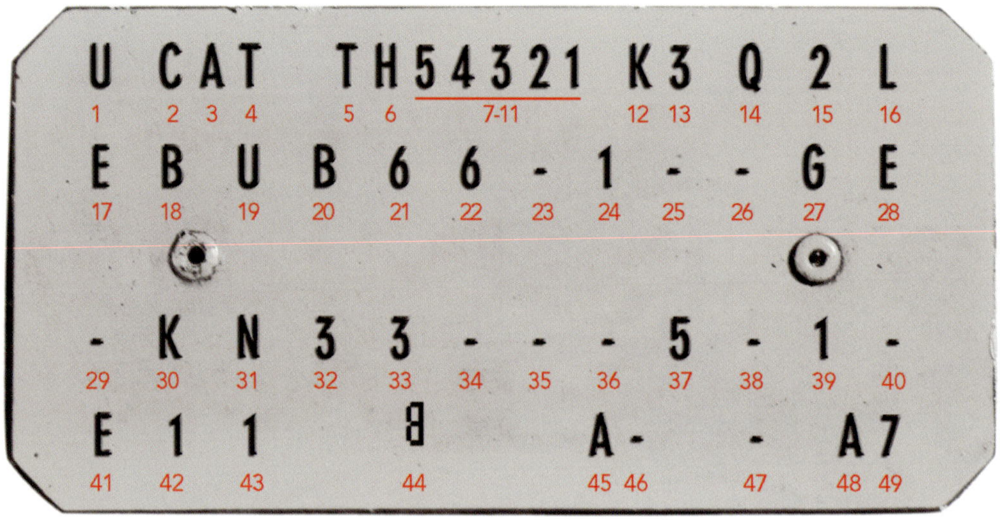

Saarlouis build plate

Mk2 Escorts assembled at West Germany's Saarlouis plant received a nice, orderly build plate riveted to the bonnet slam panel, painted the same colour as the car's bodywork. The codes contained on the plate were laid out in a pattern found on the individual car's build sheet, entitled Bauzettel PKW.

The codes reproduced here are in some cases confirmed, while others are the result of educated guesswork. As ever, pieces of this particular Escort puzzle are rather elusive.

1: Origin of order
1 or A = German Ford dealer
U = UK Ford dealer
F = Ford Germany subsidiary order
K = Austrian Ford dealer

2: Assembly plant
B = Halewood
C = Saarlouis
F = Aveley
K = Sydney
N = Amsterdam

3: Model
A = Escort

4: Body type
T = two-door saloon
F = four-door saloon
D = estate
V = van

5-6: Manufacture date
Year and month of production respectively.

Year code	Year	Jan	Feb	Mar	Apr	May	June	July	Aug	Sep	Oct	Nov	Dec
P	1974	L	Y	S	T	J	U	M	P	B	R	A	G
R	1975	C	K	D	E	L	Y	S	T	J	U	M	P
S	1976	B	R	A	G	C	K	D	E	L	Y	S	T
T	1977	J	U	M	P	B	R	A	G	C	K	D	E
U	1978	L	Y	S	T	J	U	M	P	B	R	A	G
W	1979	C	K	D	E	L	Y	S	T	J	U	M	P
A	1980	B	R	A	G	C	K	D	E	L	Y	S	T

7-11: Serial number
Unique serial number of the vehicle.

12-13: Special type
Special vehicle order for anything from taxis to towbars to sports packs and one-off colour schemes.
X0 = found on 1977 RS1800s – possibly for deletion of RS Mexico stripes
K3 = possibly SVO black

14: version
S = base
D = L
P = GL
E = Ghia
Q = Sport/RS2000/RS Mexico

15: LHD/RHD
A = LHD
1 = LHD
2 = RHD
B = RHD

16: Engine size
T = 950cc
G = 1100cc
J = 1300cc
L = 1600cc
N = 2000cc
RS1800s were built around pre-plated Sport or RS Mexico shells, so almost always had an L engine code relating to the donor model.

17: Engine rating
1 = Kent low-compression
2 – Kent high-compression
3= Kent high-compression with increased performance
5 = Kent fuel economy type
E = OHC high-compression with increased performance

18: Gearbox
B = four-speed manual
D = C3 three-speed automatic
5 = four-speed manual

19-20: Destination country package
A = Italy
2 = France
2B = USA
4 = Austria
6 = Sweden
7 = Belgium
8 = Norway
AK = Austria
B = Netherlands
BD = Belgium
CB = Canada
DB = Denmark
E = Switzerland
FD = Finland
FF = France
GK = Germany
IA = Iceland
IJ = Italy
ND = Netherlands
NQ = Norway
SK = Spain
SU = Switzerland
UB = Great Britain

21: Battery
3 = 12V, 44Ah
6 = 12V, 55Ah
8 = 12V, 66Ah

22: Heating
- = standard
4 = heavy-duty
6 = standard

23: Radio
– = no radio
2 = M32
4 = M21
6 = RST-21P
7 = RST-32P
9 = P21
H = P32
K = P42-32P or RST / RST-32P1
N = E-SRT32DPS
P = E-SRT32PS
V = P42

24: Windows
1 = clear, with laminated windscreen
2 = tinted, with toughened windscreen
A = clear, with toughened windscreen
F = tinted, with laminated windscreen

25: Roof
– = plain
1 = sliding sunroof
A = sunroof

26: Emission control specification (not required for UK cars)
– = no emission specification

27: Exterior lighting
5 = LHD sealed-beam headlamps
7 = RHD sealed-beam headlamps
G = RHD H4 headlamps
Q = RHD quad headlamps (RS2000)
R = LHD quad headlamps (RS2000)

28: special version
6 = RS2000
E = special sports package with stiffened suspension and decals (Mexico and RS1800)

29: Windows
– = standard
5 or E = opening front quarter windows

30: Wheels
– = standard
6 = 5x13in steel sports
7 = 5½x13in alloys
D = 6x13in four-spoke RS alloys
K = 5½x13in steel sports

31: Door mirrors
– = non-adjustable RH mirror
A = non-adjustable chrome mirrors both sides
C = remote-control LH mirror, non-adjustable RH
H = remote-control RH mirror, none on nearside
L = non-adjustable LH mirror
N = non-adjustable black mirrors both sides
T = remote-control RH mirror, non adjustable LH
Y = remote-control RH mirror, non-adjustable LH

32: Locks
– = standard locks
3 = locking fuel cap (possibly)

33: Brakes
– = standard brakes
3 = servo-assisted brakes
4 = standard brakes (drums and no servo)

34: Suspension
– = standard
5 = heavy-duty export pack

35: Underbody protection
– = none
A = underbody protection plates

36: Carpet
– or A = standard
3 = L version, boot carpet
4 = standard carpet plus extra insulation
8 = carpets plus boot carpet and carpeted door bottoms

37: Dashboard
– = standard fascia
5 = standard fascia

38: Bumpers
– = no bumper overriders
2 = bumper overriders

39: Centre console and clock
1 = no console
A = Ghia-type console with clock
B = RS2000 centre console with clock

40: Misc. options
– = none fitted
8 = speakers
9 = automatic aerial

41: Misc. options
– = none fitted
6 = heated rear window
E = heated rear window and RS steering wheel
F = heated rear window and soft-feel steering wheel

42: Lamps
– = no additional lamps
A = standard rear lights with reversing lamps plus rear fog lamp
1 = standard rear lights with reversing lamps

43: Warning lights configuration
1 = standard warning lights
V = standard warning lights plus brake warning indicator

44: Tyre dimensions
Not always used, but usually a B, found mainly on RS Mexicos – sometimes stamped from the front with a reversed letter. Possibly relating to fitment of 175/70HR13 radial tyres.

45: Body colour

Code	Colour	Dates
0	Signal Amber 78	Sep 1977 to Aug 1978
	Signal Orange 79	Sep 1978 to Aug 1979
	Signal Red 80	Sep 1979 to Jul 1980
1	Miami Blue	Launch to Aug 1977
	Cosmos Blue	Sep 1977 to Aug 1979
	Solar Gold	Sep 1979 to Jul 1980
2	Aquarius Green	Sep 1975 to Aug 1978
	Apollo Green	Sep 1978 to Jul 1980
3	Aero Silver 74	Launch to Aug 1976
	Jupiter Red	Sep 1976 to Aug 1979
	Sirius Red	Sep 1979 to Jul 1980
4	Bermuda Blue	Sep 1976 to Aug 1979
	Nova Green	Sep 1979 to Jul 1980
5	Jade Green	Launch to Aug 1977
	Cosmos Blue	Sep 1977 to Jul 1980
6	Aero Silver	Launch to Aug 1976
	Neptune Blue	Sep 1976 to Aug 1978
	Apollo Green	Sep 1978 to Jul 1980
7	Copper Brown	Launch to Aug 1976
	Red Velvet 77	Sep 1976 to Aug 1979
8	Nevada Beige	Sep 1976 to Aug 1977
9	Strato Silver	Sep 1975 to Aug 1976
	Signal Yellow 77	Sep 1976 to Jul 1980
A	Black	Launch to Jul 1980
B	Diamond White 73	Launch to Jul 1980
C	Sahara Beige 74	Launch to Aug 1977
	Oyster Gold	Sep 1977 to Aug 1979
	Nova Green	Sep 1979 to Jul 1980
D	Carnival Red 75	Sep 1975 to Aug 1977
	Regency Green 78	Sep 1977 to Aug 1979
	Terracotta	Sep 1979 to Jul 1980
E	Olympic Blue	Launch to Aug 1977
	Hawaiian Blue 78	Sep 1977 to Aug 1979
	Java Green	Sep 1979 to Jul 1980
F	Purple Velvet	Launch to Aug 1976
	Solar Gold	Sep 1977 to Jul 1980
G	Royal Blue 75	Launch to Aug 1975
	Strato Silver	Sep 1975 to Aug 1978
	Tuscan Beige 79	Sep 1978 to Jul 1980
H	Signal Orange 77	Sep 1976 to Aug 1978
J	Signal Green 77	Sep 1976 to Aug 1977
K	Signal Green 76	Sep 1975 to Aug 1976
	Calypso Green 79	Sep 1978 to Jul 1979
L	Signal Orange 76	Sep 1975 to Aug 1977
M	Modena Green	Launch to Aug 1977
N	Strato Silver	Sep 1975 to Aug 1976
	Saturn Gold	Sep 1976 to Aug 1977
P	Signal Green 76	Sep 1975 to Aug 1976
	Tropic Green 77	Sep 1976 to Aug 1978

P	Sierra Beige	Sep 1978 to Aug 1979
	Cordoba Beige	Scp 1979 to Jul 1980
Q	Arizona Gold 75	Launch to Aug 1977
R	Venetian Red 77	Sep 1976 to Jul 1980
S	Roman Bronze 76	Sep 1975 to Aug 1979
	Sable Brown	Sep 1979 to Jul 1980
T	Daytona Yellow 72	Launch to Aug 1976
	Peppermint Green 78	Sep 1977 to Aug 1978
	Riviera Blue 79	Sep 1978 to Aug 1979
	Nordic Blue 80	Sep 1979 to Jul 1980
U	Platinum 76	Sep 1975 to Jul 1980
V	Phoenix/Vista Orange	Launch to Dec 1975
	Strato Silver 77	
X	Midnight Blue 78	Sep 1979 to Jul 1980
Y	Special colour (SVO)	Launch to Jul 1980
Z	Primer	Launch to Jul 1980

46: Roof
– = plain
A = vinyl roof, black
D = vinyl roof, brown
K = vinyl roof, brown
M = vinyl roof, tobacco

47: Version
– = normal version

48: Trim colour
A = Night Black
B = Tan 79 or bitter chocolate/tan (Sport)
C = Cloud 74
E = Medium Blue 74
F = Marquis Blue 71 or Blue 79 or bitter chocolate/blue (Sport)
H = Red 79 or bitter chocolate/red (Sport)
J = Chocolate 76 or bitter chocolate/orange (Sport)
K = Light Tan 73
L = Saddle Brown 74
M = Green 77
N = Orange 77
P = Chocolate 76 or bitter chocolate/Indian red (Sport) or Bitter Chocolate 80
T = Saddle Brown
W = Light Tan 76
X = black
Y = non-standard

49: Upholstery
1 = cloth or vinyl
2,3,4 = cloth
5,6,7,8 = cloth – sports trim
9 = cloth – luxury trim
A,E,G,H = vinyl
Y = special upholstery

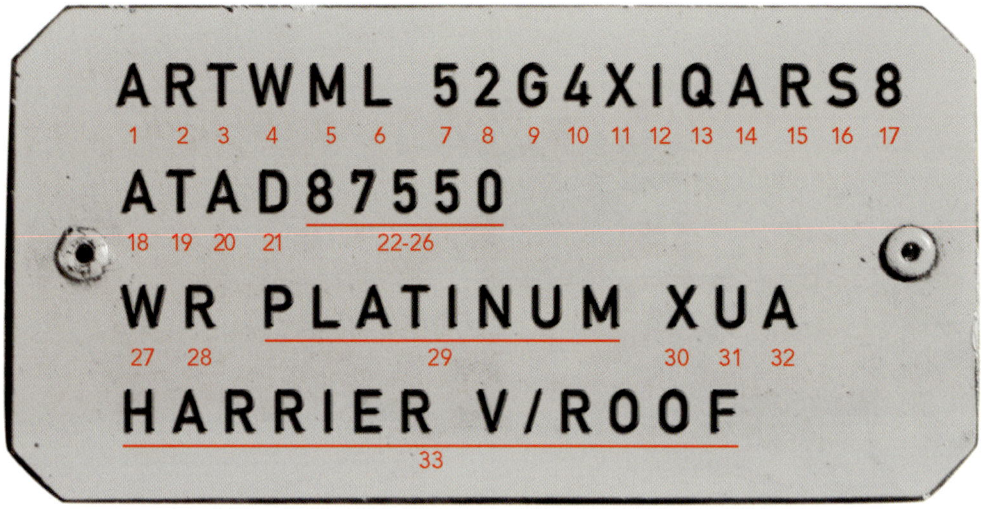

Halewood build plate

British Mk2 Escorts from the Halewood production line had a body-coloured build plate riveted to the slam panel in the same position as their German counterparts. At first glance, the British information appeared to be stamped rather randomly but closer inspection reveals an order to the codes contained on each plate. Various plate layouts were used, but all generally followed a very similar formula. Unlike Saarlouis plates, Halewood versions did not use dashes or different digits for standard specifications and non-inclusion of items.

Although some of the details on the Halewood plates are well-known, many codes are currently a mystery to anyone outside Ford Great Britain. Here, we've listed what's been confirmed as correct.

1: Model
A = Escort

2: RHD/LHD
R = RHD

3: Body type
T = two-door
F = four-door
D = estate

4: Version
B = base
C = Popular Plus
D = L
H = GL
Q = Sport
W = Harrier

5: Transmission
M = manual
A = automatic

6: Engine
H = 1100cc
J = 1300cc
L = 1600cc

7-17: Specification
A series of characters laid out (where present) in a specific order. For example…

8: Mirrors
E = fixed driver's mirror
F = fixed mirrors on both sides
2 = remote driver's door mirror, fixed passenger mirror

11: Cigarette lighter
X = cigarette lighter

12: Rear windscreen
I = heated rear window and alternator

13: Lamps
Q = hazard warning lights

16: Brakes
S = servo-assisted brakes (front discs and rear drums)

18: Model
A = Escort

19: Body type
T = two-door
F = four-door
D = estate

20-21: Manufacture date

Year and month of production respectively.

Year code	Year	Jan	Feb	Mar	Apr	May	June	July	Aug	Sep	Oct	Nov	Dec
P	1974	L	Y	S	T	J	U	M	P	B	R	A	G
R	1975	C	K	D	E	L	Y	S	T	J	U	M	P
S	1976	B	R	A	G	C	K	D	E	L	Y	S	T
T	1977	J	U	M	P	B	R	A	G	C	K	D	E
U	1978	L	Y	S	T	J	U	M	P	B	R	A	G
W	1979	C	K	D	E	L	Y	S	T	J	U	M	P
A	1980	B	R	A	G	C	K	D	E	L	Y	S	T

22-26: Serial number

Unique serial number of the vehicle.

27-28: Specification

A series of letters laid out (where present) in a specific order.

29: Colour

Name or description of the car's body colour (eg GOLD INCA or plain old WHITE).

30-32: Specification

A series of letters laid out (where present) in a specific order.

33: Special trim

Used (sometimes, but not always) to denote a special model variation (eg HARRIER) or vinyl roof, which was described alongside its colour (eg BLACK V/ROOF or TOBACCO V/ROOF).

Triplex glass dating

Triplex glass was fitted to UK-built Mk2 Escorts, and came with its own manufacturing date. So it's easy to tell if the glass matches the car's age, simply by joining the dots. Original windows were usually made one or two months before the car was built, but even six months was quite normal when dealing with tinted glass.

Triplex's code was a system of dots printed onto the glass. The year of manufacture was represented by a dot under letters in the words Toughened or Laminated, with just the last digit indicated. The month of glass manufacture was represented by a combination of dots over the letters TR and EX in the word Triplex.

Year

LAMINATED
1234567890

TOUGHENED
1234567890

Month

TRIPLEX – January
TRIPLEX – February
TRIPLEX – March
TRIPLEX – April
TRIPLEX – May
TRIPLEX – June
TRIPLEX – July
TRIPLEX – August
TRIPLEX – September
TRIPLEX – October
TRIPLEX – November
TRIPLEX – December